AF702572

SECOND EDITION

Advanced Pick™ Open Database and Operating System

SECOND EDITION

Advanced Pick™ Open Database and Operating System

Roger J Bourdon

ADDISON-WESLEY PUBLISHING COMPANY

HARLOW, ENGLAND • READING, MASSACHUSETTS • MENLO PARK, CALIFORNIA • NEW YORK
DON MILLS, ONTARIO • AMSTERDAM • BONN • SYDNEY • SINGAPORE
TOKYO • MADRID • SAN JUAN • MILAN • MEXICO CITY • SEOUL • TAIPEI

© Addison Wesley Longman Limited 1996

Addison Wesley Longman Limited
Edinburgh Gate
Harlow
Essex
CM20 2JE
England

All rights reserved. No part of this publication may be reproduced, stored in a retrieval system, or transmitted in any form or by any means, electronic, mechanical, photocopying, recording or otherwise, without prior written permission of the publisher.

The programs in this book have been included for their instructional value. They have been tested with care but are not guaranteed for any particular purpose. The publisher does not offer any warranties or representations nor does it accept any liabilities with respect to the programs.

Many of the designations used by manufacturers and sellers to distinguish their products are claimed as trademarks. Addison Wesley Longman has made every attempt to supply trademark information about manufacturers and their products mentioned in this book. A list of the trademark designations and their owners appears below.

Cover designed by Designers and Partners, Oxford.
Typeset by Pantek Arts, Maidstone, Kent
Printed and bound in The United States of America.

First printed 1996

ISBN 0-201-87696-5

British Library Cataloguing-in-Publication Data
A catalogue record for this book is available from the British Library.

Library of Congress Cataloging-in-Publication Data applied for

Trademark Notice
ACCESS, PICK and Ultimate are trademarks of Pick Systems
ADDS is a trademark of Applied Digital Data Systems
ENGLISH and Reality are trademarks of McDonnell Douglas Computer Systems
GA is a trademark of General Automation
IBM is a registered trademark of International Business Machines
Infolink is a trademark of Sables Associates
MacToPic is a trademark of Carnation Software
PFX is a trademark of Landa Systems Software
PicLan and PL-TERM are trademarks of Modular Software Corporation
PK Harmony is a trademark of Synex Systems Corporation
PRIME is a trademark of Prime Computers, Inc.
Revelation is a trademark of Cosmos, Inc.
SB+, SB/Client and W/Integrate are trademarks of Unidata Corporation
TERMiTE is a trademark of Pixel Innovations
TRW is a trademark of TRW Corporation
UNIX is a trademark of Bell Laboratories
Via Express is a trademark of Via Systems
vxConnect is a trademark of Cambridge Computer Corporation
WORD is a registered trademark of Microsoft Corporation
WordPerfect is a registered trademark of WordPerfect Corporation

To Alf and Ivy

Foreword

Roger Bourdon is to be congratulated for creating a book that remains accessible to the novice while offering ample depth to satisfy the seasoned Pick professional. *Advanced Pick: Open Database and Operating System* is well-researched and comprehensive in its coverage of the many features that have enriched Advanced Pick over its years of maturation. The two-year investment in crafting this volume is evident in the intelligent organisation and logical development of the content. The information is presented in a clear and comprehensible fashion, aided by excellent illustrative diagrams and examples.

We, at Pick Systems, sincerely appreciate the initiative Roger Bourdon has taken in writing this much-needed book. Without doubt, it will be an invaluable aid in attaining our goal of making an expanding circle of the database community familiar with the incomparable data model that is the legacy of my father.

Mark Pick
Chief Operating Officer
Pick Systems, Inc.
Irvine, California, USA

Preface

In 1986 after just four years exposure to the PICK operating system I wrote my first book entitled *The PICK Operating System: A Practical Guide*. Prior to this I had spent a dozen or so years working with many other operating systems, but as soon as I started to become involved with PICK, I turned into one of its most loyal fans and advocates. At the time I first started working with PICK it was only an operating system known as PICK R83 and there were no publications or training courses available. I had to learn PICK the hard way and my book encompassed the information I had acquired during those four foundation years. I had access to highly skilled technicians, experienced PICK users and the source code to PICK itself. I worked as the Technical Director responsible for the porting of PICK to a new British built computer system and hence was uniquely placed to write my book. I would spend many hours delving into the operational depths of PICK and then be fortunate to be able to speak to people who could answer any questions I may have had by delving into PICK source code.

I found PICK an extremely sophisticated, yet easy to use, operating system. By virtue of its internal data structure and the minimum amount of effort needed in its administration it was obviously best suited to commercial and business applications. However, PICK was labelled as being the 'best kept secret in the computer industry' and in many respects this was true. PICK was in use and still is, by most of the Times Top 1000 companies, companies like British Telecom, the BBC, local authorities and regional health authorities, yet few people knew of it by name. I hoped that PICK would gain in recognition as computer companies started promoting the product by name, but marketing by PICK Systems remained low key and UNIX won the race to become the industry standard for multi-user computer systems.

At the same time network software became more reliable and many companies solved their multi-user requirements by the introduction of network solutions. As simple peer-to-peer networks and large networks using server technology proliferated and UNIX gained in stature, PICK Systems recognized the need to re-position their product as a database system. They set about making PICK, as a database, available on as wide a variety of platforms as possible, including UNIX and mainstream networks. This started with the launch of Advanced PICK a new release of PICK which could operate as either a database or native operating system but which was fully backwards compatible with PICK R83, the operating system to which I was originally introduced.

When I first started writing this book I wrongly assumed it would simply be a case of updating a few chapters of my original book and adding a few others on the new features of Advanced PICK, but I couldn't have been more wrong! Advanced PICK is so significantly different to PICK R83 that this book has been a true labour of love, just like the first one I wrote and it has taken nearly two years to complete.

This book is for both the experienced PICK user and someone new to PICK or wanting more information on what PICK is and how it works. I have tried to ensure that it is easy to read and not like a manual. It takes the reader gradually through the facets of PICK and only after a detailed overview of the database does it start to delve into its technicalities. The book is lavish with examples, provides a practical approach in its detailed and comprehensive description of Advanced PICK and is described in terms that are both simple and easy to understand. It fully describes all aspects of Advanced PICK and throughout highlights the differences for users of PICK R83. Indeed for those already familiar with PICK R83, this book contains a chapter dedicated to the differences between the two products and explains how to upgrade a PICK R83 application to the superior Advanced PICK platform.

This book covers each of the major features of Advanced PICK in a completely practical and fully illustrated manner. It starts, therefore, with a history of its development, an overview of its main modules and takes the reader gradually into the database structure by first looking at how the system is powered up and taking an initial look around the file system. From this point it continues its step-by-step description of each aspect of PICK until the reader is able to produce management information reports and manage and control the entire system. For those interested in developing applications there are also chapters associated with system design and programming, both equally rich in examples and summarized with tips and techniques.

This book does contain a highly detailed description of the data structure, which is what sets PICK apart from other database systems, but the reader is introduced to this gradually in stages which are far less technical than they may at first appear. Subsequent chapters describe the other major elements of PICK such as the use of printers, the Update Processor, the editor, the procedure processor (PROC), Macros, Menus, file indexing and the powerful enquiry language (ACCESS). The book illustrates methods for ensuring the security and integrity of the system and advice on carrying out day-to-day management tasks. Finally, it devotes a complete chapter to the various PICK implementations for PCs, discusses the implication of fourth-generation application generators and concludes by looking at PICK's communication capability and its future in the commercial world.

This book is essential reading for anyone responsible for the management of a PICK-based system. Whilst aimed at those using or considering PICK for the first time, or moving to Advanced PICK from PICK R83, it equally provides a comprehensive and valuable reference for the more experienced user.

Acknowlegements

No technical book is the work of a single individual. This one encompasses the knowledge and experience gained from friends and users, too numerous to mention, who have been willing to share their findings with me. However, this book would not have been produced had I not been encouraged and supported to complete its predecessor and for that I wish to thank Kim Jones, John Taylor, B.Sc.(Hons), MIAP, AMBCS, and Marcus van Raaltè for their support.

The writing of this book has been a mammoth task and for technical input and support I wish to thank the Directors of APT Solutions, Peter Bowen, George Land and Stuart Shepherd and one of its talented and valuable consultants, David Beaty. In a project of this nature moral support is of equal importance and for that I have to thank both Lesley Fayers and Lyndall Hopcraft without whom this book would be more likely to be stuck in my word processor than published and out on the bookshelves!

Whilst every effort has been made to ensure the accuracy of this book, the author cannot guarantee that the book is error-free or accurate, nor can he accept responsibility for any problems associated with its use. It should be noted that there are differences of implementation on a number of manufacturers' computer systems which frequently result in minor differences of operation.

PICK is the registered trademark of PICK Systems, Irvine, California.

Roger Bourdon
APT Solutions Limited
Suite 218/219
Business Design Centre
Upper Street,
London N1 0QH, England.
February 1996

Contents

1 Introduction

If you have just taken delivery of your PICK-based computer system, you are to be congratulated for choosing one of the most powerful, yet easy-to-use multi-user operating systems available. If you have chosen PICK as the database to use on your computer system you are to be praised for astutely selecting one of the best commercial databases available.

Confused? Well PICK is available as both an operating system and database. In the 1980s PICK was vying to become the *de facto* multi-user operating system at a time when people were becoming aware of the words 'open systems' and the problems of being locked into proprietary operating systems and proprietary hardware. In the end PICK lost that race to UNIX and repositioned itself as a database. Its objective was to become the industry standard database and to that end started to make itself available on a wide range of platforms to which it had previously been unavailable. Its first move was to work as a database under UNIX. It then forged a relationship with IBM with a version of PICK that worked with AIX and from there onto many other platforms, more of which is described later on.

PICK is possibly the longest running project in the history of computers. It started around 30 years ago in 1965 under Richard Pick and up until his untimely death on 17 October 1994 at the age of 59, it still had the same project leader! As a database it provides the means to store, process and retrieve information whilst its operating system capabilities automatically take care of the use of printers, terminals and the other hardware of a computer system such as memory, disks and magnetic tapes.

Thirty years ago Richard Pick was section head at the Computation and Data Reduction Management Centre for TRW, a large computer records and project services company. I had just started work and was employed as a trainee programmer for a warehousing and distribution company that had just bought an ICT 1901 computer. I was programming in PLAN, a kind of assembler, working on commercial systems using a computer rated at just one hundredth of a mip. The computer, which had no hard disk, took its input from 80 column punched cards and had just 16 kilobytes of main memory but at today's prices cost the equivalent of around half a million pounds!

In those days there was little in the way of systems software and what was available was primarily operating systems and compilers. Applications software was largely bespoke and developed by in-house teams of analysts and programmers. The software industry was virtually non-existent and the word 'package' was just beginning to be understood. At that time with the high cost of both hardware and software, time sharing was a very common practice.

The revolution in the computing industry has been nothing short of astounding. Micro-miniaturization, the silicon chip and more and more densely populated integrated circuitry has meant that computers of phenomenal power are packaged into systems the size of a small hard-backed book. In the last four generations of Intel processor for example, the number of transistors on the processor chip alone has increased almost exponentially. The 386 contained 275,000 transistors, the 486 had a million, the Pentium (586) had 3.1

million transistors and the P6 or Pentium Pro processor around 7 million. Even so mass production techniques have dramatically affected the price of computers and today, with the price of a PC well under £1000 and running at between 50 and 100 mips, computers are no longer a luxury for a business, but an everyday tool for all of its employees. Computers are finding their way not only onto the desks of every businessman but into their homes as well.

The revolution has equally affected the software industry. Thirty years ago systems software was thrown in for 'free' when you bought a computer. In the late 1960s IBM started to unbundle their software charging for operating software and support services separately. In the late 1970s people recognized more and more that proprietary operating systems were locking them in to proprietary hardware and the computing industry started to talk about standardization. MSDOS became the industry standard for single-user PCs and PICK and UNIX fought side by side to become the *de facto* standard for multi-user systems. Both these products freed the user from any dependence on a particular hardware supplier, but UNIX won the race and gained wider acceptability, primarily because of its communication capability. In the move towards 'open systems', software developers recognized the importance of the relational database and with the increasing interest in UNIX came an equal interest in database products such as Informix, Unify, Ingres, Sybase and Oracle. No matter how good the database, the underlying operating platform being UNIX meant that operationally, the system required high level technical skills and extremely powerful hardware on which to run. Ironically it was the increasing price/performance of the minicomputer in the 1970s and the PC in the 1980s, which brought about the acceptance of UNIX in the commercial world.

Those people who come across PICK for the first time are amazed at its power and astounded by its simplicity. They find it incredible that many more users can be connected to the same hardware using PICK as the native operating system than can be connected under UNIX.

What makes PICK unique, is that it incorporates features that are found only as add-ons in other operating systems. At its heart is a database system truly integrated into the PICK environment. It is a database which handles variable length records and around which is implemented virtual memory management, a system which enables the hard disk to be used as an extension of the computer's real memory or RAM (Random Access Memory). This advanced facility removes the restriction found in most systems, that the number of tasks which can be undertaken at any one time is a function of physical memory. It also allows for a true multi-user environment in as little as 256 kilobytes (256 thousand characters) of physical memory. Indeed no new computer available today contains less than at least eight times this amount, but when it was first released, PICK was truly revolutionary. More importantly to the user, PICK includes an English-like nonprocedural enquiry language known as ACCESS. Since all data is stored in one common format then ACCESS can be used on **any** file in the system regardless of whether it contains programs, user or system data; similarly only one editor is needed. The other facilities available within the PICK environment combine to make it one of the most comprehensive and easy-to-use of any available today.

Even though PICK lost the race to become the *de facto* standard for multi-user operating systems, it has astutely and successfully repositioned itself as a leading database. Whilst PICK Systems' strategy is to provide products that allow PICK as a database to move into new markets, it remains for many an ideal operating system, being simple to use and requiring the minimum of technical knowledge to support.

In the early 1990s, PICK re-launched itself under the new name of Advanced PICK (it was formerly referred to as R83 – the version of PICK originally released in 1983) and became the only database to be widely available under a whole host of operating systems, including but not limited to UNIX, DOS, VMS and Windows NT. PICK's strength as a database was recognized by IBM with whom they have formed a strong working relationship, to the extent that IBM even actively promotes PICK. Their RS6000 systems have became a significant revenue earner for PICK, with in excess of 25% of the RS6000s sold being sold with PICK working as the database under AIX.

The strategic move by PICK to work as a database under a variety of different operating systems has ensured its future. At the beginning of 1995 there were over 3500 PICK resellers around the world resulting in more than 4 million PICK users running on over 300,000 mid-range systems and over 200,000 Intel platforms. According to the International Data Corporation (IDC) and the International Data Base Management Association Inc. (IDBMA), PICK sales are growing at the rate of over 40% per year.

Whether it operates as a database or operating system, it looks and feels the same. Hence even as a database, all the functionality described in this book is available to the user. PICK as a database is far more than just a database. It has its own enquiry language, well all databases have that, but in addition it has its own programming language, its own command language (TCL), a means to easily produce menus, job streams and much much more. What it does mean, is that if PICK is operating purely as a database, the operating system commands for control of peripherals are passed down to the native operating system, rather than being controlled by PICK directly.

Advanced PICK(AP) incorporates all the facilities of R83, so all R83 software will run under AP. However, there are fundamental differences between the two and as one would expect AP has many new additional facilities. The future of PICK is with Advanced PICK, whether it is used as a database or operating system. Development work on R83, which was only ever capable of being the underlying operating system, ceased in 1991. Whilst this book primarily deals with Advanced PICK, attention will be drawn to the differences between R83 and AP and there is a separate chapter dedicated to the conversion of R83 to Advanced Pick.

The examples in the rest of this book are illustrated using the following conventions

Convention used	**Meaning**
ACCESS	Words in all UPPER CASE are PICK terms
set-floppy	Words or characters in **bold** are commands, filenames or options and must be entered as shown. In R83 these must be in upper case only. In AP these can normally be either in upper or lower case
filename	Words in *italics* are variables which need to be substituted with actual names, e.g. *filename* with the name of the file such as ORDER or PART
{(options)}	Items contained in {} indicate optional parameters
n{-m}	The letters n and m are used to represent numbers. This example means that a number is to be input, but that a range should also include the hyphen
`to:`	Words typed in this typeface are words, prompts or outputs produced by the system
g (underlined)	Characters which are underlined and in bold indicate control characters and are produced by holding down the control key whilst pressing the underlined character. In this example ctrl/g. **Do not type the underline**
[CR]	Indicates the RETURN (↵) or ENTER key

2 Advanced PICK – an Overview

2.1 The history of PICK

Following his MBA at Berkeley University, Richard Pick started his career in data processing as a programmer with Mattel Toys. It was his interest to find better, more efficient ways to develop applications that was to bring about the PICK operating system. It started in 1965 when he joined the giant US military contractor TRW, and in conjunction with Don Nelson, was involved on a system specification that was to develop an English-based enquiry language. This system called the Generalised Information Retrieval Language System (GIRLS), developed on an IBM 360, enabled remote terminals to locate parts for rocket engines which might have been situated anywhere in the TRW organization.

Eventually the US army took an interest in the project and decided to fund a data management system to support the tracking of the Cheyenne helicopter project. This public funding had a significance later on, because public funding in the USA means that the results of a project tend to come into the public domain.

By 1972 Richard Pick and Don Nelson had produced the first commercial implementation of PICK known as the Reality operating system on the Microdata 1600 computer. In this implementation Pick put much of the operating system into micro-code which was placed in a ROM chip on the processor board. This is known as a firmware implementation and contrasts with most of the other implementations where the operating system resides on the hard disk and is known as a software implementation. This firmware implementation meant that tasks such as managing the virtual memory system and handling the terminal I/O could be carried out at very high speed.

In 1974 Microdata made its first major thrust into the end user market with Reality and went on to create a national dealer network with what was undoubtedly a revolutionary product. In as little as 32 kilobytes of real memory, 10 or more users could work satisfactorily on-line using variable length data in a true multi-user environment. Many of these features we now take for granted of course, but in those days they were truly remarkable.

Pick's natural interest in putting his product on other machines ultimately caused a breakdown of the relationship with Microdata and in 1977 a lawsuit started. This produced a counter lawsuit and it was some four years later before a settlement took place during which time both continued their developments independently. The outcome of the legal wranglings resulted in both companies having the right to the product.

During this four year period, Pick, who had set up his own company, Pick and Associates, announced the Evolution computer system, based on the Intertechnique processor built in France and also ported his system on the Honeywell Level 6. The Ultimate Corporation marketed the Level 6 product and this marked a major milestone in the history of PICK, being the first well-known computer to run the operating system. It could also run more terminals and cope with larger applications than before and hence proved to be a highly successful venture. It is likely to have been instrumental in encouraging other hardware manufacturers to offer PICK on their own systems. It is also worth noting that during this same period, in 1978, the Devcom Corporation began an emulation of PICK which they called 'Information', designed to run on Prime computers.

The first implementation on IBM equipment started in 1981 on the Series 1 and shortly after Pick and Associates adopted the name by which they are known today, that of Pick Systems. From this point on implementations flowed fast and furious. 1982 saw the start of six new ports on equipment from Altos, ADDS, Systems Management Inc. (SMI), Datamedia, General Automation and the Pertec Computer Corporation.

This saw the start of many more implementations with manufacturers queuing at Pick's door for their port of his operating system. Undoubtedly the most significant port which greatly increased the credibility of PICK was that released in 1984 for the IBM PC-XT. The PC-XT version, a full implementation of PICK for around $495, turned the PC into a multi-user micro which supported three users plus parallel printers. In addition PICK on the PC-XT supported the IBM bit-mapped screen, colour and provided an interface to MSDOS. In October 1985, PICK launched the PC-AT implementation, with two versions, one to support one–three users, the other for one–six users. Like the PC-XT implementation, the PC-AT version was R83 and not as was first planned, Open Architecture, which was rescheduled for release in 1986. This meant the operating system was made available for the personal computer right through to the large mainframes, such as IBM 4300 and 30XX products where the number of users was in the hundreds. In subsequent years, with the increased power in PCs, PICK's R83 operating system was able to support up to 33 users.

It was these developments which started to put pressure on the traditional minicomputer suppliers, the likes of ADDS, Altos and General Automation, who had been PICK Systems original source of revenue. Now with the tremendous reduction in hardware prices and with the sizeable number of users realistically being able to be supported on PCs, the minicomputer suppliers saw a large chunk of their traditional business being eroded away. With today's processors such as the Pentium processor and its successors and with Advanced PICK supporting more and more users on PC (Intel based) technology, it is obviously difficult to see how some of the traditional minicomputer companies will survive.

In 1989 PICK launched Advanced PICK (AP) for the PC to guarded enthusiasm. It was felt that AP was long overdue and its belated introduction gave its followers doubts about its stability, and sales of AP made little impact on those of R83 for a number of months. Undoubtedly computer specialists, the group used to inflicting change on others, are those least able to accept change themselves, but the enhanced facilities of AP soon won over the sceptics and nowadays whilst PICK Systems still support R83 no further developments are taking place. All future developments are taking place on AP and no sensible person is likely to consider buying anything other than AP. To influence people further, PICK Systems introduced a price differential between the two, making R83 over 20% more expensive, so R83 is all but dead for new installations.

A summary of the primary differences and improvements of AP over R83 are:

- Unlimited item size (removes the 32K limit)
- Item locking rather than group locking
- Case insensitive
- Full screen editor (Update Processor) with spell checker
- Output processor
- Phantom (background) processor
- Integrated B-Trees and indexes
- Incremental file saves
- Transaction logging
- Enhanced BASIC
- Macro processor (replacement for the PROC processor)
- Menu processor
- Level pushing (up to 16 levels)
- TCL stacker
- New processing codes
- New ACCESS facilities
- Improved security

Nowadays, AP can support up to 257 users on a standard PC and up to 512 users under AIX on the RS6000. Whilst 257 users on a PC may seem high, this is because Pick Systems launched a version of AP called 'Protected Mode' which is able to make full use of the PC's RAM above the base 640K, which formerly had only been used as disk cache.

The hardware platforms supporting PICK are numerous and Figure 2.1 shows the primary systems that support PICK.

When you consider the number of systems now running PICK it may seem strange that the system is not more widely known. In the early days of course it was being offered as Reality, Ultimate or Evolution and unlike many other operating system suppliers, Richard Pick kept close control over the implementations. We are now seeing the emergence of PICK as an industry standard database, and one that offers true portability of application software. PICK's data handling and enquiry language are the best available for the business and commercial marketplace for which they were designed. For those in the scientific and engineering industries PICK is not for you and operating systems such as UNIX or its derivatives will be best suited offering a variety of languages, in particular C and FORTRAN. However, in the commercial world PICK is unbeatable.

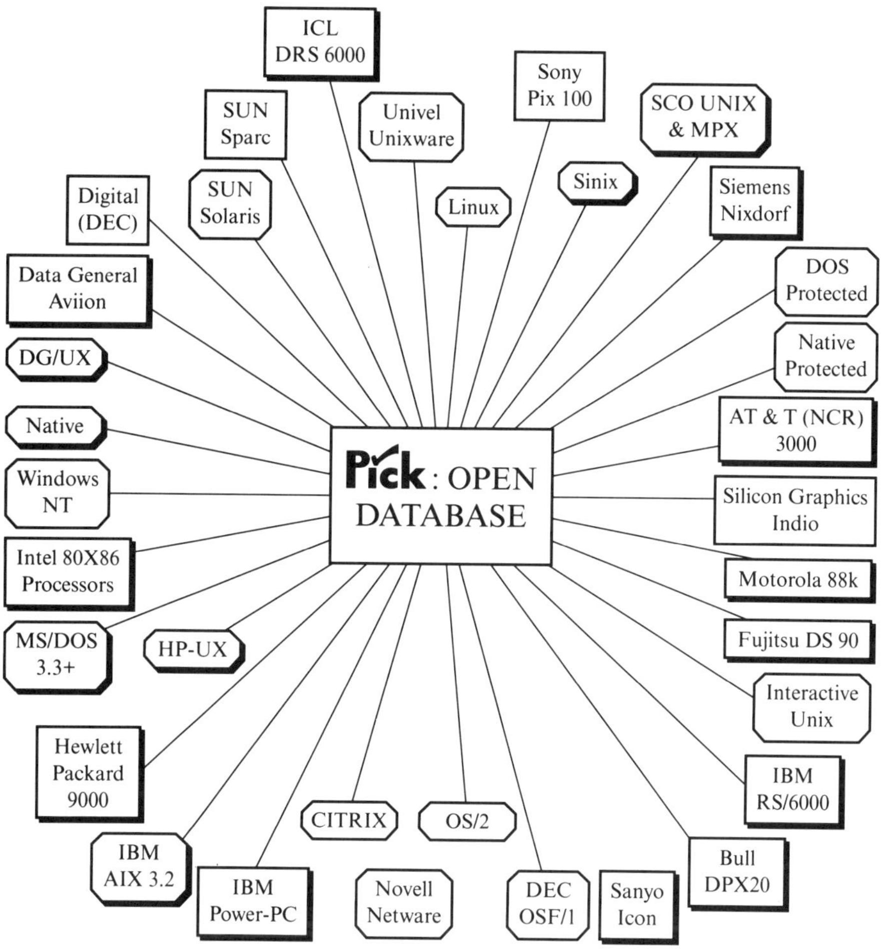

Figure 2.1 Hardware platform map.

2.2 The primary components of Advanced PICK

Whether as a database or operating system, PICK comprises a number of key components (Figure 2.2):

Terminal Control Language (TCL) forms the main interface between the user and the computer system. There are currently over 400 system utilities and procedures that can be invoked from the TCL environment as well as an unlimited number of user-defined procedures. It is from TCL that all other processes, such as the editor, Access or BASIC are invoked. It is a feature of PICK that

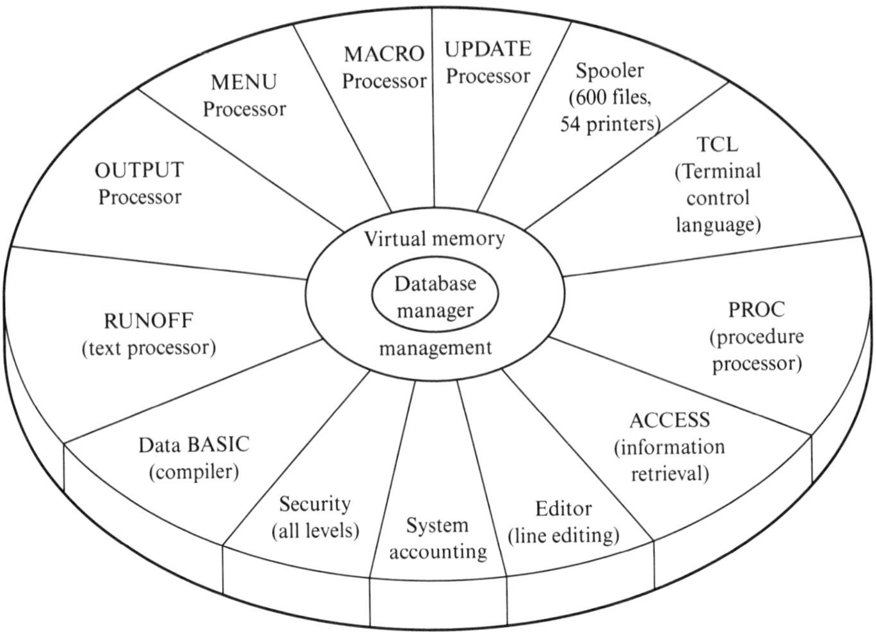

Figure 2.2 The facilities of PICK centre around a database system and virtual memory management.

these commands can be removed or renamed (possibly in a foreign language) providing a tailored environment for each user. The TCL processor is automatically entered at 'logon' and normally whenever other processes are completed. The TCL prompt is one of the first outward signs of the difference between AP and R83. In AP the familiar > prompt has been replaced with : and this symbol will be used throughout this book when TCL commands are explained.

The **EDITOR** provides for the interactive on-line modification of the database. It can access **any** element of data within any file in the system and create, modify or delete it. The editor works on the current line for making these changes and incorporates a facility to handle prestored commands for repetitive tasks. In addition data can be 'merged' from other files. Many viewed the editor as archaic and AP saw the launch of a full screen editor known as the Update Processor.

The **UPDATE** processor is a full screen editor which is available only in AP. It can be used to view, create and manipulate any element of data, but differs from the editor in that when it is used as a data file editor, it uses file dictionaries to process the data as it is entered or retrieved. It will create and maintain file relationships using local and/or remote indexing providing techniques referred to as 'cruising' and 'zooming'.

The **PROC** processor allows a sequence of operations to be executed by use of a single word command. Any sequence of operations that can be executed from a terminal can also be prestored using PROC, simplifying the day-to-day use of the system. PROC is effectively a job control language with one or two enhancements. It can control input and output from a user's terminal with validation, branching, field manipulation and links to subroutines.

The **MACRO** processor is available only in AP and is seen as a replacement for PROCs. The macro processor can perform all the tasks of the PROC processor but does it in a much more straightforward way. In early times, PROCs were used to build menu systems, but AP provides another new tool called the Menu Processor.

The **MENU** processor as its name implies is a tool for development of formatted menus, with presentation options and optional user-supplied help messages. This tool is not available under R83.

A programming language called **BASIC** (Beginners All-Purpose Symbolic Instruction Code), is an extension of Dartmouth Basic and provides a popular and easy-to-use compiler that caters for the unique PICK data structure. It is easier to use than standard BASIC removing many of its irritating constraints. It permits the use of meaningful variable names, a capability usually only found in high level languages such as Pascal or C, and permits variables to be of any length and type. BASIC features a high level interface with the database manager and consequently can access most of the functions provided by ACCESS, including selection, sorting and print formatting. The compiler provides a number of useful options including the ability to output a program listing with opcodes and 'pseudo' assembly code. The generation of variable and statement maps let the programmer accurately monitor the execution of the program to improve performance in critical areas.

ACCESS is one of the most useful and powerful features of PICK. It is a non-procedural English-like enquiry language where the user is in control and can enquire on any information in the database. Database enquiries can be made using a relatively free format language, closely related to normal English. This makes it easy to learn and simple to use, quickly inspiring confidence in users that the computer system is working for them. By using PICK's data dictionaries to define interrelationships ACCESS enables information from several files to be sorted (ascending or descending), counted or totalled. Information is selected using logical operators such as equal, not equal, less than or greater than together with the connectives AND and OR. By use of such vocabulary, people with very little training soon feel comfortable with the system and can produce their own enquiries and reports.

The **Output Management System** or **Spooler** capable of handling a wide variety of devices, including 50 serial printers, and four parallel printers is an integral part of the operating system. At any one time 600 print files (reports) may be retained and controlled. A comprehensive set of utilities are provided which allow for changes to be made to the print queue, for the examination of individual reports (including a search for a specified string of characters), and for the set up of specific printers for specified terminals. It also controls and monitors the backup processes.

RUNOFF a text processor which facilitates the preparation of documents such as memos, reports and manuals. RUNOFF uses commands embedded in the text to handle such things as justification, indenting, headings, footings and page numbering. For complex and lengthy documents it can also automatically produce the index and table of contents. With the launch of AP came a replacement for RUNOFF known as the Output Processor (OP).

The **Output Processor (OP)** is available only with AP and formats and prints text from commands embedded in the body of the text. It provides very similar capabilities to those of RUNOFF described above.

System Accounting is a means of monitoring the use of the system. The accounting history file accounts maintains a complete audit log for the system showing such details as the duration of time a user was logged on, the amount of CPU (Central Processor Unit) time used and the number of pages spooled to the printer. Users also have the option of charging specified portions of their system usage to nominated sub-accounts which permits true project costing. Various reports are available which, amongst others, show the system loading by port, the average connect time per type of user and the average number of 'sessions' per user. The information so produced can also be used to produce invoices for computer usage.

A **security** system protects sensitive information from unauthorized access. Initial system entry can be password protected and the users 'logon' profile determines his read and write capabilities on other files. Individual command files can be set up to control the entire user session from the time a user logs on, to the time they log off and such a command file can also include automatic logging of system usage.

3 The PICK Database Structure

Before we look at using a PICK system, it is essential to look at the way in which data is stored and handled. Much of PICK's strength is by virtue of the power and flexibility gained from its unique database structure. All information in the system is stored in files. There are two main types of file, data and dictionary, and these are organized in a hierarchy with four distinct levels, System Dictionary (MDS but called SYSTEM in R83), Master Dictionary (MD), File Dictionary (DICT) and Data files. Figure 3.1 shows a pictorial representation of this data hierarchy.

PICK controls data in a logical way which can be readily compared to the way in which any business handles its information. Figure 3.2 demonstrates the

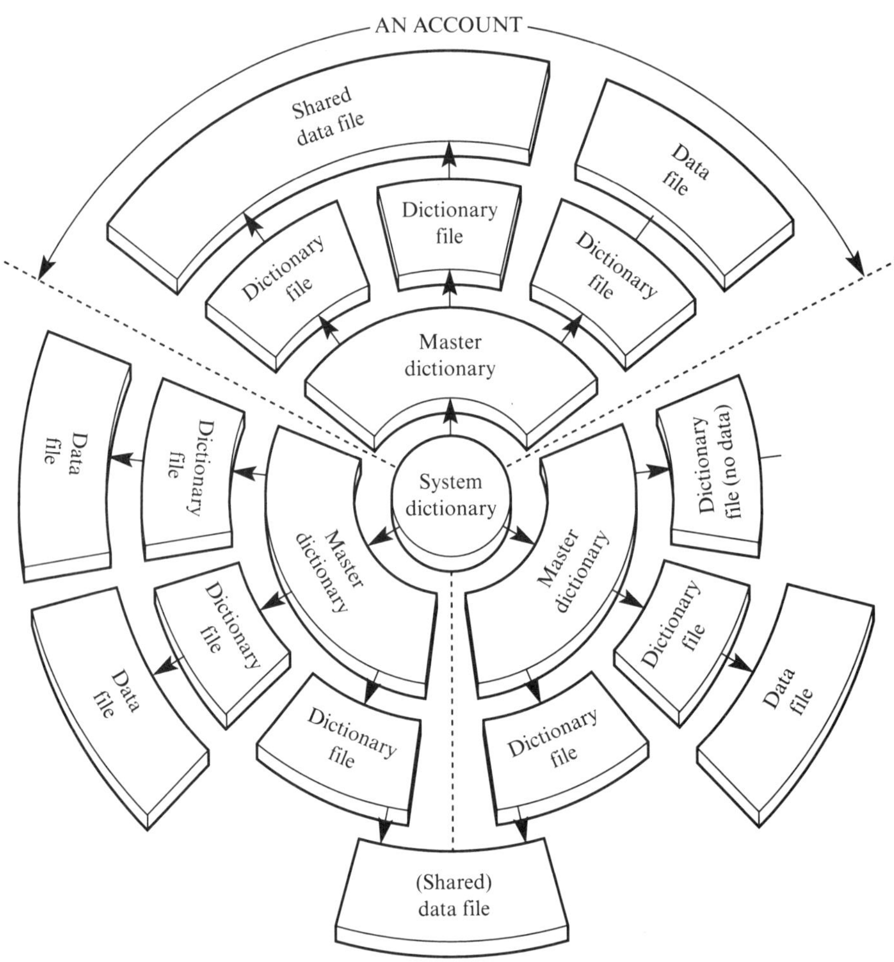

Figure 3.1 The PICK data structure.

way in which a company can be represented, with the managing director in control of a number of departments each controlling their own data files, some of which may be shared with others. PICK controls information in a similar fashion. As with a company which has files of information stored within individual departments, PICK groups together logical files of information which it calls **accounts**.

In order to keep control of these accounts, PICK assigns a the **system dictionary (mds** or **system)** which is at the top of the PICK data structure hierarchy. In our company analogy of course, this position is held by the managing director!

From this point on, a company is broken down into divisions each controlled by a single director. In PICK the system is divided into a series of

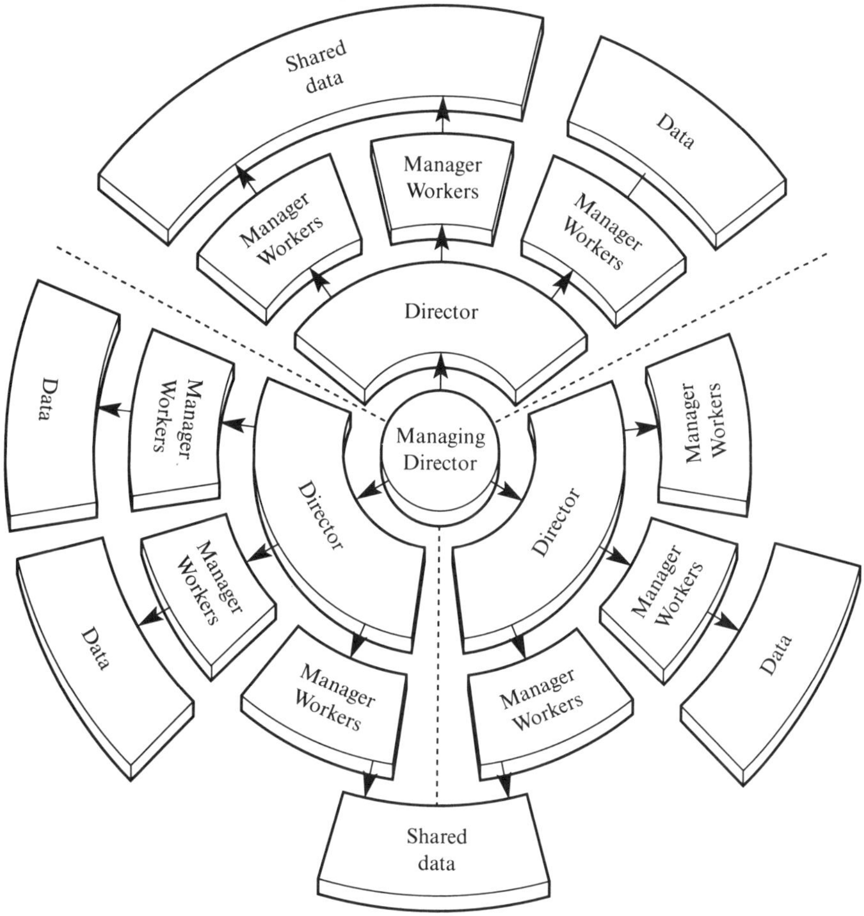

Figure 3.2 The company structure.

accounts, each controlled by a single **master dictionary**. Each director has a number of managers controlling specific departments, each of which has its own data files stored in drawers, filing cabinets and so on. In PICK each account can have a number of **data files**, each controlled by a **data dictionary**.

To look at the details of a particular stock record in a manual stock system it would be necessary to go to the stock file containing a number of records and locate the appropriate record by means of its stock code, a *unique* code used to identify the product.

PICK controls information in its files in a similar way, except that it calls records **items** and requires a key which in PICK terminology is referred to as the **item-id**.

In any office the records kept by one department are usually different both in content and format to those of another. Quite frequently the information held is clarified by having headings on the record cards which define the nature of the information held in a specific part of the record. Indeed, many parts of a record may contain a code which, whilst not always known to outside departments, are applied by known rules within the department in which the records are kept. In PICK this sort of information, the structure of the data, is held in a **file dictionary** called **DICT**, which defines the format and shape of the data itself. These 'parts' of a record are frequently referred to as 'fields' in data processing, but within PICK they are called **attributes**. Figure 3.3 represents the way in which files are broken down into items, each of which contains attributes with one of these being the item-id. In this example the filing cabinet represents the **file**, a particular stock record card, an **item**, the unique stock code used to identify the stock record card, the **item-id** and the elements of data on the stock record cards, the **attributes**.

In the same way that a departmental head is responsible for the control and security of the information in his department, PICK mirrors this by assigning one **master dictionary** to each account. Each account, therefore, has a master dictionary and a series of data dictionaries each controlling respective data files. Logging on to an Advanced PICK system consists of registering as a user to the system. Authorized user details are held in the file **USERS** and optionally the record in the users file will contain information about the account the user is to log to and by entering the user-id, the user will be validated as an authorized user and automatically logged to the specified account. If automatic logging is not defined in the user record, then the user has to log to one of the accounts of the system. In R83 the **USERS** file does not exist so the process of logging on is to log to an account. In PICK you log to an account rather than to the system in general. Without setting pointers to information held outside the account, the only information available to you is that held within the account you are logged to. The use of these pointers, known as **Q-pointers**, is fundamental to the workings of any PICK system and is described in detail in Chapter 9.

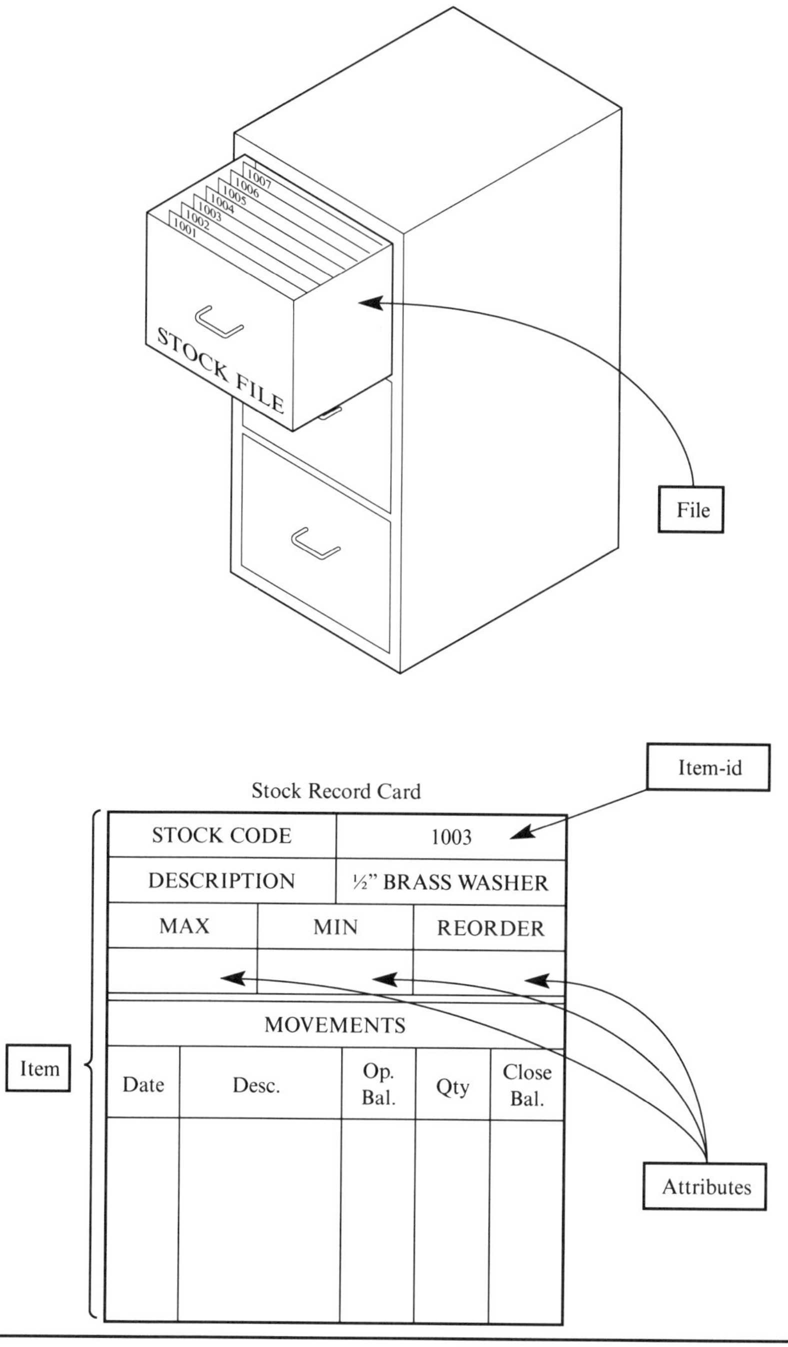

Figure 3.3 PICK terminology explained.

4 Getting Started

TCL verbs and general commands covered in this chapter

COUNT	CT	FLUSH	LIST	LISTFILES	LISTVERBS
LOGOFF		LOGON	LOGTO	OFF	SORT

4.1 Powering up and powering down

4.1.1 Powering up

PICK was designed as a multi-user operating system and requires at least one hard disk. The system will also have a backup device for the hard disk such as floppy disk, $\frac{1}{4}$ inch cartridge tape, $\frac{1}{2}$ inch reel-to-reel tape or DAT ($\frac{1}{4}$ mm digital audio tape) device. Attached to the computer will be a number of peripherals such as terminals (VDUs) and printers. None of these are usable until the PICK operating system has been loaded and is operational, assuming of course that PICK is the only operating system the computer supports. Advanced PICK can host itself as a database on many other operating systems, such as UNIX and DOS. Even as a 'host' Advanced PICK still offers most of the operating system functionality it does as a native operating system, but does so by interacting with the host operating system.

Regardless of whether or not Advanced PICK is the native operating system, Advanced PICK has to be initiated and the process is the same and the messages displayed identical. In its native form as an operating system, the day-by-day process of loading PICK is called 'booting' the system. On some R83 systems this can be handled in one of two ways, by invoking the **cold-start** or **warm-start** procedures, with Advanced PICK the only way to invoke it is with the cold-start procedure.

Advanced PICK boot procedure

One of the problems with R83 was the length of time taken to boot the system, primarily associated with the linking of workspace. The greater the number of users, the longer the time it took. Fortunately under Advanced PICK with the possibility of several hundred users this process is no longer required as the workspace for each port is allocated when Advanced PICK is first loaded and the PIB (Process Information Block) for each user cleaned out each time Advanced PICK is booted. So loading Advanced PICK takes under around 30 seconds by comparison to the many minutes it took with R83. The first step in the boot process is the initialization of the software clock. Then the spooler, scheduler and overflow processes are initiated. The PIBs for each port are set up and any tandem connections left over from a system crash are broken. Then the appropriate terminal type is established for port 0, the console port. This varies by AP platform as follows:

Platform	Terminal type
AP/RS6000	IBM 3151
AP/SCO	ANSI
AP/Native	MM-MON
AP Native	MM-MON
AP/DOS	MM-MON
AP/3B2	ATT605
Others	Wyse 50

Once this has been done all ports are set to their default values, the standard *abs* is linked in and the user's coldstart macro invoked. The *abs* area is where the PICK virtual (operating system) resides. The user's coldstart macro normally sets custom options, such as starting printers and setting baud rates. The user's coldstart macro completed, the system is set in either single or multi-user's mode (dependent on the licence purchased) and just prior to the port being logged off it spawns a background process to verify the ABS area. This causes a 'job submitted' message prior to the logon message and the ABS verified message thereafter. Figure 4.1 gives an example of a typical Advanced PICK boot session.

Early versions of Advanced PICK did not give the opportunity for a file restore using the **:files** verb and users had to reboot from the PICK floppy disks and select the file restore option. The system should also be booted from floppy when additional serial cards are added. Booting from floppy gives the following options:

OPTIONS:	**K**)ill	to delete the existing PICK partition
	F)ile	reload the file system
	A)BS	reload the ABS area
	X)execute	initialize PICK monitor

Whilst you will have to boot from floppy disk when working with Advanced PICK on the PC, some systems boot from other media such as quarter inch tapes or pseudo tapes.

R83 boot procedure

In R83, cold-start procedures vary from machine to machine and you should refer to your manual for the one specific to your system; however the tasks undertaken are very much the same. The cold-start procedure is a list of instructions that have to be performed each time a machine is powered up (without a prior 'warm save', discussed later) to set up the working environment of the system. It consists of PICK checking the number of ABS frames, and checking the availability of ports, memory, disk space, and the physical devices such as printers and tape drives. Following this the monitor, which controls all input, output and process scheduling, is loaded into memory and the spooler is started. The start-up options are then displayed. These are usually:

X for eXecute, when workspace is re-linked, following which the cold-start PROC (procedure) is executed.

F for File restore, which acts as with X but also restores the entire data area and reorganizes the disk from a tape or diskette backup.

```
Copyright (c) PICK Systems 1973-1992.
All Rights Reserved.

  WARNING, this computer program is protected by Copyright law and
international treaties. Unauthorized reproduction or distribution of
this program, or any portion of this program, may result in severe
civil and criminal penalties, and will be prosecuted to the maximum
extent possible under law. The PICK System and Flash BASIC are
registered trademarks of PICK Systems.

** End User must accept the terms and conditions of the PICK System
Software License Agreement before completing installation.


Pick O/S : 00005FC0 is explicitly licensed to :
     APT Solutions Limited
     Roger Bourdon
     0171-704 8006


Press <enter> to continue ...
Diagnostics....successfully completed
07:12:47 11 Sep 1994
[507] Scheduler started
[1138] Spooler jobs are cleared
[1139] The Spooler is started

Term setting 79,25,0,7,1,8,132,58,MM-MON
Serial Devices Configuration......completed
Boot-ABS base:24 Size: 1800 Frames added: 0

[1118] Printer 0 control block initialised



<<< 07:12:47 -- A d v a n c e d  P i c k -- 11 Sep 1994         >>>
<<<                                                              >>>
<<< Copyright (c) 1991 PICK Systems. All rights reserved.        >>>
<<< This work is property of, and embodies trade secrets and     >>>
<<< confidential information proprietary to PICK Systems. It     >>>
<<< may not be reproduced, copied, used, disclosed, transferred  >>>
<<< adapted or modified without the express written approval of  >>>
<<< PICK Systems.                                                >>>

15 Oct 1992 at-dos

[438] Job #975178053 submitted.

Logon Please
21:42:04 11 Sep 1994 from user dm line 4
ABS file 'DM,ABS,' verifies!
```

Figure 4.1 The Advanced PICK boot procedure.

Whilst you should refer to your manual for the actual procedure to follow, a typical cold-start session is shown in Figure 4.2. If no cold-start procedure exists in the main system management account (SYSPROG) on your system, PICK will try to log to an account called COLDSTART (the password is usually CS) to run the cold-start procedure. If this account is missing it will display the error message USER-ID? and take you straight to the logon prompt.

The cold-start procedure (PROC) usually prompts for date and time, and on some implementations will ask for the port the printer is attached to. These ports start at zero, so if the printer is in the third physical port you should advise PICK that the printer is 'attached' to port two. The XXXXXX in the LOGON message normally refers to the make of equipment you are using and is usually customized by your supplier.

Some manufacturers provide a controlled shutdown procedure which enables a copy of the memory of the system to be written to disk when the system is powered off and written back into memory when the machine is pow-

```
LOADER VERSION 4.0.0
R204 DD/MM/YY

512KB RAM
OPTIONS (X,F) = X[CR]

SPOOLER STARTED
LINKING WORKSPACE FOR LINE 0
****************************************************************************
LOGON TO XXXXXX AT 10:42:56mm
**********************************************************
<<<                                                    >>>
<<<                                                    >>>
<<<                                                    >>>
**********************************************************
THIS IS THE SYSTEM SETUP PROCEDURE

Now setting the default terminal type for this system

The computer's clock currently shows 10:43:03 12 MAY 1995

Enter the correct time (press RETURN if it is correct)
   (Example 13:01 sets the clock to one minute after 1PM) =[CR]

Enter the correct date (press return if it is correct)
   (Example 15MAY95 for MAY 15th 1995)= [CR]

What port is your printer plugged into?
(RETURN for no printer) =[CR]
*******************************************************
*                                                     *
*                                                     *
*******************************************************

  LOGON TO XXXXXX AT 10:43:55 :
```

Figure 4.2 The R83 cold-start process.

ered up again. The system effectively starts from where it left off, in which case the options X or F will not be presented, nor is a cold-start procedure required as the working environment is already defined. This booting facility is called a 'warm boot' of the operating system.

Once the start-up processes are complete a logon prompt will be given. This is another area where PICK systems differ, since invariably this screen will have been customized by your supplier. The message displayed at logon is held in a file called SYSTEM under the name LOGON. After you have logged on, the message LOGON from the file ERRMSG is displayed followed by another ERRMSG item called 335. The item 335, displayed each time anyone logs on, is usually used to contain day-to-day messages and forms a useful control mechanism for System Administrators.

4.1.2 Powering down

This is the procedure of closing down the system and switching off the power. There may be a controlled procedure supplied by your manufacturer, in which case it should be followed implicitly. In most Advanced PICK implementations the command is **EXIT** or **SHUTDOWN.** Figure 4.3 gives an example of the typical Advanced PICK power down process.

If you find that **EXIT**, **SHUTDOWN** or :**SHUTDOWN** are not verbs in the **dm** account (the **SYSPROG** account in R83), then you should ensure that everyone else is logged off the system and run the TCL command **FLUSH**. This verb flushes memory to disk after which it will be safe to power off the system. If you cannot carry out a FLUSH wait until *all* disk activity has stopped, normally about minute (but can be longer if your system has a large amount of RAM), before turning off the system. This ensures that any data held in memory is written to disk.

If the system is not shut down in one of these controlled ways it is possible that valuable information will be lost, and the integrity of files affected. This is because of the workings of the memory management system which is

```
Executing system shutdown procedure ....
Do you wish to continue (y/n) ?
Terminating all print jobs ....

Wrapping up process on line 1
Wrapping up process on line 2
                ↓

Wrapping up process on line nn
Wrapping up current process on line 0
Pause for wrapup processing to complete .....

Flushing memory, boot when disk is quiescent ....
```

Figure 4.3 The Advanced PICK power down procedure.

able to hold data in memory for long periods of time without updating the records held on disk. From version 6.1 Advanced PICK onwards a new feature called Halt Tolerance was introduced. This does *not* eliminate virtual memory, but does eliminate file corruption. It does so by making updates of linked overflow in a two-phase commit process. If the update does not complete, due to an improper system shutdown or hang, then it automatically 'rolls back' to the previous state. In this way the dreaded phenomenon of GFEs can be avoided.

4.2 Logging on and logging off

4.2.1 Logging on

Once the equipment is powered up, logging on consists of logging to an account (a group of logically related files), by either giving an account name or user identity. As an Advanced PICK user, you will first need to identify yourself as an authorized user. All authorized users have a record (a PICK item) in the file **USERS**. The raw Advanced PICK system comes with just two user codes, **dm** and **SYSPROG**, but you can create any number of others. It also comes with a specialized user account **dm** (in R83 it is called SYSPROG, the System Programming account). After having entered your user-id, enter the name of the account you wish to log to; you will be prompted for the name of the Master Dictionary of the account. There is no password on the **dm** account when the system is first installed, so one of the first jobs will be to set one, otherwise anyone with even a very limited knowledge of Advanced PICK will be able to gain access to your system (see Section 20.1.3 about setting passwords). It is worth noting at this point that a raw PICK system has several other accounts, but none of them are should be logged to, because in their own right they do not do anything useful, but each is an important part of the entire Advanced PICK environment. A typical logon session would be:

```
Logon Please dm[CR]
Term setting: 79,25,0,7,1,8,132,58,MM-MON

[1301] The Speller is off.

[1307] The time-date display is off.
master dictionary: dm[CR]

<<<  07:12:47 -- A d v a n c e d  P i c k  --  11 Sep 1994     >>>
<<<                                                              >>>
<<<  Copyright (c) 1991 PICK Systems. All rights reserved.       >>>
<<<  This work is property of, and embodies trade secrets and    >>>
<<<  confidential information proprietary to PICK Systems. It    >>>
```

```
<<<  may not be reproduced, copied, used, disclosed, transferred
>>>
<<<  adapted or modified without the express written approval of >>>
<<<  PICK Systems.   >>>

15 Oct 1992 at-dos
:
```

The : (colon) symbol is the command line prompt (on R83 systems this is a > (greater than) symbol). At this point you are deemed to be at TCL. If you are at the TCL prompt and wish to log to a particular account, then you can use the **LOGTO** command and under Advanced PICK you can also use **TO**, a macro which invokes the **LOGTO** verb.

4.2.2 Logging off

Logging off consists of typing **OFF** at the TCL prompt. If you need to log off another terminal, other than the one you are using, the TCL command is **LOGOFF**. The form of this command is:

LOGOFF {*port.number*}(options [CR] (remember that braces indicate options)

If no part number is entered you will be asked for the channel (otherwise known as port or line) of the terminal you want to log off:

CHANNEL:

By entering **1** (the number one) the terminal on port one will be logged off, assuming it exists and is in use. In R83 there is a **U** or unconditional option, i.e. **LOGOFF 1 (U**. If the line specified does not exist, an error message is displayed:

[535] ILLEGAL LINE NUMBER

This is just one of many messages within PICK that use the word *illegal*. It sounds a little daunting, but all it really means is that you got it wrong! The number 535 in square brackets is the reference number of the error message held in the file **MESSAGES** (in R83 the file is called **ERRMSG**). All error messages are held in the file **MESSAGES** and we will review this file later. For a full list of these messages refer to Appendix A. It is more likely that you will get the channel number correct, in which case, after logging off the requested line, a confirmation message is displayed.

```
[534] LOGOFF SUCCESSFUL
```

In this case, the **MESSAGES** file is used to display confirmation of the action taken Two other possibilities may occur when you try to use the **LOGOFF** command. Firstly, that the terminal is already logged off, in which case you are told so:

```
[536] ALREADY LOGGED OFF
```

Alternatively it may be that the terminal is not switched on, in which case the terminal being used to log off the other may 'hang', until the terminal on the appropriate line is switched on. On the occasions when the terminal to be logged off cannot be switched on, it is possible to break out of the **LOGOFF** process by using the BREAK key if your terminal has one, failing that by depressing c (CTRL (control) and C together) or another combination of keys as advised by your System Administrator. By doing so you are entering into what is called DEBUG and an exclamation mark is displayed. Any process can be terminated in this way, although use of this facility in novice hands can be exceedingly dangerous. For this reason users are frequently prevented from being able to BREAK a process in this way and enter the debugger. The display format being

```
I a.b
!
```

> where a.b refers to the operating system frame a (the term 'frame' is explained later; it is basically an area of the disk containing a fixed number of characters) and b the position within it (shown in hexadecimal), at the time of the BREAK. Typically this would look like:

```
I 278.41C
!
```

The cursor will wait by the ! for information to be typed in. Debug is one of the areas of PICK where considerable damage can be done by the inexperienced user, so frequently the ability to break into the system is restricted. If it can be used then there are two safe entries to make at this point, **END** which takes you to TCL or **OFF** which will log you off the system, displaying the system accounting information and the logon prompt, as shown in Figure 4.4.

Having established the means of logging on and off our next step is to explore the system further. The next chapter looks at the primary data files in the **dm** account.

```
<     CONNECT TIME = 3 MINS.; CPU = 20 UNITS;LPTR PAGES = 0              >
<     LOGGED OFF AT 12:23:14        ON 7 DEC 1995           >


<<<  07:12:47 -- A d v a n c e d  P i c k -- 11 Sep 1994              >>>
<<<                                                                   >>>
<<<  Copyright (c) 1991 PICK Systems. All rights reserved.            >>>
<<<  This work is property of, and embodies trade secrets and         >>>
<<<  confidential information proprietary to PICK Systems. It         >>>
<<<  may not be reproduced, copied, used, disclosed, transferred      >>>
<<<  adapted or modified without the express written approval of     >>>
<<<  PICK Systems.                                                    >>>

Logon Please
```

Figure 4.4 A typical display when logging off.

5 Looking Around Your System

In the earlier chapters we have explored the general structure of the PICK database and know how to log on and off . This chapter explores the various accounts and files which are supplied with a standard version of Advanced PICK. Not all Advanced PICK implementations are identical so you may find certain of the details given in this chapter differ from what you can find on your own system. However, the core of PICK is fundamental, so much, if not all, of what is explained here will be of value.

5.1 The prime accounts and their files

If we wish to review our system, the first step is to look at the contents of the file **mds**, which we know is the top level file. The contents can be determined with the command **SORT ONLY MDS** which reveals around 37 items. Since this is the file which controls ACCOUNTS (i.e. **M**aster **D**ictionarie**S**) it would be reasonable to assume that all these items are themselves names of accounts, but in fact that is not the case. The items in **mds** which are accounts are:

dm
pa
qa

There are two Q-pointers (or synonyms) which are provided for people familiar with R83 and to help them with the transition to Advanced PICK:

sysprog	a Q-pointer to **dm**
system	a Q-pointer to **mds**

There are two items associated with logging on:

logon	the logon banner
logon.err	the message displayed when the maximum number of users has been exceeded

The remaining items are attribute defining items which can be used when listing items from the **mds** file:

acct.name
attribute-type
base
base/dict
justification
mod/data
modulo
password

reallocation
ret-lock
syspriv
type
upd-lock
width

The most important account on your system is **dm** that of the **D**ata **M**anager (**SYSPROG** in R83). The following section describes the account in detail, explaining the files within the account and the role they play.

5.2 The dm account

Assuming you have logged to the **dm** account and are now at the TCL prompt, the : (colon) sign, or that you have been able to select TCL as one of your **dm** menu options, we can look at some simple TCL commands. At TCL we can now look at the original files supplied with your system. The list of available files is produced by using the command **LISTFILES** and is illustrated in Figure 5.1. It should be pointed out that the display you get from the command could be different to that shown in Figure 5.1 and if it is please don't be alarmed as different implementations may have some different files, but in the main the file names should be similar. The numbers following the names will more than likely differ as this indicates their physical location on the hard disk and is dependent on a number of factors about the physical hardware, so is likely to vary system by system.

```
:LISTFILES

Page 1 *** DICT DM,MD, *** File Defining Items            12 Sep 1994
DICT DM,MD,. code F/BASE... F/MOD. DESCRIPTION.......................

abs            d  3101  1
accounts       D  7461  1      System usage accounting.
block-convert  D  5542  1      Instructions for characters used by
                               block-print verb.
bp             D  5591  1
bulletin       D  2914  1
devices        D  5082  1      Legal device types.
devs           D  2955  1
errors         D  5388  7      System errors.
file-of-files  D  7398  3      Master file-of-files.
fonts          d  5502  3
funckeys       D  5561  1      Function key layouts.
gsym           d  7405  1      Global symbols.
iomap-file     D  5576  1
jobs           D  7393  1      Phantom jobs status and history.
kb.fk          D  5530  1
```

Figure 5.1 The output from **LISTFILES**.

```
kb.pc          D 5570  1
keyboards      D 2925  1        Keyboard layouts.
messages       D 2965  1        System messages.
newac          D 2830  1        Master dictionary items copied to new
                                accounts
pibs           D 7491  3        Process identification blocks.
pointer-file   D 7501  1        Stores data from save-list verb.
tcl-stack      D 5566  1        Tcl command stack.
users          D 7521  1        Authorized users
words          D 5586  1

             ***

CLASHES        DX 88044 1

             ***
acc            q                daccounts system usage accounting.
admin.bp       q bp.qa,admin
bc             q block-convert  instructions for characters used by block-
                                print verb.
dm-bp          q dm bp          system utility programs
dv             q dm devices
er             q dm errors      system errors.
errmsg         q dm messages    system messages.
ff             q file-of-files  master file of files.
files          q file-of-files  master file of files.
fk             q dfunckeys      function key layouts.
fof            q file-of-files  master file of files.
jb             q dm jobs        phantom jobs status and history.
kb             q keyboards      keyboard layouts.
m/dict         q                the item.id of a dictionary item is the
                                name of the language element being defined.
md             q                the item.id of a dictionary item is the
                                name of the language element being defined.
mds            q mds            highest level file; can be accessed from dm
                                account.
msgs           q dmessages      system messages.
pb             q dm             pibs process identification blocks.
pf             q                pointer-file stores data from save-list
                                verb.
psym           q dm gsym
stat-file      q file-of-files  master file of files.
sysprog-bp     q dm bp          system utility programs
SYSPROG-PL     Q DM BP
system         q mds            highest level file; can be accessed from dm
                                account.
system-errors  q dm errors
ts             q tcl-stack      tcl command stack.
             ***
**

[405] 51 items listed out of 948 items.
:
```

Figure 5.1 *Continued.*

This TCL verb reports on the files within the **dm** account, lists their file type (see Section 7.1.3) under the heading **CODE** and gives information about the location and size of each file under the remaining three headings. The report is broken into sections based on file type. The first section where the code is **D** shows the real data files, the section with the **CLASHES** file shows the type **DX** which means the file is a real file but is not saved when the disk is backed up to tape and the section where the file type is **Q** shows synonyms (or alternative names) for real files, but the names listed with a **Q** against them are not data files within this account. There are a number of system files listed and their function is as follows:

5.2.1 The abs file

The **abs** file contains the operating system symbols for use by technical support personnel. This file is connected to the boot ABS file by the TCL verb **set-abs**. The abs file has multiple item-ids (record keys): the item-id for the three-digit fid (frame identifier) number and the item-ids for the mode names that go into those fids.

5.2.2 The accounts file

The **accounts** file contains the history of charge units usage by user. To capture accounting data for a specific user add the character **a** to the options in attribute (9) in the **users** file. An item exists in the **accounts** file for each authorized user. The item-id from the **users** file is the item-id in the **accounts** file. Accounting may be suppressed system-wide by removing the **accounts** file. Accounting information is gathered from the **pibs** file at logoff. The **accounts** file contains items (records) with the following attributes (fields)

0	user	Item.id consists of user id
1	md	Name of md (item-id in mds file) for the accounting period data
2	l-date	Log date of the accounting information
3	l-time	Log time of the accounting data
4	acct-time	Accounting period to the second
5	cpu	Central Processing Unit (cpu) execution time in tenths of a second, used by this process for the accounting period for accounting period
6	pages	Number of printer pages output for the accounting period

5.2.3 The block-convert file

The **block-convert** file contains the instructions used by the TCL verb **block-print** to display enlarged characters. Each master dictionary has a pointer to this file that is created when the account is created.

5.2.4 The bulletin file

This file contains company messages to be displayed when a user logs on. The item-id is the date the message was created, with attribute 1 the creators name, attribute 2 the title of the message and attribute 3 the message itself. To have the message displayed add **bulletin.board** to the users logon MACRO. Bulletins over 7 days old are automatically purged.

5.2.5 The bp file

The **bp** file contains Pick BASIC programs for system utilities. The master dictionary for each account has a q-pointer item that points to this file.

5.2.6 The devices file

The **devices** file contains an item for every device (terminals and printers) recognized by the Pick System. These devices can be attached to any process. The item-ids are device codes (e.g. WY-100 for the WYSE WY-100 video display terminal). To define additional devices, use the **define-terminal** command.

5.2.7 The devs file

The file used by the **TANDEM CONVERSE** and **MIRROR** processes.

5.2.8 The errors file

The **errors** file contains error and **log-msg** messages. This file is used to determine how well the system is functioning. The item-ids are ten-digit date-time stamps (five-digit date plus five-digit time) plus an alpha character for multiple creations within a second. The specific types of errors which generate messages are:

- System errors:
  Illegal opcode, crossing frame limit, forward link zero, backward link zero, priv opcode, illegal frame reference, disk error, stack format error, overflow release error, gfe, index B-tree error.
- Logoff commands.
- Errors from the TPS (test procedure suite) in the QA account.

The attributes of this file are as follows:

ac..	attribute-name		description...........................	
0	date		Date error was logged.	
0	timedate		Item-id in errors file consists of date and time error was logged.	
1	error		Error code. Possible errors are:	
	01	phantom read	02	rtn full
	03	zero fid	04	frm lmt

05	fwd link	06	ck link
07	priv op	08	bad fid
09	disk err	0a	break
0b	stk fmt	0c	lvl push
0e	end off	0f	trace
11	gfe count	12	gfe link
13	gfe body	14	gfe hash
15	b-tree index	6	ovf mul rel
17	end	18	unused
19	logoff	1a	overflow runaway
1b	ovf abort	20	ovf signature error
21	ovf link error	22	fcb corruption
p	tps program error	s	shutdown

2	user	The user of the error logging process.
3	r	Register triggering the error.
4	mode-addr	Mode address when the error occurred.
5	abs-fid	Base fid of the abs area executed by the process.
6	pgm-ctr	Program counter when the error occurred.
7	abs-date	Creation date of the abs in which the error occurred.
8	abs-imp	Implementation type of the abs in which the error occurred.
11	pcb-fid	Process control block (pcb) frame id.
12	userpib	The user and pib of the error logging process.
20	registers	Process register image.
21	run-stack	Process execution stack.
22	last-tcl-entry	The last three tcl stack entries.
23	gfe-fid	Contains four values: (1) frame id of the group with gfe, (2) address (in storage register format) of the item in which the gfe was detected, (3) forward link of the frame in which the gfe occurred, (4) backward link of the same frame.
24	gfe-file	The path name of the file in which the gfe was found.

5.2.9 The file-of-files file

The **file-of-files** file contains statistical information for each file on the system. **file-of-files** items are created when a file is restored or created. The **file-of-files** file is also used to locate files on the disk during restores from incremental and transaction-log tapes. The item-ids are sequential file numbers assigned when the file is created. File number one is always the **file-of-files** file and file number two is always the **mds** file. The numbers of the other files are determined by the order in which they are restored or created. On a file or account restore, the files are recreated in the order in which they were saved on the file save media.

The attributes of the **file-of-files** are as follows:

ac..	attribute-name	description......................
0	f-fms	Total number of frames in the primary file space as of the last file save.
0	f-size	Total number of bytes in the primary file space as of the last file save.
0	file#	Item-id assigned in the order in which the file was created.
0	t-frames	Total number of frames in the file space as of the last file save.
1	md	Name of the md owning the file.
2	file-name	File name stored in the master dictionary (md) of the account.
3	data-name	One dictionary may have many subsidiary data files each with its own unique name. The default data section name is identical to the file name as stored in the md.
4	base	Base of file.
4	mod	Modulo of file. The number of contiguous frames comprising the primary file space concatenated.
5	items	Total number (including pointer items) of items in the file from last file save.
6	ptr-items	Number of pointer items saved in the last file save.
7	ovf-itms	Number of items which were partially or wholly stored in secondary file space during the last file save.
8	bytes	Total number of bytes in file as of last file save.
9	ptr-bytes	Total number of bytes in all pointer items as of last file save.
10	frames	Total number of frames in file as of the last file save.
11	ptr-fms	Total number of frames of pointer items as of the last file save.
12	svdate	Date when file was last saved.
13	reel#	Tape, diskette, etc. number in a multi 'reel' file save where this file begins.
14	seq#	Decimal sequence number indicating the order in which the file was saved on the file save media.
15	opendate	Date when file was last opened (update at save-time).
16	stat#	Number of last file save on which this file was saved.
18	file-code	Valid file statuses are: **c** clear file; **d** delete file; **n** new file; **r** rename file; **t** restored from tape. This attribute controls attributes 19 (timedate) and 20 (user).
19	timedate	Time-date when file activity occurred. This attribute is dependent on attribute 18 (file-code).
20	user	User-id concatenated with account-id causing the associated file action. This attribute is dependent on attribute 18 (file-code).
21	dx/dy-date	Date when dx/dy file was skipped on save.
25	save-list	Contains list of specific items to be saved for this file. Used to selectively save items in a file. Each item name is an attribute. Therefore, list extends from attribute 25 to as far as necessary. To save all items in a file, use an asterisk (*).

5.2.10 The fonts file

This is the file containing the fonts to be downloaded to a laser printer with the TCL verb DOWNLOAD.

5.2.11 The funckeys file

The **funckeys** file contains pre-set function key definition items. This file is used with the TCL verb **set-func**. Function keys can also be part of the overall keyboard definition item in the **keyboard** file selected by using the **set-kbrd** verb.

5.2.12 The gsym file

This is the file which contain global symbols which are used to reference the system-wide set of global variables. It contains in the order of 1,500 items.

5.2.13 The iomap-file file

The **iomap-file** is used by the SET-IOMAP command for one-to-one keyboard input and output translation. The data section of the file contains items that define the character translation. The dictionary level contains binary items which are compiled by the **set-iomap** program when used with the c option. The items in the dictionary have the same item-id's as the corresponding items in the data section, except that the dictionary items are preceded and followed by a %.

5.2.14 The jobs file

The **jobs** file contains data for each phantom job submitted for execution. The item-ids are ten-digit date-time stamps (five digit date plus five digit time) plus an alpha character for multiple logs within a second. An item also exists for each pib currently being used by a phantom job. The decimal pib number is the item-id.

An item also exists in the '**jobs**' file for each port currently being used by a phantom job. The various status options are

- **c** Done
- **e** Error
- **l** Logoff
- **p** Sched id
- **q** Queue
- **r** Running
- **s** Abort

The attributes of the **jobs** file are as follows:

ac..	attribute-name	description......................
0	item-id	Item-id of the jobs file.
1	status	Status of phantom job.
2	user	User who submitted the job.
3	md	Execution md of the job.
4	command	TCL command for job execution.
5	out	Output status of the job: **n** Spooler hold file number **m** Message back enabled **s** All output suppressed.
6	who	Port.number which initiated the job.
7	start	Date the job was actually started.
8	startt	Time the job was actually started.
9	tcl-command	TCL command for job execution.
11	pcb-fid	Process control block (pcb) frame id of the job.
12	pib	Pib or port.number where job is running.
15	stopd	Date the job terminated.
16	stop	Time the job finished.

The 'phantom scheduler' keeps two queues in the dictionary of the **jobs** file these being

%Q contains all jobs waiting to be run,
%R contains all finished jobs not yet released back to overflow.

5.2.15 The kb.fk file

The **kb.fk** file is used for mapping the keyboard on the console of AP/SCO of PC-class implementations only.

5.2.16 The kb.pc file

This file is used for keyboard mapping.

5.2.17 The keyboards file

The **keyboards** file contains several alternative keyboard definitions, including British, French, German, Italian, Spanish and USA. This file is used with the TCL verb **set-kbrd**.

5.2.18 The messages file

The **messages** file contains messages used by system processes to convey information to the user. The item-ids are the message numbers used by the system processes. The **newmd** item, used to create new accounts, the **logon** item, used by the logon processor, and the **bnf** item, used by the BASIC processor, are also stored in the **messages** file.

The items in the messages file use the following codes to format messages in the output buffer before displaying them:

a {(**n**)}	inserts into the output buffer the next parameter from the list of parameters passed with the message; the parameter is left justified in a field of n blanks
d	places the current date in the output buffer
e	inserts the message number (item-id in **messages** file) into the output buffer
h	places the string in the output buffer, with no carriage return or line feed; to inhibit the carriage return that is normally sent at the end of the message, use the form string
l{(**n**)}	prints the output buffer, followed by n-l blank lines
r{(**n**)}	inserts the next parameter right-justified in a field of blanks
s(**n**)	inserts n spaces in the output buffer
t	places the current time in the output buffer
x	skips a parameter in the parameter list

5.2.19 The newac file

The **newac** file contains all the master dictionary items which are copied to each new PICK account.

5.2.20 The pibs file

The **pibs** (**p**rocess **i**dentification **b**lock) file contains an item for each pib tied to a process. A pib is required for each process executing on the system. The items in the **pibs** file define the memory resident hooks of the process work spaces which, at any given time, may be in main memory or may reside solely on disk. The **pibs** file also defines the physical devices connected to the system's ports. The pib numbers are the item-ids. (Device characteristics are derived from the **pibs** file and the **devices** file. The pibs item specifies the device type and the devices item defines device characteristics and drive functions.)

Attributes for pibs:

1	location	The physical location (e.g. Mary's desk) of the devic connected to the pib.
2	device	Item-id (in **devices** file) identifying the specific device on the line (e.g. wy-50); when the line becomes active it is automatically set-up to the device type.
3	status	This is the current status of the pib. It is a display-only attribute called through a program at list-time.
4	abs-fid	This is the frame number (fid) in decimal of the first frame in the contiguously linked machine code item (abs area) being executed. It is a display-only attribute called through a program at list-time.
5	pcb-fid	This is the frame number (fid) in decimal of the process control block (pcb) linked to this pib. It is a display-only attribute called through a program at list-time.

6 pgm-ctr	This is the program location and execution stack within the machine code item (abs area) where the process is currently executing. It is a display-only attribute called through a program at list-time.
7 user	This is the item-id (in **users** file) of user logged on to this pib. It is updated at user logon and deleted at logoff. It is used in the **accounts** file if accounting is enabled.
8 u-date	This is the date the user associated with this pib logged on to this user-id. It is updated at the same time as the user and is deleted at logoff.
9 u-time	This is the time of day the user logged on. It is updated at the same time as the user and is deleted at logoff.
10 md	This is the name of the md (item-id in **mds** file) this pib is logged on to. It is updated at md logon, and deleted at logoff. This is used in the **accounts** file if accounting is enabled.
11 md-date	This is the md logon date. It is updated at the same time as the md and is deleted at logoff. It is used in the **accounts** file if accounting is enabled.
12 md-time	This is the md logon time. It is updated at the same time as the md and is deleted at logoff. It is used in the **accounts** file if accounting is enabled.
13 cpu	This is the Central Processing Unit (cpu) execution time (in tenths of seconds) used by this process since logging on to the current account. It is a display-only attribute called through a program at list-time. It is used in the **accounts** file if accounting is enabled.
14 disk	This is the number of disk reads since logging on to the account. It is called through a program at list-time.
15 pages	This is the number of printer pages output since logging on to the account. It is a display-only attribute called through a program at list-time. It is used in the **accounts** file if accounting is enabled.
16 attdev	This is the list of attached devices.
18 linkdev	This is the linked device for the pib.

5.2.21 **The** pointer-file **file**

The **pointer-file** file is the default list file containing items from save-lists. The item-id defaults to % (per cent sign) concatenated with the user-id when not specified with the list process verbs such as SAVE-LIST or EDIT-LIST.

5.2.22 **The** tcl-stack **file**

The **tcl.stack** file contains a stack item for each user on the system. A stack item stores previously executed TCL commands which may be viewed, modified, and executed from TCL. The item.ids are the user ids.

5.2.23 **The** users **file**

The **users** file contains data for every authorized user of the system. The item-id is the user id. Attributes for the **users** file are as follows:

ac..	attribute-name	description......................
1	name	User's name.
2	address	User's address.
3	zip	User's zip code.
4	phone	User's phone number.
6	keys	User's retrieval and update keys.
7	password	Optional logon password(s).
8	privilege	User privilege level.
9	options	User options:
	a (or u)	Updates accounting history file at logoff.
	d	Disables 'end' and 'off' commands from either debugger.
	r	Restarts logon procedure on any <break>+end.
	g	Stops at GFE's and offers the options to '(L)ogoff, (C)ontinue, or (Q)uit'.
	m	Invokes the automatic GFE handler at any GFE found.
12	macro	User logon macro. This is the same as a TCL macro without the macro type code, (in attribute 1) which is assumed to be 'n' (for 'non-stop'). Any number of TCL commands may be placed on attributes 12 and beyond. Each command will be executed before the user is logged on.

5.2.24 The words file

The **words** file contains all the valid words used by **UP** (Update Processor) spelling checker. An index must be created for attribute 0 of the **words** file in order to activate the spelling checker.

5.3 The pa (Personal Assistant) account

This is a working account supplied for demonstration purposes. It controls names, addresses and telephone numbers and also has a simple bank account facility enabling the logging of cheques, the production of bank statements and the preparation and printing of expense reports.

The **pa** account consists of a single menu, a couple of MACROs, two primary files and four secondary files. It also contains eight BASIC programs so all in all provides a useful reference for new users to Advanced PICK, since most processing is handled by standard system processing codes stored in file dictionaries.

Data entry is handled through screens controlled by **UP** (the Update Processor) and the reports are generated using ACCESS.

5.4 The qa (Quality Assurance) account

The **qa** account is made up of programs that are used to test system functions and commands. The account also contains an option that is used to report bugs and suggest enhancements to PICK systems.

5.5 Exploring your Master Dictionary

As described in Chapter 3, each account is controlled by its Master Dictionary (MD). There is only one MD per account and its contents dictate what can be done within the account. The Master Dictionary contains

TCL verbs
MACROs
MENUs
PROCs
ACCESS enquiry language
File pointers
Q-pointers
Catalogue entries for BASIC programs

There are a number of useful TCL verbs which will enable you to determine the contents of your Master Dictionary. The **LIST** command will list items in a file in the sequence in which they are stored (a totally random order), whilst using the command **SORT** will provide a list of the same items but in alphabetical sequence of their key (referred to in PICK as the item-id).

First try the commands

:LIST DEVICES[CR]
:SORT DEVICES[CR]

You will notice in both cases that, in addition to the item-id (key) being listed, a lot of other information relating to the item is also printed. In a large file where you are only interested in knowing which items exist in a file, this can be not only annoying and confusing, but also time wasting. If you wish to limit the information displayed to show only the item-id, then include the word ONLY in your command.

The first and most obvious command in exploring your MD is **SORT ONLY MD** which will sort the items in the MD in alphabetical order, but this will not explain what type of item each is. To determine the item type use **SORT MD V/DESC** which will provide a list similar to that shown below:

```
:assignfq        macro
:bootstrap       TCL VERB
:ccompile        Basic verb
:dcd             TCL VERB
:listabs         macro
:pmsg            Basic verb
:pxpupdate       Catalog itm
:reset-async     Basic verb
:shutdown        TCL VERB
:startspooler    macro
<                undefined
<=               undefined
```

But even so, it is not ideal to have all the types of item mixed together. There are several TCL verbs which can be used to isolate groups of items, such as MACROs MENUs and verbs and the most useful of these are listed below.

list-commands
list-files
list-jobs
list-lists
list-macros
list-menus
list-verbs

Typical output from each of these is shown below:

:list-commands md

```
   08 Oct 1994            Verb Listings            Page 1

v/name........ v/desc.... v/type v/mode  v/flags v/cat..........

!              TCL VERB   vs     17
:assignfq      macro      n      assignfq
:bootstrap     TCL VERB   vr     d
:ccompile      Basic verb VR     3        F       dm,bp, :ccompile    9
:dcd           TCL VERB   v0     2
:listabs       macro      n      sort pctl without a0 "p]" "q]" "b]" "t
:pmsg          Basic verb VR     3        F       dm,bp, :pmsg        9
:reset-async   Basic verb VR     3        F       dm,bp, :reset-async
```

:list-files

```
Page 1         dm account  MD file listing         20:05:28 08 Oct 1994
dict-name         base     mod     data-name           base       mod
abs               3348      1      abs                 3350       397
                                   dbsym               5062       307
accounts          8499      1      accounts            8501       27
block-convert     5933      1      block-convert       5935       11ds
bp                6004      7      bp                  6012       31
                                   dos                 7186       3
                                   includes            7200       3
                                   unix.h              7161       3
bulletin          3043      1      bulletin            3045       7dy
```

:list-jobs

```
PHANTOM JOBS STATUS AT 20:06:16 08 Oct 1994                         PAGE 1

user-md.... ln. pib status.... start-dt.... stop-dt.... tcl-command....

dm DM         0  4  done(23)       09/27 13:58 09/27 13:58 verify-system
dm DM         0  4  done(1)        9/23 15:37 09/23 15:37 T-REW
dm DM         0  4  done(456)      09/23 13:00 09/23 13:08 init-ovf
dm DM         0  4  done(270)      09/23 12:56 09/23 13:01 verify-system
dm DM         0  4  running(***)   09/23 12:56             init-ovf
dm DM         0  4  running(***)   09/23 11:43             verify-system
```

:list-lists
```
Page 1        dm,pointer-file,                        20:07:20 08 Oct 1994

dm,pointer-file,

cust
temp.cust

[405] 2 items listed out of 2 items.
```

:list-macros md
```
Page 1        DICT md                                 20:07:44 08 Oct 1994

DICT md..........   dc.   summary...................................

:assignfq           n     assignfq
:listabs            n     list spooler assignments for one or more
                          ports sort pctl without a0 'p]' 'q]' 'b]''t]'
                          pctl.line pctl.stat pctl.copies pctl.form
                          pctl.device hdr-supp id-supp
:startspooler       n     startspooler
?                   n     help
abs-dump-32100      n     abs-dump
abs-dump-6386       n     abs-dump
```

:list-menus md
```
Page 1        DICT md                                 20:08:30 08 Oct 1994

DICT md..........   dc.   summary...................................

admin               me
admin.control       me
admin.maint         me
admin.tape.setup    me
config.menu         me
epick.menu          me
tape-socket-menu me Tape-socket 1.2

[405] 7 items listed out of 966 items.
```

:listverbs
```
08 Oct 1994          Verb Listings For DM M/Dict            Page 1

DM,,.........  a1,,.........  a2,,.........  a3,,.........  a4,,.........

!              vs             17
:bootstrap     vr             d
:cd            VR             3              F              dm,bp, cd
:dcd           v08            2
:pmsg          VR             3              F              dm,bp, :pmsg
```

In the final sample output, the items listed are verbs found in the master dictionary, and alongside each is shown the contents of their first four attributes (fields). You will notice when you run these commands that at the end of them all is a count of the number of items. To establish the number of items in a file without listing them all out, we can use the command **COUNT** as shown below:

```
:count md
[407] 966 items counted out of 966 items.
```

LIST, **SORT** and **COUNT** are just some of the main ACCESS information retrieval commands covered in Chapter 12. Having listed the items in the MD, you can look at the contents of any individual item by the command **CT** (Copy to Terminal). In fact, the **CT** verb is just a PROC using a verb **COPY** whose workings are explained later on. Figure 5.2 shows how to display the contents of the item USER-COLDSTART in the Master Dictionary. Do not concern yourself with the contents of the item as this will be discussed later.

```
:CT MD SYSTEM-COLDSTART [CR]
system-coldstart
001  n
002  run dm,bp, setpib0
003  term-type (s
004  run dm,bp, start.rtc
005  run dm,bp, start.ss
006  initovf
007  coldstart.log
008  run dm,bp, cleanpibs
009  :reset-async
010  set-abs dm,abs, (s
011  maxusers (mql
012  rem verify.system
013  run dm,bp, start.dos.printer.p0
014  run dm,bp, clear.unix.printers
015  coldstart
016  off
```

Figure 5.2 Displaying the contents of an item using **CT**.

6 The Handling of Data

TCL verbs and general commands covered in this chapter

ACCOUNT-MAINT	CLEAR-FILE	CONV-CASE	COPY
CREATE-ACCOUNT	CREATE-FILE	CREATE-BFILE	DELETE
DELETE-ACCOUNT	DELETE-FILE	EXCHANGE	MOVE-FILE
RENAME-FILE	STEAL-FILE		

This chapter explores how to take control of the PICK database, firstly by examining the ways in which accounts can be created and deleted and then by looking at the facilities available for the creation and manipulation of files.

The first step is to log on and to gain access to the system by means of entering a user-id. Advanced PICK comes with the user-id **dm** and that of **SYSPROG** for those people used to working with PICK R83. The difference between the two is that by logging on as **SYSPROG** the TCL command **r83.setup** is executed. This is a program in the **BP** file in the **dm** account which sets up all user options to their R83 equivalents and performs the following tasks:

brk-debug	breaks will invoke system debugger
esc-data	escape keys are escape keys
speller-off	disables spelling checker
legend-off	disables pick legend on Spooler output
TCL-hdr-off	disables TCL header on Spooler output
time-date-off	disables time/date display at TCL
who (c	outputs account name, user-id
term ,,,,2	sets form feed delay at 2

To start with log on with the user-id of **dm** and the master dictionary of **dm**. This will bring you to the TCL prompt : (colon). Figure 6.1 shows how this is achieved.

Before looking at the ways of handling accounts, let's explore the creation of new users.

6.1 Creating new users

The simplest way to create a new user is to copy the profile of an existing one and change the user name. This is demonstrated in Figure 6.2 where the user **dm** is copied to the user **rjb** and the name (held in attribute 1) changed to read **Roger Bourdon**. The new user will have the same access privileges as the original one.

```
Advanced PICK O/S - Enter your PICK user id: dm
Term setting: 79,25,0,7,1,8,80,58,MM-MON

[1301] The Speller is off.
master dictionary:dm

<<< 17:20:03 -- A d v a n c e d P i c k -- 09 Oct 1994          >>>
<<<                                                              >>>
<<< Copyright (c) 1973-1993 PICK Systems. All rights reserved.   >>>
<<< This work is property of, and embodies trade secrets and     >>>
<<< confidential information proprietary to PICK Systems. It    >>>
<<< may not be reproduced, copied, used, disclosed, transferred  >>>
<<< adapted or modified without the express written approval of >>>
<<< PICK Systems.                                                >>>

15 Feb 1994 at-dos
:
```

Figure 6.1 Logging to the **dm** account.

```
:copy users dm
to :rjb
   1 dm TO rjb

[805] 1 item(s) copied


:u users rjb
users 'rjb' size = 158

name      Roger Bourdonxf
address
zip
phone
keys
password
privilege sys2
options
macro term-type
10 sp-assign
11 brk-level
12 esc-data
13 set-sym gsym
14 speller-off
users 'rjb' size = 105 filed.
```

Figure 6.2 Creating a new user from an existing user.

The alternative is to create a new user from scratch entering all the details pertinent to the user. Figure 6.3 outlines the format of the **users** file. The user code is created using the Update Processor with the command **u users *user.id*** where *user.id* is the user code. After having entered all the appropriate details the record is filed away using **xf**.

ac..	attribute-name	description
0	item-id	User-id
1	name	User's name.
2	address	User's address.
3	zip	User's zip code.
4	phone	User's phone number.
6	keys	User's retrieval and update keys.
7	password	Optional logon password(s).
8	privilege	User privilege level.
9	options	User options:
	a (or u)	Updates accounting history file at logoff.
	d	Disables 'end' and 'off' commands from either debugger.
	r	Restarts logon procedure on any <break>+end.
	g	Stops at GFE's and offers the options to '(L)ogoff, (C)ontinue, or (Q)uit'.
	m	Invokes the automatic GFE handler at any GFE found.
12	macro	User logon macro. This is the same as a TCL macro without the macro type code, (normally in attribute 1) which is assumed to be 'n' (for 'non-stop'). Any number of TCL commands may be placed on attributes 12 and beyond. Each command will be executed before the user is logged on.

Figure 6.3 The layout of the **USERS** file.

6.2 The handling of accounts

6.2.1 Creating an account

An account is created by the command **CREATE-ACCOUNT**. This invokes a MACRO, restricted to the **dm** (it is a PROC in SYSPROG with R83) account, which prompts for the information it requires. A password can be applied to the account to stop unauthorized access to the account as a whole and security codes can be set up to prevent authorized users to the system as a whole from making unauthorized access to the account. These codes are known as retrieval locks (L/RET) and update locks (L/UPD). Further it is possible to determine the initial amount of space to allocate to the account by assigning values to its MODULO (and in R83 to its SEPARATION too – remember in Advanced PICK the separation can only be one). The larger the values set, the larger the amount of initial space allocated and vice versa.

Space is allocated in units of 1024 characters each, known as frames. The separation is the number of these frames that make up a single block, whilst the modulo is the number of these blocks to be used. The next chapter explains, in detail, the terms modulo and separation and the structure and storage of items in files.

Figure 6.4 shows an example of creating an account called **TEST** using the **CREATE-ACCOUNT** command. This command is handled by a MACRO which invokes the UPDATE PROCESSOR to create a record in the **mds** file causing an account to be built. The **CREATE-ACCOUNT** process can vary between implementations, so don't be surprised if yours is not exactly the same as Figure 6.4. Please note that you should specify a system privilege, normally **SYS2**, for the account and that all the questions given in Figure 6.4 are displayed at the same time. To move around the lines, you need to use the Update Processor commands shown below, although you can move down the lines with the [CR] key. Note those underlined indicate the ctrl (control) key needs to be pressed simultaneously with the letter underlined. Hence **z** means depress the CTRL key and the Z key together. When reaching the last line, either press return to file the item and create the account or enter **xf** (the UPDATE processor command to file an item).

Bottom of current item	**ze**
Top of current item	**t**
Move cursor left	**j**
Move cursor right	**k**
Move cursor down	**n**
Move cursor up	**b**
Move cursor to next word	**u**
Move cursor to previous word	**y**

Figure 6.4 has shown how an account called TEST was created. It has no retrieval lock codes (L/RET), no update lock codes (L/UPD) and is protected by

```
:create-account test
mds,, 'test' NEW ITEM size = 35
mds,,           test
type            D
modulo          37
ret-lock        [CR]
upd-lock        [CR]
password        PICKTEST [CR] <---- Note: after entering a [CR] the password
                                          will be changed to its encrypted
                                          form of 327EB6F9
syspriv         SYS2 [CR]
justification   L [CR]
width           12 [CR]
reallocation    xf
... CREATING ACCOUNT 'test' ...

mds,, 'test' NEW ITEM size = 34 filed.
:
```

Figure 6.4 The creation of a new account.

the password PICKTEST. The account carries the highest security level or privileges (SYS2) and uses the default modulo and separation of 37 and 1, respectively. The use of L/RET and L/UPD are covered in full in Chapter 20.

For those of you who like to know a little more about what goes on internally, having created the **mds** item with an item-id of the account name, it creates the account Master Dictionary allocating the required amount of space to the account, in this case 37 blocks of data (these blocks are known as frames in PICK terminology). PICK then copies the contents of the **NEWAC** file from the **dm** account, into the MD of the newly formed account. This gives it some starting verbs and the normal MACROs and ACCESS language, for without these, when logging to the new account you would not be able to do anything, not even log elsewhere with the **LOGTO** command.

NEWAC is therefore an important file which can be customized to limit or extend the facilities made available to users when accounts are created. In reality, the creation of accounts is not a frequent occurrence in a working system anyway and often when a new account is created the System Administrator will log to the new account and customize its Master Dictionary as required. Even so it is good to know there is an alternative.

A group of users can use the same account, and are given access to the account by a series of user-ids which are stored in the file **USERS**. At the time an account is created, you should consider creating user-id in the **USERS** file. One option is to create a user-id with the same name as the account itself. This may or may not be a sensible move, because if users get to know the name of the account they use that in place of their own user-id thereby bypassing any user security you may have set up. If you do decide to create a user-id with the same name as the account, then it would be worth adding a password to it. This is achieved with the **PASSWORD** verb (described in Chapter 20 section 1.3), a TCL verb normally only available from the **dm** account.

6.2.2 Removing an account

DELETE-ACCOUNT is another MACRO and can only be run from the **dm** account. It is highly recommended that all users be logged off before running this command, since PICK removes the D-item from the system dictionary (the **mds** file) during this process not only for the account but any synonyms for that account. It does not remove any items from the **USERS** file even the user-id that is the same as the name of the account being deleted.

As a protection against removing the wrong account, an option to list the files within the account is provided and final confirmation is requested before the account is finally deleted. Figure 6.5 shows the typical dialogue in using the **DELETE-ACCOUNT** command.

With the account deleted, PICK returns you to the TCL prompt to await the next command. You will notice in Figure 6.5 two references to the file

```
:delete-account test
mds,, 'test' size = 35
type           D
base/dict      9461
modulo         37
ret-lock
upd-lock
password
syspriv
justification  L
width          12
reallocation
DISPLAY FILES BEFORE DELETING (<Y>,N)?y
        FILE              BASE      MOD      SEP
        MD                25890     29       1
        DEMOFILES         34352     11       1
        DEMOFILES         35688     101      1
            |
            v

DO YOU STILL WANT TO DELETE THE ACCOUNT (Y,<N>)?y

mds,, 'test' size = 35 deleted.
:
```

Figure 6.5 Deleting an account.

DEMOFILES. The reason for this is that there are two files with that name in the account, one containing the dictionary information for the file and the other containing its data. Hence in the normal course of events, each file in your account will have its name shown twice.

6.2.3 The ACCOUNT-MAINT verb

This is a new verb introduced with Advanced PICK for the maintenance of accounts and is not available to R83 users. The verb enables you to create, modify or delete the **mds** item. Hence this command can be used as an alternative to the **CREATE-ACCOUNT** and **DELETE-ACCOUNT** verbs. But it can also be used to modify the parameters of the account, including its name. The renaming of an account was not so easy with R83. The account had to be saved to a backup medium, restored under its new name and then the original account had to be deleted. This verb saves all that unnecessary work when such a simple change is required. Figure 6.6 shows the typical **ACCOUNT-MAINT** dialogue.

To make changes to the account via the **ACCOUNT-MAINT** enter the line number against the aspect requiring change and press [CR]. The cursor will return to the bottom of the screen and once all the details are correct, enter **FI** and the changes will be effected. The **ADMIN** verb displays a menu from which many system administration functions can be performed, including those associated with the maintenance of accounts and users.

```
:account-maint pa
Account Maintenance Workscreen      11:19:40  20 Sep 1994

 1 Account name                 -pa
 2 Modulo                       -29           Reallocation modulo -29)
 3 Privilege level              -sys2
 4 Password                     -none
 5 Accounting update            -1
 6 Retrieval lock codes                       7 Update lock codes

Enter line number to update    -
or functions EX-exit FI-file FD-delete
```

Figure 6.6 Using the **ACCOUNT-MAINT** verb.

6.3 File handling

Having looked at the various ways of creating and manipulating ACCOUNTS, let's look at how to deal with files which is the next logical step in our exploration of the Advanced PICK database.

6.3.1 Creating a file

The **CREATE-FILE** command is used to generate new dictionary and data files. These can be generated independently by the commands **CREATE-FILE DICT** and **CREATE-FILE DATA**, though more usually they are created together by the command which contains the modulo (and for R83, the separation) parameters that relate to the initial sizing of the file, for both the dictionary and data portions. Do not worry too much about the terms modulo and separation here, since they are explained fully in the next chapter.

PICK does not allow a data file to be created without first having a dictionary level file in place and if you review the PICK database diagram it is obvious why this should be so. The data file is the lowest level file in the PICK database hierarchy and its location pointer resides in the dictionary file. Without a dictionary, there can be no data file. Hence the dictionary part of the file must exist first and their modulo/separation parameters come before those for the data file in the syntax of the **CREATE-FILE** command. Even in most R83 implementations the **CREATE-FILE** command will default to a separation of 1 unless told otherwise. In Advanced PICK as has previously been stated, the separation can only be one and therefore does not need stating. However, if your implementation of PICK allows you to specify a separation, this can be shown following the modulo and separated from it with a comma. So the normal syntax for the command to create a file is as shown in Figure 6.7 with both the dictionary and data files being created at the same time, each with a default separation of 1.

:create-file *file.name dict.modulo*{*,dict.separ*} *data.modulo*{*,data.separ*} {(options}

where

file.name	is the name given to the file being created
dict.modulo	the modulo of the file's dictionary
dict.separ	the separation of the file's dictionary
data.modulo	the modulo of the file's data portion
data.separ	the separation of the file's data portion

valid options being

c	This was an R83 option to make the file a **dc** file type, indicating that the file contained binary items (program libraries and list files). In AP, any file may contain binary pointer items, so this code is no longer needed.
l	Logs any updates to this file to the transaction logger. This option is not compatible with the **x** or **y** options.
n	Negates all update protection for the given file irrespective of the global update protection setting. This option is not compatible with the **u** option.
p	Primary file space is *only* to contain 'pointer' items. These 'point' to the actual location of the data which is held outside the primary file space. This will occur regardless of the length of the records being stored.
s	Item-ids are upper/lower case-sensitive. This option is compatible with all other options.
u	Enables update protection for the given file irrespective of the global update protection setting. This option is not compatible with the **l** option.
x	Does not save the file during backup processes such as **file-save**, **account-save**, etc. This means care must be taken to back up this file prior to a restore taking place otherwise it will 'disappear' on the restored system.
y	Does not save the data stored in the file during backup processes such as **file-save**, **account-save**, etc. On a file restore, the file is recreated, but will be empty. Useful for transaction files.

Examples

Creating a file under Advanced PICK where the separation can only be 1

:create-file rbdemo 1 11

```
[417] file 'rbdemo' created; base = 8190, modulo = 1
[417] file 'rbdemo' created; base = 9461, modulo = 11
:
```

Creating a file under R83 specifying a separation other than 1

>CREATE-FILE DEMO 1,1 11,3

```
[417] FILE 'DEMO' CREATED; BASE= 24046, MODULO= 1, SEPAR= 1.
[417] FILE 'DEMO' CREATED; BASE= 24292, MODULO=11, SEPAR=3.
```

Figure 6.7 Creating a file.

Once again reference is made to the MESSAGES file, using message number 417 to confirm the file parameters. The commands in Figure 6.7 have created two files in the account you are logged to, one called RBDEMO with a dictionary size of 1 frame and a data area of 11 frames. and the other called DEMO with a dictionary size of 1 frame and a data area of 33 (11 x 3) frames. Exactly the same could have been achieved by two separate commands, one to create the dictionary (DICT) file and the other to create the data file; Figure 6.8 gives an example of this. Remember though, the dictionary file must be created first!

To create dictionary or data files with a separation other than 1, follow the modulo size, of either or both, with a comma and the separation size. Hence to provide a separation of 3 for the data file, leaving the dictionary file as a separation of 1, use the command

:CREATE-FILE DEMO 1 11,3

Remember, this format of **CREATE-FILE** command is only available for R83 users.

```
:CREATE DICT DEMO 1
[417] FILE 'DEMO' CREATED; BASE=24046, MODULO= 1, SEPAR= 1.

:CREATE-FILE DATA DEMO 11
  [417] FILE 'DEMO' CREATED; BASE= 24292, MODULO=11, SEPAR= 1.
```

Figure 6.8 Creating a file by creating dictionary and data files separately.

6.3.2 Creating multiple files with a common dictionary

Whilst every data file must have a dictionary file relating to it, it does not have to have its own unique dictionary file. There are some instances where it is helpful to split data across several data files but, since each has the same data format, to let them all share one dictionary file.

These multiple data files are created, and subsequently referred to, by following an existing dictionary file name with a comma and following that with the new data file name. Taking the example of Figure 6.8 a stage further, let's assume we wish to create the data file DEMO1 to use the existing dictionary, defined for the file DEMO. This process is explained in Figure 6.9.

```
:CREATE-FILE DATA DEMO,DEMO1 7
[417] FILE 'DEMO1' CREATED; BASE= 24303, MODULO= 7, SEPAR= 1.
```

Figure 6.9 Creating a data file to use an existing dictionary file.

From this point on, all references to the file DEMO1 must be made in conjunction with its linked dictionary file DEMO by using the words DEMO, DEMO1. It is possible to edit items in the file, use ACCESS to enquire on the file and use any of the other PICK commands to manipulate the file or its items. It is, and can be treated, just like any other file provided you refer to it by its full name DEMO, DEMO1.

6.3.3 Creating a DC type file

This is a command useful to those still using some implementations of PICK R83 or those of you who still wish to distinguish program file types by creating them with a file type **DC**. Once the file has been created, its file type given in attribute 1 of the file defining items is changed from **D** to **DC** automatically. A typical use of the command is shown in Figure 6.10.

:create-bfile rbprogs 1 11

```
[417] file 'rbprogs' created; base = 8190, modulo = 1
[417] file 'rbprogs' created; base = 9461, modulo = 11
```

Figure 6.10 Creation of a **DC** type file.

6.3.4 Removing a file

In the same way that a file's dictionary and data portions can be created separately or together, they can also be removed individually or together. Again, since the dictionary must exist before the data file, it is not possible to delete the dictionary file and leave the data file in place. To delete both dictionary and data files together you should use the following command:

:DELETE-FILE *filename*

where *filename* is the name of the file to be deleted. This command releases back to the free space manager, the OVERFLOW manager, all the frames used by the deleted file which are immediately made available to all existing applications. There are occasions when you may wish to remove the dictionary or data files independently, in which case you should use the commands:

:DELETE-FILE DATA *filename*
:DELETE-FILE DICT *filename*

6.3.5 Clearing a file

PICK provides the means to clear the contents of a file, be it dictionary or data, with the command **CLEAR-FILE**. This leaves the file empty, releases any frames that were linked to the primary file area, but leaves intact, although empty of data, the initial allocation of frames to the file. The process of clearing the contents of a file also leaves unaffected all references and pointers to the file. It is not possible to clear both the dictionary and data portions of a file at the same time. The commands to use are:

:CLEAR-FILE DICT *filename*
:CLEAR-FILE DATA *filename*

6.3.6 Moving files

There are three ways in which you can move files around the system:

- **Move file** move a file from one dictionary to another
- **Rename a file** changes the name of a file
- **Steal a file** move a file from one account to another

The** move-file **command

The **move-file** command moves a file defining item from one dictionary to another leaving its name unaltered. The dictionary file may be any dictionary file in the PICK hierarchy, from system level (**mds**) through account level (**master dictionary**) to file level (**data** dictionary). A file must be moved to the SAME LEVEL as it was created. That is, a data file to a data file, master dictionary to master dictionary, and so on.

The use of this command takes a while to get used to and you really need to have a clear grasp of the PICK database hierarchy and the way to point to a specific file in the database. It is a little like the resizing parameters in that the file you work with is the one that points to the one you wish to work with. Figure 6.11 gives some examples of the use of this command.

Another thing to be wary of is that **move-file** can change the name of a file in the 'move' process, but if this is done, a normal file (one with its **D** pointer in the **MD** and with both a dictionary and data portion) will *not* have *both* the dictionary and data portions renamed. The only file that is renamed is the one explicitly referenced by the **move-file** command. For the inexperienced user this can cause all sorts of confusion. For that reason I would use the following commands by preference:

account-maint	to rename an account
rename-file	to rename a file
steal-file	to move a file to a new account

The** rename-file **command

The **rename-file** command is much more straightforward than the **move-file** command when the name of the file is to be changed. The command renames

Example 1 – Renaming an account

:move-file mds,, *original.account.name*
`to:` ***new.account.name***

where *original.account.name* is the name of the account prior to being renamed
new.account.name is the name the account is to become after the **move-file** command

Example 2 – Renaming a dictionary file

:move-file md *original.dict.name*
`to:` ***new.dict.name***

where *original.dict.name* is the name of the dictionary prior to being renamed
new.dict.name is the name the dictionary is to become after the **move-file** command

N.B. This does not change the name of the data portion of the file, so future reference to the data file has to be with the string new.dict.name, old.file. name in the same way as you would reference one of the multiple data files of a common dictionary (see section 6.3.2).

Example 3 – Renaming a data file

:move-file dict *old.dict.name old.file.name*
`to:` ***new.file.name***

where *old.dict.name* is the name of the dict file containing the pointer to the data file to be renamed
old.file.name is the name of the data file to be renamed
new.file.name is the name to be given to the data file after the **move-file** command

N.B. This does not change the name of the dictionary portion of the file, so future reference to the data file has to be with the string *old.dict.name, new.file. name* in the same way as you would reference one of the multiple data files of a common dictionary (see section 6.3.2).

Example 4 – Moving a file to a different account

:move-file md *file.name*
`to:` ***(new.account,,***

where *file.name* is the name of the file in the account logged to which is to be moved to another account
new.account is the name of the account to contain the transferred file

N.B. This action moves both the dictionary and data portions of the file and leaves the name of both unaltered.

Figure 6.11 Examples of the **move-file** command.

both the dictionary and data portions of the file but does not work for account names (i.e. items in the **mds** dictionary). Figure 6.12 shows examples of its use.

:rename-file *original.file.name*
new name: *new.file.name*

where	*original.file.name*	is the name of the file before being renamed
	new.file.name	is the name of the file after having its name changed

---

Figure 6.12 Use of the **rename-file** command.

The steal-file *command*

The **steal-file** command is used to take a file from another account and move it to the account you are logged to. The command physically moves the file to your **MD** and requires SYS2 privileges. It also requires that the user invoking the **steal-file** command is not protected against updating the file (by checking the L/UPD codes) at any level, master dictionary, dictionary file level, or data file level.

After 'stealing' a file, there is no means of accessing the file from its original account without creating a Q-POINTER to it or by referencing it via a 'file path' (see Chapter 9).

6.4 Data handling

6.4.1 Creating data items

There is no need for a special command to create items in PICK since as soon as you refer to a new item it is created for you. Items are created in a number of ways; either through the Update Processor (refer to Chapter 10), the editor (refer to Chapter 11), via an application program written in BASIC (refer to Chapter 15) by using TCL commands like **COPY** to copy items from one file to another or through reformatting commands in ACCESS.

6.4.2 Removing data items

Apart from the PICK tools such as the Update Processor, the Editor and application programs, it is possible to delete items from a file with a TCL command. The command is **DELETE** where in addition to the file name, the item names are also given. Some licensee implementations offer a far more convenient means of deleting several items. Instead of listing the item-ids alongside the file name, it is possible to press [CR] immediately after inputting the file name, and be prompted for each of the item-ids in turn. If this is the way your system works then the process is terminated by pressing the [CR] key in response to NEXT ITEM prompt. Figure 6.13 shows both methods in action where two items with item-ids (keys) of **1001** and **1005** are removed from the file **DEMO**.

```
:DELETE DEMO 1001 1005
1001 DELETED
1005 DELETED

:DELETE DEMO
NEXT ITEM 1001
1001 DELETED
NEXT ITEM 1005
1005 DELETED
NEXT ITEM
```

Figure 6.13 Deleting items from a file.

6.5 Copying items

The **COPY** command is extremely powerful and is used to copy items to another file or to make duplicate copies of items within the original file. As discussed later, it can be used in resizing the contents of a file.

The **COPY** command can also be used to copy items to a terminal or printer and hence there are a number of different options that can be applied. Since all items in the PICK database are contained in files, the **COPY** command can be used on any file from the system dictionary (**mds**), through the **MD** (Master Dictionary) and file dictionary to the data file. Where the file dictionary is referenced, the command should include the word DICT. The general format of the command is given in Figure 6.14.

Figure 6.15 shows how to copy an existing item (**1001**) to a new item (**1005**). This duplicates the data record in the same file, but with a different key.

Figure 6.16 shows how to copy the contents of an entire file called **DEMO** (which contains five records) to a new file called **TEMP**. This assumes that the file **TEMP** already exists. If it doesn't the copying process will fail so the file must be created first (refer to the **CREATE-FILE** command). Once the file exists, the entire contents of another file can be copied to it using a wildcard facility designated by an asterisk. If the item-id of an item on the original file already exists on the destination file, PICK will display an error message, number 415, from the **messages** file. The message states that the item-id is already on file and the item will not be copied over. To overcome this use the **O** (overwrite) option.

Notice in Figure 6.16 the use of parentheses following the 'TO' prompt, which denotes the items are being copied to a different file. In Advanced PICK

COPY {DICT} *filename item.list*{(*options*)}
to:{(*filename1*} {*itemlist1*}

where

filename	is the file from which the items are being copied
item.list	the list of items to be copied (* means all items)
(*filename1*	the bracket is needed to indicate the copying is being processed to a different file to that containing the original items and *filename1* is the name of the file to which the items are being copied
item list1	is the list of item-ids to be assigned to the copied items

and the available *options* are:

nnn	an integer number which specifies the number of items to copy and is used typically for creating small versions of files for program and system test purposes
a	activates assembly **mlist** format
d	deletes the original (source) items after copying has been completed. This option is not valid with the **t** or **p** options
f	outputs a form-feed between each item and is only valid with the **t** or **p** options
i	suppresses the display of item-ids when copying between files
l	changes item to a 'list' format, if the destination file is a **DC** type file. (R83 only)
m	activates macro (assembly) format on terminal or printer output only
n	activates the nopage function on output to the terminal; only available with the **t** option
n	when used with **o** option, this prevents new items being created on copies between files. This means that the item-ids must already exist in the target file in order for the item to be copied to it
o	overwrites existing items when duplicate item-ids exist in the target file. It has no effect if used with **t** or **p** options
p	directs output to system printer, via the Spooler
s	suppresses display of line (attribute) numbers when used with **t** or **p** options
t	directs output to the terminal
u	if the item-id is in the target or destination file, the item is copied to a new item-id by creating a new item-id composed of the original item-id concatenated with a letter, starting with **a** (lowercase 'a')
x	outputs in hexadecimal; only available with **t** and **p** options

N.B. The options at the end of the command, if used, must be enclosed in parentheses with multiple options being separated by a comma.

Figure 6.14 The format of the **COPY** command.

```
:COPY DEMO 1001
TO:1005
1 1001 TO 1005
1 ITEMS COPIED
```

Figure 6.15 Copying an item within the same file.

```
:COPY DEMO *
TO:(TEMP)
1  1001
2  1002
3  1003
4  1004
5  1005
5 ITEMS COPIED
```

Figure 6.16 Copying items to a different file.

and most other implementations you will find that only the first bracket, the opening (is required, the second being completely superfluous. Figure 6.17 shows how to copy an item to a different file and to give it a different item-id. In this example the item **1003** in the file **DEMO** will be copied to the file **TEMP** and given the item-id **1022**. Once again the parentheses are needed because the destination file is different to the origination file.

The copy facility is very useful and one that you will use regularly. There are many different options (see Figure 6.14) that you can use, for example, the T option, which copies the items to the terminal, although this can equally be achieved by pressing the [CR] key in response to the TO prompt.

Like many of the TCL commands, including the majority we have used already, there is an option to direct the output of the command to the printer, the **P** option. As mentioned above, all options used need to be in parentheses with multiple options separated by a comma. Figure 6.18 shows an example of the copy command using several options and demonstrates the case of the contents of items **1002** and **1003** being listed on the printer with their contents being shown in hexadecimal format. For those of you who have not come

```
:COPY DEMO 1003
TO:(TEMP 1022
1  1003 TO 1022
1 ITEMS COPIED
```

Figure 6.17 Copying items to a different file and item-id.

```
:COPY DEMO 1002 1003 (P,X
>ENTRY # 1
```

Figure 6.18 The **COPY** command with multiple options.

across the word hexadecimal before, do not be concerned — you will probably never need to use it. It is a method of representing numbers to the base of 16, and is only used by technicians!

The COPY options, as with those on a number of TCL verbs, include some that are mutually exclusive. For example, the items copied can either be copied to a file, to the printer or to the screen. They cannot be directed to more than one device in one command. You will have to experiment with the above options to gain an understanding of which combinations are possible and which are not. Since all are fairly straightforward and should not represent any major difficulties.

6.5.1 Changing item-ids

Advanced PICK and some licencee implementations contain a useful TCL verb called **EXCHANGE**. This enables the contents of two *existing* items to be exchanged and is achieved by a BASIC program in the **bp** file in the **dm** account. In effect the process switches the item-ids of the two items.

After the exchange operation shown in Figure 6.19 the data contained in item 1002 has been transferred to item 1005 and vise versa. If your system does not contain the facility, Figure 6.20 gives details of a PROC which will achieve the same result. In the PROC, however, a temporary item %TEMP% is created and deleted once the copying is complete.

```
:exchange demo 1002 1005
Item '1002' exchanged with '1005' in file 'demo'
```

Figure 6.19 Using the **EXCHANGE** verb.

6.5.2 The CONV-CASE command

Since Advanced PICK is case insensitive (unless told otherwise), the **CONV-CASE** command enables characters within a list of items to be converted to either upper or lower case. The syntax of the command is given in Figure 6.21

EXCHANGE

```
PQ
C A PROC TO EXCHANGE THE ITEM-IDs OF TWO ITEMS IN A FILE.
C
IF A2 = DICT F
IF A F
IF A F
IF #A X
HCOPY
A2
IF A2 = DICT G 10
S3
G 11
10 A3
11 C
A
A
H%TEMP% (O,D)
STON
H%TEMP%
S2
IF A = DICT F
F
A
H
A
H<
P
```

Figure 6.20 A PROC to handle the exchange of item-ids.

:CONV-CASE *filename itemlist* {(OPTIONS)}

where

filename	is the file containing the items to be converted
itemlist	is the list of item-ids to be converted (* means all items in the file)
options	are as follows:

e	if used by itself, all characters are changed to upper-case. If **e** is used with the **q** option, it changes everything except strings in quotes that are not preceded by **CHAIN**, **TCL** or **EXECUTE**.
i	suppresses display of item-id(s).
l	converts upper case text to lower case.
o	outputs the item-ids on the same line.
q	leaves text within quotes unchanged.
u	converts lower case text to upper case (default).

Figure 6.21 The format of the **CONV-CASE** verb.

7 The PICK Database Structure in Detail

7.1 The PICK database structure explained

In earlier chapters we used terms like **frame**, **modulo** and **separation** all of which were briefly explained. In this chapter all of these terms, which describe important elements of the PICK database structure, are explained in detail.

In Chapter 3 we looked at the general philosophy of the PICK database and drew an analogy to the way an organization is structured. Figure 7.1 is a copy of the PICK data structure we referred to in that chapter.

The **System Dictionary**, referred to as **MDS**, is the highest level dictionary in the PICK hierarchy. In R83 this file was called **SYSTEM**, and the

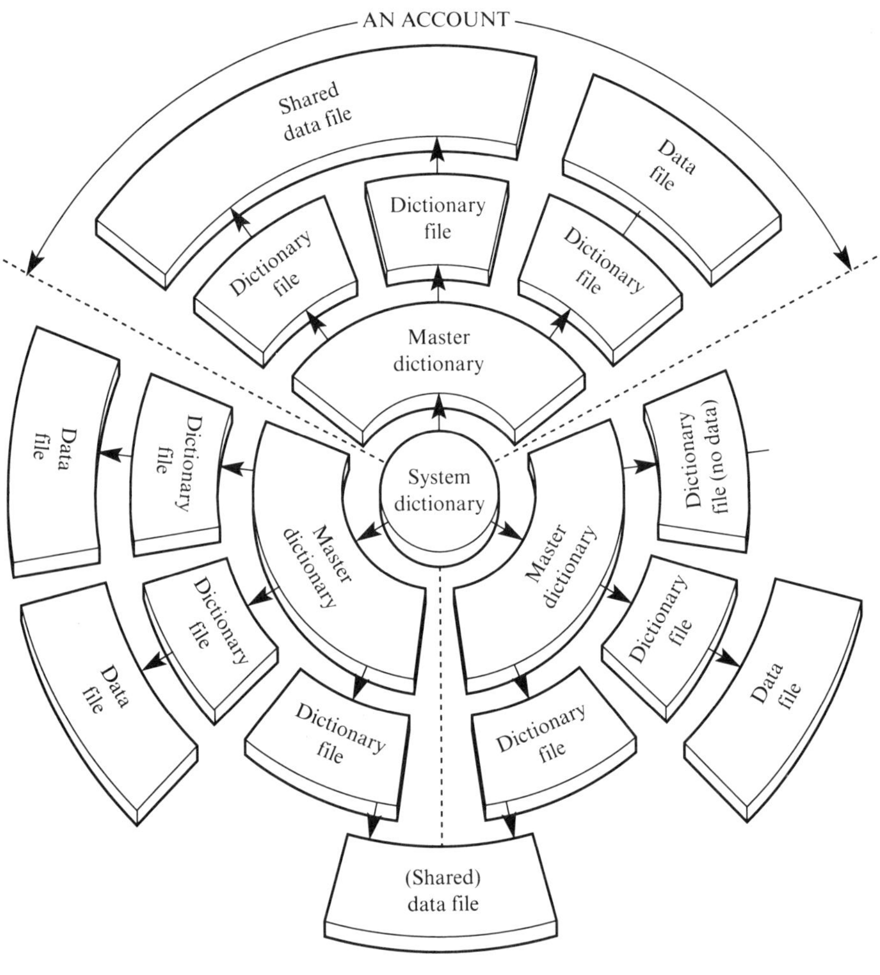

Figure 7.1 The PICK database structure.

change to **MDS** was just one of a myriad of changes made with the introduction of Advanced PICK. It controls 'the system', which itself is made up of ACCOUNTS, each of which is controlled by its own **MD** (Master Dictionary). It is understandable, therefore, why it should be renamed **MDS** but for backward compatibility, there is a synonym to it called **SYSTEM**. There can only ever be one of these files for each copy of PICK and it contains one record for each account on the system. Each record contains the location of the Master Dictionary for that account, the account password (if one has been set) and any update or retrieval locks which may have been determined. The file also contains records that have been built as synonyms or 'pointers' to an actual account.

The **Master Dictionary**, referred to as MD or M/DICT, is where information specific to the account is stored. Whilst there is no limit to the number of accounts on a system, other than the restriction of physical disk space, there can only be one master dictionary per account. The master dictionary holds definitions of the files within the account, pointers to their file dictionary together with their locking codes, the TCL and ACCESS verbs available to the account as well as its MACROs, MENUs, PROCs (procedures) and BASIC programs. It also stores pointers to files outside the account, known as 'Q' pointers, explained in detail in Chapter 9.

The **File Dictionary**, referred to as DICT, describes the structure and format of data held within the respective file and stores the pointer to the DATA file. There is always just one file dictionary for each data file, although the concept of more than one data file per file dictionary is possible. This concept whilst not common, is explained in detail in Section 6.3.2.

The dictionary file contains a record for each data field. The term **Attribute** is used in PICK to describe a field or element of a data record. Hence, in a personnel system, the dictionary of a file of employees could contain a record to describe the format of the employee name, another dictionary record to define the employee department, another the employee salary and so on.

The **Data File** is where the actual data is held and it is stored in variable length format. Hence again using the employee file as an example, the data file contains the physical data defined by its corresponding dictionary file. The data file would contain, therefore, actual names, actual departments and actual salaries of actual employees! Figure 7.2 illustrates this hierarchical relationship. Although not obvious from Figure 7.2, all elements of the database are variable length whether they reside in the system dictionary, master dictionary, the file dictionaries or data files. Hence *all* files on the PICK system are variable length.

7.1.1 Data file structure

All data held on the database is held in files; some of these files are dictionary files (system dictionary, master dictionary and file dictionaries) whilst others hold data (data files). A file is a collection of logically related information which can be of any size, subject to the amount of free disk space available.

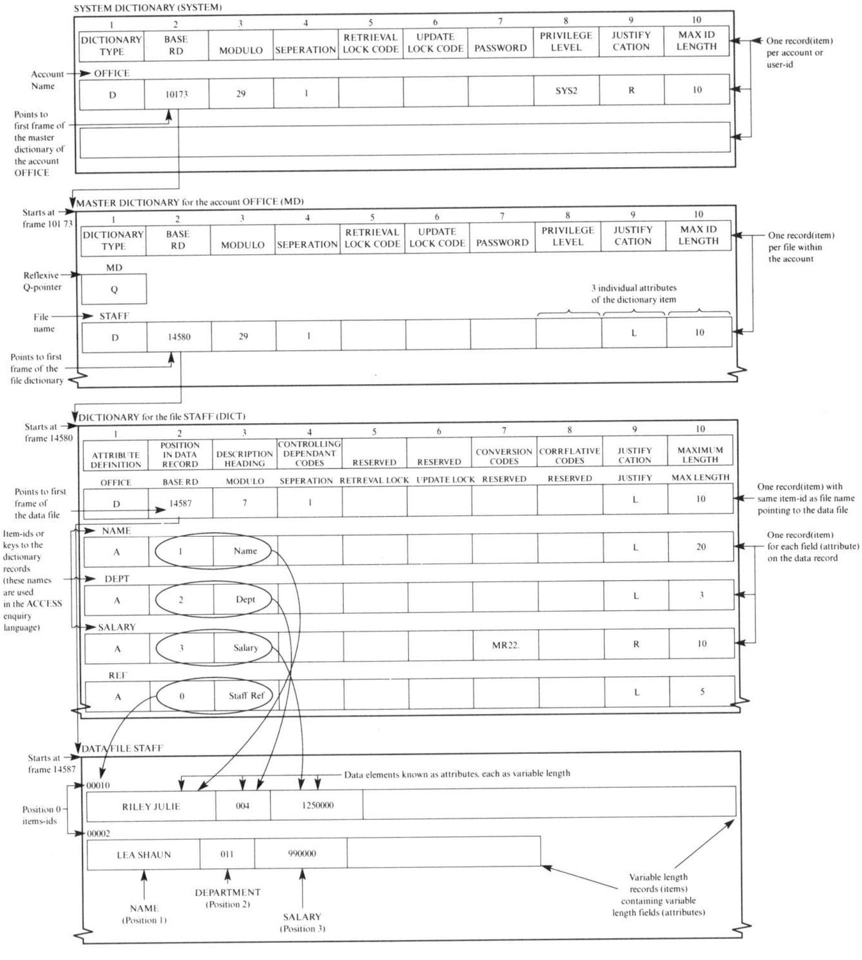

Figure 7.2 The workings of the PICK database.

Whilst the initial creation of a file requires the assigning of an amount of disk space known as the primary area, the file can grow or shrink during use without any further intervention. Note, however, that it will not shrink below the original (primary) amount of space allocated to it, so it is not sensible to define file space much larger than that expected to be used.

A file is made up of a number of **items**, PICK's term for 'records'. If you look at Figure 7.2 carefully you will see that each file in the hierarchy contains a series of items. Within PICK R83 the largest item (record) size permitted was 32K or 32,268 bytes (characters). This limit was removed completely with Advanced PICK, so there is now no limit to the size of any item. Since the number of records in a file is unlimited, restricted only by the amount of physical disk space available, the record size limit was rarely a problem anyway, but it is worth bearing in mind that if you need records this large, you probably need to re-design your database. Removing the limit is a double-edged sword. It does mean your applications will no longer fall over, but it equally means your records can grow and grow without your knowledge and large records have a detrimental effect on performance. To minimize this effect, large records are stored outside the main body of the file, as we shall discover later.

An item is subdivided into a number of **attributes**; again, to use conventional terminology, these would be called 'fields'. The key field, known as the **item-id**, is mandatory and is at the beginning of the item in attribute 0 (zero). The maximum length of the item-id is 50 characters, but seeing as these are regularly referred to you should make them as short as is reasonably possible.

So far we have tried to demonstrate the correlation between the PICK database and the conventional file system, using terms like **file**, **item** (record) and **attribute** (field). From this point on, however, the parallel to conventional systems stops and the power of the PICK data structure comes into its own.

Attributes may be divided into multiple **values,** which in turn may be further divided into **subvalues** and indeed if you wish these themselves can be further sub-divided. Any attribute, any value or any subvalue, can be of any length.

A typical application of this structure might be a personnel system where, amongst other information, it is required to monitor all the salary changes of employees. In a conventional system such as COBOL you have to define the largest, expected, number of occurrences – and that isn't always easy to determine – and then reserve that fixed amount of space for each employee in the file. In PICK, the built-in mechanism for defining data means that no fixed number of multi-values need be determined since these values (which in this case contain salary amounts) can be added and deleted dynamically. The amount of space used directly relates to the amount of data stored. Figure 7.3 shows the difference in these two methods of data storage.

PICK's data structure enables values to be broken down further into subvalues, each of which is held as variable length. This means that the multi-values of salary can themselves contain multiple entries, perhaps to show the constituent parts of salary such as tax, NHI, pension and so on. This effectively gives a three-dimensional aspect to the data, as illustrated in Figure 7.4.

The strength of PICK lies in the ease with which such a complex data structure can be changed to incorporate the requirements of a business, such as adding bonus pay as an element of salary. Once incorporated, bonus pay becomes another element of salary. However, those earlier salary values prior to the bonus scheme being introduced are unaffected; they effectively contain a null bonus pay amount. Hence it is possible to make modifications to the data structure even when the system is 'live', without affecting the existing data. This makes the PICK database flexible, capable of adapting to change with the minimum of effort and forgiving of those who don't know exactly what they want from the outset. On the other hand it can lead to systems being developed with-

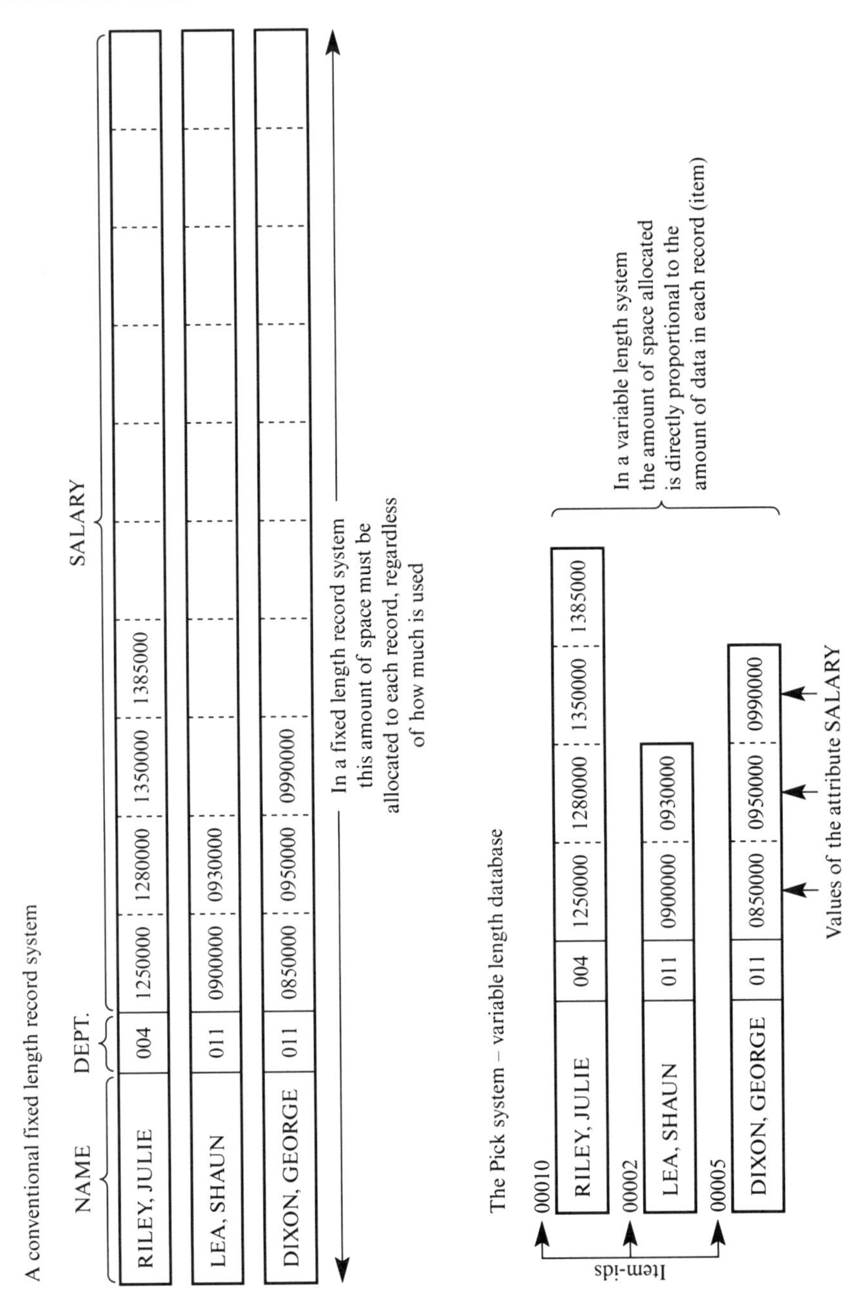

Figure 7.3 The difference between PICK and fixed length record systems.

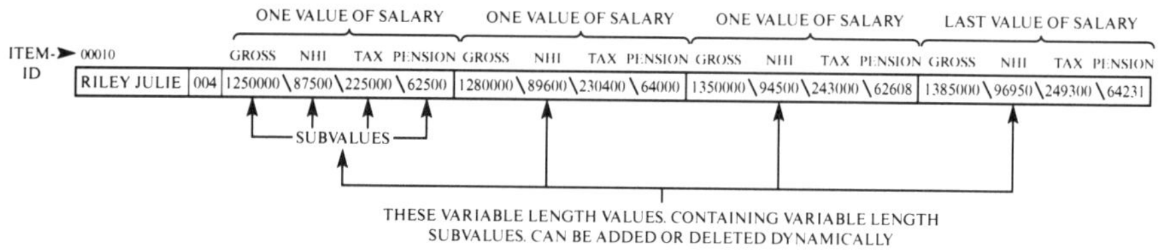

Figure 7.4 The subvalue concept.

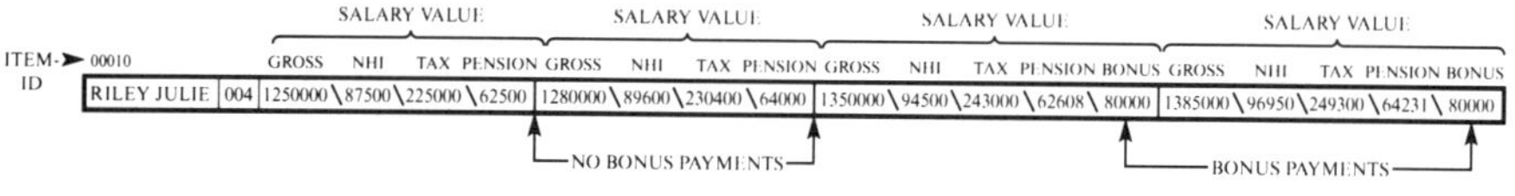

Figure 7.5 Changing the subvalue data structure.

out the requisite thought being given to the database structure, so don't take this power and flexibility for granted and don't abuse it! Figure 7.5 illustrates how bonus pay is introduced on the last two salary values.

The data structure defined by the dictionaries is extremely flexible, allowing existing attribute definitions to be changed in seconds, merely by editing the attribute definition item in the dictionary file. Previously defined attributes, even the key of the file known as the item-id, can be changed without affecting existing data, thus removing the restrictions imposed by conventional systems. It is quite feasible, having implemented such a personnel system, to change the key of the file, i.e. personnel code, from its original five digits to seven digits, just by making a simple change to the dictionary. This change is effected simply by changing attribute 10 of the dictionary item for the item-id from 5 to 7. In Figure 7.2 for example, you would change the item REF in the file dictionary of the file STAFF from 5 to 7. No more than a few seconds' effort in total! From this point on, *every* reference to the personnel code can be up to seven digits in length, i.e. for every data entry screen, every printed report, every re-printed form, every transaction process using the personnel code. The reason for this is that before PICK accesses the data it accesses the dictionary to determine the format of the data. Hence, from the time the change is made to the dictionary, it knows that the maximum length of the reference number is seven digits.

In any conventional system not using a database such a change, so simple to implement in PICK, is a nightmare and could involve hours if not days of work editing and recompiling programs.

7.1.2 The dictionaries

For those of you more familiar with conventional data processing, let me remind you that in PICK terminology records are called items and fields are called attributes. Since the dictionary is itself a file, it contains items in the same way as any data file. In this instance, however, each item defines the structure of an individual element of data contained in the files held at the next level in the hierarchy.

We have discussed the hierarchy of dictionaries in the PICK system, which start at the top level with the system dictionary with 'pointers' to the master dictionary which in turn has 'pointers' to the file dictionaries. These 'pointers' are produced automatically by PICK when accounts or files are created, and consist of an entry in the respective dictionary. Hence, when an account is created, an entry is placed in the system dictionary (**mds**) with the name of the account created. When a file is created within an account, the name of the file is an entry in the account's master dictionary. Figure 7.2 illustrates how this works.

In the case of data files, the 'pointer' in the master dictionary is to the file's file dictionary. Within this file dictionary is an entry, with the same name as the file, 'pointing' to the start of the data. The file dictionary, sometimes known as the data dictionary, and referred to as DICT, is used to define the format of the data contained in the data file. Thus a data file has two parts, one containing the data itself, the other, the file dictionary, defining the structure of the data. In a personnel system for example, the main file of personnel records might be called STAFF and would contain a number of items (records) each of which would contain a number of attributes (fields). For the purpose of this example let's assume each item comprises the following attributes:

0. Staff ref;
1. Name;
2. Department;
3. Salary;
4. Address;
5. Age;
6. Date of birth.

Notice that in PICK, attributes are numbered from zero and attribute zero is the item-id (or key). The purpose of the file dictionary is to define the structure of the item, i.e. the sequence of the attributes in the item, and the format of each these. Having pulled in a data record PICK needs to know which part of it contains salary information, which contains the name and so on. To do this the file dictionary contains an item for each attribute of the data record whose purpose is to define its format and to give such information as its length, its position in the data record, how it is to be displayed and so on. In other words, for each of the above seven components of the personnel record there is a separate item (a record) in its dictionary file which defines the attribute. Figure 7.2

shows just four of these although there are seven listed above. However, in real life a dictionary would generally contain very many more entries.

In building the dictionary item (record), a meaningful abbreviated name is given to it. This is the item-id of the dictionary item and held in attribute zero. This 'shorthand tag' is what is used from this point on within PICK to refer to the data held on the data record.

	Description	*Abbreviated name (DICT name – item-id)*
0.	Staff ref	REF
1.	Name	NAME
2.	Department	DEPT
3.	Salary	SALARY
4.	Address	ADDR
5.	Age	AGE
6.	Date of birth	DOB

It is these abbreviated names, the names of the items in the file dictionary which are used in ACCESS enquiries. Hence, if you want to list the names and salaries of all people on the database you would type in the enquiry LIST STAFF NAME SALARY where **STAFF** is the name of the file being enquired on and **NAME** and **SALARY** are items in the dictionary referred to by their item-ids. These dictionary items define where in the data record the required data is held. Having located the file, the ACCESS processor picks up the two file dictionary items from their item-ids (keys), which it interprets to find whereabouts on the data record the name and salary are held, and reads each record on the STAFF file displaying the contents of the respective attributes, in this example attribute 1 and attribute 3.

The data dictionary, therefore, will contain an item (record) for each of the above attributes (fields) with an item-id (key) of the abbreviated, dictionary name. Hence, using the above example, the dictionary (DICT) portion of the data file contains the following items (records):

```
REF
NAME
DEPT
SALARY
ADDR
AGE
DOB
```

Each of these dictionary entries serves to define the format of one attribute of the data file, STAFF, and contains such information as the description of the attribute, its maximum length, the attribute number (or the position of the data in the item) and the way the information is to be displayed, i.e. left or right justification, the number of decimal places, and so on.

In the data file the **item-id** (or key) to each data record is the 'Staff Ref' and this is stored ahead of any data on the record. In PICK the item-id is attribute 0 and all other attributes tend to be numbered sequentially thereafter (see Table 7.1). Just to complete the story, however, you should note that PICK will not complain if an attribute number is missing; it will consider the attribute to have a null value.

If you were to look at all the dictionary entries in a file dictionary you would notice one extra item which has an item-id of the same name as that given to the file itself. In our example in Figure 7.2 where the file is called STAFF, the extra item is also called STAFF. It is produced automatically by PICK when the file is created and serves to define the data file itself, containing such information as its location on disk and its retrieval and update codes.

Table 7.1 A typical dictionary format.

Position of data in record (attribute number)	*DICT name*	*Description (heading)*	*Length (in chars)*
0	REF	Staff ref	5
1	NAME	Name	20
2	DEPT	Dept	3
3	SALARY	Salary	10
4	ADDR	Address	30
5	AGE	Age	2
6	DOB	Date of birth	8

7.1.3 Dictionary item types

There are various types of dictionary item identified by the contents of attribute 1 (one). The dictionaries are hierarchical with the system dictionary defining the master dictionaries, whilst the master dictionary items define the file dictionaries which in turn define the data file.

File Definition Item – or D-pointer item

The file defining item is a record which contains the physical disk address of the file to which it relates. In the System dictionary it defines the location of the Master Dictionary, whilst the Master Dictionary D-pointers contain the location of the file dictionary, which contains D-pointers to the location of the physical data.

In addition the D-pointer contains a number of other attributes whose purpose is to define the size, access privileges and usage for the file. A detailed description of these attributes is given in Section 12.1 on dictionaries.

Attribute 0 : Item-id

Attribute 1: Dictionary code
In file defining items the first letter of attribute 1 is a **D**. If this record is in the system dictionary it defines the pointer to the master dictionary or account. In the master dictionary, the D-item defines a file dictionary and in a file dictionary it defines a data file. The file defining item is often referred to as the 'D-pointer' which can have other letters after the **D** in attribute 1 whose meaning is as follows:

C Defines the file as a 'pointer' file, mostly used to define program files (particularly in R83 where programs could only be compiled in a file of type **DC**. The file POINTER-FILE is often a **DC** type file.

L Logs any updates to the transaction logger.

N Disables update protection on a file even if global update protection is enabled, but may not be used with the **U** option. Update protection is a 'forced' write option mechanism which protects against GFE's.

P Ensures that the primary file space only contains pointer items, which means that all records are stored outside the file with pointers to them stored in the actual file. Advanced PICK does this anyway for items which are larger than 85% of the frame size. This option enables the same process for all records in the file.

S Item-ids in this file are case-sensitive.

U Enables update protection on a file even if global protection is disabled, but it may not be used with the **N** option.

X Do not save the *file contents* on a file save. The *file contents* referred to would apply to the whole account if on the D-pointer in the System Dictionary (**MDS**), the dictionary and data file files if applied to the D-pointer in the Master Dictionary (**MD**) and the data file if applied to the D-pointer in the file dictionary.

This can be a very useful means of reducing backup time, especially for accounts or files that are not frequently updated. It is not without its dangers however. Beware when restoring from a filesave tape which does not contain all the files of your system. The filesave tape overwrites the *entire* file system, so if a file is DX'd and not backed up, it will not be restored either and valuable data could be lost forever! It is therefore essential when restoring from a filesave tape to ensure it contains copies of **all** files on the system or that those accounts/file not on the tape are held on others and are able to be restored.

Y Files containing a DY in the first attribute will not be saved on a filesave tape. In this case, however, when the file restore is carried out, the file will be recreated empty, i.e. containing no records. An example of the use of this type of file would be temporary transaction files.

Attribute 2: Base
Attribute 2 contains the frame identification number (fid) of the associated file (see Section 7.2.1 for an explanation of the term fid).

Attribute 3: Modulo
Attribute 3 contains the number of contiguous frames in the primary file space of the file.

Attribute 4: Reserved and Unavailable

Attribute 5: Retrieval Lock
Determines a users access rights to records in the associated file. See Chapter 20 Section 20.1.2 for a discussion on the use of retrieval lock codes.

Attribute 6: Update Lock
Determines a users rights to update records in the associated file. See Chapter 20 Section 20.1.2 for a discussion on the use of update lock codes.

Attribute 7: Reserved and Unavailable

Attribute 8: Correlative
Processing codes specified in this attribute allow a file to function as an application by pre- and post-processing data, and are applied when an item in this file is updated. The post processing feature is not available in R83 releases.

Attribute 9: Justification
The attribute type contains codes used to specify justification for the item-id.

Attribute 10: Column Width
Attribute 11: Reserved and Unavailable
Attribute 12: Reserved and Unavailable
Attribute 13: Reallocation
Attribute 14: Input-Conversion
Attribute 15: Macro
Attribute 16: Output-Macro
Attribute 17: Description
Attribute 18: Reserved
Attribute 19: Reserved
Attribute 20 to attribute 30 inclusive: hotkeys

NB Attributes 14 onwards do not apply to R83 releases.

File Synonym Definition Item – or Q-item

In this situation attribute 1 contains a **Q**. If these occur in the system dictionary they 'point' to an actual account that a user logs to and in R83 this is the way in which user-ids are established, giving each user a unique logon name and password. In Advanced PICK of course a new file, **USERS** has been provided specifically for this purpose. In the master dictionary the Q-pointer is used to enable access to files held in another account. In the file dictionary the Q-pointer redefines or provides alternative names for existing attributes. This is either to make them shorter and easier to refer to, or to give them an alternative name to enable various departments of a company to refer to the same data by names they are familiar with. This concept of Q-pointers is fundamental to the PICK system and is discussed fully in Chapter 9.

Attribute Definition Item – or A-item

The structure of attribute defining items is described in full in Section 12.4. However these records are located in either the Master Dictionary or file dictionaries. In file dictionaries, attribute 1 usually contains an **A** to indicate the base (or initial) definition, with subsequent definitions being assigned the code **S**. Attribute definition items (ADIs) define the way in which data is to be formatted when output. It is important to bear in mind that ACCESS, the enquiry language, will use these A-items. For example, dates are held on the database as the number of days since 31 December 1967, with prior dates being held as negative numbers. The date can be displayed in various ways, dependent on the code held in the A-item. For instance, with the code D the date for 17 December 1996 will be displayed as 17 DEC 1996, but with the code as D2/ the date will be displayed as 17/12/96. Regardless of the 'output' format the date will be held on the database as a number, which for 17 December 1996 would be 10579, i.e. 10,579 days subsequent to 31 December 1967!

ADIs may also contain the code **X** which protects the ADI from being used in an ACCESS statement.

Other attribute defining items

There a many other types of item stored in the Master Dictionary (**MD**). The following is a summary of these, showing the first letter of attribute one. In most cases these can be found with additional characters following the initial letter.

C	primarily for the ACCESS enquiry language
M	for MACRO's where each command is displayed on the screen
ME	for MENU's created for use with the MENU processor
N	for MACRO's where no screen display is required of the commands executed
PQ	for PROC's
PQN	for new PROC's – a feature of McDonnell Douglas systems
Q	for Q-pointers
V	for system commands and compiled programs

7.2 File allocation and information retrieval

Before we start to use and manipulate data extensively within PICK accounts and files we need to know a little about the way in which data space is allocated and information stored and retrieved within it.

7.2.1 Disk map

Advanced PICK divides the entire hard disk into a series of equally sized blocks called **frames**, each of which is numbered consecutively from one up to the maximum FID (frame-ID) that the computer system can support. Figure 7.6 shows how the entire disk is divided into units called frames. These frames fall into a number of main sections:

Monitor frames are the 'brain' of the PICK system and reside between frame 1 and frame 23 and is the only part of PICK that is memory resident.

Boot ABS frames are reserved for the operating system and normally start at frame 24 and take anything from 1,200 to 1,800 frames depending on the hardware platform and any additional software that might be loaded.

User ABS frames are similar to boot ABS frames in that they contain operating system code which can be executed to change the functionality of the system or to add new features like special editors and communication packages. These are executed using the **EXEC** verb at TCL. User ABS are essentially special binary items that are attached to the file system and can therefore exist at any point on the disk.

PCB frames are where the root Program Control Blocks are stored for each of the users of the system. The PCB frames for normal users exist at a fixed location somewhere above the boot ABS frames, whilst the PCB frames for 'phantom' or background users are dynamically allocated and can exist at any place on the disk.

Data/overflow frames begin immediately after the PCB area and finish at the maximum FID. This section is used to build files, indexes, spooler jobs and all user-workspace attached to the PCB frames. Those frames not containing data are maintained as a pool of spare frames known as overflow.

Unlike previous PICK implementations, Advanced PICK automatically installs with a large pool of free PCBs irrespective of the number of users purchased. AP/Native for the PC for example loads with 73 PCBs and AP/Protected Mode for the PC with 257 even if the number of users purchased is as small as just one or two. This is to accommodate upgrades of the licence which increases the number of users and means that the requisite number of PCBs will already exist. In old releases of PICK, notably R83 for licencee

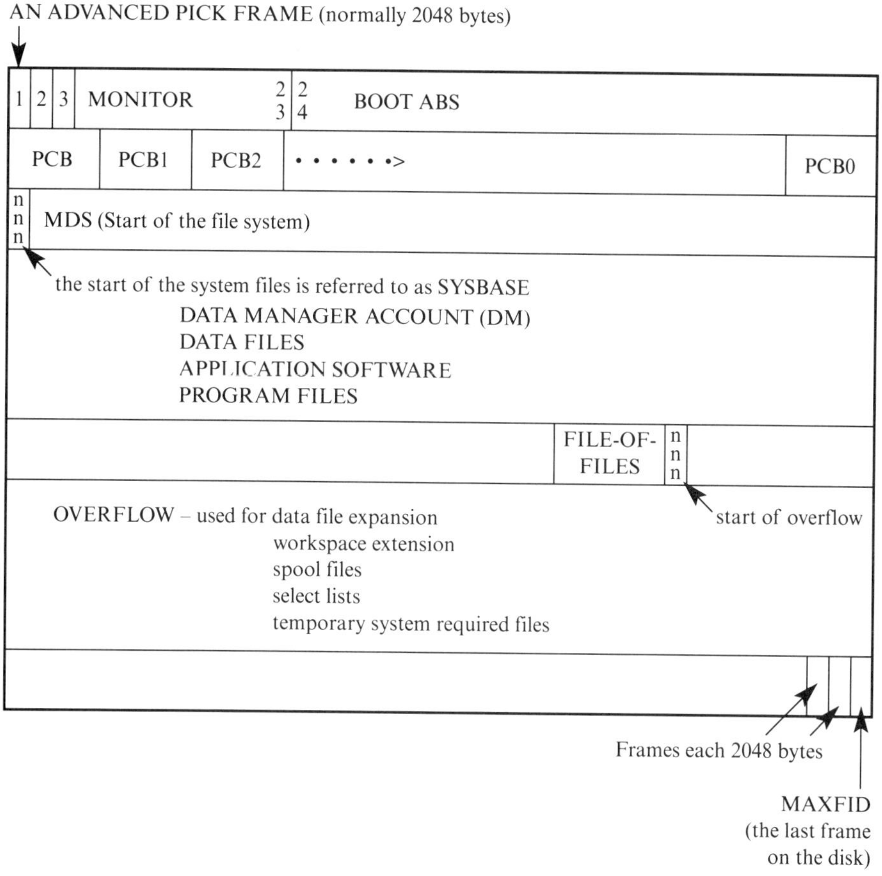

Figure 7.6 The disk map.

systems, to increase the number of users meant a full save of the system followed by a full restore during which the entire disk would be re-built and the required number of PCBs created.

In fact the number of licensed users can now be changed simply by the input of a code number supplied by PICK Systems and without even shutting down or re-booting the system.

As can be seen from Figure 7.6, the way in which the disk is laid out is dependent on the number of PCBs. However, in R83 a set number of workspace areas were built which were dependent on the number of licenced users purchased. If the number of users was subsequently increased it meant reloading the complete operating system and data files. This process caused R83 PICK to reorganize the disk and increase the number of PCB and workspace areas thus starting the system files at a new and higher frame number or FID.

7.2.2 Frame allocation

Information as we know is stored in a series of frames. On R83 the frame size is 512 bytes (i.e. 512 characters). R83 PICK uses the first 12 bytes of each frame for control information, leaving 500 bytes for user data. In AP/DOS and AP/Native the frame size was increased to 1024 byte frames with the first 24 bytes used for control purposes and the remaining 1000 for data. Most of the other Advanced PICK implementations including AP/PRO (Protected Mode) for the PC and those versions of AP that run under UNIX or AIX use 2048 byte frames. In these, the first 48 bytes are reserved for linkages and 2000 bytes for data. To determine the frame size of your system perform a **WHAT** command and look at **dfsize**. This only show the size of the data area, so if it says 2000 it means the frame size is 2K (2048) and if it says 1000 your frame size is 1K or 1024 bytes.

In creating a file it is necessary to define the initial number of frames it should have allocated to it and it is best to ensure this is large enough to handle the expected data size. This initial frame allocation is known as the file's *primary area*, and the stated number of contiguous (adjoining) frames are then allocated to the primary area for that file. Bear in mind, however, that whilst the initial amount of disk space allocated can grow or shrink during the use of the file, it will not shrink below that of the initial space allocated. This presents the dilemma of sizing your file sensibly (discussed in detail later in this chapter). If the initial space is too big, valuable disk space will be wasted. If however the initial space is too small, frames which can literally reside anywhere in the overflow are will be 'linked' to the primary file area forcing PICK to make many disk accesses to find the data and thereby lengthening response times. In the days when disk space was at a premium, this was far more of an issue than it is today. With disk space being so cheap (relatively), it is best to oversize than undersize files.

If the disk is very badly fragmented and the number of frames you need initially are scattered about the disk rather than available as one contiguous area, the file cannot be created and PICK will tell you so. Whilst this rarely happens it is worth being aware of, especially if you intend using large files. When frames are linked together to form a file, they are no longer referred to as frames, but as groups. This is because other frames can be linked into them as the storage requirements for the file increase. If we create a file containing seven frames initially, those frames will be adjoining and each now becomes the base frame of its group. The very first frame used is known as the base frame of the file. Figure 7.7 shows such a file using frames 21458 to 21464.

The number of groups a file contains is known as its modulo. Hence the file created in Figure 7.7 has a **modulo** of 7 (or primary space of seven single frame groups). If, as data is stored in the file, the initial allocation of frames is insufficient, PICK will link in others. These are not tagged onto the end of the existing file, but linked into the existing group requiring the space. Using the example of Figure 7.7, this means that the additional frames are linked into the existing frames, 21458–21464, rather than extending the original number of

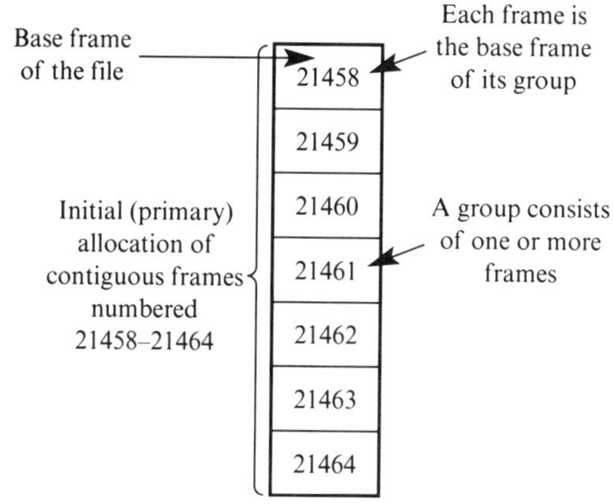

Figure 7.7 Initial allocation of frames to a file.

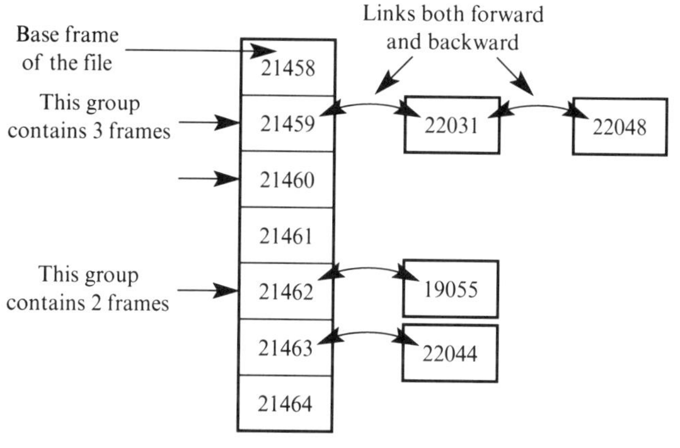

Figure 7.8 The linking of frames to a file.

base frames by adding from 21465 onwards. This is illustrated in Figure 7.8 where two linked frames have been added to group 21459 and a single linked frame added to groups 21462 and 21463.

The idea in creating a file is to optimize the time taken to read and write data to it. As is apparent from Figure 7.8, the frames subsequently linked into a group bear no relation to the original ones. They may be higher or lower and are linked in on the basis of being the 'next available' in the list of unused frames. This means that after coming to the end of one frame, to get to the next PICK will have to 'jump' to it and this generates what is known as a "frame fault".

The management of frames is handled by the only memory resident portion of Advanced PICK, the MONITOR. Just like the hard disk, real memory (RAM) is also divided into a series of blocks, known as buffers. When a frame is brought into memory it is assigned an available memory buffer by the PICK monitor and when a specific frame is requested, the Monitor will first check to see whether the frame is already memory resident. If not the Monitor generates what is known as a 'frame fault'. This is nowhere near as drastic as it sounds. It just means that PICK has to issue a command for the appropriate frame to be read from disk. Obviously a certain amount of time will be wasted in doing so, since the physical location of the frame (its track and sector) has to be determined (a calculation involving its FID) and a disk read initiated. However, any disk read will automatically terminate a users' timeslice thus suspending his processing. It may be apparent, therefore, that the continued generation of 'frame faults' will have a detrimental impact on user response. With the advance of disk caching controllers (controllers which contain their own local RAM), quite frequently whole tracks of a disk are stored at a time, so retrieving a frame is often as simple as a RAM (on the disk controller) to RAM (real memory) transfer.

In early implementations of R83 PICK there were only 500 bytes (characters) in each frame that could contain data, so any file containing records regularly over 500 bytes frequently generated frame faults. In those days the way to minimize the problem was to specify the number of frames to be allocated to each contiguous group. This number is known as the **separation** of the file. In the example of Figure 7.7, since no separation was specified, the number of frames in each group was one and new frames linked in were linked in one at a time. Its separation, therefore, is 1.

For files containing large records, the separation in R83 PICK can be increased to 2 or more but do remember that the separation in Advanced PICK **cannot** be altered and therefore will always be one. By increasing the separation of a file, the number of initial frames required by a file (its primary space) will be its modulo (the number of groups it contains) multiplied by its separation (the number of contiguous frames in a group). Once again the entire number of initial frames a file needs must be available in one contiguous area. Figure 7.9 shows how initial space is allocated to a file whose modulo is 7 and whose separation is 2. A total of 14 consecutive frames are used, 21458–21471.

Additional frames as needed are linked to the existing groups as before, except that they are linked in, in multiples of the separation. Hence if the separation is 3, three adjoining frames at a time are linked in; if the separation is 2, then two adjoining frames at a time are linked in and so on. Figure 7.10 shows how two batches of frames have been linked to group 21460, whilst groups 21466 and 21467 contain just one additional link of two frames.

Care should be exercised when increasing the separation above 1, since it could readily result in considerable wasted disk space. If the average record requires 550 bytes, to allocate two frames as the separation would mean that on average 450 bytes ((2 × 500) – 550) would be wasted in each group! It may well

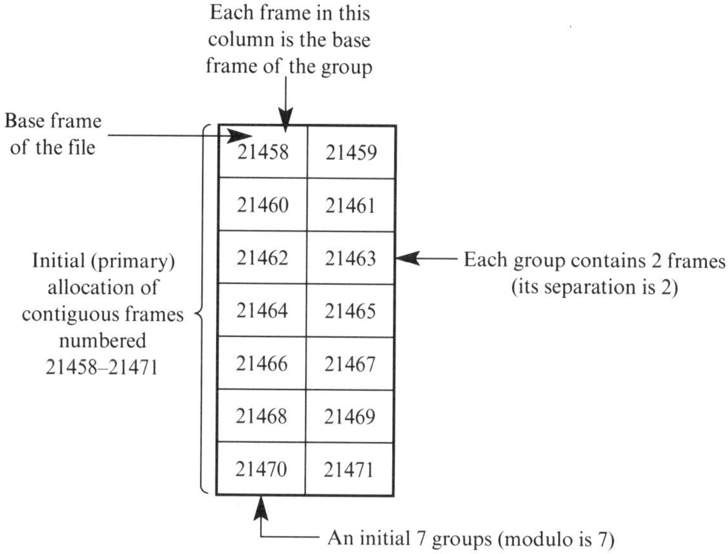

Figure 7.9 Initial allocation of frames to a file whose modulo is 7 and whose separation is 2.

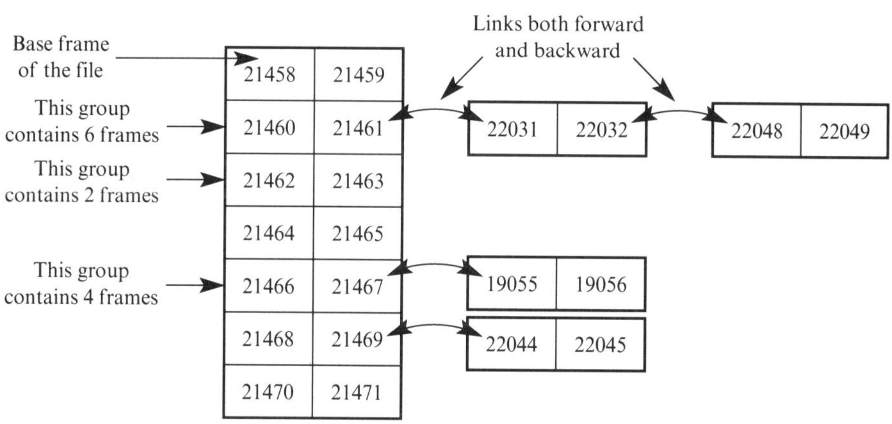

Figure 7.10 Linking additional frames to a file with a separation of 2.

be better to leave the separation at 1 and incur the frame faults. This is the dilemma to be faced when creating a file: a balance has to be struck between the speed of data access and wasted disk space.

It is important to note that Advanced PICK and indeed a number of R83 licencee implementations will not allow the separation to be altered, leaving it set to its default value of one. Having talked about frame faults and the problems it poses with response, it may seem strange to have a separation fixed at one frame. The reason for this is because in a multi-user environment, by the time PICK has determined that the data it is looking for is not in the frame being searched and generates a 'frame fault', another user has sought information from the disk causing the disk heads to be moved elsewhere. It is therefore of limited value to have the frames located together with a separation greater than one, other than in a single-user or low-activity multi-user environment. However, if your system has the ability to change the separation factor and the file mostly contains large items, it is worth doing. Whilst it may in the main not help too much, because the heads of the disk are 'elsewhere', it can never do any harm!

7.2.3 The storage and retrieval of items in a file

PICK uses a hashing technique to store and locate a specific item in a file. It uses a mathematical formula on the item-id and the file modulo and separation to compute a 'remainder' that it adds to the file base to give the starting FID (frame number) of the exact group to contain the item. When records are added to a file, therefore, they are added to a specific group but in no ordered position in the group; the item is added to the end of the other items in the group.

Whilst PICK does not know exactly where in the group a particular item resides, it normally takes very little time to search through the group's frames to find it. In a correctly sized file the hashing algorithm gives almost instant access to information, regardless of the number of records stored, and cuts out the overhead of searching through indices or B-tree structures which is how many other database systems structure their data.

Items are stored sequentially within their group, each being separated by a special character called a 'delimiter'. New items that are added to a group are added to the end of the existing chain of items within it. So as you can see there is no order *at all* to the sequence of items held in a group. Items that get changed during processing are treated as if they were a new item. They are first removed from their original position in the group with the rest of the items in the group being shuffled up to close the gap. After processing, the amended item is added to the end of all the other items of the group. When the initial allocation of frames in the group has been used up, other frames are linked into the group by a series of pointers and data continues into them. The contents of an item can therefore straddle frames.

7.2.4 Frame and group formats

A frame comprises a control and a data section. The data portion is always a multiple of 500 bytes, with the remainder of bytes in the frame being allocated to the control portion.

Frame size	*Control portion*	*Data portion*
512 bytes	12 bytes	500 bytes
1024 bytes (1K)	24 bytes	1000 bytes
2048 bytes (2K)	48 bytes	2000 bytes
4096 bytes (4K)	96 bytes	4000 bytes

In general, the larger the frame size the more efficient the system operation. Regardless of frame size the first 12 bytes contain the link information. The link information shows the frames' position by holding details of the frames to which it points both forwards and backwards. The layout of these 12 bytes is shown in Figure 7.11.

In systems where the control portion of a frame is larger than 12 bytes, the remainder is reserved by PICK and is not made accessible, even through the system debugger. The data portion of a frame is used for the storage of data. At the start of each item are 8 bytes of 'header' information which are made up as follows:

Bytes 0–3	Unused
Bytes 4–5	Item size
Byte 6	Item Flags
Byte 7	Number of saves

The function of each of these is described below:

Bytes 0–3
Item locks used to be stored in the item header, but are now stored in a LOCK table, which permits a process to lock a record and to lock it again at the same

1	2	3	4	5	6	7	8	9	10	11	12
*	NNCF	← Forward Link →				← Backward link →				NPCF	*

* – Reserved

NNCF – The count of the number of contiguous frames linked from this one (the Number of Next Contiguous Frames)

Forward Link – The FID of the frame linked forward from this one

Backward Link – The FID of the frame linked previous to this one

NPCF – The count of the number of contiguous frames linked backward to this one (the Number of Previous Contiguous Frames)

NNCF and NPCF are usually zero, except in data files whose seperation is greater than 1

Figure 7.11 Frame format – the first 12 bytes.

TCL level. However if the record is locked and TCL is pushed a level, the locking process prevents the same record being locked again. Now that item locking details are held outside the body of the item, the first 4 bytes in the header are no longer used.

Item size
The item size is the number of bytes from the start of the 8 byte header to the segment mark at the end of the stored record. The record stored will be the actual data record (if less than 85% of the frame size) or a pointer record (if the record length exceeds 85% of the frame size).

Item flags
This byte is possibly the most important in the system. It identifies the item type and other details used in the incremental save processes. The detail structure of this byte is as follows:

Byte 0	Indicates a Pointer-item, pointing to an 'out-of-line' item
Byte 1	Indicates a binary item, pointing to an 'out-of-line' item
Byte 2	Indicates a D-pointer (file definition item)
Byte 3	Indicates item-updated since last file-save
Byte 4	If bit 2 = 1, then this bit indicates file renamed since last file-save
Byte 5	If bit 2 = 0, then this bit indicates new item locked (i.e. with the Editor)
	If bit 2 = 1, then this bit indicates file cleared since last file-save
Byte 6	If bit 2 = 1 then this bit indicates file stolen from another account
Byte 7	Indicates item deleted since last full file save

Number of saves
The number of saves byte gets incremented at the beginning of a full save. When a full file-save finishes, the system goes back clearing the *updated*, *cleared* and *renamed* flags in all items and it removes the items flagged as *deleted*. This is handled when the system displays the message *clearing dirty bits* and has to be done once the file-save is known to be correct and has been validated. Thus this byte will identify whether or not the item has been updated before or during the file-save.

Directly following the header is the item-id (attribute 0) followed by an attribute mark, followed by attribute 1 and an attribute mark and so on. Between each attribute of the item is the attribute delimiter ^ (ASCII value 254). Should the attribute contain multiple values, the value mark symbol] (ASCII value 253) appears at the end of each value. A segment mark _ (ASCII value 255) is placed at the end of the item and if this ends on an odd byte number, a second segment mark is added. This is because Advanced PICK requires each item to end on an even byte boundary. Regardless of whether or not the item has one or two segment marks on it, a further segment mark is added if the item is the last in its group. So to look at a frame by 'dumping' its contents would show not only the data, but all the delimiter characters too. A typical frame format is shown in Figure 7.12.

:item myfile 3001 ◄ the **item** verb is used to locate the frame containing a particular item

```
3001
 59841.0000      00BE 3001
 59841.00BE      010A 10012
2 items 456 bytes 0/456 frames in group 59841
:
```

:dump 59841

```
  fid:    59841 :    0       0       0   0  (  E9C1 :  0     0      0  0 )
000 :........3001^This is the first attribute^This is t:
050 :he second attribute^This attribute has MULTI-VALUE:
100 :S]Next multi-value]Third multi-value]and a final m:
150 :ulti-value^This is the final attribute^_........10:
200 :012^The next item starts here and continues until :
250 :the next item is reached and so on. If the item i:
300 :s the last in the group and ends on an odd byte bo:
350 :undary then TWO additional segment marks are added:
400 :, otherwise just one additional segment mark is ad:
450 :ded^___.......2395^Aprote Systems Ltd^^Phoenix Hou:
500 :se]Sandown Road]Coulsdon]Surrey]CR3 3HR^^^0737-553:
550 :153^^PHO^D^SH^^^^MISC.ADDS*WPZYGO^8634^WPZYGO^^^13:
600 :21^1321^Y^___.......4018^WWF^^(Worldwide Fund for :
650 :Nature)]PO Box 38]Burton Upon Trent^DE14 3LP^GB^02:  ◄──
700 :83-66311]0283-67201^]^PHO]FAX^^^^^^^9446^^^^^^S^^^:
750 :^^^N^__...w...1313^KENNICK MUSIC^^11 KINGS ROAD]LO:
800 : NDON]SW3 ^^D^589-7711^^PHO^P^AM^AF^^WB4^MISC.ADDS:
850 :KMUSIC^8285^KMUSIC^^^^^Y^__.......2936^Wolseley Ce:
900 :nters Ltd^^PO Box 21]Boroughbridge Road]Ripon]N Yo:
950 :rks HG4 1SL^^GB^0765 690690]0765 690100^^PHO]FA:
```

3 segment marks on this line show the end of items in this frame

Figure 7.12 Typical output from dumping a frame.

From figure 7.12, it can be seen that the actual data store in frame 59841 ends on an odd number byte boundary, byte 453 hence it is followed by three segment marks. The information that follows the segment marks is left over from the last time the frame was used. It is therefore apparent that when PICK returns a frame to the overflow manager, it does not clear its previous contents; new information is simply written over the top of the old data. The implications for data security are obvious. So if the information you are working with is sensitive, remember to substitute the sensitive information with a dummy string of characters, such as **X**s before deleting the item.

When more than one frame is linked together in the group it is possible to see the entire contents of the group by typing the letter G (group) after the frame number. Figure 7.13 shows the output resulting from the dumping of a group of two linked frames. This follows the links forward.

7.2.5 The storage of large items

In R83 PICK all data items regardless of their size are stored in the data portion of the file. This can have an impact on system response if the file contains many large records, since locating an item means reading sequentially through its group until it is found.

```
:dump 59841 G
fid:   59841 :   0  35911       0   0  (  E9C1 :  0    8C47        0  0 )
000 :........3001^This is the first attribute^This is t:
050 :he second attribute^This attribute has MULTI-VALUE:
100 :S]Next multi-value]Third multi-value]and a final m:
150 :ulti-value^This is the final attribute^_........10:
200 :012^The next item starts here and continues until :
250 :the next item is reached and so on. If the item i:
300 :s the last in the group and ends on an odd byte bo:
350 :undary then TWO additional segment marks are added:
400 :, otherwise just one additional segment mark is ad:
450 :ded^__....Y...3404^This is the third item in the g:
500 :roup and to be found added to the end of the exist:
550 :ing items in a group. This is the first attribute:
600 : of the third record^Like so many Advanced PICK it:
650 :ems, this one also contains multi-values]this bein:
700 :g the second value]this is the third value of the :
750 :second attribute^This is the third attribute of th:
800 :e item whose item-id is 3404^When the length of th:
850 :is record exceeds the frame size, a 'free' frame i:
900 :s linked in from the overflow table and the balanc:
950 :e of the record written into the 'linked' frame un:

+ fid:   35911 :   0       0  59841   0  (  8C47 : 0       0    E9C1   0 )
000 :til the full details of the final item have been s:
050 :tored^____________________________________________:
100 :__________________________________________________:
150 :__________________________________________________:
200 :__________________________________________________:
250 :__________________________________________________:
300 :__________________________________________________:
350 :__________________________________________________:
400 :__________________________________________________:
450 :__________________________________________________:
500 :__________________________________________________:
550 :__________________________________________________:
600 :__________________________________________________:
650 :__________________________________________________:
700 :__________________________________________________:
750 :__________________________________________________:
800 :__________________________________________________:
850 :__________________________________________________:
900 :__________________________________________________:
950 :__________________________________________________:
:
```

Figure 7.13 The typical output from dumping a group of frames.

Advanced PICK introduced the concept of 'out-of-line' processing for large items; a large item being one whose size exceeds about 85% of the frame size. For these records all that is stored in the file is a 'pointer', the record itself is stored outside the file altogether. Whilst this means locating the record is a two stage process (first reading the pointer record, then retrieving the record), overall system performance is significantly improved. An example of an 'out-of-line' item is shown in Figure 7.14.

In this example, the actual data for the record whose item-id is 3404, is not stored in the data file and looking at the contents of frame 59841, we can see that all that follows the item-id is the frame number (fid) which contains the data. The frame number is stored as a hex number (to the base of 16), so the **dump** command has to be preceded with a full stop, to tell PICK that what follows is in hex.

You will notice too, that the actual data in frame 35907 (hex 8C43) does not contain an 8 byte header. All the item flags are stored against the 'pointer' record, so the actual data record is preceded with a single segment mark (hex FF) and terminated with two or three segment marks (dependent on whether or not the item ends on an even or odd byte boundary).

:dump 59841 G

```
 fid:   59841 :   0      0      0    0   ( E9C1 :  0       0      0  0 )
000 :........3001^This is the first attribute^This is t:
050 :he second attribute^This attribute has MULTI-VALUE:
100 :S]Next multi-value]Third multi-value]and a final m:
150 :ulti-value^This is the final attribute^_........10:
200 :012^The next item starts here and continues until:
250 :the next item is reached and so on. If the item i:
300 :s the last in the group and ends on an odd byte bo:
350 :undary then TWO additional segment marks are added:
400 :, otherwise just one additional segment mark is ad:
450 :ded^__........3404^008C43^___...w...1313^KENNICK M:
500 :USIC^^11 KINGS ROAD]LONDON]SW3 ^^D^589-7711^^PHO^P:
550 :^AM^AF^^WB4^MISC.ADDS*KMUSIC^8285^KMUSIC^^^^^Y^__^:
600 :^^9446^^^^^^S^^^^^^N^_....w...1313^KENNICK MUSIC^^:
650 :11 KINGS ROAD]LONDON]SW3 ^^D^589-7711^^PHO^P^AM^AF:
700 :^^WB4^MISC.ADDS*KMUSIC^8285^KMUSIC^^^^^Y^__^PHO]FA:
750 :X^^^^^^^9446^^^^^^S^^^^^^N^_....w...1313^KENNICK M:
800 :USIC^^11 KINGS ROAD]LONDON]SW3 ^^D^589-7711^^PHO^P:
850 :^AM^AF^^WB4^MISC.ADDS*KMUSIC^8285^KMUSIC^^^^^Y^__i:
900 :s linked in from the overflow table and the balanc:
950 :e of the record written into the 'linked' frame un:
```

← frame 8C43 contains the ACTUAL data for the item 3404 (line 450)

:dump .8C43 ← the frame number is stored in hex, so to dump the frame you need to preceed the fid with a full stop

```
fid: 35907 : 0 0 0 0 ( 8C43 : 0 0 0 0 )
000 :_3404^This is the third item in the group and to b:
050 :e found added to the end of the existing items in :
100 :a group. This is the first attribute of the third:
150 : record^Like so many Advanced PICK items, this one:
200 : also contains multi-values]this being the second :
250 :value]this is the third value of the second attrib:
300 :ute^This is the third attribute of the item whose :
350 :item-id is 3404^When the length of this record exc:
400 :eeds the frame size, a 'free' frame is linked in f:
450 :rom the overflow table and the balance of the reco:
500 :rd written into the 'linked' frame until the full :
550 :details of the final item have been stored^In this:
600 :example the record is too large to store in the ma:
650 :in portion of the data file as it exceeds 862 byte:
700 :s on this 1K frame implementation of Advanced PICK:
750 :.  The data file contains a pointer to this record:
800 : and the item header details in front of the point:
850 :er record are the item flags for this data record^:
900 :__________________________________________________:
```

Figure 7.14 The storage of 'large' items in Advanced PICK.

In a 1K frame system items are stored 'out-of-line' when they reach 862 bytes, whilst on a 2K frame system items need to reach 1720 bytes before they are stored 'out-of-line'.

If you wish to have all items in a file stored 'out-of-line', then create the file with the **p** option (see Section 6.3.1).

7.2.6 How to size files correctly

Having discussed the way in which items are stored in files, it is apparent that it is very important to select the correct modulo and separation for a file to minimize both the number of frame faults when accessing data and the amount of wasted space. As we have seen there is a fine balance to be taken between the two and to assist in optimizing retrieval time, it is important to spread the data *evenly* throughout the file.

The number of disk reads, which increases dramatically as the number of frames per group increases, is the factor that will contribute most to the degradation of your system. Even so, it is not wise initially to allocate the maximum number of frames you think a file will use,. This is because the original, contiguous number of frames assigned will not be reduced and a lot of space, not frequently used, will be wasted. You should aim, therefore, to allocate an initial area which takes the average file size into account, since PICK will link extra frames into a group as it needs to, and will release those frames when they are no longer needed. These 'available' frames are taken from, and returned to, a central pool called 'overflow'.

Calculation of file size in Advanced PICK

In Advanced PICK the separation is always one, so the only consideration is the modulo of the file. This is calculated as follows:

(1) Determine the average number of records that fall below the 'out-of-line' size of 85% of the frame size.

(2) Multiply this number by the average size of these records.

(3) Determine the average number of 'out-of-line' records and multiply this by the aggregation of the number of characters of the item-id and 8 (8 is the number of bytes in the header).

(4) Add together the result from points 2 and 3 and divide by 90% of the frame size.

(5) Make the result a prime number.

The result is the modulo for the file and by using 90% of the frame size as the divisor, the result allows for a certain amount of growth before overflow frames are likely to be needed.

Calculation of file size in R83 PICK

In R83, there are two considerations; for records above and below the frame size in length.

A. *For records less than the frame size*

(1) Determine the total file size by multiplying the average record length by the average number of records.

(2) Divide the result from (1) by 90% of the frame size.

(3) Make the result from (2) a prime number.

The modulo is the result of (3) and the file separation is one.

B. *For records greater than the frame size*

(1) Make a prime number out of the number of records. This becomes the modulo of the file.

(2) Divide the average record length by 90% of the frame size and round the answer. This becomes the separation.

The result ensures the best distribution of records and ensures that each frame added to the separation is more than 50% utilized.

General aspects of file sizing

In order to determine the prime number use the TCL verb **prime**. Should your system not have this function Appendix B contains a full list of prime numbers up to 32,719 the maximum supported in R83. Should you not be able to determine a prime number for whatever reason, take a guess but at least ensure the answer is an odd number. A modulo should NEVER be a multiple of 2 or 5.

In Advanced PICK the separation can not be more than one, but even with PICK R83, there are many people who will never increase the separation above one. They hold the firm belief that since PICK is a multi-user environment the disk heads will almost definitely have moved between the request for the first and subsequent frames of a group. This thus makes the importance of having these frames adjacent only marginal. Whilst this is often true, certain computers can take advantage of having the data adjacent, in which case the use of a separation greater than one, where appropriate, would improve response times. A separation greater than one can do no harm. So if your system supports it and your calculations determine you need it, apply a the appropriate separation factor in your file creation parameters.

7.3 Checking item distribution and optimizing file size

Having stressed the importance of sizing files correctly, you will be pleased to know that PICK gives you the means not only to check the distribution of items within a file using its current modulo, but to test the impact on the distribution of the items of an alternative modulo, a 'what if' process. The verb to check out the existing file modulo is **ISTAT**. This provides a histogram of the items held within each group and, at the end of the list, produces statistics which assist in deciding whether the current modulo size is correct. Figure 7.15 shows the typical output of this command on the system dictionary **mds**.

It can be seen from Figure 7.15 that there is no major problem with the file modulo. Items are distributed fairly evenly with, on average, just under seven items per group. There are no empty groups and an acceptable average number of bytes per group based on the frame size of 1000 characters.

There is a special option in Advanced PICK to review the position on 'out-of-line' items. This is the **r** option. Another option, the **s** option will suppress the histogram detail on each frame and just provide the statistics. Figure 7.16 gives and example of the difference using these options.

Determining the correct modulo first requires an analysis of the file statistics. Providing that the average number of bytes per group is in line with the frame size, the file modulo is satisfactory and does not change. However if it is higher than about 90% of the frame size it is worth considering re-sizing the file (see Section 7.4). Before you can re-size a file you need to determine the correct modulo. Whilst you can use the formula shown in Section 7.2.6 it is often difficult to get the raw data needed which is why **ISTAT** is so useful. It provides actual statistics based on actual data.

:istat mds

```
file= mds         modulo= 7                              13:45:00 25 Feb 1995
frames  bytes     items
    1       446        5 >>>>>
    1       388        8 >>>>>>>>
    1       680        7 >>>>>>>
    1       526        9 >>>>>>>>>
    1       340        5 >>>>>
    1       290        4 >>>>
    1       640        9 >>>>>>>>>
    7

                                             Hash-Test/Istat Statistics

    total item count =          47                byte count =                3310
      avg. bytes/item =       70.4                avg. items/group =           6.7
        std. deviation =       2.0                avg. bytes/group =          72.8
:
```

Figure 7.15 Output from **ISTAT** on the system dictionary file **mds**.

```
:istat admin,ad.cmp (s
file= admin,ad.cmp,          modulo= 541                   13:48:49 25 Feb 1995
frames  bytes items
   809

                                            Hash-Test/Istat Statistics

   total item count =      3443          byte count =              556414
    avg. bytes/item =     161.6          avg. items/group =           6.3
     std. deviation =        .9          avg. bytes/group =        1028.4

:istat admin,ad.cmp, (sr

file= admin,ad.cmp,          modulo= 541                   13:46:59 25 Feb 1995
frames bytes items
   809

                             Hash-Test/Istat Statistics

   total item count =      3443       byte count =                       556414
 deleted item count =         0       deleted item byte count =               0
 pointer item count =         4       pointer item byte count =            5035
                                      total byte count =                 561449

    avg. bytes/item =     163.0       avg. items/group =                    6.3
     std. deviation =        .9       avg. bytes/group =                 1037.7
:
```

Figure 7.16 The **S** and **R** options of the **ISTAT** verb.

The verb **HASH-TEST** is used to test out alternative modulos for a file, *prior* to resizing the file. It enables a 'what if' test to be done, without affecting the existing file in any way. Figure 7.17 shows **HASH-TEST** being used on the system dictionary (**mds**), with a test modulo of 3 frames.

```
:hash-test mds

test modulo: 3

Hash-test mds
file= mds        modulo= 3                         13:55:54 25 Feb 1995

frames  bytes    items
   2      1062     13 >>>>>>>>>>>>>
   2      1020     18 >>>>>>>>>>>>>>>>>>
   2      1228     16 >>>>>>>>>>>>>>>>
   6

                            Hash-Test/Istat Statistics

   total item count =       47          byte count =              3310
    avg. bytes/item =     70.4          avg. items/group =        15.6
     std. deviation =      2.5          avg. bytes/group =      1103.3
:
```

Figure 7.17 Output from **HASH-TEST** on the system dictionary file **mds.**

From Figure 7.17 we can see that the standard deviation has increased and that the average byte/group has exceeded the 1K frame size. Even though this is not such a good modulo, we can see that the number of frames used is 6, one less than when the modulo was 7 (see Figure 7.15). The standard deviation is based on the number of items/group and with the best distribution being one item per group, the ideal standard deviation for a PICK file is zero! However since the distribution of items in a file is based on their item-ids, a standard deviation of zero is difficult to achieve. You should therefore look to minimize the standard deviation, whilst at the same time trying to achieve a realistic number of items in a group. If you produce a histogram for a file, then try to

```
:hash-test mds

test modulo:11

Hash-test mds
file= mds        modulo= 11                            13:55:54 25 Feb 1995

frames  bytes items
    1      432      5 >>>>>
    1      274      3 >>>
    1       92        1 >
    1      518      7 >>>>>>>
    1      504      6 >>>>>>
    1      272      3 >>>
    1      370      6 >>>>>>
    1      470      7 >>>>>>>
    1      212      5 >>>>>
    1       72        3 >>>
    1       94        1 >
   11

                          Hash-Test/Istat Statistics

   total item count =       47         byte count =                3310
    avg. bytes/item =     70.4         avg. items/group =           4.2
     std. deviation =      2.1         avg. bytes/group =         300.9

:hash-test mds (s

test modulo:47

Hash-test mds
file= mds        modulo= 47                            13:59:27 25 Feb 1995
frames  bytes items
    47
                          Hash-Test/Istat Statistics

   total item count =       47         byte count =                3310
    avg. bytes/item =     70.4         avg. items/group =           1.0
     std. deviation =       .8         avg. bytes/group =          70.4
:
```

Figure 7.18 Output from **HASH-TEST** on the system dictionary file **mds**.

ensure that the modulo you choose gives a reasonably even distribution of items per group.

Figure 7.18 shows the results of other modulo options. As with **istat** you can use the **s** option to suppress the histogram display, which is a useful option when the modulo is large.

At first glance the results shown in Figure 7.18 seem to provide a better, more even, distribution and the standard deviation is reduced. There is obviously no point in increasing the modulo above 47 as this is the number of records in the file and a record can only be stored in one group. The maximum number of groups, and hence modulo, is therefore 47. With the modulo set this big, there are 15 empty groups and with a frame size of 1K there are 47,000 bytes allocated to the file which holds a total of just 3,310 bytes of data. As you can see there is no easy answer to determining the correct modulo, but if you have plenty of disk space you can work towards trying to achieve one record per group. Otherwise look to bringing the average bytes per group around 90% of the frame size of your system.

Do also give careful consideration to the growth of files before spending time trimming down file sizes and regularly check files to see if they need resizing. The file statistics report created at the time a full **FILE-SAVE** is taken provides the information you need for this purpose.

7.4 File sizing and resizing

The **FILE-SAVE** command, explained further in Section 20.2.3, produces a valuable statistics report on each file on the system and a careful study of this report will enable you to locate those files which need resizing. If a current file statistics report is not to hand, one can be produced with the command **LIST-FILE-STATS**.

Having decided a file needs resizing and armed with the new modulo (and if an R83 file, its separation), there are a couple of ways in which you can carry out the resizing exercise. The third is by far the most usual in practice:

(1) Create a temporary file (**CREATE-FILE**) and into it copy (**COPY**) the contents of the file to be resized. Delete the original file (**DELETE-FILE**) and recreate (**CREATE-FILE**) it with the new modulo. Then copy (**COPY**) back all the items from the temporary file and delete (**DELETE-FILE**) the temporary file.

(2) Carry out an on-line file resize using the **RESIZE** verb.

(3) Using the Update Processor (**UP**) place the new modulo and separation in attribute 13 of the file definition item in the form (*n*,*m*), where *n* is the new file modulo and *m* is the new file separation. In Advanced PICK the separation can only be 1, so either set *m* to 1 or ignore the separation altogether and enter the modulo in attribute 13 in the form (*n*). The next

time the file or account containing the file is saved and restored, either as part of a full file save (**FILE-SAVE**) or selective restore (**SEL-RESTORE**), the file will be restored (**:FILES** or **ACCOUNT-RESTORE** or **RESTORE-ACCOUNTS**) with its new modulo.

The first method has its obvious problems. Part way through the process you have to delete the original file. If at this point you have unwittingly made mistakes in the proceeding steps, then the file has gone and you will need to restore it from a backup. If the file is one which is an integral part of an application, such as a sales order file, it may not be just as simple as restoring the file itself. It is possible that many others will also have to be restored, such as the order details, customers, stock and so on. Indeed in such a scenario not only would you need to roll back files to the time of the last backup, but all subsequent transactions will need to be re-entered.

The second method is to resize a file on-line. This can be done at any time without bringing down the system or stopping processing that affects the file being resized. The **RESIZE** command changes the modulo of a file and re-hashes all the items in the file to take account of the new modulo. The file can be used normally whilst the resize takes place and since no temporary copy of the file is made, very little temporary overflow space is required. This method of resizing is most likely to be used for a small number of files when response problems are experienced. For a more thorough resizing of the files of your system, the best method is by changing the parameters held in the file definition item.

The third method is the most commonly used process for carrying out a mass change of file size parameters. Remember that PICK files are in a hierarchy, starting at the System Dictionary (**mds**) and the resize parameters must be set in the record that controls the file to be resized:

- To resize the Master Dictionary place the parameters in the file definition item in the System Dictionary (**mds**).
- To resize a file dictionary place the parameters in the file definition item in the Master Dictionary.
- To resize a data file place the parameters in the file definition item in the file dictionary.

Figure 7.19 gives an example of resizing each of these file types, by resizing the account **ADMIN** and the dictionary and data files of the file called **ADDRESS**. Note that the **D** option is used when updating a file definition item otherwise the message [433] 'ADDRESS' is a file definition item and should not be edited will be displayed. Under **NO** circumstances change the modulo and separation parameters held in attributes 3 and 4. These are used in the hashing algorithm and any change will have disastrous consequences.

```
:U MDS ADMIN (D
type            D
base            60318
modulo          31
ret-lock
upd-lock
password
syspriv         SYS2
justification   L
width           10
reallocation    (191,1) <-- Resets the size of the account ADMIN to a modulo of 191 and separation of 1

:UD MD ADDRESS
dictionary-code D
base            65740
modulo          7
structure
retrieval-lock
update-lock
output-conversion
correlative
attribute-type  L
column-width    10
input-conversion
macro
output-macro
description
reallocation    (37) <-- Resets the size of the dictionary of the file ADDRESS to a modulo of 37 and
                         a separation of 1

:UD DICT ADDRESS ADDRESS
dictionary-code D
base            65442
modulo          101
structure
retrieval-lock
update-lock
output-conversion
correlative
attribute-type  L
column-width    10
input-conversion
macro
output-macro
description
reallocation    (373) <-- Resets the size of the data portion of the file ADDRESS to a modulo of 373
                          and a separation of 1
```

Figure 7.19 Resizing files by changing their re-allocation parameters.

8 Differences Between R83 and Advanced PICK

8.1 Introduction

This chapter is aimed at introducing Advanced PICK to those people who have worked with R83 previously and want to focus on the differences between the two products. It is important to remember that Advanced PICK is totally R83 compatible so *all* R83 functions will operate under Advanced PICK, even if there are alternative or better ways of doing things under Advanced PICK.

Obviously Advanced PICK has many new major facilities which do not exist in R83 and virtually all the existing R83 tools have been enhanced and supplemented with new commands and features. Some R83 products, such as PROC hardly get a mention in Advanced PICK because new tools (in the case of PROC, MACROs and MENUs) replace the old ones. The new facilities available in Advanced PICK mean that there is no longer a need to purchase certain third party products, TCL stackers and B-Tree indexing products for example.

Probably the most significant difference is the positioning of the product. Until Advanced PICK was released, PICK was purely an operating system and hoping to become the industry standard for multi-user operating systems. That race lost to UNIX and DOS networks, PICK is now positioned as a database which can be 'hosted' on other operating systems, although it can still be purchased as a native operating system.

8.2 Primary new facilities

Advanced PICK as the name implies has many enhancements over R83 and this section outlines the key enhancements. One of the most noticeable differences is the change of the TCL prompt from a greater than symbol (>) to that of a colon (:).

Assembler

The assembler language is now symbolically referenced. You will need to buy the new assembler and may have to rewrite your assembler modes.

Background or phantom processor

AP allows for the processing of phantom tasks in the background, one phantom process being allowed per eight AP users. This means a user can spawn a process which can be set off to execute as a background or hidden task allowing the user to continue the processing of other activities on their terminal. There is a queue to handle the scheduling of phantom jobs when all the available phantom pibs are busy.

B-tree indexes

AP provides B-tree indexes implemented at the operating system level. This means that *any* change to an item, even through the Editor or Update Processor, will update the B-tree index where appropriate. Indexes may be saved and restored during a FILE-SAVE process and can be used from ACCESS, the Update Processor and BASIC. Indexes may be used to 'cruise' through a file (scan forwards and backwards through the records in the file), 'bridge' (cross reference data from another file), 'zoom' (use an attribute which refers to another file to go to that file and edit its records) and 'double clutch' (use the index in the 'zoomed' file to cruise though its records).

Case insensitivity

Generally speaking AP is case insensitive, even within BASIC programs and AP can even cope with instructions in mixed case. There are instances where this can be a problem, so if required you can force case sensitivity.

Data Manager account

This is the replacement account for SYSPROG. If you try to use SYSPROG you will be operating within the account **DM** because SYSPROG is a Q-pointer to DM in the file MDS.

Dictionary structure

The dictionary structure has changed providing a much expanded item with attributes to hold input conversions, macros, descriptions, default display definitions and hotkeys. There are new attribute definition types to invoke the transaction logger against a file and to identify a file as case sensitive.

Enhanced BASIC

The original R83 compiler has been enhanced with facilities to provide access to B-Trees and ACCESS processing. In some AP implementations, namely the UNIX ones, BASIC statements can be compiled into machine code using Flash BASIC rather than the interpreted metacode normally produced by the PICK compiler.

Error logging

All error conditions are logged in the file **ERRORS**.

File paths

AP supports the ability to define a file path without having to set Q-pointers. The file path comprises the account name and file name each suffixed with a comma.

File size

In R83 a file was limited to a modulo of 65531, but in AP this limit has been removed with file size being limited to the size of the available free disk space.

File transfer utilities

AP has two new verbs **IMPORT** and **EXPORT** to transfer files between AP and DOS and UNIX.

Frame format

R83 used the first 12 bytes for system linkage information with data starting at the 13th byte. In AP this linkage information starts at byte 0 with data starting at byte 25 (on 1K frame systems) or byte 49 (on 2K frame systems). In R83 each item starts with 4 bytes (in hex) which specifies its size whilst in Advanced PICK each item is preceded with 8 bytes of control information, specifying not only its size, but other system information, such as whether or not the record has been updated since the last save took place.

File separation always 1

In R83 the file separation was a parameter that formed part of the file sizing calculations and could be set to any number, but in AP the separation is always 1 and no longer needs to be specified when files are created.

Form queue retention.

One of the annoying features of R83 was that if you logged from one account to another, your form queue would be reset to zero (the system default). This is not the case with AP where whether you use **LOGTO** or **TO** to log to another account, your current form queue is maintained.

Frame size

The frame size is more than likely different to your R83 system. The frame size on R83 PC PICK for example was normally 512 bytes whilst on AP for the PC it is 1024. On other AP implementations you may find this increased to 2048.

Hotkeys

Up to 11 hotkeys can be defined for both file and attribute defining items that allow the calling of BASIC subroutines using the **UP** command **x***n* using attributes 20 through 30 inclusive.

Incremental file save

AP allows for both full saves (as with R83) and incremental saves (new to AP) of the database. An incremental save will save only those items that have changed since the last full FILE-SAVE.

Item locking

Under AP, individual items are locked rather than groups of records as was the case with R83.

Item size limit

In R83 the item size was limited to 32K, but this is limitless under AP, restricted only by the amount of available disk space.

Item storage in files

Items are stored differently in files. All large items are not stored in the data file, only a pointer to their physical location is stored in the data file. The item itself is stored outside the main file ensuring a much speedier response when accessing the data records. Items must now start on even byte boundaries, so items may contain two segment marks at their end and the last item in a group may contain three.

Level pushing

AP has the ability to suspend one task and start a new one by pressing the 'level pushing' key (normally the BREAK or ESC key). When a command or program is interrupted in this way the system suspends the task, displays another prompt symbol (a colon) and awaits the command to be performed. AP supports up to 16 levels.

Macro processor

The MACRO processor is a substitute for PROC allowing for multiple TCL statements to be run by executing the MACRO.

Multiple ABS files

R83 only supported a single and fixed ABS area. In AP multiple ABS are supported and different users can operate with different ABS.

Menu processor

AP has a tool to build and run menus without the need of recourse to PROC.

New device drivers

AP has many new terminal and device drivers.

New processing codes

A number of new processing codes have been introduced. These include calling BASIC subroutines, character by character updating and an IF..THEN..ELSE code.

New system accounts

There are two new accounts supplied with AP, a quality assurance account **qa** which contains a sample of the database test procedures, **pa** (personal assistant) which is a sample of application and **tutor** a tutorial account containing sample data which allows users to try the AP facilities without corrupting their 'live' data accounts.

On-line help

AP comes with an account known as EPICK (Encyclopaedia PICK) which enables an on-line version of the EPICK manual within any account. Help is invoked by typing **HELP** followed by the topic.

Output Processor

The Output Processor is a text processor with the ability to handle proportional spacing, multiple fonts and a variety of other facilities (like building of indexes and table of contents) necessary to process output. The Output Processor is an enhanced version of RUNOFF.

Overflow table

The overflow manager has been re-written to make it more robust.

Pointer-file

The **DC** pointer-file type is no longer a unique file type and can be treated like any other file. Hence you can use the standard edit, copy and delete commands on it. It also means that you no longer need to identify a BASIC program file with the type **DC** as programs can be compiled from any file.

Seamless integration

AP now works as a database under many different operating environments allowing for direct access to the native file systems and peripheral devices. PICK BASIC may directly call user subroutines written in C as well as a number of built-in functions.

TCL input buffer

In R83 the maximum input of a TCL command was 140 characters with a line continuation character of underscore. In AP the limit is in excess of 300 characters but there is no continuation character.

TCL stacker

AP has a powerful and easy-to-use TCL stacker which allows prior commands to be quickly accessed, executed or modified before re-use using the Update Processor. A TCL stack is held for each user in the file **TCL-STACK** and contains all the previously executed commands for each user. This file needs pruning from time to time to stop it growing unwieldy.

Transaction logging

AP can log changes to the file system in the FILE-OF-FILES file. The information can then be used to perform selective saves and restores.

Unlimited item size

In R83 the item size limit was 32K (32,767 bytes). In AP support for items up to 2GB (2,147,483,647 bytes) has been provided.

Update Processor

The Update Processor is a full screen editor that uses file dictionaries to define data input, output and update processing. As a data management tool it provides the mean to access items in corresponding files.

User and account logins

The first noticeable difference between R83 and AP is the login sequence. In AP the user has to first be a known user (an item in the file USERS) before being able to log to an account. By having separate user identities, users logged to the same account can be readily distinguished from each other.

User exits

There are a number of new user exits and there may be some R83 ones which are no longer supported. You should refer to EPICK for a full list of these.

Workspace

In R83 workspace was limited to 32k which often meant systems would abort with the message **Not enough workspace**, in AP there is no limit (other than the physical amount of free disk space).

8.3 File structure changes

The basic file hierarchy has not changed, however the file **SYSTEM** has been replaced with the file **mds**.

The **SYSPROG** account is now the **dm** account and all users have to first enter a user-id which is to be found in the file **users** in the account **dm**. The original AP will be supplied with the user dm. So to log on first time round when prompted for a user-id enter **dm** and when prompted for a master dictionary enter **dm**. There is a Q-pointer for **SYSPROG** which points to **dm**.

The following file changes have been made and Q-pointers for these exist pointing to their AP equivalent:

Original R83	New AP
ACC	**accounts**
ERRMSG	**messages**
KEYBOARDS	**kb.pc**
FUNCKEYS	**kb.fk**
SYSTEM-ERRORS	**errors**
STAT-FILE	**file-of-files**
TERMS	**devices**

The following new files exist in the **dm** account:

abs	boot abs
bulletin	company messages to display at logon time
clashes	the invalid items removed by UPDATE-MD process
devs	used by the TANDEM, CONVERSE and MIRROR processes
gsym	global synonyms
iomap-file	character translation for keyboard input
jobs	phantom job status and history
pibs	process information blocks
tcl-stack	user TCL stacked commands
users	valid system users
words	dictionary used by the spell checker

The **COLDSTART** PROC has been replaced with the MACRO **SYSTEM-COLDSTART** which runs the programs **coldstart.log** and **coldstart** the last of which calls the MACRO **USER-COLDSTART**.

The frame size is likely to be different and is now either 1024 or 2048 characters with the system pointer information held at the end of the frame rather than the start of the frame. Data now starts at character 0 and has to end on an even byte boundary and hence may contain two segment marks at its end. This means that the last record in the frame may have three segment marks.

Not all data records are stored in the group in the data file. If the record gets big, PICK will store the item elsewhere, grabbing whatever number of frames are required for the item and storing the pointer to the first FID where the item can be found in the group it hashes to in the data file.

8.4 New TCL commands

There have been many additions to the TCL commands and the list below gives detail of these. In many cases existing commands have been given abbreviated versions, such as **lf** for **list-files** and **cl** for **copy-list**.

!	shell out to the DOS prompt in AP/DOS or the UNIX prompt in AP/UNIX
:dcd	toggles the data carrier detect protocol on and off for a port

:reset-async	resets a port to its default values
:scrub-ovf	initializes the overflow table
:shutdown	shuts down the entire PICK system
:xonoff	toggles the use of the X-ON/X-OFF communication protocol for a port
abs.fid	displays the current 'abs' information
absdump	dumps the abs file to magnetic media
account-maint	invokes a menu to create, modify, rename or delete user accounts
admin	invokes a systems admin menu from within the **DM** account
admin.control	a menu to set the system date and time, logoff processes and send messages
admin.files	a menu for data backup and restore
admin.maint	a menu for creating and maintaining users and accounts
admin.status	a menu for information on user status and system locks
admin.tape	a menu for listing and attaching devices
admin.tape.setup	a menu to assign various tape devices for use
assignfq	assigns a printer device driver to a Spooler form queue
b/list	format and output BASIC source code
basic	the BASIC compile verb which only accepts BASIC commands in upper case
blist	format and output BASIC source code
bootstrap	reloads the PICK operating system from the currently executing system and then invokes the 'coldstart' procedure
break-key	toggles the availability of the BREAK key or displays its present status
brk-debug	force BREAK key to invoke the debugger rather than push a level
brk-level	force BREAK key to push a level rather than invoke the debugger
buf-map	displays a visual 'map' of the file system indicating which frames are currently being held in the RAM buffer area.
buffers	displays a picture of the status of memory resident buffers
buffers.g	produces a histogram of buffer usage for a range of dates and times
bulletin.board	prints bulletins from the BULLETIN file in the DM account
capt	toggles the capturing of the TCL command in the file CAPTCL
capture-off	disables the capturing of TCL commands previously invoked with **capture-on**
capture-on	enables the capture of TCL commands in the file CAPTL
case	toggles case sensitivity
case-file	converts to case of the item-ids to either upper or lower case
case-off	disables case sensitivity on the current port
case-on	enables case sensitivity on the current port
cf	create-file
chg-device	changes a tape device
chksum	calculates a checksum for an entire file or list of items
choose.term	selects one of a variety of terminal types
cl	copy list
cleanpibs	clears tandem connections for all ports logged on before port zero
clear-index	clears the index for a given file
clear-locks	clears all locks
cls	clear terminal screen leaving cursor at bottom of screen
coldstart.log	records the type of shutdown in the file **ERRORS**
compare-list	comparison of two lists

compile	compile BASIC program where case sensitivity of statements is unimportant
conv-case	converts the characters within specified items to upper or lower case
converse	links the current process to another process through a given port
create	a simplified method of creating a file and dictionary items
create-abs	sets aside a contiguous set of frames as the destination for loading abs
create-index	creates a new b-tree index for a data file
create-macro	creates a MACRO from the last TCL command processed
create-nqptrs	builds a Q-pointer for each D-pointer in the DM account and adds them to the file NEWAC which are then added to the MD of all newly created accounts
db	invokes the debug command
dcd	toggles the status of the data carrier for the specified port
dcd-off	toggles off DCD on the specified port
dcd-on	toggles on DCD on the specified port
delete-index	deletes a b-tree index for a file
dev-att	attaches an unattached port to the current process
dev-det	detaches the port currently attached to the current process
df	delete file
diag	invokes the internal system diagnostic utility
dir	displays the DOS directory or in UNIX the equivalent of **listfiles**
disc	disconnects the current process from the PICK virtual machine
display	display text on the screen
dtr-off	toggles off DTR on a port
dtr-on	toggles on DTR on a port
esc-data	specifies that the code generated by the ESCape key is to be passed through as data
esc-level	forces ESC key to push a level rather than pass through code as data
esc-toggle	toggles function of ESC between that set by **esc-data** and **esc-level**
exec	runs the current process on the specified abs
export	export PICK data to DOS or UNIX files
f-resize	recalculates the file modulos and attempts to determine the most optimum modulo for every file referenced in **FILE-OF-FILES**
fid	displays information about a memory-resident frame
fl	forms a single list from two lists
font-parms	upgrades fonts
frame-fault	diagnostic tool and randomly causes 'write frame-faults' by 'dirtying' frames in the data file space
free	displays graphical representation of the used and unused frames
gl	get list
help	interface to on-line help
import	imports DOS or UNIX files to PICK items
initovf	initiates the PICK overflow table
iselect	selects all item-ids in the group that the specified item-id hashes to using the **ITEM** verb. Useful when dealing with GFEs to determine the items to be copied out of the group
isselect	a version of **iselect** which lists the item-ids in sorted order
jobs-status	determines the status of a phantom job
l	list

ld	list dictionary – column output of dictionary items showing primary information, such as correlatives, conversions, etc.
legend	displays current legend or toggles legend on/off status
legend-off	toggles off the automatic page legend printed on every page
legend-on	toggles on the automatic page legend
lerrs	a MACRO to print a number of reports from the **ERRORS** file
lf	list files
lfd	a sorted listing of files with their description
lfs	a MACRO containing the ACCESS sentence executed by **LIST-FILE-STATS**
link-pibdev	creates a logical link between the given port and the designated device
list-abs	a report of each PICK mode in the **DM,ABS,** file
list-commands	a MACRO producing a report showing every executable command in the MD
list-jobs	a report of the status of all phantom processes (background jobs) in the file **DM,JOBS,**
list-lines	displays line details (baud rate, parity, data bits etc.) of all attached ports
list-lists	a MACRO which produces a report of all previously saved lists
list-lockq	lists the processes which are waiting to lock a frame which is currently locked by some other process
list-locks	lists the current status of all system, BASIC, spooler, group and item locks
list-logoffs	a report showing the history of logoffs reported in the file **DM,ERRORS,**
list-macros	a MACRO producing a sorted list of MACROs in the specified file
list-menus	produces a list of menu items in the MD
list-pibs	a report of each active port in the **DM,PIBS,** file
list-verbs	a list of all verbs in the MD
listc	a four column list of items in a file (unsorted order)
lm	list menus
log-msg	records date and time a particular MACRO was executed and used within the MACRO itself
log-status	displays current status of the transaction logger
loop	performs any TCL command a specific number of times (or continuously) until a key is pressed
lp	list pibs
lre	list restore errors, the errors incurred on a restore
lu	list users
maxusers	displays the number of licenced PICK users and/or sets the system in single user or multi-user mode
mirror	attaches the current port (master) to one or more other ports (slaves)
monitor-status	a listing of the memory-resident frames
move-file	moves file from one Master Dictionary to another
nframe-index	gives the total number of frames used by a specific index
node	identifies the network node unique to the specific PICK virtual machine
op	invokes the Output Processor
overflow	displays the frames in the overflow table
ovf-prot	toggles the overflow protection scheme (when on can create significant system overhead)

pitch-compile	compiles a pitch file found in the file **DM,FONTS.PITCH,**
pitch-table	builds a pitch table for a font file in the file **DM,FONTS,DESCR,**
prime	calculates the next highest and lowest prime to the given number
prompt	prompts the user with a message for which the only acceptable responses are **c** for continue or **q** for quit
r83-setup	sets up all user options to their R83 defaults
rebuild-ovf	reclaims overflow space – only works if overflow has been initialized using **init-ovf**
recover-item	recovers last item deleted by **xo** in the Update Processor
rename-file	change the name of an existing file
reset-port	a means to re-initialize a 'hung' port
ri	recover item
rnf	rename file
run-list	runs a series of BASIC programs
search	searches a file for one of a number of strings
search-file	searches a file for existence of a string and optionally creates a save-list
search-system	searches every file in the PICK system for the existence of one or more strings. If a specific account name is specified only that account is searched
send-message	sends a message (same as **msg**)
set-8mm	sets the 8 mm DAT device
set-batch	displays of changes the current sensitivity value for the interactive/batch triggers
set-batchdly	displays or changes the current sensitivity value for the interactive/batch trigger as well as the weight of the trigger and the trigger cancel value
set-device	the command to attach devices under **AP/UNIX** only
set-esc	specifies the value of the key to treat as the ESCape key, which pushes a level when pressed
set-half	attaches a half inch tape device
set-num-format	sets the currency sign, thousand mark and decimal mark for the system or a specified port
set-runaway-limit	sets the maximum number of overflow frames to be grabbed by a process
setport	sets all ports (except port 0) to 9600 baud, 8 data bits, 1 stop bit and no parity
setup-printer	downloads fonts to a laser printer attached to a form queue
sh	shell out, see ! above
shpstat	examines or changes the status of shared BASIC programs that have been compiled with Flash BASIC
sl	save-list
sortc	a four column list of item-ids in a file in sorted order of item-id
speller	displays status or toggles the spell checker on/off
speller-off	turns off the spell checker
speller-on	turns on the spell checker
stack	toggles on/off the use of the TCL stacker
stack-off	turns of the TCL stacker
stack-on	turns on the TCL stacker
startlog	activates the transaction logger for all items in files of a **DL** type

startsched	initiates the phantom processor
startshp	starts a shared printer under **AP/UNIX**
status-port	invokes **set-port**
steal-file	moves a file from another account to the current account
stoplog	turn off the transaction logger
stopsched	turn of the phantom processor
t-bsf	backspaces a given number of files on the attached device
t-bsr	backspaces a given number of records on the attached device
t-fsf	forward spaces a given number of files on the attached device
t-fsr	forward spaces a given number of records on the attached device
t-unld	physically detaches and rewinds the attached half inch tape device
tandem	links the current port to another so any input or output to either screen affects the other
tcl	suspends the process on the specified port, pushes a level then executes the TCL command
tcl-hdr	enables/disenables the display of all TCL commands on all Spooler output
tcl-hdr-off	switches off printing the TCL command output on spooled output
tcl-hdr-on	switches on printing the TCL command output on spooled output
time-date-off	turns off the automatic display of date and time at the TCL prompt
time-date-on	turns on the automatic display of date and time at the TCL prompt
timedate	toggles on/off the automatic display of date and time at the TCL prompt
timedate-off	turns off the automatic display of date and time at the TCL prompt
timedate-on	turns on the automatic display of date and time at the TCL prompt
tlog-restore	restores data from the transaction log magnetic media
txlog	initiates a menu for the administration of the transaction logger
txlog-status	displays the status of the transaction logger
type-ahead	toggles on/off the type ahead facility
type-ahead-off	turns off the type-ahead facility
type-ahead-on	turns on the type-ahead facility
u	invokes the Update Processor
unlink-pibdev	unlinks a port from another port
unlock	resets an execution lock
unlock-frame	clears the memory used by a frame by **lock-frame**
unlock group	clears group locks that haven't cleared normally
unlock-item	clears item locks that haven't cleared normally
up	invokes the Update Processor
update	invokes the Update Processor
update-accounts	updates accounts to AP format. Used when an R83 account is loaded on AP
update-logging	toggles or displays the status of the transaction logger
update-md	updates the verbs and related items in a given account MD
wherebt	invokes the **wheres** command with the **bt** option
whered	invokes the **wheres** command with the **db** option
whereindx	invokes the **wheres** command with the **in** option
wherelk	invokes the **wheres** command with the **lk** option
whereovf	invokes the **wheres** command with the **ovf** option
wherepu	invokes the **wheres** command with the **pu** option

wheres	a more readable form of the **where** command
wheresp	invokes the **wheres** command with the **sp** option
wheret	invokes the **wheres** command with the **tp** option
whoall	invokes the **wheres** command
whobt	invokes the **wheres** command with the **bt** option
whod	invokes the **wheres** command with the **db** option
whoindx	invokes the **wheres** command with the **in** option
wholk	invokes the **wheres** command with the **lk** option
whopu	invokes the **wheres** command with the **pu** option
whos	invokes the **wheres** command
whosp	invokes the **wheres** command with the **sp** option
whot	invokes the **wheres** command with the **tp** option
whovf	invokes the **wheres** command with the **ovf** option
wlist	a version of **list** that uses b-tree indexes if present
wselect	a version of **select** that uses b-tree indexes if present
wsort	a version of **sort** that uses b-tree indexes if present
wsselect	a version of **sselect** that uses b-tree indexes if present
xonoff	toggles XON/XOFF capability of a port
z *TCL command*	initiates the *TCL command* as a phantom (background) process. If invoked with **zh** or **zhs** all terminal output is placed in a hold file. With **zs** and **zhs** error messages are suppressed

8.5 Processing code changes

Processing codes are stored in attribute and file defining items in file dictionaries. More than one processing code can be specified in an attribute by separating the codes with a value mark. The codes are to be found in the following attributes

attribute 7	Output conversion
attribute 8	Correlative
attribute 14	Input conversion

Output conversion codes manipulate the display format of data and are applied just prior to output from the Update Processor, ACCESS or a BASIC call.

Correlatives are used by all the system processors and for attributes are applied by the **sort** or **select** processor when building a list of item-ids and by the Update Processor and ACCESS prior to calling output conversions. Correlative codes in file defining items are called when the item is filed, especially from the Update Processor. Some correlative codes, such as **stamps**, **item-id generation** and BASIC subroutines are only called from the Update Processor.

Input conversion codes are used by the Update Processor to validate data as it is entered. Input conversion codes define single or multiple file indexing. This allows cruising through both the current file (the file where the item resides) and other linked files.

The new processing codes are as follows:

b	**bridge correlative**	used as a correlative in file defining items to maintain a horizontal relationship (bridge) between an attribute in one item and an item in another file. This relationship may either be unidirectional or bi-directional. Bridging causes the updating of two files simultaneously. The advantage of the bridge correlative is that it performs a function which previously took significant BASIC coding.
call	**call BASIC subroutine**	calls a BASIC subroutine and is extremely useful when used in conjunction with the Update Processor. From the Update Processor, the current attribute (if not at filing time) is passed to the subroutine as a parameter and only one parameter is accepted. Other values may be obtained using the BASIC **ACCESS** statement. When called at file time the current item is passed in a dynamic array as a parameter.
callx	**callx BASIC subroutine**	a BASIC subroutine call which is specified in attribute 8 of the file defining item. This correlative differs from the **CALL** correlative in that it is called any time an item in the file is updated versus only being called when the item is updated from the Update Processor.
cu	**character update**	allows data in the attribute to be changed character by character if conversions or correlatives have been defined for the attribute. This input conversion type is used to allow character updates and changes to an attribute value when a correlative has been defined on this attribute as well. Without this input conversion the data value is erased and nulled when editing.
i	**index correlative**	indicates an index exists for the current attribute. When editing data in the attribute, users can cruise backward and forwards through the file.
i*fid*	**file index correlative**	the file index correlative is used in file defining items to maintain index keys.

i*file.ref*	**index correlative to file**	attribute is based on data indexed in another file. When editing data in this attribute, the user can cruise both forwards and backwards through the index in the specified secondary file.
id	**item id correlative**	this processing code is used by the Update Processor to create new item-ids.
mi	**must input conversion**	this conversion code forces data to be input into a field. The Update Processor does not file any item where any field in the record with an **mi** code contains a null value.
ms	**mask alter sort**	alter the normal sort sequence of the characters.
o	**ascending order**	sorts the values in the attribute in ascending order at the time the item is filed.
v*n*	**value code conversion**	used as an input conversion to specify the maximum values in an attribute. If *n* is zero than data cannot be entered and any data will be nulled.
x	**display only**	used as an input conversion and indicates the attribute cannot be modified but can only be displayed.
x*n ac*{v}**update**		stamp used as a correlative in the file defining item and provides a stamp for items that are updated giving details of the user, date and time.
zc	**zip code**	used with the file **ZCF** to display city, state and zip code. It displays a 5 or 9 digit zip code with a hyphen after the first 5.

8.6 ACCESS changes

- New connectives have been introduced. These are:

  DUPLICATE
  NI-SUPP
  SAMPLING.

- The HEADING and FOOTING modifiers have been enhanced and now have more options.
- Printed reports now show the ACCESS command (removed with TCL-SUPP or by the TCL command TCL-HDR (f).
- LIST and SORT have a new **FILL** connective.

8.7 BASIC changes

- Compiling can be case sensitive/insensitive using **COMPILE**.
- All array elements can be compared at once with the wildcard * char and the comparison is deemed true if at least one element matches the condition.
- Common variables are preserved between calls.
- Catalogued programs can be called from attr7 or attr8.
- Named common, common areas are now items and may be referenced as such.
- Source code can contain blank lines.
- Format strings have added code **d{}** for date.
- New key words or statements are as follows:

    $include
    access(1) through access(21)
    assigned()
    convert
    exit
    file
    fold
    in
    key
    occurs()
    onerr
    root
    sort()
    tclread

- New terminal cursor control codes for @(-32) through @(-300).
- IN and INPUT now support a time-out feature.
- INCLUDE now allows for a $ prefix.
- Statements which lock such as READU MATREADU etc. lock items not groups and have a LOCKED clause.
- An ONERR clause now exists for tape operations.
- A new SOUNDEX() statement has been introduced.
- The SYSTEM() function has been substantially enhanced.

- Advanced PICK BASIC object code is incompatible with R83 object code so all programs must be recompiled.
- You can compile a program in any file; the **DC** file type is no longer mandatory for program files.
- The R83 string limit of 32K has been increased to 4GB.
- DIM statements must be declared before use of variables to which they refer.
- The undocumented feature of **GOTO000 GOSUB000** now needs a space before 000.
- The undocumented syntax **IF condition THEN ELSE statements** acceptable in R83 now requires **NULL** between **THEN** and **ELSE**.
- AP no longer inserts the date and time in the object code.

8.8 Changes in File-Saves and File-Restores

- An new facility to only save changed items known as incremental file save.
- A new facility to record file updates to another device known as the transaction logger.
- The SAVE verb no longer needs a **D** option to save data and
  accepts a save list
  has an option for incremental saves
  has an option to save indexes.
- The account save and restore process has a different display.
- SET-FLOPPY no longer supports the **S** option it is now the **L** option.
- SET-DEVICE will soon to replace the SET-XXXX verb.

8.9 Converting an R83 account to Advanced PICK and vice versa

In general converting from an existing R83 account to Advanced PICK is very straight forward. Do an **ACCOUNT-SAVE** on the R83 machine, an **ACCOUNT-RESTORE** on the Advanced PICK machine, run the verb **UPDATE-ACCOUNTS** within the account **DM** on the restored account, then log to the account and recompile and recatalogue all BASIC programs. To reverse the process do an identical set of operations except that the **ACCOUNT-SAVE** must have the **C** option set.

However, there are some details to consider and some hints which might prove useful and the remainder of this chapter is devoted to them.

8.9.1 Considerations

There are a number points to consider before launching into the conversion to Advanced PICK. Firstly when performing the conversion to Advanced PICK for the first time, it is quite possible you will be using the same computer to run the converted application, thus overwriting the R83 version completely. The implications are obvious. You need to ensure that should anything go wrong, you can recover and return to the working R83 system. The first step is therefore to ensure you have at least two **verified** file saves of the R83 system, a simple precaution but often overlooked in the excitement of moving to something new. Taking a **verified** file save will be time consuming and taking a second may seem like an eternity, but it may take more than an eternity to recover your data if you don't have it well secured!

Next ensure you have **all** the source code to your applications. All programs need to be recompiled under Advanced PICK, without exception so the lack of just one program will ruin the conversion.

If you are using third party products, you will need to upgrade to Advanced PICK versions of these. In most cases this will not be a problem, other than the cost involved, as any vendor wishing to retain their market share will have an Advanced PICK version of their application. However, do take care to ensure that the Advanced PICK version of the third party product will run with your chosen Advanced PICK platform. For example, JET (word processor), whilst available for AP as the native operating system on a PC, is not available under AP/DOS (the version of PICK which runs as a DOS application).

Make sure you have saved the special characteristics of your R83 system which may have taken you quite some time to set up. Here I am referring to your coldstart procedures and user log ons. To that end it is worth dumping the **SYSTEM** file which will contain your user ids and your logon banner and the **SYSPROG-PL** file which will contain your coldstart procedures.

The final consideration is to check that your R83 PICK diskettes are still working. It may be quite a while since you used them and they may have parity errors. If possible check these out by testing them on another machine. If you do not have another machine, check them out immediately prior to loading AP on your system, because if you need to return to R83 because of unexpected difficulties you'll need the original R83 diskettes.

If you have taken all the above precautions you are now ready to start the conversion process.

8.9.2 Conversion procedure from R83 to Advanced PICK

Saving your R83 system

All your in-house developed BASIC source code and your PROCS are fully compatible but since you object code is not, it is worth decataloguing the object code from your program files with the command **DECATALOG *prog.file.name*** * (where ***prog.file.name*** is the name of your program file). This will save you the time and trouble of saving data that will not work in the new environment.

Next check that you do not have any files **DX**ed or **D**yed (i.e. with **DX** or **DY** in attribute 1, the file defining attribute) that should not be. You can check the **MD** entry for all files by performing a **LIST MD WITH *A0 = "DX" "DY"** but this does not check for the status of the data portion of the file which can only be checked by looking at each individual file defining item with the command **CT DICT *file.name file.name*** (where ***file.name*** is the name of the file in question). Providing attribute 1 is **D** the contents of the file will be saved. If it is **DX** the contents of the file will not be saved and if it is **DY** then the file will be reconstituted on the target system, but as an empty file.

Take a copy of the **SYSTEM** and **SYSPROG-PL** files. First attach the media (**SET-FLOPPY**, **SET-SCT**, or **SET-HALF**), then use the commands

T-REW
T-DUMP SYSTEM
T-DUMP SYSPROG-PL

Take a separate account save of the account **SYSPROG** and take a separate **T-DUMP** of the PROCS in your SYSPROG account, using **T-DUMP SYSPROG WITH *A1 = "PQ"**.

Now take at least two **verified** full file-saves (using the command **FILE-SAVE**). For any account that straddles a volume of the backup media it is worth taking a copy of the account separately using the **ACCOUNT-SAVE** verb, because occasionally the restore process has trouble with accounts split across different volumes.

If you have difficulties creating a PICK compatible FILE-SAVE you will need to perform a series of PICK compatible ACCOUNT-SAVE tapes. If both of these prove problematical you will need to perform a series of T-DUMPs of both the dictionary and data portions of all the files you wish to transfer, but if you reach this stage I would strongly recommend you perform your upgrade to a completely separate system so you can return to the original system if you need to.

Equally, if you are able to use a separate system to perform the upgrade this is by far the most ideal situation as you can always recover data from the old system that you might have overlooked.

Bear in mind that tape labels and blocking factors vary across implementations of PICK and if you are experiencing problems this is the most likely cause. Advanced PICK only supports a diskette blocking factor of 500, whilst on tapes the blocking factor can be varied up to a maximum of 16384.

If securing your system on a compatible medium is still a problem you could consider using the RS232 port using a PICK to PICK communication product such as InfoLinke or Mainlink or even consider using a PICK to DOS communication package (TERMiTE, ViaDuct, PK Harmony and the Laguna

Connection are the most popular) to first transfer the data to DOS and then from DOS transfer the data into Advanced PICK. Data transfer using this method will not be quick (around 7 MB per hour) and it would be best to look for a data transfer bureau if possible. Once the data is in DOS you can use these products to import it into PICK.

Another alternative particularly where the target computer is a PC is to use the IMPORT verb to pull the data from DOS or a DOS floppy into Advanced PICK. Not all AP platforms can support a PC format floppy disk, so this option will not be available on all AP systems.

Load Advanced PICK

The next step is to load Advanced PICK. Where you have purchased a system with Advanced PICK already loaded the next step is obviously restoring the R83 system described in the next section. Loading Advanced PICK is a relatively straightforward task and Chapter 24, which deals with PICK on the PC, covers the loading task in detail. Perhaps the trickiest part is the configuration of the serial ports and it is worth remembering that each time serial ports are added it will be necessary to reload the operating system to force it to reconfigure the serial ports.

Reloading the R83 system to Advanced PICK

Dependent on the backups taken, restoring the original R83 system will comprise of one of the following:

- restoring the accounts from a file-save tape;
- individual account restores from account save tapes;
- creating the required account and its files and rebuilding the files from the 'dumped' files;
- creating the required account and its files and populate the files from data uploaded from the serial port or imported from the DOS partition or DOS diskettes.

If your save is from an R83 system which is version 2.1 or earlier, then prior to restoring the data you will need to set the device with the **R** option (i.e. **SET-SCT (R**) to ensure reverse compatibility with older tape versions.

If the tape contains a full file-save or multiple account saves you can tell AP to load all new accounts (i.e. those not already on the system) with the RESTORE-ACCOUNTS verb. This verb has some options to assist with file-save tapes from Ultimate systems. The C option is used with tapes created on Ultimate systems, whilst the **U** option indicates the tape is in 'Ultimate' format rather than PICK compatible format.

Making the R83 account accessible within AP

The first step is to log to the **dm** account and run **update-account** which will prompt you for the names of the accounts to update. The process will scan through the account's files and inserts the new expanded information into the dictionaries. As it scans through the MD it will find verbs, PROCs and subroutines it cannot resolve into an equivalent AP version. These are placed into the file **CLASHES** in the **dm** account. This file is a multi-level data file, with a separate data files created for each account 'updated'. This file contains a list of all the problem items encountered which are generally caused for the following reasons:

Licencee verbs that don't exist in AP
Licencee **HUSH/NO HUSH** which does not exist in AP (use **ECHO**)
Licencee **PERFORM** which does not exist in AP (use **EXECUTE**)
Unsupported user exit calls
IF..THEN..ELSE correlatives

Since this file can only be used as a reference, once the account is working don't forget to remove the file using **DELETE-FILE CLASHES,*account.name*** (where ***account.name*** is the name of the R83 account that has been 'updated'.). The comma following the word CLASHES is important and denotes the file is a multi-level data file.

Set up the system environment

First set up users in the file **users**. When the accounts were restored you would have been given the opportunity to create users with the same name as the restored accounts. This obviously would not have created user records for individuals but as a starting point you could use, as a base, the one you have created with the same names as the account that has been restored. Where a user is to use a specific account, copy the user record for the account to the required user-id. Assuming the user-id is the users initials, then use the command

: **COPY USERS *account.name***
TO: ***user-id***

The users record format is as follows:

ac..	attribute-name	description....................
1	name	Name of authorised user of the Pick System.
2	address	User's address.
3	zip	User's zip code.
4	phone	User's phone number.
5	unused	n/a
6	keys	The retrieval and update keys for this user.
7	password	Optional logon password.
8	privilege	User privilege level. May be **sys0**, **sys1**, or **sys2**.

9	options	User options. Valid options are: **a** (or u) Updates accounting history file at logoff. **d** Disables 'end' and 'off' commands from either debugger. **r** Restarts logon procedure on any <break>+end. **g** Stops at GFEs and offers the options to '(L)ogoff, (C)ontinue, or (Q)uit'. **m** Invokes the automatic GFE handler at any GFE found.
10	not used	n/a
11	not used	n/a
12	macro	User logon macro. This is the same as a TCL macro without the macro type code, (in attribute 1) which is assumed to be 'n' (for 'non-stop'). Any number of TCL commands may be placed on attributes 12 and beyond. Each command will be executed before the user is logged on.

Copy the user coldstart PROC from the file SYSPROG-PL to the MD of the account **dm**, using the command **SEL-RESTORE DM USER-COLDSTART** (**O** from the account save tape of SYSPROG of the T-DUMP of the SYSPROG-PL file.

If you created any PROCs in the SYSPROG account these should be copied to the MD of the **dm** account. This can be done either with the **T-LOAD** or **SEL-RESTORE** verbs. Do bear in mind that these PROCs may have the same name as items already in the MD, so using a simple T-LOAD runs the risk of omitting some of your PROCs and using the **O** (overlay) option runs the risk of overwriting crucial AP-supplied PROCs.

If you had any new programs in the SYSPROG BP file copy these to the account **dm** and file **BP** and then compile the programs. Similarly for any terminal drivers in the SYSPROG CURSOR file copy them to the **dm devices** file.

Recompile all R83 source code

Once the system environment is set up, log to the account that has been transferred and determine the program files. Since the account has come from an R83 system, the program files will contain **DC** in attribute 1 and will be listed separately in the output from the **LISTFILES** command. Having identified the program files, compile all the programs using **BASIC** ***program.file*** * (where ***program.file*** is the name of the program file). There may be some compilation errors caused by licencee specifics such as:

HUSH/NO HUSH	***replace with***	**ECHO ON/ECHO OFF**
PERFORM	***replace with***	**EXECUTE**
INCLUDE item FROM file	***replace with***	**INCLUDE *file item***

You should now find you have successfully upgraded to Advanced PICK!

8.9.3 Moving an Advanced PICK account back to an R83 system

Once an account has been transferred to Advanced PICK it can readily transferred back to R83, by first saving the account using the **C** option, which creates an R83 compatible save, using **ACCOUNT-SAVE *account.name*** (where ***account.name*** is the name of the account to be transferred).

To load the account back onto the R83 system, using **ACCOUNT-RESTORE *account.name*** and then update the MD using either **UPDATE-ACCOUNTS** (only available on R83 version 3.1 onwards) otherwise copy the contents of **NEWAC** to the account MD using

SET-FILE *account.name* MD
COPY QFILE * (O
to : **(QFILE**

Then log to the account and compile all the programs.

9 Q-Pointers and File Paths

The TCL verbs and general commands covered in this chapter

ED	PASSWORD	SET-FILE

9.1 Introduction

No discussion of PICK would be complete without detailed reference to one of its fundamental features, the Q-pointer. We have already seen that logging on in PICK is handled by logging to an account, rather than the system as a whole. An account, an environment containing a logical grouping of files, is analogous to a company department. Whilst people working within a department are primarily using the information held within their department, there are many occasions when they need information held elsewhere.

Within PICK the account is the working area and the files and data in that account are all that are immediately accessible. There are two means of accessing data held outside the account:

- Q-pointers
- File paths

There are many reasons why you might want to access information held in other accounts. A typical example of this is where a number of accounts use the same program file. Rather than duplicate the program file and hold it within each account, a Q-pointer can be set up to 'point' to the account that holds the program file. A Q-pointer is an item in a file that points to another so that it can be used time and time again. The file path is included as part of the TCL command at the time it is executed, so to in that respect is only temporary. Hence in our example of a program file being accessed from multiple accounts, a file path would be inappropriate and a Q-pointer to the location of the program file would need to be set up in each of the accounts requiring access to the programs.

9.2 Q-pointers

A Q-pointer is an item which resides in a file and contains a **Q** in attribute one to identify it as such. It can be used to give an alternative or shorter name to a file, often referred to as its synonym but can equally be used to provide alternative names to accounts and TCL verbs. Its other use is to provide access to files held outside the account.

In the same way as different people within a department need to work with differing parts of their manual files, some of which may be highly confidential, PICK, by using Q-pointers provides the same capability. When placed in the **mds** file (**SYSTEM** in R83) the Q-pointer provides an alternative name for an account, enabling different users access to the same account, but with different security levels and passwords. Since R83 does not have a **USERS** file this mechanism is the only way to set up different users with an R83 PICK system since this effectively gives the user a user code or user-id to the PICK system which tells PICK the facilities and files the user can freely access, the account the user has access to and the user's password. Figure 9.1 shows how to achieve this with R83 PICK and Figures 9.2 and 9.3 demonstrate the setting up of users with Advanced PICK.

```
:ED SYSPROG MIKE            <-- Create a new item in SYSPROG called MIKE
NEW ITEM
TOP
.I[CR]                      <-- Insert
001 Q[CR]
002 SYSPROG[CR]
003 .[CR]                   <-- Use a '.' for attributes that should contain a null value
004 .[CR]
005 .[CR]
006 .[CR]
007 .[CR]
008 SYS1[CR]
009 LU[CR]
010 10[CR]
011[CR]
TOP
.F[CR]                      <-- Flip buffers
TOP
.RU10/.//[CR]               <-- Replace all '.' with a null
003
004
005
006
007
EOI 010
.FI[CR]                     <-- File the item MIKE
MIKE FILED

:PASSWORD                   <-- Set a password for MIKE
ENTER ACCOUNT NAME?MIKE[CR]
ENTER NEW PASSWORD?MJBUI[CR]
ENTER PASSWORD [CR]
:
```

Figure 9.1 Creating a new user and password under R83 PICK.

9.2.1 User identification (user-id)

Before generating user-ids in the **mds** file make sure that the accounts they use exist and, if not, create them. User-ids are created with the Update Processor or the Editor in the **dm** account and by editing entries into the **mds** dictionary.

The item-id created in the **mds** dictionary becomes the synonym to the account (or user-id if using R83) and the other attributes define the user's profile when accessing the real account. The format of a **mds** dictionary Q-pointer is shown in Figure 9.2 and for these items attribute one must contain a **Q**. In general only the first four attributes (attributes 0–3 inclusive) are used for Q-pointer items, but in the case of the creation of user-ids in the **mds** file then it can contain all the attributes available in a normal file defining item.

Figure 9.1 shows the creation of another user who accesses the **SYSPROG** account with SYS1 privileges (see Chapter 20 for information on privilege levels). The user was created using the editor, (for details on how to use the Editor refer to Chapter 11). Since it is not usual to directly edit 'null' into an item, the attributes that are to be set to null are first set to a nominated

Item-id attribute	User name
000	User-id
001	Q
002	Account name to which the user will have access
003	Reserved and unavailable
004	Reserved and unavailable
005	Retrieval locking code
006	Update locking code
007	Password
008	Privilege level code
009	Justification code and to show whether the system accounting file is to be updated — value of **L R T U W** or **WW** (**X** can be used in conjunction with **L R** or **T**)
010	Length
011	Reserved and unavailable
012	Reserved and unavailable
013	Null
014	Null
015	Null
016	Null
017	Description

Figure 9.2 The format of a Q-pointer in the system dictionary to set up a user profile.

character, in this case a full stop, which is then replaced by null. Notice too that the password is not set through the editor, but from the TCL command **PASSWORD**, which encrypts the password **MJBUI** so that anyone looking through the system dictionary cannot readily interpret the passwords.

In Figure 9.3 we can see the difference in using the more up-to-date tools provided with Advanced PICK, where a user is created in the **mds** file using the Update Processor. There is no need to use the **PASSWORD** command afterwards, because as the password is entered it is immediately replaced with its encrypted version.

Chapter 20 explains the way to secure your system and covers, in detail, locking codes and privilege level codes and the use of system accounting.

```
:u users mike
users          'rjb' size = 158

name           Mike Brownxf
address
zip
phone
keys

password MJBUI  <----------  after entering the password, the encrypted version
                             93B7E2E8 is displayed in its place

privilege      sys2
options
macro term-type
10 sp-assign
11 brk-level
12 esc-data
13 set-sym gsym
14 speller-off
users 'rjb' size = 105 filed.
```

Figure 9.3 Creating a new user and password.

9.3 Q-pointers to files

File Q-pointers either point to files held in other accounts or are used to provide alternative and often shorter names to files in any account. Q-pointers are edited into the master dictionary of the account that uses them. It is worth noting here that anyone with the use of the editor or Update Processor can readily point create a Q-pointer to ***any*** file in the system, and hence access to these tools needs to be carefully controlled. All aspects of security are discussed further in Chapter 20. The format of a file Q-pointer is shown in Figure 9.4.

Item-id attribute	User name
000	The name by which the item being referenced by the Q-pointer is to be called
001	**Q**
002	The account name in which the file being referenced is to be found
003	The name of the file being referenced

Figure 9.4 The format of Q-pointers.

Should you wish to change certain other aspects of the synonym then you can change other attributes of the Q-pointer and Figure 9.2 explains the other attributes to which you have access. However, it is much more common for Q-pointers just to contain four attributes (including its item-id) as shown in Figure 9.4.

Figure 9.5 shows the format of a Q-pointer that points to a file called **CUSTOMER** in an account called **ACCOUNTS**. The Q-pointer is called **CUST**. As soon as the Q-pointer is created, any action taken on the file **CUST** such as listing customers, or printing details of specific customers, will actually be referring to the data held in the **CUSTOMER** file in the account **ACCOUNTS**. Every part of the file is available to the account containing the Q-pointer just as though the file itself was resident in that account.

The Q-pointer **CUST** would be created by using either the Update Processor or the editor and is illustrated in Figure 9.6. The Q-pointer is edited

000	Item-id	**CUST**
001	Dictionary code	**Q**
002	Account name	**ACCOUNTS**
003	File name	**CUSTOMER**

Figure 9.5 A Q-pointer example.

```
:U MD CUST
MD 'CUST' NEW ITEM
01 Q[CR]
02 ACCOUNTS[CR]
03 CUSTOMER[CR]
04 xf[CR]
md  'cust' NEW ITEM
md  'cust' NEW ITEM size = 34 filed.
```

Figure 9.6 Using the Update Processor to create a Q-pointer.

into the master dictionary with its first attribute as 'Q' and the remaining attributes defining the account and file to which the Q-pointer relates.

There are several permissible variations. Firstly, what is known as the reflexive form, is where the Q-pointer references the file in which it is stored. This is to be found for the entry **MD** in the master dictionary of any account and in dictionary-only files where the item-id is the file name. If you refer back to Figure 7.2 you will see such an entry in the file **MD**. In this case attribute 1 contains the **Q** and attributes 2 and 3 are empty (see Figure 9.7). This is a technical, but essential, requirement which is automatically taken care of by PICK and which enables PICK to make access to the master dictionary, which it would be unable to do if the reflexive Q-pointer was not present.

Item-id	**MD**
Attribute 1	**Q**
Attribute 2	
Attribute 3	

Figure 9.7 The content of the MD Q-pointer in the master dictionary.

9.4 Temporary Q-pointers

The above examples leave permanent entries in either the system, master or File dictionaries. There are many instances where a temporary pointer is needed. This is handled by the command **SET-FILE**, which updates the item QFILE in the master dictionary. Each time the command **SET-FILE** is used, the item QFILE is updated. Since there is only one item in the MD called QFILE, it is obviously not possible to have more than one temporary Q-pointer in any one account at any one time.

The **SET-FILE** facility is often used where it is necessary to make a change to a file in another account or where a file from another account is to be copied into your own account and where reference to that file is unlikely to be needed again.

Once the Q-pointer is set up, the file being pointed to is referenced by the name QFILE. Figure 9.8 shows how a temporary Q-pointer is set up to the **CUSTOMER** file in the account **ACCOUNTS** and how a list of the item-ids within the **CUSTOMER** file can be produced by reference to the temporary Q-pointer QFILE.

The example given by Figure 9.8 shows the typical use of a temporary Q-pointer. It is important to realize that the temporary Q-pointer exists as the item QFILE in *each* master dictionary. As such, anyone with access to the account and the command SET-FILE can change the file it points to. PICK will not stop two people using the command SET-FILE in the same account at the same time. Hence the last person to update the Q-pointer QFILE by the com-

```
:SET-FILE
ACCOUNT NAME ?ACCOUNTS[CR]
FILE NAME ?CUSTOMER[CR]
QFILE UPDATED

:SORT ONLY QFILE
PAGE 1                              17:58:00   7 JUN 1994
QFILE...........
A01
B01
B02
B03
D02
S01
T01
W01
W02
9 ITEMS LISTED
```

Figure 9.8 The use of the temporary Q-pointer, QFILE.

mand SET-FILE will determine its contents and for this reason the temporary pointer should be seen as such and treated with care.

9.5 File paths

A new concept was introduced with Advanced PICK, that of file paths, a mechanism of referring to a file by specifying its location from the **mds** file. This makes available to the user *any* file in *any* account providing they have the appropriate retrieval and update codes (see Chapter 20 on security).

The file path is designated by placing a comma at the end of each file in the path. Hence all the following formats are allowable:

mds,*account.name*,	**to access another account**
account.name,,	**to access another account**
dict *account.name*,*filename*,	**to access a dictionary in another account**
account.name,*filename*	**to access the data file in another account**

Note the ',' at the end of the file path is mandatory. Referencing the file without the comma will cause the following error to be displayed

[201] '*account.name*' is not a file name

It takes a while to remember about file paths when first introduced to Advanced PICK after working with R83 and undoubtedly you will find yourself setting permanent and temporary Q-pointers instead of using file paths. Indeed since the file path is only 'active' at the time the file is referenced there are many occasions in which setting Q-pointers is the right approach. However, once you get used to file paths you will find them extremely useful. Figure 9.9 gives some useful examples of the use of file paths.

Whilst Figure 9.9 gives some examples of the use of file paths, there are numerous places in which you will be able to address files in other accounts. Equally there are places where this type of reference is not permitted, primarily in the creation and deletion of files, but it is worth experimenting when the need arises!

:sort only sb+,,	produces a sorted list of the contents of the Master Dictionary in the sb+account
:sort only sb+,dmprogs,	produces a sorted list of the programs in the file **dmprogs** in the account **sb+**
:listfiles sb+,md,	list the files in the account **sb+**
:copy progs * `to:` **(sb+,progs,**	copy all the programs in the file **progs** in the current account to the **progs** file in the **sb+** account

Figure 9.9 Examples of the use of file paths.

10 The Update Processor

The TCL verbs and general commands covered in this chapter

U UP

10.1 Introduction

The Update Processor (**UP**) is one of the new main modules to be released with the introduction of Advanced PICK. It is a dictionary driven, full screen editor which can be used to view, create, amend and manipulate *any* item in *any* file in the same way that is possible using the EDITOR. The primary difference between the two is that the EDITOR works on a line by line basis, whereas the Update Processor is a full screen editor. You can also file, compile and catalog BASIC programs whilst using **UP**, with just two keystrokes; a great time saver over use of the editor when after filing the program you have to perform compilation and cataloguing through two further TCL commands. The other important difference is that the Update Processor provides the ability to 'cruise' through items in the same file and to 'zoom' to records in other file if a 'bridge' or link to that file exists in the item being edited. For example if you are editing records in a customer file and you choose a particular record, whilst in that record you can move forwards and backwards to other customer records. This is known as 'cruising' . Equally whilst in a customer record and whilst positioned on the salesman code for example, you can view the salesman's record in the salesman file, the function known as 'zooming'.

PICK's intention in providing this new facility is for it to be used in conjunction with the OUTPUT processor and form a word processor/data processor. Certainly whilst it is a considerable step forward from the EDITOR, the combination of the two do not realistically form what most people would accept as a word processor and it is certainly not something to be put in the hands of naive users used to working with industry standard word processors such as Word and Word Perfect. But in truth it was never intended to replace these products, but to satisfy the PICK community who demanded more sophisticated development and editing tools within PICK itself.

Used as a data processor, **UP** uses file dictionaries to process the data as it is entered or retrieved. With the use of B-tree indexes users can scan forwards and backwards through the records in a file. With the ability to call BASIC subroutines from dictionaries, **UP** can be used to execute these subroutines through various dictionaries and carry out other data manipulations transparent to the user. If no attributes are specified, **UP** functions purely as a full screen editor.

UP also contains a spell checker although it is biased towards American spelling. Needless to say you can add words to your systems dictionary so you can gradually build a dictionary suited to your own requirements.

The biggest problem with **UP** is that all commands start with a control character formed by simultaneously pressing the control key and one of the 26 alphabetic characters, known as the command character. In some cases a second command character is required and can be input whether or not the key is depressed. The early versions of Advanced PICK had a fixed keyboard layout to perform these functions and this led to PICK issuing a keyboard layout chart with each system they supplied. A copy of this is shown at Figure 10.1. In this book, the way in which control characters are shown is by the underlining of the character. Thus **xe** means hold down and depress the control key and **x** simultaneously release keys and then press **e**.

From release 6.1 of Advanced PICK, users have been able to define their own keyboard layout, but control characters cannot be used for data, so defining keyboards is a skill requiring careful thought.

10.2 Update Processor concepts

UP works with a temporary version of the data which it manipulates until the record is filed or abandoned. Changes made using **UP** have no effect on the actual item in the file, just on the item contained in **UP** workspace, until the item is filed with **xf**. No changes will be made to the item if it is abandoned using **xe**.

UP accepts characters as they are typed. Since control keys are used as commands, they cannot be used for data.

UP works in two modes, insert and overtype. When **UP** is initially invoked it is put in overtype mode and the characters typed replace the character at the cursor position. Insert mode is switched on by using **r**. During input words typed over the end of the screen 'wrap' to the next line and if the spell checker is switched on it will beep and not display the last letter typed if it does not find the current string in its dictionary, although obviously you can force **UP** to accept what has been typed and switch off the spell checker if you wish, but more about the spell checker later.

There is a prestore command capability, just as there is with the EDITOR, except under **UP** there is no limit to the number of prestored commands and they can be stored in a file and recalled later as needed.

Whilst in command mode, the top line of the screen is used to display messages and when the **UP** is invoked the letter **O** appears on the far right of the top line to indicate that the mode is overtype. This can be changed to insert mode by **r** in which case the letter changes to an **I**.

10.2.1 Invoking the Update Processor

The **UP** is invoked by use of either of the following commands, **Update UP U** but since U is the shortest, the remainder of the section will use **U**. The general format of the command is as follows:

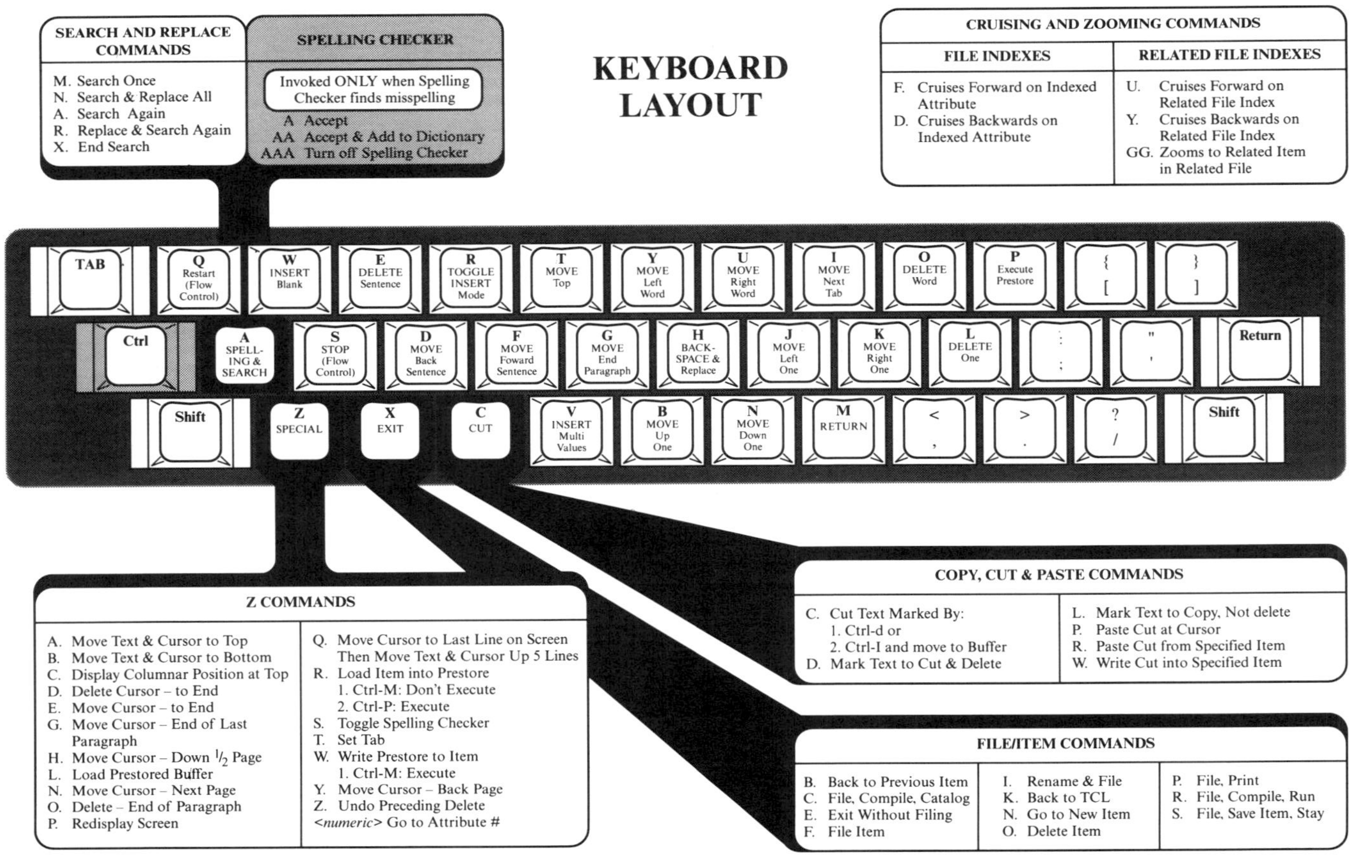

Figure 10.1 Keyboard layout.

U *file* {*item.list*} {*attr.list*} {(*options*)}

where

file	is the file name containing the items to be processed
item.list	the item-ids of the items to be processed. A * signifies all items in the file
attr.list	the dictionary name of the attributes to be processed
options	the options are

C	clears the screen before bringing up the display of the data to be processed.
I	includes the item-id on the display of data and enables the item-id to be modified. Modifying the item-id and filing it away has the effect of creating a new item, leaving the original untouched.
L	'Look only' option which precludes the data from being changed.
S	toggles off the spell checker.

If you are using **UP** to create new items in a file and wish to avoid having to type in a long list of item-ids after the **UP** command, then follow the command with **DATA-ENTRY**. This will enable you to enter, file items and remain in the **UP** until you file an item with the 'kill' option to return to TCL i.e. **xk**. Remember that if you want to determine the item-ids using the **DATA-ENTRY** facility you also need the (**I** option set.

10.3 A summary of the Update Processor commands

Cursor movement

Bottom of current item	**ze**
Top of current item	**t**
Refresh screen	**zp**
Goto line *nnn*	**z***nnn*
Move down ½ page	**zh**
Redisplay screen	**zp**
Move to next page	**zn**
Move to previous page	**zy**
Move cursor left	**j**
Move cursor right	**k**
Move cursor down	**n**
Move cursor up	**b**
Move cursor to next word	**u**
Move cursor to previous word	**y**
Move cursor to next tab stop	**i**
Move cursor to start of current sentence	**d**
Move cursor to start of next sentence	**f**

Move cursor to start of next paragraph	**m**
Move cursor to end of current paragraph	**g**
Move cursor to end of previous paragraph	**zg**

Other cursor controls

Redisplay screen	**zp**
Redisplay screen with current line at top	**za**
Redisplay screen with current line at bottom	**zb**

Text deletion

Delete character at cursor	**l** (lower case L)
Delete character left of cursor (backspace)	**h**
Delete word	**o**
Delete current item	**xo**
Delete from cursor to end of current paragraph	**zo**
Delete from cursor to end of current sentence	**e**
Delete from cursor to end of item	**zd**
Undo last delete	**zz**

Insert, Search & Replace

Insert new line	**m**
Insert space at cursor	**w**
Insert value (multi-)	**v**
Insert/Overlay toggle	**r**
Search once for *string*	**a***string***m**

Once the search string has been found the options are

- **a** Do not replace this occurrence, search for the next one and then stop.
- **n** Replace this occurrence and then all others without further pause.
- **r** Replace this occurrence then search for the next one and then stop.
- **x** Do not replace this occurrence and stop searching further.

Search for a *string*	**a***string*
Search for a *string1* and replace with *string2*	**a***string1***r***string2***n**

If *string2* is null it has the effect of deleting *string1*

string1 is replaced with *string2* as entered. However if the replacement is at the beginning of a sentence the initial letter is replaced in upper case. To specify an exact replacement enclose the *string2* in single or double quotes

Repeat last search	**a**
Replace all *str1* with *str*	**a***str1***r***str2***n**
Replace chosen *str1* with *str2*	**a***str1***r***str2***m**

Save & exit

Save item & remain in UP	**xs**
Save item & exit	**xf**
Save, compile & catalog BASIC	**xc**
Save, compile & run BASIC	**xr**
Exit without save	**xx**
Exit from a list of items	**xk**

10.4 Using the Update Processor

10.4.1 Moving around the screen

The **UP** is a full screen editor and one of the first exercises in becoming proficient in its use is to be able to freely move around the item being edited and be able to position the cursor where you wish. In **UP** the cursor is moved to the required position in the text, through use of its cursor movement commands and then changes, deletions and insertions are made at the cursor position through a further set of commands.

When you have positioned the cursor to the appropriate position in your text or data item, you then need to enter a valid Update Processor command to tell **UP** what you want to do. Figure 10.2 shows you how to move around an item within **UP**.

Remember that **UP** will word wrap. You should not press [CR] or **m** when you reach the end of a line. The following are the remainder of cursor movement commands not shown in Figure 10.2:

Goto line *nnn*	z*nnn*
Move down $\frac{1}{2}$ page	**zh**
Move down $\frac{1}{4}$ page	**zq**
Move to next page	**zn**
Move to previous page	**zy**
Move cursor to next tab stop	**i**
Move cursor to end of previous paragraph	**zg**
Refresh screen	**zp**
Redisplay screen	**zp**
Redisplay screen with current line at top	**za**
Redisplay screen with current line at bottom	**zb**

10.4.2 Adding, amending and deleting text

UP operates in either overtype or insert mode. In overtype mode, characters are replaced at the cursor position with the new characters that are typed. In insert mode, characters are inserted at the cursor position. When insert mode is

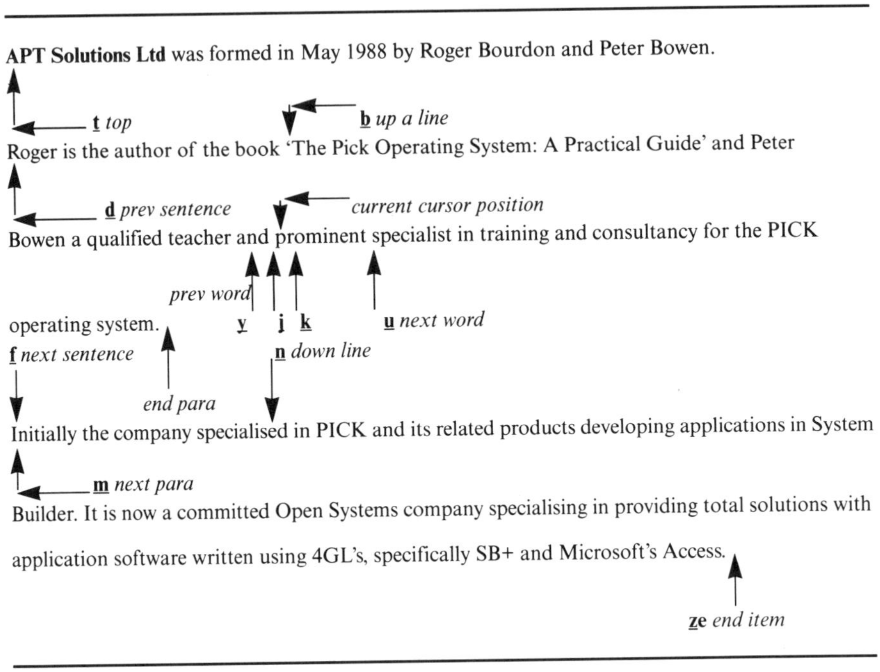

Figure 10.2 Cursor movement with **UP**.

invoked, text following the cursor is moved down a line and is moved back to the end of the inserted text as soon as another **UP** command is invoked. To insert a space, whether in insert or overtype mode enter **w**.

The following is the list of commands for deleting text. Deleting blocks of text will be dealt with in the next section.

Delete character at cursor	**l** (lower case L)
Delete character left of cursor (backspace)	**h**
Delete word	**o**
Delete current item	**xo**
Delete from cursor to end of current paragraph	**zo**
Delete from cursor to end of current sentence	**e**
Delete from cursor to end of item	**zd**
Undo last delete	**zz**

10.4.3 Block text

The text you wish to manipulate is not always a single character, word, sentence or paragraph. Often there is a block of text you wish to handle, to either delete, copy or move. The first step is to identify the block by marking its beginning and its end. This is done with the commands **cd** or **cl** and **cc** respectively. The beginning of the text block is denoted by **cl** if the text block is to be left in tact, or **cd** if the text block is to be deleted.

Move the cursor to the first character of the block and press either **cd** or **cl**; the system inserts a symbol at this point (a small solid square). Now move the cursor to one character beyond the last character of the block and press **cc** and immediately the marked block is saved in an internal cut buffer and deleted if the start of it was marked with **cd**.

Once a block of text is cut in this way you have the following options:

cp copy the contents of the cut buffer into the item at the cursor position

cw copy the contents of the cut buffer into an item in the current file. The message CUT SAVE-ID is displayed on the top line of the screen. Enter the item-id where the cut buffer is to be stored

cg copy data from another item into the displayed item. This can be an item saved using **cw** or any other item in this or any other file.

When you enter **cr** the **UP** responds with PASTE FROM to which you may respond as follows:

item-id	copies the entire item into the current record at the cursor position
item-id attr1	copies attributes from *attr1* to the end of the item of the item given by *item-id* into the current record at the cursor position
item-id attr1-attr2	copies the attributes from *attr1* to *atttr2* of the item into the current record at the cursor position
(filename item-id	copies all the data of the item given by *item-id* in the different file given by *filename* into the current record at the cursor position
(filename item-id attr1	copies the attributes from *attr1* to the end of the item given by *item-id* in the different file given by *file-name* into the current record at the cursor position
(filename item-id attr1-attr2	copies the attributes from *attr1* to *attr2* of the item given by *item-id* in the different file given by *file-name* into the current record at the cursor position.

10.4.4 Searching and replacing

UP can be used to locate any individual character or any character string. You can use **UP** just to locate the string or if required to both find and replace the string. When using the replace feature, all or selected replacements can be made.

The first step is to position the cursor at the place from which the search or search/replace is to be made. This doesn't mean you have to locate the cursor at the first occurrence of the search string, because this function will locate the string wherever it exists in the record. However, you should be aware of where you want the search to start from, and that is not always the start of the document.

Provided the cursor is above the text to be searched enter **a** and you will be prompted at the top of the string for the search screen. Respond with the character string you wish to locate. **UP** will find the first match regardless of case, but if case is important, enclose the search string in single or double quotes.

If you want to replace the located string with a different string, after entering search string enter **r** rather than [CR]. In this case you will be prompted for the replace string. Again to force an exact replacement enter the replace string in single or double quotes. To replace all occurrences type **n** otherwise to check each occurrence individually and decide on whether or not replacement is required enter **m** or [CR]. Once the first occurrence is dealt with, **UP** will move to the next and so on. A summary of the search and replace commands is as follows:

Search once for *string* **a***string***m**

Once the search string has been found the options are

- **a** Do not replace this occurrence, search for the next one and then stop.
- **n** Replace this occurrence and then all others without further pause.
- **r** Replace this occurrence then search for the next one and then stop.
- **x** Do not replace this occurrence and stop searching further.

Search for a *string* **a***string*

Search for a *string1* and replace with *string2* **a***string1*r*string2***n**

If *string2* is null it has the effect of deleting *string1*

string1 is replaced with *string2* as entered. However if the replacement is at the beginning of a sentence the initial letter is replaced in upper case. To specify an exact replacement enclose the *string2* in single or double quotes

Repeat last search **a**

Replace all *str1* with *str2* **a***str1***r***str2***n**

Replace chosen *str1* with *str2* **a***str1***r***str2***m**

If the string does not exist you will get the message STRING NOT FOUND otherwise **UP** will stop at the first match it finds.

10.4.5 The spell checker

The spell checker uses a file called **WORDS** that is located in the account **DM**. In order to make use of the spell check facility, you must either be operating in the **DM** account or have a Q-pointer to that file in the account you are operating within and an index must be generated on attribute 0 of the **WORDS** file.

Whilst using **UP** the spell checker can be toggled on and off by use of **zs**. The spell checker can be switched on and off at TCL using the commands **SPELLER-ON** and **SPELLER-OFF**. There is also an option, the **S** option when calling **UP** which will toggle the spell checker. Obviously it is possible to use a combination of these options, so you will need to know what state the spell check is in. Using **zs** within **UP** will display the message SPELLER ON or SPELLER OFF dependent on the current state of the toggle.

If the spell checker is active, then each character typed in will be compared to the words in its dictionary. A string of characters is valid if it is a word, or is the first part of word in its dictionary. If, by adding a character to a valid string the total string cannot be found in the dictionary, the terminal will beep and the character will not be displayed. When this happens you can take one of the following courses of action:

a	ignore the spelling checker and accept what is being typed until the word is complete. The spelling checker will be active from the start of the next word
aa	add the word to the dictionary and accept the word being typed
aaa	accept the typing and switch off the spell checker altogether
u	search the dictionary starting at the nearest word and move forward through the dictionary towards the letter **Z** each time **u** is entered
y	search the dictionary starting at the nearest word and move backwards through the dictionary towards the letter **A** each time **y** is entered
zs	toggle the spell checker on and off.

10.4.6 Prestored commands

A prestored command is a sequence of **UP** commands which are stored for use at any time. The prestored command can be created 'on-the-fly' or you can run one that has previously been created and stored. You can write as many prestored commands as you wish. They are stored as an item in any file, though mostly they are stored in the Master Dictionary.

When you execute a prestored command, the whole sequence of commands is executed. To run a prestored command it is first loaded from its item into the prestore buffer where it remains until it is overwritten with another or until you return to TCL. Only one prestored command at a time can be held in the prestore buffer. We will now look at the two ways of writing prestored commands.

Creating a prestored command as a file item

The prestored item can be created by **UP**, the editor or any other editing tool available. After deciding where the item is to be stored, use the editing tool to create the item. Once the item is created it can be executed by referring to its item-id.

The first attribute of the item should contain a **P** which defines the item as a prestored item. The remaining attributes should contain the **UP** commands to be executed in the order in which they are to be executed. The difference between the prestored commands and the execution of the commands outside a prestored command is that *no* control characters are entered into the prestored command. Since AP recognizes the item as a prestored command (attribute 1 contains a **P**), AP automatically applies the equivalent of a control key to each of the first characters of each command. Figure 10.3 gives some examples of prestored commands.

In these examples the command performs one or a series of tasks that can be invoked when using **UP** to edit a single item. However there are occasions when you wish to perform a series of tasks across a number of items or indeed in all of the items in a file. This is achieved by re-executing the prestored command in an automated way. Figure 10.4 shows how this is achieved.

Example 1

```
:U MD REP.PICTURE
MD 'REP.PICTURE' NEW ITEM
P
A'PICTURE'R'PAINTING'N
```

This prestored command locates each occurrence of the word **PICTURE** and replaces it with the word **PAINTING**

Example 2

```
:U MD DEL.PARA
MD 'DEL.PARA' NEW ITEM
P
M CD
G CC
```

This prestored command deletes a whole paragraph

Figure 10.3 Examples of the prestored command.

```
:U MD REP.PICTURE
MD 'REP.PICTURE' NEW ITEM
P
A'PICTURE'R'PAINTING'N
XF
P
```

This prestored command locates each occurrence of the word **PICTURE** and replaces it with the word **PAINTING**. It files the item and then re-executes the prestored command on the next item in the file until all the items in the file have been examined

---

Figure 10.4 Re-executing the prestored commands.

To make this work, we need to identify the items to be updated and then invoke the appropriate prestored command. The steps involved are:

(1) Invoke **UP** for the appropriate items.

(2) Load the prestored command in the prestore buffer with the command **zr**.

(3) Execute the prestored command with the command **p**. (Note in a prestored command to be re-executed, the last two commands file the item **xf** and the re-execute the prestored command with **p**.)

Figure 10.5 gives an example of the execution of a prestored command which changes the word **PICTURE** with the word **PAINTING** in all items in the file **ARTWORK**.

When loading a prestored command, if the item is stored in the Master Dictionary, then after the **zr** all that is required is the item-id of the item in the MD. If the item is stored in another file after executing **zr** the system will respond PRESTORED ID to which you should respond

(filename item-id

where

filename is the name of the file in which the prestored command resides

item-id is the item-id of the item containing the prestored command in *filename*

:U MD REP.PICTURE
MD 'REP.PICTURE' NEW ITEM
P
A'PICTURE'R'PAINTING'N
XF
P

:U ARTWORK *
ARTWORK '940998' size = 103
01 This is a picture painted by Miss Hopcraft
02 It was painted in the summer of 1994
03 The colours are very vivid

position the cursor at the start of the first character of the first item then

zr you are prompted with PRESTORED ID to which you should respond with the name of the prestored command, in our example **REP.PICTURE**. This will load the command in the prestore buffer which can then be executed. Next enter:

p this executes the prestored command which will go through all the items in the file and replace all occurrences of the word **PICTURE** with the word **PAINTING**

Figure 10.5 Using a prestored command to change all items in a file.

Building a prestored command in the prestore buffer

In many instances the prestored command is not likely to be required again and to save it in a file is unnecessary. In these situations the prestored command can be loaded directly into the prestore buffer and executed. Before this can be done you must have already invoked **UP** and have an item being processed.

When in **UP** you can build a prestored command using the command **zl** after which the system prompts with P: at the top of the screen and will display the existing contents of the prestore buffer if it already contains a prestored command.

To build up the commands in the prestore buffer, enter the commands using the normal update letter, but without using the <ctrl> key in the same way as you would if the command was being saved in an item. Each command should be separated with a space and any text should be enclosed in single or double quotes. When you have finished entering the commands, press [CR] or **m**.

If after having created the prestore command you decide you do wish to save it after all, then use the command **zm** in which the case **UP** will respond with PRESTORE ID and you can either enter the item-id if the item is to be stored in the MD or (*filename item-id* if the prestored command is to be stored as a named item in a named file.

10.5 Cruising, zooming and double-clutching

These facilities are dependent on the existence of AP indexes on the file. If you are working on an item in a file and an index exists for the file, you can cruise forwards and backwards through the file. Position the cursor on the attribute that is indexed and use the following commands:

f	Display the next item based on its position in the index
d	Display the previous item based on its position in the index

Hence if **UP** was positioned on the name field in an address file and the name field had its own index enabling records to be directly located by name, then **f** would work alphabetically forwards through the file and **d** would work alphabetically backwards though the file. This method of working through the file is known as *cruising*.

If the attribute is indexed to another file you can display the next record in the file with the command **u** and the previous record with the command **y**.

11 Using the Editor

TCL verbs and general commands covered in this chapter

ED	EDIT

11.1 An introduction to the editor

An editor is an essential ingredient of any operating system, and prior to the release of Advanced PICK, the editor was the only tool available. The Update Processor has superceded the editor and for those of you new to PICK this chapter is really redundant.

However, for those of you still using R83 rather than Advanced PICK the editor is the only editing tool available. Whilst the PICK editor is a line rather than full screen editor, it provides a powerful tool to access and modify any piece of information within the database. As we have seen PICK comprises a series of files of just one format and hence only one editor is required.

Whilst the editor can freely make changes throughout the database, it is not the common form of file updating which is routinely handled by application programs written in BASIC. The editor is most frequently used to make entries in dictionaries, to set up Q-pointers and to create or modify PROCS and BASIC programs. It is the ability to access and change anything within the PICK database that makes the editor so powerful and obviously a security hazard! The aspects of security are discussed fully in Chapter 20, but obviously one aspect to the management of any PICK system is controlled access to the editor.

The editor works on what is called the current line concept, which means that at any given time there is a current line which is addressed and against which information is added, changed, deleted or displayed. Once the simple editor concept is understood, all that is required to make full use of the editor, is access to its list of commands.

11.2 Editor concepts

The editor works with a temporary version of the data which it manipulates in two variable length work buffers. The original and permanent version held on disk is *only* altered when the changes made with the editor are filed away. When the editor is invoked, a copy of the record is read into buffer 1. Each attribute of the item is assigned a sequential number starting at 1, with the current line pointer pointing to the current line, initially the top of the item and an End-of-Item (EOI) pointer pointing to the last line of the item.

As changes are made in buffer 1 (Current Buffer), a new version is built up in buffer 2 (Update Buffer) and hence, for fairly obvious reasons, updating can only continue in ascending line number sequence. To view the 'current' state of the edited item, the contents of buffer 2, the update buffer, have to be made available. This is handled by an **F** (Flip buffer) command which resequences the attributes within the update buffer and switches the functions of the buffers. From this point on, until another **F** command is executed, changes are made to the contents of buffer 2, now the Current Buffer, which are written away in buffer 1, the update buffer. This process of toggling the buffers can continue indefinitely until the item is filed away or the edit abandoned.

Figure 11.1 provides a pictorial representation of the editor, showing a typical editing session. It explains how a two-line item on disk is updated to a three-line item. The original record is first copied to the current buffer. The text of the record in the current buffer is changed to upper and lower case and a third line added. However, a spelling mistake is made in line two, which can only be corrected by flipping the buffers, making buffer 2 current. The spelling correction is then made and the record filed back on disk.

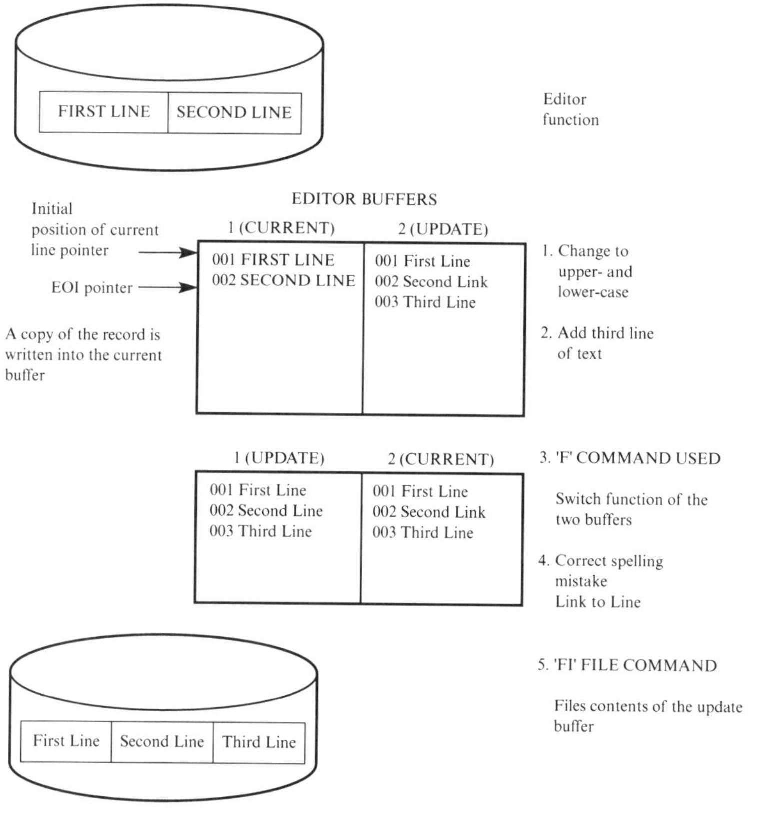

Figure 11.1 The editor concept.

11.3 A summary of the editor commands

The editor commands and their functions are as follows:

Options	Description
[CR]	Next line
^	Toggle 'wildcard' function
?	Status – displays filename, item-id and current line number
n	Go to line n
A	Again – repeats last locate or search command
AS	Toggles display of data in assembly format
B	Go to the bottom of the item
C	Display column numbers
DE	Delete current line
DEn	Delete n lines starting at current line
DEn/X	Delete lines containing string X in the next n lines starting at the current line
EX	Exit, do not change the existing record. It is the equivalent of ABORT
EXK	As with EX, but return immediately to TCL. Useful if you want to abandon the list of edits being processed
FD	Delete the item being edited from the file
FDK	As with FD, but return immediately to TCL
FI	File item, including changes made
FI n	File item, including changes, with the item-id n
FIK	File current item, including changes made and return immediately to TCL
FI (f i	File the item in file **f** with an item-id **i**
Note. Any of the above FI options can include the K option to return immediately to TCL, an 0 option to overwrite any item found with the same item-id or L which converts files to list format	
FS	File current state of edited item on disk, but continue with the edit session. A useful way of saving current work when processing a large item
FS n	As with FS, but save to item n
FS (f i	As with FS, but save on file **f** as item **i**
Note. Any of the above FS options can include the 0 option to overwrite an existing item with the same item-id or L, which converts the item to list format	
Gn	Go to line **n**
I	Insert after current line
Ln	List **n** lines from current line
L/X	Locate string **X** from current position in current line
Ln/X	Locate string **X** in **n** lines starting at current line

Ln/X/a-b	Locate string **X** in **n** lines starting at current line and occurring between columns **a** and **b**
L:X	Locate string **X** which starts in column 1
M	Toggle macro expansion
MEn//	Merge **n** lines from current item from line I
MEn//m	Merge **n** lines from current item from line **m**
MEn/i/	Merge **n** lines from item **i** in current file starting at line 1
MEn/ i /m	Merge **n** lines from item **i** in current file starting at line **m**
MEn (f i	Merge **n** lines from file **f** item **i** starting from line 1
MEn (f i)p	Merge **n** lines from file **f** item **i** starting from line **p**
N	Redisplays current line
Nn	Moves down **n** lines
P	Execute prestored command 0 (zero)
Pn	Execute prestored command **n**
Pn X[Y[Z	Set prestore command **n** to perform task **X** followed by task **Y** followed by task **Z**. The ESC key delimits each command
PD	Display contents of all prestored commands
R	Replace contents of current line
Rn	Replace contents of next **n** lines from current line
R/X/Y	Replace string **X** with string **Y**
R/X//	Replace string **X** with null
R//X	Insert string **X** at the beginning of current line
Rn/X/Y	Replace the first occurrence of string **X** in the next **n** lines with the string **Y**
Rn/X/Y/a-b	Replace the first occurrence of string **X** in the columns **a** to **b** in the next **n** lines with the string **Y**
RU...	Used in place of **R** to indicate that every, rather than just the first, occurrence of a string in a line, is to be replaced
S	Toggles suppression of line numbers
S?	Displays the size of the item in bytes and is only accurate if the buffer has been flipped
T	Go to the top of the item
TB n,m...	Sets tab stops at position **n**, **m** and so on
Un	Go up **n** lines
X	Cancels effect of last insert, replace or delete commands
XF	Cancels the effect of all commands since the last **F** command
Z a-b	Set zone between columns **a** and **b** and only display data within these columns

11.4 Using the editor

The editor is invoked by the TCL command EDIT, normally abbreviated to ED. Either of these commands will call up the editor which then needs to be told the file and item in the file to be edited. The format of the command is:

:EDIT {DICT} *filename itemlist*

or

:ED {DICT} *filename itemlist*

where

filename	is the name of the file containing the items to be edited
itemlist	is the list of item-ids of the items to be edited. These should be separated by a space and if the item-id contains a space, the entire item-id should be enclosed in quotes, otherwise quotes are unnecessary.

The editor, which can either edit an existing item or create a new one, is simple and easy to use. Once you have grasped the concept of the way it works, i.e. the use of its buffers, the rest is plain sailing and just a case of learning the commands. Probably the easiest way of learning the editor is to spend time in a test file creating and amending items, merging data from other items and trying out all the other options.

By way of an introduction and to show the features of the editor we will create and then modify a list of the names of the months of the year in an item called MONTHS in a file called DEMO. The editor will not create a file if it does not already exist, so if the file does not exist it should first be created with the **CREATE-FILE** command (see Section 6.3.1).

11.4.1 Adding new items with the editor

To explain in detail the workings of the editor we will first create the item MONTHS in the file DEMO with just the first six months in it. Figure 11.2 shows how this is achieved.

```
:ED DEMO MONTHS
NEW ITEM     <------ Shows that the item does not already exist
TOP
.I[CR]<------------- Editor prompt is . (full stop) and the I is the insert command
001+JANUARY [CR]
002+FEBRUARY [CR]
003+MARCH [CR]
004+APIL [CR]
005+MAY [CR]
006+JUNE [CR]
007+ [CR]
 TOP
.FI <--------------- The 'file away' command
'MONTHS' FILED.
```

Figure 11.2 Creating a new item with the editor.

The final command in Figure 11.2 files away the item MONTHS in the file DEMO. You can see that each line entered is given a unique number by the editor so that it can be referred to at any time. As you may have noticed in Figure 11.2, the item is only half complete and one of the months is spelt incorrectly. The next section shows how to use the editor to add the rest of the months and to correct the spelling mistake.

11.4.2 Changing the details of an item

Editing changes into an existing item is handled by adding new lines (attributes), replacing all or part of an existing line or by deleting lines. All of these functions are shown in Figure 11.3.

```
:ED DEMO MONTHS
TOP
.L2O[CR]              <--- List 20 lines
001 JANUARY           <--+
002 FEBRUARY             |
003 MARCH                |
004 APRIL                +--- Current buffer contents
005 MAY                  |
006 JUNE              <--+
EOI 006               <--- End of item pointer, line 6
.G4[CR]               <--- Go to line 4
004 APRIL             <--- The editor displays current contents
.R[CR]                <--- Replace the line
004 APRIL[CR]         <--- Type in new contents
.B                    <--- Go to bottom
EOI 006
.I                    <--- Insert command
006+JULY[CR]          <--+
006+JULY[CR]             |
006+AUGUST[CR]           |
006+SEPTEMBER[CR]        +--- new details added to the update buffer
006+OCTOBER[CR]          |
006+NOVEMBER[CR]         |
006+DECEMBER[CR]      <--+
006+[CR]
EOI 006
.T[CR]                <--- Go to top of item
TOP
.L2O[CR]              <--- List 20 lines
```

Figure 11.3 An editor session n an existing item.

```
001 JANUARY
002 FEBRUARY
003 MARCH
004 APIL
005 MAY
006 JUNE
007 JULY
008 JULY          Current buffer contents
009 AUGUST
010 SEPTEMBER
011 OCTOBER
012 NOVEMBER
013 DECEMBER
EOI 018
.8[CR]            Goto line 8
008 JULY
.DE[CR]           Delete line
.FI[CR]           File item away
MONTHS FILED
```

Figure 11.3 *continued*

Figure 11.3 demonstrates a number of editor functions and shows the way in which you can readily move around the item: **T** for top, **B** for bottom, ***n*** or ***Gn*** for line *n* and so on. In addition changes had to be made in ascending sequence, hence the contents of line 4 are replaced before other lines are added at the bottom. If we tried to do it the other way round the editor would have complained with the error message **SEQN?**, which is always a signal to flip the buffers using the **F** command and to look at the current state of the item before going further.

The other commands used, as with a number of others, can be applied to more than one line by including the number of lines with the command, such as **L** for list which on its own lists just one line, whereas **L2O** lists 20 lines. In the same way **DE** deletes the current line, but **DE5** will delete five lines starting at the current line.

Hopefully the principles are now clear. Changes are applied in ascending line number sequence by moving the current line pointer to the appropriate line and then applying the required command. Once a change is needed to be made to an earlier line or to new lines added, the **F** command must be used to flip the buffers and make the current state of the item available for editing.

11.4.3 The principles of replacing data

In the last example we saw one way in which information can be replaced. By completely re-inputting the line – the word **APIL** was replaced by **APRIL**. This is not too difficult when the amount of information to type in is small, but on a long line this is not only time-wasting but prone to error. Hence the editor provides a way of replacing part of a line. This is done by identifying a sequence or string of characters in the original line to be replaced by a different string. The general format is shown in Figure 11.4.

R{**U**}{*n*}/*Current string*/*Update string*/{*c*{*-d*}}
where:

R	stands for the replace command
U	means universal or every occurrence in a line
n	means that the string replacement is made in the next n lines from the current line. Unless the U option is taken, only the first occurrence of the current string is replaced with the update string in each of these lines
/	known as the 'delimiter' and used to separate the two character strings. Whilst the / (oblique symbol) is the usual delimiter, any character not contained in either character string, (the current string or update string) can be used
c	starting column position
d	ending column position The start and end column positions are used to restrict the location of the data to be replaced.

Figure 11.4 The format of the editor replace command.

Hence, to correct the spelling of **APIL** in Figure 11.3 we could have used:

R/PI/PRI/[CR]

or, as explained in Figure 11.4 any character not in the current or update string can be used as the delimiter. Hence using an asterisk as a delimiter would provide an alternative command string to correct the spelling of **APIL**

R*I*RI*[CR]

Replacing strings becomes a lot more difficult when the text string occurs several times in the line. Take the following example:

003 sdfsdfsdfsdfsdfsdfsdfsdfsdfsdfsdfsdfsdf

where we want to replace the sixth occurrence of **sdf** with **xxx**. Without typing in the full 18 characters it would seem impossible to point at the specific part of the line to be replaced. However there is a way in which you can replace the first occurrence of a string from a particular column by stating the column position and to make life easier the **C** command will produce a column ruler. Let's see this in action in Figure 11.5 to replace the string **sdf** in column 16 with thc string **xxx**.

The replacement command is of particular value in reproducing the null character, quite frequently needed when defining dictionary items. In these cases a special character not used elsewhere is placed on these lines and then the special character is replaced with the null value. Figure 11.6 shows how to create a new user record called MIKE where those lines needing null values are first given a value of' a full stop, each of which is then replaced by a null value.

```
:ED DEMO DUMMY
TOP
.3[CR]
003 sdfsdfsdfsdfsdfsdfsdfsdfsdfsdfsdfsdfsdf
.C
         1         2         3         4          5
12345689012345678901234567890123456789012345678901 234567890123456
R/sdf/xxx/16  <------  Replace first occurrence from column 16
.FI  <---------------  It is not necessary to flip buffers before filing if you are certain
                       of your actions
'DUMMY' FILED
```

The data string now looks like this: sdfsdfsdfsdfsdfxxxsdfsdfsdfsdfsdfsdfsdf

Figure 11.5 Replacing a character string with the editor.

```
:ED USERS MIKE
NEW ITEM
TOP
.I[CR]  <-----------------  Create a new item in the system dictionary
001+ Mike Stewartson [CR]
001+ . [CR]
001+ . [CR]  <---
001+ . [CR]      |
001+ . [CR]      |-------  Assign the value '.' to
001+ . [CR]      |         all items requiring a
001+ . [CR]  <---          null value
001+ SYS2[CR].
001+ .[CR]
001+ .[CR]
001+ .[CR]
```

Figure 11.6 Creating a user-id with the editor.

```
001+ TERM-TYPE [CR]
001+ SP-ASSIGN [CR]
001+ BRK-LEVEL [CR]
001+ ESC-DATA [CR]
001+ SET-SYM GSYM [CR]
001+ SET-SYM GSYM [CR]
001+ SPELLER-OFF [CR]
001+ LOGTO ADMIN [CR]
001+ [CR]
TOP
.F [CR]           <-------- Flip buffers
.RU99/.// [CR]    <-------- Replace up to 99 occurrences of a '.' with a null value
002 <-
003
004
005
006
007              --  Editor responds with the line
009                  number of those lines that have been changed
010
011 <-
EOI 10
.FI <------------------ File away the item in its current state
'MIKE' FILED
```

Figure 11.6 *continued*

Another way of editing in a null value is by pressing the control key and up-arrow key simultaneously. This combination of keys generates an attribute mark. The symbols which are used to represent the special PICK data marks, sub-value mark (\), value mark (]) and attribute mark (^), can be edited into an item by holding down the control key and depressing the key representing the symbol.

Hence the normal representation of an attribute mark the caret symbol (^) is generated using the control key and caret key together, the value mark, represented by the right square bracket (]) is generated using the control key and right square bracket key together and the sub-value mark represented by the backslash (\) is generated by holding down the control key and depressing the backslash key.

11.4.4 Merging data with the editor

The command **ME** will allow data from the existing or a totally different PICK file and/or item to be included in the item being edited. The data merged is not removed from the originating file, but copied from it and hence the original file and item remains intact. The line number of the information held in the originating file is used to determine what is to be merged. The general format of this command is shown in Figure 11.7.

Take care to ensure you have flipped the buffers and have studied the current state of the item before carrying out the merge command, particularly where you are merging lines from the item itself. Having merged the data the editor only responds with its command prompt, a full stop, so you should flip the buffers after a merge to ensure the correct data has been merged.

Figure 11.8 shows how an item containing a list of the months of the year is changed using the merge command. Firstly lines 3 and 4 of the item are merged within itself at line 6, and then one line is merged from another item, (**DUMMY**) in the same file (**DEMO**) as the item being edited. Finally three lines are taken from a completely different file and item and merged in.

ME{*n*}*itemid*/{*m*} ◄── where the item is in the file being edited, or
ME{*n*}({**DICT**} *filename itemid*/{*m*} ◄── where the item is in another file
where

n	represents the number of lines to be merged
m	represents the starting line number; when omitted line 1 is assumed
filename	is the name of the file containing the item whose contents are to be merged with the current item being edited
itemid	is the item-id of the item whose contents are to be merged with the current item being edited

To merge lines from the item being edited, use null as the item-id. This is usually represented by two backslash (\) characters, although any character not in the character string can be used as the delimiter.

Figure 11.7 The format of the editor merge command.

```
:ED DEMO MONTHS
TOP
.6[CR]
006 JUNE
.ME2//3[CR] ◄──── Merge two lines from this item starting at line 3
.F[CR]
TOP
.L10[CR]
001 JANUARY
002 FEBRUARY
003 MARCH
004 APRIL
005 MAY
006 JUNE
```

Figure 11.8 Examples of the editor merge command.

```
007 MARCH
008 APRIL
009 JULY
010 AUGUST
.ME1/DUMMY/3[CR]   Merge 1 line from the item DUMMY held in this file, i.e. the
.F [CR]            file called DEMO
TOP
.7 [CR]
007 MARCH
.ME3(TEST TEST1) [CR]<—Merge 3 lines from the item TEST1 in the file TEST
.F [CR]                starting with attribute 1
TOP
.6 [CR]
006 JUNE
.L10 [CR]
007 MARCH
008 FIRST LINE FROM TEST1
009 SECOND LINE FROM TEST1
010 THIRD LINE FROM TEST1
011 APRIL
012 JULY
013 AUGUST
014 sdfsdfsdfsdfsdfsdfsdfsdfsdf
015 SEPTEMBER
016 OCTOBER
.FI [CR] <————————— File item away
MONTHS FILED
```

Figure 11.8 *continued*

11.4.5 Using the search facility

Looking for a particular string of characters in an item is handled by the locate command **L**. Having found the string the editor displays the line it was found on. The **A** command will carry out the search again.

Like the replace command, the search command can look for the first *n* occurrences of the string and can limit its search to a range of specified columns, giving the general format of the command as shown in Figure 11.9. If however the search requires that the string start in column 1, then the format of the command is **L/***String*.

11.4.6 Using the wildcard facility

The up-arrow input on the command line toggles the wildcard facility. When switched on the up-arrow (^) indicates a wildcard character, i. e. any character. This enables you to determine the same course of action for strings of characters which are similar, but not the same. Figure 11.10 shows how this is used.

L{*n*}/*String*/{*c*{-d}}

where:

- *n* — means that the string search is made in the next n lines from the current line.
- / — Known as the 'delimiter' and used to separate the character string. Whilst the oblique symbol (/) is the usual delimiter, any character not contained in the character string can be used
- *c* — starting column position
- *d* — ending column position

Figure 11.9 The editor locate command.

```
:ED DEMO TEST
top
.L20 [CR]
001 MY NAME IS TOM
002 I HAVE A FRIEND CALLED TIM
003 TIM HAS A VERY BAD TEMPER
eoi 003
.T [CR]
top
.RU999/T^M/XXX[CR]   <----  The wildcard facility starts off being active
001 MY NAME IS XXX
002 I HAVE A FRIEND CALLED XXX
003 XXX HAS A VERY BAD XXXPER
eoi 003
.F [CR]
top
.^ [CR]   <----  Contrary to displayed message, this switches OFF the
/^\ on    <----  wildcard facility
.RU999/X^X/MMM/ [CR]   <----  The wildcard facility no longer works
eoi 003
.^ [CR]   <----  Switch on wildcard facility again
/^\ off
.F [CR]
top
.RU999/X^X/MMM/ [CR]
001 MY NAME IS MMM
002 I HAVE A FRIEND CALLED MMM
003 MMM HAS A VERY BAD MMMPER
eoi 003
.FI [CR]   <----  File item away
TEST FILED
```

Figure 11.10 The use of the wildcard facility.

11.4.7 The use of prestored commands

The editor has the means to store one or a number of editor commands in one of ten command buffers numbered from 0 to 9. The commands held within them are executed by requesting use of the prestored command facility, denoted by the letter P followed by the appropriate command buffer number. Hence by typing in P0 the editor would execute the commands found in prestored buffer 0; likewise P1 would perform the commands found in prestored buffer 1.

On entering the editor you will find that the prestored command P0, usually referenced simply as P, has been automatically is set to **L22**. Hence by typing **P** at the editor prompt, the next 22 lines will be displayed.

The contents of the prestored commands are listed using the command **PD** (prestored display commands) at the editor prompt. It should be noted however that all command buffers other than P0, i.e. P1 to P9, are cleared as soon as the edit session has been terminated. The prestored command buffers are temporary and only apply to the edit session in progress.

These buffers need first to be given the appropriate command sequences, which is achieved by entering the prestored command number followed by the string of commands. The general format for building a prestore command is shown in Figure 11.11.

P*n Command 1***|** *Command 2***|** *Command 3*

where:

n	represents the prestored command buffer number
Command	is the editor command that would be typed in manually at the editor command prompt (.)
|	is the special character that separates the commands. This is achieved by pressing the ESC key (on some implementations this may be a value mark (control/]). Note that whilst this displays as a left square bracket, it is not one and the left square bracket key on its own will not achieve the correct result.

Figure 11.11 The format of editor prestored commands.

The prestored command facility is of particular value when you need to make a change within a number of records in a file, for example to correct spelling. In Figure 11.12 all records in an address file which have the name DERBY spelled as DERBBY are corrected.

In Figure 11.12 an entire file, albeit of five records, was searched looking for a misspelt word. In real life of course this could be working on a file of many hundreds if not thousands of records. The process works automatically and at remarkable speed, through all the records in the file without the need for any manual intervention. The only way to stop the process is to 'break' it using the break key sequence. Figure 11.12 shows that the spelling mistake was found in two records, and that overall a total of three corrections had to be made.

After the corrections were made control was returned to the TCL prompt. Another common use of this editor feature is to search through the master dictionary to change Q-pointers that point to one account and to change them to point to another. This would typically occur when new programs need to be tested. In this situation, typically a copy of the live account would be restored to a test account and the Q-pointers within the test account changed to point at the account containing the programs for testing. This is illustrated in Figure 11.13, using exactly the same principles as described in Figure 11.12.

Screen	Comment
:ED ADDRESS `*[CR]`	Edit all records in the file
`10012`	Item-id of first record found
`TOP`	
.P2 R99/DERBBY/DERBY/[F1[P2[`[CR]`	Replace occurrences of DERBBY with DERBY, file the item and re-execute command P2
.P2	Execute the commands held in the prestore command buffer
`EOI 016`	
`'10012' FILED.`	No change made to this record
`10160`	
`TOP`	
`EOI 017`	
`'10160' FILED`	No change made to this record
`10101`	
`TOP`	
`012 DERBY`	Line 12 of this record changed
`018 County of DERBY`	Line 18 of this record changed
`E01 020`	
`'10101' FILED.`	
`10114`	
`TOP`	
`011 DERBY`	Line 11 of this record changed
`EOI 015`	
`'10114' FILED.`	
`10115`	
`TOP`	
`EOI 016`	
`'10115' FILED.`	No change made to this record
`:`	

Figure 11.12 The use of prestored commands in the editor.

```
:ED MD * [CR]  <----  Edit all records in master dictionary
SET-TAPE-TYPE  <----  Item-id of first record found
TOP
P1 R999/LIVE/TEST/[FI[P1 [CR]  <----  Replace up to 999 occurrences of LIVE
                                      with TEST, file the item and re-execute
                                      command P1
P1 [CR]  <----  Execute the commands held in the prestore
                command buffer number 1
EOI 010
'MEHELP' FILED.  <----  No change made to this record
T-REW
TOP
EOI 003
'T-REW' FILED.  <----  No change made to this record
DM13
TOP
002 TEST  <----  Line 2 of this record changed
EOI 003
'DM13' FILED.
DM1S
TOP
002 TEST  <----  Line 2 of this record changed
EOI 003
'DM15' FILED.
   |
   |
   v
:
```

Figure 11.13 The use of editor prestored commands to change Q-pointers in the Master Dictionary.

In operation this command is so quick that it is impossible to read what is being displayed on the screen. If you wish to temporarily stop the screen display press S̲ (CTRL/S). Once you are ready for the operation to proceed, type Q̲ (CTRL/Q). These commands can be used to stop and restart any screen output which displays too fast to read.

12 Information Retrieval Using ACCESS

TCL verbs and general commands covered in this chapter

CHECK-SUM	COPY	COPY-LIST	COUNT	DELETE-LIST
EL	EDIT-LIST	GET-LIST	HASH-TEST	ISTAT
NSELECT	LIST	LIST-ITEM	LIST-LABEL	QSELECT
REFORMAT	SAVE-LIST	SELECT	SORT	SORT-ITEM
SORT-LABEL	SREFORMAT	SSELECT	STAT	SUM
S-DUMP	T-DUMP	T-LOAD		

12.1 An introduction to ACCESS

It is within ACCESS that users start to recognize the power, the flexibility and virtue of buying a PICK system and, for those of you *still* unsure whether PICK is for you, I am sure this section will finally convince you!

ACCESS is a general-purpose information retrieval language and typically consists of a relatively free format sentence using an English-like language. An ACCESS sentence contains the name of the file on which to enquire, the selection criteria and the information to be printed and its format. It is known by other names within some PICK implementations, e.g. ENGLISH, INFORM, INFO/ACCESS or RECALL, to name just a few, but they all relate to the same facility.

Whilst it is an exaggeration to say you will never need to write a report program it is not far from the truth. The bulk of both the regular and *ad hoc* reports any business uses can be produced using ACCESS. ACCESS provides the means to selectively or conditionally retrieve information from the database and to report on it. Output reports can be produced on the printer or terminal and may be formatted and sequenced in a variety of ways. ACCESS features:

- relatively free form of input of the ACCESS sentence;
- generalized selection of information using logical and arithmetical relationships;
- the means to sort information in ascending or descending sequence;
- the creation and retention of lists of selected items for use in subsequent TCL processes or BASIC programs;
- the ability to search, select, sort, total, to break on a change of like items and to output based on items defined in the dictionary;
- the ability to produce automatic reports from a file, or user-defined reports with their own optional headings and footings, in columnar or non-columnar form;
- the generation of statistical information relating to files.

The general steps of the ACCESS processor are shown in Figure 12.1.

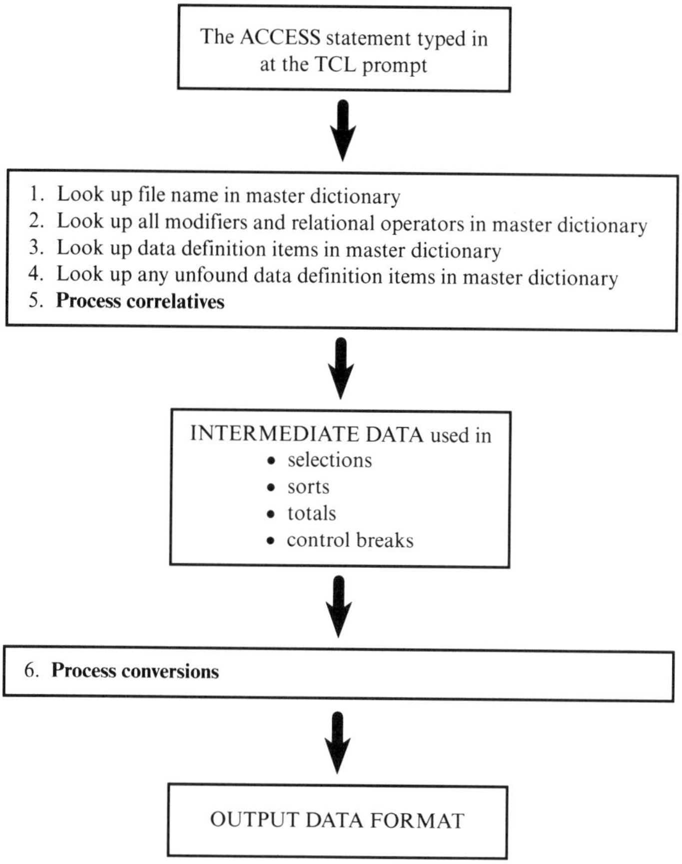

Figure 12.1 The steps of the ACCESS processor.

ACCESS is a dictionary-driven language in the sense that the file dictionary contains the names of the data elements to be used in the enquiry language and defines the way in which that data is to be presented. The Master Dictionary contains the vocabulary of the ACCESS enquiry language, such as COUNT, LIST, SORT, TOTAL and so on. Much of PICK's strength, and what sets it aside from the traditional databases, comes from the capability of its dictionaries. Do bear in mind, as you read on, that what we are discussing is an integral and functional part of Advanced PICK whether used as a database or as a native operating system.

Where PICK is the native operating system, ACCESS is not a database management system that has been 'bolted on', but a functional and extremely important part of it. Other multi-user operating systems, such as UNIX, do not offer these facilities and it is incumbent on the user to locate and purchase a database of their own choice and then integrate it with their applications.

Such is the importance of the dictionaries to the ACCESS language that the next chapter is devoted to their structure and capabilities.

12.2 ACCESS enquiry language – some important rules

As already discussed, ACCESS is a dictionary-driven language in that it is the dictionary that contains the names of the data elements to be used in the enquiry language and defines the way in which data is to be presented. It is the master dictionary (MD) in each account that contains the vocabulary of the ACCESS enquiry language, such as COUNT, LIST, SORT, TOTAL and so on. In the next chapter we discuss the various ways in which the dictionary definition items can be manipulated to reduce the amount of data stored and to enable data to be presented in a suitable form. In the following sections we will see how to use the ACCESS processor to retrieve information from the database.

In developing ACCESS reports be careful not to fall into the trap of wasting a considerable amount of time trying to get ACCESS to produce a report it is incapable of doing – it is quicker to write a program! There are a few simple rules to follow which will ensure your success. These are:

(1) ACCESS enquiries must be entered either at TCL, as part of a MACRO (see Chapter 17) or within the Primary Input Buffer of a PROC (see Section 18.2).

(2) The first word of the ACCESS statement must be one of the ACCESS verbs contained in the master dictionary.

(3) At TCL the statement must be terminated by a carriage return.

(4) In Advanced PICK the TCL input buffer is sufficient to take the longest ACCESS statement, but in R83 the limit is 140 characters. To input multiple line statements in R83 type CTRL/SHIFT/0 at the end of each line followed by a carriage return. A : will be prompted by the ACCESS processor awaiting subsequent input.

(5) Only one file name can be used within an ACCESS sentence. To report on data held in more than one file, it will be necessary to set up correlatives.

(6) The word **DICT** can precede the file name to enable ACCESS enquiries on dictionary files.

(7) Any number of attribute names can be used in an ACCESS statement. If the amount of data to be displayed exceeds the printer (or screen) width, the report will be printed down the page, one attribute to a line.

(8) Any number of modifiers and relational operators, which are defined in the MD, may be used.

(9) ACCESS verbs, file names, attribute names, modifiers and relational operators are separated by either blanks, quotes (“ or ‘) or backslashes (\). It is rare to use anything other than a blank.

(10) Specific items to be listed are enclosed in backslashes (\) or quotes (“ or ‘) and *must* appear immediately following the file name. With Advanced PICK version 6.1 these delimiters are no longer required.

(11) Specific values are enclosed in double quotes (“) or backslashes (\) and apply to the previous attribute name. With Advanced PICK version 6.1 these delimiters are no longer required.

12.3 The structure of an ACCESS sentence

Whilst ACCESS is generally a free-format enquiry language, the sentence created is made up of a number of different functional sections, the first two of which **must** be the ACCESS verb and the file name. The following shows the general form of the ACCESS command:

Verb	File reference	Sort criteria	Item list	Selection criteria { Print limiters}	Output specifications	Modifiers	Options

12.3.1 Verb

The ACCESS sentence **must** start with a verb. These indicate the course of action to be taken by the system and comprise any one of the following

CHECK-SUM	COPY-LIST	COUNT	DELETE-LIST
EDIT-LIST	GET-LIST	HASH-TEST	ISTAT
LIST	LIST-ITEM	LIST-LABEL	NSELECT
REFORMAT	SAVE-LIST	SELECT	SORT
SORT-ITEM	SORT-LABEL	SORT-LIST	SREFORMAT
SSELECT	STAT	SUM	T-DUMP
T-LOAD			

The two most commonly used verbs are **LIST** which produces a list of data in random order, and **SORT** which produces a report of data in a sorted order. The function of the ACCESS verbs is as follows:

CHECK-SUM	calculates a hexadecimal checksum for a specified attribute or the entire item if no attribute is specified
COPY-LIST	creates a copy of an existing list with either a new name or to an output device
COUNT	produces a total of the number of items that meet the specified selection criteria
DELETE-LIST	deletes a list previously saved with the **SAVE-LIST** command
EDIT-LIST	retrieves an existing list and enters the line editor
GET-LIST	retrieves an existing list
HASH-TEST	produces a histogram of item distribution for a test modulo of an existing file
ISTAT	produces a histogram of item distribution in a file

LIST	lists the contents of a file (the results are unordered)
LIST-ITEM	displays items in their internally stored format
LIST-LABEL	produces selected output in label format (the results are unordered)
NSELECT	selects items which would fail the selection criteria of a 'select' statement
REFORMAT	takes the values from the attributes specified in the ACCESS command and places them either in another file or to magnetic media, in the order in which the attributes are specified
SAVE-LIST	saves a list of item-id's specified by a SELECT, SSELECT, QSELECT or GET-LIST command
SELECT	selects the item-id's that meet a given selection criteria (the results are unordered) and makes this list 'active' to the next TCL command executed
SORT	sorts the items selected by the ACCESS statement into a nominated order. This command is the 'sorted' version of LIST
SORT-ITEM	produces a sorted list of items displaying their internally stored format. This command is the 'sorted' version of LIST-ITEM
SORT-LABEL	produces a sorted list of output in label format (the sorted version of LIST-LABEL)
SORT-LIST	retrieves a previously saved list, sorts it, then rewrites it to the file from which it was retrieved
SREFORMAT	takes the values from the attributes specified in the ACCESS command and places them either in another file or to magnetic media, in the order of the specified sort keys. This command is the 'sorted' version of REFORMAT
SSELECT	selects the item-ids that meet a given selection criteria makes this list 'active' to the next TCL command executed. The items are sorted in accordance with the sort criteria of the ACCESS statement
STAT	outputs certain file statistics based on the given selection criteria
SUM	produces the numeric total of a given attribute for all items meeting the selection criteria
T-DUMP	copies the selected items to the 'attached' magnetic media device
T-LOAD	loads the selected items from the 'attached' magnetic media device

12.3.2 File reference

This is the file name and **must** follow the verb. The data portion of a file will be used unless the word **DICT** precedes the file name. Where the only output required by the ACCESS processor is a list of item-ids, then precede the file name with the word **ONLY**. Hence the sentence **SORT ONLY MDS** will produce a list of all the accounts on the system (i.e. a list of the item-ids in the file **mds**).

After the file name has been specified, the remaining parts of the ACCESS statement can be listed in any order.

12.3.3 Sort criteria

This section of the ACCESS statement specifies the order in which the selected data is to be compiled for the report. Each sort field is preceded with the word **BY** and a maximum of 16 sort fields are permitted. The items are sorted in ascending order unless the modifier **BY-DSND** is used, in which case the items are sorted in descending order. Where more than one sort key is used, the primary sort key must be specified first. Hence to sort data by name within department order, the sort criteria would look something like **BY DEPARTMENT BY NAME**.

If the field being sorted is a multi-value and it is required to include each of the multi-values then use the 'by-exploded' modifier **BY-EXP** (see Section 12.4.4). This will sort in ascending order unless the descending option **BY-EXP-DSND** is specified.

12.3.4 Item list

This section allows a list of specific items to be identified. If an item list is specified ACCESS will perform a direct read on the file to locate the specific items because it knows their item-ids. Without such a list being specified, ACCESS will read through the entire file. The item list may be as long as is required.

12.3.5 Selection criteria

The selection criteria is where the complex processing of an ACCESS report is carried out. Selection criteria are preceded with the word **WITH** and are the conditions an item must satisfy to be included in the report. Any number of conditions can be specified and linked together by the connectives **AND** and **OR**. It is possible to select items based on just part of an attribute such as whether they begin with a specific string (e.g. **xxx]**), end with a specific string (e.g. **[xxx**) or contain a specific string (e.g. **[xxx]**).

12.3.6 Print limiters

Print limiters are used to suppress the printing of details unless they satisfy specific conditions. Hence it is possible to display a column which contains the price of an item, but only print the price if it is above a certain value, otherwise the record will be listed but with its actual price not shown. This is useful to highlight exception values on a report. Print limiters differ from selection criteria in that print limiters do not limit the records that are chosen, rather whether or not the contents of an attribute will be printed or not. Print limiters do not contain the **WITH** modifier.

12.3.7 Output specifications

The output specifications section specifies the data attributes to be listed in the report and starts with the word **WITH** or **IF**. The **WITH** or **IF** is followed by an attribute name which in turn can be followed by a logical operator and control value. Any number of selection conditions can be specified and each is linked with the connectives **AND** and/or **OR**. Breaks can be produced on a change of values in an attribute and sub-totals and grand totals produced. An option exists to produce a totals only report and facilities exist for the inclusion of user defined headings and footings. Where a user heading is defined it will replace the default heading produced by the ACCESS processor. Separate messages can be displayed at control total breaks, whether these be sub-totals or grand totals.

12.3.8 Modifiers

A modifier is a word that modifies the normal operation of the ACCESS processor, such as suppressing item-ids, suppressing column headings or sending the report to the printer. These are just some examples and we will look at them all in detail later on.

12.3.9 Options

These come at the end of the ACCESS sentence, just like they would with any other TCL command. They are preceded with an open round bracket symbol '('. There is a modifier for each option although the reverse is not true. A full list of options and modifiers is shown in Section 12.4.17.

12.3.10 Stopping output from the ACCESS processor

Since an ACCESS report can be many hundreds of pages long, it is useful to know what to do to either completely abandon a report, or, if it is being displayed to the screen, how to temporarily halt the display and then re-start it.

There are two useful ways to abort the ACCESS processor. The first is *x* (CTRL/X), the pressing of the CTRL key together with the X key. This will terminate the display at the current page of the ACCESS report on the screen and return you to the TCL prompt.

The other, if you are just wanting to stop the display from scrolling up the screen, rather than terminate it completely, is to use **s** (CTRL/S). This will hold the display on the screen until a **q** (CTRL/Q) is entered, after which time the output will restart and the report will scroll up the screen. This will only apply if you use the **N** (Nopage) option which does not require the return key to be pressed at the end of each page output.

Obviously you could also use the BREAK key or **c** (CTRL/C). This will terminate the ACCESS processor whilst it is compiling its report and is useful when an incorrect statement has been entered to save wasted processing time. Use of this function can be dangerous since it gives access to the system debugger and an exclamation mark is displayed to denote this. At this point the *only* command that should be entered is END to return to the TCL prompt. In extreme cases where the system does not respond to END, type OFF to log off the system.

The remainder of this chapter will reference data held on the files **STAFF** and **DEPT**. The contents of both the dictionary and data portions of these files are described below for reference.

Staff file dictionary

Item-id →	KEY	NAME	FNAME	SNAME
Attribute				
001	A	A	A	A
002	0	1	1	1
003	Ref	Name	First Name	Surname
004				
005				
006				
007				
008			G1,1	G,1
009	R	L	L	L
010	3	20	20	20
011				
012				
013				
014				
015				
016				
017				
018				
019				
020				

Item-id →	FULL	ADDRESS	TEL
Attribute			
001	A	A	A
002	1	2	3
003	Full Name	Address	Tel
004			
005			
006			
007			
008	A;N(FNAME)": :"N(SNAME)		
009	L	L	L
010	20	30	15
011			
012			
013			
014			
015			
016			
017			
018			
019			
020			

Item-id ⟶	DEPT	DEPTDESC	INTERESTS	SALARY
Attribute				
001	A	S	A	A
002	4	4	5	6
003	Dept	Description	Interests	Salary
004				
005				
006				
007	S;*;'NO'			MR22,
008		TDEPT;C;;1		
009	L	L	L	R
010	3	20	20	10
011				
012				
013				
014				
015				
016				
017				
018				
019				
020				

Staff file data

Item-id	001
Name	DIXON, GEORGE
Address	21 GROVE LANE CRAYTHORNE LEICS LE1 1QS
Tel No	0116 30303
Department	02
Interests	SQUASH BADMINTON BRIDGE
Salary	£15,500
Item-id	002
Name	LEA, SHAUN
Address	55 LYNDON WAY LONDON NW1 7SZ
Tel No	0171 346 2456
Department	11
Interests	SAILING SWIMMING READING
Salary	£13,250
Item-id	003

Name	PIKE, JOHN
Address	74 WASHWOOD HEATH ROAD BIRMINGHAM B7 7RR
Tel No	0121 359 6009
Department	13
Interests	BRIDGE SQUASH CHESS
Salary	£11,350

Item-id	004
Name	HARLOW, MICHAEL
Address	58 FOUNTAIN LANE BILLERICAY ESSEX CM12 3HF
Tel No	01474 344255
Department	11
Interests	SQUASH MUSIC
Salary	£12,900

Item-id	005
Name	MORRIS, JIM
Address	33 MILL LANE REIGATE SURREY RH3 8VX
Tel No	0181 345 5454
Department	13
Interests	SQUASH BRIDGE RALLYING
Salary	£15,500

Item-id	006
Name	BRIGHT, IAN
Address	121 JOINERS LANE WELWYN HERTS SG1 1DD
Tel No	01244 99933
Department	02
Interests	KARATE MARTIAL ARTS
Salary	£15,400

Item-id	010
Name	RILEY, JULIE
Address	2 HIGHMEAD SUTTON COLDFIELD BIRMINGHAM B12 1TT
Tel No	0121 355 6060
Department	11
Interests	SWIMMING SAILING
Salary	£14,550

Dept. file dictionary

Item-id →	KEY	DESC
Attribute		
001	A	A
002	0	1
003	Code	Description
004		
005		
006		
007		
008		
009	L	L
010	3	20
011		
012		
013		
014		
015		
016		
017		
018		
019		
020		

Dept. file data

Item-id (Attribute 0)	*Description (Attribute 1)*
01	ACCOUNTS
02	ADMINISTRATION
06	MAINTENANCE
11	SALES
13	SW SUPPORT

12.4 The ACCESS processor in detail

12.4.1 Producing unsequenced reports

LIST is one of the prime ACCESS verbs. It can be used with just a file name to produce a simple enquiry, or can additionally include selection criteria, output format specifications, item lists and other options to deal with a more complex enquiry. In its basic form **LIST** will list the contents of a file or file dictionary as is illustrated in Figure 12.2.

:LIST STAFF ← Lists the contents of the data portion of the STAFF file

```
Page  1   STAFF                         16:43:48 12 Mar 1995

STAFF.....

002
003
001
004
005
010
006

[405] 7 items listed out of 7 items.
```

:LIST DICT STAFF ← Lists the contents of the dictionary portion of the STAFF file

```
DICT STAFF       SALARY
 1                A
 AMC              6
 3               Salary
 CONVERSION       MR22,
 TYP              R
 MAX              10

DICT STAFF       STAFF
 1                D
 AMC              82646
 3                1
 TYP              L
 MAX              10

DICT STAFF       NAME
 1                A
 AMC              1
 3                Name
 TYP              L
 MAX              20

DICT STAFF       KEY
 1                A
 AMC              0
 3                Ref
 TYP              R
 MAX              3

        ↓

DICT STAFF       SNAME
 1                A
 AMC              1
 3                Surname
 CORRELATIVE      G,1
 TYP              L
 MAX              20

[405] 12 items listed out of 12 items.
```

Figure 12.2 Simple enquiries using **LIST**.

You will notice from Figure 12.2 that although in both cases we used the simple **LIST** command, in the case of the data file we were only shown the item-ids whilst for the dictionary we were shown a great deal more information. In a large file where you are only interested in finding out which items exist in a file, this extra information is not only annoying, sometimes confusing, but it can also be time-wasting. If you wish to limit the information displayed to show only the item-id then the word **ONLY** (one of the ACCESS modifiers as discussed in Section 12.4.17) should be included in the statement immediately after the **LIST** verb as shown in Figure 12.3.

There is another useful list verb called **LIST-ITEM** which combines the action of the **COPY** or **CT** verbs with the selection capability of ACCESS. The beauty of this command is that it shows you the format of each item *exactly* as stored on the hard disk; that is to say it contains all value and sub-value marks and the internal format of any data items, such as dates and financial amounts. A typical **LIST-ITEM** report is shown in Figure 12.4 where all items whose department code is 11 are listed.

:LIST ONLY DICT STAFF

```
Page  1   DICT STAFF                    17:12:26 12 Mar 1995

DICT STAFF

SALARY
STAFF
NAME
KEY
INTERESTS
DEPT
FNAME
DEPTDESC
FULL
ADDRESS
TEL
SNAME

[405] 12 items listed out of 12 items.
```

Figure 12.3 Listing item-ids using the **ONLY** modifier.

12.4.2 Default output specifications

Whilst we have now restricted the displayed information for the dictionary items to the item-id by use of the **ONLY** modifier it does not explain why the two lists shown in Figure 12.2 differed so greatly in the original amount of information displayed when the command used effectively looked the same.

:LIST-ITEM STAFF WITH DEPT = "11"

```
Page  1         STAFF                                    17:14:05 12 Mar 1995

002
001 LEA,SHAUN
002 55 LYNDON WAY]LONDON NW1 7SZ
003 0171 346 2456
004 11
005 SAILING]SWIMMING]READING
006 1325000

004
001 HARLOW,MICHAEL
002 58 FOUNTAIN LANE]BILLERICAY]ESSEX CM12 3HF
003 01474 344255
004 11
005 SQUASH]MUSIC
006 1290000

010
001 RILEY,JULIE
002 2 HIGHMEAD]SUTTON COLDFIELD]BIRMINGHAM  B12 1TT
003 0121 355 6060
004 11
005 SWIMMING]SAILING
006 1325000

[405] 3 items listed out of 7 items.
:
```

Figure 12.4 The output from **LIST-ITEM**.

When we listed the data position of the STAFF file we were just presented with a list of item-ids, but when we listed the dictionary we were shown the contents of the first 10 attributes. So why should this be?

The reason is not obvious, but as you might have guessed is associated with the dictionaries controlling these files. By now you should be familiar with the PICK file hierarchy and know that the master dictionary controls the file dictionary, whilst the file dictionary controls the data. Normally within the master dictionary are dictionary definition items with the item-ids **1**, **2**, **3**, through to **10** each defining its respective attribute. Hence the MD item **1** defines attribute position **1**, item **2** attribute **2** and so on. This sequential set of ten item-ids will be referenced where no specific output specifications are quoted and the contents of the first 10 attributes displayed by default. If the sequential list of items is broken, then ACCESS will list the first *n* sequential attributes providing the sequential dictionary items in the MD start at **1**.

Hence when listing the contents of a file dictionary the ACCESS processor will include in its output any number of sequential item-ids starting at **1** as default output specifications where no specific output requirements are defined.

Since there are no similar dictionary items in the file dictionary of STAFF, no default output was produced from the simple **LIST** command. If, for example, we felt it would be useful to see the name and telephone number listed as defaults each time a simple LIST enquiry was processed, we could create two new entries, 1 and 2, in the dictionary of the file STAFF. This can be achieved very simply by copying the dictionary items NAME and TEL and naming them 1 and 2. The **LIST** command would then reflect their presence. The total exercise is shown in Figure 12.5.

This is the only way of defining default output specifications within PICK R83, but in Advanced PICK you can define these in attribute 15 (the MACRO attribute) of the file dictionary. So to achieve the same result as that given in Figure 12.5 just add the words **NAME TEL** to the MACRO attribute as shown in Figure 12.6.

```
:COPY DICT STAFF NAME TEL
TO :
1 2[CR]
1 NAME TO 1
2 TEL TO 2
[805] 2 item(s) copied
:LIST STAFF


Page 1          STAFF                        17:12:49 12 Mar 1995

STAFF..... Name                Tel

002         LEA,SHAUN           0171 346 2456
003         PIKE,JOHN           0121 359 6009
001         DIXON,GEORGE        0116 30303
004         HARLOW,MICHAEL      01474 344255
005         MORRIS,JIM          0181 345 5454
010         RILEY,JULIE         0121 355 6060
006         BRIGHT,IAN          01244 99933

[405] 7 items listed out of 7 items.
```

Figure 12.5 Creating default reports using **LIST**.

```
:delete dict staff 1 2
[435] Item '1' deleted
[435] Item '2' deleted

:ud staff
DICT staff 'staff'  size = 57
dictionary-code     D
base                21706
modulo              1
```

Figure 12.6 Creating default reports using the MACRO attribute of a file's dictionary.

```
structure
retrieval-lock
update-lock
output-conversion
correlative
attribute-type       L
column-width         10
input-conversion
macro                name tel
output-macro
description
reallocation
hotkey.all
hotkey1
hotkey2
hotkey3
hotkey4
hotkey5
hotkey6
hotkey7
hotkey8
```

:LIST STAFF

```
Page  1        STAFF                     17:12:49 12 Mar 1995

STAFF..... Name             Tel

002        LEA,SHAUN        0171 346 2456
003        PIKE,JOHN        0121 359 6009
001        DIXON,GEORGE     0116 30303
004        HARLOW,MICHAEL   01474 344255
005        MORRIS,JIM       0181 345 5454
010        RILEY,JULIE      0121 355 6060
006        BRIGHT,IAN       01244 99933

[405] 7 items listed out of 7 items.
```

Figure 12.6 *continued*

12.4.3 Producing reports in sorted sequence

The reports we have produced so far have been in random sequence and are in the order that they are stored within the file. Whilst this is acceptable for small reports, it is far from satisfactory for management reports and reports that are used as reference documents, for example where you need to look up a telephone number. If today's telephone directories were not in alphabetical sequence we would never be able to use them! Sorting is another major ACCESS function and is handled by the verb **SORT**. Using **SORT** as we did **LIST**, without any further qualification, will produce a report in ascending sequence of item-ids as is shown in Figure 12.7.

The data can be sorted in any other sequence by adding the dictionary name of the attribute on which to sort preceded by the word **BY**. To sort in descending sequence use **BY-DSND**. Examples of these two functions are given in Figure 12.8. Additionally there is a **SORT-ITEM** verb to perform a sorted **LIST-ITEM** function.

:SORT STAFF

```
Page  1         STAFF                                  17:14:24 12 Mar 1995

staff.....  Name              Tel

001         DIXON,GEORGE      0116 30303
002         LEA,SHAUN         0171 346 2456
003         PIKE,JOHN         0121 359 6009
004         HARLOW,MICHAEL    01474 344255
005         MORRIS,JIM        0181 345 5454
006         BRIGHT,IAN        01244 99933
010         RILEY,JULIE       0121 355 6060

[405] 7 items listed out of 7 items.
```

Remember default output specifications have been defined.

Figure 12.7 Using an unqualified **SORT** verb.

:SORT STAFF BY NAME

```
Page  1         STAFF                             17:14:36 12 Mar 1995

STAFF.....  Name              Tel

006         BRIGHT,IAN        01244 99933
001         DIXON,GEORGE      0116 30303
004         HARLOW,MICHAEL    01474 344255
002         LEA,SHAUN         0171 346 2456
005         MORRIS,JIM        0181 345 5454
003         PIKE,JOHN         0121 359 6009
010         RILEY,JULIE       0121 355 6060

[405] 7 items listed out of 7 items.
:
```

:SORT STAFF BY-DSND NAME

```
Page  1         STAFF                             17:14:59 12 Mar 1995

STAFF.....  Name              Tel

010         RILEY,JULIE       0121 355 6060
003         PIKE,JOHN         0121 359 6009
005         MORRIS,JIM        0181 345 5454
002         LEA,SHAUN         0171 346 2456
004         HARLOW,MICHAEL    01474 344255
001         DIXON,GEORGE      0116 30303
006         BRIGHT,IAN        01244 99933

[405] 7 items listed out of 7 items.
:
```

Figure 12.8 Using the **SORT** verb.

Sorting need not be limited to one attribute, since PICK is capable of sorting by up to 16 keys. Hence it would be possible to produce a report giving an alphabetical list of people broken down by departments using the command **SORT STAFF BY DEPT BY NAME**. Notice that the primary sort key is specified first followed by the secondary sort key, tertiary sort key and so on. Notice too, that each attribute to be sorted is preceded with the word **BY**.

Using the command as shown, however, will not list the department number as is it not one of the defaults items listed in the dictionary. (Remember **1** defines the name and **2** the telephone number.) In order to list other attributes it is necessary to switch off the defaults which is achieved by requesting the specific attributes by name, even if one of them is a default attribute.

12.4.4 Specifying the data to be output

Specifying the data to be output switches off the display of the default attributes and displays only those attributes listed in the ACCESS statement. Figure 12.9 shows how this is used to produce a sorted report showing the department, its description and the name of the staff member in the department.

So far, the data we have listed has not been multi-valued. If we were to list people's interests (which is multi-valued) in place of the department name we would convert the report to look like that illustrated in Figure 12.10.

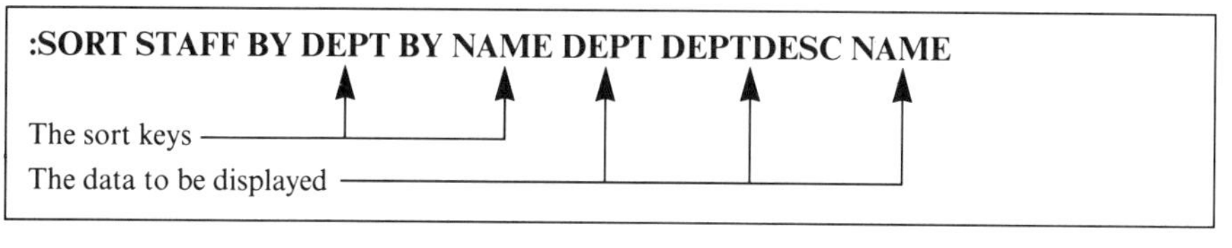


```
Page  1   STAFF                          17:15:26 12 Mar 1995

STAFF..... Dept Description      Name

006      02 ADMINISTRATION    BRIGHT,IAN
001      02 ADMINISTRATION    DIXON,GEORGE
004      11 SALES           HARLOW,MICHAEL
002      11 SALES           LEA,SHAUN
010      11 SALES           RILEY,JULIE
005      13 SW SUPPORT        MORRIS,JIM
003      13 SW SUPPORT        PIKE,JOHN

[405] 7 items listed out of 7 items.
```

Figure 12.9 Selecting the data to be output.

:SORT STAFF BY DEPT BY NAME DEPT NAME INTERESTS

```
Page  1          STAFF                              17:15:26 12 Mar 1995

STAFF..... Dept Name               Interests

006          02 BRIGHT,IAN         KARATE
                                   MARTIAL ARTS
001          02 DIXON,GEORGE       SQUASH
                                   BADMINTON
                                   BRIDGE
004          11 HARLOW,MICHAEL     SQUASH
                                   MUSIC
002          11 LEA,SHAUN          SAILING
                                   SWIMMING
                                   READING
010          11 RILEY,JULIE        SWIMMING
                                   SAILING
005          13 MORRIS,JIM         SQUASH
                                   BRIDGE
                                   RALLYING
003          13 PIKE,JOHN          BRIDGE
                                   SQUASH
                                   CHESS

[405] 7 items listed out of 7 items.
```

Figure 12.10 A report containing multivalues.

As you can see from Figure 12.10, multi-values are listed underneath each other with a line being devoted to each value. In the case of this report, it would be easier to read if it were double spaced, with a blank line following the last interest shown. This facility is just one of a number of options and modifiers that are available. A full list is shown later, but for the sake of completing this example, we will use the option that will double space a report, the **DBL-SPC** option (Figure 12.11).

12.4.5 Sorting multi-values using BY-EXP or BY-EXP-DSND

ACCESS has a powerful feature enabling multi-values to be 'exploded' to effectively become items in their own right and is handled by the **BY-EXP** or **BY-EXP-DSND** verbs. In our example this feature will enable the sorting of the multi-valued 'interests' attribute in ascending (**BY-EXP**) or descending (**BY-EXP-DSND**) sequence. Figure 12.12 gives an example of this facility and uses the I option which suppresses the item-id.

12.4.6 Print limiters

Print limiters are used to suppress the printing of details unless they satisfy specific conditions. Hence it is possible to display a column which contains the

```
:SORT STAFF BY DEPT BY NAME DEPT NAME INTERESTS DBL-SPC

Page  1           STAFF                          17:15:26 12 Mar 1995

STAFF..... Dept Name              Interests

006          02 BRIGHT,IAN        KARATE
                                  MARTIAL ARTS

001          02 DIXON,GEORGE      SQUASH
                                  BADMINTON
                                  BRIDGE

004          11 HARLOW,MICHAEL    SQUASH
                                  MUSIC

002          11 LEA,SHAUN         SAILING
                                  SWIMMING
                                  READING

010          11 RILEY,JULIE       SWIMMING
                                  SAILING

005          13 MORRIS,JIM        SQUASH
                                  BRIDGE
                                  RALLYING

003          13 PIKE,JOHN         BRIDGE
                                  SQUASH
                                  CHESS

[405] 7 items listed out of 7 items.
```

Figure 12.11 A report containing multivalues using the DBL-SPC option.

price of an item, but only prints the price if it is above a certain value, otherwise the record will be listed but with its actual price not shown. This is useful to highlight exception values on a report. Print limiters differ from selection criteria in that print limiters do not limit the records that are chosen, rather whether or not the contents of an attribute will be shown or not. Print limiters do not contain the **WITH** modifier.

In Figure 12.13 we will list all staff members, but only print out their salary if it is above £14,000.

The print limiter is part of the output specification section and is applied to the attribute against which print limiting is required. The print limited attribute does not have to be the first specified.

12.4.7 Print limiters and multi-value attributes

The action of print limiters on multi-value attributes differs to the way they act on single value attributes. As we saw in Figure 12.13, all items were listed, but the value contained in the attribute was only printed where it satisfied the print limit criteria.

With multi-value attributes, where no print limiter is specified, providing any one of the values meets the selection criteria, *all* values will be shown in the

:SORT STAFF BY-EXP INTERESTS INTERESTS NAME TEL (I

```
Page  1          STAFF                          08:13:05 13 Mar 1995

Interests        Name               Tel

BADMINTON        DIXON,GEORGE       0116 30303
BRIDGE           DIXON,GEORGE       0116 30303
BRIDGE           PIKE,JOHN          0121 359 6009
BRIDGE           MORRIS,JIM         0181 345 5454
CHESS            PIKE,JOHN          0121 359 6009
KARATE           BRIGHT,IAN         01244 99933
MARTIAL ARTS     BRIGHT,IAN         01244 99933
MUSIC            HARLOW,MICHAEL     01474 344255
RALLYING         MORRIS,JIM         0181 345 5454
READING          LEA,SHAUN          0171 346 2456
SAILING          LEA,SHAUN          0171 346 2456
SAILING          RILEY,JULIE        0121 355 6060
SQUASH           DIXON,GEORGE       0116 30303
SQUASH           PIKE,JOHN          0121 359 6009
SQUASH           HARLOW,MICHAEL     01474 344255
SQUASH           MORRIS,JIM         0181 345 5454
SWIMMING         LEA,SHAUN          0171 346 2456
SWIMMING         RILEY,JULIE        0121 355 6060

[405] 18 items listed out of 7 items.
```

:SORT STAFF BY-EXP-DSND INTERESTS INTERESTS NAME TEL (I

```
Page  1          STAFF                          08:15:13 13 Mar 1995

staff.....  Interests      Name              Tel

002         SWIMMING       LEA,SHAUN         0171 346 2456
010         SWIMMING       RILEY,JULIE       0121 355 6060
001         SQUASH         DIXON,GEORGE      0116 30303
003         SQUASH         PIKE,JOHN         0121 359 6009
004         SQUASH         HARLOW,MICHAEL    01474 344255
005         SQUASH         MORRIS,JIM        0181 345 5454
002         SAILING        LEA,SHAUN         0171 346 2456
010         SAILING        RILEY,JULIE       0121 355 6060
002         READING        LEA,SHAUN         0171 346 2456
005         RALLYING       MORRIS,JIM        0181 345 5454
004         MUSIC          HARLOW,MICHAEL    01474 344255
006         MARTIAL ARTS   BRIGHT,IAN        01244 99933
006         KARATE         BRIGHT,IAN        01244 99933
003         CHESS          PIKE,JOHN         0121 359 6009
001         BRIDGE         DIXON,GEORGE      0116 30303
003         BRIDGE         PIKE,JOHN         0121 359 6009
005         BRIDGE         MORRIS,JIM        0181 345 5454
001         BADMINTON      DIXON,GEORGE      0116 30303

[405] 18 items listed out of 7 items.
```

Figure 12.12 The use of **BY-EXP** and **BY-EXP-DSND**.

report. Figure 12.14 shows an ACCESS statement where although it appears only squash players have been requested, the report also shows the other interests of the squash players, in other words we have not limited the report just to show the interest 'squash'. Figure 12.15 shows the effect of print limiters on the report given in Figure 12.14.

:SORT STAFF BY DEPTDESC BY NAME DEPTDESC NAME SALARY > "14000" (I

```
Page  1           STAFF                                08:15:44 13 Mar 1995

Description         Name               Salary

ADMINISTRATION      BRIGHT,IAN         15,400.00
ADMINISTRATION      DIXON,GEORGE       15,500.00
SALES               HARLOW,MICHAEL
SALES               LEA,SHAUN
SALES               RILEY,JULIE        14,550.00
SW SUPPORT          MORRIS,JIM         15,500.00
SW SUPPORT          PIKE,JOHN

[405] 7 items listed out of 7 items.
:
```

Figure 12.13 The use of print limiters.

:SORT STAFF BY DEPTDESC BY NAME BY-EXP INTERESTS WITH INTERESTS = "SQUASH" DEPTDESC NAME INTERESTS

```
Page  1           STAFF                                08:21:38 13 Mar 1995

STAFF.....  Description       Name              Interests

001         ADMINISTRATION    DIXON,GEORGE      BADMINTON
001         ADMINISTRATION    DIXON,GEORGE      BRIDGE
001         ADMINISTRATION    DIXON,GEORGE      SQUASH
004         SALES             HARLOW,MICHAEL    MUSIC
004         SALES             HARLOW,MICHAEL    SQUASH
005         SW SUPPORT        MORRIS,JIM        BRIDGE
005         SW SUPPORT        MORRIS,JIM        RALLYING
005         SW SUPPORT        MORRIS,JIM        SQUASH
003         SW SUPPORT        PIKE,JOHN         BRIDGE
003         SW SUPPORT        PIKE,JOHN         CHESS
003         SW SUPPORT        PIKE,JOHN         SQUASH

[405] 11 items listed out of 7 items.
:
```

Figure 12.14 The **BY-EXP** function with selected output.

12.4.8 Selection criteria

As we have seen in some of the previous examples it is not necessary to report on the entire database when producing an ACCESS report. The data shown is determined by the use of selection criteria which is handled in ACCESS by the use of logical connectives and relational operators.

:SORT STAFF BY DEPTDESC BY NAME BY-EXP INTERESTS = "SQUASH" DEPTDESC NAME INTERESTS

```
Page  1           STAFF                                     08:22:23 13 Mar 1995

STAFF.....  Description         Name              Interests

001         ADMINISTRATION      DIXON,GEORGE      SQUASH
004         SALES               HARLOW,MICHAEL    SQUASH
005         SW SUPPORT          MORRIS,JIM        SQUASH
003         SW SUPPORT          PIKE,JOHN         SQUASH

[405] 4 items listed out of 7 items.
:
```

Figure 12.15 The use of **BY-EXP** with print limiters.

Connective	*Description*
AND	Both parts linked by the AND must be true
OR	Either or both parts linked by the OR must be true

Note: **if a connective is not used, *OR* is assumed**

Operator	*Description*
= **EQ**	Equal to
£ **NE** **NOT** **NO**	Not equal to
> **GT** **AFTER**	Greater than
>= **GE**	Greater than and equal to

Operator	*Description*
< **LT** **BEFORE**	Less than
<= **LE**	Less than and equal to
Note: **if a relational operator is not used,** ***EQ*** **is assumed**	

12.4.9 String and substring selection

Within the ACCESS selection criteria, it is possible to carry out string searches. These are handled in one of five ways:

- the full string
- begins with a string
- ends with a string
- contains a string
- a string with one or more wild card characters, either the full string, start string, ending string or containing string

The full string ("xxxx")

Selection of records based on the full string is handled by getting ACCESS to compare the value in an attribute to that in the ACCESS statement and to ensure an exact and total match. In this situation the string is normally enclosed in quote marks. The quote marks became unnecessary in release 6.2 onwards of Advanced PICK and in AP/Protected mode. They are shown here for completeness and for compatibility for those of you with other PICK versions. It should also be borne in mind that if you are looking to ensure your software works with the widest number of PICK implementations, strings in ACCESS statements which are executed from BASIC programs should always be contained in quotes. A typical example of the full string selection is **WITH SURNAME = "WATSON"** in which records will only be selected where the surname is **WATSON** and nothing else.

Begins with substring ("xx]")

To select records that begin with a specified set of characters, the substring is followed by a closing square bracket and the entire string contained in quotes. Hence **WITH SURNAME = "WA]"** would select people whose surname begins with the letters **WA** such as **WATSON**, **WALMER**, **WAINWRIGHT** and so on.

Ends with substring ("[xx")

To select records that end with a specified set of characters, the substring is followed by an opening square bracket and the entire string contained in quotes. Hence **WITH SURNAME = "[SON"** would select people whose surname ends with the letters **SON**, such as **CARSON**, **WATSON** and **ROBINSON**.

Contains substring ("[xx]")

To select records that contains a specified set of characters anywhere within it, the substring is enclosed in square brackets and the entire string contained in quotes. Hence **WITH SURNAME = "[ER]"** would select people whose surname contained the letters **ER** such as **BERNARD**, **SHEPHERD** and **PALMER**.

The wildcard option (^)

The caret (^) symbol is the wildcard symbol and denotes *any* character. Hence if you want to select records based on certain known characters in specified character positions, but with other character positions unknown and of no importance you can use the wildcard facility. The wildcard option can be used with any of the four previous string/substring selection options. Hence

WITH SURNAME = "DYS^N" would select any surname containing five letters where the first three are **DYS**, the last is **N** and the fourth character is any character and not limited to just letters. Hence this selection would find the people called **DYSAN** and **DYSON** but it would equally select **DYS;N** and **DYS6N**.

WITH FORENAME = "^O^" would select three letter forenames where the middle letter is an **O** hence it would chose **TOM, ROB** and would also select **6O!** if such a name existed. In other words the wild card makes *no* assumptions about the characters and neither should you.

WITH SURNAME = "^O]" selects surnames where the second letter is an **O**, such as **HOGAN** and **BOURDON**.

These features combine to provide a powerful and flexible interrogation facility. It enables the majority of *ad hoc* as well as regular reports to be produced using ACCESS. Figure 12.16 shows a number of different reports to illustrate the string and substring searches.

The four selections reflect the following:

(1) select all staff with an interest in squash in order to set up a squash ladder;
(2) select those people living in the London or Birmingham telephone areas with a view to setting up a social club;
(3) the selection criteria of both previous examples i.e. those people living in the London or Birmingham telephone areas who are interested in squash;
(4) select all those working in departments from 10 through to 19.

Example 1

:SORT STAFF BY DEPT BY NAME WITH INTERESTS = "[SQUASH]" DEPT NAME TEL INTERESTS (I

```
Page  1          STAFF                           21:50:39 15 Mar 1995

Dept Name                 Tel                Interests

 02 DIXON,GEORGE          0116 30303         SQUASH
                                             BADMINTON
                                             BRIDGE
 11 HARLOW,MICHAEL        01474 344255       SQUASH
                                             MUSIC
 13 MORRIS,JIM            0181 345 5454      SQUASH
                                             BRIDGE
                                             RALLYING
 13 PIKE,JOHN             0121 359 6009      BRIDGE
                                             SQUASH
                                             CHESS

[405] 4 items listed out of 7 items.
```

Example 2

:SORT STAFF BY TEL WITH TEL = "0171]" OR "0181]" OR "0121]" NAME ADDRESS TEL DBL-SPC ID-SUPP

```
Page  1          STAFF                           21:53:38 15 Mar 1995

Name             Address                    Tel

RILEY,JULIE      2 HIGHMEAD                 0121 355 6060
                 SUTTON COLDFIELD
                 BIRMINGHAM B12 1TT

PIKE,JOHN        74 WASHWOOD HEATH ROAD     0121 359 6009
                 BIRMINGHAM B7 7RR

LEA,SHAUN        55 LYNDON WAY              0171 346 2456
                 LONDON NW1 7SZ

MORRIS,JIM       33 MILL LANE               0181 345 5454
                 LONDON
                 SURREY RH3 8VX

[405] 4 items listed out of 7 items.
```

Example 3

:SORT STAFF BY TEL BY NAME WITH TEL = "0171]" "0181]" "0121]" AND WITH INTERESTS "[SQUASH]" NAME TEL INTERESTS (I

```
Page  1          STAFF                           21:55:25 15 Mar 1995

Name             Tel                  Interests

PIKE,JOHN        0121 359 6009        BRIDGE
                                      SQUASH
                                      CHESS
MORRIS,JIM       0181 345 5454        SQUASH
                                      BRIDGE
                                      RALLYING

[405] 2 items listed out of 7 items.
```

Figure 12.16 The use of selection criteria with strings and substrings.

Example 4
:SORT STAFF BY DEPT BY NAME WITH DEPT "1^" DEPT NAME ADDRESS TEL (I

```
Page  1          STAFF                          21:56:06 15 Mar 1995

Dept Name              Address                    Tel

 11 HARLOW,MICHAEL     58 FOUNTAIN LANE           01474 344255
                       BILLERICAY
                       ESSEX CM12 3HF
 11 LEA,SHAUN          55 LYNDON WAY              0171 346 2456
                       LONDON NW1 7SZ
 11 RILEY,JULIE        2 HIGHMEAD                 0121 355 6060
                       SUTTON COLDFIELD
                       BIRMINGHAM B12 1TT
 13 MORRIS,JIM         33 MILL LANE               0181 345 5454
                       LONDON
                       SURREY RH3 8VX
 13 PIKE,JOHN          74 WASHWOOD HEATH ROAD     0121 359 6009
                       BIRMINGHAM B7 7RR

[405] 5 items listed out of 7 items.
```

Figure 12.16 *continued*

12.4.10 The use of the AND and OR connectives

In Figure 12.16 we saw the use of both the **AND** and **OR** connectives. We also saw the use of the implied **OR** connective in Example 3. In this section we will look at the rules associated with the use of these connectives in an ACCESS statement.

The first point to note is that your ACCESS statement can contain any number of conditions and these have to be linked with either the **AND** or **OR** connectives. Where a selection has multiple choices each can be shown next to each other in which case **OR** is implied as in the case of Example 3 in Figure 12.16 where the statement **WITH TEL = "0171]" "0181]" "0121]"** is the equivalent of **WITH TEL = "0171]" OR "0181]" OR "0121]"**. Both statements are correct and will achieve the same result, the first is just simpler and much shorter!

Care has to be taken when using the **OR** condition with the 'not equal' operator. In this situation the 'not equal' operator will need to be repeated. For example if you want to select all people who do not have a London telephone number the statement **WITH TEL NE "0181]" "0171]"** will select all people whose telephone number does *not* start with **0181** and also all those whose number *does* start with **0171**. This is because the operator **EQ** is assumed in between the two values. In order to get the required result you need to include another **NE** in your statement which should therefore read **WITH TEL NE "0181]" OR NE "0171]"**.

As already stated, it is not necessary to include **EQ** or = in an ACCESS statement, because this is the logical operator assumed if one is not specified. This was mentioned in the previous paragraph and we saw an example, Example 4 of Figure 12.16 with the statement **WITH DEPT "1^"** which could also have been written **WITH DEPT = "1^"**. Once again both statements are correct and will give the same answer.

To select items that fall within a range of values you need to link the selection criteria with the **AND** connective. As an example **WITH SALARY > "11000" AND WITH SALARY < "15000"** will select all people whose salary is in the range £11,001 to £14,999. Connecting these two conditions with the **OR** connective would select everyone, since every salary must either be above £11,000 or below £15,000!

The final issue revolves around the interpretation of a statement with multiple **AND** and **OR** connectives. The rule here is that **AND** is given a higher priority than **OR** so care needs to be taken when constructing a sentence to ensure the items selected are those required. Hence a statement such as **WITH TEL = "012]" AND WITH SALARY > "14000" OR WITH DEPT "02" "11" AND WITH INTERESTS "[SQUASH]"** would select the people with a telephone number beginning with **012** whose salary is greater than **£14,000** and those people whose department code is either **02** or **11** who have an interest in **SQUASH**.

In summary a statement where you have the condition ***A*** **AND** ***B*** **OR** ***C*** is ambiguous and can be read in several ways. The structure of the ACCESS statement for these is as follows:

(*A* AND *B*) OR *C* **WITH *A* AND WITH *B* OR WITH *C***

e.g. WITH MAKE = "FORD" AND WITH EXTRAS "[CD]" OR WITH EXTRAS "[A/CON]"

selects all FORDs with a CD player and any make of car with air conditioning

A* AND (*B* OR *C*)** **WITH *A* AND WITH *B C

e.g. WITH MAKE "FORD" AND WITH EXTRAS "[CD]" "[A/CON]"

selects all FORDs with either a CD player or air conditioning

but if *B* and *C* relate to two different attributes you need to repeat the *A* condition as follows

e.g. WITH MAKE "FORD" AND WITH EXTRAS "[CD]" OR WITH MAKE "FORD" AND WITH COLOUR "BLUE"

selects all FORDs with a CD player regardless of colour and all blue FORDs regardless of whether or not they have CDs

12.4.11 The use of throwaway connectives

Throwaway connectives are used to add clarity and naturalness to the ACCESS statement. In the examples used so far, where we have specified the data to be output, we have just included the dictionary names to be output. To some people ACCESS may be easier to use if it were possible to include the words **SHOW ME** in the statement. These additional words are known as throwaway connectives and whilst they aid the clarity, they add no functionality. Some throwaway connectives are already provided by PICK, these being

A	ANY	IN	OR
AN	FILE	ITEMS	THE
ARE	FOR	OF	

Others can readily be created by copying any of the above entries in the master dictionary to the new throwaway connective required. Figure 12.17 shows this working by creating the new throwaway **SHOW ME**, which is used in a subsequent ACCESS enquiry.

```
:COPY MD AN
to :SHOW
   1 A TO SHOW

[805] 1 item(s) copied

:COPY MD AN
to :ME[CR]
   1 A TO SHOW

[805] 1 item(s) copied

:SORT STAFF BY DEPT BY NAME SHOW ME THE DEPTDESC NAME TEL

Page  1          STAFF                          22:59:09 15 Mar 1995

STAFF..... Description       Name             Tel

006        ADMINISTRATION    BRIGHT,IAN       01244 99933
001        ADMINISTRATION    DIXON,GEORGE     0116 30303
004        SALES             HARLOW,MICHAEL   01474 344255
002        SALES             LEA,SHAUN        0171 346 2456
010        SALES             RILEY,JULIE      0121 355 6060
005        SW SUPPORT        MORRIS,JIM       0181 345 5454
003        SW SUPPORT        PIKE,JOHN        0121 359 6009

[405] 7 items listed out of 7 items.
```

Figure 12.17 Using throwaway connectives.

12.4.12 Selecting attributes which contain dates or monetary amounts

Since ACCESS recognizes that dates and monetary amounts are stored internally in a different format to the way they are referred to by the user, when selection is carried out on an attribute which is either a date or money attribute, the selection value is converted to internal format according to the conversion code held in attribute 7 (conversion codes are explained fully in the next chapter). After conversion, the resulting value is compared to the data held on file *after* any correlatives have been applied but *before* any conversions.

Hence in date selection the value in the ACCESS statement need not be in the same form as that output by the attribute definition. By way of explanation, the date 15/03/95 is held on the database in internal format as the number of days since 31/12/67 i.e. 9936. If the attribute is holding the date as a **D2-** conversion code, then the date would be displayed in the form **15-03-95**. However when selecting on this date attribute *any* format of date could be used as all of them when converted to internal format will give the result **9936** the actual data stored on the database. Hence the statement could read any of the following and each would produce the same selection result.

WITH DATE = "15.03.95"
WITH DATE "15 MAR 1995"
WITH DATE "15/03/1995"

For the reasons explained above trying to select on parts of a date will not work, thus

WITH DATE = "[DEC]"	selection based on the description of the month
WITH DATE "01]"	selection based on the day number
WITH DATE "[95"	selection based on the year number

will not produce the desired result. However, if you do want to select records based on parts of a date, create a separate item in the dictionary without a conversion code in attribute 7, but with the appropriate processing code in attribute 8 (the correlative attribute). Correlatives get processed prior to the selection process, so put a **DMA** processing code in attribute 8 if you wish to select a month by its description of use the standard **D2/** if you want to perform a selection based on the day number or year number.

Similar principles need to be used with monetary fields. ACCESS converts the selection value to internal format and compares it to the actual value on the database which is also in internal format. The internal format does not hold currency symbols, commas or decimal points. Whilst you should ignore the currency symbol and commas in your selection value, you should include the decimal point for selections which are not whole numbers, because the conversion code is applied to the actual data to determine its scaling factor. So the number **£1,234.56** will be stored on the database as **123456** and it will have a conversion code which will indicate the number is to be shown to 2 decimal places. Hence the statements

WITH AMOUNT "1234.56"
WITH AMOUNT > "1000"

will select the record with the amount of £1,234.56, whilst the statements

WITH AMOUNT "£1,234.56"
WITH AMOUNT "123456"

will not.

12.4.13 The spreadsheet connective SS

There spreadsheet connective **SS** enables information to be output in table form, providing the data is analysed by date. The table shows the value of one attribute for dates in a given range. The general format is **SS** *date.field "start.date" "end.date" total.field* where

date.field	is the date field on which start and end dates are to be selected
start.date	is the start date for item selection
end.date	is the end date for item selection
total.field	is the name of the attribute to be totalled and placed in each cell

There is one option you can apply to your statement, the **G** option which suppresses row and column totals. Remember too that the date conversion in the date attribute needs to be in attribute 7 on the dictionary item for the spreadsheet connective to work properly.

A typical statement might read

SORT SALES BY REGION BREAK-ON REGION SS SALES.MONTH "01/01/95" "31/12/95" TOTAL ORDER.VALUE DET-SUPP (P

12.4.14 Comparing attributes with others

A common requirement is the need to compare the contents of attributes. For example a stock re-order report would be based on the comparison of actual stock with minimum stock requiring a statement such as **LIST STOCK WITH ACTUAL < MINIMUM ...** but in ACCESS such comparisons are not permitted since the second operand must be a literal. The way of achieving the same result is to create a dictionary item that takes the minimum value from the actual value and use that in the ACCESS statement selecting those records where the surplus stock is greater than zero, i.e. **LIST STOCK WITH SURPLUS > "0" ....** Since so much of the functionality of ACCESS is based around the capabilities of dictionary items, the next chapter is devoted to them. Arithmetic processing of the type described here is performed using the **A** or **F** processing codes.

12.4.15 The use of breaks and totals

Reports can be divided into sections by means of the **BREAK-ON** verb. This will cause a break to be established in a report as soon as the value in the attribute following the **BREAK-ON** verb changes. In fact it is not the entire value which is compared for a change, but *the first 24 characters only* and the check is made by working from left to the right in the string.

When a control break occurs, ACCESS will automatically print three asterisks (***) underneath the attribute causing the change, unless told otherwise. Further, a maximum of 15 control breaks can be specified, the highest level being the first one to be specified in the ACCESS statement. When a control break occurs numeric attributes can be totalled using the **TOTAL** verb. Any attribute specified as a control break (with **BREAK-ON**) or a total field (using **TOTAL**) will automatically be listed in the report so should not be specified separately as an attribute to be displayed. Figure 12.18 illustrates the use of both the **BREAK-ON** and **TOTAL** verbs.

Frequently the default of *** on the break line is perfectly good enough. However if you wish you can replace them with something more meaningful.

:sort staff by dept by name break-on dept deptdesc name total salary (i

```
Page  1            STAFF                                  22:43:26 15 Mar 1995


Dept Description         Name                   Salary

 02 ADMINISTRATION       BRIGHT,IAN          15,400.00
 02 ADMINISTRATION       DIXON,GEORGE        15,500.00

***                                          30,900.00

 11 SALES                HARLOW,MICHAEL      12,900.00
 11 SALES                LEA,SHAUN           13,250.00
 11 SALES                RILEY,JULIE         14,550.00

***                                          40,700.00


 13 SW SUPPORT           MORRIS,JIM          15,500.00
 13 SW SUPPORT           PIKE,JOHN           11,350.00

***                                          26,850.00

                                             98,450.00

[405] 7 items listed out of 7 items.
:
```

Figure 12.18 The output using **BREAK-ON** and **TOTAL**.

This is achieved by including the text to be printed in double quotes immediately following the **BREAK-ON** attribute name. This text can include a number of options and these need to be enclosed in single quotes. The possible options are as follows:

b Outputs the value causing the break in either the heading or footing output field where the **b** option is found in the heading or footing option string. It is not meaningful to specify this option within more than one **break-on** specification.

d Suppresses the break data line if only one detail line has been output since the last control break.

l Suppresses the blank line preceding break data line. This option is ignored when the **u** option is used.

n Resets the page counter to one on each break.

p Issues a form feed (page eject) after the data associated with this break has been output.

r Inhibits page 'rollover'. Outputs any occurrence of one or more control break lines at the end of the page, rather than at the top of the next page, thus forcing all the data associated with this break to be current on the same page.

u Underlines all total fields.

v Outputs the value causing the control break in the **break-on** label.

'' (two single quotes) Inserts a single quote in text.

Similarly, text can be added against the grand total line which may include any of the options **U** (underline), **L** line suppress, **P** (page eject) and '' (single quote mark). The underline will produce underlining as a row of equals signs whilst the page eject option is extremely useful where the final total is meaningless. It means that the final total will be produced on a separate page which can then be thrown away! Figure 12.19 demonstrates the use of these options.

The **DET-SUPP** modifier enables the detail lines of the report to be suppressed, giving a totals only report. In this situation a correlative will not be evaluated unless it is the control break attribute. The result of adding **DET-SUPP** to the statement used in Figure 12.19 is shown in Figure 12.20.

:sort staff by deptdesc by name break-on deptdesc "'VLU' Total" name total salary grand-total "Total salaries for the company"

```
Page  1          STAFF                            22:51:46 15 Mar 1995

staff..... Description             Name                Salary

006        ADMINISTRATION          BRIGHT,IAN          15,400.00
001        ADMINISTRATION          DIXON,GEORGE        15,500.00
                                                       ---------

           ADMINISTRATION Total                        30,900.00

004        SALES                   HARLOW,MICHAEL      12,900.00
002        SALES                   LEA,SHAUN           13,250.00
010        SALES                   RILEY,JULIE         14,550.00
                                                       ---------

           SALES Total                                 40,700.00

005        SW SUPPORT              MORRIS,JIM          15,500.00
003        SW SUPPORT              PIKE,JOHN           11,350.00
                                                       ---------

           SW SUPPORT Total                            26,850.00

Total salaries for the company                         98,450.00

[405] 7 items listed out of 7 items.
```

Figure 12.19 Including text on control breaks.

:SORT STAFF BY DEPTDESC BREAK-ON DEPTDESC TOTAL SALARY DET-SUPP

```
Page  1          STAFF                            22:52:34 15 Mar 1995

Description              Salary

ADMINISTRATION        30,900.00
SALES                 40,700.00
SW SUPPORT            26,850.00
                      98,450.00

[405] 7 items listed out of 7 items.
```

Figure 12.20 A summary report using **DET-SUPP**.

12.4.16 Headings and footings

Text to be printed at the top or bottom of each page can be defined with the modifiers **HEADING** and **FOOTING**, each of which must be followed by text enclosed in double quotes. Within the text of each of these a number of options can be included, which if used must be enclosed in single quotes. These are as follows:

''	(Two single quotes). Outputs (one) single quote.
'attr.name'	Inserts the value of 'attr.name'. Processes any conversion codes, but not correlatives in the attribute defining item.
b	Inserts the attribute name causing the break if the **b** option has been specified with 'roll-on' (in AP) or 'break-on' (R83 only).
c	Centres the output line.
d	Retrieves the current date (format dd mmm yyyy).
f{n}	Inserts the file name; {in a field of 'n' blanks}.
j	Right-justifies the rest of the line. (AP only)
l	Issues a carriage return and line feed.
n	Prevents the pause at the end of each page (like **NOPAGE** modifier). (AP only)
p	Retrieves the current page number, right-justified in a field of four blanks.
pn	Retrieves the current page number, left justified. (R83 only)
p{n}	Retrieves the page number, right-justified in a field of 'n' blanks (default 'n'=4). (AP only)
r	Retrieves the Roman numeral page number. (AP only)
s	Toggles on italics mode. (AP only)
t	Retrieves the current time and date (format hh:mm:ss dd mmmyyyy).
u	Toggles on underline mode. (AP only)
v	Toggles on boldface mode. (AP only)
xc	Used with 'c' to centre a segment. The 'xc' delimits the end of the segment. (AP only)
xs	Toggles off italics mode. (AP only)
xu	Toggles off underline mode. (AP only)
xv	Toggles off boldface mode. (AP only)

Figure 12.20 gives an example of an ACCESS statement making use of some of these options. Notice now that the length of the statements being used is gaining

in size the further we progress through this chapter. Whilst typing in such a lengthy statement is perfectly satisfactory for *ad hoc* requests, it is not the best way to handle ACCESS reports that become standard reports. In R83 where there was no TCL stacker and TCL statements could not be modified as they can using the Update Processor commands in Advanced PICK, any typing mistake meant retyping the whole statement again. Even so for regular reports re-typing an ACCESS statement is laborious, so store the ACCESS sentence as a MACRO or, if you are using R83, as a PROC. Remember that if the ACCESS statement is complete and you have just run it, it can be converted to a MACRO using the **CREATE-MACRO** verb. For building simple PROCs refer to Section 18.2.

12.4.17 Modifiers and options

Modifiers and options can be used to further enhance the ACCESS statement. A modifier is included in the statement as part of the statement, whilst the options (most of which have an equivalent modifier) are included at the end of the statement enclosed in parentheses. The modifiers and options available are shown in Figure 12.21.

Modifier	*Option*	*Description*
BREAK-ON		Specifies a break will occur when the value of a specified attribute changes
BY		Designates the attribute immediately following as a sort key
BY-DSND		Specifies sorting by the attribute immediately following to be in descending sequence
BY-EXP		Sorts by exploding multi-valued attributes in ascending sequence
BY-EXP-DSND		Sorts by exploding multi-valued attributes in descending sequence
COL-HDR-SUPP	C	Suppresses the output of the time/date heading, the column headings and the end-of-list message
DBL-SPC		Double spacing
DET-SUPP	D	Suppresses the detail lines when used with **TOTAL** or **BREAK-ON**
DICT		Specifies interrogation of the dictionary
DUPLICATE		Selects items which have duplicate index keys. The attribute must have an index specified (an i on attribute 14 of the dictionary item)
EVERY or EACH		Modifies a selection criterion requiring every value of an attribute to meet the specified condition for the criterion to be true for the item. It must immediately follow the modifier **WITH**
FILL	R	Forces listings into an 'across the page' format if the listing would otherwise not be shown in columns

Figure 12.21 The use of modifiers and options.

Modifier	*Option*	*Description*
FOOTING		Specifies the text string to appear at the bottom of each page output
	F	Specifies that a new page is to be started for each item when using the **LIST-ITEM**, **COPY** and **SORT-ITEM** verbs. Note, there is no equivalent modifier
GRAND-TOTAL		Specifies the text to be printed alongside the grand total
HEADING		Specifies the text to appear at the top of each page output
HDR-SUPP or SUPP	H	Suppresses the output of the time/date heading and the end-of-list message
ID-SUPP	I	Suppresses the list of item-ids for **LIST** and **SORT** functions
LEG-SUPP	K	Suppresses the output of the legend message for **LIST** and **SORT** operations
LPTR	P	Sends output to the spooler for printing
NI-SUPP	B or J	Suppresses the 'number of items listed' message at the end of most ACCESS reports
	S (R83 only)	
ONLY		Suppresses default report attributes. It must precede the file name
NOPAGE	N	Stops display halting at the end of each page, when report being displayed on the terminal
SAMPLING n		Limits the number of items processed by the ACCESS sentence to a specific number
TAPE		Sends report to tape in T-DUMP format
TCL-SUPP		Printed reports now show the ACCESS statement, but this can be suppressed with this modifier
TOTAL		Produces totals for the attributes following this modifier
USING		Causes the attributes to be obtained from a file other than the dictionary-level file
WITH or IF		Specifies the attribute name immediately following is part of a selection criterion
WITHOUT		A synonym for **WITH NOT** or **WITH NO**
WITHIN		Specifies a special form of processing in which items may contain additional item-ids relating to the primary item-id
	S	Suppresses the normal action of attribute defining items with an attribute-type of 'w', thus preventing any embedded Output Processor commands from being applied to the data being processed (AP only)
	Y	The Y option displays the Access 'compiled' string to the terminal. This string contains information about the attributes to display on the report in an internal representation for the list processor. If any attribute defining items being output contain 'A' (algebraic) processing codes, each one is translated into an 'F' (function) processing code and the 'F' code is displayed
	Z	The Z option prints the Access 'compiled' string to the printer. (See Y option for more information.)

Figure 12.21 *Continued*

In some of our earlier examples we have seen the use of some of the modifiers and options listed above. Figure 12.22 shows the use of a couple of others.

:sort staff by dept by name break-on deptdesc full interests dbl-spc col-hdr-supp (I

```
ADMINISTRATION          IAN BRIGHT          KARATE
                                            MARTIAL ARTS

ADMINISTRATION          GEORGE DIXON        SQUASH
                                            BADMINTON
                                            BRIDGE

***

SALES                   MICHAEL HARLOW      SQUASH
                                            MUSIC

SALES                   SHAUN LEA           SAILING
                                            SWIMMING
READING

SALES                   JULIE RILEY         SWIMMING
                                            SAILING

***

SW SUPPORT              JIM MORRIS          SQUASH
                                            BRIDGE
                                            RALLYING

SW SUPPORT              JOHN PIKE           BRIDGE
                                            SQUASH
                                            CHESS

***

[405] 7 items listed out of 7 items.
:
```

Figure 12.22 The use of modifiers and options.

12.5 Producing output in label format

There are functions in ACCESS which enable the information to be produced in label format. It is just one of the winning features of PICK as anyone who has tried writing a label printing program confirm. Producing labels makes use of all the ACCESS statement functions already described, but it uses special verbs, **LIST** is replaced with **LIST-LABEL** and **SORT** with **SORT-LABEL**.

After the ACCESS statement has been processed and prior to the output being produced, a **?** will appear on the screen, which is the prompt requesting the label parameters. If the ACCESS statement has been produced in a either a MACRO or PROC, these additional parameters will have to be 'stacked' into the ACCESS statement within the MACRO or PROC. If the

ACCESS statement has been entered manually then you will need to enter the label parameters manually. These can either be entered one at a time, in which case a **?** will be displayed after each parameter has been entered until all parameters are input, or if you prefer you can enter all the parameters in one go, each separated by a comma. The parameters are in the following format:

?*count*,*rows*,*skip*,*indent*,*size*, *space* **{,C}**

where

count	represents the number of labels across each page
rows	represents the depth of the label in number of print lines
skip	represents the number of print lines between the bottom of one label and the top of the one beneath it
indent	represents the number of spaces to indent from the left margin, invaluable for certain printers
size	represents the width of the label in number of print positions (or print characters)
C	compresses (removes) any blank lines within the output

N.B. One of the problems regularly encountered with label production is if the parameters are wrong. Rather than displaying a meaningful message you will see the message 'the range of the parameter *n* is unacceptable' (where *n* is a number, more often 1). This message occurs when the total width of the labels, including spaces between each column, is greater than the width of the output device, as determined by the **TERM** command. If problems exist with the formatting of the **list-label** output, try using the **tcl-hdr-off** command first and then re-try using the **k** option.

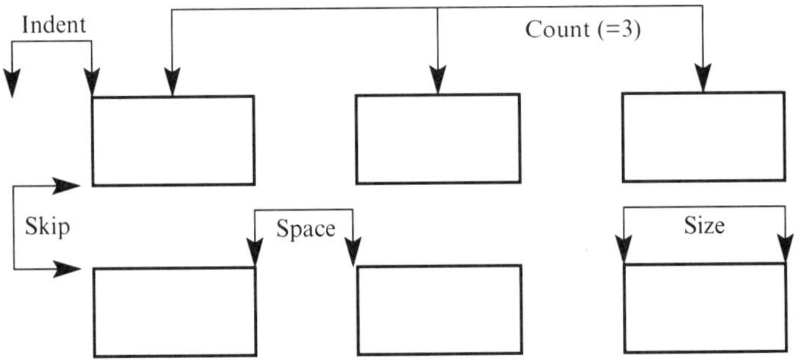

Figure 12.23 gives an example of the production of labels with the parameters being input manually.

:sort-label staff by dept by name name address col-hdr-supp ni-supp
?2,6,2,0,30,2,c

```
006                        001

BRIGHT,IAN                 DIXON,GEORGE

121 JOINERS LANE           21 GROVE LANE

WELWYN                     CRAYTHORNE

HERTS SG1 1DD              LEICS LE1 1QS

004                        002

HARLOW,MICHAEL             LEA,SHAUN

58 FOUNTAIN LANE           55 LYNDON WAY

BILLERICAY                 LONDON NW1 7SZ

ESSEX CM12 3HF

010                        005

RILEY,JULIE                MORRIS,JIM

2 HIGHMEAD                 33 MILL LANE

SUTTON COLDFIELD           LONDON

BIRMINGHAM B12 1TT         SURREY RH3 8VX

003

PIKE,JOHN

74 WASHWOOD HEATH ROAD

BIRMINGHAM B7 7RR
```

Figure 12.23 Label production using ACCESS.

12.6 The principles and uses of lists

As we have discovered, ACCESS provides an extremely powerful and flexible enquiry language which in conjunction with the strength of the dictionaries enables ready access to the database to produce a variety of reports. In the examples shown in the earlier sections, ACCESS has had to scan the entire file selecting the required records, sorting them in order and producing them in the form of a report. In true life applications databases can be extremely large and we will want to limit the number of times ACCESS has to read through the entire file. We can do this through the use of lists.

Lists are of two types, the **explicit list** where the item-ids of the required records are identified or the **implicit list** in which the item-ids for a certain group of records are selected and then used in a subsequent process. The explicit list is straightforward in that the item-ids of the required records are given in the ACCESS statement. In the case of an explicit list ACCESS does a direct read for each item and does not read through the entire file. An example of an explicit list is given in Figure 12.24.

:SORT STAFF BY NAME '002' '004' '006' NAME ADDRESS

```
Page  1          STAFF                              23:05:40 15 Mar 1995

STAFF.....    Name                Address

006           BRIGHT,IAN          121 JOINERS LANE
                                  WELWYN
                                  HERTS SG1 1DD
004           HARLOW,MICHAEL      58 FOUNTAIN LANE
                                  BILLERICAY
                                  SSEX CM12 3HF
002           LEA,SHAUN           55 LYNDON WAY
                                  LONDON NW1 7SZ

[405] 3 items listed out of 3 items.
```

Figure 12.24 An explicit list.

But what happens when we do not know all the item-ids in question, or indeed there are too many of them to type in individually. In those circumstances we can create an **implicit list** which is a list of item-ids of records which meet certain specified criteria. In other words we can still use all the capability of ACCESS, but instead of outputting the results in the form of a report, we can hold onto the list of item-ids for future use.

To build lists you will need to use one of two new ACCESS verbs **SELECT** (instead of **LIST**), which selects items holding the item-ids in random sequence, and **SSELECT** (instead of **SORT**) which selects items in a sorted sequence. These two verbs can be looked on as equivalents to **LIST** and **SORT** except they do not directly produce output.

The **SELECT** and **SSELECT** statement is the first step in a two-stage process. These verbs generate a list of item-ids that meet specified selection criteria, a list which can then be used by a second and *immediately following* process. It is worth stressing here that unless steps are taken to save the list of item-ids from the select commands, the list produced is destroyed as soon as the next command has completed execution. Hence list processing is always a two-stage process – the first to produce the list and the second to make use of it.

There are also commands to save, edit, copy and retrieve lists all of which are described further on.

Lists which are saved are stored in a special system file called POINTER-FILE. This file is always resident in the **dm** (in R83 the **SYSPROG**) account and is 'pointed' to within other accounts by a Q-pointer in their master dictionary. If such a Q-pointer does not exist you should establish it before saving any lists. Without it, using R83, you will only be able to use **SELECT** and **SSELECT** to create temporary lists. In AP you can store lists in any file, although the are still normally stored in POINTER-FILE. Since lists can take up a lot of space, and people tend to be careless in tidying up behind themselves, the POINTER-FILE and any other file storing lists should be checked from time to time and all unwanted lists removed.

12.6.1 The SELECT and SSELECT verbs

The **SELECT** and **SSELECT** verbs equate to **LIST** and **SORT** except they do not directly produce output. Their purpose is to produce a temporary list containing the item-ids of the records which meet specified criteria. This list of item-ids is in random sequence if **SELECT** is used and in sorted sequence if **SSELECT** is used. All the selection criteria described above, which can be used with the **LIST** and **SORT** verbs can be used with the select verbs. Since the purpose of these select verbs is to generate a list of item-ids, facilities for control breaks, report formatting and totalling are inapplicable and if used will give spurious results.

The temporary list is referred to by the original file name that was interrogated by the select commands. To all intents and purposes it can be considered to be a subset or restricted version of the original file – for use by the next command only. Hence the list can next be processed by:

- an ACCESS command using any data dictionary name defined in the original and interrogated file;
- another **SELECT** or **SSELECT** statement;
- a BASIC program;
- the **SAVE-LIST** command to save the list for later use;
- the **T-DUMP** command to dump the items to diskette or tape;
- any **TCL** command;
- the Update Processor;
- the editor;

An example of the use of these commands is given in Figure 12.25. These select verbs are frequently used to generate sorted lists for use by a BASIC program. As is discussed in Chapter 15, PICK BASIC has no **sort** statement and hence

:sselect staff by dept by name with dept > "05"

```
[404] 5 items selected out of 7 items.
```

>list staff name break-on deptdesc total salary

```
Page  1          STAFF                           23:07:20 15 Mar 1995

staff.....  Name              Description          Salary

004         HARLOW,MICHAEL    SALES             12,900.00
002         LEA,SHAUN         SALES             13,250.00
010         RILEY,JULIE       SALES             14,550.00

                              ***               40,700.00

005         MORRIS,JIM        SW SUPPORT        15,500.00
003         PIKE,JOHN         SW SUPPORT        11,350.00

                              ***               26,850.00

**                                              67,550.00

[405] 5 items listed out of 5 items.
```

Figure 12.25 The use of the **SELECT** verb.

the selecting and sorting of data to be processed by a BASIC program is handled by the ACCESS processor and is either handled by executing the ACCESS statement within the program or by encompassing the ACCESS statement in a MACRO or PROC immediately prior to the execution of the program.

There are some points to be aware of which are demonstrated by Figure 12.25. Firstly when a list is 'active' (i.e. a **SELECT** or **SSELECT** statement has just been executed) the TCL prompt is changed from a colon (:) to a chevron (>). The next TCL command will use the list and is typed in at the chevron prompt. Also since we used the **SSELECT** command, the list of item-ids is already in order (in the case of Figure 12.25 in the order of name within department) so when we produce the ACCESS report it is only necessary to use the **LIST** verb. This saves sorting the items more than once.

This leads to the next useful function of lists, which is the ability to use them time and time again. If for example you had a very large file of transactions and needed to produce several different reports on the current months transactions, it would obviously be very time consuming to produce these reports from the transaction file each time. A better method would be to select this months transactions, save them in a list and use this list for each report. In this way ACCESS will perform a direct read on the transaction file for each record in the list prior to the production of the relevant report.

12.6.2 The verbs for manipulating lists

There are a number of commands which will manipulate lists and these are as follows:

COPY-LIST	copies a saved list to either a new item-id, a new file or to the specified output device
DELETE-LIST	deletes a saved list
GET-LIST	retrieves a saved list and makes it 'active'
SAVE-LIST	saves a list of item-ids to a list with a nominated list name
SORT-LIST	retrieves a saved list, sorts it and then re-writes it back to the file from which it was originally retrieved

The SAVE-LIST *verb*

A list item is an item, normally held in POINTER-FILE, which has as each attribute one of the item-ids of the selected records and itself has as its item-id the name given to it from the **SAVE-LIST** command. Lists required for later use are saved using the **SAVE-LIST** command. This saves the list of item-ids and writes an item in the POINTER-FILE but will *only* work if the **SAVE-LIST** command is issued *immediately* following the **SELECT** or **SSELECT** statement. The name of the list is a functional part of the **SAVE-LIST** command and is the name to be used from then on when referring to that specific list. There are two things about list names to bear in mind:

- the list name need not bear any relation to the file used in the **SELECT/SSELECT** statement;
- no warning is given if you save a list with the name of an existing list. In this situation the old list is just overwritten with the new one;
- if no list name is specified one of **%user.name** is created.

The format of the **SAVE-LIST** command is given in Figure 12.26.

SAVE-LIST {{ *file.reference* } { *listname* }}

where:

file.reference is the file in which to save the list. If no reference is given, the list is saved in POINTER-FILE.

listname is the name of the list-item. If there is already an item with the specified item-id, it automatically overwritten by the new list. If no listname is specified, the default name, "%user.name", is used.

Figure 12.26 The format of the **SAVE-LIST** command.

The GET-LIST verb

Once saved, the list can be retrieved as frequently as you wish using the **GET-LIST** command. One valuable use of saving and retrieving lists in this way is to use a select list to feed another, in effect gradually reducing the records being manipulated. For the less experienced ACCESS user this can be a practical way of handling what would otherwise be a highly complicated ACCESS statement and Figure 12.27 shows this in action. Notice that the first selection is not the same as that in the initial ACCESS statement. Since you will undoubtedly be processing large files, you should always make your first selection one that will take the smallest number of records into the next selection stage. In Figure 12.27 we are looking for the details of retired men in the London area who worked in departments 01 to 10 at the time they retired. Since the number of people over the age of 65 is likely to be significantly less than the number of men or the number of Londoners the first select statement chooses people over 65. Notice too that the sorting process is left until last. This keeps the processing requirements to an absolute minimum.

Since the list is just a list of item-ids it can be used to process data on any file, not just the file on which the original **SELECT** was performed. Hence if you have your data split into multiple files each keyed on the same attribute then you can select a certain group of records from one file and use this list to display data on those records from another. Figure 12.28 gives an example of this in which the payroll details of London based employees are reported.

Once a select list has been created it can be used time and time again and can be particularly time saving where the initial file is sizeable and Figure 12.29 show this in action where the list of Londoners is processed through a variety of management information reports.

The ACCESS statement

```
:SORT STAFF BY DEPT BY NAME WITH DEPT >= "01" AND WITH DEPT <=
"10" AND WITH SEX "M" AND WITH AGE > "65" AND WITH TEL = "0181]"
"0171]" NAME ADDRESS TEL (IP
```

The alternative – using multiple SELECT statements

```
SELECT STAFF WITH AGE > "65"
[404] 137 items selected out of 2991 items.
>SELECT STAFF WITH DEPT >= "01" AND WITH DEPT <= "10"
[404] 68 items selected out of 137 items.
>SELECT STAFF WITH SEX "M"
[404] 27 items selected out of 68 items.
>SORT STAFF BY DEPT BY NAME WITH TEL "0181]" "0171]" NAME ADDRESS TEL (IP
```

Figure 12.27 Using select lists in the place of complex ACCESS statements.

```
:SELECT STAFF WITH TEL "0181]" "0171]"
[404] 1203 items selected out of 2991 items.
>LIST PAYROLL NAME TAX.CODE NHI.NUMBER TOTAL TAX.TO.DATE (P
```

Figure 12.28 The processing of select lists against multiple files.

```
:SELECT STAFF WITH TEL "0181]" "0171]"
[404] 1203 items selected out of 2991 items.
>SAVE-LIST LONDONERS
List 'LONDONERS' in file 'pointer-file' saved.

:GET-LIST LONDONERS

[404] 1203 items selected out of 1 items.
>SORT STAFF BY DEPT BY NAME BREAK-ON DEPT NAME TEL TOTAL SALARY

:GET-LIST LONDONERS
 [404] 1203 items selected out of 1 items.
>SSELECT STAFF BY NAME WITH SEX "M"
 [404] 839 items selected out of 1203 items.
>LIST PAYROLL NAME TAX.CODE NHI.NUMBER

:GET-LIST LONDONERS

[404] 1203 items selected out of 1 items.
>RUN BP REPORT1
```

Figure 12.29 The use of a select list for the production of multiple reports.

So far we have seen that the select list is a list of item-ids, but it is possible to have the list to contain details of one of the attributes of the records being selected so that the list can be used against a file which is not keyed on the item-id of the original file, but on one of its attributes. Let's assume that we have a list of orders and we have a problem with a particular product. We would want to select the orders for a particular product and then list all the customers involved to advise them of the problem. Figure 12.30 shows how this could be achieved by first creating a select list which instead of the item-id of the order holds the customer codes and then uses the select list to list out the customer details.

```
:SSELECT ORDERS BY CUST.NO WITH PRODUCT.CODE "ST543" CUST.NO
[404] 12 items selected out of 241 items.
:LIST CUSTOMER NAME TEL (P
```

Figure 12.30 Processing select lists with attributes from the original items.

The EDIT-LIST verb

The **EDIT-LIST** command enables you to edit and amend the list and invokes the Editor. The format of the **EDIT-LIST** command is given in Figure 12.31.

EDIT-LIST {*file.name* } {*itemlist*} {(*options*}

If no file.name is given, the list is retrieved from POINTER-FILE and an itemlist is not specified, the default list item will be presented.

valid *options* being

A Activates the assembly formatter. Equivalent to the as editor command

D Allows editing a 'd-pointer'

M Activates the macro expansion function. Equivalent to the m editor command.

P Directs the output to the system printer, via the spooler.

S Suppresses the display of line numbers, in normal edit mode, or suppresses object code display when the assembly formatter is on.
Equivalent to the 's' editor command.

Z Suppresses the 'top' and 'eoi' messages.

Figure 12.31 The format of the **EDIT-LIST** command.

The DELETE-LIST verb

Once the list is finished with it can be removed using the **DELETE-LIST** verb whose format is given in Figure 12.32.

:DELETE-LIST {{ *file.name* } *list.name* }{(*options*

Deletes list from specified *file.name*, otherwise defaults to POINTER-FILE". and if no *list.name* is provided, the default list name of '%user.name' is deleted. The only option is **i** which suppresses the 'item deleted' message.

Figure 12.32 The format of the **DELETE-LIST** command.

The** COPY-LIST **verb

If you wish to make a copy of an existing list, the command **COPY-LIST** will do this for you. The format of the command is given in Figure 12.33.

COPY-LIST {{*file.name*} {*itemlist*} {(*options*}
`to:` {(*file.name1* } {*itemlist1*}

where:

file.name	is the file containing the list. If not specified POINTER-FILE assumed
itemlist	is the list name, but if not specified %USERNAME is used
file.name1	is the name of the file to contain the copy of the list. In Advanced Pick any file can hold lists. In R83 *only* POINTER-FILE (or any file with a **DC** file type) is used for lists. Equally since there is no differentiation in Advanced PICK between 'pointer' and 'non-pointer' files, the verb **COPY** could be used instead of **COPY-LIST**.
itemlist1	is the name of the new copy of the list, but if not specified %USER-NAME is used

options are as follows:

n (integer number) Copies only the first 'n' items.

d	Deletes the source item(s) from the source file after copying.
f	Issues a form-feed between items; each item starts on a new page. This option is only valid with **t** and **p** options.
i	Suppresses display of item-ids.
n	Activates nopage function on output to the terminal.
o	Overwrites duplicate item-id{s}.
p	Copies list to printer, via the Spooler.
s	Suppresses display of line numbers when used with **t** or **p** options.
s	Suppresses error message output on a file copy.
t	Copies list to terminal.
u	If item-id is in destination file, copies item, but renames it by concatenating current item-id with a character, starting with lower case **a**
x	Lists output in hexadecimal.

Figure 12.33 Format of the **COPY-LIST** command.

The** NSELECT **verb

So far in all our examples we have looked at lists which are selected from records that exist on the file. On occasions it is useful to use an existing list to select all records in a file which are NOT in the list. To achieve this use the verb **NSELECT** in place of **SELECT**. In a similar way to the **SELECT** verb, if output specifications are defined with **NSELECT** statement the list is built from the contents of the specified attributes rather than the item-ids. One thing to bear in mind is that there is no 'sorted' version of this command, i.e. a replacement for **SSELECT**. The general format of the **NSELECT** statement is shown in Figure 12.34.

NSELECT *file.name* {*itemlist*} {*selection*} {*outlist*} {*modlist*}

where:

file.name	is the name of the file being interrogated
itemlist	is a list of specific item-ids
selection	the selection criteria
outlist	the output specifications. If this exists, the list is built from the contents of the specified attribute(s) rather than the item-ids
modlist	list of modifiers/options.

Figure 12.34 The format of the **NSELECT** statement.

The QSELECT verb

The **QSELECT** verb is used build files which can be used to provide secondary access to a file. The **QSELECT** verb builds an inverted list which is held in a normal file(rather than POINTER-FILE) and can be readily maintained by your applications. The format of the verb is shown in Figure 12.35

QSELECT *file.name.* {*itemlist*} {(*attr.ref*}

where

file.name	is the name of the file being interrogated
itemlist	a list of specific item-ids
attr.ref	The attributes specified here are used to construct the list. Each attribute, value and sub-value becomes a single attribute in the list and if no *attr.ref* is specified, all attributes are used.

Figure 12.35 The format of the **QSELECT** verb.

12.6.3 Miscellaneous ACCESS verbs

There are a number of other verbs which are can be used at the start of an ACCESS statement, which do not need much explanation. The following section is devoted to them.

The COUNT verb

The ACCESS verb **COUNT** counts the number of items that meet specific criteria. If no selection criterion is stated it will count all the items in a file and examples are shown in Figure 12.36.

:COUNT STAFF
```
[407] 7 items counted out of 7 items
```

:COUNT STAFF WITH TEL = "0171]" "0181]" "021]"
```
[407] 2 items counted out of 7 items
```

Figure 12.36 The **COUNT** verb.

The SUM verb

The ACCESS verb **SUM** generates the total of all the values of one attribute name for a selected set of items in a file. ACCESS selection options can also be applied if required. Figure 12.37 gives examples of this verb.

:sum staff
```
[423] Total of staff = 758
```

758 is the number of characters in the file. This includes attribute marks, value marks and the 8 byte item header. It does not include segments marks.

:sum staff salary
```
[423] Total of Salary = 98,450.00
```

:sum staff with dept "11" salary
```
[423] Total of   Salary = 40,700.00
```

Figure 12.37 The **SUM** verb.

The STAT verb

The **STAT** verb works in the same way as the **SUM** verb except it produces additional statistical information. Figure 12.38 gives examples of the use of this verb.

The HASH-TEST and ISTAT verbs

Whilst these verbs have been covered in earlier sections of this book relating to item distribution, it is worth noting that they are part of ACCESS. To review their function further refer to Section 7.3.

```
:stat staff
statistics of staff :
total =    758 average =    108.28 count =     7

:stat staff salary
statistics of Salary :
total = 98,450.00 average = 14,064.2857 count =     7

:stat staff with dept "11" salary
statistics of   Salary :
total = 40,700.00 average = 13,566.6666 count =     3
```

Figure 12.38 The **STAT** verb.

The T-DUMP ***and*** *T- LOAD* ***verbs***

These verbs are covered fully in Sections 20.2.9 and 20.2.10 which discuss the various ways in which data can be secured and recovered. It is worth noting, however, that these verbs are part of ACCESS.

The REFORMAT ***and*** *SREFORMAT* ***verbs***

The **REFORMAT** and **SREFORMAT** verbs are equivalent to, respectively, **LIST** and **SORT** except that the output is directed to another file or magnetic tape or diskette instead of to the terminal or printer. Figure 12.39 demonstrates the use of these verbs.

Example 1

```
:SREFORMAT STAFF BY DEPT BY NAME DEPT NAME ADDRESS SALARY
FILE NAME : TEMP[CR] <------ The file TEMP must exist otherwise an error condition will occur
```

Example 2

```
:t-att 500
Block size: 500
:set-floppy (ah
Block size: 500
[1088] Tape device is assigned to 3 1/2" high density (1.44M) floppy using
drive 'A '.
:reformat staff name address salary
File Name? :tape
Block size: 500
[802] 7 items dumped.
```

Figure 12.39 The **REFORMAT** and **SREFORMAT** verbs.

12.7 Summary

We are now at the end of the chapter on ACCESS, and I am sure you will agree that the PICK system has given real consideration to **users'** needs to retrieve and report on stored data. The ACCESS enquiry language is relatively straightforward for even the most naive user and since enquiries are written in an English-like form, most people need less than a day's training to become proficient in its use. Through the use of dictionary definition items and synonyms the PICK system can readily be made to understand the terminology used throughout a company which greatly increases its ease of use and acceptability. The next chapter is dedicated to the most important files of the PICK system, the dictionaries.

13 PICK Dictionaries

In the previous chapter we explored the interrogation of our database with an English-like language called ACCESS. In the construction of the ACCESS statements we used dictionary names to specify the parts of the database we wanted listed and totalled. Data dictionaries are just one of the three types of dictionary in the PICK system This section talks about the these levels of dictionary and focuses on the data dictionary, the file which defines the structure of your data records.

As we have seen, the PICK database hierarchy comprises three levels of dictionary files before arriving at the *actual* data. These are:

The System Dictionary	**mds** (called SYSTEM in R83 PICK)
The Master Dictionary	**MD**
The file dictionaries	

Everything in PICK is stored as an item in a file. The dictionary is just one such file and contains records in the same format as the records stored in the data files. There are two types of dictionary record, the file defining item and the attribute defining item. File defining items, as their name suggest control files and to that end affect the display of attribute 0 of the items in that file. In addition they contain the fid (frame address) of the location of the file they control together with other system information. File defining items can be found in all three dictionaries of the PICK database hierarchy.

Attribute defining items are to be found in both Master Dictionaries and file dictionaries. These items define a specific attribute of a data record and provide such information as its position within the data record, its maximum length, the display justification and any processing codes that apply. Whilst we will take a look at both the System and Master dictionaries, most of this chapter is devoted to attribute defining items and in particular the use of processing codes (conversions and correlative codes) which is where much of PICK's power comes into play.

13.1 File defining items

13.1.1 File Definition Item – or D-item

The file defining item is a record which contains the location of the file on your computer's hard disk. The file defining item contains the base frame id and modulo of the file which PICK converts to a drive, cylinder, sector and head address. In the System Dictionary these records define the location of the Master Dictionary, whilst in the Master Dictionary pointers contain the location of the file dictionary and those in file dictionaries point to the start of the physical data.

In addition the D-pointer contains a number of other attributes whose purpose is to define the size, access privileges and usage for the file. A detailed description of the file defining item follows but it should be noted that in R83 the file defining item comprises the first 13 attributes only.

Attribute 0 : Item-id

The name of the file 'pointed' to. In the System Dictionary this is the account name (or the name of a Q-pointer to an account). In the Master Dictionary this is the name of the file dictionary and in the file dictionary this is the name of the data file.

Attribute 1: Dictionary code

In file defining items the first letter of attribute 1 is a **D**. If this record is in the system dictionary it defines the pointer to the master dictionary or account. In the master dictionary, the D-item defines a file dictionary and in a file dictionary it defines a data file. The file defining item is often referred to as the 'fid' or 'D-pointer' can have other letters after the **D** in attribute 1 whose meaning is as follows:

C Defines the file as a 'pointer' file, mostly used to define program files (particularly in R83 where programs could only be compiled in a file of type **DC**. The file POINTER-FILE is often a **DC** type file.

L Logs any updates to the transaction logger.

N Disables update protection on a file even if global update protection is enabled, but may not be used with the **U** option. Update protection is a 'forced' write option mechanism which protects against GFEs.

P Ensures that the primary file space only contains pointer items, which means that all records are stored outside the file with pointers to them stored in the actual file. Advanced PICK does this anyway for items which are larger than 85% of the frame size. This option ensures all records in the file are stored outside the file itself.

S Item-ids in this file are case-sensitive.

U Enables update protection on a file even if global protection is disabled, but it may not be used with the **N** option.

X Do not save the *file contents* on a file save. The *file contents* referred to would apply to the whole account if on the D-pointer in the System Dictionary (**MDS**), the dictionary and data file files if applied to the D-pointer in the Master Dictionary (**MD**) and the data file if applied to the D-pointer in the file dictionary.

This can be a very useful means of reducing backup time, especially for accounts or files that are not frequently updated. It is not without its dangers however. Beware when restoring from a filesave tape which does not contain all the files of your system. The filesave tape overwrites the *entire* file system, so if a file is DX'd and not backed up, it will not be restored either and valuable data could be lost forever! It is therefore essential when restoring from a filesave tape to ensure it contains copies of **all** files on the system or that those accounts/file not on the tape are held on others and are able to be restored.

Y Files containing a DY in the first attribute will not be saved on a filesave tape. In this case, however, when the file restore is carried out, the file will be recreated empty, i.e. containing no records. An example of the use of this type of file would be temporary transaction files.

Attribute 2: Base
Attribute 2 contains the frame identification number (fid) of the associated file (see Section 7.2.1 for an explanation of the term fid).

Attribute 3: Modulo
Attribute 3 contains the number of contiguous frames in the primary file space of the file.

Attribute 4: Reserved and unavailable

Attribute 5: Retrieval lock
Determines a users access rights to records in the associated file. See Chapter 20 Section 20.1.2 for a discussion on the use of retrieval lock codes.

Attribute 6: Update lock
Determines a users rights to update records in the associated file. See Chapter 20 Section 20.1.2 for a discussion on the use of update lock codes.

Attribute 7: Password/reserved and unavailable
In the System Dictionary, this attribute contains the password to the account. Passwords are encrypted and may be multi-valued (although they rarely are). In any other file this attribute is reserved and unavailable.

Attribute 8: Reserved and unavailable/processing code
In the System Dictionary this attribute is reserved and unavailable. In all other files this attribute of the File Defining Item can contain a processing code (Not in PICK R83). Processing codes specified in this attribute allow a file to function as an application by pre- and post-processing data, and are applied when an item in this file is updated.

Attribute 9: Justification
The attribute type contains codes used to specify justification for the item-id.

Attribute 10: Column width
The column width is used to define the number of characters to be allocated when displaying the item-id on ACCESS reports.

Attribute 11: Reserved and unavailable

Attribute 12: Reserved and unavailable

Attribute 13: Reallocation
This attribute holds the new file size parameters which will be applied when the file is restored.

Attribute 14: Input-conversion
This attribute contains the processing codes to be applied prior to data entry.

Attribute 15: Macro
Contains the attribute names to be used as the default input specifications for the Update Processor. These are also used as the default output specifications for an ACCESS report where no alternative list is given in attribute 16. The contents of attribute 15 and 16 override the normal ACCESS output specifications of **1 2 3** etc. if they exist in the file dictionary (see Section 12.4.2).

Attribute 16: Output-macro
If present this becomes the default output specifications for ACCESS reports on the file.

Attribute 17: Description
A free text field to describe the function of the current file.

Attribute 18: Reserved

Attribute 19: Reserved

Attribute 20 to attribute 30 inclusive: hotkeys

Attribute 20 Hotkey.all
Attribute 21 Hotkey 1
Attribute 22 Hotkey 2
through to
Attribute 30 Hotkey 0

Hotkeys

There are 11 dictionary attributes in both the File and Attribute Defining Items related to 'hotkeys'. Attribute 20 is defined as 'hotkey.all', with attribute 21 onwards known as 'hotkey0', 'hotkey1', and so on.

Hotkeys enable the calling of PICK BASIC subroutines from dictionaries using the Update Processor command **x***number*(**CTRL/x***number*), where *number* is a number between **0** and **9**. Hotkey subroutine calls are available in addition to subroutine calls from the 'output-conversion', 'processing code' or 'input-conversion' attributes.

To call a PICK/BASIC subroutine while in the Update Processor on a particular attribute, type **x***number*. Only the program(s) from one dictionary will be executed by each command although you may call more than one subroutine per attribute by multi-valuing the call statements. (Use **v** to multi-value call statements). The subroutine that gets executed is dependent on the following set of priorities:

If there is a subroutine called on 'hotkey.all' (attribute 20) in the current attribute defining item, it will be executed, regardless of the value of *number*. If there is not a subroutine on attribute 20, the subroutine called on attribute 20 + *number* of the current attribute defining item will be executed and if number is zero it will look for a subroutine on attribute 30.

If there are no subroutine calls in the attribute defining item itself, the same order of priorities are applied to the file defining item, i.e. first look at 'hotkey.all' before looking for a subroutine on a specific hotkey.

13.2 System Dictionary

The System Dictionary **(mds** in Advanced PICK and **SYSTEM** in R83) contains file defining items (D-pointers) which point to all Master Dictionaries and synonym records for these Master Dictionaries (or accounts) i.e. Q-pointers. In addition there are a few D-pointers to 'system level' files. There are no attribute defining items, because the System Dictionary controls files not attributes.

13.3 Master Dictionary

The Master Dictionary contains TCL verbs, PROCS, Macros, Menus, the ACCESS language, attribute defining items, file defining items and synonyms (Q-pointers). In essence the Master Dictionary determines what is possible and accessible from within the account and hence as it controls the account, there is only one Master Dictionary per account. If you list your MD and look at the contents of attribute 1 you will see all the different types of record that are stored.

a	attribute defining items
c*x*	ACCESS language
d	file defining items
m	macros
me	menus
n	macros
pq*x*	PROCs
q	synonym items
v	TCL verbs
vr	compiled BASIC programs

13.4 Attribute defining items

The dictionary records of a file dictionary define an individual element of data. In PICK terminology, therefore, each item in a file dictionary defines an attribute of the data item and hence they are called attribute defining items (ADIs). Dictionary items are created using the Update Processor, the Editor or any piece of software provided by your supplier for the purpose. All 4GL products (fourth generation languages or application generators) for example, contain routines for building dictionaries. In the absence of such software it is a simple enough task with either the Update Processor or Editor. Assuming the dictionary for the file **STAFF** has already been created, to create the dictionary items **SNAME** and **FNAME** you would type in, at the TCL prompt:

:U DICT STAFF SNAME FNAME

The Update Processor would create two new items in the dictionary file of the file **STAFF** for the items **SNAME** and **FNAME**. Then for each you would need to define the relevant attributes, up to 30 in total (the first 10 only in R83). One of the important features of the dictionaries is the ability to re-define the same attribute by different names. This enables different departments of a company to refer to the data in terms they understand. Hence the Sales department could refer to 'models', the Production department to 'products' and the Service department to 'parts' each using names they are familiar with but each referring to the same element of the data record. These synonyms are created by copying one dictionary definition item to another, and then changing attribute 3 the heading attribute within the newly created item. It is necessary to change the headings, and only the headings, thus enabling the description to agree with the name to which the data attribute is referred. Figure 13.1 shows this happening with the existing dictionary item, **MODEL**, the term in current use on the **STOCK** file, being copied to new dictionary items **PRODUCT** and **PART**, with the respective headings of these new dictionary items being changed.

13.4.1 The structure of file dictionary records

The dictionary record consists of a number of separate attributes, the total of which fully define each element of data in a data file. In Advanced PICK these attributes can number up to 30, but in R83 only the first 10 apply. Figure 13.2 shows the format of these dictionary (or attribute defining) items and explains the function of each of its attributes.

```
:COPY DICT STOCK MODEL MODEL
to : PRODUCT PART[CR]
     1 MODEL TO PRODUCT
     2 MODEL TO PART

[805] 2 item(s) copied

:U DICT STOCK PRODUCT PART
DICT STOCK 'PRODUCT' size = 50
01 An
02 1n
03 Productxf
04
05
06
07
08
09 L
10 20
DICT STOCK    'PRODUCT' size = 51 filed.
DICT STOCK    'PART' size = 49
01 An
02 1n
03 Partxf
04
05
06
07
08
09 L
10 20
07
08
09 L
10 20
DICT STOCK    'PART' size = 45 filed.
```

Figure 13.1 Creating dictionary synonyms.

Attribute 0 : Item-id
The name of the record found in the dictionary. It is this name which is used in ACCESS statements.

Attribute 1: Dictionary code
This attribute can contain one of three values.

- **a** indicates the original definition
- **s** indicates a synonym definition. In practice there is no difference between the treatment of an **a** or **s** item.
- **x** defines a 'protected' attribute

In AP only, an optional description can follow the dictionary code without affecting any normal operation of the ADI

Figure 13.2 The format of attribute definition items.

Attribute 2: Attribute mark count
Defines the attribute position of this element of data within the entire data record

Attribute 3: Heading
Attribute 3 contains the description to appear at the top of the column in ACCESS reports

Attribute 4: Structure
Used to define the controlling and dependent relationships of which this attribute is a part

Attribute 5: Reserved and unavailable

Attribute 6: Reserved and unavailable

Attribute 7: Output conversion processing code
A code which is used to convert data between the internally stored format and the format to be displayed and printed (the external or output) format

Attribute 8: Processing code
A pre-processing code which denotes a special function that needs to be performed on the data. Information defined in this way can be considered as 'derived' data

Attribute 9: Justification
The attribute type contains codes used to specify justification for the item-id

Attribute 10: Column width
The column width is used to define the number of characters to be allocated when displaying the item-id on ACCESS reports

Attribute 11: Reserved and unavailable

Attribute 12: Reserved and unavailable

Attribute 13: Reserved and unavailable
This attribute holds the new file size parameters which will be applied when the file is restored

Attribute 14: Input-conversion
This attribute contains the processing codes to be applied prior to data entry when using the Update Processor. These codes can be used for data validation and are executed even if there is a null entry

Attribute 15: Macro
Contains the attribute names to be passed as an attribute list to the Update Processor when zooming to another item. The attribute names are separated with a space

Attribute 16: Reserved and unavailable

Figure 13.2 *Continued*

Attribute 17: Description
A free text field to describe the function of the attribute. The text in this attribute will be displayed by the Update Processor when a **?** is entered as the first and only character of data in the data attribute defined by this attribute definition item

Attribute 18: Reserved and unavailable

Attribute 19: Reserved and unavailable

Attribute 20 to attribute 30 inclusive: hotkeys

Attribute 20	Hotkey.all
Attribute 21	Hotkey 1
Attribute 22	Hotkey 2
through to	
Attribute 30	Hotkey 0

Figure 13.2 *Continued*

Attribute 1 – attribute definition

Attribute 1 defines the type of item. Where the item provides the main definition, this attribute generally contains **A**. Where the item is a redefinition or synonym of the main definition this attribute generally contains an **S**. Since PICK treats both these types identically, the **S** code is not generally used. An **X** indicates the attribute is not to be printed and/or displayed.

Attribute 2 – the attribute mark count (amc)

This attribute defines the position of the dictionary item in the data record. Hence, if in a personnel system, a record has as the item-id a personnel code, which is followed by the surname, then the first name and so on. The item-id is located in position 0 (the key field), the surname in position 1, the first name in position 2 and so on. Hence, in this example, the attribute mark count would be 0, 1, or 2, respectively.

There are two special location definitions which are useful. If attribute 2 of a dictionary item contains 9999 it will provide the size of the selected item in bytes. If it contains 9998 it will produce a sequential item count of the items selected.

Attribute 3 – heading definition

This attribute contains the text for the heading to be used in the ACCESS report. If this attribute contains a null value, the item-id of this attribute is used as the heading. If this attribute contains a backslash (\), no heading text is shown. In all cases if the heading text is less than the maximum number of characters defined in attribute 10, the heading text is padded out with full stops. If the text of the heading is greater than the maximum number of characters, the full heading is displayed.

It is possible to have multiple line headings, achieved by placing multi-value marks](CTRL/]) at the end of each line of text. In this instance each heading line follows the previous one. If the second or subsequent lines of the heading are greater than the first, the first line will be padded out with full stops to the length of the longest heading. The multi-line heading only works where the headings appear above columns of data.

It should be noted that data will only be output in columns providing the total length of each data line is less than 80 characters for screen output or 132 characters for printed reports. Where the length exceeds these values the report is produced down the page with each element of each item of data appearing on a separate line.

Figure 13.3 gives examples of these for the dictionary item SNAME which defines the surname in a personnel system.

Attr. **10** *(Size)*	**Attribute** **3** *(Description)*	**OUTPUT** **REPORT** *(Output)*
5	Surname	Surname
10	Surname	Surname...
5	Surname]of]Staff member	Surname........ Of Staff member
5	\	.....
5		SNAME

Figure 13.3 The heading definition attribute.

Attribute 4 – controlling and dependent

The fourth attribute of a dictionary definition item defines the controlling and dependent relationship. For example, in an order-processing system each line of an order contains information dependent on each other, the product code, unit price, quantity ordered and so on. Whilst each of these is dependent on each other in that each line of the order requires all these elements to be present, they are controlled and hence will only be present where a new line of the order is completed. In this situation the order line number controls the other elements of data which are dependent on it.

Attribute 4 is where this kind of relationship is defined. The controlling dictionary item contains a **C** in this attribute, followed by ;*nn* for each data element it controls, where *nn*, defines the location (amc) of the dependent element in the record. A dependent element contains a **D** in this attribute followed by a single ;*nn* where nn defines the location of the controlling attribute. Figure 13.4

DICT Name	---- Dictionary Attributes ---- 1 2 3	4
ORDNO	A 0 Order Number	
LINENO	A 1 Line Number	C;2;3;4;5
PRODNO	A 2 Product Number	D;1
LISTPRICE	A 3 List Price	D;1
QTY	A 4 Quantity Ordered	D;1
LINEVALUE	A 5 Line Value	D;1

Figure 13.4 The controlling and dependent attribute.

shows how this works for an order-processing system containing a number of data elements used for each order line.

Attributes 7 and 8 – conversion and processing code processing codes

Processing codes are used to manipulate data in some way. In general a conversion code is used to display data in a given form and appears in attribute 7, whilst processing codes are used to derive data in some way and appear in attribute 8. The important difference in using these processing codes is the way in which ACCESS itself works. During the execution of an ACCESS statement, data is first taken from the database in its raw form and any processing code applied to it. This provides an intermediate format which is used whenever:

1. The attribute name is part of a sort key.
2. The data is *compared* in selection criteria.
3. The data is used in producing totals.
4. The data produces a control break.
5. The data is printed, *except* on break lines.

Once any of the above steps have been taken, the conversion code is applied to produce an output format of the data. This reformats the data into the format provided in the ACCESS report, which can either be shown on the screen or produced on the printer. A summary of the possible conversion and processing code codes is shown in Table 13.1.

Such is the importance of these processing codes that an entire section (Section 13.5) of this chapter is devoted to them.

Attribute 9 – justification

Attribute 9 of a dictionary definition item determines the justification required. The options available are as follows:

Table 13.1 Summary of conversion and processing code codes.

Code	*Description*
A	**Arithmetic** computes mathematical expressions and is converted to an 'F' code at runtime
B	**Bridge** to maintain a relationship between an attribute in one item and an item in another file
C	**Concatenate** concatenates attributes together
CALL	**Call** a BASIC subroutine
CALLX	**Call** a BASIC subroutine an time an item is filed (only valid in attribute 8)
CU	**Character update** allows data in the attribute to be changed attribute by attribute. (valid in attribute 14 only)
D	**Date** converts dates to external format
F	**Function** computes mathematical and relational operations on attributes
G	**Group** extracts data elements from a group of elements by specifying a delimiter that separates them
I	**Index** processing code indicating the existence of an index for the attribute
ID	**item-id** used by the Update Processor to create new item-ids
L	**Length** specifies output length constraints
MC	**Mask character** has various options to convert string to upper and lower case or to extract numeric or alphabetic characters from strings
MD & MR	**Mask decimal** performs output conversions, literal insertions and currency formatting on numeric fields held in internal format
MI	**Must input** ensures that items created in the Update Processor contain data in this attribute (valid in attribute 14 only)
ML	**Masked decimal** As MD/MR but with left justification
MS	**Mask alter sort** alters the normal sort sequence of the characters
MT	**Mask time** converts time of day into external format
MX	**Mask hexadecimal** converts ASCII strings to hexadecimal format
MY	**Mask hexadecimal** converts hexadecimal strings to ASCII format
O	**Ascending order** sorts the values in an attribute into ascending order when item is filed(valid in attribute 14 only)
P	**Pattern match** limits items selected to those of a specific pattern of characters (including literals)
R	**Range** restricts items selected to those that fall within a particular range of values
S	**Substitution** allows other data to be substituted where a zero or null value is found
T	**Text extraction** extracts any number of characters from any position in the attribute
T*file*	**File translation** enables a file look-up facility based on the value held in the attribute
U	**User-defined** A means to invoke user routines written in assembly to perform special conversions or processing codes
V	**Maximum values** specifies the maximum number of values permitted in an attribute (valid in attribute 14 only)
X	Display only prevents an attribute from being modified or will provide audit trail of modifications that are made
ZA	Displays a PICK item in assembly source code format
ZC	**Zip Code** used with the file **ZCF** to display city, state and zip code

- **L** left-justified. Where data exceeds the maximum length specified in attribute 10, the data is folded, at the first character after the maximum, onto the next line
- **R** right-justified, which overlays the column(s) to the left if the data is longer than the column width
- **T** left-justified, but where the data exceeds the maximum length specified in attribute 10, the data is folded into multiple lines, starting at a space
- **U** left-justified (no data is folded onto new lines)
- **W** data is processed though the Output Processor (OP) before being output and the justification code can be followed by any valid OP command. This option is only valid for non-columnar output
- **WW** processes all attributes from this attribute onwards through the OP before output. Once again this is only valid for non-columnar output. A form feed occurs after the processing of the final attribute
- **X** used with **L R** or **T** to expand the display field to fill the report

These codes are also used when sorting takes place. Right-justified data is sorted into numeric sequence, whilst left-justified text is sorted into alphabetical sequence. Figure 13.5 demonstrates the effect of these codes where the column width is defined as nine characters.

Attribute 10 – maximum data length

This attribute specifies the maximum number of characters to be used when data is displayed. Remember too that attribute 2 of a dictionary definition item contains the text for the column heading. If this contains a heading which is less than the maximum number of characters as defined by attribute 10, the heading text is padded out with full stops. This padding only applies to the heading and does not affect the data listed.

Attribute 14 – Input-conversion processing code

This attribute can contain a processing code which is applied by the Update Processor immediately after entry. The codes can be used for data validation as well as data formatting. These codes will be applied regardless of whether or not data is entered into the attribute. Typically entries here are those to indicate a local and/or remote index, but equally it could contain the **mi** code which indicates mandatory input and would prevent the item being saved with a null value. The input conversion attribute can contain any processing code with the exception of the **U** (user exit) code. However there are a number of processing codes which can **only** be used here and are not able to be placed in attribute 7 or 8. These are

- **cu** character update
- **i** index
- **o** ascending order

Justification code = L

```
STAFF..... Desc.....

001        ADMINISTR
           ATION
002        SALES
003        SW SUPPOR
             T
004        SALES
005        SW SUPPOR
             T
006        ADMINISTR

010        SALES
007        MARKETING
           AND PR
```

Justification code = R

```
STAFF..... Desc.....

001        ADMINISTRATION
002        SALES
003        SW SUPPORT
004        SALES
005        SW SUPPORT
006        ADMINISTRATION
010        SALES
007        MARKETING AND PR
```

Justification code = T

```
STAFF..... Desc.....

001        ADMINISTR
           ATION
002        SALES
003        SW
           SUPPORT
004        SALES
005        SW
           SUPPORT
006        ADMINISTR

           ATION
010        SALES
007        MARKETING
           AND PR
```

Justification code = U

```
STAFF..... Desc.....

001        ADMINISTRATION
002        SALES
003        SW SUPPORT
004        SALES
005        SW SUPPORT
006        ADMINISTRATION
010        SALES
007        MARKETING AND PR
```

Justification code = RX

```
STAFF..... Desc.................................................
001                                               ADMINISTRATION
002                                                        SALES
003                                                   SW SUPPORT
004                                                        SALES
005                                                   SW SUPPORT
006                                               ADMINISTRATION
010                                                        SALES
007                                             MARKETING AND PR
```

Figure 13.5 Justification using attribute 9.

mi	must input
v*n*	value code
x	display only

Attribute 15 – Macro

This attribute contains the default attributes which are passed to the Update Processor when 'zooming' to another item. The values named here should be separated by spaces.

Attribute 17 – Description

This attribute is free text for the developer to use to define the function of the current attribute. The text this attribute contains will be displayed to the user as help text when inputting data via the Update Processor and being uncertain of what to do. Entering a **?** as the first and only character in the field will cause this text to be displayed.

Attributes 20–30 – Hotkeys

These 'hot keys' provide access to BASIC programs whilst operating within the Update Processor. Attribute 20 is defined as 'hotkey.all', with attribute 21 onwards known as 'hotkey0', 'hotkey1', and so on.

Hotkeys enable the calling of PICK BASIC subroutines from dictionaries using the Update Processor command **x***number*(**CTRL/x***number*), where *number* is a number between **0** and **9**. Hotkey subroutine calls are available in addition to subroutine calls from the 'output-conversion', 'processing code' or 'input-conversion' attributes. It should be borne in mind that no parameters can be passed to the subroutine.

To call a PICK/BASIC subroutine while in the Update Processor on a particular attribute, type **x***number*. Only the program(s) from one dictionary will be executed by each command although you may call more than one subroutine per attribute by multi-valuing the call statements. (Use **v̲** to multi-value call statements). The subroutine that gets executed is dependent on the following set of priorities:

If there is a subroutine called on 'hotkey.all' (attribute 20) in the current attribute defining item, it will be executed, regardless of the value of *number*. If there is not a subroutine on attribute 20, the subroutine called on attribute 20 + *number* of the current attribute defining item will be executed and if number is zero it will look for a subroutine on attribute 30.

If there are no subroutine calls in the attribute defining item itself, the same order of priorities are applied to the file defining item i.e. first look at 'hotkey.all' before looking for a subroutine on a specific hotkey.

13.5 Processing codes

Processing codes are a powerful PICK facility providing database links and data calculation and manipulation capability. These codes can be held on both file defining items and attribute defining items in one or more of the three attributes

attribute 7	the output conversion code (attribute defining items only)
attribute 8	the correlative code
attribute 14	the input conversion code

The remainder of this chapter is dedicated to a discussion on each of these processing codes and gives examples of their use. Table 13.2 which follows

Table 13.2 Processing codes and their usage.

Processing code	*File Defining Items*			*Attribute Defining Items*		
	Attr 7	*Attr 8*	*Attr 14*	*Attr 7*	*Attr 8*	*Attr 14*
A arithmetic				√	√	√
B Bridge		√				
C Concatenate				√		√
CALL BASIC subroutine		√	√	√	√	√
CALLX BASIC subroutine		√				
CU Character update						√
D Date				√	√	√
F Function				√	√	√
G Group				√	√	√
I Index		√				√
ID item-id		√				
L Length				√	√	√
MC Mask character				√	√	√
MD & **MR** Mask decimal				√	√	√
MI Must input						√
ML Masked decimal				√	√	√
MS Mask alter sort					√	
MT Mask time				√	√	√
MX Mask hexadecimal				√	√	√
MY Mask hexadecimal				√	√	√
O Ascending Order		√			√	
P Pattern match				√	√	√
R Range				√	√	√
S Substitution				√	√	√
T Text extraction				√	√	√
T*file* File translation				√	√	√
U User-defined				√	√	
V Maximum Values						√
X Display only						√
X Update stamp		√				
ZA assembly source code format			√		√	
ZC Zip Code				√	√	√

shows the full list of processing codes and which can be used where in both file defining items and attribute defining items.

13.5.1 The A (Arithmetic) processing code

This processing code is used to carry out arithmetic calculations and, whilst all its functions can be performed using an **F** processing code, the syntax of the **A** processing code is simpler and hence easier to understand and maintain. Even so, **A** processing codes are translated by ACCESS into **F** processing codes. The **A** processing code is generally placed in attribute 8 of the dictionary definition item. The **A** proccssing code can use dictionary names, dictionary positions or literals in its calculations. It can use the logical operators **AND** and **OR**, the **IF..THEN..ELSE** construct and a wide range of relational operators. Its general format is as follows:

A{*number*}{;}{*expression*}

where

number	is used to indicate the number of decimal places (between 0 and 4 inclusive) to retain during calculations involving a mixture of fractions and whole numbers. This number can be omitted and zero is implied.
expression	the expression which produces the required result.

Do not be fooled by the simplicity of the general construct of this processing code. It can become extremely complex and is very powerful. **A** processing code expressions are created in a form similar to those of PICK BASIC and consist of operands, operators, conditional statements and special functions.

In expressions where dictionary names are used, the name is enclosed in parentheses and proceeded by the letter N. Attributes are referred to by specifying their position (amc) and literals (whether numbers or alphabetic strings) are enclosed in single or double quotes. Care must be taken in deciding whether to use attribute names or attribute positions in processing codes since they are handled differently. If the position is used, the value used is that as stored in the appropriate position on the disk. If, however, the name is used, the ACCESS processor will look this up in the file dictionary and will apply any conversions or processing codes associated with that name. In some cases this would cause significantly different results.

A processing codes are dummy fields in that the result they produce does not generate data which actually exists on the disk. The information is calculated or 'derived' using existing data. As such **A** processing code dictionary items are mostly assigned the attribute position 0 or the attribute position of the attribute on which a calculation is being performed. If you are uncertain which to give it use zero and see if that provides the right result. If not change it to that of the attribute it redefines.

Operators and functions

The operators for concatenation, addition, subtraction, multiplication and division, respectively :,+, –, * and /, can be used in calculations although it should be noted that the result of a division will always return an integer result. Hence **"5"/"2"** will return a result of 2 and not 2.5. If you require the decimal positions you will need to carry out a multiplication in the formula to factor the result. Thus to produce two decimal places in the result, the formula of **("5"*"100")/"2"** that produces the answer 250 will require a conversion code of **MR2** applied to it to give the output result 2.50. In order to define the precedence of operations up to 20 levels of parentheses can be used.

The **A** processing code has two arithmetic functions, these being the **R** (remainder) function and the **S** (sum) function. Examples of these functions and some other simple **A** processing codes is given in Figure 13.6 including one that will accumulate the contents of all the multi-values of an attribute, the **S** (sum) function. This could be used where a customer's aged balances are held as multiple values in a single attribute, and you wish to know the total balance outstanding. The final example of Figure 13.6 shows how the remainder from a calculation can be computed.

A;6+7+"35"	Adds together the contents of attribute 6 with the contents of attribute 7 and adds the constant 35 to the result
A;N(GROSS)-N(TAX)	Subtracts the contents of the attribute called TAX from the contents of the that called GROSS. Any processing codes contained in the dictionary items GROSS and TAX will be applied prior to the calculation taking place
A;S(9)	Sums together all the amounts contained in each of the values of the multi-valued attribute of attribute 9
A;"0171":4	Prefixes the contents of attribute 4 with the literal "0171".
A;R(3/"4")	Provides the remainder of the contents of attribute 3 divided by the constant 4

Figure 13.6 Examples of some simple **A** processing codes.

The use of relational operators

The arithmetic processing code can also use the relational operators, greater than (>), less than (<), equal to (=), not equal to (£), greater than or equal to (>=), less than or equal to (<=). Where these are used, each operator takes two expressions as operands and the result evaluates to 1 if the relationship is true and 0 if the relationship is false. Figure 13.7 gives examples of the use of relational operators and the way in which you an simulate the use of **AND** and **OR** operations.

A;N(BONUS)*(N(GROSS)<10000))

If GROSS is less than £10,000 then the last part of the processing code will equate to one and the bonus payment will be equal to the contents of the attribute BONUS multiplied by one otherwise it will equate to zero and the bonus payment will be nil, i.e. the contents of the attribute BONUS multiplied by zero

A;((3>5)*(N(AGE)>"21"))*N(BONUS)

In this statement, only if the contents of attribute 3 is greater than the contents of attribute 5 **AND** the contents of the attribute **AGE** is greater than 21 will a bonus be paid

A;(((3>5)+(N(AGE)>"21"))>"0")*N(BONUS)

In this statement, if the contents of attribute 3 is greater than the contents of attribute 5 **OR** if the contents of the attribute **AGE** is greater than 21 will a bonus be paid. Notice that the results of the two comparisons are added together and then compared to zero

Figure 13.7 The use of relational operators in the **A** processing code.

Special operands

The **A** processing code has some special operands and functions which are listed in Table 13.3.

Table 13.3 Special operands and functions for the **A** processing code.

Operand	*Description*
D	The system date in internal format
LPV	Load previous value
NB	The break-level counter; it is zero at detail time and increases by one for each break level encountered. It is 255 for the grand total. Use in attribute 7 only
ND	The detail line counter; it is 1 at detail time and is only valid at break time. Use in attribute 7 only
NI	The item counter; it is zero during select time and only active during the output stage. Can be used in attribute 7 or 8
NS	The secondary value counter; it is equal to 1 for the total line. Use in attribute 8 only
NV	The value counter; it is equal to 1 for the total line. Use in attribute 8 only
T	The system time in internal format

The D **operand**

The **D** operand returns the current internal date held within the computer and can be used to perform calculations which involve the difference between 'today's' date and that held in an attribute on a file. As an example:

A;(D-N(DUE.DATE))

will calculate the number of overdue days of an invoice from the date it was due to be paid which is calculated by taking it's due date from today's date.

The LPV **operand**

The 'load previous value' operand takes the value of the last column output in an ACCESS as its input. Hence for a general calculation of VAT the processing code would be

A;(LPV*"175")/"10"

Hence if such a dictionary item called VAT were to be set up, this could be called several times in the same ACCESS statement to calculate VAT on several different price elements as shown below:

:LIST STOCK LIST.PRICE VAT DISCOUNT.PRICE VAT (ID-SUPP

```
Page 1            STOCK              16:57:36 08 Apr 1995

List Price        VAT.......         discount..         VAT.......
                                                        price

15500.00          2712.50            2440.80            427.00
13250.00          2318.75            2086.20            365.05
11350.00          1986.25            1787.40            312.72
12900.00          2257.50            2031.30            355.42
15500.00          2712.50            2440.80            427.00
15400.00          2695.00            2425.50            424.37
14550.00          2546.25            2291.40            400.92
10000.00          1750.00            1575.00            275.62

[405] 8 items listed out of 8 items.
```

But do be aware of the effect a conversion code with a comma will have on this operand. In essence only the digits prior to the comma are passed to the **LPV** operand and hence will give spurious results as can be seen from the example shown at the top of page 244:

The NB **operand**

The **NB** operand is known as the break-level counter. It is zero at detail time and increases by one for each break level that is encountered. The operand is only valid when placed in attribute 7 (the conversion attribute) and contains 255 for the grand total.

```
:LIST STOCK LIST.PRICE VAT DISCOUNT.PRICE VAT (ID-SUPP
Page 1              STOCK              16:57:36 08 Apr 1995

List Price        VAT.......        discount..        VAT.......
                                    price

15500.00          2712.50           2,440.80          0.35
13250.00          2318.75           2,086.20          0.35
11350.00          1986.25           1,787.40          0.17
12900.00          2257.50           2,031.30          0.35
15500.00          2712.50           2,440.80          0.35
15400.00          2695.00           2,425.50          0.35
14550.00          2546.25           2,291.40          0.35
10000.00          1750.00           1,575.00          0.17

[405] 8 items listed out of 8 items.
```

The ND **operand**

The **ND** operand is used to determine the number of individual detail lines between breaks and this information can then be used to calculate averages. The detail line counter is set to 1 at detail time and is only valid at break time. Since **ND** only has a meaning at the total line, this dictionary item can only be used in conjunction with the **BREAK-ON** and **DET-SUPP** modifiers which must be included in the ACCESS statement. The **ND** operand, like that of **NB**, can only be used in attribute 7 as a conversion code. We will now define and use two new dictionary items, **AVE.SALARY** and **NO.STAFF**.

AVE.SALARY	**NO.STAFF**
001 A	001 A
002 0	002 0
003 Ave.]Salary	003 No. Staff
004	004
005	005
006	006
007 A;6/ND]MR2,	007 A;ND
008	008
009 R	009 R
010 10	010 10

Note that these] are value marks and that used in attribute 7 demonstrates the use of multiple processing codes

To find the average of the contents of a multi-value it is necessary to perform two operations. The first is to sum the contents of the multi-values and the second to divide the total by the number of values. If an average is required for the multi-values of attribute 4, the processing code would be

A;(S(4)/S(4=4))

```
:sort staff by dept break-on deptdesc total salary
ave.salary no.staff (det-supp

Page 1        STOCK                    16:57:36 08 Apr 1995

Desc................        Salary   Ave....... No. Staff.
                                     Salary

ADMINISTRATION           30,900.00   15,450.00          2
SALES                    40,700.00   13,566.66          3
SW SUPPORT               26,850.00   13,425.00          2
MARKETING AND PR         10,000.00   10,000.00          1
                        108,450.00

[405] 8 items listed out of 8 items.
```

The NI **and** NS **and** NV **operands**

The **NI** operand is used to provide a count of the number of items and can be used in attribute 7 or 8. **NS** can only be used in attribute 8 and returns the sequential number of the sub-value being processed. **NV** is also only able to be referred to in attribute 8 and is the value counter which is applicable with a **BY-EXP** sort. It is equal to 1 for the total line and returns a sequential number of the value being processed.

S.NI	**S.NS**	**S.NV**
001 A	001 A	001 A
002 0	002 0	002 0
003 s.ni	003 s.ns	003 s.nv
004	004	004
005	005	005
006	006	006
007	007	007
008 a;ni	008 a;ns	008 a;nv
009 R	009 R	009 R
010 4	010 4	010 4

The IF..THEN..ELSE *condition*

The **IF..THEN..ELSE** condition, although a part of many licencee implementations for many years, was first introduced to the generic implementation of PICK with the advent of the first release of Advanced PICK. In Section 13.5.1, on arithmetic processing codes, we saw how to achieve **IF..THEN..ELSE** conditions with relational operators, but to the uninitiated the processing code is not so easy to understand. The **IF..THEN..ELSE** condition makes the whole issue of condition testing much easier to implement and much clearer to interpret but you should be aware it is not a valid code in PICK R83. The general format is as follows:

:sort staff by-exp interests interests s.nv s.ni s.ns

```
Page 1        staff                      17:33:51 08 Apr 1995

staff.....    Interests         s.nv  s.n1  s.ns

007           BADMINTON            1     1     1
001           BADMINTON            2     2     1
001           BRIDGE               3     3     1
003           BRIDGE               1     4     1
005           BRIDGE               2     5     1  <--
003           CHESS                3     6     1
006           KARATE               1     7     1
006           MARTIAL ARTS         2     8     1
004           MUSIC                2     9     1
005           RALLYING             3    10     1
002           READING              3    11     1
002           SAILING              1    12     1
010           SAILING              2    13     1
001           SQUASH               1    14     1
003           SQUASH               2    15     1
004           SQUASH               1    16     1
005           SQUASH               1    17     1
002           SWIMMING             2    18     1
010           SWIMMING             1    19     1
[405] 18 items listed out of 8 items.
```

BRIDGE is the second value of the attribute INTERESTS of staff record 005

IF *condition* **THEN** *algebraic function* {**ELSE** *algebraic function*} {**END**}
IF *condition* **ELSE** *algebraic function*} {**END**}
IF *condition* **THEN** *algebraic function* {**END**}

Any condition which evaluates to zero is considered false whilst those evaluating to 1 are considered true. If the condition is false and the **ELSE** clause is missing a null is returned. If the condition is true the **THEN** clause (if present) is taken. If it is not present a null is returned.

If an **END** is not specified the **ELSE** is paired off to the nearest previous **IF**. The **END** is used to complete the current **IF** and tie it to the associated **ELSE**. In the following example the word 'high' is printed against salaries greater than £14,000 and 'low' against the remainder

HIGH.LOW
001 A
002 0
003 High/Low
004
005
006
007
008 if N(SALARY) > "1400000" then "high" else "low"
009 L
010 10

```
:LIST STAFF SALARY SAL.HIGH

Page  1          staff       17:33:51 08 Apr 1995

STAFF.....        Salary       High/Low

001             15,500.00      high
002             13,250.00      low
003             11,350.00      low
004             12,900.00      low
005             15,500.00      high
006             15,400.00      high
010             14,550.00      high
007             10,000.00      low

[405] 8 items listed out of 8 items.
```

13.5.2 The B (Bridge) processing code

This processing code undertakes the task of maintaining the relationship between an attribute in one item and an item in the other. This could be where one file contains a list of item-ids of related records in another file such as in an order processing system or where an attribute in a related file needs to be updated, such as the total order value each time a new line of an order is added or amended. The general format of the bridge code is as follows:

B*file;attr1;attr2*{;{*attr3*;+/–}/**d**}

where

attr1 contains the attribute number of the attribute in the current item that contains the item id(s) of the item(s) in the 'bridged to' file. If the attribute is multi-valued, all items in the 'bridged to' file are updated

attr2 contains the attribute in the 'bridged to' item that is to be processed. Unless the + or – operators are used this attribute contains the item-id of the current item as a cross-reference to the current file

\+ or – adds to or subtracts from the value contained in *attr3* in the current item with the value contained in *attr2*. The reverse process takes place where the current item is being deleted

d allows for the current item to be deleted even if *attr1* is not null

The **B**ridge processing code maintains the cross-reference integrity between two files which previously took significant PICK BASIC code. Figure 13.8 gives examples of the use of this code.

Example 1

Assume we wish to correlate the orders received by customer. In the orders file, attribute 5 contains the customer number of the customer who placed the order and in the customer file attribute 1 is a multi-value list of orders placed by the customer. To get PICK to maintain this cross reference list automatically, we need to place a bridge correlative in the orders file. To do so we need to modify the file definition item held in the file dictionary (not the MD entry) and add the bridge code to attribute 8, the correlative attribute.

:ud order {or **:ed dict order order (d** }

```
dictionary-code      D
base                 27739
modulo ·             1
structure
retrieval-lock
update-lock
output-conversion
correlative          bcustomer;5;1
attribute-type       L
column-width         10
input-conversion
macro
output-macro
description
reallocation
hotkey.all
```

Adding an order whether using the Editor, Update Processor or a program, will place the item-id of the order in attribute 1 of the customer file as a multi-value list. Deleting an order will remove the item-id from the list. If you have a many-to-many relationship, such as trying to monitor the customers who order specific products, then you should place the bridge correlative on both files. In the above example this would involve adding the code **border;1;5** to attribute 8 of the file defining item of the customer file.

Example 2

Assume we wish to keep a running total of the quantity of a products ordered. We need to increase this figure each time an order line is raised and decrease this figure each time an order line is cancelled and deleted. On the order detail file we need a bridge correlative which adds the quantity ordered held in attribute 3 on the order line to the total ordered held in attribute 16 on the product file. The bridge code is once again placed in attribute 8 of the DICTIONARY record of the file defining item for the order line file. Assuming the product code on each order line is held in attribute 1 the bridge code would be **bproduct;1;16;3;+**

Figure 13.8 The Bridge processing code.

13.5.3 The C (Concatenate) processing code

The **C** code provides the means to concatenate attributes and literals together. It is a simple processing code to use and has the format:

C;*exp1* {*x exp2*}...
where

exp1	is the first of the attributes or literals in the concatenated string
exp2	is the second of the attributes or literals in the concatenated string and so on. In this processing code you cannot specify attributes by name, only by their position
x	is the character to be inserted between the attributes or literals. The reserved character is a semicolon which means no separation character is to be used and an asterisk will concatenate the item-id

Assume attribute 6 contains '0181' and attribute 7 contains '440 0906'

C;6;7 Concatenates the contents of attribute 6 with the contents of attribute 7
Result 0181440 0906

C;6-7 Concatenates the contents of attribute 6 with the contents of attribute 7, separated with a hyphen
Result 0181-440 0906

C;"BARNET";6-7 Concatenates the contents of attribute 6 with the contents of attribute 7, separated with a hyphen and prefixes the result with the word "BARNET"
Result BARNET 0181-440 0906

13.5.4 The CALL processing code

The **CALL** processing code is used to call a PICK BASIC subroutine from either the file defining item or attribute defining item (dictionary record). The general format is as follows:

CALL *subroutine*

where
subroutine is the name of a catalogued BASIC subroutine

When called from a file defining item the entire item is passed to the subroutine as a dynamic array and when called from an attribute defining item the value contained in the attribute is passed to the subroutine. The subroutine must therefore contain a parameter, even though one is not specified in the **CALL** processing code.

There are some rules to remember:

(1) When a subroutine is called from attribute 14 of the *file defining item* control is passed to the subroutine immediately after the Update Processor has been invoked but before the first item has been displayed.

(2) When a subroutine is called from attribute 14 of the *attribute defining item* control is passed to the subroutine immediately after input to the attribute.

(3) When a subroutine is called from attribute 8 of the *file defining item* control is passed to the subroutine immediately prior to the record being filed away. If the statement **INPUTERR** is executed within the subroutine the item will not be filed and control is returned to the Update Processor.

(4) When a subroutine is called from attribute 8 of the *attribute defining item* control is passed to the subroutine immediately prior to processing.

(5) When a subroutine is called from attribute 7 on either the file defining item or attribute defining item control is passed to the subroutine on output.

(6) The contents of the parameter passed to the subroutine can only be altered when the subroutine is called from attribute 14 (the input conversion code) of an attribute defining item.

The **ACCESS** function of PICK BASIC is described in detail in Section 15.20. To assist with examples of the **CALL** statement the syntax of the statement is included here. The syntax of the function is **ACCESS(***n***)** where *n* is a number in the range 1–24 whose values mean the following:

1 data file file variable.
2 dictionary file file variable.
3 item from the associated file as a dynamic array and contain null if the item is new.
4 item count (the number of items processed to the current point).
5 attribute count (the number of attributes processed to the current point).
6 value count (the number of values processed to the current point).
7 sub-value count (the number of sub-values processed to the current point).
8 detail line count (the number of lines processed to the current point).
9 break-on level counter (the number of break levels pushed to the current point).
10 the item-id.
11 the file name.
12 item delete flag. Returns 1 if the item is being deleted.
13 root variable.
14 returns current cursor column position in the Update Processor.
15 returns current cursor row position in the Update Processor.
16 new item flag. Returns 1 if item is new.
17 returns 1 if processing an input-conversion.
18 used in the input-conversion attribute of the file 'd-pointer' to specify which value of attribute 15 ('macro' attribute) to use.
19 returns the character which ended the last input, usually a [CR], **u**, etc.

20 item changed flag (0-item not changed, 1-item changed).

21 used from a PICK/BASIC subroutine called by UP to place characters in the UP command string. For example, access(21) = 'xe' in a subroutine called from the input-conversion causes the Update Processor to exit after the attribute calling the subroutine is re-entered. **BEWARE**: This function will overwrite any prestore previously set; any **p** will execute the value assigned to ACCESS(21).

22 spelling checker flag. Returns non-zero (usually 1) if the spelling checker is enabled, and 0 if it is not. Access(22) may be assigned a '1' in a subroutine called by the input conversion of a file defining item. Even if the spelling checker is disabled for the user session, this invokes the spell checker for the editing of this item or list of items. **NOTE**: the speller will only work on attributes with an attribute type of 'w'. Available in AP releases 5.2.5 and above.

23 Returns the calling environment. It returns
- 0 if the function was called from FlashBASIC or PICK/BASIC
- 1 if the function was called from a callx or from an index
- 2 if the function was called from the update processor (except for a callx or index)
- 3 if the function was called from ACCESS. Access(23) is available in AP releases 6.1.0 and higher only.

24 Returns the actual attribute number of the attribute definition.

ACCESS(3) and **ACCESS(10)** can be used to pass data both ways between a PICK/BASIC program and a data file. When either of these two statements appear on the right of the assignment (= sign), data is passed to the program. When they are used to the left of the assignment, data is passed from the program to the file. **ACCESS(3)** can only be updated from an input-conversion of a dictionary item. It cannot be updated as a conversion, correlative or in a 'd-pointer' input-conversion.

By way of an example (see Figure 13.9) let's use a personnel system in which information is to be entered into the file **STAFF** and the following tasks need to be addressed.

(1) The user **RJB** can input salary and grade details whilst all other users will not have these attributes presented to them. Each user view is held as a multi-value list in the MACRO attribute (attribute 15) of the file defining item and **ACCESS(18)** is set to which of these values is to be used.

(2) The office location code is to be validated to comprise one of just three codes only

L (London)
T (Telford)
S (Sheffield)

and after the code has been entered the town for the office is to be stored in the record. This is handled by a processing code on the input conversion of the attribute **LOCATION**.

(3) The NHI number is mandatory and must be nine characters. It is to be input without formatting characters. The nine characters are to be formatted and tested against the pattern 2A2N2N2N1A and formatted with hyphens between each section. This is handled by the **CALL** on the output conversion of the attribute **NHI.NUMBER**.

(4) No records can be deleted from the **STAFF** file. This is checked from a **CALL** processing code on the correlative attribute (attribute 8) of the file defining item.

```
             STAFF
dictionary-code     D
base                29739
modulo              1
structure
retrieval-lock
update-lock
output-conversion
correlative         call staff.check
attribute-type      L
column-width        10
input-conversion    call initiate.staff
macro           name address phone dob location nhi
                name address phone dob location nhi salary grade
output-macro
description
reallocation
hotkey.all


                        LOCATION          NHI.NUMBER
dictionary-code            A                 A
attribute-count            5                 12
substitute-header          Location          NHI Number
structure
output-conversion                            call format.nhi
correlative
attribute-type             R                 L
column-width               1                 14
input-conversion           call format.location
macro
output-macro
description
hotkey.all


subroutine initiate.staff (record)
if system(29) then system.type = 3 else system.type = 2 ;*check to
see whether R83 or AP in use as
      * the output from WHO is different
execute "who" capturing cap returning ret
user=field(cap," ",system.type)
if oconv(user,"mcu") = "RJB" then
   access(18) = 2
end else
   access(18) = 1
end
return
```

Figure 13.9 The use of the **CALL** processing code.

```
subroutine format.location(location)
record=access(3)
location=item<5>
begin case
   case oconv(location,"mcu") = "L"; location="London"
   case oconv(location,"mcu") = "T"; location="Telford"
   case oconv(location,"mcu") = "S"; location="Sheffield"
   case 1; location = ""
   inputerr "location code incorrect. Must be L, T or S"
   goto 999
end case
   item<5>=""
   access(3)=record
999   return


subroutine format.nhi(nhi)
item=access(3)
nhi=item<6>
if nhi matches "2A2N2N2N1A"then
   nhi=oconv(nhi,"mr(#2-#2-#2-#2-#1)
end else
   inputerr "Enter the NHI number as 9 characters in the format 2A2N2N2N1A
without hyphens"
    goto 999
end
999 return


subroutine staff.check (record)
if access(12) then inputerr "no items can be deleted from this file"
return
```

Figure 13.9 *Continued*

13.5.5 The CALLX processing code

The **CALLX** processing code is only valid on attribute 8 (the correlative attribute) of a file defining item and is called when an item in that file is updated regardless of how the updating is processed. Hence while **CALL** only worked with the Update Processor, **CALLX** works with any process, whether a TCL command, within the Editor, the Update processor or a BASIC program.

If a routine writes, deletes or modifies an item in a file using a **CALLX** subroutine to validate the data and the validation fails, the item will not be written to the file. Use **INPUTERR** to indicate error conditions.

13.5.6 The CU (Character Update) processing code

This is only valid on the input conversion attribute (attribute 14) and allows data with either an output conversion code (in attribute 7) or a correlative code (in attribute 8) to be changed character by character when the record is processed with the Update Processor. If **CU** is not specified the existing data is erased and nulled first.

The code is **only** required when there is another conversion code present, typically where the attribute is a date field and contains a **D** type conversion code.

13.5.7 The D (DATE) processing code

The date conversion code provides the means of converting the date, held on the disk in internal format, to a variety of output formats. Dates are stored on the disk in internal format, this being the number of days since 31 December 1967. If the date being stored is earlier than this date, it is held as a negative number. This compact way of storing dates not only saves space but enables arithmetic and sorting on any date field. The general format of the **D** conversion code is:

D{*yr*}{xm}{o}

where

yr	is the number of digits in the year (0, 1, 2, 3 or 4). The default is 4
x	any single non-numeric character specifying the delimiter between fields for group extraction. If omitted a space is assumed
m	specifies the number of fields to skip for group extraction
o	either the special single non-numeric character that separates the day, month and year on output, or a special code being one of the following:

D	numeric day of the month (1-31)
F	full external date with alphabetic month, day of month and 4 digit year
I	typically used in attribute 8 (processing code) to convert an external date to internal form in the pre-processing stage of an ACCESS sentence
J	julian day of the year (1-366)
M	numeric month number (1-12)
MA	alphabetic month
Q	numeric quarter (1-4)
W	numeric day of the week
Y	for year (default is 4 digits)

The following are examples of the conversion of the date 7th January 1995 held internally as 9869.

Conversion	*Format displayed*	*Comments*
D	07 Jan 1995	
D/	07/01/1995	
D-	07-01-95	
D0	07 Jan	

Conversion	*Format displayed*	*Comments*
D0/	07/01	
D2/	07/01/95	
D2+	07+01+95	Any character can be the delimiter
DD	07	Day number
DWA	Saturday	Alphabetic day
DM	01	Month number
DMA	January	Alphabetic month
DY	1995	
D2Y	95	
DQ	1	Quarter number

13.5.8 The F (Function) processing code

The **F** processing code is a very powerful processing code, which enables arithmetic functions to be performed. It encompasses all of the features of the **A** processing code and offers a great deal more. All its operations are performed on the last two entries in a push-down stack and it is access to this stack that expands its power over the **A** processing code.

To its detriment calculations must be specified in Reverse Polish notation, a notation not too many people are familiar with! This makes it far more difficult to understand, to apply and to maintain and for this reason the **A** processing code was introduced. Another disadvantage of the **F** processing code is that it cannot use dictionary names.

In Reverse Polish notation, as an attribute number, constant or character string are encountered they are pushed onto the top of the stack, pushing all the other values on the stack down by one. When an operator is encountered, the specified operation is performed on the top one or two entries on the stack (usually the top two), these operands are removed from the stack and the result placed at the top of the stack. When all the operations have been performed, the result is what is at the top of the stack.

Elements of an **F** processing code are scanned from left to right and like the **A** processing code, its general format is quite straightforward, but the processing code itself can be extremely complex.

F;*element*{;*element*}...

where
element is an operand or operator separated by a semicolon

Since the **F** processing code performs very similar operations to that of the **A** processing code many of the operands, operators and relational operators are the same between the two types of processing code. Indeed all **A** processing codes are translated to **F** processing codes prior to processing and the **Y** option at the end of your ACCESS statement will produce the 'compiled' string which is then processed by ACCESS and includes all arithmetic operations as **F** processing codes.

To demonstrate the workings of the stack, Figure 13.10 shows the processing involved in multiplying the sum of 4 and 5 by 3 (i.e. (4+5)*3). In an **F** processing code, constants are preceded with the letter **C**.

The **F** processing code **F**; **C3;C4;C5;+;***

Steps →	1	2	3	4	5
Value processed →	**C3**	**C4**	**C5**	+	*
Stack level 1	3	4	5	9	27 ← The result
Stack level 2		3	4	3	
Stack level 3			3		
Stack level 4 ↓					

Figure 13.10 Processing an **F** processing code using the stack.

Operands

The following list shows the operands available to you and gives some examples of their use:

*N***R** where *N* is an attribute number and **R** is a 'repeat' function which specifies that the first value of an attribute is to be used repeatedly when using it against a multi-value or sub-value. Hence **F;2;3;+** would add together the contents of attribute 2 and attribute 3

The **R** option is used when working with multi-values. If both attributes are multi-valued, then the **F** processing code works with corresponding values within each attribute. Hence **F;2;3;*** multiplies the first value in attribute 2 with the first value in attribute 3, then it multiplies the second value in attribute 2 with the second value in attribute 3 and so on. However, what happens if one of the attributes is multi-valued and the other is not. In this case you need to *repeat* the use of one attribute against each multi-value of the other. Hence if attribute 2 is not multi-valued the same expression would be given by the code **F;2R;3;***

"string" a literal string. Hence **F;"Interests ";5;:** would concatenate the word **Interests** in front of the contents of attribute 5

C*n* where *n* is a number. **F;C2;C3;+** adds together 2 and 3 with a result of 5

D the system date in internal form

LPV Load previous value

NB The break-level counter; it is zero at detail time and increases by one for each break level encountered. It is 255 for the grand total. Use in attribute 7 only

ND The detail line counter; it is 1 at detail time and is only valid at break time. Use in attribute 7 only

NI The item counter; it is zero during select time and only active during the output stage. Can be used in attribute 7 or 8

NS The secondary value counter; it is equal to 1 for the total line. Use in attribute 8 only

NV The value counter; it is equal to 1 for the total line. Use in attribute 8 only

T The system time in internal format

Operators

Many of the operators in **F** processing codes are the same as those for **A** processing codes. Hence the operators for concatenation, addition, subtraction, multiplication and division, respectively :,+, –, * and /, can be used in calculations although it should be noted that the result of a division will always return an integer result. It is up to you to multiply numbers where necessary to ensure you are then able to descale them to give you the required number of decimal positions. To assist you, the multiplication operator (*) can have a descaling factor placed after it. Hence **F;"100";"20";*2** would produce the result 200 (not 2000), because the descaling factor is one less than the number stated!

The full list of operators is as follows:

(*conv*) where *conv* is any valid ACCESS conversion code. If it appears on its own it is applied to the top element on the stack, otherwise it can appear immediately following an attribute number which forces the conversion to be applied to the contents of the attribute prior to it being moved to the stack. Hence **F;D;3;-;(D2/)** will subtract the contents of attribute 3 from today's date and convert the result to a date in the format DD/MM/YY

*{*n*} Multiplies stack level 1 by stack level 2. The optional *n* is used to descale the result by 10 to the power of (*n*-1)

/	Divides stack level 2 by stack level 1, and returns result to stack level 1. Be aware that the results of division operations are rounded down. For example **F;C11;C3;/** would provide the result 3 in stack level 1
R	This is the same as / except the remainder of the division is placed on stack level 1. Hence **F;C11;C3;R** would place 2 in stack level 1
+	Adds the top two entries in the stack and returns the sum to stack level 1
–	Subtracts stack level 1 from stack level 2 and returns the result to stack level 1
:	Concatenates the contents of stack level 1 to the end of the contents of stack level 2 and places the result in stack level 1
[ ]	Extracts a substring from string value in stack level 3, using stack level 2 as the starting character position and stack level 1 as the number of characters to extract. The result is placed in stack level 1. Hence **F;"ABCDEFGH";C3;C4[ ]** would place the characters **CDEF** in stack level 1
S	Adds together the multi-values in stack level 1 (if any) and returns the sum to stack level 1
_	The underscore operator exchanges the top two positions in the stack, so stack level 2 is placed in stack level 1 and stack level 1 is placed in stack level 2
P	Pushes the top stack value back on the stack, resulting in the same value in stack level 1 and stack level 2

Relational operators

The **F** processing code can also use the relational operators, greater than (>), less than (<), equal to (=), not equal to (£), greater than or equal to (>=), less than or equal to (<=). Where these are used, each operator takes two expressions as operands and the result evaluates to 1 if the relationship is true and 0 if the relationship is false. The result, either a 1 or 0 is placed on the top of the stack at stack level 1. All comparisons take place between stack level 1 and stack level 2 with the expression being:

stack level 1 *relational operator* stack level 2

Hence a 1 (or true) condition will be returned to stack level 1 where:

=	stack level 1 equals stack level 2
£	stack level 1 is not equal to stack level 2

>	stack level 1 is greater than stack level 2
<	stack level 1 is less than stack level 2
>=	stack level 1 is greater than or equal to stack level 2
<=	stack level 1 is less than or equal to stack level 2

The IF..THEN..ELSE *condition*

The **IF..THEN..ELSE** condition is available to handle complex condition. The general format is as follows:

IF *condition* **THEN** *f.processing code* {**ELSE** *f.processing code*} {**END**}
IF *condition* **ELSE** *f.processing code*} {**END**}
IF *condition* **THEN** *f.processing code* {**END**}

Any condition which evaluates to zero is considered false whilst those evaluating to 1 are considered true. If the condition is false and the **ELSE** clause is missing, a null is returned. If the condition is true the **THEN** clause (if present) is taken. If it is not present a null is returned.

If an **END** is not specified the **ELSE** is paired off to the nearest previous **IF**. The **END** is used to complete the current **IF** and tie it to the associated **ELSE**.

Branching

A facility of **F** codes which does not exist in **A** codes is the concept of branching. It is possible to label stack entries and then use the branch option to use a particular stack entry. The branch options available are:

~label	where *label* is the label name containing any ASCII character with the exception of the semi-colon
J *~label*	branches to the stack entry with the label *label*
JF *~label*	if the top stack entry is zero, branch to the specified *label*
JT *~label*	branch to the specified *label* if the top stack entry is not zero

As an example if we run the **IF..THEN..ELSE** condition given in the earlier section on **A** processing codes an switch on the **Y** option in the ACCESS processor it will convert the condition to an **F** processing code using the branch options. Figure 13.11 shows this in operation.

How to write F *processing codes*

Whilst at first glance **F** processing codes look quite daunting, there are some simple rules that will help you build them. However it is generally much easier to write **A** processing codes, particularly as these can contain parenthesis to group together functions in a logical way. However if you fancy a challenge use

The dictionary item containing the **IF..THEN..ELSE** condition

HIGH.LOW
001 A
002 0
003 High/Low
004
005
006
007
008 if N(SALARY) > "1400000" then "high" else "low"
009 L
010 10

The ACCESS statement

:list staff salary high.low (y

The output from the ACCESS processor with the **Y** option

```
Dstaff^^^^L^10^_
A Salary^6^mr2,^^R^10^_
A Salary^0^^F;6;"1400000";<;JF %01;"high";J %02;~%01 "low";~%02^R^10^_
```

The resulting report when the **Y** option is switched off

```
:LIST STAFF SALARY SAL.HIGH

Page   1        staff                              17:33:51 08 Apr 1995

STAFF.....       Salary    High/Low

001           15,500.00    high
002           13,250.00    low
003           11,350.00    low
004           12,900.00    low
005           15,500.00    high
006           15,400.00    high
010           14,550.00    high
007           10,000.00    low

[405] 8 items listed out of 8 items.
```

Figure 13.11 The use of branches in **F** processing codes.

F processing codes or if you wish to cheat as I did in some of the above examples, write the **A** processing code first and let ACCESS (with the **Y** option) do the work for you!

To write an **F** processing code first write down the expression you are trying to achieve. Then for each step take each logical group and place its operator to the right of the second operand and then perform the same step within each logical group. Then write up the result with the correct syntax.

As an example with the expression **(3*8)/(12-6)** which results in 4 (24/6) after having written down what you want to achieve move the / to the end of the second operand where each bracketed group is deemed an operand. This gives **(3*8) (12-6)** / and so we now have to do the same to each bracketed group, leading to **3 8 * 12 6 - /** which produces the processing code **F;C3;C8;*;C12;C6;-;/**.

13.5.9 The G (Group extraction) processing code

Group extraction enables the extraction of parts of a character string containing delimiters. The delimiter used in the group extraction syntax can be any character, including space, provided it is not a number, a minus sign or one of the reserved special characters used to define the attribute mark, the value mark or subvalue mark. The general format of the **G** processing code is:

G{*n*}*xm*

where

n	is the number of groups to skip. If omitted zero is assumed
x	any single non-numeric character defining the delimiter, provided it is not a number, minus sign or a reserved character
m	a number signifying the number of contiguous groups to be extracted

In this context therefore it is possible to extract one or a number of words from a sentence, in which case the delimiter is obviously a space. Figure 13.12 shows how a group extraction could be used to extract the first name and surname from a file whose names are held in attribute 1 in the format 'surname, first name', where the delimiter is a comma. Notice that in this instance we create new dictionary items where the attribute position (amc) is **not** zero, but takes the position of the attribute it redefines, in this example an attribute position of 1.

Having done this it may be useful to be able to concatenate these two dictionary items together. In order to concatenate the first name onto the surname, we need to concatenate the dictionary items FORENAME and SURNAME which can only be done by specifying them by name. This ensures that any conversion or processing code, in this case the **G** processing code, is applied before the data is retrieved from disk. Since it is not possible to use dictionary names with **C** (concatenate) processing code it is necessary to concatenate them together within the **A** processing code. This is achieved by defining a new dictionary item, a further redefinition of the name attribute and

```
NAME              FORENAME          SURNAME
001 A             001 A             001 A
002 1             002 1             002 1   <--- the same attribute
003 Name          003 Name          003 Name     position as that
004               004               004          of NAME, the one
005               005               005          it redefines
006               006               006
007               007               007
008               008 G1,1          008 G,1
009 L             009 L             009 L
010 20            010 20            010 20
```

Assuming the data held on file for NAME was:

DIXON,GEORGE
LEA,SHAUN
PIKE,JOHN
HARLOW,MICHAEL
MORRIS,JIM
BRIGHT,IAN
RILEY,JULIE

Then defining the dictionary items FORENAME and SURNAME would enable the data to be listed showing the forename and surname separately as follows:

:list staff forename surname

```
Page 1          staff                                  18:05:43 08 Apr 1995

staff.....   First Name          Surname

001          GEORGE              DIXON
002          SHAUN               LEA
003          JOHN                PIKE
004          MICHAEL             HARLOW
005          JIM                 MORRIS
006          IAN                 BRIGHT
010          JULIE               RILEY
007

[405] 8 items listed out of 8 items.
```

Figure 13.12 Using the **G** group extract processing code.

hence with an attribute position (amc) of 1, containing the following arithmetic processing code in attribute 8.

A;N(FIRSTNAME):" ":N(SURNAME)

Equally we could have used the **F** processing code:

F;1(G1,1);" ";:;1(G,1);:

Figure 13.13 shows the creation of a new dictionary item to concatenate these tow parts of the name together and shows the output from its use.

```
FULL.NAME
01 A
02 1
03 Full name
04
05
06
07
08 a;n(forename):" ":n(surname)
09 L
10 30
```

:list staff full.name

```
Page  1         staff                          18:08:09 08 Apr 1995

staff.....    Full name....................

001           GEORGE DIXON
002           SHAUN LEA
003           JOHN PIKE
004           MICHAEL HARLOW
005           JIM MORRIS
006           IAN BRIGHT
010           JULIE RILEY
007

[405] 8 items listed out of 8 items.
```

Figure 13.13 Concatenating group extracted data.

It is worth reflecting for a moment what has been achieved in doing all this. The most important thing to understand is that the data has been stored once only in the format 'Surname, First name'. Through the group extraction using the **G** processing code we have been able to extract at will the first names and surnames and have been able to concatenate them together. This concatenation, using the arithmetic processing code, enables us to refer to the names in the usual form, with the surname appearing after the first name. All of these new dictionary definitions were defined as synonyms to the original dictionary definition item, being given, as their attribute position, that allocated to the original attribute, i.e. position 1. All of which I am sure you will agree is really clever. It demonstrates the power and flexibility provided by this unique database system and further explains why people once exposed to the PICK database soon become won over by it!

13.5.10 The I (Index) processing code

In it's simplest form the letter **i** is placed in the input conversion attribute (attribute 14) of the attribute definition item. This indicates the existence of an index and enables 'cruising' through the items in the file either with **f** (control/f) to cruise forwards of **d** to cruise backwards. The same commands are used to peruse the TCL stack when at the TCL prompt.

13.5.11 The I*fid* (Index) processing code

This is another version of the index processing code in which the **I** code is suffixed with the frame number of the root node of the index. It is built by PICK from the **CREATE-INDEX** function run at TCL and the **I***fid* will automatically be placed in attribute 8 of the file definition item as shown below:

```
:ED DICT STAFF STAFF (D
top
.p
001 D
002 82646
003 1
004
005
006
007
008 I27647a1
009 L
010 10
```

13.5.12 The I*file.ref* (Index) processing code

This is another version of the **I** processing code which is used as an input conversion (attribute 14) in an attribute definition item. It indicates the contents of the attribute are based upon data which is indexed in another file. In our earlier examples we saw how the **STAFF** file contained a department code which had to be a code on the **DEPT** file. In entering new records in the **STAFF** file it may be useful to scan through the records in the **DEPT** file and carry out searches for specific records. We can do this by putting an **I***file.ref* processing code in attribute 14 of the attribute definition item and adding a **T***file* translation code (see section 13.5.26) in attribute 8 as shown below:

```
:ed dict staff dept
top
.p
001 A
002 4
003 Dept
004
005
006
007
008 tdept;x;;1
009 R
010 3
011
012
013
014 idept;a1
```

13.5.13 The ID (assign ID) processing code

This processing code is used specifically by the Update Processor to create new item-ids. The general format of the code which is only valid in attribute 8 of the file defining item is

> **id**{*code*}
>
> where
>
> *code* is a code to indicate how the id is to be constructed. This can be an **A** processing code, a number (which is the starting number for item-ids) or **T** in which case the item-id comprises the concatenation of the internal date and time (in seconds). Should an item be created at exactly the same second as another it will have a unique alphabetic character (starting at **A**) appended to it.

If no code is specified, the item is created using the current date concatenated with a system wide sequence number.

13.5.14 The L (Length) processing code

The **L** code processing code is used test the length of data and take the appropriate action. The general format is

> **L**{*length*{,max.length}
>
> where
>
> *length* indicates that data will only be output if it is exactly the length specified by *length*. Anything longer or shorter will be output as a null. If *length* is specified as zero, then the length of the data (in characters) is displayed instead.
>
> *max.length* indicates that data whose length falls between that specified by *length* and *max.length* will be output. Anything longer or shorter will be output as a null.

Figure 13.14 gives examples of the use of this code, which can either be placed in attribute 7 or attribute 8.

As you can see, with **L5** it only lists the forename where the length is exactly five characters, whereas a code of **L1,5** lists all names whose length is up to and including five characters long. In the examples in 13.14 the processing code was alternatively used in attribute 7 and 8. In certain instances the

```
FNAME               FNAME1                 FNAME2
001 A               001 A                  001 A
002 1               002 1                  002 1
003 Name            003 Name               003 Name
004                 004                    004
005                 005                    005
006                 006                    006
007 L5              007                    007 L0
008 G1,1            008 G1,1]L1,5          008 G1,1
009 L               009 L                  009 L
010 20              010 20                 010 20
:LIST STAFF FNAME FNAME1 FNAME2
Page  1        STAFF                              18:15:50 08 Apr 1995

STAFF..... First Name        First Name          First Name

001                                               6
002          SHAUN             SHAUN              5
003                            JOHN               4
004                                               7
005                            JIM                3
006                            IAN                3
010          JULIE             JULIE              5
007

[405] 8 items listed out of 8 items.
```

Figure 13.14 The **L** processing code.

location of the code is extremely important as those in attribute 8 are use in selections, sorts, totals, etc., whilst those in attribute 7 just modify the format of the data on output. In this case as you can see, it does not matter which attribute contains the code.

It is possible to put more than one processing code on the same line and each should be separated by a value mark (ctrl/])]. The dictionary definition FNAME1 shows an example of this,

13.5.15 The MC (Mask Character) conversion code

There are a variety of character conversion codes that can be applied to convert your physical data to different output form. The format of this processing code is as follows:

> **MC**{*/*}*code*
>
> where
>
> *code* is one of the conversion codes. Multiple codes can be used and each must be delimited with a value mark (ctrl/]) **]**.

There are conversion codes which will show strings in upper, lower or upper and lower case. Some of the conversion codes will remove the numbers from an alphanumeric string of characters, others will remove the alphabetic characters. All of these 'masks' are applied to the physical data on output only. They do *not* affect or change what is held on disk. The conversion codes are shown in Table 13.4 and should be edited into attribute 7 of the dictionary definition item.

As can be seen from this table, the conversion code of **MCT** is extremely valuable for displaying names and addresses for mailing, when no consistent form of input has been used. It only has one drawback in that it will not print the Scottish 'Mc...' properly, so 'McBride' comes out as 'Mcbride'. The only way to overcome this is to put a space between 'Mc' and 'Bride' when keying in data, or hold the surname as two individual components, using the **MCT** conversion on both and then concatenating them together.

Table 13.4 The MC conversion codes.

Code	*Description*
MC/A	Removes all alphabetic characters from a string
MCA	Retrieves only alphabetic characters from a string
MC/AN	Removes all alphabetic and numeric characters from a string
MCAN	Retrieves only alphabetic and numeric characters from a string
MC/N	Removes all numeric characters from a string
MCN	Retrieves only numeric characters from a string
MCDX	Converts all decimal numbers to their hexadecimal equivalent
MCL	Converts all characters in a string to lower case
MCP	Replaces all non-printable characters in a string to full stops
MCS	Capitalizes the first word after each full stop
MCT	Capitalizes the first letter of each word
MCU	Converts all characters to upper case
MCXD	Converts all hexadecimal characters to their decimal equivalent

Data on disk	*Code*	*Output displayed*
John Pike is 36	MCU	JOHN PIKE IS 36
JOHN PIKE IS 36	MCL	john pike is 36
John Pike is 36	MCA	JohnPikeis
John PIKE iS 36	MCN	36
JOHN PikE	MCT	John Pike

13.5.16 The MD, ML and MR (Mask Decimal) conversion codes

Mask conversion codes are used to carry out the formatting of alphabetic or numeric strings. The general format of the conversion code, which is placed in attribute 7 of the dictionary definition item, is as follows:

M{*just*}{{*m*}{*n*}}{*Z*}{,}{*sign*){$}{*format string*}

where

just	is the justification code, where **L** indicates the data should be left-justified **R** indicates the data should be right-justified **D** indicates the data should be right-justified (identical to **R**)
m	is the number of decimal places (0–9). When omitted defaults to zero
n	is the scaling factor to be applied. To descale by 10 set to 1; to descale by 100 this should be set to 2; and so on. Numbers are rounded up
Z	suppresses leading zeros
,	inserts comma in every thousands position
sign	indicates how negative numbers are to be treated. These further editing symbols can be one of the following **C** means follow negative numbers by CR **D** means follow positive numbers by DR **E** causes negative numbers to be enclosed in pointed brackets **M** negative numbers are followed by a minus sign **N** causes the minus sign to be suppressed
$	causes a $ sign to be appended to the start of the number. Some implementations also support the pound sign.
format.string	the format string may be any combination of literals or one of the following special 'fill' characters **£***n* displays data in a field of *n* spaces %*n* displays data in a field of *n* zeros **n* displays data in a field of *n* asterisks (the fill character can

The two conversion codes **MD** and **MR** are identical and carry out conversions of numbers to decimal numbers with right justification of the result. The **ML** conversion code also carries out decimal conversion but with left justification. Numbers are stored on the database as numbers without any decimal point or indication of scaling. The **MD**, **ML** and **MR** codes indicate not only the scaling and justification to be applied, but also enable commas to be placed to represent thousands, millions and so on. These codes also allow other editing characters to be included, such as CR and DR.

Numbers are handled through this conversion code in exactly the same way as they are handled in BASIC (see Section 15.4.4). Table 13.5 gives examples of these mask conversion codes which should be placed in attribute 7 of the dictionary definition item.

Table 13.5 Examples of MD, ML and MR mask codes.

Data on disk	*Conversion code applied*	*Result*	
123456	MR2	1234.56	
123456	MD2	1234.56	
123456	MR26	0.12	← rounded
123456	MR24	12.35	← (rounded)
123456	MR2,	1,234.56	
-123456	MR2,E	<1,234.56>	
-123456	MR46,C$	$12.3456CR	
123456	MR2(%8)	01234.56	
123456	MR2(*9)	**1234.56	
123456	MR(###-##-##-#)		
or	MR(3#-2#-2#-#)	1-23-45-6	
123456	ML(###-##-##-#)	123-45-6 -	
Roger	MR2	Rog.er	

13.5.17 The MI (Must Input) processing code

This is used as an input conversion code (in attribute 14) and prevents an item processed by the Update Processor from being filed if any attribute defined with a **mi** code is null.

13.5.18 The MS (Mask alter Sort) processing code

The **MS** processing code indicates that data in this attribute is to be sorted into some sequence other than the standard ASCII sequence. It is only meaningful on an attribute used in the sort criteria of an ACCESS statement and if used can **only** be used in attribute 8 (the correlative attribute).

The required sequence must be specified by an item called **SEQ** held in the **messages** file (**ERRMSG** in R83).

13.5.19 The MT (Mask Time) processing code

The time of day is held on the system as a number of seconds since midnight. The **MT** conversion code converts this number to a time of day, optionally displaying this using the 24-hour clock system. The general format is:

> **MT**{{*H*}{*S*}}
>
> where
>
> *H* if present, specifies use of the 12-hour clock
> *S* if present, specifies that the number of seconds is to be displayed

Examples of this conversion code follow:

Value on disk	*code*	*Conversion Result*
53600	MTHS	02:53:20PM
53600	MTH	02:53PM
53600	MT	14:53
53600	MTS	14:53:20

13.5.20 The MX and MY (Hexadecimal) conversion codes

The **MX** code enables character strings to be converted to hexadecimal characters and the **MY** code reverses the process. Although not greatly used, it can be helpful for specialized work, and for finding the non-printable characters in a data string. It is simple to use and represented by placing the code **MX** or **MY** in attribute 7 of the dictionary definition item.

13.5.21 The O (ascending order) processing code

This code is used to sort the values in an attribute in ascending order. Whilst this can be used as a correlative (in attribute 8) of an attribute defining item it will cause the screen to refresh on each value added. For this reason the code is best placed in attribute 8 of the file defining item which will only sort the values in sequence once the item is filed. The format of this processing code is:

> **O**{;}{*attr.no*}{*attr.no1*}....
>
> where
>
> *attr.no* is the attribute number containing values to be sorted
> *attr.no1* is the attribute number containing values to be sorted

13.5.22 The P (Pattern matching) processing code

The **P** code processing code enables data to be restricted to that which matches a specific pattern of characters. As an input conversion (in attribute 14) this code will validate data input via the Update Processor otherwise this code is valid in attribute 7 as an output conversion. The general format being:

> **P**(*pattern*){;(*pattern*)}....
>
> where
>
> *pattern* is a series of characters denoting the pattern match

The characters that can be tested for are:

A	for alphabetic
N	for numeric
X	for alphanumeric
"abc"	a literal string tests for an exact match to the literal string

The first three options (A, N and X) can have a number placed before them to indicate the number of characters. Hence 2N means to two numeric characters and 4A four alphabetic characters. Combinations of alphabetic, numeric, alphanumeric and literals can be mixed together in the pattern code. Pattern codes are enclosed in parentheses with multiple tests separated by a semicolon.

Hence P(4N-3N-4N) tests for a string of four numbers, followed by a hyphen, followed by three numbers, followed by a hyphen, followed by four numbers. Using this pattern test 0171-387-9233 would pass and 061-334 8798 would fail the test, so 0171-387-9233 would be printed and a null value output for the other.

To allow combination testing a semicolon is used. Hence to allow either the pattern of numbers 2N-33N-4N or 6A6N, i.e. nine numbers broken into three groups separated with a comma, or six alphabetic characters followed by six numbers, use the notation **P(2N-3N-4N);(6A6N)**.

If the pattern type is preceded by the number 0 such as **P(0N)** the length of the data being tested is irrelevant. In this example it means output the data providing it is totally numeric or null. The codes **P(0A)** and **P(0X)** work the same way but for alphabetic and alphanumeric characters respectively.

13.5.23 The R (Range) processing code

The **R** processing code enables data that is displayed to be restricted to that which falls within a specific range of values. The general format of the processing code is:

R*min,max*{;*min,max*}

where

min	the minimum value of the range
max	the maximum value of the range

Multiple ranges can be specified each of which is separated with a semicolon. Hence **R10,50** will test the data to be in the range 10 to 50 inclusive. A range code of **R10,50;100,150** will print data which is in the range 10 to 50 inclusive or 100 to 150 inclusive. Any data found outside these ranges will have a null value sent to the ACCESS processor and hence will be shown as blank. It is important to note that multiple ranges must be in ascending sequence. If this code is used as an input conversion (attribute 14), data entered with the Update Processor can be validated as being within the appropriate range(s).

It is important to specify the lower range value first, so remember with negative numbers that –100 is a lower number than –10.

13.5.24 The S (Substitution) processing code

The substitution processing code enables data to be substituted if a null or zero value is found. The data substituted can either be the contents of another attribute or a literal string. The general format of the code is as follows:

S;*param1*;*param2*

where

param1	is either an asterisk (*), attribute number or literal string enclosed in quotes to be used as substitute text if the attribute being tested **is not** null or zero
param2	is either an attribute number or literal string enclosed in quotes to be substituted if the attribute being tested **is** null or zero

In the **S** processing code, two substitution parameters are used, one for when a null or zero is encountered, and one for when it is not. For example **S;2;"NIL PAID"** will print the words NIL PAID if the data encountered is null or zero, otherwise it will print the contents of attribute 2. The attribute being tested is the attribute position of the dictionary item containing the **S** processing code.

An asterisk can be used as the first parameter to print out the original value if it is not null or zero.

13.5.25 The T (Text extraction) processing code

This is used to extract a specified number of characters from a string. The general format is

T{*start.pos,*}*length*

where

start.pos	the number of characters from the left-hand end of the string from which extraction is to commence
length	the number of characters to extract

Hence **T3,4** always takes the first four characters after the first three starting at the leftmost character in the string. If this were applied to the string ABC1234 it would extract 1234.

If the first parameter denoting start position is omitted, then extraction starts from the first character of the string, either from the right or left hand end dependent on the justification in attribute 9 of this dictionary definition item. If attribute 9 is L, counting starts from the left. If it is R, counting starts from the right.

13.5.26 The Tfile (Translation) processing code

This processing code enables powerful look-up facilities across data files and minimizes the duplication of data. For example, in a personnel system we would hold details of our staff and the departments they work in. Rather than have the description of the department held on each staff record, it is far better to put a department code on the record to look up the description from a separately maintained file. In such a situation if a department changes its title only the department file is affected. If the department name were held on *every* individual staff record, it would be necessary to identify and change that department description on all affected staff records!
The format of this command is shown at the top of page 274.

To demonstrate the use of this processing code, we will assume that there are three files which are linked together: the **STAFF** file, which contains details of all personnel, the **DEPT** file which contains information about departments and the **CC** file which contains details of cost centres. The format of these files is as given in Table 13.6. The **STAFF** and **DEPT** files contain a code linking it to the next in the chain.

As can be seen from Table 13.6, the department code held on each staff record is what can be used to find the correct department record on the department file. The department file contains a cost centre code which can be used to

T{DICT}*file*;*sc*{*n*};*i-amc*;*o-amc*{;*b-amc*}

where

- DICT — is when the dictionary file is used as the look-up file
- *file* — is the name of the look-up file
- *sc* — is a subcode denoting the action to be taken if the record being looked up does not exist:
  - **C** returns the item-id (the look-up key)
  - **I** inputs verify only
  - **O** outputs verify only
  - **V** it must exist, otherwise abort
  - **X** returns a null value
- *n* — optional value mark count. If this is **N** it returns the value mark count in the target, an * takes the same value mark count as the source, otherwise it contains the value number of the value whose contents are to be returned
- *i-amc* — the attribute number used for input translation. It is not used by ACCESS and may be null or the same as the *o-amc*
- *o-amc* — the attribute number used for output translation being the attribute whose value is to be passed as the translated value
- *b-amc* — the attribute number whose value is to be used in break-on and total lines in place of *o-amc*

Table 13.6 File layouts showing linked files.

	← *File names* →		
Attribute number	**STAFF**	**DEPT**	**CC**
0	Staff no.	Dept. code	Cost centre code
1	Name	Dept. description	Cost centre description
2	Address	Annual budget	Annual budget
3	Tel Number	Cost centre code →	
4	Dept. code →		

look up the correct cost centre record. These codes are the 'links' that enable ***any*** attribute of the linked file to be made accessible to the other. This only works in a 'forward' direction. In other words since there is a department code in the **STAFF** file, all attributes from the **DEPT** file can be accessed from the **STAFF** file, but ***not*** the other way round.

These file translations are performed by creating a dictionary synonym of the attribute containing the data that will be used for the file translation. It is important to note that the attribute position of the synonym *must* be the same as that of the look-up data and the synonym contains the T-file code. So, to be able to refer to the department description on the **STAFF** file, we would create a synonym on the **STAFF** file with the same attribute position as the department code, i.e. 4, and to be able to reference the cost centre description on the **CC** file, we would create a synonym on the **DEPT** file whose attributes position (AMC) would be 3. Each of these synonyms would contain a Tfile processing code. This would provide the situation illustrated in Table 13.7.

Table 13.7 The Tfile processing code.

	← *File names* →		
Attribute number	**STAFF**	**DEPT**	**CC**
0	Staff no.	→ Dept. code	→ Cost centre code
1	Name	Dept. description	Cost centre description
2	Address	Annual budget	Annual budget
3	Tel Number	Cost centre code	
3		Cost centre desc. →	
4	Dept. code		
4	Dept. description →		

```
DEPT.DESC
001 A
002 4
003 Description
004
005
006
007
008 TDEPT;X;;1  <-
009 L
010 30
```

Return the contents of attribute 1 on the file **DEPT** using the contents of attribute 4 as the key to the **DEPT** file

```
CC.DESC
001 A
002 3
003 Description
004
005
006
007
008 TCC;X;;1  <-
009 L
010 30
```

Return the contents of attribute 1 on the file **CC** using the contents of attribute 3 as the key to the **CC** file

In both cases in Table 13.7 the processing code would use the contents of the appropriate attribute of each record as the key to access the file name contained in the Tfile processing code. If the record was found, it would return the contents of attribute 1 from the target file, i.e. the description. If the record was not found it would return a null value (as a result of the **X** in the middle of the Tfile code).

In Table 13.7 two separate processing codes were established. The first from the staff file to the department file, the second from the department file to the cost centre file. It is possible to set up a processing code on the staff file to carry out both operations, thereby making the cost centre description (and any other data from the cost centre file) accessible from the staff file. In this case the department code on the staff record is used to access the department record from which the cost centre code is used to access the cost centre file and the description of the cost centre returned. In this case the synonym, which again takes the same attribute position as the department code (i.e. attribute 4), contains a multiple Tfile processing code separated by a value mark] (CTRL/]) as shown in Table 13.8.

Sample data files are shown in Figure 13.15 as the basis for the examples shown in Figure 13.16.

In order to demonstrate the use of the Tfile processing codes, the output from a simple ACCESS report is shown in Figure 13.16. This uses the data in Figure 13.15 with the processing codes given in Tables 13.7 and 13.8.

Attribute number	**STAFF**					
0	001	002	003	004	005	006
1	Hopcraft, L	Smart, P	Bourdon, R	Farmer, L	Jones, K	Walters, E
2	.....	.....	.....	.....	.....	....
3	.....	.....	.....	.....	.....	....
4	001	011	009	009	010	002

Attribute number	**DEPT**				
0	001	002	004	009	011
1	Sales	Admin	Accounts	R & D	Costing
2	.....	.....	.....	.....	.....
3	02	01	06	03	06

Attribute number	**CC**		
0	01	02	06
1	Administration	Sales & Mkting	Accounting

Figure 13.15 Sample data used in Figure 13.16.

Table 13.8 The use of multiple Tfile processing codes.

	← *File names* →		
Attribute number	**STAFF**	**DEPT**	**CC**
0	Staff no.	Dept. code	Cost centre code
1	Name	Dept. description	Cost centre description
2	Address	Annual budget	Annual budget
3	Tel Number	Cost centre code	
3		Cost centre desc.	
4	Dept. code		
4	Dept. description		
4	Cost centre descr		

```
CC.DESC
001 A
002 4
003 Description
004
005
006
007
008 TDEPT;X;;1]TCC;C;;1
009 L
010 30
```

The contents of the department code on the staff file is used to look up the cost centre code held as attribute 3 on the department record. The cost centre code on the department record is then used to extract the department description (attribute 1) from the cost centre file. If the department record is not present a null value will be returned. If however the cost centre record is not found, the cost centre code from the department record will be displayed instead – this being the purpose of the **C** option in the processing code, used in place of the **X** in previous examples.

13.5.27 The U (User defined) processing code

The **U** processing code specifies an entry point into a user-written piece of software, known as a user exit. It is only for experienced PICK users and should not be used unless you are fully conversant with its effects. There are a wide number of user exits described in the PICK manual and those who wish to explore the use of these should refer to their manual. Each user exit starts with **U** and is followed by the frame address in which the assembly language code can be found. The most common user exits are:

U50BB returns line number, user-id and account of the current process
U20B9 converts £ sign to $ symbol

```
DEPT.DESC
001 A
002 4
003 Description
004
005
006
007
008 TDEPT;X;;1
009 L
010 30


CC.DESC
001 A
002 4
003 Description
004
005
006
007
008 TDEPT;X;;1]TCC;C;;1
009 L
010 30
```

A typical ACCESS enquiry

:LIST STAFF NAME DEPT.CODE DEPT.DESC CC.DESC

This requests a list from the STAFF file showing staff names, their department codes, department names and cost centre names.

The output

```
PAGE 1

                              10:20:11 10 NOV 1995

STAFF.... Name....... Dept   Dept Name  CC Name.........

001       HOPCRAFT,L  002    Admin      Administration
003       BOURDON, R  009    R & D      03
006       WALTERS, E  002    Admin      Administration
005       JONES, K    010
002       SMART, P    011    Costing    Accounting
004       FARMER, L   009    R & D      03
```

The effect of a processing code returning a null value when the look-up record is not found

The effect of a processing code returning the item-id when the look-up record is not found

---

Figure 13.16 Examples of output from Tfile processing codes.

13.5.28 The V (Value limit) processing code

This code is used as an input conversion to limit the number of values to be created within an attribute whilst within the Update Processor. The general format is

> **V***number*
> where
> *number* is the maximum number of values permitted. If this is zero no data can be entered in the attribute

13.5.29 The X (display only) processing code

This is used in attribute 14 of an attribute definition item to stop it being amended within the Update Processor. The **X** code can be used with other codes in the file definition item as an update stamp as described in the next section.

13.5.30 The X (update stamp) processing code

This code is placed in attribute 14 (the input conversion code) of a file defining item in order to provide an audit trail of items that are updated. The valid options are:

XA*n* puts the user name in attribute *n* of the updated item
XD*n* puts the current date in attribute *n* of the updated item
XS*n* puts the accumulated time (in seconds) taken to update the item attribute *n* of the updated item
XT*n* puts the current time in attribute *n* of the updated item

If **V** is added to the end of the code the stamp will be appended to the end of the existing contents of the attribute containing the stamp, otherwise the new stamp will overwrite the old one.

Multiple combinations are possible. Hence **XA20D21T22** will put the user-id in attribute 20, the date in attribute 21 and the time in attribute 22.

13.5.31 The ZC (Zip Code) processing code

This processing code uses the files **ZCF**, **STATE** and **COUNTY** to display the city, state, postal zip code and country during zip code entry or output. The **ZC** code can be placed in any of the three processing code options in the attribute defining item. It is not applicable for a file defining item.

13.5.32 Multiple processing codes

Whilst we have seen some examples of the use of multiple processing codes, it is worth mentioning that you are not limited to the number of processing codes you can use at any one time. To use more than one code ensure that each is separated with a value mark] (CTRL/]); an example of which is shown in Figure 13.16.

14 Systems Design Techniques for the PICK Database

14.1 Introduction

This chapter is aimed at providing help to those people responsible for the design and implementation of PICK-based solutions. Those of you not involved in the design of systems or just interested in the facilities available within PICK can skip this chapter. It covers the control and development of projects, the techniques for analysis and the subsequent considerations for the efficient design of accounts and files to produce the most effective PICK-based solutions.

The development of large computer systems is one of the most complex activities undertaken by organizations and the number of staff involved and the resources consumed often make it one of the most costly of all projects undertaken by a business. Everyone has heard of projects which grossly exceed their projected development costs and timescales and even then they may fail to provide the facilities the user requires!

Today's users have high expectations for their systems. They expect instant response, even to the most elaborate request and have no concern, nor interest in the technical issues involved. Whilst many suffer major disappointment in the performance of their system, the potential for fast and effective data retrieval is a key to the success of the PICK system.

The PICK database was designed primarily to enable users with little computing experience to access information quickly and easily. It requires the minimum of hardware resource and transforms a normal PC into a highly effective multi-user system.

Poor system performance in a PICK environment is not an inherent problem, but one most commonly caused by poor file design and insufficient data analysis resulting in a database which is inappropriate for the requirements of the intended application and development environment.

One of the reasons for poor design under PICK is an analyst used to alternative databases and operating systems applying those techniques to the design of a PICK system. It is not appropriate to assume that methods applicable to one environment will work efficiently and effectively for another.

The simplicity of PICK, although largely an asset can work as a disadvantage when DP professionals move from more complex environments. This simplicity hides the necessity of understanding the mechanics and implications of PICK data retrieval and leads to development of applications which may be inherently unsuitable for PICK development and which may become unmaintainable and dreadfully slow in operation.

Poor design is often the result of too much emphasis being placed on what to do with the data rather than the information requirements of the system. Computer systems are all about the control and production of information from the data input. The design of a system should reflect its data flow and the increase in expected data volumes.

Design of the database is crucial for efficient application development. Data analysis should be carried out using traditional tools and the resultant

PICK database design based on a thorough understanding of the PICK file structure, accounts organization, data retrieval methods and its available tools for accessing and updating information.

14.2 The stages of project development

The key stages in the life-cycle of the development of a system are:

- **Terms of reference including business objectives**
  The terms of reference are set by the company department to receive the system or by the financial management of the company and possibly the Board of Directors. The document outlines the requirements of the system and the business objectives to be achieved by the system, financial and administrative.
- **Feasibility study**
  A feasibility study is required to determine if the objectives are realistic and must address the technical, economic and social areas of concern. The study must therefore present a detailed specification of the objectives together with an analysis of the impact on the organization of any project aimed at meeting them. Techniques such as cost benefit analysis, discounted cash flow and return on investment are used to establish economic feasibility. Technical feasibility needs to be established by estimation of processing and data requirements while social feasibility can only be determined by discussions with the proposed user. At the end of a feasibility study, a decision as to whether or not to proceed has to be taken.
- **Investigation**
  The investigation stage is a detailed study of the existing system looking at how the current system works, its processes and how the data is processed, including its volume. It should identify all known problems of the current system and any special requirements of the new system should be documented.
- **System analysis**
  System analysis is the organization of information gathered during the investigation stage into a logical and meaningful form. The analysis stage will first produce a model of the existing system, which is enhanced to reflect the improvements identified and results in a statement of requirements.
- **System and database design**
  During this stage the design of the system is considered. This has to take into account the chosen hardware and software, in the case of this chapter, the design for a PICK database solution. This is a two-stage process, first logically breaking the system down into modules then identifying from this the physical operations required and the physical database structure.

- **Implementation**
  This is the stage where the completed system is imposed on the user in the form of a working system and the user is expected to operate with what has been developed. The tested software may well be run in parallel with the existing system and control totals between the new and old systems compared for correctness and to prove the new system.
- **Training**
  This is a very essential part of any successful system and is one of the implementation requirements. The introduction of new systems will impose new technology and new disciplines on existing and new users. Their training needs to be identified and training provided to enable them to take control and be confident of, their new system.
- **Maintenance and modification**
  The system should be reviewed regularly and audited after its implementation to ensure it has achieved its original objectives. These steps will undoubtedly result in changes to the system; even if the user hasn't already decided on the changes he would like resulting from his operational use of the new system.
- **Support**
  This is an important stage of any system at any point in its development, but far more so after the system is operational. It requires providing the user with access to suitability qualified staff to handle ongoing problems of both an operational and IT nature.

14.2.1 Project control

Dependent of the size of the project it may be necessary to set up a Project Steering Committee, which could comprise a number of IT staff as well as those from the user departments. Generally one of the users will take overall project responsibility.

The purpose of the Project Steering Committee is to develop the Project Plan and control all the stages from inception to implementation of the Project. The Project File will contain all the documents associated with the Project, starting with the initial System Proposal and ending with the system testing data and results and any control papers associated with any parallel run.

The Project Plan is produced at the beginning of the Project and breaks it down into manageable tasks. Each task should be analysed separately to determine the:

- Tools to be used
- Documentation required
- Resource allocated, man-days and people
- Resource taken. man-days

- Scheduled start and end days
- Task dependency
- Slippage

The system requirements then needs to be analysed and this chapter will explain how to use the following tools:

- Document flow diagrams
- Data flow diagrams
- Data structure diagrams
- Normalization
- Process outlines
- File/Process matrix

Once the requirements have been analysed and the database designed, consideration will have to be given to systems implementation.

Whilst this chapter focuses on data analysis and database design techniques for completeness it is worth remembering that there are many other aspects involved in the implementation of a new system and the key aspects requiring consideration are listed below.

- Access security
- Application specific non-processal requirements
- Archiving requirements
- Audit trails
- Data security/resilience
- Data conversion
- Development standards
- Fallback and recovery
- Hardware requirements (including cabling)
- Implementation plan
- Performance
- Support (including support modem)
- System testing
- Technical documentation
- User documentation and training
- User acceptance

14.3 Structured systems analysis

Structured systems analysis is a technique to carry out an organized and ordered analysis of requirements which comprises several techniques and a formalized system of documentation. There are many very good books written purely on the subject of Structured Systems Analysis and Design and on SSADM (Structured Systems Analysis and Design Method) so this chapter aims to outline some useful principles. It does not represent nor purport to represent formal SSADM techniques which are considerably more detailed and involved and equally it should be recognized that pure SSADM does not cater for the special PICK database structure, in particular it has no concept of multi-values.

The techniques described here have been found most useful and practical in the analysis of new systems and limit the amount of documentation needed. They here have proved invaluable within our software company (APT Solutions Ltd), which concentrates on developments using 4GL products and in particular SB+, where the lowest level function is called a process.

All of the tools produce standardised documentation which serves several purposes:

- To assist in performing the task itself.
- To assist in interfacing between tasks.
- To facilitate good communications between the various parties involved with the development of the system (e.g. user and development team, designer and programmer).
- To provide standardized product documentation.

14.3.1 Standard tools

The standard tools defined within a structured design methodology are:

- **Document flow diagrams**
  Identifies the source and destination of data, whether internal or external.
- **Data flow diagrams (DFDs)**
  Identifies, documents and confirms the various processes required by the application and produces a view of the system understandable to the user.
- **Data structure diagrams (DSDs)**
  These are used to model the data held within the application and to design and specify the physical file structure.
- **Normalization**
  Normalization is a technique of analysing relationships and follows mathematically derived rules to identify the logical entities in the system, the key of each entity and results in a list of the data items contained within each entity or physical file. At a physical level they also contain sizing information.

- **Process outlines**
  Process outlines are used to specify the detail of the functional requirements of each task and ultimately form the final program specifications.
- **File/Process matrices**
  File/Process matrices provide a cross-reference of the files used within each process.

Process documentation and program listings serve as final documentation of the software produced and a list of problems and additional requirements provides an indication of problems experienced with new requirements identified together with their source and the process/DFD affected.

14.3.2 The Project Plan

The Project Plan is a very important document and should be developed very early on in the life of a project. The plan should identify tasks which ideally should be sized to last for between one day and four weeks to enable a reasonable level of control in the monitoring of the task.

The analysis section of the final plan should always contain at least:

- Lowest level proposed physical DFD
- Physical DSD
- File definitions
- Process maps
- File/Process matrices

In addition it is desirable to include physical process outlines for each process on the proposed physical DFD.

14.3.3 SSAD diagram conventions

Before looking at some examples of DFDs, familiarize yourself with the following diagram conventions which will be used through the remainder of this chapter.

- **Symbols**
  - ☐ A process not broken down at next level

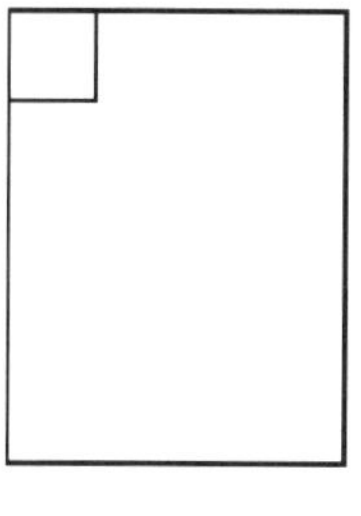

☐ A process which is broken down at the next level

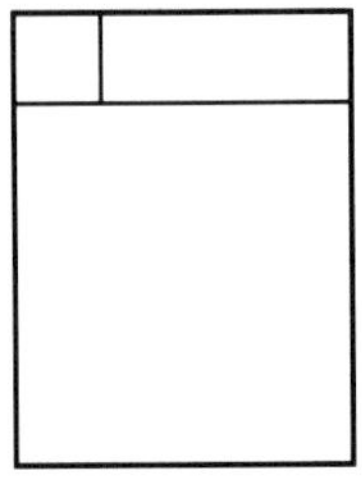

☐ An external entity

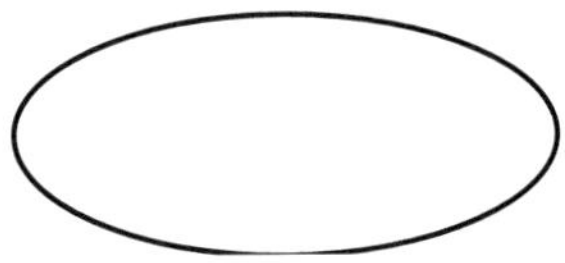

☐ An external entity appearing elsewhere on the same diagram

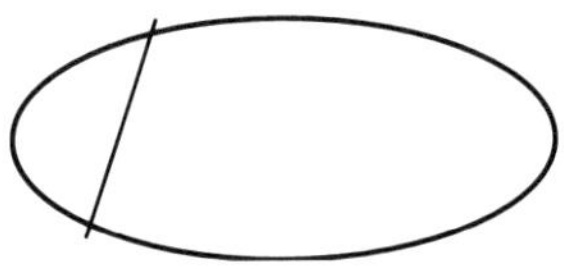

☐ A data store

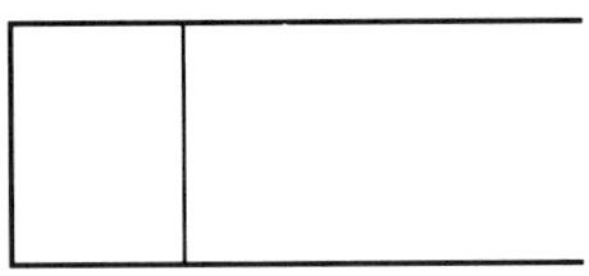

☐ Data store appearing elsewhere on the same diagram

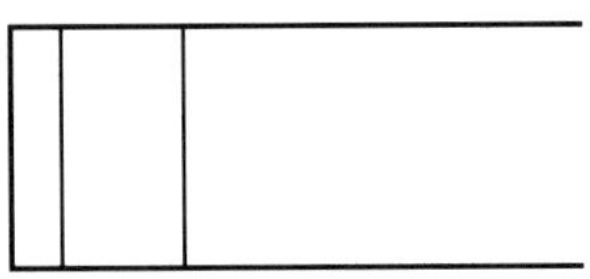

☐ One way data flow

☐ Two way data flow, same data going both ways

☐ Two way data flow, different data going each way

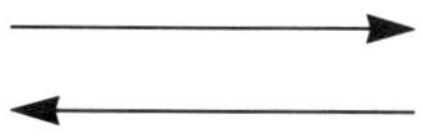

- **Labels**
  Each component should be named in terms related to the application so that the user can verify the correctness of the analyst's understanding of the system. Processes are numbered using:

  ☐ A single alphabetic character at the system level.

  ☐ The appropriate sub-system identifier (for multi sub-system systems) followed by an integer at overview level.

  ☐ The appropriate higher level identifier followed by a '.' and an integer for process that are broken down to lower levels.

  Data stores are numbered using an integer prefixed by an alpha code:

D	Computer file
M	Manual file
T	Temporary computer file

14.3.4 Document flow diagrams

The use of document flow diagrams is optional but at an Overview level they can provide an extra and simply read diagrammatic representation of the flow of information and objects between the various entities inside or outside the system. Each entity is depicted as a labelled box and all data and objects are drawn as, suitably annotated, data flows. For examples of document flow diagrams refer to Figures 14.1–14.6 at the end of Section 14.3.

14.3.5 Data flow diagrams

Data flow diagrams (DFDs) are a diagrammatic representation of a system drawn in user understandable terms and are used to:

- Identify the various processes that exist within the users view of the application.
- Show the main flows of data through the system.
- Show the inputs and outputs from each process.

DFDs are used to gain agreement with the user that the correct facilities have been identified and can be used to document both the current system and the proposed system. They form the basis of the processal design of the system and are a useful tool to aid processal analysis and design. DFDs are not generally a precise tool but are drawn in a way that is most clear to the user. The final diagrams should be accurate and complete within the level of detail used but must retain readability by those who know the application.

The prime objective of the DFD is the identification of the processes required of the system in order to fulfill the processal requirements of the application. To that end it is therefore essential that time is taken to produce accurate and comprehensive DFDs.

DFDs depict a system by breaking it down into:

- **Processes**
  A process corresponds to a single processal area within the system taken at a similar level to that of the DFD. On the System Level DFD each process corresponds to a sub-system; on an Overview DFD each process corresponds to a major processal area within the sub-system and at the lowest level a process corresponds to a single process.
- **External entities**
  An external entity is a source or destination of data which resides outside the physical bounds of the system.
- **Data stores**
  A data store is a storage place for the data held within the physical bounds of the system.
- **Data flows**
  A data flow is a movement of data between the other components of the DFD. Data may flow between:
  - □ an external entity and a process, depicting an input or output into or out of the system
  - □ a process and a data store, depicting an update or retrieval to or from the filing system.

There are various forms of DFD which represent models of the system during its respective phases of refinement and these are:

- Current physical — *how the existing system operates*
- Current logical — *what the current system achieves*
- Proposed physical — *how the required system will operate*
- Proposed logical — *what the new system will achieve*

Current physical DFD

This is the DFD which shows a picture of the system as it is performed now in terms of:

- processes – the operations that are actually performed in the current system;
- data stores – these correspond to storage areas that are actually used (e.g. Cash Book, Card Indexes, etc.);
- data flows – these correspond to actual movements of information within the system (usually on paper).

The current physical DFD is used to confirm with the user that the analyst has established a complete understanding of the current system.

Current logical DFD

This is the DFD which shows the requirements of the current system in terms of:

- the processes which are necessary to have the same logical effect as the current physical system. Tasks that are duplicated are removed, tasks that have been split for operational reasons but are logically part of a single larger task are combined;
- the data stores that are necessary to support the logical process data stores that are purely physical (i.e. necessary for operational reasons) are removed.

The current logical DFD is used to aid the analyst in identifying the true logical processing of the current system and basically reduces the current physical DFD to just those elements that are necessary to achieve the business requirement. Any duplication of processing or information storage that exists in the current system would appear on the current physical DFD but would be removed on the current logical DFD.

Proposed logical DFD

This is the DFD which shows the logical view after the proposed system boundaries have been established and any new requirements have been added in. The proposed logical DFD takes the current logical DFD as a base and is then reduced to take account of the computer system/manual boundary and modified to take account of new requirements.

Proposed Physical DFD

This is the DFD which shows the user's view of the proposed system using processes which correspond to facilities in the computer system. The proposed physical DFD represents the users view of the system in terms of the actual facilities that will exist. Ultimately the proposed physical DFD will become the basis of the functional specification of the system.

The proposed logical DFD is used as the base by the designer and the operational aspects of the system are then applied. Usually each lowest level process on the proposed physical DFD will become a lowest level menu option in the computer system.

DFDs may be constructed at three primary levels:

The SYSTEM level DFD
which is used where the application can be regarded as several sub-systems. Each sub-system is represented together with its major inputs and outputs and the interfaces with the other sub-systems.

The OVERVIEW level DFD
which is used to break down each sub-system into its major processing areas.

The LOW level DFD
which is used to progressively break down each processing area on the overview DFD until the lowest level has been reached corresponding to the processes that exist within the application.

Data flow diagrams are derived from a process known as Processal Analysis. Processal analysis is a technique whereby the purely logical facilities required by a system are identified by removing all physical considerations. The physical aspects of the required system are then applied to the logical system to produce the required physical system. This involves

- Constructing the current physical DFD showing an exact 'plan' of the current system. This will depict the processes involved exactly as the user sees them and is therefore a good tool to use to gain user confirmation that the analyst has a complete and accurate picture.
- The current physical DFD is then reduced by removing any duplication and by amalgamating tasks which are separate for purely operational reasons (e.g. task performed jointly by two geographically apart sites). This produces the current logical DFD which shows the processing requirements rather than the physical operation of the system.
- The boundaries of the required system are incorporated and new requirements are added in to produce the proposed logical DFD. Processes on the current logical DFD which are outside the proposed system boundaries are converted to external entities. New requirements will often result in new processes but may simply modify existing processes (by modifying data flows or data stores).
- The operational aspects of the proposed system are incorporated into the proposed logical DFD to produce the proposed physical DFD.

The two main outputs coming from the processal analysis are:

- The proposed logical DFD showing the facilities required in the new system, each lowest level process corresponding to a facility which must be provided by the development team. Each different facility will probably require its own code with little overlap of code between facilities.

- The proposed physical DFD showing the user view of the new system, each lowest level process will correspond to a lowest level menu option and the DFD hierarchy will probably be very similar to the menu hierarchy.

Facilities are identified by looking at the different types of trigger driving the system which will either be real-time or batch.

A real-time facility can be identified because it falls into one of the following categories:

- The facility is triggered by the receipt of data from a single external entity; the data which constitutes the trigger is usually input by an operator using a screen. The receipt of data requiring real-time processing is termed an 'EVENT', the data itself is often termed a 'TRANSACTION'.
- The facility to be used to process a particular event is determinable from the data itself and is normally chosen by selecting a menu option.

A batch process is usually triggered by something other than the receipt of data, possibly time of day, size of workload or selected database update. The data that drives the process is taken from a single data store and the process is performed once for every item selected. Each item in the driving data store that is selected for processing should require similar processing at the logical level (i.e. on the proposed logical DFD), but several batch processes operating on the same data store might be combined for physical reasons (e.g. performance) on the proposed physical DFD.

For examples of DFDs refer to the following figures at the end of Section 14.3:

Figure 14.1 System level DFD
Figure 14.2 Overview level DFD
Figure 14.3 Low level DFD
Figure 14.4 Physical DFD
Figure 14.5 Logical DFD

- **General format**

System level and overview DFDs are drawn in landscape orientation whilst lower level DFDs are drawn in portrait orientation with a single DFD representing one higher level process broken down to the lower level.

By definition, external entities are outside the system and data stores are inside the system. On overview DFDs external entities are drawn around the outside of the diagram with data stores drawn centrally and the processes drawn between the two as an interface.

The lowest level processes on the DFD correspond to the various facilities required to perform all of the different types of task required within the application. This provides a break-down analysing an application by its PROCESSALITY not by its detail even when going to a lower level. The lowest level process must involve either real-time or batch processing.

- ☐ Real-time processing must be driven by a single data flow usually triggered from an external entity or another in rare circumstances by a process. It must respond immediately to the trigger and is usually driven by data entered through a keyboard if the system is computerized. The external influence that triggers real-time processing is termed an EVENT. All occurrences of a particular event should require broadly similar processing and should all be handled by the same facility.
- ☐ Batch processing is almost always driven by data previously stored in a data store, and is performed once for each logical record selected. In rare circumstances data may be generated internally without pre-stored data driving the process.

The data flow that drives a lowest level process is identified on a DFD by encircling the arrow-head at the process end. If the data flow comes from an external entity it indicates a real-time process but if it comes from a data store it indicates batch processing.

Every lowest level process should have exactly one such data flow, and such a data flow cannot exist on higher level process.

14.3.6 Data structure diagrams

Data structure diagrams (often referred to as Entity Models) are a very important part of the analysis process and are a means of defining relationships that exist amongst the data entities in a system in terms of:

- the logical or physical groupings of data
- the interrelationship between groupings
- the types of cross-referencing mechanisms used

DSDs show the relationship between FILES, describe the data structure in a mathematically precise format and as such have little meaning to the end user. The final versions must be complete and accurate since they form the basis of the database design in the final system.

Two types of DSD can be constructed the logical DSD and the physical DSD.

Logical DSD

This DSD shows the relationships between the strictly logical data groupings without any consideration of the physical implementation. These are drawn to aid the analyst in identifying a normalized data structure.

On a logical DSD, a file is a group of like data, each item of which is similar both in content and processing to all others in the same file but each item of which must be uniquely identifiable.

The entities are identified initially by looking for 'user keys' – these are items which in the user's view of the application are allocated an identifier which enables the user to uniquely identify the item – each of the item types then become first cut entities.

As the processing requirements become clearer the logical DSD is modified to ensure that the logical data structure can support the processality required in the application, so by this stage an intuitive data structure diagram has been produced.

As a separate exercise all data flows (i.e. source documents, reports, etc.) are analysed using Third Normal Data (TNF) analysis. This will produce a mathematically derived DSD and a list of contents for each file. The DSD derived from TNF is compared to the logical DSD and any differences are reconciled and amended to produce a composite DSD.

Physical DSD

This DSD uses the logical DSD as a base and applies the modifications necessary to implement it on the chosen file handler, showing cross referencing mechanisms and, optionally sizing information. These serve as final documentation of the physical data structure.

On a physical DSD a file corresponds to an actual file in the final system and probably to a file on the logical data structure.

Physical data design takes the final composite DSD and applies the characteristics of the particular file handler to produce a data design suitable for implementation. In a PICK environment each file on the logical DSD becomes a candidate for a file on the physical DSD and ultimately a file in the physical system. Logical entities may however be split for physical reasons such as performance or data security into two or more physical entities.

Each crows-foot on the logical DSD must be examined to investigate the need for use of one of the three standard downwards cross-referencing mechanisms:

- normal one-to-one
- optional one-to-one
- one-to-many

The aim is to keep record sizes as small as is possible. The most common cause of large records in a PICK environment is the inclusion of multi-valued attributes in the file item definitions.

Large records should be split into multiple files where possible with establishment of one-to-one relationships. This is achieved by grouping the together the attributes that are required by particular processes. In this way only the attributes that are needed are ever loaded into the users workspace.

This technique is particularly useful when a logical master file contains multi-valued cross-references or sub-files. Each sub-file is made into its own file with a one-to-one relationship set up with the master. A process requiring a particular sub-file then reads only the appropriate file and hence minimizes unnecessary system overheads.

Data structure diagrams – entity relationships

Two entities may be directly related in only one of two ways:

- one-to-one
- one-to-many

but circumstances will exist where there is a many-to-many relationship between entities. However, direct many-to-many relationships are not allowed to exist. In these situations the many-to-many relationship is identified by an intermediary file.

The one-to-one relationship

Each item in one of the entities is related to one item in the other file and vice versa. At logical level a one-to-one relationship usually indicates that the two entities can be combined into one. At a physical level the existence of a one-to-one relationship implies that the record from one file can be identified directly from its corresponding record in the other file. This is achieved by holding the key of one record somewhere in the item of its corresponding record on the other file. Mostly, but not always, both items have the same item-id. One-to-one relationships at the physical level usually occur as a result of some physical design considerations, perhaps the breaking down of a large item into several small ones or for security reasons.

There are two one-to-one relationships: the normal one-to-one relationship drawn as follows:

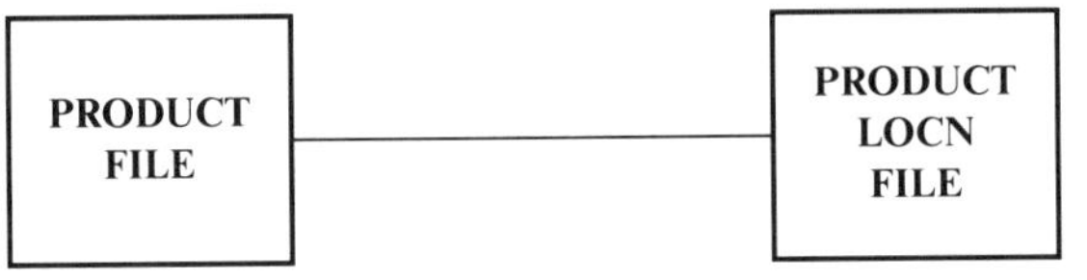

and the optional one-to-one relationship in which the letter **O** is written through the line joining the entities.

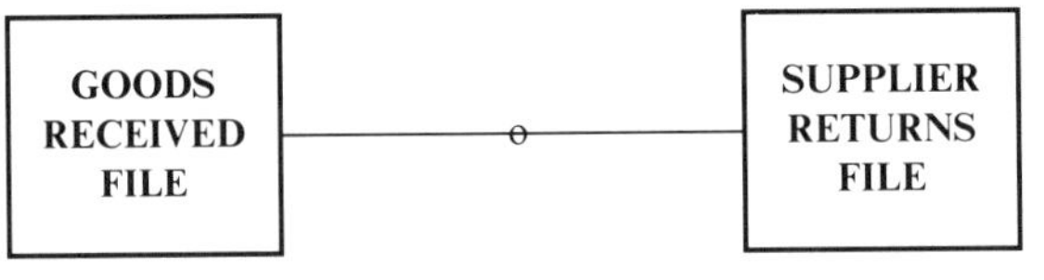

The one-to-many relationship

This type of relationship exists where each item in a 'Master' file may have many items related to it and held in a 'Detail' file, but where each item in the detail file only has a relationship to one item in the master.

The most commonly understood example is that of an order processing system in which an order can have many lines associated to it, but the order line can only relate to one order. The order owns its order line which itself cannot exist without the order. Hence the ORDER is the master and the ORDER LINE is the detail. The drawing convention is for a crows foot to be drawn on the 'many' end of the relationship. Hence for one order, there can be many order lines (a one-to-many relationship) with the order lines being at the 'many' end. Do note that 'many' includes the special cases of one or none and does not by itself imply any limits to the number of detail records belonging to its parent.

The many-to-many relationship

This type of relationship can exist in a logical view of entities. For example a part can be purchased from many different suppliers and a supplier can provide many different parts. However the DSD is not drawn by joining each entity together and drawing a crows foot at each end, it is drawn by linking each of the entities together through a third entity. Hence the logical view is drawn in the following way:

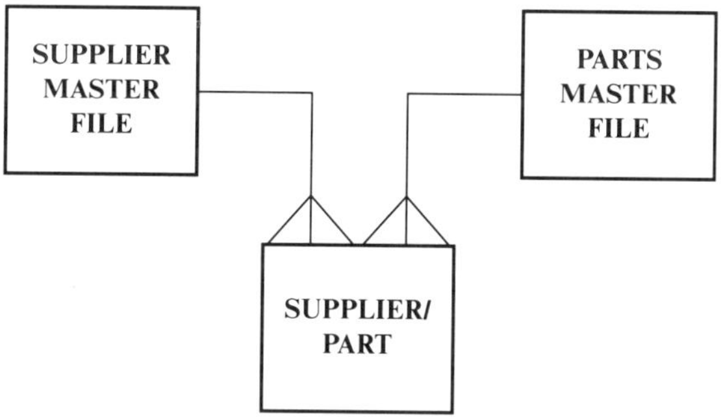

Each item in one file can be related to many items in the other file and vice versa. This type of relationship cannot be implemented using PICK multi-values on both the supplier and part file. It equally couldn't be implemented in most other file handlers unless there is data stored concerning the link itself.

The physical DSD is constructed by taking into account the nature of the particular file handler to be used and any other non-processal considerations that may affect the data structure (e.g. item length, security etc.). In the PICK environment there are three basic cross referencing methods to consider:

- **Paging detail file**
  by making the detail page off the master file.
- **Paging cross-reference file**
  using another file to cross-reference downwards by paging off the master.
- **Cross-reference file with multi-valued attributes**
  by using another file to store the keys of the detail as a multi-valued attribute.

These three methods are described in full further on in this chapter in Section 14.4.3 which looks in detail at file structure.

In the one-to-many relationship it should always be possible to access an item by key or from any other item in the structure by using indexes to go down the structure or by keys stored in the detail items to go up the structure. Access to a file by an attribute that is not a key elsewhere can only be achieved by performing a serial pass through the entire file which is often unacceptable.

An alternative to this is to use an INVERSION of the file on the attribute by which access is required. Two types of inversion are possible depending on the type of attribute being inverted. If the attribute uniquely identifies the item in which it appears a one-to-one inversion is used which is implemented by keying the inverted file on the attribute being inverted and holding the key of the main file as an attribute.

Whereas if the attribute being inverted can take the same value in many different items a one-to-many inversion is used, implemented in the same way as an ordinary one-to-many relationship with the same considerations concerning cross-referencing (see Section 14.4.3).

Sizing information may optionally be included on a DSD and would normally only apply to physical DSDs. The top-right-hand corner of the entity box takes the total number of records in the file, the top-left-hand corner of the box is used to hold the average record length in bytes, including byte counts and delimiters while the bottom-left-hand corner takes the total file size (product of top-left and top-right corners).

The crows-feet can be annotated with the average number of records in the detail file for each record in the master. Hence the top-right-hand corner (total number of records in file) of detail entities is derivable from the product of top-right-hand corner of master (number of records in master) and number on crows-foot (average occurrence of detail for each record in master). Cross-reference and inverted file sizes may also be calculated by using this method.

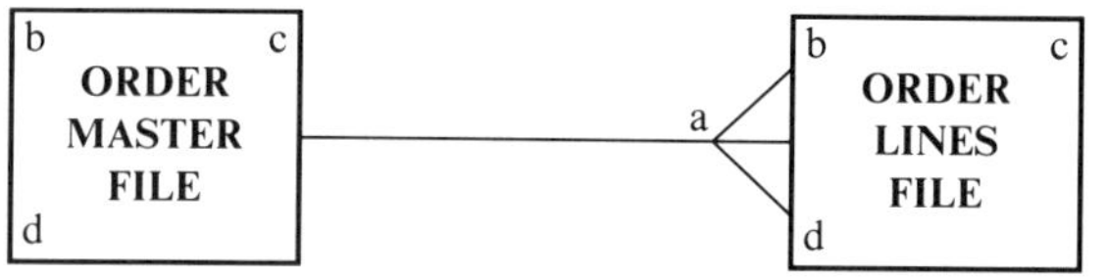

where

a is the average number of records in detail for each record in master
b is the average record length in bytes
c is the total number of records in file
d is the total file size in bytes.

An example of a logical DSD can be found in Figure 14.7 and a physical DSD in Figure 14.8, both of which can be found at the end of Section 14.3.

14.3.7 Third normal form data analysis (normalization)

Third normal form (TNF) analysis is a fundamental analysis technique which analyses RELATIONS and which follows mathematically derived rules to identify:

- the logical entities in the system;
- the key of each entity;
- the contents of each entity.

In physical terms a relation would normally be derived from information held on paper documents and used in the current manual system. Where the existing system is computerized, relations could be derived from the existing file definitions, the input screens and the reports.

It is important to base TNF analysis not only on existing relations but also on the features required in the new system and to this end the proposed documents and the existing documents suitably modified should be used in this stage of analysis.

TNF analysis is performed in five stages on each of the documents available:

- The unnormalized relationships (UNF) are derived directly from the document.
- Repeating groups are removed from the UNF relation to create new relations, this is first normal form (FNF).
- Part-key dependencies are removed from the FNF to create new relations, this is second normal form (SNF).
- Mutual data dependencies are resolved from SNF to create new relations, this is third normal form (TNF).

- Once TNF has been reached for all the unnormalized relations in the system the entire set of relations is optimized by amalgamating relations with exactly the same key.

Each relation in the optimized TNF set of relations then becomes an entity (suitably named) on a logical data structure. The DSD so derived should be the same as the one derived earlier in the analysis from the much less formal approach used at that stage. Any differences must be reconciled in terms of the error in deriving either or both structures or the error in understanding user requirements.

As an example of the TNF analysis technique, we will undertake the five stages using the following Customer Order History Report:

Customer Order History Report

Customer Code : HACK1
Customer Name : Hackney Engineering Ltd
Address : Unit 3
Hackney Business Park
Leabridge Road
London E5

Order No	Order Date	Prod Code	Product Description	Price	Quantity	Value
0236	18/1/95	3507	Bolt, Large, Alloy	2.51	100	251.00
		8428	Rod, Small, Brass	6.78	50	339.00
		6224	Screw, Small, Steel	5.76	200	1152.00

				Order Value		1742.00
043	1 8/2/95	4007	Bolt, Large, Steel	1.67	250	417.50
		2509	Bolt, Small, Alloy	.87	500	435.00
		9012	Cover, Small, Alloy	.86	350	301.00
		9029	Vent, Large, Steel	2.28	100	228.00

				Order Value		1381.50
051	2 14/3/95	9109	Rod, Large, Steel	1.63	200	326.00
		9072	Vent, Large, Alloy	2.28	300	684.00

				Order Value		1010.00

Step 1. The unnormalized relationships (UNF) are derived directly from the document

The first step is to look at the entire document and to treat is as a single relation. The next step is to identify a suitable key for the relation which for this report is obviously the Customer Code. Any unique field or combination of fields will do as a starting point as the natural keys will appear as part of the later normalization process.

Finally list all the fields as a single relation, headed by the chosen key and ensure that each field listed is different to all the others. The key field is underlined to highlight it as the chosen key. Hence for the Customer Order History Report the UNF analysis would give:

Customer Code
Customer Name
Customer Address
Order No
Order Date
Product Code
Product Description
Price
Quantity
Line Value
Order Value

Step 2. Repeating groups are removed from the UNF relation to create new relations, this is first normal form (FNF)

Now the single UNF relation is separated into new relations by removing the repeating groups. We need to analyse the UNF and determine whether any of the data fields from the UNF relation have more than one value on the document. Careful study reveals two of them, one of orders (nested within customer) and one of order details (nested within order). Each repeating group is therefore removed and becomes a new relation, suitably keyed as follows:

Customer Code	Line Number	Order Number
Customer Name	Order Number	Order value
Customer Address	Product Code	
	Product Description	
	Price	
	Quantity	
	Line Value	

Step 3. Part-key dependencies are removed from the FNF to create new relations, this is second normal form (SNF)

In this phase each FNF relation is checked for part-key dependency and new relations are created where appropriate. Each field is reviewed to see whether it is dependent on the whole key or just part of it. Where it is dependent on part of the key the field is pulled out into a new relation keyed on the part key.

In our example the Product Description is dependent only on the Product Code part of the key so that a new relation is created to hold this field.

Customer Code	Product Code	Order Number	Line Number
Customer Name	Product Description	Order Value	Order Number
Customer Address			Product Code
			Price
			Quantity
			Line value

Step 4. Mutual data dependencies are resolved from SNF to create new relations, this is third normal form (TNF)

At this point each SNF relation is checked for mutual data dependency and new relations are created where appropriate. The question is whether any two fields in the relation relate to each other. In other words can the value of one field be directly derived from another?

In our example the price is derived from the Product Code field. Hence given the Product Code it is possible to determine the Price – the price can be directly extracted from the Product relation. This gives the TNF relations

Customer Code	Product Code	Order Number	Line Number
Customer Name	Product Description	Order Value	Order Number
Customer Address	Price		Product Code
			Quantity
			Line value

Once TNF has been reached for all the unnormalized relations in the system the entire set of relations is optimized by amalgamating relations with exactly the same key

Steps 1 to 4 are repeated for every form in the system after which the many resulting relations are optimized by combining those that have exactly the same keys. Each of the optimized relations is given a name and now correspond to a single logical entity on a DSD. In our example we have arrived at the following entities

CUSTOMER
PRODUCT
ORDER HEADER
ORDER DETAIL

If we examine the relationships we can establish the following:

Entity	Relationship	Entity
CUSTOMER	places many	ORDERS
ORDER	contains many	ORDER LINES
PRODUCT	appears on many	ORDERLINES

The logical DSD shows how these entities are linked together

Logical DSD

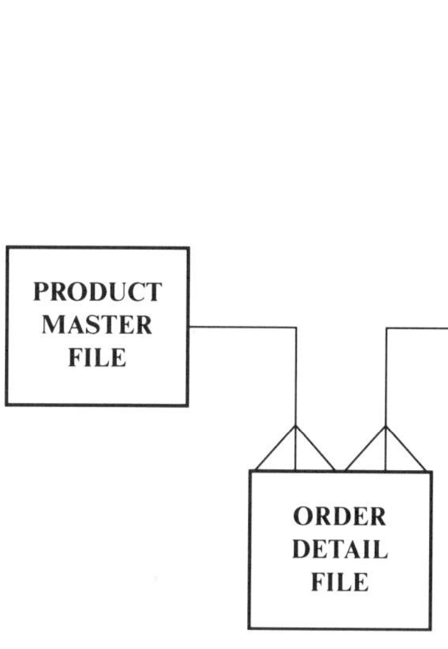

14.3.8 Process outlines

The process outline provides a means of specifying the requirements of each process on the DFD. Process outlines can be used at a logical level to communicate ideas to the user or at a physical level as a detailed program specification.

A full process outline comprises of four sections:

- a free text description outlining the requirements of the process
- a specification of the inputs required from the user, perhaps with a screen format if appropriate
- a specification of the outputs produced by the process, if any, including reports that may actually be produced at some point in the future by a batch run
- a structured English description of the requirements of the process, comprising a structured English description of each of the steps involved

together with a list of the files accessed by each step and the attributes required or affected.

Physical process outlines

Physical process outlines are used to specify detailed requirements to the programmer. They should contain all of the sections outlined above with the possible exception of the screen format. They must be written in sufficient detail to allow the programmer to code the module correctly and must accurately and unambiguously specify the requirements of the module.

Accuracy is vital since it will be against these requirements that the functionality of the process module will be tested.

Logical process outlines

Logical process outlines are used to communicate the requirements of a process to the user. They must therefore be written in clear, easily understandable language which is accurate and unambiguous. They can be used to agree the functional requirements of each facility in the proposed system with the user before any physical design has been carried out. They should consist of the free format description, a screen format, the output specifications and a reduced form of the structured English section showing data stores instead of files.

The sections of a process outline

Process outlines comprise the following sections

- Free text description
- Specification of required inputs
- Specification of outputs
- Structured English description with conditional steps

Free text description

The descriptions used are dependent on whether the process outline is logical or physical. In logical process outlines the description is of a general nature and describes the overall requirements of the process in user-related terms.

In physical process outlines the requirements are described in technical terms and in a way specifically for a programmer to use (structured English). It should outline the overall operation and include any information that helps to explain anything which could be unclear elsewhere (that is, use of flags and so on).

Specification of required inputs

This section is only needed if the process is driven by input from the user, and therefore usually relates to real-time processes. It should list the data fields entered by the user and the characteristics of each should be specified in terms of:

- its name as it appears in the file definition
- any default value which applies
- the validation rules in accordance with the following syntax:

MI	Mandatory Input
EQ	Equal to
NE	Not equal to
LT	Less than
LE	Less than or Equal to
GT	Greater than
GE	Greater than or Equal to
NUMERIC	Must be numeric
ALPHA	Must be alphabetic
TIME	Valid time
DATE	Valid date
IN-RANGE	Must be between the two numbers specified
IN-ALPHA	Must be in string specified
ON-FILE	Must be on file specified
NOT-ON-FILE	Must not be on file specified
Free Format	

A screen format may also be included if thought appropriate. Logical process outlines should always include a format but would probably not include the detailed field specification as outlined above.

Specification of outputs

The outputs from the process are specified in terms of the fields on the report or screen enquiry, and an example of the layout should be included. Where the method of writing to report files is adopted (for batch printing at some time in the future) the names of such files and the relevant fields should be given. Each report is given a reference, which is cross-referred to in the structured English section.

Structured English description

Structured English is a means of describing the process in discrete steps each of which comprises:

- a step number
- a precise but brief description of the step using structured English
- a list of the files accessed by the step denoting
  - ☐ the type of access (direct, paging or serial)
  - ☐ the file access mode (add, modify, delete or look-up)
  - ☐ a list of the attributes required from the file read or by the step

Each step must be one of the following types with nesting shown by giving the step a lower level step number and by indenting it:

- a pure operation which is free format, but should be kept simple. Any operation which is complex should be broken down into a series of simple ones. An operation step must not contain any conditional or looping functionality and where it produces an output, the report reference should be given in the description;
- a pure condition which always triggers a nesting condition and must start with **IF**. No operational logic is allowed in the conditional step itself but must follow on subsequent steps, indented by one level. An **ELSE** step is permitted following the steps executed if the condition is true. This should be indented on the same level as the **IF** step and the operation steps for the **ELSE** clause should be indented to the same level as those for the true condition;
- a pure loop structure which always triggers a nesting condition and should start with a **FOR EACH**. Following this is the loop specification indented one level. Where the loop step specifies a serial pass through the file, the order of processing of the records should be given as part of the loop step, e.g. *unsorted* or *sorted by name within department*. The last step should start with **END** followed by any optional free text.

An example of a logical process outline is shown in Figure 14.9 and that for a physical process outline in Figure 14.10, both of which can be found at the end of Section 14.3.

14.3.9 File/function matrices

A file/function matrix is a list of all the process and files in the system with a reference for each process against the file it uses, indicating the way in which it uses the file. The method of use is determined by the following:

A Add
D Delete
L Look
M Modify
I Insert

The matrix serves two very useful and important tasks. It provides, at a glance, a cross-reference of the files used by each process and it can help validate the design stage by highlighting files which are created, but never used or enquired upon by other processes.

An example of a file/function matrix can be found in Figure 14.11 immediately following this section.

SYSTEM LEVEL DFD		
System: APT administration	**Level:** 1	**Date:** 17 September 94
Sub-system: Accounts		**Page:** 1 of 1

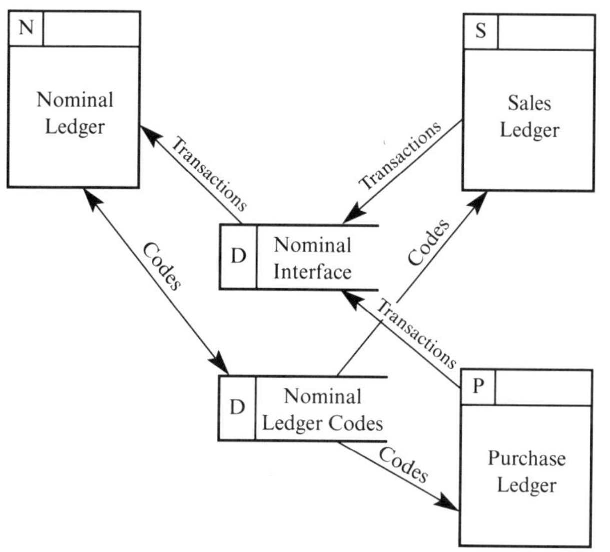

Figure 14.1

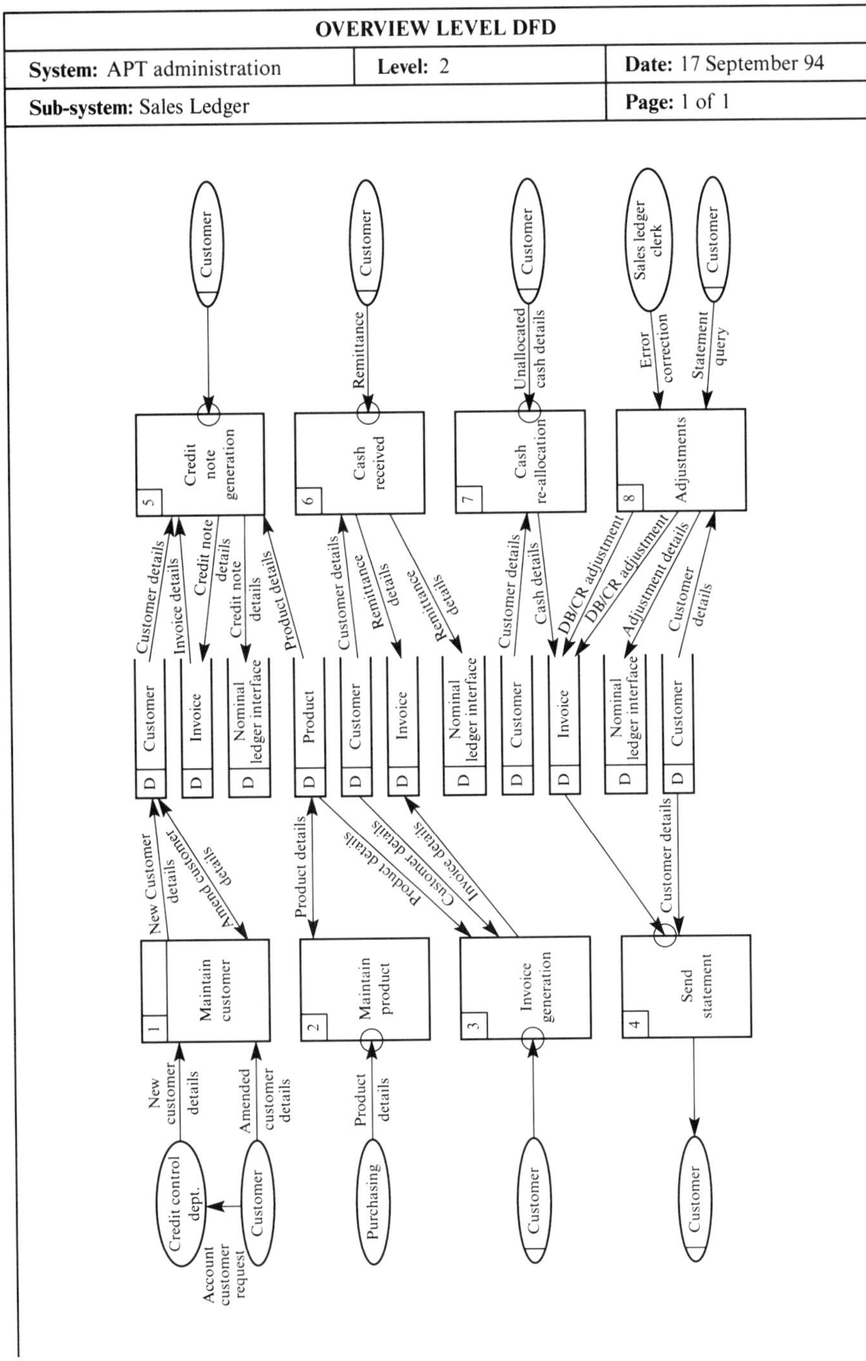
OVERVIEW LEVEL DFD
System: APT administration
Level: 2
Date: 17 September 94
Sub-system: Sales Ledger
Page: 1 of 1
Customer
Credit note generation
Cash received
Remittance
Unallocated cash details
Cash re-allocation
Sales ledger clerk
Error correction
Statement query
Adjustments
Customer details
Invoice details
Credit note details
Product details
Remittance details
Cash details
DB/CR adjustment
Adjustment details
Invoice
Nominal ledger interface
Product
New Customer details
Amend customer details
Invoice generation
Send statement
Maintain customer
Maintain product
New customer details
Amended customer details
Credit control dept.
Account customer request
Purchasing

Figure 14.2

LOW LEVEL DFD

System: APT administration	**Level:** 3	**Date:** 17 September 94
Sub-system: Sales Ledger – Adjustments		**Page:** 1 of 1

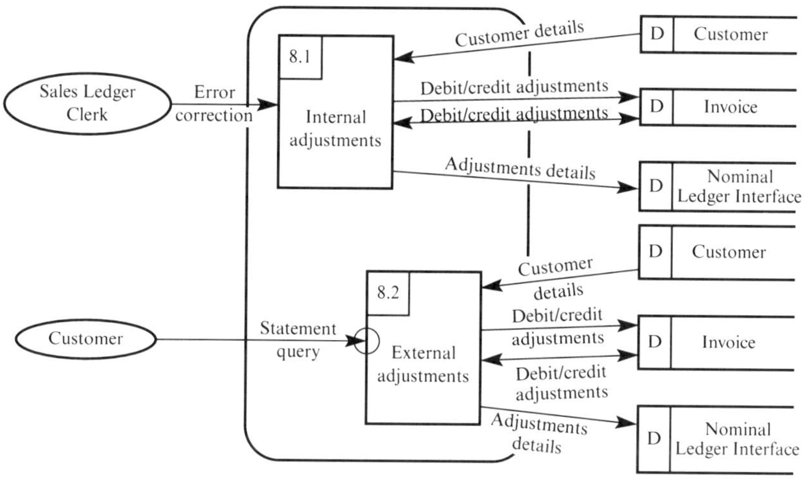

Figure 14.3

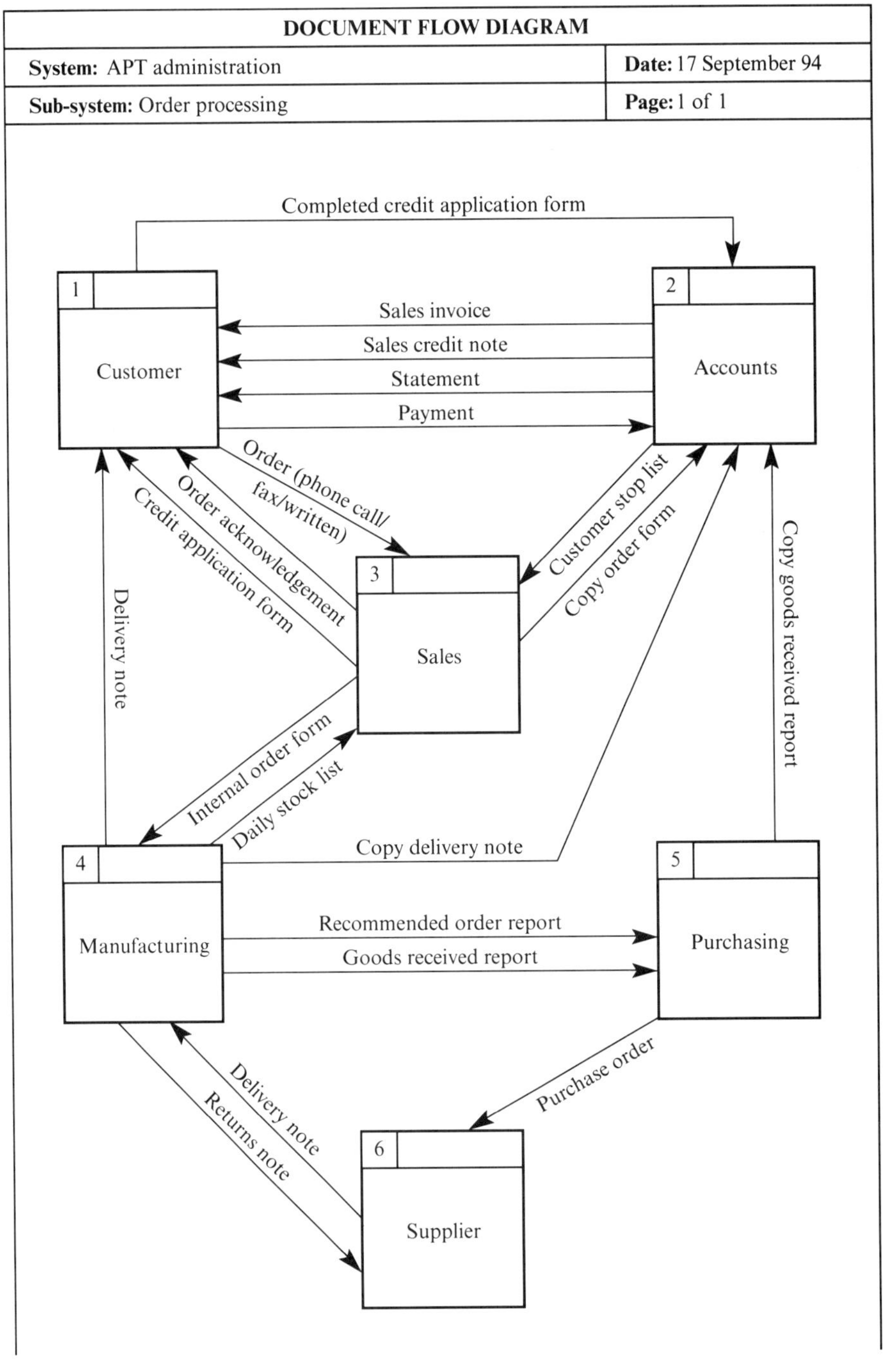
DOCUMENT FLOW DIAGRAM
System: APT administration
Date: 17 September 94
Sub-system: Order processing
Page: 1 of 1
Completed credit application form
1
Customer
2
Accounts
Sales invoice
Sales credit note
Statement
Payment
Order (phone call/ fax/written)
Order acknowledgement
Credit application form
Delivery note
Customer stop list
Copy order form
Copy goods received report
3
Sales
Internal order form
Daily stock list
Copy delivery note
4
Manufacturing
5
Purchasing
Recommended order report
Goods received report
Purchase order
Delivery note
Returns note
6
Supplier

Figure 14.4

DATA FLOW DIAGRAM	
Current: Physical	**Level:** 2
Sub-system: APT administration	**Date:** 17 September 94
Sub-system: Sales	**Page:** 1 of 1

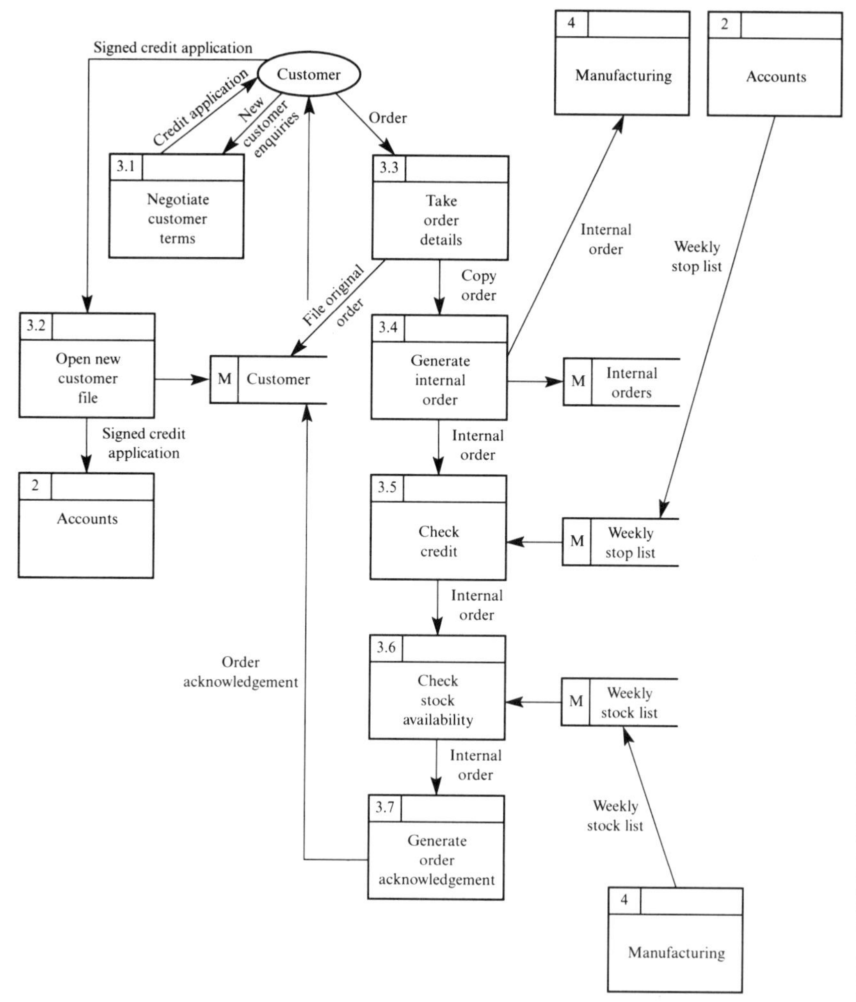

Figure 14.5

DATA FLOW DIAGRAM	
Required logical	**Level:** 2
Sub-system: APT administration	**Date:** 17 September 94
Sub-system: Sales	**Page:** 1 of 1

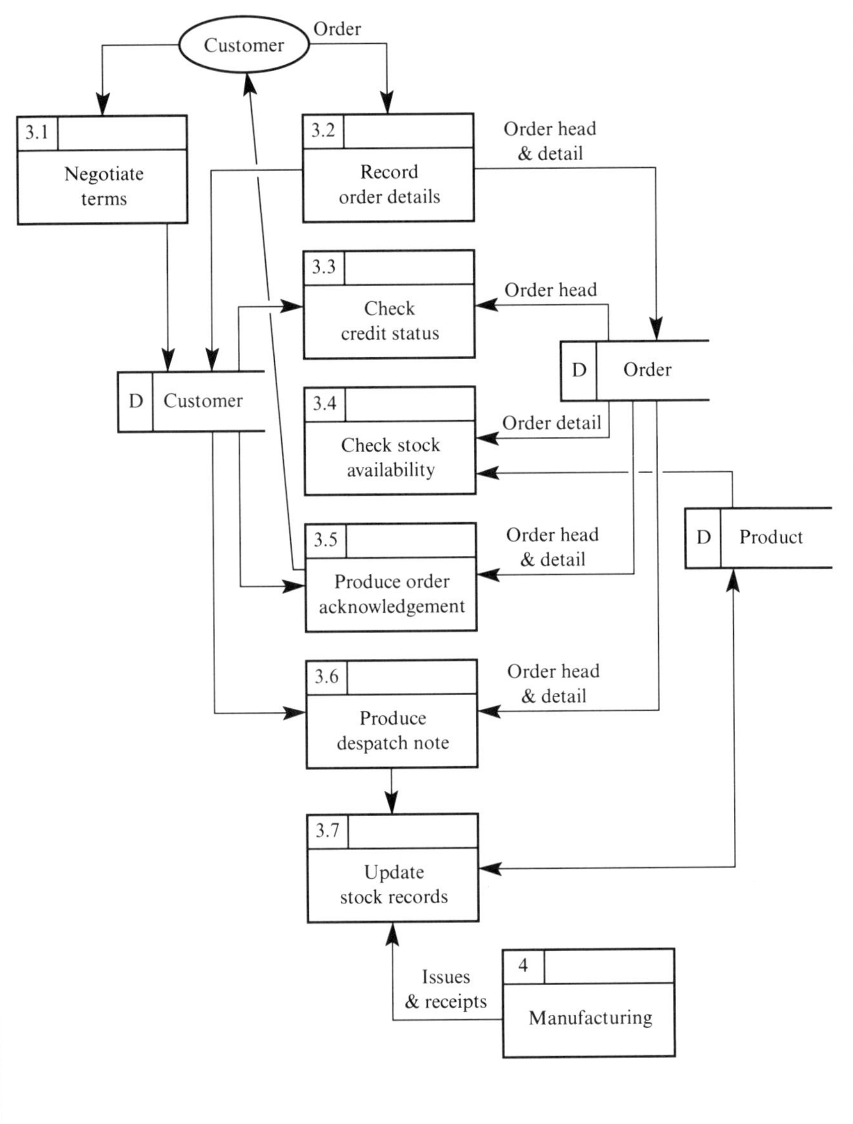

Figure 14.6

DATA STRUCTURE DIAGRAM	
Current Logical	**Level:** 2
System: APT administration	**Date:** 17 September 94
Sub-system: Sales	**Page:** 1 of 1

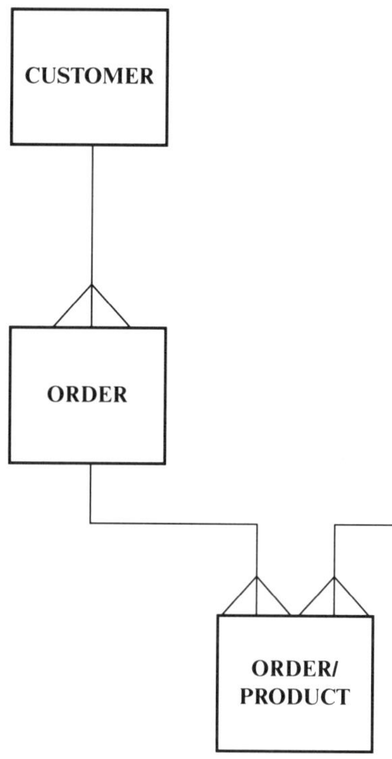

Figure 14.7

DATA STRUCTURE DIAGRAM	
Required Physical	**Level:** 2
System: APT administration	**Date:** 17 September 94
Sub-system: Sales	**Page:** 1 of 1

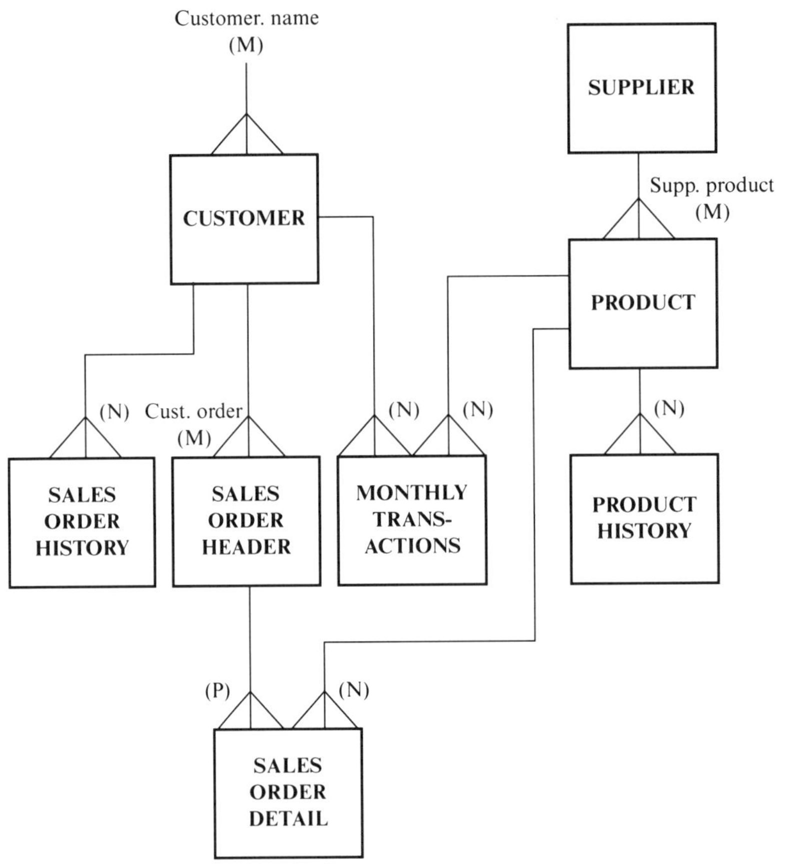

Figure 14.8

LOGICAL PROCESS OUTLINE	
System: APT administration	**Date:** 17 September 94
Sub-system: Sales	**Page:** 1 of 1
Title: Take an order	**Process Ref:** 3.3

Description of function:

This option is where new customer orders are entered into the system. The order received is checked as complete and the order is checked to be from an existing customer. Any problems with the order are referred to the Sales Manager and once a completed order is ready to process the details are entered into the system. The original customer order is then filed and a copy of the order used to process the order through the remaining stages within the company.

Figure 14.9

PHYSICAL PROCESS OUTLINE

System: APT administration	**Date:** 17 September 94
Sub-system: Sales	**Page:** 1 of 1
Title: Take an order	**Process Ref:** 3.3

Step	Description	Action	Entity	Access	Attribute
1.	For each order entered	MI	ORDER		
1.1	Get customer number		CUSTOMER	L	CUST.NUMBER
1.2	If valid customer	EQ	CUSTOMER	L	CUST.NUMBER
1.2.1	Display customer details				
1.2.2	If customer details correct				
1.2.2.1	Enter order details	I	ORDER	A	ORDER.NUMBER
1.2.3	Else (wrong customer chosen)				
1.2.3.1	Enter at step 1.1				
1.2.4	End of if				
1.3	Else (not known customer)				
1.3.1	Prompt user whether to create				
1.3.2	If create customer required				
1.3.3.1	Display customer entry details				
1.3.3.2	Validate customer details				
1.3.3.3	If details valid				
1.3.3.3.1	Add record to file	I	CUSTOMER	A	CUST.NUMBER
1.3.3.4	Else				
1.3.3.4.1	Display error message(s)				
1.3.3.4.2	Enter at step 1.3.3.2				
1.3.3.5	End of if				
1.3.4	Else (do not create customer)				
1.3.4.1	Enter at step 1.1				
1.3.5	End of if				
1.4	End of if				

Figure 14.10

FILE/FUNCTION MATRIX

System: APT administration | **Date:** 17 September 94

Sub-system: Sales | **Page:** 1 of 1

	3.1 Negotiate terms	3.2 Record order details	3.3 Check credit status	3.4 Check stock availability	3.5 Produce order acknowledgement	3.6 Produce despatch note	3.7 Update stock records
Customer	M	M	L		L	L	
Product		M		M	L	L	M
Order header		I	L		L	L	
Order detail		I		L	L	M	

Figure 14.11

14.4 File design considerations

14.4.1 The virtual memory environment

The primary consideration of virtual memory management is to minimize the number of disk reads required to bring relevant data into main memory. In addition care should be taken to ensure that only data pertinent to the particular process is read into main memory. If the main memory fills quickly with redundant data, frame faults will occur and it is to access to the hard disk, one of the slowest parts of a computer system, that slows down the overall performance of the system. When designing a database for the PICK operating system the following points should be considered.

- A batch processing function such as an ACCESS report often involves the processing of a great many items. If each of these items is small, more items will fit into a frame and fewer disk reads will be necessary. Indeed it is always possible that the information read into main memory during the early stages of the processing may still be there.
- Transaction processing generally involves header and detail records with the detail records being individual items. On very large transactions, this may have a similar effect as batch processing. in that many items brought into memory from disk, will be used subsequently. Hence the file design needs to reflect a careful balance between optimum retrieval and updating.
- Large items need more memory for efficient processing.

Hence the moral is to keep items as small as possible and to limit the information in an item to that required for processal processing.

14.4.2 Timeslice

PICK is a multi-user system which is controlled by each user having a given time slot for processing all of which is controlled by the PICK monitor. Processes are queued according to their priority with batch processes given a lower priority than the interactive ones. A task can lose its time allocation for a number of reasons and this will slow down its processing. The prime causes for this are

- a disk read
- the disk record is locked
- an RQM in a PICK/BASIC program
- I/O is roadblocked
- the process is sleeping.

If processes constantly lose their timeshare, prematurely, they will take longer to complete and system thrashing will be more likely. It is important that this be recognized and file design should take PICK locking into account and once again should minimalize disk reads.

14.4.3 File structure

Physical one-to-one file design

To minimize record size, large records should be split into many files with one-to-one relationships between them. This is achieved by grouping attributes together based on their processal use. The existence of a one-to-one relationship implies that a record in one file can be identified directly from the other with the item-id of one file being held somewhere in the other. This creates a simple one-to-one relationship capable of being dealt with by the ACCESS processor, particularly if the item-id itself is common.

Normal one-to-one

A typical example is the case of a PARTS file where the data is split into processal areas. In the case of the example below, the static information is stored in the primary parts file, with information on locations stored in the PART.LOCN file. In both instances the files contain the same key, the part number.

PART FILE	PART. LOCN FILE
0 Part number	0 Part number
1 Description	1 Location (mutli-valued)
2 Product group	2 Quantity in stock (mutli-valued)
3 Unit of measure	

This technique is particularly useful when a master file contains multi-valued details. These may be split up into other files which maintain a one-to-one relationship with the master. A process requiring particular details then reads only the appropriate file and hence minimizes unnecessary system overheads. The rule for this type of relationship is that you must easily be able to get from one file to the other and vice versa.

In the above example the relationship is permanent, but this is not always the case. Optional one-to-one relationships can occur in file design and in these instances it is rare to have them keyed with the same item-id. In optional one-to-one relationships the key to one file is generally an attribute in the other.

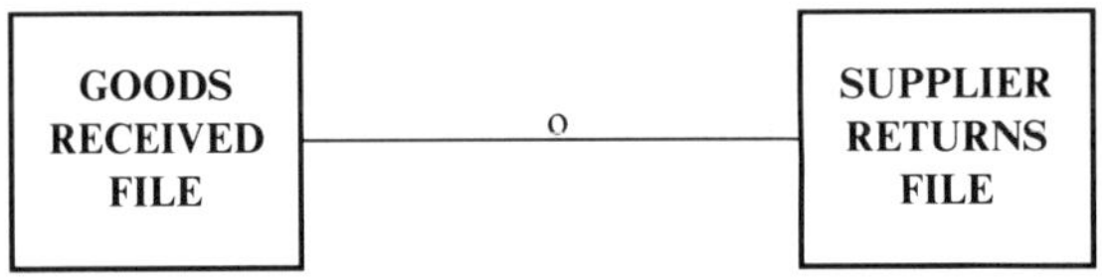

Goods received file	Supplier returns file
0 GRN number	0 Supplier return note number
1 Supplier code	1 Supplier code
2 Purchase order number	2 Quantity returned
3 Qty received (good)	3 Date returned
4 Qty received (rejected)	
5 Supplier return note number	

Normal one-to-many relationships

A one-to-many relationship implies that the items in the detail file can be readily identified from its master and vice versa. This one-to-many relationship typically exists where the master and detail are held in separate files and is typical of a transaction processing data structure. Since it is necessary to derive the detail item-ids directly from the master without performing a serial read on the detail file, it implies that all detail items must relate to its master. Similarly, the item-id of the master will need to be held somewhere in the detail record which makes available the data held in the master record for the purposes of sort and selection processes.

In principle there are three basic methods of building these cross reference mechanisms and we will look at each in turn.

- **Paging detail file** where the detail record pages off the master file.
- **Paging cross-reference file** which uses another file to cross-reference downwards by paging off the master.
- **Cross-reference file with multi-valued attributes** which uses another file to store the keys of the detail records as a multi-valued attribute in the master record.

Paging detail file

In the paging detail file structure, the primary key of the paging detail file is generally the key of the corresponding master record concatenated with a sequence number. This concatenation of keys ensures a unique item-id for the paging detail file. Bear in mind that since the item-id of the master item may be derived from the detail's key it is not necessary to store the item-id of the master in the detail record in order to go up the structure.

Consider an order processing system where the order comprises a fixed element in the master item with each order line comprising a record in the detail file.

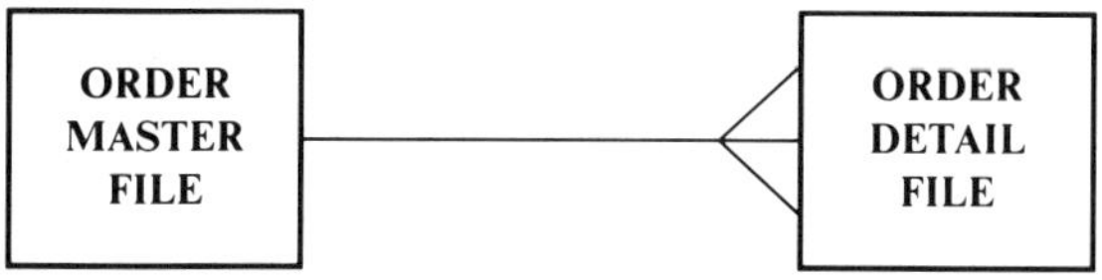

0 Order number
1 Customer code
2 Order date
3 Total order value

0 Order number
0 Line number (sequence number)
1 Product code
2 Order quality
3 Unit price
4 Line value

This structure is not without its problems, particularly if you need to know how many lines there are on any given order, although this could obviously be added as an attribute in the order master. However if an order line needs to be deleted it can cause a potential break in the sequence of numbers, making the processing of detail records quite complicated. It does, however, offer the advantage of breaking the total order information into small records and minimizes the data being handled at any one time.

Paging cross-reference file

This indirect paging method involves a cross reference file which sits between the master and detail file. The cross-reference file is indexed on a concatenation of the master item-id and sequence number and holds the unique product code section of the detail item-id. In the order processing example, the order cross-reference file contains the product code as an attribute and the product code concatenated with the order number forms the key to the detail file.

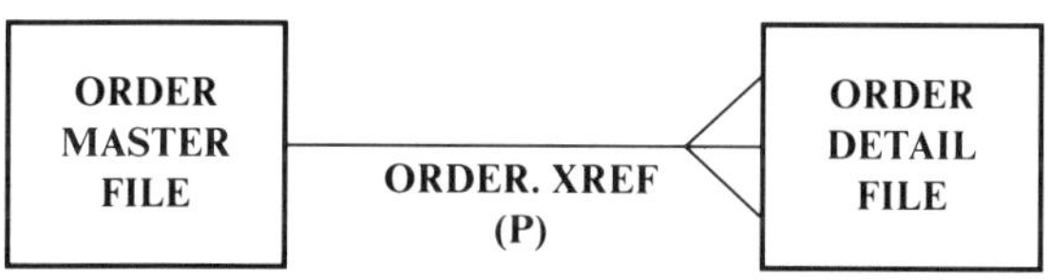

0 Order number
0 Sequence number
1 Product code

0 Order number
1 Customer code
2 Order date
3 Total order value

0 Order number
0 Product code
1 Order quality
2 Unit price
3 Line value

This method has difficulties when dealing with the transfer of a detail record from one master to another. In this situation a sequential pass on the index file is carried out using the master record id and when the index record is located and deleted, the others need to be resequenced and the new index record added to the appropriate master with the appropriate sequence number.

Cross-reference file with multi-valued attribute

This form of one-to-many relationship structure can only be emulated by PICK, which has the unique concept of multi-values and there are three possibilities to consider.

The first is to store in the master a multi-value list of keys to the detail file. This could be the order line number, a sequential number or the product code (assuming it to be unique to an order).

0 Order number
1 Customer code
2 Order code
3 Total order value

0 Order detail key
1 Product code
2 Order quantity
3 Unit price
4 Line value

The second option is to create a cross-reference file keyed on order number which contains a multi-value list of product codes.

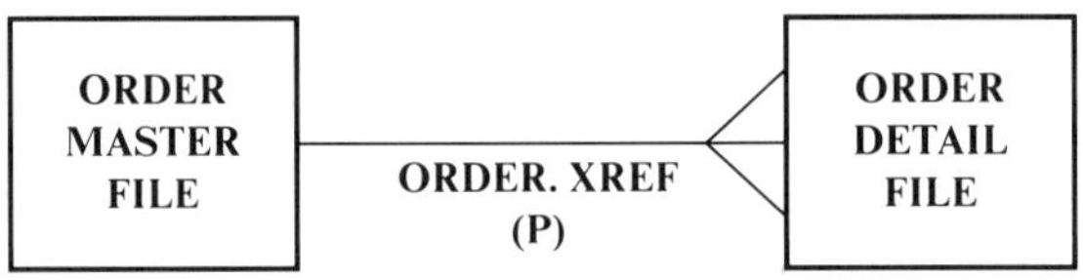

0 Order number
1 Product code (mutli-valued)

0 Order number
1 Customer code
2 Order date
3 Total order value

0 Order number
0 Product code
1 Order quantity
2 Unit price
3 Line value

An alternative for master/detail relationships

The final alternatives in processing master/detail relationships are to consider including all the detail in one record. In this case there is no detail file and the master contains a series of multi-value attributes containing the data which would normally be held in the detail file.

0 Order number
1 Customer code
2 Order date
3 Total order value
4 Product code (multi-valued)
5 Quantity ordered (multi-valued)
6 Unit price (multi-valued)
7 Line value

A compromise between a fully detailed master and the one-to-many relationship structure with index files is to create a one-to-one relationship where all the details are held in one record in the associated file (see the section on normal one-to-one files).

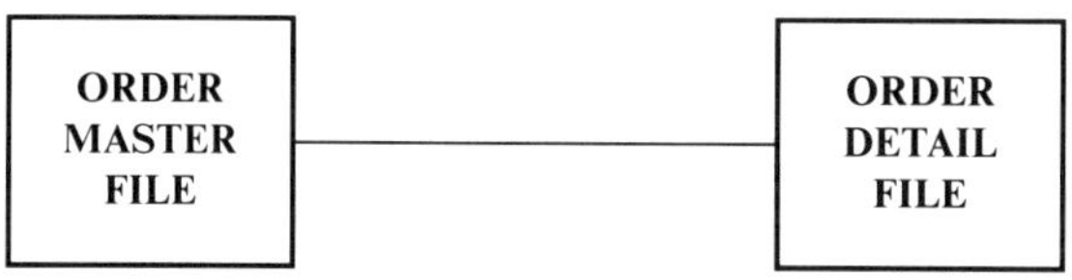

0 Order number
1 Customer code
2 Order date
3 Total order value

0 Order number
1 Product code (multi-valued)
2 Order quantity (multi-valued)
3 Unit price (multi-valued)
4 Line value (multi-valued)

These last two file designs can run into serious problems with item size and remember that with R83 PICK the maximum record size is 32K. However, whilst these structures can be appropriate in certain instances, you should ensure that record size is limited to a maximum of around 5K otherwise system performance will be affected.

Multi-valued downward pointers have the advantage that they are readily handled within the ACCESS processor and can be used to directly access detail records with although this requires a serial pass through the detail file.

14.4.4 Item structure in file design

People used to working on traditional systems are aware of a considerable overhead in the processing of large numbers of different files and for that reason have tended to group as much information as possible into one file.

However PICK works better with smaller items since performance problems occur with data structures growing too big and with data strings within records becoming too long. Hence it is far more efficient in a PICK environment to process multiple files containing small items.

The information held together should reflect its use. It should not be grouped together if it is being used by different sets people in different ways. Only data which is necessarily processed together should be held in the same file. Ideally a PICK item should comprise:

- homogenous records
- no more than 200 bytes
- maximum of 30 attributes
- maximum of 30 multi-values.

As we saw in the above section, the normalization process will group information which has like keys but that does not determine whether information should be put in one file or divided into separate files.

After normalization is complete, group together data fields which will be accessed together for either update or retrieval purposes. This ensures that only information pertinent to a particular process or report is grouped together and therefore will tend to reflect the purposes of different users. It also means that only the attributes that are needed at any one time are read into main memory. Sometimes this will result in very large items, however, in the long term disk reads will be reduced, even though items may be forced into overflow. In R83 large separations may help minimize overflow but remember that on Advanced PICK the separation is 1 and cannot be altered.

This technique will also help deal with the perennial archiving problem as dynamic information will tend to be grouped together, as will static and historic data. Now let's consider the content of an item.

The body of an item

In general the following guidelines should be followed.

- Fields which are mandatory should occupy the earlier attributes as trailing attribute and value marks are generally not held.
- Fields most commonly accessed should be held in the early attributes of an item.
- Single values should be held at the top of the item with multi-valued fields lower down.

- Code fields should be stored and these should reference lookup tables for their descriptions. Apart from helping with consistency of input, it also reduces item size.
- Null values should be used wherever possible to represent the most likely or default value.
- Multi-value fields should only be used to hold repeated information of the same type and the position of the value should have no meaning other than its entry in terms of date or sequential order. The most common cause of large records is the inclusion of multi-valued attributes and in R83 systems this is the most common cause of the item size limit being broken.
- Separate fields should be used to hold separate information.

Adopting these rules has the effect of minimizing item size which in turn simplifies file sizing, ensures memory is not filled with redundant data and reduces the number of sequential searches. You should always question your design when an item contains more than 70 or so attributes and in particular when it calls for multi-values and even more so, sub-values. You need to carefully review files containing header/detail or master/history combinations.

14.4.5 Item-id structure

Quite frequently you have no control over the structure of the item-id, but for internal files, the format of the item-id can have a significant effect on processing. The following rules will help to optimize performance.

- Where update and retrieval is frequent and the size of the file is large, use sequential keys to ensure an even distribution of items.
- Where items are not sequentially keyed, always use a prefix rather than a suffix and aim at uniform length. This will encourage uniform distribution as the most significant character is rightmost in the item-id and there is different weighting given to each character, dependant on its position in the item-id.
- The weighting of the hashing algorithm ensures that the last twenty characters have most significance so keep item-ids less than this.

The length of the item-id should be kept to a minimum. On some systems, notably R83, the limit is 50 characters. Equally, keys should hold a minimum of information so the idea of concatenating several fields together to help in sorting and selections is entirely misplaced.

Multiple information in a key may be useful, but keep the length of the item-id to a minimum and hold the information in the order which it will most likely be accessed. Where the fields being concatenated are not of a fixed length, separate the fields with a separator, such as an asterisk. This will enable group extractions to be performed (see Section 13.5.9).

Eliminate redundancies within item-ids, especially to the right-hand side which is the most significant part of the item-id. Doing so will help flatness and distribution, thereby improving hashing and so accessibility.

14.4.6 ACCESS and its implications on file design

The ACCESS retrieval language is a very powerful tool which enables users with very limited data processing experience to generate their own enquiries and reports from the PICK database. Given a well designed file system, ACCESS should be able to cater for a large proportion of an organization's reporting requirements.

When designing a PICK database, consideration should be given to the way in which ACCESS works. Indeed relationships between files can be tested by ensuring that ACCESS can generate the required standard reports. If the files for a particular application have been designed in accordance with third normal form data analysis using the methods suggested in this chapter, the application will have a more stable and flexible base from which ACCESS reports can readily be generated.

The following aspects need to be considered if the files are to be interrogated using ACCESS:

- **TFILE correlatives/conversions** create problems when used to access multi-values in the file being referenced. The multi-values are returned as a single string with the value marks replaced by spaces. This is probably one of the most frustrating problems with the **Tfile** processing code. The only way around it is to define a separate dictionary item for each specific value of the multi-value string. However where the number of values is unknown (such as in the case of an address, the number of lines in an order etc.) this is not always practical or possible.
- **Multi-values** should be used only for like data, where the number of values may vary. Any other use can make reporting with ACCESS quite difficult
- **Sub-values** are not supported in the ACCESS processor and should not be used. A file that seems to need sub-values probably needs a design rethink!

14.4.7 The organization of files

Files are logically grouped together into accounts which traditionally emulate the organizational structure of a company and often represent a specific application area. Whilst this is an understandable approach, with the changes that can occur within an organization, this grouping is not always appropriate. The following are some ideas for consideration for the organization of your files.

- All files updated on a daily basis should be held on a separate account.
- Files updated on a monthly and yearly basis should be similarly separated.
- All files containing live MACROs, PROCs and programs should be held on a separate account.
- MACROs, PROCs and programs currently under development should be held on a separate development account and transferred across to the live software account when testing is complete.
- Where there are many different users each with their own version of software, it may be useful to have separate accounts for each.
- A further software account containing recently changed versions of live software should also be created.
- If it is necessary to keep other versions of previous software, these should also be held in a historical software account.

14.5 Software development standards

Software development standards are essential, particularly in an organization where multiple projects are being undertaken concurrently and need to integrate together at some future point. The following details are aimed at pointing you in the general direction of the areas to consider, rather than providing a definitive set of standards to operate from.

Program file naming

Programs should be grouped together by application area and held in a file XXXX.PROG where XXXX indicates the application of the file, e.g. ORDER.PROG for an order entry system and CUSTOMER.PROG for customer maintenance and enquiry programs.

Some people prefer to use the file name BP (Basic Programs) for program files and again a prefix can be helpful. Whatever file naming convention you choose, try to remember to put **DC** in attribute 1 of the file definition item in the MD. This makes identifying program files with the TCL **LISTFILES** command much easier as the files are listed by file type with the **DC**s showing up separately.

Program naming

Program names should indicate the logical data file they process and the primary nature of their process, i.e. 'A'dd, 'C'hange, 'D'elete or 'E'nquiry. There should also be an indication of its position within a suite of programs. Hence:

CUSTOMER.C1 To indicate the first (or only) program in a suite of Customer amendment programs.

ORDER.A2	The second (or subroutine call) in a suite of order entry programs

File naming

File names should be in the singular, e.g. CUSTOMER, PART. The various physical files which together form a logical entity should have a common name indicating the nature of that entity. Further, a suffix should be used to identify the type of data held in the file. For clarity, a dot should be used to separate the prefix and file name:

CUSTOMER.MASTER	Main (static) customer details
ORDER.HEADER	Current order header details
ORDER.DETAIL	Order line details
CUSTOMER.ORDER	Customer/orders cross reference
ORDER.HISTORY	Completed orders master

Q-pointers should have a **.Q** suffixed to them, i.e. CUSTOMER.MASTER.Q.

Field naming

Field names should be consistent throughout the system and should be meaningful. Where the same field is to be found in more than one file (this should normally only apply to foreign keys) the same name, prompt and/or description should be used. Field names should be prefixed with a suitable abbreviation of the file name they belong to. Once again a dot should be used to separate words.

CUST.CODE	Customer item-id
CUST.NAME	Customers name
ORDER.NO	Order number
ORDER.VALUE	Order Value

Menus

Menus should be limited to one page only and pull down menus should wherever possible leave on display the calling menu option.

Screens

Ensure the screen has a heading and that matches the menu option name. Ensure that screens are of a consistent size and that pop-up windows appear in a consistent place. Where an application uses process keys, standardize the use of these keys wherever possible, i.e. F1 for on-line help, F2 to save, etc. Avoid abbreviations wherever possible and try to adopt a standard colour scheme where colour is used in applications, nothing is worse than having the foreground and background colours change each time a different menu option is chosen. Ensure that all error messages are displayed in a common format in a consistent part of the screen.

Reports and enquiries

Wherever possible provide the option for user run-time selection criteria and provide for output to optionally go to the screen and printer. Limit the output to 80 characters wherever possible, but keep the maximum below 132 characters, the standard width of most printers.

BASIC code

Always start the program with a section containing a description of the processality of the program. Clearly document any subsequent changes to the program in the same section. Be careful not to use any machine specific syntax and always use the full form of a process. Include as many comments as possible within the program (you may find them invaluable if you have to modify your program at some future date – others will undoubtedly find them invaluable!). At a minimum include comments at the beginning of the program, at the start of each subroutine, after each CALL or GOSUB and particularly where the program logic may be difficult to understand. When assigning variable names use ones that are meaningful and do not re-use variables unless absolutely essential, it can make understanding a program more difficult. Determine a common block for your programs and control the allocation of its variables carefully to minimize conflict.

15 Programming in PICK BASIC

TCL verbs and general commands covered in this section are

BASIC	CATALOG	COMPILE	DECATALOG	RUN

15.1 An introduction to PICK BASIC

When the first PICK systems were supplied PICK BASIC did not exist. In those days people used ACCESS and PROC and any application programming that was needed was written in assembler. It didn't take long to realize that a procedural programming language was needed and Ken Simms was charged with the responsibility of developing it and the result was the PICK BASIC compiler. Although enhanced, the fundamentals are very much the same as he originally developed. Ken sadly died at the very early age of 38 in November 1988, but the compiler remains a tribute to a very talented individual.

PICK BASIC is an extended and enhanced version of Dartmouth BASIC, on some systems it is called Data BASIC, and it is the language most widely used for developing application software. There is an assembler language which is only for the experienced and competent programmer, and not readily distributed. Such is the power of the assembler that any company that uses it voids their operating system warranty and indeed some manufacturers refuse to distribute it altogether!

Needless to say PICK BASIC contains all the necessary features to develop complete and comprehensive applications based around the special PICK database structure without the need to resort to assembler. It works with variable names of any length allowing sensible programmers to give them meaningful names! It also encourages structured programming by providing multi-line IF statements, a CASE statement for the conditional selection of BASIC statements, a 'LOOP..UNTIL..DO..REPEAT' facility and the means to call external subroutines.

PICK BASIC is a compiled BASIC protecting the original source code which can be removed from any 'live' system. The object code produced by the compiler, however, is not native machine code and therefore has to be interpreted at runtime. This explains the frequently used, but often confusing statement that PICK BASIC is a compiled interpretative BASIC. Another important feature is that the compiled program is re-entrant. This means that if more than one person is using the same program only one copy of its logic is kept in memory which everybody uses although each user will naturally be assigned their own data area.

BASIC programs are held in a file. Each progam is an item in that file and normally each program statement is an attribute of the item. Since the compiler writes an object code pointer in the file dictionary of the item there are two important aspects to every BASIC program file which need to be borne in mind. Firstly it ***must*** contain a dictionary portion and secondly its Master Dictionary entry in R83 systems ***must*** contain DC in attribute one indicating it to be a pointer file. Whilst it is not necessary to define a program file any differently than a normal data file under AP, you might find it useful to change the file definition item in the Master Dictionary to DC anyway. It just makes identifying program files that much easier as the **LISTFILES** command will separate files by their file type.

15.2 Creating, compiling and running BASIC programs

The first stage in programming is to create a file to hold the programs. This file is often given the name BP (Basic Programs) but obviously can be called any other name you choose. You may find such a progam file already exists since it is frequently part of the **DM** account. If you cannot find this file, try the LISTFILES (or LF) command and look for a file containing DC under the heading CODE. Any file with the DC code, other than POINTER-FILE whose special purpose is discussed in Section 5.2.21, can be used as the program file. If no program file exists you must first create one using the CREATE-FILE command as discussed in Section 6.3.1. Having created the file, ensuring it has a dictionary portion, the next step is to edit its MD entry and change the first attribute, which defines the file type, to DC. Remember whilst this is optional in Advanced PICK it is essential in R83. Figure 15.1 explains how these two important steps are handled.

Having created the program file the next stage is to create a program. A program contains source code which is lines of PICK BASIC instructions the last

```
:CREATE-FILE BP 3 27

[417] FILE 'BP' CREATED BASE= 29576, MODULO=3, SEPAR=1.
[417] FILE 'BP' CREATED BASE= 31985, MODULO=27, SEPAR=1.

:ED MD BP
TOP
.[CR]
001 D
.R[CR]
001 DC[CR]
.FI[CR]
'BP' FILED.
```

Figure 15.1 Creating a file to hold BASIC programs.

of which should be a **STOP** statement. Each program requires a name which uniquely identifies it. The program is created using the Editor or Update Processor and once created has to be compiled to generate the object code which is interpreted at run time. Compilation is handled by the TCL command BASIC or COMPILE, both of which carry out the same task. However AP programs can contain lower case statements and lower case variables which are not permitted in R83. Programs containing any lower case letters can only be compiled using the COMPILE verb; the command BASIC will not work with lowercase syntax.

In order to know what program to compile these TCL commands have to be told the program file name and program name. When the program has been compiled successfully, it can be run by typing the TCL verb RUN followed by the program file name and program name. Figure 15.2 shows the development of a small program called PROG1 through these various stages. Do not worry too much at this stage about the syntax of the program.

The program in Figure 15.2 displays on the screen four random numbers between 0 and 100. The RND function generates random numbers between 0 and one less than the number contained in brackets. You may have noticed that following the instruction to compile the program, and the command COMPILE could have been used in place of BASIC, there followed a series of asterisks. If you count these you will find that one asterisk is displayed for each

```
:ED BP PROG1
NEW ITEM
TOP
.I
001+*THIS PROGRAM PRINTS 4 RANDOM NUMBERS[CR]
002+PRINT "FOUR RANDOM NUMBERS BETWEEN 0 & 100 ARE "[CR]
003+FOR I=1 TO 4[CR]
004+NUM=RND(101)[CR]
005+PRINT NUM[CR]
006+NEXT I[CR]
007+END[CR]
008+STOP[CR]
009+[CR]
EOI 007
.FI[CR]
'PROG1' FILED.

:BASIC BP PROG1

 ********
SUCCESSFUL COMPILE! 1 FRAMES USED.
:RUN BP PROG1
FOUR RANDOM NUMBERS BETWEEN 0-100 ARE
22
26
47
90
```

Figure 15.2 The development stages of a program.

line in the program, hence as our program was eight lines long, eight asterisks were shown. In some implcmentations with very high speed processors one asterisk may denote many lines of BASIC code; on the Sequoia for example each asterisks represents 10 lines of code.

A number of compiler options are available and these are shown in Figure 15.3.

:BASIC *'Program file name' 'Program name'* {(OPTIONS
:COMPILE *'Program file name' 'Program name'* {(OPTIONS

where the possible options are:

A The assembled code option which generates a listing of the source code line numbers, the labels and the BASIC opcodes used by the program. This is a 'pseudo' assembly code listing which allows the user to see what BASIC opcodes his program has generated
B Turns on array bounds checking when used with the 'o' option
C The catalog option for fully debugged programs. It suppresses the End-Of-Line opcodes from the object item. Since the compiler uses the EOL opcodes to count lines for error messages it means the compiler can only show error messages as being on line 1. The advantage of this option being that it saves 1 byte for each source code line
D Prevents the runtime 'd' option from entering the debugger
E Lists error lines only
H Hides Flash BASIC object code from other users
I Lists lines from any included program as part of the listing. If used with the 'L' option the included lines are indicate by a '+'
K Keeps a shared Flash BASIC module loaded. The TCL command **SHPSTAT** gives detailed information about shared loading
L Lists each line of the program as it is compiled
M Produces a variable map and a statement map both of which are printed after compilation. These maps show where the program data has been stored in the user's workspace
N No pause; suppresses the need to press [CR] at the end of each terminal display
O *{lvl* Produces Flash BASIC native code. This option can be followed by a number indicating the desired optimization level
P All compilation output goes to the printer
R Generates R83 compatible arithmetic (i.e. truncate precision) when using the **O** option
S Supresses the symbol table which is normally generated during compilation and which is used exclusively by the Debugger
X Generates a cross-reference of all variables and labels which it stores in a file called **BSYM** which normally has to be created by the user
W Optimizes without source when used with the **O** option

Figure 15.3 Compiler options.

In Figure 15.2 a lot of typing was required to run the program. We had to include the program file name and the program name so that PICK could identify the program to execute. There is a much easier way to execute a compiled program. Any compiled program can be catalogued using the TCL verb **CATALOG**. This places an entry of the program name in the Master Dictionary and from this point on the program can be run by just typing in the program name. There is just one potential problem with this process which is not so obvious but which can be time consuming to resolve and that is the cataloguing of programs of the same name in different program files.

PICK will allow you to catalogue programs even if they have been catalogued before and will not complain if the program was previously catalogued and from a different program file. All that will happen when you go to run the program is that it will run the last program to be catalogued under that name. So if one of your programs or subroutines is doing wildly outrageous and inexplicable things, you may find this to be the reason. There is an obvious moral to this story which is that no program name should be duplicated and certainly not in the same account. It may sound obvious and without doubt it is common sense. However since all subroutines **HAVE** to be catalogued before they can be called from a program problems of this nature have been known to occur.

Please note too, that some implementations of PICK require that programs be catalogued each time a change is made although not a feature of standard PICK. Having shown the way in which a program can be catalogued, it is worth mentioning that programs can also be decatalogued. This is achieved with the **DECATALOG** command, which not only removes the entry in the Master Dictionary but removes the object code as well. To reuse the program in any way after it has been decatalogued it will need to be recompiled! Like the **CATALOG** verb, **DECATALOG** requires the program file name and the program name. To catalogue or decatalogue all programs in a program file you can use the wildcard, asterisk, facility as shown in Figure 15.4.

Whatever the implementation of PICK any change to the source code will obviously require the recompilation of the program in order to generate new object code. Figure 15.5 illustrates how program changes are handled. In this example the program is changed to reflect the following requirements:

- clear the screen before displaying any data
- request the upper limit number of the random number to be chosen by the user
- check the user entered number does not exceed 32,767.

```
:CATALOG BP *
:DECATALOG BP *
```

Figure 15.4 Cataloguing and decataloguing all programs in a program file.

```
:ED BP PROG1
TOP
.[CR]
001 *THIS PROGRAM PRINTS 4 RANDOM NUMBERS
.I[CR]
001+LOOP[CR]
001+PRINT @(-1) ; *THIS CLEARS SCREEN[CR]
001+PRINT "RANDOM NUMBER PROGRAM"[CR]
001+PRINT "CHOOSE A NUMBER BELOW 32,767"[CR]
001+INPUT MAXNO[CR]
001+UNTIL MAXNO > 32767 DO[CR]
001+PRINT "CHOOSE A NUMBER BELOW 32,767"[CR]
001+PRINT "PRESS RETURN TO CONTINUE"[CR]
001+INPUT DUMMY [CR]
001+[CR]
.[CR]
002 PRINT "4 RANDOM NUMBERS BETWEEN 0 & 100 ARE"
.R[CR]
002 PRINT "THESE ARE 4 RANDOM NUMBERS 0 TO ":MAXNO[CR]
. I[CR]
002+MAXNO=MAXNO+1[CR]
002+[CR]
.[CR]
003 FOR I=1 TO 4
.[CR]
004 NUM=RND(101)
.R/101/MAXNO/[CR]
005 NUM=RND(MAXNO)
.FI[CR]
'PROG1' FILED.
```

Figure 15.5 Changing an existing program with the editor.

Do not worry if the changes in Figure 15.5 have been difficult to understand since the entire new source code is shown in Figure 15.6. Figure 15.6 shows how the new program is compiled, catalogued and run. In the first section of Figure 15.6 a format program is used. The purpose of this program is to format the program into logical blocks making it easier to understand and hence easier to maintain. This is achieved by indenting the source code to make it more readable. To consider the worth of this program, compare the original program in Figure 15.2 with that of Figure 15.6. Since not every implementation has this facility, a copy of the source to the format program is given in Appendix F.

```
:FORMAT

DATA/BASIC FILE NAME -?BP
DATA/BASIC PROGRAM NAME - ?PROG1

*THIS PROGRAM PRINTS 5 RANDOM NUMBERS
LOOP
   PRINT @(-1) ;*THIS CLEARS SCREEN
   PRINT "RANDOM NUMBER PROGRAM"
   PRINT "CHOOSE A NUMBER BELOW 32,767"
   INPUT MAXNO
UNTIL MAXNO > 32767 DO
   PRINT "PLEASE CHOOSE A NUMBER BELOW 32,767"
   PRINT "PRESS RETURN TO CONTINUE"
   INPUT DUMMY
REPEAT
   PRINT "THESE ARE 4 RANDOM NUMBERS BETWEEN 0 & ":MAXNO
   MAXNO=MAXNO+1
FOR I=1 TO 5
   NUM=RND(MAXNO)
   PRINT NUM
NEXT I
END
STOP

-DONE-

:BASIC BP PROG1
 *****************
SUCCESSFUL COMPILE  1 FRAMES USED.

:CATALOG BP PROG1
'PROG1' CATALOGUED!

:PROG1
RANDOM NUMBER PROGRAM
CHOOSE A NUMBER BELOW 32,767
?7535
THESE ARE 4 RANDOM NUMBERS BETWEEN 0 & 7535
1695
921
6776
5936
```

Figure 15.6 Formatting, compiling, cataloguing and running a BASIC program.

15.3 PICK BASIC conventions

We have already started to work with the PICK BASIC in the above examples to get a feel for the language. Those of you already familiar with other BASICs will undoubtedly have understood much of the source so far. Before we start to move more seriously into BASIC let's look at some of its conventions.

A BASIC statement comprises two parts; the statement number and the statement itself. The statement number though, is optional and is normally only included when the statement is itself the destination of another statement.

Using statement numbers in this way certainly saves the headache of renumbering programs to incorporate new code, but remember when used statement numbers must be numeric and unique within the program.

Although it is usual to have one statement on one line, it is possible to include several statements on one line, in which case each is separated by a semi-colon. Figure 15.6 gave an example of this.

Variables can be assigned names of any length (actually restricted to 32,267 characters in R83). They must begin with a letter and can contain any combination of letters, numbers, full stops and dollar signs. They cannot be one of the command words nor one can they comprise one of the following reserved words:

AND	ELSE	GOSUB	LT	ON	THEN
AT	END	GOTO	MATCHES	OR	TO
CASE	EQ	GT	MATCH	REPEAT	UNTIL
CAT	GE	IF	NEXT	SETTING	WHILE
DO	GO	LE	NE	STEP	

Variables sensibly should be given meaningful names to assist others who may need to maintain or debug your program. Avoid the trap of being 'ultra-efficient' and using variables names as short as possible, particularly those just one letter long. Just imagine how difficult it would be to locate all the occurrences of a single letter variable in a program!

Alphanumeric literals or constants consist of a string of or characters surrounded either by single quotes, double quotes backslashes. Numbers can exist on their own. Hence the all following literals are valid:

A="123"	A=123.99	A="NAME"	A='NAME'
A=/NAME/	A="B7 4BJ"	A='Say "Hello"'	

A number can be represented in virtually any way, with or without signs or decimal points. The largest number that can represented is 147037488350000, the smallest is the negative of the same number. PICK traditionally holds numbers to four places of decimals, although this can be altered in the program by use of the **PRECISION** statement.

Arithmetic expressions are formed using arithmetic operators, each of which is given an order of precedence. These are:

Operator	Operation	Precedence
+	Unary plus	1 (high)
–	Unary minus	1
*	Multiplication	2
/	Division	2
+	Addition	3
–	Subtraction	3

This means that expressions like 6+4/2+3*2 are acceptable to PICK BASIC although quite frankly it is hardly clear to most people what the result might be! For the sake of completeness in this book it should be noted that where two or more operators appear that have the same precedence, the leftmost is evaluated first. I trust, however, that most people will use parentheses in formula, not just for the sake of clarity but in respect of the sanity of the person who has to maintain your program. The use of brackets transforms the previously stated equation to the expression (6+(4/2)+(3*2)), which makes it completely unambiguous and gives the same result, 14.

Within BASIC statements a series of logical and relational operators can be used. These being:

Operator	*Operation*
<	Less than
LT	Less than
>	Greater than
GT	Greater than
<=	Less than or equal to
LE	Less than or equal to
>=	Greater than or equal to
GE	Greater than or equal to
=	Equal to
EQ	Equal to
#	Not equal to
NE	Not equal to
MATCH	Matching a pattern
MATCHES	Matching a pattern
:	Concatenation
CAT	Concatenation

Any statement commencing with either of the two symbols * ! or the word **REM** will be considered to contain user-defined remarks and thus will be ignored by the compiler.

15.4 The control of terminals in BASIC

15.4.1 Terminal input

The **INPUT** statement provides the means of collecting information keyed in by the user at a terminal. The word **INPUT** is followed by the name of a data area in the program, called a variable, in which the BASIC compiler will place the typed in data so that the program can make use of it.

The BASIC functions covered in this section are

[ ]	Assign part of a string
CRT	Send data to the terminal
IN	Input a single character from the type-ahead buffer
INPUT	Input data from the terminal
PRINT	Send data to the output device
PROMPT	Assign the prompt character

The general format of the **INPUT** statement is shown in Figure 15.7.

Without any enhancement to the statement, as shown in Figure 15.8, the program will print a question mark on the screen and place the cursor immediately after it awaiting the input of data.

INPUT {@(*col,row*){:}} *var* {=*expr*}{,*len*}{*mask*}{_}{:}

where

col	column position of input
row	row position of input
:	suppresses the carriage return/linefeed
var	the variable to which terminal input is assigned
expr	the value to which the variable is initially assigned. This value is displayed on the screen for the user to modify or accept
len	the maximum length in characters that can be input. If **len** evaluates to 0 or 1 then only one character is accepted. When the maximum number of characters has been input a [CR] is issued automatically unless followed by a : in which case the user has to input the [CR]
mask	an expression equating to the construct of the input. If the input does not match the structure defined by the mask the operator is re-prompted for the input. **N.B.** the mask function can only be used with the @ function
_	outputs a "beep" for each character typed that exceeds the maximum defined in **len**
:	suppresses the carriage return/linefeed

Figure 15.7 The format of the **INPUT** statement.

INPUT QTY would cause the terminal to respond with a question mark as shown below

?

any information typed in after the '?' would be written in the variable 'QTY' accessible to the program

---

Figure 15.8 The **INPUT** statement.

Input statements of this type are not very satisfactory since they only prompt the user with a question mark and do not explain what is being requested and a program full of these would be most confusing! It is a regular need to ask the user for information but far better to do this by first explaining what the user is expected to input. This is achieved by combining the **INPUT** statement with the **PRINT** statement, as shown in Figure 15.9. (The **PRINT** statement is described in Section 15.4.2 on terminal output.)

PRINT 'WHAT IS THE QUANTITY SOLD'
INPUT QTY ← Program statements

```
WHAT IS THE QUANTITY SOLD
?
```
← the result displayed on the terminal

Figure 15.9 **INPUT** and **PRINT** statements.

In Figure 15.9 the words WHAT IS THE QUANTITY SOLD appear on one line whilst the question mark appears on the next. To improve the statement further, it is possible to ensure that input is made on the same line by placing a ':' at the end of the print statement. In order to control the number of characters permitted to be input, the maximum digits allowed can be specified in the **INPUT** statement. Figure 15.10 shows these improvements.

PRINT 'WHAT IS THE QUANTITY SOLD ':
INPUT QTY,4 ← Program statements

```
WHAT IS THE QUANTITY SOLD ?
```
← display on screen which allows a maximum of 4 digits to be input

---

Figure 15.10 **INPUT** and **PRINT** statement.

In Figure 15.10 we saw that the ':' on the **PRINT** statement prevented the automatic carriage return and linefeed which caused the ? to be displayed on the following line. The ':' can also be applied to the input statement, again to prevent an automatic carriage return and linefeed. In Figure 15.10 as soon as the fourth digit is input the program will execute the next statement of the program and any subsequent input will assume a carriage return and linefeed has taken place. If a ':' is placed at the end of the **INPUT** statement, i.e. **INPUT QTY,4:** the user will either have to press the RETURN key to send his input to the program or input the exact number of characters as specified in the **INPUT** statement before the next statement of the program is executed.

PICK BASIC automatically uses the '?' as a prompt unless told otherwise. The statement to change the prompt is **PROMPT** followed by the appropriate character. Hence:

PROMPT ":"	will change the prompt to a ':' and
PROMPT ""	will remove the prompt character altogether

The prompt character will remain in effect until another **PROMPT** statement is encountered. Input or print statements of this nature will assume that information is to be input or displayed on the current line or the line following the current line. In many programs, however it is necessary to input information at a specific column and row of the screen. To accept or display information at a specific position on the screen the @ function is added to the statement. The starting position is the top left of the screen addressed by the co-ordinates 0,0. The @ is followed by parameters, contained in parentheses, that specify the column and row position, for example:

INPUT @(41,2):QTY would position the cursor at column 41, row 2 and await data input

It is important to note that had the variable 'QTY' already contained a value that value would have been displayed first, after which the cursor would have been repositioned at the start of the displayed data awaiting to receive input from the user. If the return key is pressed, the variable will remain unchanged containing the value of the displayed data. Any other data keyed in by the user will change the variable, 'QTY', to the value of that input.

The **INPUT** command is extremely powerful as it can optionally contain a format mask against which the data input is displayed and/or verified. This is makes the **INPUT** statement extremely powerful. If a mask is specified the @ function ***must*** be used. The mask is there to verify and reformat the actual input data . The structure of the format masks is detailed in Section 15.4.4. If a mask is used, the data input is verified according to the mask, then stripped of its output characteristics and stored in internal format. Hence if a number was being input and the mask specifies a decimal digit and/or a scaling factor, then numeric checking is performed.

The problem with input masks are that they only format the data on the screen and hence if you are working with numbers containing decimal points, and the user enters a decimal point, unless this is subsequently stripped out by the program the decimal point will remain and PICK does not store decimal points when storing numbers. The internal format of a number is the number itself, the external or display format being that modified by a mask or conversion code either processed by a program or held in the data dictionary. Hence the statement **INPUT @(10,10):NUM"R2"** will prompt the user for input at row 10, column 10 and if the number 12.3 is input this will be redisplayed as 12.30 (the mask asks for the data to be formatted as right justified to two decimal positions) but the actual input, i.e. 12.3 will be stored in the variable.

Many special characters cannot be captured by the standard **INPUT** statement since control characters are stripped out. This means that as the programmer you cannot capture the fact that a [CR] has been pressed nor can you detect that the user has pressed a function key. To overcome this problem, BASIC has a function **IN** which accepts single character input from the keyboard without displaying a prompt character or requiring a [CR] until the end of the entire string. The characters are retrieved from the type-ahead buffer without being processed and are converted to their equivalent ASCII format before being assigned to the variable. The general format of the **IN** statement is given in Figure 15.11 and examples of its use in Figure 15.12

IN *var* {**for** *time* }{**then/else** *statements*}

where

var	the variable containing the characters input
time	the maximum time in tenths of a second that the system waits for input before returning to the program. If *time* is zero and there is at least one character in the input buffer, the character is returned and the *then* clause is taken. If *time* is zero and there is no character available the *else* clause is taken. If *time* is negative no time-out applies and the system waits indefinitely for character input
then	specifies the subsequent *statements* are to be executed if the conditional statement evaluates to true
else	specifies the subsequent *statements* are to be executed if the conditional statement evaluates to false
statements	the BASIC statements to be executed based on the use of **then/else**

Figure 15.11 The format of the **IN** statement.

15.4.2 Terminal output

Information is displayed on the terminal by use of the **PRINT** or **CRT** statement. The **PRINT** statement will print information either on the printer or terminal dependent on whether or not the printer has been assigned in the program. Printers are assigned with the **PRINTER ON** and **PRINTER OFF** statements. If the **PRINTER ON** statement is used all subsequent **PRINT** statements will print to the printer until a **PRINTER OFF** statement is encountered. All information produced by the **CRT** statement is sent to the terminal regardless. Most people adopt the **PRINT** statement for both terminal and printer output and it is worth noting here that unless told otherwise, the **PRINT** statement automatically produces its output on the terminal.

The **PRINT** statement also contains the information to be printed, which may be a string of characters contained in single or double quotes, or a variable which is given by its name as assigned in the program.

As with the **INPUT** statement, the @ function determines cursor positioning hence:

Example 1

```
LOOP
   IN ONECHAR
UNTIL ONECHAR = 13 DO REPEAT
```

Inputs characters until a [CR] detected

Example 2

```
LOOP
   IN ONECHAR
   X=CHAR(ONECHAR)
   BEGIN CASE
        |
   Program Statements to check for special characters
        v
   END CASE
UNTIL ONECHAR = 13 DO REPEAT
```

Inputs characters one at a time, checking for their content, until the input string has been processed

Figure 15.12 Examples of the **IN** statement.

PRINT @(20,1):"WHAT IS THE QTY"	will print the message in row 1 column 20
PRINT @(30):"WHAT IS THE QTY"	will print the message at column 30 on the current row

The **PRINT @** statement uses cursor control to position the cursor at a specified position on the screen However you should be aware that some terminals will not accept implicit cursor addressing (as given in the last example **PRINT @(30)**) and it is therefore recommended that the column and row positions are specified in each case to eliminate any possible difficulty in the future when the software may have to be transported to another PICK system.

Again, as with the **INPUT** statement, format masks can be used to specify how the information is to be printed. These masks can specify scaling factors, justification, the suppression of leading zeros and so on. See Section 15.4.4. for further details on these masks.

15.4.3 Special screen control functions

The @ function can be used to carry out special screen controls, such as clear screen, clear from cursor position to end of line, backspace one character and so on. These screen control functions are shown in Figure 15.13. It should be noted that many of the functions will not behave properly unless the term type (part of the **TERM** verb) corresponds to the emulation of the users terminal. To test this out you may find a program in your BP file in the DM account. On the implementation for the PC there is a program called **TEST-CURSOR** which is shown below courtesy of PICK Systems.

```
!
 * cursor test utility
 *
 *** (c) copyright 1986, 1987, 1988, 1989, 1990 pick systems ***
 *
 casing off
 sc = '';ec = ''
 * clear screen *
 print @(-1):
* test cursor addressing *
 print @(25,23):'CURSOR ADDRESSING':
 gosub 100
 gosub 1000
 * test cursor home *
 print @(-2):'* HOME SWEET HOME *':
 gosub 1000
 * test erase to end of screen
 sc = @(-3)
 if sc = '' then goto 20
 print @(-1):
 print @(25,23):'ERASE TO END OF SCREEN':
 gosub 200
 gosub 1000
 print @(0,10):sc:
 gosub 1000
 20 * test erase to end of line
 sc = @(-4)
 if sc = '' then goto 30
 print @(-1):
 print @(25,23):'ERASE TO END OF LINE':
 gosub 300
 gosub 1000
 print @(40,0):sc:
 *gosub 1000
 print @(40,22):sc:
 gosub 1000
 30 * test cursor back
 print @(-1):
 print @(25,23):'CURSOR BACK':
 gosub 100
 gosub 1000
 print @(60,11):
 for i = 1 to 41
   print @(-9):'<':@(-9):
 next i
 gosub 1000
 * test cursor up
 print @(25,23):'CURSOR UP ':
 print @(39,21):
 for i = 1 to 21
   print '^':@(-10):@(-9):
 next i
 gosub 1000
```

```
* test cursor forward
 sc=@(-19)
 if sc="" else
   print @(25,23):'CURSOR FORWARD':
   gosub 1000
   print @(18,11):
   for i = 1 to 41
     print sc:'>':@(-9):
   next i
   gosub 1000
 end
 * test cursor down
 sc=@(-20)
 if sc="" else
   print @(25,23):'CURSOR DOWN ':
   gosub 1000
   print @(39,1):
   for i = 1 to 21
     print 'v':sc:@(-9):
   next i
   gosub 1000
 end
 * blinking
 sc = @(-5);ec = @(-6)
 if sc = '' then goto 40
 print @(-1):
 print @(25,23):'BLINKING':
 gosub 200
 gosub 1000
 gosub 300
 gosub 1000;gosub 1000
 40 * protect *
 sc = @(-7);ec = @(-8)
 if sc = '' then goto 50
 print @(-1):
 print @(25,23):'PROTECT':
 gosub 100
 print @(-11):
 gosub 300
 gosub 1000
 print @(-1):
 gosub 1000
 print @(-12):
 gosub 1000
 50 * reverse video *
 sc = @(-13);ec = @(-14)
 if sc = '' then goto 60
 print @(-1):
 print @(25,23):'REVERSE':
 gosub 100
 gosub 1000
 gosub 300
 gosub 1000
 60 * underline *
 sc = @(-15);ec = @(-16)
 if sc = '' then goto 70
 print @(-1):
 print @(25,23):'UNDERLINE':
 gosub 100
 gosub 1000
 gosub 300
 gosub 1000;gosub 1000
 * check for inputerr and @(column)
 print @(-1):"* CLEAR SCREEN *":
 gosub 1000
```

```
print "** CHECKING @(COLUMN) ADDRESSING ***"
print @(0,5):"AT COL-0 ROW-5":@(40):"AT COL-40"
gosub 1000;gosub 1000
inputerr "* INPUTERR LINE CHECK *":
gosub 1000;gosub 1000
print @(-1):""
70 * end here *
stop
100 * star *
print @(39,11):'*':
for i = 1 to 10
  print @(39,11-i):'I':
  print @(39+2*i,11-i):'/':
  print @(39+2*i,11):'=':
  print @(39+2*i,11+i):'\':
  print @(39,11+i):'I':
  print @(39-2*i,11+i):'/':
  print @(39-2*i,11):'=':
  print @(39-2*i,11-i):'\':
next I
print @(-2):
return
200 * circle *
for i = 0 to 350 step 10
  x = 39 + int(25 * cos(i))
  y = 11 + int(11 * sin(i))
print @(x,y):'+':
next i
print @(-2):
return
300 * box *
z = str('=',41)
print @(18,0):sc:'+':z:'+':ec:
for i = 1 to 21
  print @(18,i):sc:'I':ec:
  print @(60,i):sc:'I':ec:
next i
print @(18,22):sc:'+':z:'+':ec:
print @(-2):
return
1000 * delay *
rqm
return
end
```

Figure 15.13 provides a complete and comprehensive list of the @ functions, but is should be borne in mind that these can vary from implementation to implementation. Also there is a wide variety of terminals supporting a wide range of features and not all terminals will support all the features listed whilst most modern terminals most likely will. If you have any doubts about your terminal or these aspects of video attributes refer to your terminal manual or your supplier. If your terminal is not responding properly to these attributes and/or cursor control then it probably means that your terminal type is wrong.

15.4.4 Format masks

These masks provide a convenient and clever means of formatting and validating data and are discussed in detail in Chapter 13 which deals with the

@(-1) Clears the screen and places the cursor in what is known as the home position, i.e. column 0 row 0
@(-2) Positions the cursor in the home position
@(-3) Clears from the cursor position to the end of the screen
@(-4) Clears from the cursor position to the end of the line
@(-5) Starts blinking of data subsequently printed
@(-6) Ends blinking
@(-7) Starts a protected field, which is one that cannot be overwritten
@(-8) Ends the protected field
@(-9) Backspace by one character
@(-10) Up one line

@(-11) Enables Protect Mode. Enables the terminals ability to accept 'protected-field' mode commands @(-7) and @(-8)
@(-12) Disables Protect Mode
@(-13) Starts Reverse Video
@(-14) Stops Reverse Video

@(-15) Begins 'underline' mode. All characters written after this command will be underlined
@(-16) Terminates 'underline' mode
@(-17) Begins 'slave-printer' ('transparent') mode
@(-18) Terminates 'slave-printer' mode
@(-19) Cursor Forward
@(-20) Cursor Down
@(-21) Graphics Character Set On
@(-22) Graphics Character Set Off
@(-23) Keyboard Lock
@(-24) Keyboard Unlock
@(-25) Control Character Enable
@(-26) Control Character Disable
@(-27) Write Status Line. Positions the cursor to the 'status line', and writes the text that follows on that line
@(-28) Erase Status Line
@(-29) Initialise Terminal Mode. Resets (initializes) the terminal back to its original power-on settings
@(-30) Download Function Keys
@(-31) Non-Embedded Stand-Out On
@(-32) Non-Embedded Stand-Out Off

Functions @(-33) through @(-40) set colour terminals background colours.
See also the TCL "colour" command.

@(-33) Set Background Colour = WHITE
@(-34) Set Background Colour = BROWN

Figure 15.13 Screen and printer control function codes.

@(-35) Set Background Colour = MAGENTA
@(-36) Set Background Colour = RED
@(-37) Set Background Colour = CYAN
@(-38) Set Background Colour = GREEN
@(-39) Set Background Colour = BLUE
@(-40) Set Background Colour = BLACK

Functions @(-41) through @(-48) set colour terminals foreground colours to a full-intensity colour.

@(-41) Set Foreground Colour = WHITE
@(-42) Set Foreground Colour = BROWN
@(-43) Set Foreground Colour = MAGENTA
@(-44) Set Foreground Colour = RED
@(-45) Set Foreground Colour = CYAN
@(-46) Set Foreground Colour = GREEN
@(-47) Set Foreground Colour = BLUE
@(-48) Set Foreground Colour = BLACK
@(-49) through @(-56) (Reserved)

Functions @(-57) through @(-64) set colour terminals foreground colours to a low-intensity colour.

@(-57) Set Foreground Colour = WHITE
@(-58) Set Foreground Colour = BROWN
@(-59) Set Foreground Colour = MAGENTA
@(-60) Set Foreground Colour = RED
@(-61) Set Foreground Colour = CYAN
@(-62) Set Foreground Colour = GREEN
@(-63) Set Foreground Colour = BLUE
@(-64) Set Foreground Colour = BLACK
@(-65) through @(-88) (Reserved)
@(-89) Activate monochrome monitor to 80x25 mode
@(-90) through @(-92) (Reserved)
@(-93) Activate colour monitor to 80x25 mode
@(-94) Activate colour monitor to 80x25 B&W mode
@(-95) through @(-99) (Reserved)
@(-99) Embedded Visual Attributes
'0' = Visual Attributes are 'hidden'
'1' = Visual Attributes are 'embedded'
@(-100) Sets the foreground brightness to half-intensity
@(-101) Sets the foreground brightness to full-intensity

The next section details the @ commands to handle printer features.
@(-102) Italics On
@(-103) Italics Off

Figure 15.13 *Continued*

@(-104) Shift half-line Downwards
@(-105) Shift half-line Upwards
@(-106) through @(-109) (Reserved)
@(-110) Resets the printer back to its original power-on settings
@(-111) (Reserved)
@(-112) (Reserved)
@(-113) Set Vertical Motion Index
@(-114) Set Lines Per Inch
@(-115) Set enlarged character printing
@(-116) Set condensed character printing
@(-117) Set proportional character printing
@(-118) Perf Skip On. Enables the printer's ability to 'skip over' the page perforation on continuous forms
@(-119) Perf Skip Off
@(-120) through @(-124) (Reserved)
@(-125) Set Horizontal Motion Index
@(-126) Set Default Font

The @(-127) through @(-241) functions involve selecting /downloading fonts to a LASER printer.

@(-127) Specifies or downloads Font #1
@(-128) Specifies or downloads Font #2
@(-129) Specifies or downloads Font #3

and so on until

@(-239) Specifies or downloads Font #105
@(-240) Specifies or downloads Font #106
@(-241) Specifies or downloads Font #107
@(-242) Font Parameter – Point Size
@(-243) Font Parameter – Point Size
@(-244) Font Parameter – Pitch
@(-245) Font Parameter – Pitch
@(-246) Font Parameter – Style – Reverse-Off & Italics-Off
@(-247) Font Parameter – Style – Reverse-Off & Italics-On
@(-248) Font Parameter – Block
@(-249) Font Parameter – Reverse
@(-250) Font Parameter – Black
@(-251) through @(-255) (Reserved)
@(-256) Font Parameter – Stroke – 1 (L. Light)
@(-257) Font Parameter – Stroke – 2 (M. Light)
@(-258) Font Parameter – Stroke – 3 (H. Light)
@(-259) Font Parameter – Stroke – 4 (L. Medium)
@(-260) Font Parameter – Stroke – 5 (M. Medium)
@(-261) Font Parameter – Stroke – 6 (H. Medium)
@(-262) Font Parameter – Stroke – 7 (L. Bold)
@(-263) Font Parameter – Stroke – 8 (M. Bold)
@(-264) Font Parameter – Stroke – 9 (H. Bold)

Figure 15.13 *Continued*

@(-265) Font Parameter – Stroke -10 (V. Bold)
@(-266) Font Parameter – Spacing – Proportional
@(-267) Font Parameter – Spacing – Fixed
@(-268) (Reserved)
@(-269) Inter-Job Sequence. (For Shared Printers on UNIX Systems)
@(-270) Font Parameter – Orientation – Portrait
@(-271) Font Parameter – Orientation – Landscape (sideways)
@(-272) through @(-300) (Reserved)

Figure 15.13 *Continued*

conversion codes associated with PICK dictionaries (see Sections 13.5.15 – 13.5.20). The intention of this section is to give an example of some of them and how they can be applied. The format string comprises of two sections, the numeric mask and the format mask and on some implementations the format mask needs to be enclosed in brackets. These masks immediately follow a variable name and comply to the format shown in Figure 15.14.

Please note that whatever the format characters used, the **entire** format string must be enclosed in single or double quotes. Format masks present a convenient way to present information in a format we are familiar with. Masked input, for example, can be used to collect information in a specific form, such as a date or money field where the input contains 2 decimal places. With masked output it is possible to specify, amongst others, that the information should be left or right justified, filled with asterisks or show commas between the thousands positions. Examples of format masks are shown in Figure 15.15.

variable = variable "{j}{n}{m}{Z}{,}{c}{$}{(format mask)}"

where for the numeric mask

j	justification which defaults to left. R is right and L is left
n	number of digits to print following the decimal point. If n equals zero, no decimal point will be printed
m	optional scaling factor, which de-scales the converted number by the mth power of 10. Since BASIC assumes 4 decimal places unless changed by PRECISION statement, to de-scale by 10, m should equal 5 and to de-scale by 100, m should equal 6
Z	specifies the suppression of leading zeros
,	specifies the inserting of commas between every thousands position of a value
c	the credit indicator. The options being:

Figure 15.14 The general format of format masks.

C causes letters CR to follow negative values and two spaces to follow positive values
D causes letters DB to follow positive values and two spaces to follow negative values
E causes negative values to be enclosed in pointed brackets <...>, whilst a blank follows positive values
M causes a minus sign to follow negative values whilst a space follows positive values
N causes the minus sign of negative values to be suppressed
$ causes a dollar sign to be appended to the leftmost position of the value prior to conversion

For the format mask

$	outputs a dollar sign in the leftmost position of the field
#n	fills data on a field of n blanks
%n	fills data on a field of n zeros
*n	fills data on a field of n positions of the character * where the asterisk can be any specified character

Figure 15.14 *Continued*

INPUT @(10,1):VAR.DATE 'D'	Input is only valid if it is in date format DD/MM/YY. Input is taken from the screen at column 10 row 1, and if it conforms to the date format mask **D**, which requires the date to be entered in the format DD/MM/YY then what is entered is put in the variable VAR.DATE
INPUT @(10,1):AMT.DUE 'R2,'	Input a number and decimal point where appropriate. Number will be displayed to 2 decimal places with commas in the thousands positions. The format mask of **R2**, means that a number input as **1234.5** will be displayed as **1,234.50**
INPUT @(10,1):QTY "R26(%15)"	Input a number (ignore decimal positions input) and redisplay number to 2 decimal positions right justified on a field of 15 zeros

Figure 15.15 Format masks for INPUT statement.

The input format masks validate the input and will display a message on the last line of the terminal, if the validation fails. The output format masks for numeric data are a little more complicated in that the format mask code is enclosed in parentheses prior to the information regarding justification, the number of decimal places and the scaling required. Figure 15.16 explains the way in which numeric format masks can be used.

Value of NUM	PRINT statement	Output result
1234	**PRINT NUM "R26"**	12.34

Justification ——— R
Decimal Places ——— 2
Scaling Factor ——— 6

The number is right justified to 2 decimal places. The number is de-scaled to the 6th power of 10, but since BASIC assumes 4 decimal places the number is de-scaled by 100

1234567	**PRINT NUM "R26,"**	12,345.67
As previous example but with commas printed		
12.35	**PRINT NUM "1"**	12.4
Print rounded to 1 decimal place		
123456	**PRINT NUM "R26,M(*15)**	*******1,234.56
Print right justified, with commas and two 2 decimal places on a 15 character field of asterisks		
123456	**PRINT NUM "L(%10)"**	1234560000
Print left justified in a field containing 10 zeros		
123456	**PRINT NUM "R(#10)"**	123456
Print right justified in a field containing 10 spaces		

Figure 15.16 Examples of numeric format masks.

15.4.5 Limiting the data printed

Sometimes it is necessary to print part of a string, or perhaps just the first *n* characters. This is handled by referring to the starting position of the first character and the number of characters required, separated by a comma and enclosed in square brackets.

Hence if the variable **NAME** contained BOURDON, ROGER JAMES and there was only room on the report to print the first ten characters, the statement **X=NAME[1,10]** would assign BOURDON, R to X.

15.5 The control of printers in BASIC

The BASIC functions covered in this section are

HEADING	Specify heading for output device
FOOTING	Specify footing for output device
PAGE	Advance to head of page on output device
PRINTER OFF	Directs output from subsequent **PRINT** statements to the terminal
PRINTER ON	Directs output from subsequent **PRINT** statements to the printer
PRINT ON	Directs output to one of a number of print files
PRINTER CLOSE	Closes the report on the spooler causing it to be printed

As was discussed earlier, the **PRINT** statement is used to direct information to the printer provided that the **PRINTER ON** statement has been declared in the program. From this point on, and until a **PRINTER OFF** statement is used, the output from the **PRINT** statement will be produced on the printer.

At the start of a program printers are unassigned and hence all output from the **PRINT** statements will be produced on the screen. If a printer is assigned using the **PRINTER ON** statement, all printed output is written to a spool file which is closed and printed out when the program completes its execution. If it is necessary to force printing earlier than at the end of the program, the spool file must be 'forced' closed, which is achieved by issuing a **PRINTER CLOSE** statement.

It is frequently necessary to compile more than one report at a time within a program and PICK BASIC handles this by use of the **PRINT ON** statement. This allows the programmer to specify up to 255 printed reports to be printed simultaneously. Each report has to be given a unique number so that the **PRINT ON** statement can identify which report is being addressed. As with the output for a single printer , none of the reports will be printed until the **PRINTER CLOSE** statement is encountered or until the program finishes. Figure 15.17

```
PRINTER ON
PRINT "This is a line for report 1"
PRINT ON 1 "This is a line for report 2"
PRINT ON 2 "This is a line for report 3"
```

Writes separate report lines to three separate reports

Figure 15.17 Producing more than one report from a program.

shows how three separate reports are produced from the same program. Notice that **PRINT** assumes report number 0, so a **PRINT ON 0** is not needed.

In order to produce several reports from a program, which are to be printed on separate printers, all reports need to be spooled with the *hold* option and manipulated to the various printers using **SP-EDIT** (refer to Section 22.3). The assignment of the *hold* status would have to be handled before the program was executed and would be achieved by use of the **SP-ASSIGN** command. In this situation the **SP-ASSIGN** command can either be typed in at TCL before the program is run, or can be included in a **MACRO** or PROC that runs the program subsequent to the **SP-ASSIGN** command. Eventually these can be **EXECUTED** with in the program.

Where several **PRINT ON** statements are used and it is required that the reports produced go to the same printer, only one **SP-ASSIGN** is necessary. If the reports are to be sent to different printers then several **SP-ASSIGN**s are required in the form **SP-ASSIGN FnRm** where n is the printer form number and m is the number given by the **PRINT ON m** statement in the program.

15.5.1 Headings, footings and page throws

To make life easy PICK BASIC will print automatic headings and footings (lines at the top and bottom of each page), with special commands which do not require control by the programmer. Once the commands have been encountered within the program, each page of output will automatically include the heading and/or footing without the programmer having to check the number of lines already produced by the program and issue a command to print the heading and/or footing.

There is a separate function **PAGE** which will force the printer to throw to the top of a new page. This ends the output at the point the **PAGE** statement is encountered, prints any appropriate footing, throws a new page and prints any appropriate heading.

Headings and footings are handled with the special statements **HEADING** and **FOOTING**. Within these it is possible to have multiple lines, to have the text centred or to include the date, time or page number. Figure 15.18 shows the possible options that can be included within the text of the heading or footing. In all cases the options chosen must be enclosed in single quotes.

Headings or footings can be more than one line long. Typically a heading may include a line of text for the title of the report followed by one or two blank lines and then text lines which give a heading to each column of information printed. Multiple line headings or footings are performed by including the 'L' option at the end of each line of text. Let's assume a report with a title of 'Staff List' which prints out a list of staff showing their names, department number, age and telephone number. Figure 15.19 shows typical BASIC statements for headings and footings and their effect.

Figure 15.19 has introduced extensions to some of the features already discussed. You will notice that the heading contains a number of options which

Option	Meaning
P	Current page number, right justified
PN	Current page number, left justified
L	Carriage return/line feed
T	Current time and date (HH:MM:SS DD MMM YYYY) e.g. (21:53:11 21 1985)
D	Current date (DD MMM YYYY) e.g. (21 1985)
C	Centre the text

Figure 15.18 HEADING and FOOTING options.

Statements from the BASIC Program

HEADING "STAFF LIST AS AT 'DC'   PAGE 'PLL'FULL   DEPT TEL'L'NAME   CODE   AGE   NUMBER 'L'"
PRINT NAME "L(#20)":DEPT "L(#10)":AGE "L(#8)":TEL "L(#20)"

N.B. The # shown above is the symbol given by holding the SHIFT key and pressing the 3 key on the main keyboard (not the numeric section of the keyboard). On some terminals this may display as a £ rather than #

The printed report output from the Program

```
       STAFF LIST AS AT 21 OCT 1995        PAGE 1

FULL               DEPT                         TEL
NAME               CODE      AGE                NUMBER

D H Houghton       004       22          0171-455 1211
M Hynes            009       28          0181-236 4680
     |
     |
     v
       STAFF LIST AS AT 21 OCT 1995        PAGE 2

FULL               DEPT                         TEL
NAME               CODE      AGE                NUMBER

L L Leech          001       34          0171-236 1987
     |
     |
     v
```

Figure 15.19 Use of HEADING and FOOTING.

have been combined together and contained in single quotes. The first two **DC** incorporates the date (D) into the title and centres (C) the entire title, including the date. The second group of options is **PLL** which prints the page number (P) and spaces up two lines (L). Notice that the first word of the column heading **FULL** appears immediately after the options **PLL** and on the report appears in the first column of the first line of column headings.

Apart from the standard options shown in Figure 15.18, headings and footings can contain variables and/or variables using conversion codes. Suppose a program requested period start and end dates which you wanted to be included in a heading. The dates would be held in the program as two variables in internal format (the number of days since 31.12.67), let's call the variables **FROM.DATE** and **TO.DATE**. These could either be assigned to other variables in output format, such as **DISP.DATE=OCONV (FROM. DATE,'D')** after which **DISP.DATE** could be included in the heading, or the could be converted in situ, enabling:

HEADING"PERIOD":OCONV(FROM.DATE,'D'):"TO":OCONV(TO. DATE, 'D')

The **OCONV** statement is very powerful and handles the conversion of data held in internal format to a format for output, i.e. to a format the user will understand. Hence on dates, which are held in the PICK database as the number of days since 31/12/67, can be displayed in any format suitable for management reports. Indeed a date such as 12 July 1994, is held in the PICK database as 9690 but the **OCONV** can convert it to many external formats based on the conversion code used, for example you could display just the year, the month (both numerically and alphabetically), the quarter number and so on. These conversion codes are detailed in Section 13.5.7 in the chapter on PICK dictionaries.

The **PRINT** statement of Figure 15.19 shows how items of information can be printed across a page one after the other. This is denoted by the colon which means concatenate. However had we not applied a format mask to the information printed, (the format mask is what appears in double quotes after each of the variables, e.g. **L(#20)**), the pieces of information printed would be bunched together, without any spaces between them and without appearing under the headings – see Figure 15.20. The purpose of the format mask, therefore is to give a fixed length to each of the columns by effectively overlaying the data to be printed on a fixed number of spaces. Hence **L(#10)** or **L#10** requests that the information be printed left justified on a data area containing 10 blanks.

There are times when it is necessary to force the printer to throw a page and this is achieved using the **PAGE** statement. This causes the current heading to be printed at the top of the new page if one has been defined. The **PAGE** statement can optionally be followed by a number which then becomes the next page number to be used. This resetting of the page number can be useful where control totals are printed on separate pages.

Statements from the BASIC PROGRAM

HEADING "STAFF LIST AS AT 'DC' PAGE 'PLL'FULL DEPT TEL'L'NAME CODE AGE NUMBER 'L'"
PRINT NAME:DEPT:AGE:TEL

The printed report output from the program

```
    STAFF LIST AS AT 21 OCT 1985    PAGE 1

FULL                DEPT      TEL
NAME                CODE      AGE          NUMBER

D H Houghton004220171-455 1211
M Hynes009280181-236 4680
```

Figure 15.20 A report printed without format masks.

15.6 File control in PICK BASIC

The BASIC functions covered in this section are

DELETE	Delete a record from a file
FILE	Open a file, both data and dictionary portion allowing attributes to be referenced by their dictionary names
OPEN	Open a file
READ	Read a record from a file
READV	Read a single attribute from a file
WRITE	Write a record to a file
WRITEV	Write a single attribute to a file

If you are new to PICK, it is worth refreshing your mind on the special PICK data structure in Chapter 3, before proceeding too far with this section. From this point on we will be using PICK terminology, explained in that chapter, to describe the file handling facilities of PICK BASIC.

15.6.1 The OPEN statement

Before you can use any file it must first be opened, and made known to the program. This is achieved using the **OPEN** statement, which can enable access to either the dictionary or data sections of the file, remember that both the dictionary and data portions of a file are files in their own right and if you wish to access both then you must have two **OPEN** statements in your program, one to open the dictionary file and one to open the data file. You can open as many files as you like at any one time, but unlike other systems BASIC does not require, nor does it provide for, the closing of files. Files are automatically closed when the program finishes.

The filename given in the **OPEN** statement must be the name of an **existing** file, which would previously have been created using the **CREATE-FILE** command unless of course it came with the original system such as files like **ERRMSG**.

There is no BASIC command that will create a file, although you can **EXECUTE** the TCL command **CREATE-FILE**. The format of the **OPEN** statement is shown in Figure 15.21.

The statements following the **ELSE** used to be mandatory and told the compiler how to handle the exception condition of the file not existing. Whilst they are no longer mandatory, you should not ignore this possibility in a 'live' application and you should consider what action should be taken if the file cannot be found. If you do not provide an alternative, the program will abort saying the file is not a known file name. It is quite feasible to tell the program to stop if such a condition occurs. Whilst this is a simple and easy option to take, it is unhelpful in 'live' operation when a program just stops and it is therefore more usual to pass control to an exception routine or to display a message on the terminal stating which file is missing. Figure 15.22 shows various forms of **OPEN** statement.

OPEN '{DICT}','*FILENAME*' {**TO** '*var*'} {**ELSE** *statements*}

where

DICT	appears in single quotes if the dictionary section of the file is to be maintained and if omitted the data portion is assumed. A variable can be used here which equates to **DICT** in which case the quotes would not be needed. If the data portion is being maintained, the entire expression, including the single quotes can be ignored
FILENAME	is the name of the file as held in the MD
var	is the name used from this point on in the program to refer to the file
statements	are those BASIC statements that will be executed should the file specified by *FILENAME* not exist in the Master Dictionary (MD)

Figure 15.21 The **OPEN** statement format.

```
OPEN "OPORDERS" TO ORD ELSE ◄──────── Open data section of
   PRINT "OPORDERS NOT FOUND"          the file OPORDERS
   STOP
END
OPEN 'DICT', 'OPORDERS' TO ORD ELSE STOP ◄── Opens the DICTionary
                                              of the OPORDERS
                                              file

OPEN "OPORDERS" TO ORD ◄───────────────────── No error processing

OPEN "OPORDERS" TO ORD ELSE GOSUB 900 ◄────── Open data section of
                                              OPORDERS ELSE
                                              perform subroutine 900
```

Figure 15.22 Use of the **OPEN** statement.

It should be noted that the variable assigned to the file is not treated as a normal variable, hence it cannot be assigned a value or have its contents displayed or printed. It is assigned to enable a program that handles several files, to uniquely identify the file to be updated. In a program that uses external subroutines, all files should be opened in the main program with the file variable being passed as a parameter. Alternatively the file variable should be passed to the subroutine in a special part of the program called the COMMON area as defined by the **COMMON** statement. The COMMON area is an area that is common between programs and subroutines, enabling the value of variables to be stored and interpreted by any program or subroutine that has the COMMON block defined within it.

15.6.2 The READ statement

The **READ** statement reads from the specified and **already opened** file and places the entire item (record), with the exception of the item-id (key), in the specified variable. The format of the **READ** statement is shown in Figure 15.23.

The statements following the **ELSE** used to be mandatory and told the compiler how to handle the exception condition caused by the record not existing. This is no longer the case, but in the tradition of good programming, this exception condition should be catered for. Figure 15.24 shows the various forms of the **READ** statement.

In each of the cases in Figure 15.24 assuming the record exists, an entire item (record) is read from a file called ORDREC, the filename as given in the original CREATE-FILE command. In the first example in Figure 15.24, the item-id or key of the record was held in a variable called ORDNO in the

---

READ *var* **FROM** {*file var,*} *item-id* {**LOCKED** *lstatements*} {**THEN/ELSE** *statements*}

where

var	contains the contents of the record
file var	is the name assigned in the **OPEN** statement
item-id	is the key of the record
lstatements	the statements to be invoked if the record is locked by another user. SYSTEM(0) returns the port number which has the item locked
statements	are those BASIC statements that will be executed should the record specified by item-id exist in the file (in the case of the use of **THEN**) or not exist (in the case of the use of **ELSE**)

Figure 15.23 The **READ** statement format.

READ ORDREC FROM ORD,ORDNO ELSE PRINT "RECORD NOT FOUND": ORDNO; STOP

Read a record with a key of that held variable ORDNO into the variable ORDREC otherwise display the words RECORD NOT FOUND followed by the contents of the variable ORDNO and then stop the program

READ ORDREC FROM ORD,"123" ELSE PRINT "RECORD NOT FOUND '123'"; STOP

Read a record with the key of 123 into the variable ORDREC otherwise display the message RECORD NOT FOUND 123 and stop the program

READ ORDREC FROM ORD,ORDNO ELSE GOSUB 900

Read a record with a key of that held in the variable ORDNO into the variable ORDREC otherwise then execute the statements in the subroutine 900

READ ORDREC FROM ORD,ORDNO LOCKED GOSUB 100 ELSE GOSUB 900

Read a record with a key of that held in the variable ORDNO into the variable ORDREC otherwise display the words RECORD NOT FOUND followed by the contents of variable ORDNO and then execute the statements in the subroutine 900. If the record is locked by another user then execute the statements in subroutine 100.

Figure 15.24 The **READ** statement.

second example the item-id was known and a specific record with the key 123 was read. The final example showed how an error subroutine is invoked if the record is not found. In this case a separate section of the program must have a series of statements that begin with the label **900** and ends with the statement **RETURN**. A similar series of instructions that begin with the label **100** and ends with the statement **RETURN** will deal with the actions to be taken if the record is in use and therefore locked by another user.

This version of the read statement will read an entire item which is fine if you need to work on several attributes (fields) of the item. However you may just want to read a single attribute which can achieved with the **READV** statement. In this statement since you require a specific attribute, you need to provide the position of the attribute within the item as well as its' item-id. The **READV** statement reads the entire item into temporary workspace and then extracts the required attribute and resets the temporary workspace. A series of **READV** statements against different attributes in the same record forces the system to continually re-read the same item. It is therefore far more efficient to read an entire record if more than two attributes need to be referenced. The general format of the **READV** statement is shown in Figure 15.25, whilst Figure 15.26 gives examples of its use.

READV *var* **FROM** {*file-var*,} {**LOCKED** *lstatements*} *exp1,exp2* {**THEN/ ELSE** *statements*}

where

var	is the name of the variable which is to contain the contents of the specified attribute
file-var	is the name of the file variable
lstatements	the statements to be executed if the record is locked by another user
exp1	specifies the item-id of the record
exp2	specifies the attribute number
statements	are those BASIC statements that will be executed should the record specified by item-id exist in the file (in the case of the use of **THEN**) or not exist (in the case of the use of **ELSE**)

Figure 15.25 The **READV** statement format.

15.6.3 The FILE statement

Advanced PICK introduced the **FILE** statement for the first time, so you will not be able to make use of this statement on R83 PICK, nor on many licensee implementations. For that reason it is worth bearing in mind that if you do use this function, you are likely to run into problems when porting your software to a different hardware platform.

However, using **FILE** means that you open both the data and dictionary portions of the file at the same time and means that you can use dictionary names in your program. The general format of the statement is given in Figure 15.27 and examples of its use are given in Figure 15.28.

READV VAT FROM ORD,ORDNO,12 ELSE PRINT "RECORD NOT FOUND": ORDNO; STOP

Read attribute 12 of the record with a key of that held in variable ORDNO, into the variable VAT from the file whose file variable is ORD otherwise display an error message and stop the program

READV VAT FROM ORD,"123",12 ELSE PRINT "RECORD NOT FOUND '123'"; STOP

Read attribute 12 of the record with a key of 123 into the variable VAT from the file whose file variable is ORD

READV VAT FROM ORD,"123",12 LOCKED GOSUB 100 ELSE PRINT "RECORD NOT FOUND '123'"; STOP

Read attribute 12 of the record with a key of 123 into the variable VAT from the file whose file variable is ORD. If the record is locked, execute the subroutine 100

Figure 15.26 The **READV** statement.

FILE *file1* {*file2,file3* ....}
where

file1 the name of the file to be opened
file2 the name of the file to be opened

Figure 15.27 The **FILE** statement.

FILE MS.MEMBER
MEMNO = "000330"
READ MS.MEMBER MEMNO ELSE STOP
IF MS.MEMBER(AGE) < 24 THEN MEM.TYPE = "U24"

If the member's age is under 24, set the membership type to U24

IF NOT(ASSIGNED(MS.MEMBER)) THEN FILE MS.MEMBER

If the file variable **MS.MEMBER** has not been previously assigned, then the **FILE** statement is executed

Figure 15.28 Examples of the **FILE** statement.

The compiler scans through the program looking for reference to the files' dictionary names and determines the size of the dimensioned array required by taking the highest attribute position (defined by the amc part of the dictionary record) and adding one to it.

After an item is read from the file, attributes within the record (item) may be referenced using the dictionary record item-ids. Correlative processing codes within the dictionary record are executed but output conversions are not. It is also possible to determine whether the file has previously been opened using the **FILE** statement and Figure 15.28 shows examples of this and other uses of the statement.

15.6.4 The WRITE statement

As with the read statement, there are two variants of the write statement, **WRITE** to write the entire record and **WRITEV** to write a specific attribute of a record. Again, it is far better to write away an entire record if you have more than two attributes to update than to write them away individually. If the record or attribute specified in these statements already exists it will be overwritten if not a new record or attribute will be created. A **WRITEV** therefore can itself write a new record but only to a file that already exists. The format of these commands is given in Figure 15.29.

You will probably have noticed that there is no **THEN/ELSE** clause in these statements. This is because it is always possible to write data. If the record being written to does not exist, a new one will be created. The only possibility for error here is that the file has not been opened first. In both the case of the read and write statements, a runtime error will be displayed if the file has not been opened, normally:

```
[B12] LINE n FILE HAS NOT BEEN OPENED
```

where **n** is the statement number in the program trying to read or write to a non-opened file. You may remember that all error messages are held in the **MESSAGES** file and in this case the message has the item-id **B12**. Figure 15.30 shows examples of these write statements.

WRITE *var1* **ON** {*file-var,*} *expr1*

WRITEV *var2* **ON** { *file-var,*} *expr1,expr2*

where

var1	contains the contents of the record
file-var	is the file variable
expr1	contains the item-id of the record
var2	contains the contents of the attribute
expr2	specifies the attribute number

Figure 15.29 The **WRITE** and **WRITEV** statement format.

WRITE ORDREC ON ORD,ORDNO
Write a record whose contents are held in the variable ORDREC, on the file assigned to the variable ORD the key being that held in the variable ORDNO

WRITE "DATA RECORD" ON ORD, "123"
In this case the record written has a key of 123 and has literal string DATA RECORD stored in attribute 1

WRITEV VAT ON ORD,ORDNO,12
Write the contents of variable VAT in attribute 12 of the record on the file assigned to the variable ORD whose key is given by the contents of variable ORDNO

WRITEV "15" ON ORD,"123",12
Here attribute 12 of the record on the file assigned to the variable ORD, and whose key is 123, is assigned the value 15

Figure 15.30 The **WRITE** and **WRITEV** statements.

The variable containing the entire record to be written away and which reflects the format of the PICK database, is referred to as a dynamic array. The subject of dynamic arrays is discussed fully in Section 15.11.

The **WRITEV** statement has the facility to insert information at the beginning of the record and to append information to the end of the record by defining the attribute number as **0** or **-1**, respectively. Figure 15.31 shows the use of these two versions of **WRITEV**.

Assuming the item **MONTHS** in the file **DEMO** contains the following 3 attributes :

```
001 FEB
002 MAR
003 APR
```

Then:

WRITEV "JAN" ON DEMO,"MONTHS",0
Inserts the literal string JAN at beginning of the item MONTHS

WRITEV "MAY" ON DEMO,"MONTHS",-1
Appends the value MAY to the end of the item MONTHS

The result of a program containing both these statements would be an item containing:

```
001 JAN
002 FEB
003 MAR
004 APR
005 MAY
```

Figure 15.31 Using **WRITEV** to add to the start and end of the attributes in a record.

15.6.5 The DELETE statement

The **DELETE** statement is used to remove records, attributes and values from the database. Nothing will happen if the record or attribute does not exist so there is no need for an **ELSE** clause. However, a runtime error will be displayed if the file has not been opened. This section deals with how records are deleted, whilst Section 15.11.2 explains how attributes and multi-values are removed. The format of the statement for deleting records from the database is shown in Figure 15.32 whilst Figure 15.33 gives examples of its use.

DELETE *{file-var,} expl*

where

file-var	is the name assigned in the **OPEN** statement
expl	specifies the item-id of the record

Figure 15.32 The **DELETE** statement format.

DELETE ORD,ORDNO

Delete the record from the file assigned to the file variable ORD, whose key is held in the variable ORDNO

DELETE ORD,"123"

Delete the record with the key of 123, held on the file assigned to the file variable ORD

Figure 15.33 The **DELETE** statement.

15.7 Using the AP indexes in BASIC

The BASIC functions covered in this section are: KEY, search index for a specific value; ROOT, open index file. Using an index really speeds up access to a file where the item-id is not known and access to a record is via one of its attributes which has been indexed. The B-tree indexes are a fundamental feature of Advanced PICK (they do not exist at all in R83) being implemented at the operating system level. Hence there is no need to worry about updating the indexes if a record is added, modified or deleted. The only time you will need to access the indexes is for searching purposes and to do so could not be made more simple.

There are two new BASIC functions in Advanced PICK associated with the use of the B-Tree indexes, the **ROOT** function which is the equivalent of an **OPEN** statement and the **KEY** function which enables the reading of records via the index.

15.7.1 The ROOT function

The **ROOT** function is similar to the **OPEN** statement for normal files in that it makes the index file available for use by assigning a variable, known as the root variable. It is called the root variable because when PICK creates an index it puts the root frame address (the top level frame in the B-tree) in the file defining attribute on the correlative attribute (i.e. attribute 8). Any number of indexes may be 'open' at once, provided that each has a unique 'root.variable'. Once defined in the **ROOT** function, the index is available to the program and can be scanned through using the **KEY** function. The general format of the **ROOT** function is given in Figure 15.34.

ROOT *file.reference,a.code* **TO** *root.variable* {**THEN | ELSE** *statements*}

where

file.reference	is the name of the file which has the index associated with it
a.code	is the a-correlative code in the same format as was used in **CREATE-INDEX**
root.variable	the variable name assigned to this index and used in subsequent **KEY** statements
statements	the statements that are executed with the **THEN | ELSE** clauses

The optional **THEN** clause is executed if the specified index is found and the **ELSE** clause is executed if it is not.

Figure 15.34 The general format of the **ROOT** function.

15.7.2 The KEY function

The **KEY** function is the statement in BASIC that allows the index to be searched for a specific value or the 'closest' value. Once a specific record is located, the **KEY** function can be used to 'browse' forwards or backwards through the index. The **ROOT** statement whose format is shown in Figure 15.35 ***must*** precede the **KEY** function.

Figure 15.36 gives an example of a program using the **ROOT** and **KEY** functions. It assumes that an index has been created on attribute 1 of the file **CUSTOMER** where the customer name is held. This would have been created using the command **CREATE-INDEX CUSTOMER A1**. The program asks the user to input a partial name and then displays a screen of 10 names, 5 before and 5 after the partial name in the index.

KEY(*operator, root.variable, index.key, item-id* {*,vc.expression*}) {**THEN | ELSE** statements}

where

operator indicates the type of search, and may take one of the following values:

- **c** Compares, left-to-right, against the *index.key* and returns the first *item-id* whose index matches. If no match is found, the next sequentially higher index and first associated item-id are returned.
- **n** Returns the next *index.key* and *item-id*. If more than one *item-id* exists for an *index.key*, this option returns the next *item-id*. After all *item-ids* for an *index.key* have been returned, or if the *item-id* is null it returns the next *index.key* and *item-id*.
- **p** Returns the previous *index.key* and *item-id*. If more than one *item-id* exists for an *index.key*, this returns the previous *item-id*. After the first *item-id* for an *index.key* has been returned, or if *item-id* is null, it returns the previous *index.key* and the last *item-id*.
- **r** Returns the *index.key* and *item-id* only on an exact match with the *index.key*.
- **v** Verifies the index. Locates the given *index.key* and *item-id* and verifies that an exact match can be found.

root.variable is the b-tree root fid associated with the target index. It first must be initialized by the **ROOT** statement, and must be defined prior to using the **KEY** statement.

index.key specifies a mandatory variable containing the search string. The variable must be defined before using the **KEY** statement. The actual string found is returned into *index.key* when using the **c**, **n** or **p** operators. The **r** and **v** operators expect an exact match.

item-id is the variable that contains the *item-id* of the item that contains the *index.key*. The *item-id* need not be pre-assigned when using the **p** or **n** operators, but it must be pre-assigned when using the **v** operator.

vc.expression is the value number of the key attribute containing the *index.key*, returned to the *vc.expression* by the **KEY** statement. This only works with the **c**, **n**, **p** and **r** operators.

statements the statements that are executed with the **THEN | ELSE** clauses.

The optional **THEN** clause is executed if the specified *item-id* is found or if the *index.key* verifies with the **v** operator and the **ELSE** clause is executed either of those conditions are not satisfied.

Figure 15.35 The general format of the **KEY** statement.

```
FILE CUSTOMER
ROOT "CUSTOMER","A1" TO CUST.ROOT ELSE
      PRINT "The customer index is missing!"
      GOTO 999
      END
PROMPT ""
PRINT @(10,10): "Enter the name of the customer to find" :
INPUT NAME
INDEX.KEY = NAME
*
*Display 5 previous names
*
FOR X=1 TO 5
      KEY("P",CUST.ROOT,INDEX.KEY,CUST.ID) THEN
          READ CUSTOMER FROM CUST.ID THEN
            PRINT CUSTOMER(NAME)
          END
      END
NEXT X
*
*Look for an exact match
*
INDEX.KEY = NAME
KEY("R",CUST.ROOT,INDEX.KEY,CUST.ID) THEN
      READ CUSTOMER FROM CUST.ID THEN
          PRINT CUSTOMER(NAME)
      END
END
*
*Display 5 subsequent names
*
INDEX.KEY = NAME
FOR X=1 TO 5
      KEY("N",CUST.ROOT,INDEX.KEY,CUST.ID) THEN
         READ CUSTOMER FROM CUST.ID THEN
            PRINT CUSTOMER(NAME)
         END
      END
NEXT X
```

Figure 15.36 Using the **ROOT** and **KEY** functions.

15.8 Handling arrays in BASIC

The BASIC functions covered in this section are

DIM	Declares a specific number of storage locations for a matrix of variables
MAT	Initialize all elements of a dimensioned array
MATBUILD	Create a dynamic array from a dimensioned array
MATPARSE	Create a dimensioned array from a dynamic array
MATREAD	Reads a record assigning each attribute to an element of a dimensioned array
MATWRITE	Writes a record to a file using the elements of a dimensioned array

A variable is an entity in a program we can give a name to, but whose value varies. It varies because different values can be assigned to it and the values within it adjusted. When we read a record from the database we know it will comprise of a number of attributes. PICK BASIC allows the record to be read into a set of variables called an array which comprises of a number of elements, each of which can be addressed individually. Hence when the record is read into the array, element one of the array will contain attribute one, element two of the array attribute two and so on.

Arrays can be one dimensional, when they are known as a vector, or two dimensional when they are known as a matrix. The handling of records involves single dimensional arrays. Before an array can be used, its maximum dimensions have to be defined, which is handled by the **DIM** statement. Figure 15.37 shows how arrays are defined and addressed.

Once the array has been defined, records can be read in, and written from, using the special read and write commands: **MATREAD** and **MATWRITE**. Although they perform special array handling functions, the format of these statements, as shown in Figure 15.38, is the same as the normal **READ** and **WRITE** statements.

Where there are fewer attributes in the record than elements in the array, the remaining elements are given a null value. The problem that may occur with *real arrays* (as these arrays are called) is that the record may contain more attributes than the **DIM** statement has defined. In these cases most PICK implementations will place the remainder in the final element of the array.

A one-dimensional array – Vector

DIM A(5)

Each element is referred to by specifying its offset position contained in parenthesis

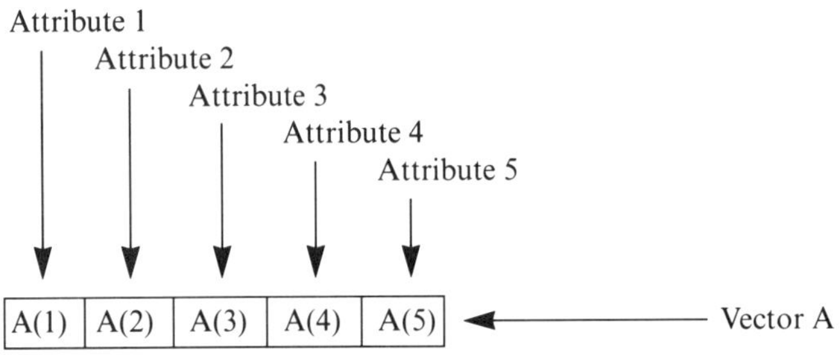

A two-dimensional array – Matrix

DIM B(4,5)

Each element is referred to by specifying its position in the array, row then column, contained in parenthesis

Matrix B

B(1,1)	B(1,2)	B(1,3)	B(1,4)	B(1,5)
B(2,1)	B(2,2)	B(2,3)	B(2,4)	B(2,5)
B(3,1)	B(3,2)	B(3,3)	B(3,4)	B(3,5)
B(4,1)	B(4,2)	B(4,3)	B(4,4)	B(4,5)

Figure 15.37 The VECTOR and MATRIX.

However, do beware, since in some implementations it doesn't and the final elements will be lost! Another way of handling record processing is to use dynamic arrays, where the length of them is assigned dynamically by BASIC at the time the record is read in order to reflect the exact length of the record being processed.

15.9 The handling of variables in BASIC

A variable is an entity in a program we can give a name to, but whose value varies. It varies because different values can be assigned to it and the values within it adjusted. Already within this chapter we have seen considerable refer-

MAT *array1 = expr*
which assigns the evaluated value of *expr* to all elements of the array *array1*

{MAT} *array1* = **{MAT}** *array2*
which assigns each element of the array *array2* to the corresponding element of *array1*. The arrays thus become equivalent. Remember that each array must first be dimensioned with the **DIM** statement and must have the same number of elements, although the actual dimensions do not have to be identical. The elements are assigned in consecutive order regardless

MATBUILD *string* **FROM** *array, delimiter*
where

string	the string or dynamic array to be created
array	the dimensioned array from which the elements are read
delimiter	an expression evaluating to the characters used to delimit elements in *string*

MATPARSE *array* **FROM** *string, delimiter* {**SETTING** *var*}
where

array	the dimensioned array to be created
string	an expression evaluating to the string or dynamic array from which to read the elements
delimiter	an expression evaluating to the characters used to delimit elements in the *string*
var	assign to *var* the number of fields separated by *delimiter* in the *string*. The contents of *var* can be tested to determine if it is greater than the dimensions of the array

MATREAD *var* **FROM** {*file variable*}, *item-id* {**LOCKED** *lstatements*} **ELSE** *statements*

where

var	contains the contents of the record
file variable	is the name assigned in the **OPEN** statement
item-id	is the key of the record
lstatements	those BASIC statements that will be executed if the item is locked by another user
statements	are those BASIC statements that will be executed should the record specified by item-id not exist in the file

MATWRITE *var* **ON** {*file-var,*} *item-id*

where

var	contains the contents of the record
file-var	is the file variable
item-id	contains the item-id of the record

Figure 15.38 The **MAT MATBUILD**, **MATPARSE**, **MATREAD** and **MATWRITE** statements.

ence to the use of variables, including the ability to assign arrays to a variable and to reference the individual elements by subscripting.

By far the most efficient way to handle variables is by use of the **EQUATE** or **EQU** statement. The general format of the command is shown in Figure 15.39.

The **EQUATE** statement offers a number of advantages in that no storage location is generated for the variable, since its immediate value is compiled into the object code of the program at each point in which it is referenced. This means that it does not have to be reassigned and its variable location computed and accessed each time the variable is used which is the case with variables which are not **EQU**ated. A further advantage is that by using meaningful names, readability of the program is improved.

The use of **EQUATE** cannot be too highly recommended for program efficiency and clarity. Examples of the use of **EQUATE** are given in Figure 15.40.

EQU{ATE} *var1* **TO** *var2*{,*var3* **TO** *var4*)

var1 is a simple variable
var2 can be a literal number, string, character or array element, **CHAR** function or any combination thereof
var3 repeat of *var1*
var4 repeat of *var2*

Figure 15.39 The **EQUATE** statement.

EQUATE PI TO 3.142
Assigns the literal value 3.142 to the variable PI

EQUATE AM TO CHAR(254), VM TO CHAR(253)
Assigns the attribute mark value to the variable AM and that for a value mark to variable VM using the **CHAR** function

EQUATE NAME TO REC(1), ADDRESS TO REC(2), TEL TO REC(3)
Assigns the elements of an array, specifically the contents of REC(1) to the variable NAME, that for REC(2) to the variable ADDRESS and that for REC(3) to the variable TEL

Figure 15.40 Examples of the use of the **EQUATE** statement.

15.10 Multi-user aspects of file control

PICK is a multi-user database system which means that more than person can use the some database at any one time. It also means that it is possible for more than one person to be using the same program at the same time. In this sort of environment, the multi-user systems environment, steps have to be taken to protect the integrity of the database. It would be foolish to enable two or more people access to the same record for updating at the same time. In such a case, as each person finished their updating their record would be written away overwriting what was there previously and the final state of the record would reflect only the changes made by the last person to finish.

PICK provides for control in a multi-user environment by use of a locking mechanism that prevents more than one person accessing a record to be updated. In BASIC this is handled by adding a **U** (Update) to the end of each of the file handling commands. Hence **READ** becomes **READU**, **READV** becomes **READVU** and so on. The read with lock commands will remain effective until released with the **RELEASE** statement or until a write statement is encountered that also ends in **U**, such as **WRITEU**, or **MATWRITEU**.

Within the early PICK implementations locking was at the group rather than item level and this is the case with the R83 implementation of PICK. One of the major changes with the introduction of Advanced PICK is the implementation of item locking. If your PICK implementation only has group locking remember that a group can consist of one or a number of frames and hence a number of items. The important thing to bear in mind, therefore, is that by locking a group you have also locked other records not necessarily associated with the transaction. This rarely becomes a problem even in a very busy multi-terminal system, but when locking the group locks records another user requires their terminal will bleep, to signify the data they need is locked. This bleeping will continue until the group is unlocked and the other user can then continue with their work.

Sensible file sizing reduces the problems of group locking to a minimum. However most PICK implementations now include true record (item) locking, which is obviously far preferable. There are a number of TCL commands within the ***dm*** account to assist in lock situations should they become a problem. Firstly **LIST-LOCKS** which displays the location of the locks, **CLEAR-BASIC-LOCKS** which clears file locks set in BASIC and **CLEAR-LOCKS** which clears all locks, or specific locks according to the TCL options.

Whether or not your implementation uses group or item locking, one very important consideration is the handling of records which are used to control your application. If your application assigns item-ids, for example the issue of sequential numbers for order numbers, goods received numbers and so on, it would be madness to have a single control record with each attribute referring to the next sequential number for each type of record (Sales Orders, Goods Received Notes, etc.). If this were the case, locking problems would be very likely to arise. Far better for each to have its own record and if appropriate for them to be in unique files.

One of the biggest worries in programming in a multi-user environment is that of conflict during updating. A process known as *deadlock* or *deadly embrace* can occur. This is a situation where one user has locked file *A* and now wants access to file *B* and a second user has locked file *B* and now needs access to file *A*. Neither can obviously progress forward and the only way out is then to use the **CLEAR-BASIC-LOCKS** command to free up both terminals.

PICK does not recognize a deadlock situation so it is up to the programmer to take the utmost precaution to ensure the possibility is minimized. Sensibly, therefore, as few a number of files as possible should be opened for updating at any one time. Not only that, but the number of instructions between locking data and releasing the lock should be kept to an absolute minimum. It is also sensible to ensure that when files are updated, they are updated in the same sequence in each transaction. This means that if file *A* and file *B* are used in a number of different transactions, file *A* is always updated before file *B* in each transaction.

Some application software will handle its own locking mechanisms by using one attribute of the record to indicate whether or not the record is locked.

There is another facility within BASIC to help overcome these problems, and that is the **LOCK** statement. The **LOCK** statement sets an execution lock of which there are 48 (0–47), which prevents another program setting the same lock number until the current process that set it has freed the lock number using the **UNLOCK** statement. Setting locks in this way has the advantage of being able to program exception conditions since the **LOCK** statement has an **ELSE** condition not available with the read statements (**READU**, **MATREADU**, etc.), and which enables other statements to be executed should the lock be already set.

15.11 Handling dynamic arrays in BASIC

The BASIC functions covered in this section are

COUNT	Counts the number of occurrences of a substring
DCOUNT	Return the number of fields separated by a delimiter
DELETE	Delete an element from an array
EXTRACT	Return an attribute value or sub-value from an array
INSERT	Insert an attribute, value or sub-value in an array
LOCATE	Find an attribute, value or sub-value in an array
REPLACE	Replace an attribute, value or sub-value in an array

We have seen how a complete record can be read into a variable using the **READ** statements. Unless defined by a **DIM** statement the variable will be called a ***dynamic array***. Hence **READ ORDREC FROM OPORDERS, ORDNO** without a previous **DIM** statement will create the dynamic array **ORDREC**. Having a complete record available in this way means that we need to have the means of accessing and manipulating specific attributes, multi-values and sub-values. We can refer to a specific part of the record by surrounding its positional reference within pointed brackets rather than the standard parenthesis used for real arrays as discussed in Section 15.11. Hence to refer to attribute 1 of the dynamic array, ORDREC, we would use the form **ORDREC<1>** and to refer to the first multi-value of attribute 2 we would use **ORDREC<2,1>** and for the second sub-value of the first multi-value of attribute 3 **ORDREC<3,1,2>** and so on.

This same notation is used when building up a dynamic array. However whilst they need no dimensioning, dynamic arrays have to be assigned a value, albeit a null value, before they can be referenced in any way which enables the compiler to locate the start point of the array in its table of variables (known as the descriptor table). Figure 15.41 gives an example of building up a record in the dynamic array ORDREC which is first assigned a null value.

There are a number of BASIC statements used to handle dynamic arrays. These statements are able to handle attributes, multi-values and secondary values and provide powerful string handling facilities. We have looked at two already, **READV** and **WRITEV**, and will now consider the others in the next few sections looking at the ways in which dynamic arrays can be manipulated.

ORDREC=""	The dynamic array is assigned a null value
ORDREC<1>=NAME	Attribute 1 is assigned the value of variable NAME
ORDREC<2,1>=ADDR1	Attribute 2, multi-value 1 is given the value of variable ADDR1
ORDREC<2,2>=ADDR2	Attribute 2, multi-value 2 is given the value of variable ADDR2
ORDREC<2,3>=ADDR3	Attribute 2 multi-value 3 is given the value of variable ADDR3
ORDREC<3>=TELNO	Attribute 3 is assigned the value of variable TELNO
ORDREC<4>=TLX	Attribute 4 is assigned the value of variable TLX

Figure 15.41 The dynamic array.

15.11.1 The INSERT and REPLACE statements

The format of these commands are the same, but obviously the **INSERT** statement will insert information into a dynamic array whilst **REPLACE** will replace it with some new data. The general format for these statements is shown in Figure 15.42.

INSERT(*var,exp1,exp2,exp3;new*)
REPLACE(*var,exp1,exp2,exp3;new*)

where

var is the name of the dynamic array
exp1 is the attribute position
exp2 is the multi-value position
exp3 is the sub-value position
new is the new data to insert or the data used to replace the existing data

Figure 15.42 The **INSERT** and **REPLACE** statement format.

It is not necessary to specify multi-value and sub-value positions where they don't apply, so in order to make this apparent to BASIC the new data must be preceded by a semicolon. Figure 15.43 gives examples of the use of these statements.

Using the value **–1** for *exp2* or *exp3* in either of these commands will append to the end of the multi-value or sub-value string being updated. Notice too that it is possible and equally valid to make a direct assignment rather than use the **REPLACE** statement. Hence in Figure 15.43, we could have substituted **REC<2,3>="YYY"** for the **REPLACE** statement.

```
OPEN "OPORDERS" TO ORD ELSE
   PRINT "OPORDERS NOT FOUND"
   STOP
   END
REC=""
* Read record whose item-id is 123
READ REC FROM ORD,"123" ELSE
   PRINT "RECORD NOT FOUND '123'"
   STOP
   END
* Insert the string XXX as multi-value 2 on attribute 2
REC=INSERT(REC,2,2;"XXX")
* Replace multi-value 3 on attribute 2 with the string YYY
REC=REPLACE(REC,2,3;"YYY")
* Write away new contents of record 123
WRITE REC ON OPORDERS,"123"
END
```

Figure 15.43 The use of **INSERT** and **REPLACE** in dynamic arrays.

15.11.2 The DELETE and EXTRACT statements

The **DELETE** statement will delete information from a dynamic array. **EXTRACT** will extract information from a dynamic array for use in the program, but will leave the original data in the array. Data extracted from an array can be used in conditional statements or assigned to variables leaving the array untouched.

The general format of these two commands is shown in Figure 15.44 whilst examples of their use are shown in Figure 15.45.

Once again, reference to **–1** in *exp2* or *exp3* will point to the last multi-value or sub-value and zero the first multi-value or sub-value.

It is also possible and just as accurate to replace the **EXTRACT** command in Figure 15.45 with a direct assignment such as **IF REC<2,3>=" XXX" THEN GOTO 999**. Many programmers prefer the use of direct assignment as is makes the program easier to write and maintain.

DELETE(*var,exp1,exp2,exp3*)
EXTRACT(*var,exp1,exp2,exp3*)

where

var is the name of the dynamic array
exp1 is the attribute position
exp2 is the multi-value position
exp3 is the sub-value position

Figure 15.44 The **DELETE** and **EXTRACT** statement format.

```
OPEN "OPORDERS" TO ORD ELSE
   PRINT "OPORDERS NOT FOUND";STOP;END
REC=""
* Read record whose item-id is 123
READ REC FROM ORD,"123" ELSE
   PRINT "RECORD NOT FOUND '123'";STOP;END
* If multi-value 3 of attribute 2 is XXX then exit program
IF EXTRACT(REC,2,3)="XXX" THEN GOTO 999
* Delete multi-value 3 of attribute 2
REC=DELETE(REC,2,3)
* Write away new contents of record 123
WRITE REC ON OPORDERS,"123"
999 END
```

Figure 15.45 The **DELETE** and **EXTRACT** statement.

15.11.3 The LOCATE statement

This is an extremely valuable statement which enables you to locate specific information. It is used not only to determine whether a particular value is present or not, but to maintain values in ascending or descending sequence within the array, whether these values be attributes, multi-values or sub-values. The format of the statement is shown in Figure 15.46.

If neither *exp1* or *exp2* are included in the statement, the **LOCATE** statement will search down each attribute of the record in turn looking for the appropriate value. It will look at the *ENTIRE* contents of each attribute and will not pay attention to the fact that some of may contain multi-values or sub-values nor that string to be located is a part of the attribute. Figure 15.47 gives an example of a **LOCATE** statement, looking for the string XYZ within in a record. Whilst the character string appears within several attributes, the **LOCATE** statement will not recognise it as being present because XYZ is not the complete value of any of the attributes.

The same string XYZ does exist as an exact value of one of the multi-values of attribute 3. To search a specific attribute, the attribute number is included in the **LOCATE** statement as *exp1*. Hence using the same record shown in Figure 15.47, the variable **POS** would contain 3 after use of the statement:

LOCATE("XYZ",ORD,3;POS) ELSE POS=0

LOCATE(*value,var{,exp1,exp2};var1{;seq}*) **ELSE** *statement*

where

value	contains the string to be located. A literal must be enclosed within single or double quotes
var	is the name of the dynamic array
exp1	is the attribute position
exp2	is the multi-value position
var1	is the variable containing the position number of the string
seq	defines the sequence where appropriate (see Figure 15.45) The sequences permitted are **A** ascending order left justified **AL** ascending order left justified **AR** ascending order right justified **D** descending order left justified **DL** descending order left justified **DR** descending order right justified
statement	is the BASIC statement to be executed should the string contained in value not be present

---

Figure 15.46 The **LOCATE** statement format.

Item-id = 123 as contained in dynamic array ORD is the record being searched and contains:

```
001 PO123
002 WATFORD HQ
003 ABC]DEF]XYZ]ZZZ
004 XYZ445
```

LOCATE("XYZ",ORD;POS) ELSE POS=0

would not find the string XYZ so the variable POS would contain 0

Figure 15.47 The **LOCATE** statement.

since the string XYZ is the third multi-value of attribute 3. Similarly to search through a specific multi-value, looking for a string, the multi-value number must be included in the **LOCATE** statement as *exp2*.

If we were to use a format of the statement where following **ELSE** was the word **NULL**, meaning take no action, then if the string to be located was not found the variable **POS** would contain a number one greater than the number of attributes or multi-values or sub-values searched. Hence in the case of Figure 15.48, the value of **POS** is first set to 5 by the **LOCATE** statement but then set to 0 (zero) by the **ELSE** portion of the statement.

The **LOCATE** statement can be made to abandon its search part way through if you specify a sequence for the search. In this case the data it is searching is assumed to be in sequence (ascending or descending), and the position variable **POS** will be given a number one more than the number items it passed when it finally found the string to be out of sequence. Figure 15.49 shows how this facility can be used to maintain a series of multi-values in ascending sequence. It shows how the string GHI is added in the correct position in attribute 3 to maintain its ascending sequence of multi-values.

Item-id = 123 as contained in dynamic array 'ORD'

```
001 PO123
002 WATFORD HQ
003 ABC]DEF]XYZ]ZZZ  <----------  Contains 4 multi-values
004 XYZ445
```

LOCATE("AAA",ORD,3;POS) ELSE NULL

would not find the string AAA in attribute 3 so the variable POS will contain 5 (4 attributes + 1)

Figure 15.48 The **LOCATE** statement for multi-values.

15.11.4 The COUNT and DCOUNT statements

The **COUNT** statement will count the number of occurrences of a specified string of characters within another string, returning a value of zero if the

Item-id = 123 as contained in dynamic array 'ORD'

```
001 PO123
002 WATFORD HQ
003 ABC]DEF]XYZ]ZZZ  <-------  Begins with 4 multi-values (GHI is now to be
004 XYZ445                     input to follow DEF)
```

*Locate the string "GHI" held in ascending sequence in attr 3
LOCATE("GHI",ORD,3;POS;"AL") ELSE NULL

* The variable POS now contains 3
*Insert the string 'GHI' in the correct sequence in attr. 3
ORD=INSERT(ORD,3,POS;"GHI")

Figure 15.49 Maintaining a string sequence with **LOCATE.**

string is not found. This function will return a number equivalent to the number of characters in the string if asked to look for a null character. Figure 15.50 shows the general format of the **COUNT** statement whilst Figure 15.51 gives some examples of its use.

COUNT(*string1,string2*)

where

string1 is the string being examined
string2 is the string to look for

Figure 15.50 The **COUNT** statement format.

ANS=COUNT('INITIALLY IT IS LIMITING','IT')
ANS will show result of COUNT which is 3 (the string IT exists in INITIALLY, **IT** and LIMITING)

ANS=COUNT('THE MISSISSIPPI IS A RIVER','I')
ANS will contain 6

A='THE MISSISSIPPI IS A RIVER'
B='IS'
ANS=COUNT(A,B)
ANS will contain 3

ANS=COUNT('THE THAMES','')
ANS will contain 10 (the number of characters in the original string)

Figure 15.51 The **COUNT** statement.

The **DCOUNT** statement is used to count the number of values in a variable separated by a specified delimiter. It is a very useful command and is used to count the number of attributes in an item, or the number of multi-values or sub-values in an attribute. A value of zero is returned if the entire string is null. Counting of attributes, multi-values and sub-values is handled by use of the **CHAR** conversion function which converts a number to its respective ASCII value. The values for **CHAR** which can be used to count attributes, multi-values and sub-values are as follows:

Attribute mark	ASCII value 254
Value mark	ASCII value 253
Sub-value mark	ASCII value 252

Figure 15.52 gives examples of the **DCOUNT** statement.

The contents of item-id = 123 as contained in dynamic array ORD

```
001 PO123
002 WATFORD HIGH STREET
003 ABC]DEF]XYZ]ZZZ
004 XYZ445
```

ANS=DCOUNT(ORD,CHAR(254))

ANS will contain 4 (the number of attributes)

ANS=DCOUNT(ORD<3>,CHAR(253))

ANS will contain 4 (the number of multi-values in attribute 3)

A=ORD<2>
B=' '
ANS=DCOUNT(A,B)

ANS will contain 3 (the number of words in attribute 2) (Variable B contains a space)

Figure 15.52 The use of **DCOUNT.**

15.12 Structured programming

The BASIC functions covered in this section are

CALL	Call an external subroutine
CASE	Perform conditional statements
CHAIN	End the program and execute a TCL command
COMMON	Declare data elements to be shared amongst different BASIC modules

ENTER	Transfer control to another program
EXECUTE	Execute a TCL command and return to the program
EXIT	Force an early exit from a loop
FOR..NEXT	Repeat a series of instructions a specific number of times
GOSUB	Branch to an internal subroutine
IF	Conditionally execute a series of statements
LOOP	Iterative loop of statements until an ending condition is met
RETURN	Return control from a subroutine back to the main program
TCL	Execute a TCL command
THEN/ELSE	Decision path operations

PICK BASIC provides the means to produce well structured programs, a structured program being one that reflects the structure of the problem it solves. In this environment use is made of subroutines and loops and the word **GOTO** is frowned on as four-letter word! Subroutines which are routines written to handle specific tasks, can be part of the main program or completely external to it. When external the subroutine is compiled and catalogued totally independent of the main program and just called in by the main program as required, with control then returning to the main program once the subroutine has finished.

In a structured programming environment, each task to be performed represents a separate program or subroutine, with the overall control of these functions being handled by the main program.

15.12.1 Internal subroutines

An internal subroutine is an area within a program which performs a task that is required to be repeated frequently within the program. In this situation, or one where an exception or error routine is required, an internal subroutine is used since it is not considered appropriate for the exception or error routine to be coded at exactly the place it occurs in the program.

A subroutine is defined by the **GOSUB** statement which specifies a label at which the start of the subroutine is to be found. Control is returned to the program at the instruction following the **GOSUB** statement, just as soon as a **RETURN** statement is encountered in the subroutine.

Since the return addresses of subroutine calls are held in a stack, one on top of the other, it is possible to call a subroutine within a subroutine, as required, with confidence of returning to the right part of the program afterwards, providing each has only one entry and exit point. The maintenance and understanding of such a process is another matter entirely and the 'nesting' of subroutines is not a recommended practice! Figure 15.53 shows the workings of subroutine calls.

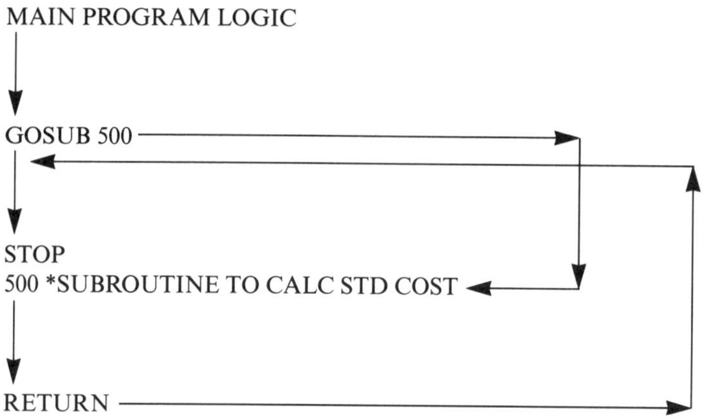

Figure 15.53 Subroutine logic.

An extension of the **GOSUB** statement allows for the evaluation of an expression first. This permits one of a number of subroutines to be called dependent on the value of a variable. Hence:

ON ANS GOSUB 500,600,700,800

would cause the program to branch to one of the subroutines at label 500, 600, 700 or 800 dependent on the value of **ANS**. If **ANS** contains *one* then the subroutine at label 500 will be executed, if it is *two* then the subroutine at label 600 will be used and so on. If the value of **ANS** is less than one or greater than the number of statement labels, no action will be taken, so care must be taken when using this command to cater for this possibility.

15.12.2 The IF statement

The **IF** statement allows for the appropriate action to be taken on the results of a test. In its simplistic form the statement format is:

IF *exp* **THEN** *statements*

where *exp* is the test expression and *statements* are the statements executed as a result. Figure 15.54 gives examples of the simplistic form of the **IF** statement.

An extension to the **IF..THEN** statement adds the **ELSE** condition and enables complex conditions to be handled. The general format of this statement is :

IF *exp* **THEN**
statements

↓

END ELSE
statements

↓

END

IF A THEN GOSUB 500
If **A** is not zero then subroutine 500 is performed

IF A = B THEN GOSUB 500

IF A > 12 THEN X = 2

IF A = "BLUE" THEN PRINT X

Figure 15.54 The simplistic **IF** statement.

Figure 15.55 gives examples of the complex form of the **IF..THEN..ELSE** statement.

The various relational operators that can be used within an **IF** statement are given in figure 15.56

N.B. The # symbol shown in the *NOT EQUAL* option in Figure 15.56 is achieved by pressing the SHIFT key and 3 key (on the main keyboard) together. On certain keyboards this will generate a £ symbol

15.12.3 The CASE statement

Since the **IF** statement can become complicated and difficult to understand even by the person who first wrote it, BASIC provides a simpler way of coding multiple **IF** conditions by use of the **CASE** statement. As many **CASE** statements as needed can follow each other, but they must all be bound within two statements, a **BEGIN CASE** at the beginning and an **END CASE** at the end. The general format being

BEGIN CASE
  CASE *exp*
  statements
  CASE *exp*
  statements
END CASE

Example 1

```
IF A > 0 THEN
  X=X-1
END ELSE
  X=X+1
END
```

If A is greater than zero then X=X–1 otherwise X=X+1

Example 2

```
IF FLD<12> = X THEN
   PRINT @(10,3):"ERROR CODE ":FLD<12>
   STOP
END ELSE
   IF X = "BLUE" THEN ◄——— This IF statement will ONLY be executed if
                           FLD<12> does not = X
     A="RIGHT"
   END ELSE
     A="WRONG" ◄——— Variable A contains WRONG when X not = "BLUE"
  END
END
```

Figure 15.55 The **IF..THEN..ELSE** statement.

< or LT	means LESS THAN
> or GT	means GREATER THAN
= or EQ	means EQUALS
# or <> or NE	means NOT EQUAL
<= or LE or =<	means LESS THAN OR EQUAL TO
>= or GE or =>	means GREATER THAN OR EQUAL TO
MATCH or MATCHES	means match pattern

Figure 15.56 The relational operators for the **IF** statement.

It is important to realize that each **CASE** statement is tested only *until* a true one is found. Once a true one is found, all statements relating to the true **CASE** statement are processed until the next **CASE** statement and then the remainder of the statements are ignored with control being passed to the statement immediately following the **END CASE** statement. For this reason to optimise the efficiency of your program you should ensure that the most frequently true condition is the first in the list. Figure 15.57 gives examples of the use of these statements.

```
LOOP
  PRINT @(10,10):;INPUT ANS,1;
BEGIN CASE
  CASE ANS = 'Y' OR ANS = 'y'
    ANS = 'Y'
  CASE ANS = 'N' OR ANS = 'n'
    ANS = 'N'
  CASE 1;* RETRY
    ANS = 'X'
    PRINT @(10,10):" ":
END CASE
UNTIL ANS = "Y" OR ANS = "N" DO
  NULL
REPEAT

  statements
999 STOP
  END
```

A test expression of 1 means *always true* hence if the previous **CASE** statements are inappropriate, **CASE 1** will force the subsequent statements to be processed setting **ANS** to an invalid response of **X** and causing the loop to be restarted

Figure 15.57 The **CASE** statement.

CASE statements can be nested to handle highly complex conditions. It is obviously important in this situation to think carefully about where the **BEGIN CASE** and **END CASE** statements should go. Figure 15.58 gives an example of nested **CASE** statements.

```
BEGIN CASE
  CASE X = 1
    BEGIN CASE

  statements

    END CASE
  CASE X = 2
    BEGIN CASE

  statements

    END CASE
END CASE
```

Figure 15.58 Nested **CASE** statements.

15.12.4 Various methods of programming loops

The FOR...NEXT *loop*

A loop is a set of instructions which are executed several times before the program continues further. Within the loop and for each successive iteration of the loop a variable is increased. Once the variable reaches a specified value, the loop is exited and the program continues. The **FOR..NEXT** loop is one of the most common loops of the BASIC language which can be enhanced by the addition of the **WHILE** or **UNTIL** clauses and Figure 15.59 gives examples of these.

Example 1

```
FOR I=1 TO 5 <---- First time round sets I = 1
PRINT I
NEXT I <--------- Increments I by 1
```

Example 2

```
X="10"
FOR I=1 TO 12 WHILE X < 50  ----> This loop will continue until I = 12 or X >=
   PRINT X*X                      50 whichever  comes first. It actually loops
X=X+5                             8 times
NEXT I
```

Example 3

```
*Read order number 123
READ ORDREC FROM OPORDERS,"123"
*Count the number of multi-values in attribute 30 of ORDREC
X=DCOUNT(ORDREC<30>,CHAR(253))
*Process loop for as many occurrences as there are multi-values
FOR I=1 TO X
*Build attribute 60 of ORDREC to contain same number of
*  multi-values as attribute 30 , each being twice that held
*  in the original multi-values in attribute 30
   ORDREC<60,I>=ORDREC<30,I>*2
*Increment loop
NEXT I
*Write record away
WRITE ORDREC ON OPORDERS,"123"
```

Figure 15.59 Examples of the **FOR..NEXT** loop.

In each of the examples in Figure 15.59 the counter variable was automatically incremented by 1 simply by asking for the next. In some cases it is necessary to increment by more than one at a time, which is handled by adding the **STEP** clause to the statement. Hence

```
FOR I=1 TO 40 UNTIL X > 50 STEP 2
   |
 statements
   |
   v
NEXT I
```

means that each time the **NEXT I** statement is encountered, the variable **I** will be increased by two.

15.12.4.2 The EXIT *function*

If it is necessary to terminate a **FOR..NEXT** or **LOOP..REPEAT** loop early, it can be achieved using the **EXIT** statement a function not available to R83 users. The typical reason to perform an early exit is if the user enters a termination value in response to an input question or even if a known value is encountered in the loop. If the **EXIT** function is not embedded in a loop statement it is ignored. Figure 15.60 gives examples of its use. It should be mentioned that the use of an **EXIT** in the middle of a loop like this is not considered good practice for those who practice structured programming.

```
FOR X = 1 TO 10
      PRINT "Choose a number between 1 and 100"
      INPUT NUM
      IF NUM = "END" THEN EXIT
      RANDOM.NO=RND(NUM+1)
      PRINT "Next random number = ":RANDOM.NO
NEXT X
```

Figure 15.60 Use of the **EXIT** function.

15.12.4.3 The LOOP..UNTIL/WHILE..DO..REPEAT *loop*

This kind of loop, often referred to as the **DO loop**, differs from the **FOR..NEXT** loop in that the loop is not executed a pre-set number of times. In the **FOR..NEXT** loop a variable is set equal to the number of occurrences the loop is to executed, for example **FOR I=1 TO 5** and the loop process started. In the **LOOP** statement, the loop is executed **UNTIL** a specific condition occurs, or **WHILE** a specific condition occurs. So this kind of loop enables execution of the series of commands following the **DO** statement **UNTIL** a test condition proves positive or **WHILE** a test condition prevails. Whilst these conditions apply program control will loop back to the top of the loop. Once the test condition is satisfied, control is passed to the first statement following the **REPEAT** statement and Figure 15.61 gives examples of these.

The main program in the first example of Figure 15.61 could easily have been the first program we encountered in this chapter which generated random numbers. To insert the loop routines around this program would mean that rather than finishing after running through the program once, the program could optionally be rerun until the user, rather than the program decided to stop.

Example 1

```
LOOP
  PRINT @(1,20):"DO YOU WANT ANOTHER GO? (Y or N) ":
  INPUT ANS
  WHILE ANS NE "N" DO <-- Process the main program until N is input by the user
   |
    main program statements
   v
REPEAT
```

Example 2

```
I=0
LOOP
  I=I+1
  UNTIL ORD<3,I> = '' DO <-- Process the program routine for each multi-value
   |                         of attribute 3 of the dynamic array ORD and
   |                         stop when it is null
program routine statements
   v
REPEAT
```

Figure 15.61 The **LOOP..WHILE/UNTIL..DO..REPEAT** statement.

15.12.5 The handling of external routines

As was discussed earlier, in structured programming each task becomes a separate program controlled from the main program. This is the right approach to programming but presents a problem of how to link all these routines together. There are four ways in which your program can interface to other programs and other parts of the system.

(1) The preferred way is via a **CALL** to an external subroutine where data is passed between the two processes. Once the external subroutine has finished control returns to the calling program.

(2) The program can **ENTER** another program. In this case although data can be passed to the entered program control is not returned to the calling program.

(3) The **EXECUTE** statement enables the program to execute any TCL command, after which control is returned to the calling program.

(4) The **CHAIN** statement enables the program to execute any TCL command but control is not returned to the program.

One undocumented statement which might prove useful when using a series of external subroutines is the **X=ERROR()** statement, where the variable **X** is assigned the entire contents of the TCL statement that called the program. This makes it possible to develop a program which performs several functions dependent on the options keyed in. Beware using this technique when the program is called from a PROC, since on some PICK implementations (but not under Advanced PICK) it is the PROC name which will be assigned to the variable.

15.12.5.1 The external subroutine and CALL *statement*

An external subroutine is one that has been written, compiled and *catalogued* outside and separate to the main program. It is called into use by the **CALL** statement within the main program. Once the subroutine has finished execution control is returned to the main program at the instruction following the **CALL** statement. The external subroutine cannot be used unless it has been catalogued and if you have forgotten to do so, the program will go into debug displaying the message, **PROGRAM 'XXX' HAS NOT BEEN CATALOGUED**. Another important point to bear in mind with subroutines is that they must use the same arithmetic precision as that used within the main program.

The external routine must start with the **SUBROUTINE** statement and end with the **RETURN** statement. When using external subroutines it is often necessary to pass them data collected by the main program, such as information keyed in by the user. Such information, known as the parameter list or argument list, can be passed in two ways. If the amount of information is small and limited to a few arguments, reference to these can be made following the **CALL** statement in the main program. If the amount of information is substantial, both the main program and external subroutine can declare a common area between them in which information can be passed. This common area can be of any size and is defined by the **COMMON** statement. Figure 15.62 shows how external subroutines are used, by demonstrating the calling of a program *CALC* within a main program.

The **CALL** statement can include the list of variables to be passed to the subroutine, by containing these, each separated with a comma, within parentheses. If the argument list is used for the **CALL** statement the same feature ***must*** apply to the **SUBROUTINE** statement. These arguments may be called by a different name in the main program to those used within the subroutine,

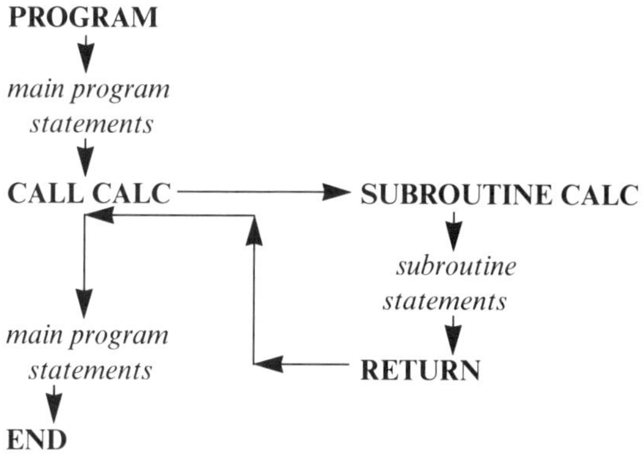

Figure 15.62 The use of external subroutines.

provided that the ***number*** of arguments in the **CALL** statement and **SUBROUTINE** statement are the same. Figure 15.63 gives an example of argument passing where prior to calling the subroutine the arguments passed, **A**, **B** and **C** are given values. Whilst the names of the arguments are not the same in the external subroutine, the number of arguments is identical and the values of the arguments are therefore assigned in the same order as the list in the **CALL** statement. Hence in Figure 15.63 **X** has the same value as **A**, **Y** the same value as **B** and **C** the same value as **Z**.

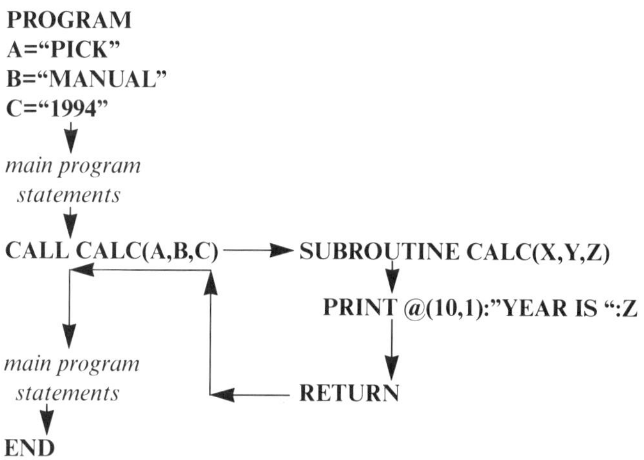

The message displayed by the subroutine is `YEAR IS 1994`

Figure 15.63 Passing arguments between subroutine and main program.

Arrays may be passed to a subroutine by identifying them as such which requires using **MAT** prior to the variable name. The variable must first be dimensioned with the **DIM** command in the calling program, and the external subroutine must also dimension its variable before making use of its contents. It is quite feasible to change the array dimension providing that the total number of elements in the array remain the same. Hence a vector (single dimensioned array) of 8 elements can be changed into a matrix (two dimensional array) of 2×4 elements and Figure 15.64 gives an example of this.

With argument-passing the parameters are copied from the data area of the main program to the data area of the subroutine. If the amount of information to be passed is large, this not only wastes space but time. A far more efficient way of passing information in these circumstances is through the common area. This is a common data area which both the main program and any subroutine can access and can update. If this concept is adopted, then ***both*** the subroutine and main program must contain a common area, defined by the **COMMON** statement. Once again there is complete independence between the names used to described these variables in the main program and subroutine(s) although it is good programming practice to use the same names in both.

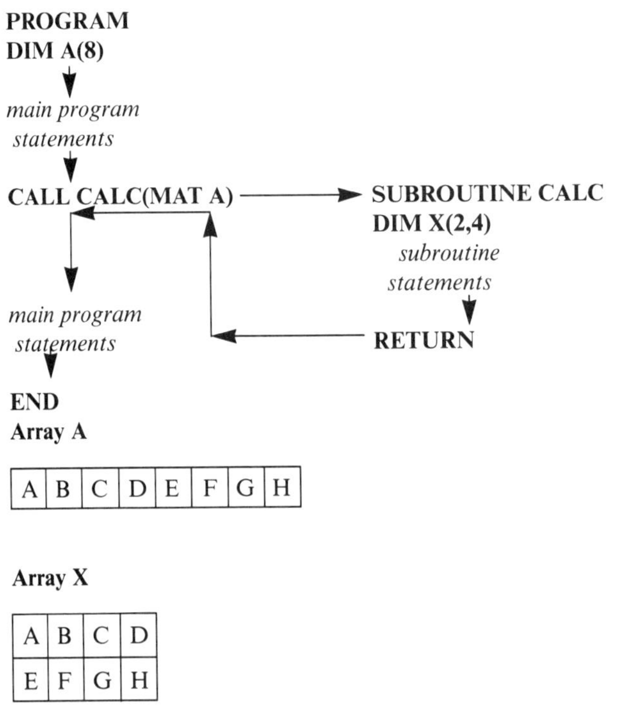

Figure 15.64 Passing arrays as arguments to external subroutines.

The **COMMON** statement does impose some disciplines that should be borne in mind. Firstly the **COMMON** statement must appear before the use of any of the variables contained in it. Whilst this does not dictate that it has to be placed at the start of the program or subroutine, it is generally found there. Arrays can be declared by specifying their dimensions within parentheses. Any arrays declared in this way should not be declared again in a **DIM** statement.

As with argument lists, the elements defined by the **COMMON** statement in the main program 'mask' those defined in the external subroutine. Hence where the main program defines a common statement with the variables **A**, **B** and **C** and the subroutine declares the common statement with **X(2)** and **Y**, **X(1)** refers to **A**, **X(2)** refers to **B** and **Y** refers to **C**. Figure 15.65 shows how the **COMMON** statement is used to define a single variable, **A**, and a single-dimensional array of 8 elements, **B**, in the main program which is defined as variable **X** and the two-dimensional array **Y** in the subroutine.

One useful aspect of the **CALL** statement is that it can be used to make indirect calls. This applies in the situation where one of a number of external subroutines is to be used, dependent on the result of test condition. In this form a variable is set to contain the subroutine name and the call statement calls the variable. To indicate that the name being called is a variable, it is preceded with an @. Hence the general format of the command is :

CALL *@subroutine {(arguments)}*

where

subroutine is the subroutine name
arguments are the arguments to be passed

Figure 15.66 shows how the indirect call to an external subroutine is made.

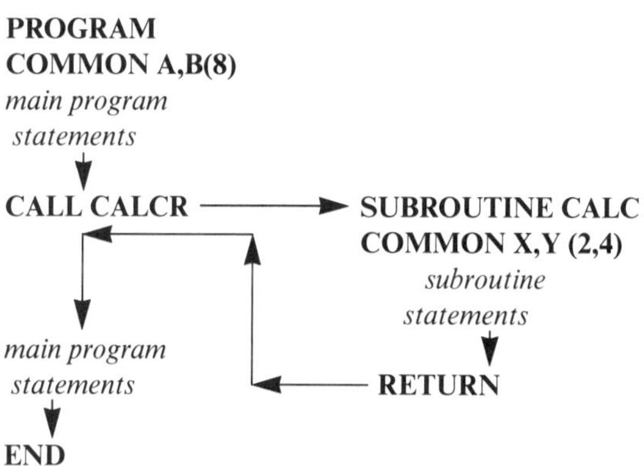

Figure 15.65 Use of the **COMMON** statement.

```
COMMON A,B,C(8)
    |
    v
BEGIN CASE
  CASE ANS = 1
    SUBNAME = 'SUBR1'
  CASE ANS = 2
    SUBNAME = 'SUBR2'
  CASE ANS = 3
    SUBNAME = 'SUBR3'
END CASE
CALL @SUBNAME
    |
    v
END
```

Figure 15.66 The indirect subroutine call.

15.12.5.2 The external routine and ENTER *statement*

Use of external routines using the **ENTER** statement are similar to the **CALL** statement except for two major differences. Firstly no argument list can be used so data ***must*** be passed using the **COMMON** statement. Secondly and most importantly control is ***not*** returned to the calling program once the external routine has finished execution. It is permitted to **ENTER** a program that calls a subroutine, but is obviously illegal to enter a subroutine from a program because on reaching the **RETURN** statement in the subroutine and being unable to return to the calling program, the program would have nowhere to go! Figure 15.67 shows the use of the **ENTER** statement which enters another program which itself calls a subroutine. Again as with the **CALL** statement the indirect form of **ENTER** is permitted.

15.12.5.3 External routines and the EXECUTE *statement*

The **EXECUTE** statement was a late addition to the R83 version of PICK and as such was not available from every licensee. Nowadays only the really old versions of PICK suffer the lack of **EXECUTE**. This statement provides extremely powerful facilities to the programmer, enabling the execution of any TCL command from within BASIC. After the execution of the TCL command control is returned to the program at the statement following the **EXECUTE** statement. It is the introduction of this statement which lead to a significant reduction in the use of **PROC**s. Prior to its introduction the only way to execute a TCL command from a BASIC program was to use **CHAIN**, a statement which does not return control to the calling program.

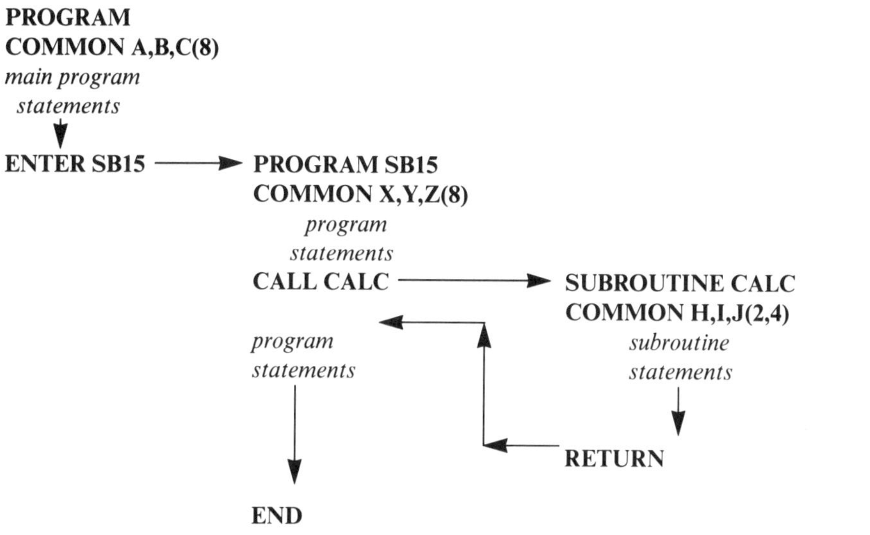

Figure 15.67 Using the **ENTER** statement.

The only disadvantage with **EXECUTE** is that it requires additional workspace in which to operate. These workspaces, each 413 frames, are taken from overflow and maintained in a special workspace table for use by the **EXECUTE** process. When an **EXECUTE** is complete, the workspace it used is returned to this table and not to system overflow. If sufficient space is not available in this table and more needs to be constructed the process can incur a noticeable delay.

This issue of workspace becomes important in a multi-user environment, and even more important in a heavily loaded system using nested **EXECUTE** statements. It could become very serious indeed in a heavily loaded multi-user system using nested **EXECUTE** statements on a system with limited free disk capacity, such as 10 or 20 megabytes.

In general, the **EXECUTE** statement preserves the current working environment before executing the TCL command and restores it after the execution is complete. However, there are certain parameters that are not restored before resuming the BASIC program, these being:

(1) The terminal characteristics are not restored if they are changed by a **TERM** command.
(2) The spooler assignment is not restored if altered by a spooler command, such as **SP-ASSIGN, SP-OPEN**, etc.
(3) Terminal output suppression (**P** verb) is not restored if the current execution does not have output capturing.

(4) Current CPU usage statistics are not restored.
(5) Tape attachment and tape record size changes when the **T-ATT** and **T-DET** verbs are not restored.

Certain TCL verbs will not return after 'execution', namely **OFF** and **LOGTO** and from the debugger **END** or **OFF** will not continue with the **EXECUTE**.

EXECUTE has a number of general formats given in Figure 15.68, and examples of its use are given in Figure 15.69.

Input can be passed to the TCL command by means of the **DATA** statement although no data can be passed to a **PROC**. Once the TCL command is complete, the data stack is reset.

Output from the executed command may be captured and redirected back to a variable in the calling program by use of the **CAPTURING** clause. If output is being redirected in this way, carriage return/linefeed pairs are converted to attribute marks and 'clear screen' sequences are removed.

In 15.69, the TCL statement **COPY** was used to copy the contents of the file **MASTER** to the file **BACKUP**. The variable **ERR** will contain **805** if the copy is successful, which is the message passed from **messages**. A complete list of the message numbers and their meanings contained in the file **messages** is listed in Appendix A.

15.12.5.4 Performing a TCL command with the TCL *function*

The **TCL** function is an alternative to **EXECUTE** for the execution of a TCL command, but is not available to users of R83. Once the command has completed the BASIC program will continue from the statement immediately following the **TCL** function. As with **EXECUTE** data can be passed to the **TCL** statement prior to the TCL statement being execute. The format of the function can be seen opposite:

EXECUTE *expr*
EXECUTE *expr* **RETURNING** *var1*
EXECUTE *expr* **CAPTURING** *var2*
EXECUTE *expr* **RETURNING** *var1* **CAPTURING** *var2*
EXECUTE *expr* **CAPTURING** *var2* **RETURNING** *var1*

where

expr is a complete TCL statement
var1 is a variable that will contain error messages numbers after the execution. The variable will contain a string of error messages numbers each separated by a space
var2 is a variable to capture the output from the executed command

---

Figure 15.68 The format of the **EXECUTE** statement.

```
DATA "(BACKUP)"
ITEMS = " *"
FILE = " MASTER"
OK = 805

EXECUTE "COPY ":FILE:ITEMS RETURNING ERR CAPTURING LIST
IF ERR # OK THEN
   PRINT "COPY FAILED. ERROR WAS":ERR
END ELSE
   PRINT "COPY SUCCESSFUL. ITEMS COPIED WERE":LIST
END
```

Figure 15.69 Using **EXECUTE** and **DATA** statements in BASIC.

TCL *tcl.command* {**TO** *dim.array*}

where

tcl.command	is the TCL command to execute
dim.array	is the dimensioned array holding the output from the TCL command

Multiple 'data' statements may be passed if they are separated by value marks and multiple TCL statements may be passed when they are separated by attribute marks. If an active select list is generated by the **TCL** command it is passed back to the program and can be used by the **READNEXT** statement or it can be assigned to a specific variable using the **SELECT TO** statement. As with **EXECUTE**, if the TCL verb **OFF** is executed control does not return to the BASIC program. If the results of the **TCL** function are to be analysed they can be determined by examining the dimensioned array *dim.array* as shown in Figure 15.70

15.12.5.5 EXECUTE *with select lists*

The **EXECUTE** statement can be used to generate select lists which can then be used in a **READNEXT** statement in your program. This would typically be used where you wanted to process a certain selected group of records from a file, for example those with a particular payment code. If you use the BASIC statement **SELECT** the **READNEXT** would work its way through every record on the file, so you can use the **EXECUTE** to select the records to pass to the **READNEXT** statement.

```
DIM CAPTURE.VAR(3)
TCL 'COUNT CUSTOMER WITH COUNTY = "ESSEX"' TO CAPTURE.VAR
NUMBER.CUST = CAPTURE.VAR(3)
NUMBER.CUST.IN.COUNTY = CAPTURE.VAR(2)
```

The format of the variable **CAPTURE.VAR** is that in the first element it contains the message number from the **MESSAGES** file and the others contain the values which would be output from the message itself. Hence in the above example if the output from the **COUNT** statement was

```
[407] 33 items counted out of 3429 items
```

the array **CAPTURE.VAR** would contain the following

```
CAPTURE.VAR(1)    407
CAPTURE.VAR(2)     33
CAPTURE.VAR(3)   3429
```

Figure 15.70 Use of the **TCL** statement.

When using **EXECUTE** to build select lists, you are executing an **ACCESS** statement and these often contain both single and double quote characters. For this reason it is best to use the \ (backslash) character to delimit the **ACCESS** statement. However you can use the single quote or double quote characters to delimit the **ACCESS** statement providing they are not needed in the **ACCESS** statement itself.

Figure 15.71 gives examples of the use of select-list processing with the **EXECUTE** statement.

It should be noted that certain implementations of PICK handle **EXECUTE** differently to the generic version of PICK (R83 and Advanced PICK). The result is that the active select list is made available to the **READNEXT**

<u>Example 1</u>

```
SENTENCE = \SSELECT CUSTOMER BY NAME WITH PAY.CODE = "DD"\
```

<u>Example 2</u>

```
PAY.CODE = "DD"
SENTENCE = \SSELECT CUSTOMER BY NAME WITH PAY.CODE = "\
SENTENCE = SENTENCE : PAY.CODE : \" \
```

<u>Example 3</u>

```
SENTENCE = 'SSELECT CUSTOMER BY NAME WITH PAY.CODE = "DD"'
```

Figure 15.71 Select-list processing using the **EXECUTE** statement.

statement but not to the next **EXECUTE** statement. One of the main versions that works this way is Ultimate and this results in a different syntax being required. If the standard version of **EXECUTE** is giving compiler errors, refer to your manual for the correct construct of the statement.

15.12.5.6 External routines and the CHAIN *statement*

Prior to the introduction of the **EXECUTE** statement, the **CHAIN** command was the only way in which a TCL command could be executed directly from BASIC. The **CHAIN**ed program, can therefore, by definition also execute a **PROC** or run another program using the TCL command **RUN**. Once the command is initiated full control is passed to the TCL command so there is no ability to return to the BASIC program.

Any data to be passed to the TCL command must be done via the **DATA** statement in the same way as shown in Figure 15.69 using the **EXECUTE** statement. The general format of the statement is:

> **DATA** *expression*
> **CHAIN** *"TCL command"*

Figure 15.72 shows an example of this command.

---

main program	**TCL processor**
↓	
CHAIN "LISTU"	**LISTU**
	CH# PCBF NAME...... TIME ....
	*00 0400 SYSPROG 10:39
	01 0420 SYSPROG 10:39
	↓
The TCL prompt ——→	:

Figure 15.72 The **CHAIN** statement.

15.13 String handling

A string in simplistic terms is any expression that evaluates to, or can be converted to a string of characters. Frequently it is necessary to manipulate strings of characters and there are many functions available. In dynamic array processing we saw the use of functions such as **DELETE**, **EXTRACT**,

INSERT and **REPLACE** powerful statements, which are dependent on the standard PICK delimiters (Value Mark, Attribute Mark and Segment Mark), but how can we handle strings that don't contain these delimiters? Fortunately PICK BASIC has a number of string processing functions and this section is dedicated them.

The BASIC functions covered in this section are

[ ]	Assign a substring
:	Concatenate (performs the same task as the CAT function)
ALPHA	Tests for all alphabetic characters
ASCII	Convert a string from EBCDIC to ASCII
CAT	Concatenate (performs the same task as the : function)
COL1()	Return the preceding column position (used with the FIELD function)
COL2()	Return the following column position (used with the FIELD function)
CONVERT	Converts one string within a variable into another string
COUNT	Count the number of occurrences of a substring
DCOUNT	Return the number of fields separated by a specified delimiter
EBCDIC	Convert a string from ASCII to EBCDIC
FIELD	Returns a delimited substring of a string
FOLD	Breaks a string into a string of given lengths, each delimited
INDEX	Return the position of a substring within a string
LEN	Return the length of a string
MATCHES	Checks the string for a specific pattern of characters (can also use MATCH)
NUM	Tests for all numeric characters
OCCURS	Searches a string for attributes or values that occur consecutively
SORT	Sorts a string delimited by attribute or value marks in ascending order
SOUNDEX	Returns the 4 digit soundex code for the phonetic string
SPACE	Generate a specified number of spaces
STR	Generate a string of a specified number of a specified character
TRIM	Removes extraneous blank spaces from a string

15.13.1 [ ] *Assign a substring*

This function enables the definition of a part of a string by specifying the start position and length of the substring within the string. The format of the statement is *string*[*startpos,len*]

where

string	is the string from which a substring is to be extracted
startpos	the starting position in characters of the substring within the *string* starting from character position 1 of the *string*
len	the length of the substring to be assigned

The substring can also be assigned to a variable. Hence if the string **NAME** is in the format of an initial followed by a space followed by a surname (such as R BOURDON), the surname could be extracted by using **SURNAME = NAME[3,999]** where **999** is a catch-all with **SURNAME** ending up containing BOURDON. Hence the statement means assign to the variable **SURNAME** up to 999 characters starting at character 3.

15.13.2 : *or* CAT *Concatenate*

The **:** and **CAT** perform exactly the same function that of concatenating string expressions together. The format of the expression is as follows:

str1:str2 or *str1* **CAT** *str2*

Hence the format to concatenate the two variables FIRST.NAME and SURNAME with a space in between would be **FIRST.NAME:" ":SURNAME** or **FIRST.NAME CAT " " CAT SURNAME**.

15.13.3 ALPHA *Tests for all alphabetic characters*

The **ALPHA** function tests whether a string is alphabetic or not. The characters A to Z and their lower case equivalents a to z are considered alphabetic. The expression which returns a 1 (one) for true and 0 (zero) for false is of the following form:

ALPHA(*string*)

and is typically used in **IF** and **CASE** statements such as **IF ALPHA (FULL.NAME) THEN** ..... or **IF NOT (ALPHA(FULL.NAME)) THEN** ...

15.13.4 ASCII *Convert a string from EBCDIC to ASCII*

The **ASCII** function converts a string in EBCDIC code to ASCII code. This is not a commonly used function but is invaluable where data conversion between these two formats is required and many IBM files are still held in EBCDIC format. The structure of the statement is

ASCII(*string*)

Again the function would be used in conjunction with the assignment of a variable, such as **REC<1>=ASCII(FULL.NAME)**.

15.13.5 FIELD, COL1() *and* COL2() *To locate substring within a string*

The **FIELD** function returns a substring from a string specifying a delimiter character and is used in conjunction with the **COL1()** and **COL2()** functions which return respectively the column position before and after the string returned to the **FIELD** function.

The **FIELD** function is useful when a value has been sub-divided by a program into a number of sub-values with a user-defined delimiter and the sub-values need to be addressed. The general format of the function is:

FIELD(*string,delimiter,occurrence*)

where

string is the string being searched
delimiter the character which separates the substrings
occurrence the number of occurrences minus 1, of the delimiters to be skipped prior to extraction of the string

Figure 15.73 shows how the **FIELD** function works with those of **COL1()** and **COL2()**.

```
ADDRESS = 15 HIGH STREET*BOW*LONDON*E3 3AB
ANS=FIELD(ADDRESS,"*",3)          ANS = LONDON
START.COL=COL1()                  START.COL = 16
END.COL=COL2()                    END.COL = 23
```

Figure 15.73 The use of **FIELD**, **COL1()** and **COL2()**.

15.13.6 CONVERT *Replace a character with another*

The **CONVERT** statement searches a variable for a specific character and replaces it with another. It can either convert all occurrences of the specified character to the replacement character or can be made to do so based on the corresponding positions of the characters in the specified and replacement strings. This is best explained by example and Figure 15.74 illustrates its general format whilst Figure 15.75 gives examples of its use. This function is not available in R83.

15.13.7 COUNT *Count the number of occurrences of a substring*

The **COUNT** statement counts the number of occurrences of a specified string of characters within another string, returning a value of zero if the string is not found. This function will return a number equivalent to the number of characters in the string if asked to look for a null character. Figure 15.76 shows the general format of the **COUNT** statement whilst Figure 15.77 gives some examples of its use.

CONVERT *string1* **TO** *string2* **IN** *variable*

where

string1 is the string of the specified character(s)
string2 is the string of the replacement character(s)
variable the variable containing the string to be searched

Figure 15.74 The **CONVERT** statement.

Example 1

CONVERT CHAR(253) TO " " IN INVOICE.NUMBERS
This converts all value marks in a multi-valued string called **INVOICE.NUMBERS** to spaces.

Example 2

CONVERT "ABC" TO "XYZ" IN MESSAGE
This converts all **A** to **X** all **B** to **Y** and all **C** to **Z**; hence if the variable **MESSAGE** originally contained **ABACUS** then after conversion it would contain **XYXZUS**.

When the *specified* and *replacement* strings are the same length then there is no problem, but if they or different lengths then all characters beyond the length of the *specified string* are deleted. Hence:

Example 3

CONVERT "ABC" TO "X" IN MESSAGE
This converts all occurrences of the three character string **ABC** in the variable **MESSAGE** to the single character **X**.
However the reverse is not quite the same.

Example 4

CONVERT "A" TO "XYZ" IN MESSAGE
This converts all occurrences of the character **A** in the variable **MESSAGE** to the single character **X**.

Figure 15.75 Examples of the **CONVERT** statement.

COUNT(*string1*,*string2*)

where

string1 is the string being examined
string2 is the string to look for

Figure 15.76 The **COUNT** statement.

ANS=COUNT('INITIALLY IT IS LIMITING','IT')
ANS will show result of COUNT which is 3 (the string IT exists in INITIALLY, **IT**, and LIMITING)

ANS=COUNT('THE MISSISSIPPI IS A RIVER','I')
ANS will contain 6

A='THE MISSISSIPPI IS A RIVER'
B='IS'
ANS=COUNT(A,B)
ANS will contain 3

ANS=COUNT('THE THAMES','')
ANS will contain 10 (the number of characters in the original string)

Figure 15.77 The use of the **COUNT** statement.

15.13.8 DCOUNT *Count the number of fields separated by a delimiter*

Whilst the **DCOUNT** statement is mostly used in the processing of dynamic arrays, it really offers functionality to string processing. Its function is to count the number of values in a variable separated by a specified delimiter. The delimiter can be any character, so in text strings for example, the delimiter is

The contents of item-id = 123 as contained in dynamic array ORD

```
001 PO123
002 WATFORD HIGH STREET
003 ABC*DEF*XYZ*ZZZ
004 XYZ445
```

ANS=DCOUNT(ORD<1>," ")
ANS will contain 2 (the number of words)

ANS=DCOUNT(ORD<2>,"T")
ANS will contain 4 (the number strings delimited by the letter T)

A=ORD<3>
B="*"
ANS=DCOUNT(A,B)
ANS will contain 4 (the number of words in attribute 3)

Figure 15.78 The use of **DCOUNT.**

often the space character. The function will return value of zero if the entire string is null. Figure 15.78 gives examples of the **DCOUNT** statement.

15.13.9 EBCDIC *Convert a string from ASCII to EBCDIC*

The EBCDIC function converts a string in ASCII code to EBCDIC code. This is not a commonly used function but is invaluable where data conversion between these two formats is required and many IBM files are still held in EBCDIC format. The structure of the statement is

EBCDIC(*string***)**

Again the function would be used in conjunction with the assignment of a variable, such as **REC<1>=EBCDIC(FULL.NAME)**.

15.13.10 FOLD *Divide a string into multiple strings of a given length*

The **FOLD** statement is used to divide a string into multiple strings of a specified number of characters. If the fold length is not specified it defaults to

---

FOLD(*string,fold.length,delimiter***)**

where

string	is the string being examined
fold.length	is the maximum length of the 'folded' string
delimiter	is the delimiter to be used in the folded text to delimit each 'fold' point. If null a value mark is used

---

Figure 15.79 The **FOLD** statement.

Value of string input to the following example: This is a test string to demonstrate the 'fold' function

```
EQU SVM TO CHAR(2520
INPUT STRING
STRING=FOLD(STRING,10,SVM)
```

Value of string after the **FOLD** function: This is a\test\string to\demonstrat\e 'fold'\function

---

Figure 15.80 The use of the **FOLD** statement.

25 characters and where possible the 'fold' takes place on a space character. Figure 15.79 shows the general format of the **FOLD** statement whilst Figure 15.80 gives some examples of its use. This function is not available in R83.

15.13.11 INDEX *Search a string for a specific character or substring*

The **INDEX** statement is used to search through a string looking for the occurrence of a character or string of characters. If the search string is found,

---

INDEX(*string,substring,occurrence*)

where

string	is the string being examined
substring	is the string to locate in *string*
occurrence	is the number of occurrences of *substring* within *string*

Figure 15.81 The **INDEX** statement.

INDEX returns the position at which the *n*th occurrence is found, where *n* is a number specified in the statement itself. Figure 15.81 shows the general format of the **INDEX** statement whilst Figure 15.82 gives some examples of its use.

POS=INDEX("ABCABC,"A",2)	**POS** is assigned the value 4
X="MISSISSIPPI" **Y="I"** **POS=INDEX(X,Y,3)**	 **POS** is assigned the value 8

Figure 15.82 The use of the **INDEX** statement.

LEN(*string*)

NAME="Roger James Bourdon" **X=LEN(NAME)**	 **X** contains 19
NUM=12 **X=LEN(NUM*100)**	 **X** contains 4 i.e. the length of 1200

Figure 15.83 The **LEN** statement.

15.13.13 MATCHES String pattern matching

The **MATCH** or **MATCHES** function checks a string against a specific pattern. Three pattern operators are available:

- **A** alphabetic
- **N** numeric
- **X** wildcard (any character)

These operators are preceded by a number to indicate the number of characters of each operator to match against. A number of 0 (zero) indicates any length. In addition any literal enclosed in quotes may be used in the pattern match. The format of the command is

string1 **MATCHES** *string2*

The result of the comparison is either 1 (true) or 0 (false) and for this reason the **MATCHES** function is used in conditional checks, such as the **IF** or **CASE** statement. Some examples follow.

IF TEL.NO MATCHES "3N'-'3N'-'4N" THEN .....
Checks for a telephone number in the form three numbers, a hyphen, three numbers, a hyphen and four numbers. Hence a telephone number of 071-288-6222 matches the pattern, whilst a number of 0956-70-6222 does not.

IF DATE = "2NX2NX2N" THEN ....
Checks for a date in the form NN?NN?NN where ? can be any character. Hence a date of 24.07.94 will match the pattern, as will 24/07/94, but a date of 24 JUL 94 will not.

It is worth noting that the functions **ALPHA** and **NUM** are more efficient ways of testing for alphabetic and numeric characters in a string than the function **MATCHES "0A"** and **MATCHES "0N"**. However, where the hyphen and decimal point will pass as numeric under the **NUM** function, they will not using **MATCHES "0N"**.

15.13.14 NUM *Tests for all numeric characters*

The **NUM** function tests whether a string is numeric or not. The characters 0 to 9, the minus symbol, plus symbol and decimal point are considered numeric. The expression which returns a 1 (one) for true and 0 (zero) for false is of the following form:

NUM(*string*)

and is typically used in **IF** and **CASE** statements such as **IF NUM(SALARY) THEN** ..... or **IF NOT (ALPHA(SALARY)) THEN** .....

NUM(*string*)

and is typically used in **IF** and **CASE** statements such as **IF NUM(SALARY) THEN** ..... or **IF NOT (ALPHA(SALARY)) THEN** .....

15.13.15 OCCURS *Search for consecutive occurrences of a string*

The **OCCURS** statement is used to determine the consecutive number of occurrences of a string delimited by either a value or attribute mark. The general format of the function is given in Figure 15.84 with an example in Figure 15.85. This function is not available in R83.

15.13.16 SORT *Sort a delimited string in ascending order*

The **SORT** statement will sort values or attributes in ascending left-justified order only. The string being sorted must be delimited by either an attribute or value mark, no other delimiter is acceptable. Equally, the only order the string can be sorted in is ascending order. The general format of the function is given in Figure 15.86 with an example in Figure 15.87. This statement is not available in R83.

OCCURS(*string,occurrences*)

where

string	is the string being examined
occurrences	is the number of occurrences of any string of characters

---

Figure 15.84 The format of the **OCCURS** statement.

```
X="22]11]11]11]22]11]11]22]11]11"          where ] represents a value mark
FOR N=1 TO 4
     FOUND.STRING=OCCURS(STRING,NUM)
     PRINT FOUND.STRING : "the string(s) occurring" : NUM : " times"
NEXT N
```

The output from the above would be as follows:

```
22]11]22]11]22]11 the string(s) occurring 1 times
11]11]11 the string(s) occurring 2 times
11 the string(s) occurring 3 times
the string(s) occurring 4 times
```

Figure 15.85 Using the **OCCURS** statement.

---

string1 = **SORT**(*string2*)

where

string1 is the original string (containing unsorted values)
string2 is the sorted value of *string1*

Figure 15.86 The format of the **SORT** statement.

```
EQU VM TO CHAR(253)
INTERESTS="SQUASH":VM:"BADMINTON":VM:"SWIMMING":VM:"BRIDGE"
SORTED.INTERESTS = SORT(INTERESTS)
```

After the above, the variable **SORTED.INTERESTS** will contain
BADMINTON]BRIDGE]SQUASH]SWIMMING
where] is a value mark

Figure 15.87 Using the **SORT** statement.

15.13.17 SOUNDEX *Soundex code for a phonetic expression*

The **SOUNDEX** statement is used produce a four digit soundex code for a phonetic string expression. The format of the function is:

SOUNDEX *(string{,code})*

where

string is the string for which a soundex code is required
code is the option which provides compatibility with R83 user exit **U00B9**, where
code = 0 (the default) for the original census soundex (R83 compatible)
code = 1 English language soundex

15.13.18 SPACE *Generate a specified number of spaces*

The space command generates a string of a specified number of spaces and has a simple form:

SPACE(*expr*)

where *expr* is the number of spaces to be generated.

This command is most frequently used when printing output to either the screen or printer, typically

```
PRINT "Ref ":REC<1>"L(%6)":SPACE(3):"Salary ":REC<2>"R26,"
```

which prints the word Ref followed by attribute 1 of the array REC masked left justified on a field of 6 zeros, followed by 3 spaces, followed by the word **Salary** followed by attribute 2 of the array REC masked to 2 places of decimals.

15.13.19 STR *Generate a string of a specified character*

The **STR** function is very similar to the **SPACE** function in that a string of a number of a specified character is generated, except that the character string it generates can be of any character and is not limited to the space character. Its construct is as follows:

STR(*expr,num*)

where *expr* is the character to be generated and *num* is the number of the *expr* character to be generated.

This command is most commonly found in output statements. The following shows three ways in which a string of 20 asterisks can be printed.

```
PRINT "********************"
PRINT STR("*",20)
PRINT STR(PRINT.CHAR,NO.TIMES)
```

where **PRINT.CHAR** equates to an asterisk and **NO.TIMES** equates to 20.

15.13.20 TRIM *Removing extraneous blank spaces from a string*

This function removes extraneous blanks from a string of characters. This means all leading and trailing blanks and then any occurrences of two or more blanks are replaced by a single blank. The construct is

TRIM(*string*)

The normal use of **TRIM** is to equate either a new variable or the string itself to the 'trimmed' version, for example

```
NEW.SENTENCE=TRIM(OLD.SENTENCE)

OLD.WORD.STRING=TRIM(OLD.WORD.STRING)
```

The BASIC functions covered in this section are

ABS	Returns the absolute value of a given expression
CHAR	Returns the ASCII value of a decimal value
COS	Returns the cosine of the expression
EXP	Returns e to the specified power

INT	Returns the integer portion of an expression
LN	Returns the natural log of an expression
MOD	Returns the remainder of one expression divided by another
PRECISION	Determines the decimal precision of numeric values
PWR	Returns an exponential value
REM	Returns the remainder of one expression divided by another
RND	Returns a random number
SEQ	Returns the decimal value of an ASCII character
SIN	Returns the sine of the expression
SQRT	Returns the square root of an expression
TAN	Returns the tangent of an expression

15.14 Arithmetic operations

In Section 15.3 we touched on the principles of arithmetic processing and the precedence of arithmetic operations. This section looks at these in detail together with the primary arithmetic statements.

A number can be represented in virtually any way, with or without signs or decimal points. The largest number that can be represented is 147037488350000, the smallest is the negative of the same number. PICK traditionally holds numbers to 4 places of decimals, although this can be altered in the program by use of the **PRECISION** statement.

Arithmetic expressions are formed using arithmetic operators, each of which is given an order of precedence.

Precedence

Expressions in a BASIC program are evaluated according to a set of rules for the evaluation of its components. The rules of precedence are based on the operation involved, the top level of which is when parentheses are present. With parentheses, the innermost set have the highest priority. Thereafter the next highest priority is for the exponential function followed by multiplication and division. Since multiplication and division have equal priority they are evaluated from left to right. Next with equal priority is addition and subtraction (with the same left to right evaluation as with multiplication and division). At the next level is print masking followed by concatenation, the relational operators (e.g. **EQ**, **NE**, etc.) and finally the logical operators of **AND** and **OR**.

For the sake of clarity, if not for yourself for the person who may need to modify your program, parentheses should always be used and two operators may not be used in succession unless they are separated by parentheses.

The following table gives a complete list of operations and their precedence and where applicable whether those with equal precedence are evaluated from left to right (shown with the word **left**) or whether they are evaluated from right to left (shown with the word **right**).

Operator	Operation	Precedence	
()	Parentheses	0 (highest)	
[ ]	Substring extraction	1	
< >	Dynamic array	1	
^	Exponentiation	2	left
* *	Exponentiation	2	left
*	Multiplication	3	left
/	Division	3	left
\	Remainder	3	left
+	Addition	4	left
–	Subtraction	4	left
+	Unary plus	4	right
–	Unary minus	4	right
"mask"	string masking	5	left
cat	concatenation	6	right
:	concatenation	6	right
EQ/=	logical equal	7	
NE/£	not equal	7	
< >/> <	not equal	7	
LT/<	less than	7	
LE/<=	less than or equal to	7	
GT/>	greater than	7	
GE/>=	greater or equal to	7	
match(es)	pattern match	7	
AND/&	logical and	8	left
OR/!	logical or	8	left

There is no doubt that parenthesis should be used in complex mathematical expressions, rather than relying on the precedence of the operator, for the sake of your own sanity if not for that of others who may need to maintain your program.

There are a number of mathematical functions, most of which are straightforward in use and the remainder of this section is dedicated to them.

15.14.1 ABS *Return the ABSolute value of an expression*

The absolute value of an expression is the number itself regardless of whether the number is positive or negative. Hence if a variable contains the number –3.142 the absolute value of the variable would be 3.142. The format of this function is **ABS**(*expr*) where

expr is the expression evaluating to a numeric value

An example of the ABS function is as follows:

INV.VALUE = "–123.50"
INV.VALUE=ABS(INV.VALUE)
PRINT INV.VALUE

which would print the result 123.50.

15.14.2 CHAR *Returns the ASCII value of a decimal value*

The **CHAR** function returns the ASCII value of the supplied decimal value and is the opposite of the **SEQ** function. The format of this function is

CHAR(*expr1*)

where

expr1 is the expression evaluating to a numeric value

The **CHAR** function is particularly useful for accessing characters like attribute marks and value marks (**CHAR**(254) and **CHAR**(253) respectively). The **CHAR** function is commonly used in **EQUATE** statements and **CHAR**(7) when sent to the terminal will sound the terminals error beep.

Hence **CRT CHAR(7)** will sound the terminal beep
PRINT CHAR(12) issues a form feed or page eject to the printer
EQU AM TO CHAR(254) assigns a constant for the attribute mark symbol

15.14.3 COS *Return the COSine of the expression*

This function simply returns the trigonometric cosine of the expression. The format of this function is

COS(expr)

15.14.4 EXP *Return the EXPonential of an expression*

This function returns the value of the base number *e* raised to the power of the given expression. It is the inverse of the **LN** function. The format of this function is

EXP(*expr*)

where

expr is a number or an expression evaluating to a number

15.14.5 INT *Returns the INTeger portion of an expression*

The **INT** function returns the integer portion of a given expression, which means the numbers following the decimal point (the fractional portion of a number) is truncated. Hence if a variable contained 3.142 the **INT** function would return the value 3. The format of this function is

INT(*expr*)

where

expr is the expression evaluating to a numeric value

An example of the INT function is as follows:

```
INV.VALUE = "–123.50"
INV.VALUE=INT(INV.VALUE)
PRINT INV.VALUE
```

which would print the result 123.

15.14.6 LN *Returns the natural log of an expression*

The **LN** function returns the log base *e* of a given expression and is the inverse of the **EXP** function. The format of this function is

LN(*expr*)

where

expr is the expression evaluating to a numeric value

15.14.7 MOD *Returns the remainder of a division calculation*

The **MOD** function divides one expression by another and returns the remainder. It is identical in function to the **REM** function. The format of this function is

MOD(*expr1*,*expr2*)

where

expr1 is the expression evaluating to a numeric value of the number to be divided
expr2 is the expression evaluating to a numeric value of the number to divide by

The expressions can evaluate to any value with the exception that *expr2* cannot be zero.

An example of the **MOD** function is as follows:

```
OLD.VALUE = "19"
REM.VALUE=MOD(OLD.VALUE,3)
PRINT REM.VALUE
```

which would print the result 1.

15.14.8 PWR ***Returns the value of a number raised to the power of another***

The **PWR** function returns the value of one number raised to the power of another. The format of this function is

PWR(*expr1,expr2*)

where

expr1 is the expression evaluating to a numeric value of the number to be raised by the power of *expr2*
expr2 is an expression evaluating to the exponent that *expr1* is to be raised to

Note: if *expr1* is zero, the **PWR** statement will return zero
if *expr2* is zero, the **PWR** statement will return 1

15.14.9 REM ***Returns the REMainder of a division calculation***

The **REM** function divides one expression by another and returns the remainder. It is identical in function to the **MOD** function. The format of this function is

REM(*expr1,expr2*)

where

expr1 is the expression evaluating to a numeric value of the number to be divided
expr2 is the expression evaluating to a numeric value of the number to divide by

The expressions can evaluate to any value with the exception that *expr2* cannot be zero.

An example of the **REM** function is as follows:

```
OLD.VALUE = "19"
REM.VALUE=REM(OLD.VALUE,3)
PRINT REM.VALUE
```

which would print the result 1.

15.14.10 RND ***Returns a random number***

The **RND** function generates a random number between 0 and one less than the value specified in the statement. The value of maximum number that can be used in this statement is 32,000. The format of this function is

RND(*expr1*)

where

expr1 is the expression evaluating to a numeric integer value of the range from zero to *expr1-1* which the random number is to be generated

An example of the **RND** function is as follows:

```
HIGH.VALUE = "134"
RANDOM.N=RND(HIGH.VALUE)
PRINT "A random number from 0 to 133 is ":HIGH.VALUE
```

which would print the result

```
A random number from 0 to 133 is 47
```

15.14.11 SEQ *Returns the decimal value of an ASCII character*

The **SEQ** function returns the decimal value of the supplied character and is the opposite of the **CHAR** function. The format of this function is

SEQ(*expr1*)

where

expr1 is the expression evaluating to a single character. If *expr1* evaluates to a string of characters, the **SEQ** function is only performed on the first character of the string

15.14.12 SIN *Returns the SINe of the expression*

The **SIN** function returns the trigonometric sine of the expression. The format of this function is

SIN(*expr1*)

where

expr1 is the expression evaluating to a numeric value in the range 0 to 360. Values outside this range are treated as 360

15.14.13 SQRT *Returns the SQuare RooT of an expression*

The **SQRT** function returns the square root of an expression, given that the expression evaluates to a positive number. The format of this function is

SQRT(*expr1*)

where

expr1 is the expression evaluating to a numeric value

If *expr1* evaluates to a negative value the **SQRT** function returns a value of zero.

15.14.14 TAN *Returns the TANgent of the expression*

The **TAN** function returns the trigonometric tangent of the expression. The format of this function is

TAN(*expr1*)

where

expr1 is the expression evaluating to a numeric value in the range 0 to 360. Values outside this range are treated as 360.

15.15 Conversions using ICONV and OCONV

Data is often stored on the database in a form different to how it may be represented to a user, in which case the data is held in what is known as internal format. Dates for example, are held as a physical number representing the number of days in relation to 31 December 1967 and monetary amounts are held without their decimal point. There are two functions which enable the interchange between the internal form and the external form or form in which the data is presented to the user. The **ICONV** converts the data to internal format whilst the **OCONV** converts the data to external form. These expressions use the ACCESS conversion and correlative codes shown in Section 13.4.1 in Chapter 13.

15.15.1 ICONV – Converting data from external to internal format

The **ICONV** function converts data which is held in external format to the internal format ready for storage in a file on the database, or to compare to information held on the database. The general format of the statement is as follows:

ICONV(*expr,conv.expr*)

where

expr is an expression containing the data to be converted
conv.expr an expression evaluating to the conversion code to be used in the conversion process

When storing dates, it is much better to store them in internal format, although of course you can store them in external format if you which. Whilst this makes them 'readable' if you ever need to edit the file, it makes them useless when wanting to do anything remotely arithmetical with them, i.e. adding a couple of weeks to the date or seeing how many days exist between two dates.

The most commonly used conversion codes are

D	Convert date to internal format
G	Group extraction
MT{**H**}{**S**}	Convert time to internal format where **H** is for 12-hour format **S** is where seconds are to be included
MR*xx*	Mask conversion
MX	Convert hexadecimal to ASCII representation
P	Pattern matching

Among the ACCESS codes that cannot be called by **OCONV** are the '**F**', '**A**' and '**S**' conversions. Figure 15.88 gives examples of its use.

15.15.2 OCONV – Converting data from internal to external format

The **OCONV** function converts data which is held in internal format to that in external format. The general format of the statement is as follows:

OCONV(*expr,conv.expr*)

where

expr is an expression containing the data to be converted

conv.expr an expression evaluating to the conversion code to be used in the conversion process

Whilst data is stored in internal format for consistency and flexibility, the **OCONV** function converts it to a format suitable for use and understanding by the user.

The most commonly used conversion codes are

D	Convert date to internal format
G	Group extraction
MT{**H**}{**S**}	Convert time to internal format where **H** is for 12-hour format **S** is where seconds are to be included
MR*xx*	Mask conversion
MX	Convert hexadecimal to ASCII representation
P	Pattern matching
Tfile	File translation

Among the ACCESS codes that cannot be called by **OCONV** are the '**F**', '**A**' and '**S**' conversions.

OCONV is not the most efficient way of providing output conversions and you should avoid using **OCONV** where alternatives are possible. Some examples are shown over:

Example 1

PRICE = "24.50"
INT.PRICE = ICONV(PRICE,"MR2")

After the **ICONV** statement, **INT.PRICE** would contain the value 2450.

Example 2

DATE = "07/08/94"
I.DATE = ICONV(DATE,"D")
After the **ICONV** the variable I.DATE would contain 9716, the date in internal form.

Example 3

```
PRINT @(10,1):"Select invoices due for payment"
PRINT @(10,2):"========================"
PRINT @(10,5):"Input FROM date ":
INPUT ANS
FROM.DATE=ICONV(ANS,'D')
PRINT @(10,6):"Input TO date ":
INPUT ANS
TO.DATE=ICONV(ANS,'D')
IF FROM.DATE > TO.DATE THEN ERR = "FROM date cannot be less than TO
date"; GOSUB 1OOO
IF FROM.DATE = TO.DATE THEN ERR = "FROM date cannot be same as TO
date";GOSUB 1000
```

Example 4

```
INPUT ANS,1
IF ICONV(ANS,"P('Y');('N')") THEN GOSUB 1000
```

The subroutine 1000 will be executed if the answer input is either **Y** or **N**.

Figure 15.88 Examples of the **ICONV** function.

Instead of	**Use**
INV.DATE=OCONV(INV.DATE,"D2/")	**INV.DATE=INV.DATE"D2/"**

MC type conversions used as masks simply require the M to be dropped.

WHERE.TO=OCONV(WHERE.TO,"MCU")	**WHERE.TO=WHERE.TO"CU"**

MR type functions should be handled as follows, as masking is considerably faster.

Instead of	Use
TOTAL=OCONV(TOTAL,”MR2,$”)”R#15”	**TOTAL=TOTAL”R26,$#15”**
OCONV G1*1	**FIELD**
OCONV MX	**DTX**
OCONV Tx,y	**[x,y]**

Figure 15.89 gives examples of the use of the **OCONV** statement.

Example 1

PRICE = REC<1>
The variable contains 2450 at this point
OUT.PRICE = OCONV(PRICE,”MR2”) or OUT.PRICE = OCONV(REC<1>,”MR2”)

After the **OCONV** statement, **OUT.PRICE** would contain the value 24.50

Example 2

DATE = REC<2>
The variable contains 9716
O.DATE = OCONV(DATE,”D2/”) or O.DATE=OCONV(REC<2>,”D2/”)

After the **OCONV** the variable O.DATE would contain 07/08/94. Do bear in mind the same internal date can be displayed in many different forms, including the alphabetic representation of the month, the alphabetical representation of the day of the week and the quarter; all achieved by using different conversion codes on the same variable. See Section 13.5.7.

Example 3

CUST.ID = REC<3>
The variable CUST.ID contains the key to a record in the file CUSTOMER
CUST.NAME=OCONV(CUST.ID,”TCUSTOMER;X;;1”)
or **CUST.NAME = OCONV(REC<3>,”TCUSTOMER;X;;1”)**
The variable CUST.NAME contains the contents of attribute 1 from the customer record from the file CUSTOMER whose key is given by the variable CUST.NAME

Figure 15.89 Examples of the **OCONV** function.

15.16 The date and time

The date and time can be displayed using the commands **DATE(),** for the date, **TIME(),** for the time and **TIMEDATE()** for the combined date and time.

The **DATE()** statement returns the date in internal form, i.e. a number of days in relation to 31 December 1967. If the date is prior to this date the internal date is a negative number, if subsequent to it the number is positive. In this way arithmetic can be carried out on dates. In order to display dates in a meaningful way a conversion code has to be applied to them using the **OCONV** statement.

Chapter 13, PICK dictionaries, discusses conversion codes in detail. For the purpose of this section the conversion codes and their result is given in Figure 15.90 without further explanation, together with an example of displaying the date.

The **TIME()** statement returns the time since midnight converted to seconds. As with the date an output conversion code has to be applied to display the time in a meaningful way. Figure 15.91 shows how this would be used in a program and shows the conversion codes that apply.

↓
main program
↓

INT.DATE=DATE()
O.DATE=OCONV(INT.DATE,'D') ◄── where D is the conversion code
PRINT O.DATE ◄── displays date as DD MMM YYYY

Conversion	Format displayed	--------Comments-------
D	07 DEC 1985	
D/	07/12/1985	
D-	07-12-85	
D0	07 DEC	
D0/	07/12	Useful with US date format
D2/	07/12/85	
D2+	07+12+85	Any character can be delimiter
DD	07	The day
DM	12	The month
DY	1985	Four digit year
D2Y	85	Two digit year
DQ	4	The quarter

Figure 15.90 The **DATE()** statement and its conversion codes.

main program

↓

```
INT.TIME=TIME()
O.TIME=OCONV(INT.TIME,'MTS') ◄── where MTS is the conversion code
PRINT O.TIME ◄── displays time as HH:MM:SS
```

Conversion	Format displayed	--------Comments-------
MT	13:15	
MTS	13:15:33	
MTH	01:15PM	
MTHS	01:15:33PM	

Figure 15.91 The **TIME()** statement and its conversion codes.

The **TIMEDATE()** statement returns the current time and date in external format: HH:MM:SS DD MMM YYYY. The general format being *Var*=**TIMEDATE().**

15.17 The SYSTEM statement

The **SYSTEM** statement will provide details of some of the system parameters. For example it will return the current page number or line number if the **HEADING** or **FOOTING** commands are in use or return a code to signify whether or not the system printer is on. The general format of the command is:

Var=**SYSTEM(n)**

where **n** represents the function to be tested.
The possible functions are :

Code Function

0 Context-oriented status information.

After a tape-handling error, system(0) returns:
1 if not attached.
2 null variable.
3 attempt to write null string.
5 EOT encountered.
6 tape not write-enabled.
7 tape unit not ready.

8 unrecoverable parity error.
9 block transfer error.
10 binary item read (see note below).
11 record truncated.

After a **READU**, **READVU** and **MATREADU** statement which contains a 'locked' clause, system(0) returns the port.number that has the item locked.

Value 10 actually has nothing to do with tape and is relevant to all 'read'-type statements. It is set when an 'indirect' (or 'pointer') item is read.

On AP/UNIX implementations, system(0) returns the value of 'errno' after a C function call.

All statements which allow the **ONERR** clause provide a 'hook' to system(0).

(1) Returns 1 if the system printer is 'on', meaning that a **PRINTER ON** statement has been issued or that the program was activated with a **(P)** option. Otherwise, a 0 (zero) is returned, meaning that output is being directed to the terminal.

(2) Returns the current output device page width as defined by the **TERM** command.

(3) Returns the current output device page length as defined by the **TERM** command.

(4) Returns the number of lines remaining to print on the current page, based on the current terminal characteristics previously defined with the **TERM** command.

(5) Returns the current page number.

(6) Returns the current line number (not the 'port' number but the actual print line number).

(7) Returns the terminal 'type' code, as defined by the **TERM** command.

(8) Returns the block size at which the tape was last attached.

(9) Returns the current CPU millisecond count.

(10) Checks the current stack (STON) condition. Returns 1 (one) if the stack is on, or 0 (zero), if not.

(11) Checks for an externally-generated active list. Returns the number of items in the list, or 0 (zero) if no list is active. This does not have anything to do with the internal **SELECT** statement, which needs a **READNEXT** to determine if any items were selected.

(12) Returns the system time in milliseconds.

(13) Forces an rqm (terminates timeslice) and returns a 1. Deactivates the process in the scheduling queue until its next turn.

(14) Returns the number of bytes in the terminal type-ahead input buffer.

(15) Returns the TCL verb option{s} that are in effect.

(16) Returns the current process level.

(17) Returns the message numbers (item-ids) returned by the previous **EXECUTE** statement, separated by attribute marks.

(18) Returns the number of ports on the system.

(19) Returns a unique item-id consisting of the current system date in internal format, followed immediately by the current system time in seconds. If more than one item-id is generated in a second, an alpha character is appended to the item-id.

(20) Returns the most recent Spooler entry number generated by the current process.

(21) Returns today's date in internal format with a sequential number suffix.

(22) Returns the port.number of the current process.

(23) Returns the current process privilege level. (In R83, this returns 1 if the current process has a **SYS2** privilege level, otherwise it returns 0 (zero).)

(24) Returns 1 if the current process is a phantom. Otherwise it returns 0 (zero).

(25) Checks for an active secondary list. Returns the number of items in the secondary list, or 0 (zero) if no secondary list is active.

(26) Returns 1 if 'capturing on' is in effect. Otherwise, it returns 0 (zero).

(27) Returns 1 if TCL case-sensitivity is in effect for the current process. Otherwise, it returns 0 (zero).

(28) Returns 1 if the current PICK/BASIC program is data case-sensitive, or 0, if not. The first time a PICK/BASIC program is entered, the PICK/BASIC case flag is set to the current process's case flag. Any subsequent 'casing' statement modifies the PICK/BASIC flag but not the current process' flag. Only the current process's flag is passed between levels.

(29) Returns 1 if R83-format **WHO** is in effect (port.number,account name, user-id) or 0 (zero) if AP-format is in effect (port.number, user-id, account name). (Note that in R83, there was no user-id.)

(30) Returns the port.number of the process which has the item locked.

(31) Returns the current Spooler form queue number most recently assigned with an **SP-ASSIGN**.

(32) Returns the data frame size for the system.

(33) Returns the name of the PICK/BASIC program which called the subroutine.

(34) Returns the total number of physical ports on the system, excluding phantom ports.

(100) Returns the system identification in the form

system;filename: name;release;version;hardware; date

where

system	The system name, which may contain spaces.
filename	Configuration file name.
name	Contents of the 'name' statement in the configuration file.
release	The current release level.
version	The current version level.
hardware	The type of hardware.
date	The date of the release.

On AP/UNIX implementations, the format returned by system(100) is as follows:

AP/UNIX: system; o/s name; filename:name; release; version;hardware; boot monitor version; date

where

system	The system name, which may contain spaces.
o/s name	'SCO', 'AIX', etc.
file name	Configuration file name.
name	Contents of the 'name' statement in the configuration file.
release	UNIX system release.
version	UNIX system version.
hardware	Machine hardware name, or serial number.
boot monitor version	The release level of the monitor.
date	Boot monitor date.

15.18 Special INPUT functions

There are three **INPUT** functions which might prove useful:

INPUTERR	Display an error message on the bottom line of the terminal
INPUTNULL	Establish character as null input
INPUTTRAP	Transfer program control according to data input

15.18.1 The INPUTERR function

The **INPUTERR** function prints the specified text on the last line of the terminal and is used in conjunction with the INPUT statement. The format of the statement is

INPUTERR *expr*

where

expr an expression evaluating to the message to be displayed on the last line of the terminal

An entry to the next **INPUT @** statement erases and messages previously sent to the bottom of the screen.

15.18.2 The INPUTNULL function

The **INPUTNULL** function defines a character to be interpreted as the null string if sent as a response to an **INPUT @** statement. The **INPUTNULL** statement must precede the **INPUT @** statement, only works with single character input and only one **INPUTNULL** statement can be active at any one time. If there is an **INPUTTRAP** active for the same character, the **INPUTNULL** takes precedence. The format of the function is as follows

INPUTNULL *expr*

where

expr an expression evaluating to a single character. Any extraneous characters are ignored

Normally the **INPUT @** statement continues to prompt the user until a value is input which matches the format expression. The only exceptions are the characters specified by the **INPUTRAP** and **INPUTNULL** statements which provide an exit from the **INPUT @** function.

In the following example the user is allowed to specify a zero, by inputting an **X**:

```
INPUTNULL "X"
PRINT @(10,10): "Enter the cost price "
INPUTERR 'Enter "X" to denote zero'
INPUT @(10,32): COST.PRICE"L2,"
```

15.18.3 The INPUTTRAP function

The **INPUTTRAP** function determines characters which when input as a full response to the **INPUT @** statement force a branch to specified labels. The general format of the command is

INPUTTRAP *expr* {**GOSUB** or **GOTO**} *label1, label2 .....*

where

expr an expression evaluating characters to be searched for in the input

GOTO branch to the specified label and do not return

GOSUB branch to the specified subroutine and return to the line following the **INPUTTRAP** statement

labeln statement labels to be branched to. If the input is the *n*th character in *expr*, the *n*th label is branched to

An example of its use is as follows:

```
INPUTTRAP "YN" GOSUB 1000,2000
INPUT @(10,10): ANS
```

If the user inputs **Y** then the program will branch to subroutine 1000, if they enter **N** then the subroutine with the label 2000 will be invoked.

15.19 Other program statements

PICK BASIC provides a number of other commands the most useful of which are summarized below. None of them require a great deal of explanation as their use is fairly straightforward. Should you require further information you should consult your BASIC manual.

Command	Function
ABORT	Aborts the program returning the user to TCL regardless of the environment in which the program executed The ABORT statement differs from the STOP statement as the STOP statement returns to the controlling environment
ASSIGNED	This function interrogates a variable to determine if it has previously been assigned a value. If the variable has a value assigned a non-zero value (true) is returned otherwise a zero is returned. This is of particular help in PICK/BASIC subroutines called from the 'call' Access processing code where it can prevents files from being repeatedly opened and variables from continually being re-initialized
BREAK ON	Enables the use of the 'BREAK' key on the VDU to interrupt the program and enter the debugger
BREAK OFF	Disables the use of the 'BREAK' key. The BREAK ON reverses the last executed BREAK OFF. If multiple BREAK OFF statements are executed an equal number of BREAK ON statements must be executed to return to a 'breakable' state
CLEAR	Initializes all variables throughout the program assigning them all a value of zero. In a subroutine only local variables are affected and named variables will remain unaffected regardless
CLEARFILE *{file var}*	Removes all data from the file specified by the file variable
DEBUG	Enters the PICK BASIC debugger at the point the statement is encountered

ECHO ON	Enables the characters types in at the keyboard to be 'echoed' back to the VDU so what was typed in can be seen
ECHO OFF	Turns off the character echo on the screen. Used where passwords are entered, that have to be interpreted by the program, but for security reasons should not be shown on the terminal The function **ECHO** without the ON or OFF following it can be used to toggle the terminal character echo
FOOTING	Specifies the text to be printed at the bottom of each page of output and is in the format **FOOTING** *expr* where *expr* is the expression evaluating to the text to be printed
HEADING	Specifies the text to be printed at the top of each page of output and is in the format **HEADING** *expr* where *expr* is the expression evaluating to the text to be printed
LET	An optional word that can be placed in front of the syntax for assigning the value of an expression. Hence although it is most common to assign variables by use of **A** = **X** it is equally correct to say **LET A** = **X**
NULL	A **NULL** statement results in no action and is used in places where BASIC requires statements, but where there is no operation to be performed
ONERR	Identifies the statements to be executed when an error occurs during the operations on peripheral devices using commands such as **READT**
READT	Read a record from the tape device specified by the most recently executed **T-ATT** command
REM *comment*	Places a comment line in the program. It is functionally identical to the **!** or * which signifies the text which follows should be ignored by the compiler
SLEEP n	Stop program for n seconds, then continue. The function **RQM** ***n*** performs the same task
SLEEP *HH:MM:SS*	Stop program until time reaches the time given by *HH:MM:SS,* then continue. This function uses the 24 hour clock
TCLREAD	Loads into a variable the TCL command used to initiate the program
WEOF	Write an End-Of-File mark at the current position of the currently attached magnetic media
WRITET	Writes a tape record to the attached magnetic media

15.20 BASIC with ACCESS and the Update Processor

A completely new function, **ACCESS(*n*)** was introduced with Advanced PICK which provides access to the information processed by ACCESS or the Update Processor and is intended for those who need to take control in either of these environments to process and control the records being accessed. The function can ***only*** be used in subroutines that are called from dictionaries, again a new concept in Advanced PICK. In generic R83, it was not possible to put BASIC code in a dictionary item, even though some licensees have had this facility for a long time. First let's look at the places at which BASIC subroutines can be called from both the file definition item and the attribute definition item.

The file definition item

000	Item-id	
001	Dictionary-code	
002	Base fid	
003	Modulo	
004	Reserved and unavailable	
005	Retrieval-lock	
006	Update-lock	
007	Reserved and unavailable	
008	Correlative	**call** *file.time.subroutine*
009	Justification	
010	Column-width	
011	Reserved and unavailable	
012	Reserved and unavailable	
013	Reallocation parameters	
014	Input-conversion	**call** *before.update.subroutine*
015	Macro (default input specifications)	
016	Output-macro	
017	Description	
018	Reserved and unavailable	
019	Reserved and unavailable	
020 – 030	Hot keys	

- Subroutines called from the CORRELATIVE attribute are executed immediately prior to the item being filed.
- Subroutines called from the INPUT-CONVERSION attribute are executed immediately prior to the item from the file being accessed.

From attribute defining items, PICK/BASIC subroutines can be called from the output-conversion, correlative, and input-conversion attributes.

Attribute defining item

000	Item id	
001	Dictionary-code (**a**, **s** or **x**)	
002	Attribute mark count	
003	Substitute-header	
004	Structure	
005	Reserved and unavailable	
006	Reserved and unavailable	
007	Output-conversion	**call** *output.subroutine*
008	Correlative	**call** *preprocessing.subroutine*
009	Attribute-type	
010	Column-width	
011	Reserved and unavailable	
012	Reserved and unavailable	
013	Reserved and unavailable	
014	Input-conversion	**call** *after.input.subroutine*
015	Macro	
016	Reserved and unavailable	
017	Description	
018	Reserved and unavailable	
019	Reserved and unavailable	
020 – 030	Hot keys	

- Subroutines called from the OUTPUT-CONVERSION attribute are executed on output.
- Subroutines called from the CORRELATIVE attribute are executed prior to processing.
- Subroutines called from the INPUT-CONVERSION attribute are executed after input.

The **ACCESS**(*n*) function is used within the called subroutine. The number given within the brackets of the **ACCESS**(*n*) function determines the information made available. In some instances this is the physical data, such as the entire body of the item or its item-id, but it can also provide other useful information such as whether the item is a new item or whether it has changed.

The syntax of the function is **ACCESS**(*n*) where *n* is a number in the range 1–24 whose values mean the following:

1 data file file variable.
2 dictionary file file variable.
3 item from the associated file as a dynamic array and contain null if the item is new.
4 item count (the number of items processed to the current point).
5 attribute count (the number of attributes processed to the current point).

6 value count (the number of values processed to the current point).
7 sub-value count (the number of sub-values processed to the current point).
8 detail line count (the number of lines processed to the current point).
9 break-on level counter (the number of break levels pushed to the current point).
10 the item-id.
11 the file name.
12 item delete flag. Returns 1 if the item is being deleted.
13 root variable.
14 returns current cursor column position in the Update Processor.
15 returns current cursor row position in the Update Processor.
16 new item flag. Returns 1 if item is new.
17 returns 1 if processing an input-conversion.
18 used in the input-conversion attribute of the file 'd-pointer' to specify which value of attribute 15 ('macro' attribute) to use.
19 returns the character which ended the last input, usually a [CR], **u**, etc.
20 item changed flag (0-item not changed, 1-item changed).
21 used from a PICK/BASIC subroutine called by UP to place characters in the UP command string. For example, access(21) = 'xe' in a subroutine called from the input-conversion causes the Update Processor to exit after the attribute calling the subroutine is re-entered. **BEWARE:** This function will overwrite any prestore previously set; any **p** will execute the value assigned to ACCESS(21).
22 spelling checker flag. Returns non-zero (usually 1) if the spelling checker is enabled, and 0 if it is not. Access(22) may be assigned a '1' in a subroutine called by the input conversion of a file defining item. Even if the spelling checker is disabled for the user session, this invokes the spell checker for the editing of this item or list of items. **NOTE:** the speller will only work on attributes with an attribute type of 'w'. Available in AP releases 5.2.5 and above.
23 Returns the calling environment. It returns
- 0 if the function was called from FlashBASIC or PICK/BASIC
- 1 if the function was called from a callx or from an index
- 2 if the function was called from the update processor (except for a callx or index)
- 3 if the function was called from ACCESS. Access(23) is avail able in AP releases 6.1.0 and higher only

24 Returns the actual attribute number of the attribute definition.

ACCESS(3) and ACCESS(10) can be used to pass data both ways between a PICK/BASIC program and a data file. When either of these two statements appear on the right of the assignment (= sign), data is passed to the program. When they are used to the left of the assignment, data is passed from the program to the file. ACCESS(3) can only be updated from an input-conversion of a dictionary item. It cannot be updated as a conversion, correlative or in a 'd-pointer' input-conversion.

The item-ids as well as the remainder of the attribute values within those items can be modified directly through the Update Processor using input conversions or correlatives and the function **INPUTERR** can be used to advise the Update Processor of any errors detected. It also displays a message on the bottom line of a terminal. Do note that all of the ACCESS() routines share a common buffer and for that reason it is not currently possible to combine references to ACCESS() elements on the same line such as:

```
COMMAND = "LIST ":ACCESS(11):" ":ACCESS(10)
```

but the required effect can be achieved by assigning separate variables thus:

```
FILE = ACCESS(11)
ITEM = ACCESS(10)
COMMAND = "LIST ":FILE:" ":ITEM
```

Be aware that although the syntax for these subroutines does not specify any parameters, when a subroutine is called from the file defining item, the entire item body is passed as a parameter. It is also worth being aware there can be considerably more overhead when calling a PICK/BASIC routine from a dictionary item than using an intrinsic processing code, obviously dependent on its complexity. For that reason the ACCESS() function should be used sparingly and only where a standard PICK processing code will not provide the

```
SUBROUTINE NEW.CUST(CUST.REC)
CUST.REC=ACCESS(3)
IF ACCESS(16) THEN CUST.REC<1> = "NEW"
ACCESS(3)=CUST.REC
RETURN


SUBROUTINE VAL.AMOUNT(INV.AMOUNT)
INVOICE.REC=ACCESS(3)
INV.AMOUNT=INVOICE.REC<2>
IF INV.AMOUNT THEN
    IF INV.AMOUNT < 0 THEN
        NEW.FORMAT.OF.AMT=INV.AMOUNT"R26,C(%10)"
    END ELSE
        INPUTERR "Credit note amounts must be negative"
        INV.AMOUNT=""
        RETURN
    END
END
RETURN
```

Figure 15.92 Examples of the **ACCESS(*n*)** function.

required result. For example a 'simple' processing (conversion/correlative) code such as **A3+4** or **AN(PRICE)*N(QUANTITY)** is much faster than doing the same thing by calling a PICK/BASIC program.

A useful function that can be used in these subroutines is the **ASSIGNED** function. It is used to determine whether or not a variable has previously been assigned and is typically used to prevent files from being opened more than once and to prevent variables from being continually initialized.

The format of the function is **ASSIGNED**(*variable*) where *variable* is the variable to test. If the variable has already been assigned a value *variable* will be non-zero (true) otherwise it will be zero (false). An example of its use is as follows:

```
IF NOT(ASSIGNED(CUSTOMER)) THEN FILE CUSTOMER
```

Hence if the file variable **CUSTOMER** has not been assigned, open the file **CUSTOMER** and assign its file variable.

15.21 Batch processing

All the discussion so far has revolved around interactive data processing, where the keys of the records to be processed have been known or input at runtime. Whilst most of the programs will fall into this category, there is still a need for batch processing, where a batch of records are to be processed at a time. Typically this happens at the end of a month when special routines need to be applied, like ageing debts and clearing out and producing a report from the months transactions. Another typical use of batch processing is when the entire or part of the database has to be updated to handle a special situation, such as increasing the price list by x% to account for inflation or changing the price list to reflect a change in VAT.

All these processes require a series of routines to be applied to a selection of records from the database and sometimes requiring the records to be input in a given sequence. The first point to note here is that, unlike some programming languages PICK BASIC does not contain a SORT command. Whilst all Advanced PICK implementations overcome this problem with the **EXECUTE** statement, the previous means of handling this requirement was to include the program in a PROC which has previously handled the selection and sorting of records using an ACCESS statement. Not only does ACCESS handle sorting but it has extremely powerful selection facilities which provide the programmer with great flexibility and obviates the need to develop complex programs for record selection.

Where ACCESS is not used, BASIC provides the means to select and process every record in a file by use of the **SELECT** statement, whose general format is shown in Figure 15.93.

SELECT *{file-var}* {**TO** *variable*}

where

file-var	is the name of the file variable as defined in the **OPEN** statement. If omitted, the last file opened, is assumed.
variable	is the name used from this point on in the program to refer to the file

Figure 15.93 The **SELECT** statement.

The **SELECT** statement builds a list of item-ids which can then be processed within a program using the **READNEXT** statement, whose format is shown in Figure 15.94. The **READNEXT** statement will retrieve each item from the selected list which can be used in the standard **READ** statement to enable processing of each record to take place. The loop for processing each record must be constructed by the programmer with the **READNEXT** being at the top.

Figure 15.95 shows these statements in action. In this example the entire price list contained in the file, OPPRICE, is increased by 8% with a report on the changes being listed on the printer.

In order to repeat the process shown in Figure 15.95 but on a selected group of items, and to produce the report in alphabetical sequence the program must either be incorporated into a PROC or MACRO containing an ACCESS statement that carries out the selection and sorting process, or the program must contain an **EXECUTE** statement performing the sort. Figure 15.96 shows how this is handled where the ACCESS statement called in a PROC and as an alternative a MACRO selects all records whose price is less than £10 and sorts them into alphabetical sequence of their description before running the same program shown in Figure 15.95. The third example in Figure 15.96 shows the modified version of the program to perform the same task using the **EXECUTE** statement.

READNEXT *var* {**FROM** *sel-var*} **ELSE** *statements*

where

var	contains the contents of the 'next' record
sel-var	is the name assigned in the **SELECT** statement
statements	are those BASIC statements that will be executed after the last record in the file has been processed

Figure 15.94 The **READNEXT** statement.

The program

```
FLG=""
OPEN "OPPRICE" TO PRICE ELSE STOP 201,"OPORDERS"
PRINTER ON
SELECT PRICE
HEADING "'C'PRICE LIST INCREASES AS AT 'D' 'LL'DESCRIPTION ORIGI-
NAL INCREASE NEW 'L'OF GOODS PRICE IN PRICE PRICE 'L'"
LOOP UNTIL FLG DO
10  READNEXT RECID ELSE
       PRINT
       PRINT "---------END OF REPORT---------"
       STOP
    END
    READ PRICEREC FROM PRICE,RECID ELSE
       PRINT "ID NOT FOUND ":RECID
       GOTO 10
    END
    DESC=PRICEREC<1>
    ORIG=PRICEREC<2>
    INCR=ORIG*(8/100)
    NEW=ORIG+INCR
    PRINT DESC"L(#17)"ORIG"R26(#10)":INCR"R26(#10)":NEW"R26(#10)"
REPEAT
```

The output from the program

```
PRICE LIST INCREASES AS AT 25 NOV 1985

DESCRIPTION          ORIGINAL       INCREASE       NEW
OF GOODS             PRICE          IN PRICE       PRICE

SAW                  12.25          0.98           13.23
SCREWS               0.24           0.02           0.26
HAMMERS              8.76           0.70           9.46
SCREWDRIVER 1"       3.33           0.27           3.60
:
-------END OF REPORT--------
```

Figure 15.95 Using the **READNEXT** statement.

As you may have now realized, the combination of ACCESS with PICK BASIC and its incorporation into PROCs and MACROs provide a complete and flexible systems environment. In many older and more established application systems, programs are run from behind a menu system built completely using PROC, with a master PROC which then calls other PROCs, ACCESS statements or BASIC programs. A complete hierarchy can be built up, typically starting with a procedure at the top level and ending with programs at the bottom levels.

Example 1 (Using a PROC)

```
PQ
HSSELECT OPPRICE BY DESC WITH PRICE < “10”
STON
HRUN BP PROG10
P
```

Example 2 (Using a MACRO)

```
N
SSELECT OPPRICE BY DESC WITH PRICE < “10”
RUN BP PROG10
```

Example 3 (Using EXECUTE in the program)

```
FLG=“”
OPEN “OPPRICE” TO PRICE ELSE STOP 201,”OPORDERS”
PRINTER ON
EXECUTE ‘SSELECT OPPRICE BY DESC WITH PRICE < “10”’ CAPTURING
CAP RETURNING RET
HEADING “‘C’PRICE LIST INCREASES AS AT ‘D’  ‘LL’DESCRIPTION  ORIGI-
NAL  INCREASE  NEW  ‘L’OF GOODS  PRICE  IN PRICE  PRICE ‘L’”
LOOP UNTIL FLG DO
10  READNEXT RECID ELSE
      PRINT
      PRINT “---------END OF REPORT---------”
      STOP
    END
    READ PRICEREC FROM PRICE,RECID ELSE
      PRINT “ID NOT FOUND “:RECID
      GOTO 10
    END
    DESC=PRICEREC<1>
    ORIG=PRICEREC<2>
    INCR=ORIG*(8/100)
    NEW=ORIG+INCR
    PRINT DESC”L(#17)”ORIG”R26(#10)”:INCR”R26(#10)”:NEW”R26(#10)”
REPEAT
```

Figure 15.96 The use of ACCESS with BASIC.

15.22 The PROCREAD and PROCWRITE statements

The **PROCREAD** and **PROCWRITE** are valuable and frequently undocumented statements. They allow for reading and writing to the PROC PIB (Primary Input Buffer). The **PROCREAD** statement assigns the contents of the PIB to a variable whilst **PROCWRITE** writes the contents of a variable to the PIB. The general format of these commands is as follows:

> **PROCREAD** *var* **ELSE** *statements*
> **PROCWRITE** *var*

Notice the **PROCREAD** statement has an **ELSE** clause which is invoked if the program has not been run from a PROC. Figure 15.97 gives an example of the use of **PROCREAD** together with the PROC that called it, both of which you might find useful. The purpose of the PROC is to produce an analysis of catalogued programs from any account. It the procedure is run without the name of an account (i.e. by typing **CATA**), the account to which the user is logged will be used and catalogued programs within it analysed. If analysis is required of a different account, the account name must follow the procedure name (e.g. **CAT OFFICE** will produce an analysis of catalogued programs in the account **OFFICE**).

The PROC to produce a list of catalogued programs

```
PQ
C LIST CATALOGUED PROGRAMS
IF #A2 IHMD <-------- If no parameter follows CATA when the PROC is called A2 is
HSSELECT              set to MD
A2
HWITH *A2 = "E6" BY *A0 BY *A6
STON
HRUN BP CAT
P
```

The program CATA

```
*CATALOGUED PROGRAM ANALYSIS
*READ PROC PIB
*
```

Figure 15.97 The use of **PROCREAD**.

```
PROCREAD MDNAM ELSE MDNAM="MD"
*
*CHECK TO SEE WHETHER A PARAMETER EXISTS AFTER THE WORD
*'CAT' WHICH SPECIFIES AN ACCOUNT NAME, AND IF SO CAPTURE IT
*IN THE VARIABLE 'MDNAM'
*
IF INDEX(MDNAM," ",1) THEN MDNAM=MDNAM[INDEX(MDNAM,"
",1)+1,32767]
*
*OPEN THE MD OF THE ACCOUNT
*
OPEN MDNAM TO MDID ELSE STOP 201,MDNAM
OPEN "MD" TO MMD ELSE STOP 201,"MD"
PAGENO=0
LINENO=100
DUM=""
START=1
*
*SELECT THE CATALOGUED ITEMS IN THE ACCOUNT
*
EXECUTE 'SSELECT ':MDNAM:' WITH *A2 = "E6" BY *A0 BY *A6' CAPTURING
DUMMY2
FINAL=0
LOOP
*
*READ THROUGH SELECT LIST, WHEN COMPLETE DELETE ANY DUMMY
*'Q' POINTER THAT MAY HAVE BEEN USED. 'Q' POINTER GIVEN
*ID OF 'CCCBBBCCCBBB'
*
READNEXT KEY ELSE
DELETE MMD,"CCCBBBCCCBBB"
IF LINENO=24 THEN PRINT "PRESS RETURN TO CONTINUE":;INPUT
DUMMY
PRINT;FINAL=1
END
UNTIL FINAL DO
READ ITM FROM MDID,KEY ELSE STOP 203
FLAG=0
*
*OPEN DICT VALUE OF ATTRIBUTE 6. CHECK TO SEE IF IT IS A
*'Q' POINTER
*
OPEN "DICT", ITM<6> TO ITMID ELSE
Q=""
```

Figure 15.97 *Continued*

```
READ Q FROM MMD,MDNAM ELSE FLAG=1
IF Q<1> # "Q" THEN FLAG = 1 ELSE
  PROC=""
  PROC<1>="Q"
  PROC<2>=Q<2>
  PROC<3>=ITM<6>
  WRITE PROC ON MMD,"CCCBBBCCCBBB"
  OPEN "DICT","CCCBBBCCCBBB" TO ITMID ELSE FLAG=1
END
END
IF FLAG=0 THEN READ OBJ FROM ITMID,KEY ELSE FLAG=1
IF LINENO > 23 THEN
  LINENO=2
  PAGENO=PAGENO+1
    IF START THEN START=0 ELSE PRINT "PRESS RETURN TO CONTINUE":;
    INPUT
DUMMY
  IF SEQ(DUM)=24 THEN PRINT;STOP
  PRINT @(-1)
    PRINT     "PROGRAM"L#20":"FILE""L#20":"B/FID""L#9":"N/F""L#5":"
COMPILE DATE"
END
PRINT
LINENO=LINENO+2
PRINT KEY"L#20":ITM<6>"L#20":
IF FLAG THEN PRINT "**** NO OBJECT CODE FOUND ****":ELSE
  PRINT OBJ<2>"L#9":OBJ<3>"L#5":OBJ<5>
END
REPEAT
END
```

Figure 15.97 *Continued*

Figure 15.98 shows a typical output produced by the procedure of Figure 15.97.

```
PROGRAM          FILE       B/FID     N/F    COMPILE DATE

BMRK.DYNAMIC     BENCH      4474      1      21:29:43 29 APR 1995
BMRK.ICONV       BENCH      4477      1      21:29:45 29 APR 1995
BMRK.MATH        BENCH      4475      1      21:29:44 29 APR 1995
BMRK.OCONV       BENCH      4476      1      21:29:45 29 APR 1995
BMRK.R/W         BENCH      4472      1      21:29:41 29 APR 1995
```

Figure 15.98 Example of the use of **PROCREAD** and **PROCWRITE.**

15.23 The interactive debugger

No chapter on BASIC would be complete without discussion of its debugger, the means to debug programs and find out what is going wrong. The PICK debugger enables full control of the execution of the program allowing you, amongst other things, to step line by line through the program, to display the original source code and to list and change variables.

The BASIC debugger can be entered on demand at runtime by pressing the **BREAK** key (if your terminal has no **BREAK** key, press **CTRL** and **C** together), or by taking the debug option (**D** with the **RUN** command. In some cases the program will automatically go into debug where it encounters a situation it cannot understand. In all cases the BASIC debugger is represented by an asterisk prompt.

Having arrived at the debugger prompt a number of options are available. The most likely initial requirement will be to display a part or all of the source code of the program. Whilst all manuals explain that the **L** command handles this function, they do not clearly explain that unless the **Z** function is used first the debugger will display the words NO SOURCE. The **Z** function makes available to the debugging session the source of any program held within the account and providing that the program has not been compiled with the **S** option, then you can review and change the contents of your program variables. (The **S** option is used to suppress the symbol table during compilation and is denoted by the display of a double rather then single asterisk when in the BASIC debugger.) Figure 15.99 gives an example of using the debugger on the program shown in Figure 15.96. The example shows how to list the first ten lines of source code of the program being debugged. Following this the pro-

```
: RUN BP PROG10 (D          <---- Initiate the debugger

*I1        <---- The current line number
*Z[CR] FILE/PROG NAME? BP PROG10 <----The program whose source is to be
                                      displayed
*L1-7 <---- List lines 1-7 of the program
FLG=""
OPEN "OPPRICE" TO PRICE ELSE STOP 201,"OPORDERS"
PRINTER ON
SELECT PRICE
HEADING "'C'PRICE LIST INCREASES AS AT 'D'       'LL'DESCRIPTION   ORIGINAL
INCREASE        NEW    'L'OF GOODS     PRICE    IN PRICE     PRICE 'L'"
LOOP UNTIL FLG DO
10 READNEXT RECID ELSE
*G <---- resume execution of program from current line number until the end of
         the program
```

Figure 15.99 The **Z** and **L** commands of the debugger.

gram is allowed to finish normally using the **G** command. Figure 15.99 gives just one use of the **L** command. A full summary of all debugger commands is given at the end of this section.

Having established the way to list out a program in the debugger, the next likely requirement is to look at and possibly change the contents of variables at a particular point in the program. To effect this requires stopping the program at a given line number. Stopping the program at a specific line number is handled by setting a 'breakpoint' equal to the line number using the command **B$=***nn* where *nn* equals the line number. There are four breakpoints that can be set at any one time (1–4). Any one of them can be removed with the **K***n* command to kill a specific breakpoint (between 1 and 4), or **K** which will remove them all.

The contents of a variable are displayed by preceding the variable name with a forward slash, i.e. /. When the contents are displayed they will be followed by an equals sign. If the content of the variable is to remain unchanged, press the [CR] key, otherwise enter the new value of the variable and press the [CR] key.

Figure 15.100 shows the setting of a breakpoint at line 20 of the program, which enables the description on the first line of the report to be changed. The breakpoint is then removed to enable the rest of the program to complete as usual.

```
:RUN BP PROG10 (D  <—— Initiate the debugger

*I1                <—— Current line number
*B$=20[CR] +       <—— Set breakpoint on line 20, system responds with + to indicate OK
*G                 <—— Continue program until breakpoint reached

DESCRIPTION        ORIGINAL        INCREASE        NEW
OF GOODS           PRICE           IN PRICE        PRICE

*B1 20             <————————————— Breakpoint 1 reached, program halted at line 20
*/DESC[CR] SAW=NUTS 3mm [CR] <— Display contents of variable DESC and
                                 change it from SAW to NUTS 3mm
*K1[CR] -          <———————————— Remove breakpoint 1, system responds with - to
                                 indicate OK
*G [CR]            <———————————— Continue with program until its end

SAW                 12.25           0.98            13.23
SCREWS               0.24           0.02             0.26
HAMMERS              8.76           0.70             9.46
SCREWDRIVER 1"       3.33           0.27             3.60
:
------END OF REPORT------
```

Figure 15.100 The use of breakpoints to change variables in the debugger.

There is a further use of the breakpoint which is extremely useful and that is in setting conditional breakpoints. In this situation the logic to be applied is written at the debugger prompt. Hence to stop the program as soon as the variable RECID equals 1009, the following would be input at the debugger prompt :

BRECID="1009"

It is all well and good setting a breakpoint in a program providing you reach the condition or the line of the program specified. In some programs, however, when the program just aborts for no apparent reason or enters a part of the program it has no reason to be in, you need to trace what is going on by looking at the sequence of program statements that are being executed. The command **E***n* is used to step through the program *n* statements at a time each time a **G** command is executed. The step by step process is turned off by entering an **E** followed by [CR] at the debug prompt. Figure 15.101 shows the use of the **E** command which is first used to step a single statement at a time, then two statements at a time through the program until the exercise is abandoned and the program run to completion using the **G** command.

```
:RUN BP PROG10 (D  <-- Initates the debugger

*I1                <-------- Current statement number in program
*E1[CR]            <-------- Execute a statement at a time
*G[CR]             <-------- Proceed
*I2                <-------- Current statement number in program
*G[CR]             <-------- Proceed
*I3                <-------- Current statement number in program
*E2[CR]            <-------- Execute two statements at a time
*G[CR]             <-------- Proceed
*I5                <-------- Current statement number in program
*G[CR]             <-------- Proceed

PRICE LIST INCREASES AS AT 25 NOV 1995
*I12               <-------- Current statement number in program
*E[CR]             <-------- Turn off the E command
*G[CR]             <-------- Proceed to end of program

DESCRIPTION        ORIGINAL      INCREASE      NEW
OF GOODS           PRICE         IN PRICE      PRICE

SAW                12.25         0.98          13.23
SCREWS              0.24         0.02           0.26
HAMMERS             8.76         0.70           9.46
SCREWDRIVER 1"      3.33         0.27           3.60
:
-------END OF REPORT------
```

Figure 15.101 The **E** and **G** command in the BASIC debugger.

These are the main debug commands, but there are several others which are summarized here for completeness. For full details of their use refer to your BASIC manual.

Command	**Function**
B*exp*	Set breakpoint based on expression *exp*
B$*nn*	Set breakpoint when line number *nn* reached
D	Display breakpoint and trace tables
DE	Enter system debugger (denoted by an exclamation mark **!**)
DEBUG	As with DE above
E*n*	Execute *n* statements at a time. **E[CR]** turns it off
END	End execution of program and return to TCL
G	Proceed from breakpoint
G*n*	Go directly to line *n*. Do not execute other statements in between
K	Kills all breakpoints
K*n*	Kills breakpoint *n*
L*n-m*	List program lines from line *n* to line *m*
LP	All output forced to printer
N*n*	Ignore the next *n*+1 breakpoints
N	Resets the **N***n* command above. Breakpoints are processed
OFF	Log off
P	Toggles whether output is displayed or not
PC	Force printer closed and send report to spooler
R	Removes address from top of stack, forcing program to return from current subroutine as though a **RETURN** statement had been encountered
S	Display subroutine stack
T	Toggle trace function
T*var*	Sets variable *var* in trace table
U	Remove all variables from trace table
U*var*	Remove variable *var* from trace table
Z	Use symbol table (including source code) from specified program
$	Current statement number
/*var*	Display value of variable *var*
/*a*(*x*)	Print value of point *x* in array *a*
/*a*(*x*,*y*)	Print value of point *x*,*y* in array *a*
/*a*	Print the entire array *a*
/*	Display entire symbol table
[*x*,*y*]	Set left margin *x* and right margin *y* for debugger display
[	Remove limits from [*x*,*y*] command

15.24 BASIC optimization techniques

The prime considerations in optimising BASIC programs are

- Operational efficiency
- Minimizing disk reads
- Efficient variable management (optimising use of the descriptor table)

The effective control of these aspects of BASIC programs will have a significant effect on system performance. Needless to say, structured programming is not simply an exercise in improving program maintainability and clarity, it has a significant effect on program performance as it helps to optimize use of the descriptor table and reduce the number of frame faults required.

Do also remember that there is little point in spending significant time optimizing a small portion of code which is not routinely run, when other broader programming issues continue to contribute more significantly to system overheads. This section concentrates techniques for improving runtime efficiency.

15.24.1 Variable management and the descriptor table

The purpose of the descriptor table is to maintain the contents of the variables during the running of a BASIC program. The descriptor table either holds the actual value contained in the variable or, if the variable contents exceed eight bytes, a pointer to its location in free workspace.

The free workspace area is used to store strings which exceed eight characters in length. The free workspace area begins as one contiguous block, somewhat like the overflow table and is divided into buffers. These buffer areas are normally 50, 150, 250 and multiples of 250 bytes. As a string outgrows its buffer it is allocated a new buffer in the next increment and the space previously used is freed up for use by a new variable. Hence the original contiguous block of workspace becomes fragmented and a process known as 'garbage collection' may become necessary to reorganise the fragmented blocks into one contiguous block. In R83, if after garbage collection, a sufficiently large enough contiguous space cannot be found the BASIC program will abort with the message:

```
[B28] Not enough workspace.
```

Advanced PICK does not have this problem because it has what is known as 'floating workspace' which means that more workspace is added to the process as required. However, the more frequently garbage collection is required, the slower the program will run and the volume of large strings is a major factor in determining the frequency of garbage collection. It perhaps also explains why reusing a variable, wherever practical, is recommended.

In R83, the maximum size of the descriptor table was 32,000 bytes, with a maximum number of entries of 3,200, i.e. 10 bytes per variable. Advanced PICK has all but removed that limitation with a maximum of 214,748,363 variables but unpredictable results can occur with variables above about 32,000 in number.

Descriptor entries are held in the following order:

- Common block variables
- Default file variables
- Default active list

- Simple variables
- Dimensioned variables

The first two bytes of a descriptor designate its type, the remainder varies according to what type it is, and is as follows:

- a numeric variable is held as a 6 byte binary number
- file variables are held as base, modulo and separation
- subroutine names are held as 6 byte pointers to the first frame of their object code
- select variables are 6 byte pointers to where the list is held on disk
- ASCII strings of 8 bytes or less are held in the descriptor table otherwise they are held in free workspace with the descriptor entry holding a 6 byte pointer to it.

Whilst BASIC variables can be declared in a program at any time, and can be assigned at the time they are first needed, any variable referenced on the right side of an equals sign prior to initialization, will cause the error message

```
[B10] VARIABLE HAS NOT BEEN ASSIGNED A VALUE; ZERO USED
```

It makes sense, therefore, and is a recommended practice that variables be initialized at the start of the program. Variable allocation may be examined by compiling the program with the (M option. This will provide a map of variable usage and may be sent to the printer using the following option (MP.

PICK/BASIC does not require specific declaration of variable types but it is important to define variables correctly for intended use. The variable type is indicated in the first two bytes of its descriptor entry and may be one of the following:

- Numeric
- File variable
- Subroutine name
- ASCII string
- Select variable

Consider the following:

```
NUMBER=100
PRINT NUMBER
```

The variable NUMBER is used in two separate ways. In the first statement as a number stored as in 6 bytes. In the second statement it is used as an ASCII string taking up 3 bytes. It therefore has to be converted from numeric to ASCII. The reverse exercise takes place in the following example:

```
NUMBER='255'
NUMBER=NUMBER+0
```

If a variable requires conversion from one state to another for the purposes of a particular function or statement, PICK/BASIC will generally handle the conversion very efficiently. However, careful thought can minimize this conversion need.

Every time a variable is referenced the system must check to see if the descriptor is in memory. To ensure optimum variable management and minimal garbage collection the following measures should be taken.

- Reuse variables wherever possible, especially where they hold long strings.
- Use Boolean logic wherever possible when testing the value of conditions.

15.24.2 Reducing disk reads in BASIC programs

Frame distribution is indicated on the variable map after the listing of variables. This will indicate whether frames are being crossed during critical points of the program, for example, in the middle of loops. The effect of frame crossing will have greater impact in batch processing than on-line processing where generally speaking disk access will perform faster than human input. Where thrashing of the system is occurring then this will be of critical importance.

Structured programming will increase the likelihood of discrete subroutines occurring within frames. Structured programming within PICK should attempt to keep as much of the repeated main stream logic memory resident, during program execution with any special processing held as subroutines.

15.24.3 Structured programming

Structured programming uses small subroutines or code segments as the means to build a program. Each part will ultimately constitute a subroutine. with one entry point and one exit point.

Variables, wherever possible, should be defined locally and only truly global variables should be defined in the initialization subroutine passed through the COMMON block. This is because subroutines at the same level are effectively independent of each other and are dependant only on higher level subroutines.

There are various arguments as to the maximum length of each subroutine. Some suggest that the figure should be 20 lines on the basis that a whole subroutine should be visible on a screen. Where subroutines are determined on the basis of conditions the problem should not arise. If a subroutine is longer than 20 lines but is conditionless, any further breakdown would be arbitrary and so be of little use.

The advantages of modularized code are:

- Optimization of disk reads is more likely.
- Variable management is more easily controlled.
- Commonly used routines may be held as one piece of code.
- Special processing may be taken away from the main logic.
- Where changes of software are required, maintainability is easier. Testing and implementation is quicker, as compilations are speedier and test plans more reliable.
- Portability of software is enhanced.

A subroutine should not be repeatedly called from within a loop. The difference will not be significant in intensively used data, but in batch processing situations, however, this may significantly increase the occurrences of disk reads during program runtime.

Additionally, by way of warning, indirect external calls may be nearly ten times slower than direct calls. **GOTO**s out of subroutines should never be used as they not only break the fundamental tenants of structured programming listed above but they may also may corrupt the RETURN stack. Without doubt **CHAIN** should never be used from a subroutine. It is like a system-wide **GOTO**.

15.24.4 Sharing code segments

One of the most important aspects of PICK/BASIC programming is the ability to have the same segment of code shared by many programs, each with its own workspace containing the contents of its variables. Use of code segments allows programs to be shorter and maintenance requirements to be simplified.

One very useful method is using **INCLUDE**d code segments. These are compiled in-line with the object code generated by the original source program. Included segments of code are effectively merged into the object of the main program at runtime. The syntax may vary, but it will be something of the form:

INCLUDE *filename itemid*

dependent on the PICK implementation you may find that the statement uses one of the following three alternatives **$INCLUDE INSERT** or **$INSERT**

where

filename is the name of the file where the included code can be found
itemid the item id of containing the included code

Often **INCLUDE**d are common block variables, standard constants and data structures. Such practices not only enhance efficiency, but ensure that standards become adopted. The example below gives you an idea of the type code that could be designated for program inclusion.

```
EQUATE AM TO CHAR(254)
EQUATE VM TO CHAR(253)
EQUATE SVM TO CHAR(252)
EQUATE BELL TO CHAR(7)
EQU TRUE TO 1
EQU FALSE TO 0
FALSE=0
GOOD=FALSE
OK=FALSE
CLEAR.SCREEN=@(-1)
```

The fixed structure of files should be reflected in programs processing them which will ensure that variable names used in suites of programs accessing remain constant.

```
DIM COMPANY.REC()
EQUATE COMPANY.NAME TO COMPANY.REC(1)
etc.
```

The advantage of **INCLUDE**d code is that it only exists once, so if a change has to be made it is only made once, rather than in every program that uses it. However, if the included code is changed then all programs using the code would have to be recompiled.

Included code should be used whenever there is a common set of instructions used by many program, for example **COMMON** statements. **COMMON** statements should always be used for sharing globally used variables amongst suites of programs. Common variables are stored separately, at the beginning of the descriptor table and are shared by the main program and all called routines. They may on some implementations be stored in a named common area. On the variable map, common variables are indicated by a C prefix.

When programs are called and parameters are passed across locally, their own variables are added to the descriptor table and workspace. Where variables are passed across, the descriptors are copied over to another level in the descriptor table.

15.24.5 Condition testing

Where the truth of one condition mutually excludes the truth of other values, always use the CASE construct for the following reasons:

- It is easier to maintain and change without changing the logic flow
- It is more in line with the structured approach of programming
- It is more efficient if used properly – when using **IF**s every possible **IF** condition has normally to be tested even if the correct one is found first

CASE statements used in conjunction with indexed branching is probably the most efficient method of all in cutting down on the overhead caused by lengthy **CASE** statements and an example is as follows:

```
INPUT ANS,1
ON INDEX('ABCD',ANS,1) GOSUB 100,200,300,400
```

15.24.6 Reading and locking

READUs are time consuming and will leave locks if not released. Therefore, never use **READU** when the is no chance that the record will be updated. Remember **READU**s do not lock out **READ**s and if groups remain unintentionally locked and the lock table becomes full, the system will hang.

The **LOCKED** statement is also very useful in preventing the system beeping at users when there desired record has been locked. The following format can be used to ensure modularised code is maintained, using this facility:

```
READU REC FROM FILE,ITEM.ID LOCKED
      GOSUB 10 ; * RECORD LOCKED
END THEN
      GOSUB 20 ; * PROCESS EXISTING RECORD
END ELSE
      GOSUB 30 ; * PROCESS RECORD NOT ON FILE
END
```

15.24.7 Presentation conventions

Good consistent presentation not only adds to program clarity but improves maintainability.

Statement labels should always be positioned in the first column and be consistently structured so that subroutines may be easily localized. They should be succinctly commented on the same line to express their function as should the **CALL** statement to the subroutine. This practise minimizes the mistake of calling the incorrect subroutine and certainly makes it much easier to identify.

Numeric statement labels can include decimal points or contain leading zeros. Hence the following are valid statement labels:

```
1  10  0100  01001.5
```

Take care in using alphanumeric labels, because although Advanced PICK supports them, not all implementations do – R83 does not for instance. Alphanumeric statement labels ***must*** start with an alphabetic character and must be followed by a : (colon). If a statement is to be placed on the same line it must be separated from the statement label with one or more spaces.

Since Advanced PICK allows null statement lines, a statement label can stand by itself on a line of the program. This is not the case in R83 where the statement label had to be on the same line as a valid BASIC statement.

Scatter comments as liberally as possible through the program.

Another great aid to readability is the use of indentation. Indenting should be used for all loops and **THEN/ELSE** constructs. Two characters for each indentation level should be quite sufficient.

Multiple statements on the same line should only be used for simple assignment or equate statements but even then it should be avoided, except where it is necessary to add clear comments by way of explanation. Do remember multiple statements are difficult to debug both at compile and run-time.

Where spaces are not a mandatory, as in the case of =, > or < comparisons, ***be consistent*** in their use as this makes using editing facilities such as global locates and replace easier to control..

Open all files in the same place, near the logical beginning of the program and never in external subroutines, except perhaps a specific subroutine which opens all files.

Initialize all global variables next, again at the logical beginning but not necessarily the physical beginning of the program.

Neither of these subroutines need to be placed at the physical beginning of the program as they rarely have to be changed, so let the programmer see the mainstream of the code when examining the program. This mainstream code will tell the programmer exactly where they need to go to find the code requiring changing.

File variables should have a common prefix, indicating their role in the program.

Keep all lines, including commented ones to a maximum of 80 characters.

15.24.8 Array handling

A dynamic array replicates a PICK data item, using system delimiters and takes up one variable location in memory and has a single entry in the descriptor table.

There are certain BASIC intrinsic file-handling functions associated with dynamic arrays, for example, insertion, deletion, extraction and location

Dimensioned arrays have a descriptor element for each array entry and do not have these intrinsic file-handling functions associated with them.

When reading data into a dimensioned array, if the array is not large enough, the final attributes will all be read into the last element. No problems will be encountered, unless it is required to extract data from this last element. Where the array may be written back to the file, a **MAT** statement should be used to initialize the array to null. This will avoid zeros being written to trailing null values, especially if the number of elements exceeds the number of attributes in the item.

The difference in the way dynamic and dimensioned arrays hold data causes access time of individual entries to vary. Retrieval from a dimensioned array is direct whilst retrieval from a dynamic array involves a sequential search through the whole item. Therefore when dealing with large items dynamic arrays can involve a massive overhead. Using dimensioned arrays to compensate for this involves losing the intrinsic file update facilities of dynamic arrays.

Writing and reading from dimensioned arrays also takes about twice as long. A read is quicker using a dynamic array as the item can be read directly from disk to a variable item. A dimensioned array must be parsed out to each individual variable location making up the item.

The following guidelines should be considered:

- keep item sizes below a frame size;
- where a value in an array is to be referenced more than once, extract the value and store it in a variable. Process the variable rather than the element in the array. This is particularly important in the case of numbers held in dynamic arrays as considerable overhead will be saved in the conversion processes required;
- if your program updates a few attributes near the beginning of the item use a dynamic array, however if many attributes are being updated or retrieved, dimensioned arrays will always perform faster than dynamic arrays particularly where the item size is large.

15.24.9 Other handy hints

(1) To reduce frame faults during program execution

(a) Reduce the number of run-time lines of code
(b) Maximize the efficient use and organisation of internal storage
(c) Reduce the amount of data handled

(2) GOSUBS

(a) Subroutines called only once should be incorporated into the main body of the program
(b) Small subroutines executed two or three times should be incorporated into the main body of the program
The run-time code generated for a **GOSUB** statement is small compared to the reduction in program size created by its use
(c) Careful placement of the **GOSUB** statement can help to reduce frame faults

(3) CALL

(a) The **CALL** statement generates a large overhead and therefore should be used sparingly
(b) It should be used to reduce the run-time code of large programs widely used in a multi-user environment
(c) It should be used where the program size exceeds the maximum item size
(d) When passing parameters, use the **COMMON** statement rather than an argument list

(4) GOTO

- (a) The use of **GOTO** is widely recognised as poor programming practice and hence the use of them should be kept to a minimum
- (b) Where possible replace them with **ON...GOTO** statements
- (c) Reduce the number of instructions skipped between the **GOTO** and its destination to a minimum

(5) REM

- (a) Remarks should be placed at the end of a statement line rather than on a separate line

(6) Stack-related statements

- (a) Stack related statements should be kept on the same statement line

(7) Assignment statements

- (a) Do not assign any constants to variables within loops
- (b) Do not re-evaluate expressions, assign them once only to a variable
- (c) Initial values should be assigned in the initialization section
- (d) Eliminate all variables that are not used
- (e) Concatenation is time consuming and should be kept to a minimum

(8) Literals

- (a) Literals are not stored in the descriptor table which contains the contents of variables
- (b) Descriptor tables of only one frame tend to remain in main storage
- (c) Literals appear in run-time code, exactly as they appear in the source code
- (d) String literals (value enclosed in quotes), require 2 bytes plus the length of the literal in runtime code
- (e) Numeric literals (value not enclosed in quotes), are converted to 6 byte binary numbers and require 7 bytes of run-time code
- (f) It takes only 3 bytes of run-time code to reference a variable
- (g) A frame fault is normally required to access a variable
- (h) In order to maximize the chance of variables being located in the descriptor table in main memory, re-use variable names wherever possible, providing the clarity of the program is unaffected

(9) Dynamic arrays

- (a) Use dynamic arrays when dealing with data files
- (b) Use standard arrays for internal tables
- (c) If the same information is needed more than once assign it to a variable rather than continually **EXTRACT**ing it
- (d) Use the **REPLACE** statement for replacing two or three values in large dynamic arrays
- (e) Use **MATREAD** and **MATWRITE** statements when building, accessing or updating large dynamic arrays

(f) Use standard arrays only when necessary since the object code it creates is greater than for simple variables

(g) Do not enlarge source code by using arrays simply to avoid using subscripted variables

(10) Space

(a) For six spaces or less use **bb.b** where **b** is the number of blanks needed

(b) For more than six spaces use **SPACE(n)** where **n** is the number of blanks needed

(11) STR

(a) Where the string is nine characters or less use **cc..c** where **c** is the character desired

(b) Where the string is greater than nine characters use **STR('c',n)** where **c** is the desired character and **n** its number of occurrences

(12) ICONV/OCONV

(a) These conversions are executed quite rapidly in most cases

(b) When a definite field width is desired, use the format masks

(c) If the format is to be used often, assign it to a variable

(13) Position curser

(a) Each parameter takes up 7 bytes of runtime code and therefore these statements should be used sparingly

(14) IF

(a) Multiple **IF** statements containing **AND** and/or **OR** conditions are not optimized

(b) There is an overhead associated with every **IF**

(c) Use the complex **IF** statement wherever possible

(15) FOR...NEXT and LOOP

(a) **FOR...NEXT** statements execute faster than building a **FOR/NEXT** with the **LOOP** statement

(b) If the index variable is not used within the loop use the **LOOP** statement with the **WHILE** or **UNTIL** clause

(c) Avoid repetition of deriving the same value for both the **UNTIL/WHILE** test within the loop

(d) **FOR/NEXT** have initial and terminal conditions – make use of them!

(16) EQUATE

(a) The immediate value is compiled into object code
(b) They do not access variable locations during runtime
(c) The array address is computed during compilation
(d) They should be used to pre-define:
  Attribute marks
  Value marks
  Sub-value marks
  Array elements
(e) Extensive use of the **EQUATE** statement is highly recommended to improve program efficiency and program clarity

(17) ENTER

(a) **ENTER** is faster than **CHAIN** to execute a BASIC program
(b) The programs executed must be **CATALOG**ued
(c) Use caution as **ENTER** does not initialize the variables used in the **ENTER**ed program

(18) CASE
(a) Ensure that the condition most frequently expected to be found true is tested first

16 File Indexing using B-Trees

16.1 Introduction

The introduction of B-trees in Advanced PICK, one of its major features, can make significant performance improvements to applications. Indeed in its own right, this feature should provide the necessary incentive for the traditionalists still entrenched in R83 to move up to Advanced PICK.

The great thing about these indexes is their integration at the operating system level. This means that ***any*** change made to the data will update the index.

In Advanced PICK, therefore, if you make a change to the data, either through application program, the Update Processor or the Editor the B-tree indexes will be updated. Similarly TCL processes like **COPY DELETE** and **T-LOAD** will also update the index.

The word B-tree means a 'balanced tree' and is essentially a system-maintained access method. It provides an ordered-list based on any attribute or combination of attributes of the items in a file and it allows quick retrieval of items based on this secondary key.

An index would be used where data needs to be accessed on an attribute other than its item-id. An example would be a customer file, where access would be via the customer name. Without a B-tree index direct access to the record could only be made by its item-id. If you needed to locate a record using the customer name you would need to search sequentially through the file, which on a file with many thousands of records would be unworkable as finding the record could take several minutes and we all know that users find waiting more than a couple of seconds unacceptable!

The alternative and preferential way to sequential searching through a file is to use an alternative access method, that is to say to use an index. Hence the means to find a customer record without knowing the customer code, but knowing the name is to create an individual index on the customer name attribute. Once done, the PICK system will maintain it and access to a specific record is virtually instantaneous. With minor modifications, existing PICK applications can make use of B-trees and once in existence ACCESS will also use the indexes greatly enhancing the speed in which reports are produced.

16.2 The building and maintenance of indexes

16.2.1 Creating an index

An index is created using the **CREATE-INDEX** verb. This command will create an index file based on a nominated data attribute which is defined using the **a** processing code. The index needs only to be created once and thereafter Advanced PICK will maintain it. The syntax for this TCL statement is shown in Figure 16.1.

create-index *file.name a.code*

where

file.name	is the name of the file containing the attribute to be indexed
a.code	is the **a** processing code defining the attribute to be indexed (an asterisk in place of the **a** code means create all indexes)

Figure 16.1 The format of the **CREATE-INDEX** verb.

There is no physical limit to the number of attributes in a file that can be indexed, although the more there are the larger the amount of disk space required and the longer it will take to process file updates. However in reality there are not normally more than two or three attributes that need indexing. Figure 16.2 gives some examples of the way in which the **a** processing code can be used to create indexes.

There are two ways to create multiple indexes on a file, either to run the verb **CREATE-INDEX** several times or to use the * or wildcard option to get the system to generate all the indexes associated with the file. In order to do this you first need specify the indexes required, which is achieved by modifying the D-pointer of the file in question and placing the references to the indexes in attribute 8. The index references are separated by a value mark, but traditionalists beware, these have to be entered using the UPDATE Processor, ***not*** the EDITOR. Whilst there should be no difference which edit processor you use, entering multiple index references using the EDITOR just simply does not work. Figure 16.3 gives you an example of a typical procedure.

Example 1

:create-index customer a1	This creates an index on the contents of attribute 1 in the file **customer**. This is a simple example and assumes something like the customer name is in attribute 1

Example 2

:create-index hire.det a3(tcars;x;;2)	In this example for a car rental system, attribute 3 of the rental agreement (the car registration number) is used to access the second attribute of the cars file (the colour of the vehicle). The resulting index enables access to the rental agreements based on colour of the vehicle

Example 3

:create-index cars a1:2	In this example the index is created based on a concatenation of two data attributes, attribute 1 and attribute 2

Figure 16.2 Examples of the use of **CREATE-INDEX.**

```
:u dict cars cars (d
DICT cars 'cars' size = 36
DICT cars cars
01 D
02 92002
03 7
04
05
06
07
08Ia1 v
  Ia2 v
  Ia1:2 v xf
09 L
10 10
DICT cars 'cars' size = 47 filed.

:create-index cars *
```

Figure 16.3 Using **CREATE-FILE** to create multiple indexes.

Once the index has been created, PICK changes the contents of attribute 8 to indicate that an index is available and to denote its physical location. If you look at the D-pointer you will see something like I06374a2 indicating an index exists on attribute 2 of the file items and the index is physically located starting in frame number 6374.

16.2.2 Deleting an index

Removing an index is simple to do by using the command **DELETE-INDEX**. In the same way as creating the index, the delete command needs to have the **a** processing code specified if an individual index is to be deleted and an * (asterisk) where all indexes for a given file are to be deleted. The following are the commands to delete the indexes built in Figure 16.2.

```
:delete-index customer a1
:delete-index hire.det a3(tcars;x;;2)
:delete-index cars a1:2
```

Whilst it should be obvious, never delete an index processing code directly from the File Defining Item as this is the equivalent of deleting a 'd-pointer', in that the space for the index is NOT returned to the overflow table. You should also, never alter a pre-existing root fid in an index, as this can cause data corruption.

16.2.3 Verifying an index

If you suspect an index to be corrupt, it can be easily checked out with the **VERIFY-INDEX** verb, which like all the index processing commands we have met so far, also needs the **a** processing code or an asterisk to be specified as shown in the following examples:

```
:verify-index customer a1
:verify-index hire.det a3(tcars;x;;2)
:verify-index cars a1:2
:verify-index customer *
```

During the process a file called **VI.DUMP** is created, but so as its contents are not saved unnecessarily it is created by PICK as a **DX** type file. There is another alternative format, which is to follow the command with a question mark (**verify-index ?**), which causes on-line help to be displayed.

Unlike the other index commands discussed so far, the verify process has a number of options which can be invoked and these are as follows:

c	compare the file to the index only.
f	Verify the file to the index only.
i	Displays item-id's.
k	Verifies links and nodes.
l	Locks each data item as it is verified.
m	Suppresses all messages.
o	Reports missing item-id's and locates items indexed in the wrong place. While using this option makes the process run slower, it increases the reliability and effectiveness of the process.
p	Directs report to system printer, via the Spooler.
r	Inhibits index recreation on link error.
s	Suppresses display of item counter.
v	Verifies that the data exists for the given indices. This is used in the unusual case where the index contains pointers to item-id's which have been deleted.
x	Suppresses automatic fix of bad indices. This option produces a report only.

16.2.4 Rebuilding an index

INDEXER is the TCL verb called at the end of the file and account restore processes and is used to build indexes on part or all of the files of the system. The verb on its own will rebuild the indexes on all files on the system. If you want to re-build the indexes on just one account, follow the verb with the account name. If you want to re-build the indexes on multiple accounts, perform a **SELECT** function on the **mds** file thereby creating an active select list of the appropriate account names. This can then be passed for re-indexing using the **INDEXER** verb. There are just three options available with this command as follows:

- **a** the select list is a list of file names rather than account names
- **n** when outputting information on the screen, do not pause at the bottom of each screen
- **p** prints the output from the command to the printer rather than screen

Figure 16.4 gives examples of index re-building.

If there are just specific files in an account for which you wish to have indexes re-built, then you need to first build a select list of the file names, and pass this to the **INDEXER** verb, using the **a** option. Figure 16.5 gives an example of this.

:indexer
Rebuilds the indexes for all files in all accounts on the system

:indexer sbdemo
Rebuilds the indexes for all files in the account SBDEMO

:select mds "sbdemo" "apt.pc" "stratum"
[404] 3 items selected out of 44 items
:indexer
Rebuilds the indexes for all files in the accounts SBDEMO APT.PC and STRATUM

Figure 16.4 Rebuilding indexes using **INDEXER.**

:select md "customer" "cars"
:indexer (a
Rebuilds the indexes for the files CUSTOMER and CARS in the current account

---

Figure 16.5 Rebuilding specific files within an account.

16.2.5 Determining the size of the index

If you dump a frame of the index you will see that it consists of a header of 16 bytes, followed by multiple sets of three components, a 4 byte control block, the key and the item-ids with that key. To find the number of frames used in an existing index, use the command **nframe-index** whose syntax is as follows:

nframe-index *filename a.code* (an * can be substituted for the *a.code* to find the size of every index on a file)

16.2.6 Saving indexes

In initial releases of AP there was no option to save the indexes on the assumption it took time to save and the time saved could be best put to use by re-generating the indexes to ensure they were not corrupt. However, from release 6 onwards the indexes can be saved by using the **B** option on a file-save.

16.3 Using indexes in the Update Processor

The indexing capabilities of Advanced PICK can be put to good use in the Update Processor to perform tasks known as 'cruising', 'zooming' and 'double clutching'. Whilst these terms may seem daunting at first they simply mean using a local index (cruising), using a remote index (zooming) or using both (double clutching). Let's explore these definitions further.

16.3.1 Cruising

Cruising is the ability to scan forwards and backwards through the items in a file based on an index created on one of the attributes in a file. Typically on a customer file where the item-id is numeric and the customer name is one of the data attributes, let's say attribute 1. If an index is created on the name field in attribute 1, then you would be able to browse forwards and backwards through the records in the file using **f** (control/f) and **d** (control/d), respectively. You could either enter a full or partial name them follow it by one of these control sequences and advanced PICK will locate the nearest record to it that it can find. If that record is not correct, you can cruise through the file, either forwards or backwards, record by record until the beginning or end of the index is reached.

16.3.2 Zooming

Zooming uses what is called a remote index which links to records in another file. The process of zooming allows direct access to the related record in the remote file which can itself be modified by the Update Processor, before exiting back to the original record. Zooming to the related record is achieved with **gg** (control/g g) whilst exiting from the record (with or without filing it) takes you back to the original record (the one from which the zoom command was executed). The remote index also facilitates a table look up capability, without having to traverse to the remote file. Browsing through the remote index is achieved using **u** (control/u) to browse forwards and **y** (control/y) to browse backwards. More by way of an explanation and examples later.

16.3.3 Double-clutching

Double-clutching means the combined abilities of zooming and cruising. This means there is both a local and remote index and the user can either search a remote file index for valid values and/or search the local (current) file index for specific items. Once having zoomed through the 'doorway' to another file the user has the option to cruise from item to item in the new file and return to the original file or zoom to yet another file and cruise through that one.

16.3.4 Setting up the input conversion code for local indexes

Whilst PICK at the operating system level will maintain the index as soon as it is created, it will not be active for 'cruising' and 'zooming' until you have notified PICK which dictionary item controls the index. PICK looks at the input conversion code (attribute 14) of the attribute defining item and if you wish to use the index capabilities to the full you need place an **i** in attribute 14 of the dictionary record on which the index is built. Hence if you wish to access a customer file indexed on customer name, by the customer name, after having created the index, put an i in attribute 14 of the dictionary record which defines the customer name. Even having done this, the cruising and zooming facilities will only work if you specify the index attribute as part of the Update Processor command, i.e. **u customer name** whereas just using the Update Processor on the entire item (i.e. **u customer** *) will not give you access to the cruising and zooming functions.

Hence you cannot automatically use the Update Processor cruise and zoom commands without either addressing the index attribute specifically, such as **u customer name** (assuming the attribute **name** is the one with the index) or by specifying in the file defining item, the attributes to be displayed as one of the default attributes when processing the file with the Update Processor. The default attribute names are placed in attribute 15, each separated with a space. Providing one of these attributes is an attribute on which the file is indexed, then whilst in the Update Processor and pointing to that attribute, the cruise and zoom commands will be available to you. By way of an example, Figure 16.6 shows an index being set up on attribute 2 (the colour) of a file called **cars** and this attribute is then marked as an indexed attribute by the addition of the processing code **i**. Then in the final stages, attribute 15 of the file defining item is updated with the list of attributes to display when the Update Processor is active and the Update Processor is invoked to show the effects of the cruising commands.

16.3.5 Setting up the input conversion code for remote indexes

Remote indexes are used when 'zooming' and again involve setting an input conversion code in attribute 14 of the dictionary item of the data element in question. Hence in a car hire application, whilst reviewing the list of vehicles it

Step 1 – create an index on the attribute containing the cars' colour

:create-index cars a2

Step 2 – activate the index on the attribute by placing an **I** in attribute 14

:u dict cars colour
DICT cars 'colour' size = 46
01 A**ze** (**ze** (ctrl/z e) moves cursor to end of data)
02 2
03 Colour
04
05
06
07
08
09 L
10 15[CR]
11[CR]
12[CR]
13[CR]
14 **ixf** (**xf** (ctrl/x f) files the item)
DICT cars 'colour' size = 51 filed.

Step 3 – set up the macro of default attributes for the Update Processor

:u dict cars cars (d
DICT cars 'cars' size = 63
01 D**ze**
02 91503
03 1
04
05
06
07
08 I93165a2
09 L
10 10[CR]
11[CR]
12[CR]
13[CR]
14[CR]
15 **colour book.price miles hire.no xf**
DICT cars 'cars' size = 77 filed.

Figure 16.6 The stages for setting up indexes for use in the Update Processor.

Step 4 – Use the Update Processor to 'cruise' the index on the colour of the vehicle

```
:u cars ERT931
cars 'ERT931' size = 77
Colour        NAVY BLUEd
Book Price       18000.00
Mileage      3029
Hire No       218
cars 'ERT931' size = 77 exited.
cars 'DKT531' size = 77
Colour        NAVY BLUE
Book Price      15000.00
Mileage      34256
Hire No      339
```

By using the index, although the original Update Processor verb addressed only a single car, registration **ERT931**, others can be accessed using the index. In this example we use the 'cruise' command **d** (control/d) to access the previous record, equally **f** would access the next record

Figure 16.6 *Continued*

may be useful to look at the hire agreements registered against the cars and to 'zoom' across to the full detail of an individual agreement. We will now take the example in Figure 16.6 a stage further and switch on the 'zoom' feature for the attribute HIRE.NO by setting up the appropriate indexes and input conversion codes.

The first step is to create and index on the attribute (HIRE.NO) containing the hire agreement number, in our example this is attribute 20. Having done this we need to set the input conversion code in attribute 14 of the dictionary record HIRE.NO. The input conversion code has to be a little more than the **i** we used for local indexes, because Advanced PICK needs to know the name of the remote file and which attribute in that file it is to use when cruising through the records in the remote file. This is normally the item-id, but in the instances where this is not the case then a 'Tfile' processing code must also be specified. The final stage is to create an index on the remote file for the attribute which links the two files together and is used for cruising through the remote file.

In the example under discussion, the file **CARS** contains a multi-valued list of hire agreements in attribute 20. The hire agreements are in a separate file called **HIRE.DET** which has as its item-id the hire agreement number. Figure 16.7 shows the stages involved in enabling a zoom facility when accessing the hire agreement number in the cars file.

Once these steps have been undertaken everything is set to permit access the to **HIRE.DET** file from within the **CARS** file . Figure 16.8 gives an example of how this works.

Now that a remote index exists, it would be possible to use the table facility to determine what other hire agreement numbers exist without having to zoom to them. This is done by entering **u** (control/u) to get the next agree-

Step 1 – create an index on the attribute containing the cars' hire agreement number
:create-index cars a20

Step 2 – activate the remote index by setting up the input conversion code in attribute 14
:u dict cars hire.no
DICT cars 'hire.no' size = 47
01 A**ze** (**ze** (ctrl/z e) moves cursor to end of data)
02 20
03 Hire No
04
05
06
07
08
09 L
10 15[CR]
11[CR]
12[CR]
13[CR]
14 **ihire.det;a0xf** (**xf** (ctrl/x f) files the item)
DICT cars 'hire.no' size = 59 filed.

Step 3 – create an index on the remote file for the cross-referenced attribute
:create-index hire.det a0

Figure 16.7 Setting up a remote index.

ment number and **y** (control/y) to get the previous one and Figure 16.9 shows this is operation. At first glance this may not seem too useful and perhaps in the context of the example given it is not. However, there are instances where this could be very useful, for example if you were working with customer records and wished to browse through the other customers by name.

Both an **i** (local index) and an **i***file.reference;a.code* (remote index) processing code can be specified in attribute 14, the input conversion attribute. When these two processing codes are specified in the same attribute defining item, **d** (control/d) and **f** (control/f) function differently depending on the order of the index codes specified. If the **i***file.reference;a.code* code is specified before the **i** code, and if either **d** (control/d) or **f** (control/f) is pressed, the Update Processor accesses the index specified by the first code in the secondary file and gets the previous or next attribute value for the specified index key. The Update Processor uses the index in the secondary file as it would use an index in the primary file. If the **i** code is specified first, the index in the primary file is used when **d** (control/d) or **f** (control/f) is pressed.

```
:u cars ERT931
cars 'ERT931' size = 77
Colour        NAVY BLUEd
Book Price        18000.00
Mileage       3029
Hire No       218
cars 'ERT931' size = 77 exited.
cars 'DKT531' size = 77
Colour        NAVY BLUE
Book Price       15000.00
Mileage      34256
Hire No       339gg
hire.det '339' size = 69
Deposit 174.50
Payment
From Date 06/04/90
To Date 13/05/90 xx
cars 'DKT531' size = 77
Colour             NAVY BLUE
Book Price           15000.00
Mileage            34256
Hire No 339 xx
:
```

By using the index, although the original Update Processor verb addressed only a single car, registration **ERT931**, others can be accessed using the index. In this example we use the 'cruise' command **d** (control/d) to access the previous record, equally **f** would access the next record

This is the 'zoom' command to bring up the details of the hire agreement number 339

The details of hire agreement number 339
When exiting the record **xx** (control/x x) you are taken back to the original record in the **cars** file

Figure 16.8 Zooming using remote indexes.

```
:u cars ERT931
cars 'ERT931' size = 77
Colour        NAVY BLUEd
Book Price        18000.00
Mileage       3029
Hire No       218
cars 'ERT931' size = 77 exited.
cars 'DKT531' size = 77
Colour        NAVY BLUE
Book Price          15000.00
Mileage       34256
Hire No       339u
```

By using the index, although the original Update Processor verb addressed only a single car, registration **ERT931**, others can be accessed using the index. In this example we use the 'cruise' command **d** (control/d) to access the previous record, equally **f** would access the next record

As soon as the **u** executed, the number 339 will be replaced with the next hire number on the file **HIRE.DET** and you can use **u** and **y** freely at this point to cruise forwards and backwards through the records on the **HIRE.DET** file.

Figure 16.9 Browsing through the remote index as a table of records.

16.4 Using indexes in PICK BASIC

Once indexes have been established you can access them from within your BASIC applications. The impact can be dramatic. Users will experience instant response, the application will provide immediate updating and retrieval of data and you will have no more complex cross-reference files or inverted lists to maintain or regenerate. Equally you will have no further need for any third party B-tree software with its associated cost implications.

Using the Advanced PICK indexing facilities is very straightforward. There are two new BASIC functions in Advanced PICK associated with the use of the B-tree indexes, the **ROOT** function which is the equivalent of an **OPEN** statement and the **KEY** function which enables the reading of records via the index.

16.4.1 The ROOT function

The **ROOT** function is similar to the **OPEN** statement for normal files in that it makes the index file available for use by assigning a variable, known as the root variable. It is called the root variable because when PICK creates an index it puts the root frame address (the top level frame in the B-tree) in the file defining attribute on the correlative attribute (i.e. attribute 8). Any number of indexes may be 'open' at once, provided that each has a unique 'root.variable'. Once defined in the **ROOT** function, the index is available to the program and can be scanned through using the **KEY** function. The general format of the **ROOT** function is given in Figure 16.10.

ROOT *file.reference,a.code* **TO** *root.variable* {**THEN** | **ELSE** *statements*}

where

file.reference	is the name of the file which has the index associated with it
a.code	is the a-correlative code in the same format as was used in **CREATE-INDEX**
root.variable	the variable name assigned to this index and used in subsequent **KEY** statements
statements	the statements that are executed with the **THEN** | **ELSE** clauses

The optional **THEN** clause is executed if the specified index is found and the **ELSE** clause is executed if it is not.

Figure 16.10 The general format of the **ROOT** function.

16.4.2 The KEY function

The **KEY** function is the statement in BASIC that allows the index to be searched for a specific value or the 'closest' value. Once a specific record is located, the **KEY** function can be used to 'browse' forwards or backwards through the index. The **ROOT** statement whose format is shown in Figure 16.11 ***must*** precede the **KEY** function.

KEY(*operator, root.variable, index.key, item-id* {,vc.expression}) {**THEN** | **ELSE** statements}

where

operator indicates the type of search, and may take one of the following values:

- **c** Compares, left-to-right, against the *index.key* and returns the first *item-id* whose index matches. If no match is found, the next sequentially higher index and first associated item-id are returned.
- **n** Returns the next *index.key* and *item-id*. If more than one *item-id* exists for an *index.key*, this option returns the next *item-id*. After all *item-ids* for an *index.key* have been returned, or if the *item-id* is null it returns the next *index.key* and *item-id*.
- **p** Returns the previous *index.key* and *item-id*. If more than one *item-id* exists for an *index.key*, this returns the previous *item-id*. After the first *item-id* for an *index.key* has been returned, or if *item-id* is null, it returns the previous *index.key* and the last *item-id*.
- **r** Returns the *index.key* and *item-id* only on an exact match with the *index.key*.
- **v** Verifies the index. Locates the given *index.key* and *item-id* and verifies that an exact match can be found.

root.variable is the b-tree root fid associated with the target index. It first must be initialised by the **ROOT** statement, and must be defined prior to using the **KEY** statement.

index.key specifies a mandatory variable containing the search string. The variable must be defined before using the **KEY** statement. The actual string found is returned into *index.key* when using the **c**, **n** or **p** operators. The **r** and **v** operators expect an exact match.

item-id is the variable that contains the *item-id* of the item that contains the *index.key*. The *item-id* need not be pre-assigned when using the **p** or **n** operators, but it must be pre-assigned when using the **v** operator.

vc.expression is the value number of the key attribute containing the *index.key*, returned to the *vc.expression* by the **KEY** statement. This only works with the **c**, **n**, **p** and **r** operators.

statements the statements that are executed with the **THEN** | **ELSE** clauses

The optional **THEN** clause is executed if the specified *item-id* is found or if the *index.key* verifies with the **v** operator and the **ELSE** clause is executed either of those conditions are not satisfied.

Figure 16.11 The general format of the **KEY** statement.

Figure 16.12 gives an example of a program using the **ROOT** and **KEY** functions. It assumes that an index has been created on attribute 1 of the file **CUSTOMER** where the customer name is held. This would have been created using the command **CREATE-INDEX CUSTOMER A1**. The program asks

```
FILE CUSTOMER
ROOT "CUSTOMER","A1" TO CUST.ROOT ELSE
        PRINT "The customer index is missing!"
        GOTO 999
        END
PROMPT ""
PRINT @(10,10): "Enter the name of the customer to find" :
INPUT NAME
INDEX.KEY = NAME
*
*Display 5 previous names
*
FOR X=1 TO 5
        KEY("P",CUST.ROOT,INDEX.KEY,CUST.ID) THEN
            READ CUSTOMER FROM CUST.ID THEN
                PRINT CUSTOMER(NAME)
            END
        END
NEXT X
*
*Look for an exact match
*
INDEX.KEY = NAME
KEY("R",CUST.ROOT,INDEX.KEY,CUST.ID) THEN
        READ CUSTOMER FROM CUST.ID THEN
            PRINT CUSTOMER(NAME)
        END
END
*
*Display 5 subsequent names
*
INDEX.KEY = NAME
FOR X=1 TO 5
        KEY("N",CUST.ROOT,INDEX.KEY,CUST.ID) THEN
            READ CUSTOMER FROM CUST.ID THEN
                PRINT CUSTOMER(NAME)
            END
        END
NEXT X
```

Figure 16.12 Using the **ROOT** and **KEY** functions.

the user to input a partial name and then displays a screen of ten names, five before and five after the partial name in the index.

16.4.3 Indexes and the enquiry language ACCESS

There is nothing to do to invoke the use of the indexes within ACCESS. The standard verbs **LIST**, **SORT**, **SELECT** and **SSELECT** automatically utilize the index if it is present.

ACCESS retrieves keys from the index when an associated attribute defining item is used in a **by** clause, such as **sort customer by cust.name** where **cust.name** is an indexed attribute with an **i** in attribute 14 of its dictionary item. Only one index may be used during any ACCESS **sort** or **select** statement; therefore, only one sort or selection criterion may be used within the ACCESS statement if you wish to take advantage of the index. Similarly no wildcard selections (e.g. **cust.name = 'brow]'**) are allowed if you want ACCESS to use the index. However, a **with** clause with no **by** clause will also use the index.

You can tell whether or not ACCESS has used the index by the structure of the number of items message at the conclusion of the ACCESS report. If it says X of items selected out of Y of items then it has selected X records from the total of Y records contained in the file and the index was not used. If the index is used, then the message X items selected will be displayed and the index will have been used. To force a sort or select of the whole file and not use the index, use the **W** option which will force ACCESS to traverse the whole file even though an index may be present.

17 Macros and Menus

The MACRO and MENU processors were only introduced with the advent of Advanced PICK. Prior to that time, PROCs were used to perform these tasks. Whilst PROCs are all but dead in Advanced PICK and indeed do not feature in their description of the product, PROCs remain in a wide number of PICK installations. For that reason a full explanation of the workings of PROC are given in Chapter 18.

17.1 Macros

Macros are multiple TCL commands that can be executed by a single command, that of the name of the macro. In the same way as PROCs, the macro contains each of the TCL functions be to performed in the sequence in which they are to be performed.

A macro is a very useful time saver, in that it can execute, if required, completely without user intervention. Hence a typical end of month process which performs many different tasks can be set into motion by invoking the end of the month macro and can be left to run unattended and even overnight if required.

Macros can be as long as you wish, but in honesty they were not intended to be complicated or act as a substitute for tasks better performed by BASIC programs. Hence a macro cannot call another macro, cannot validate user input and does not handle conditional statements and branching. This contrasts directly with PROC which can handle all these tasks, but is a very complicated language to understand for the naive user.

If you wish to add comments to your macro so that others may understand your intentions, then comments can be added at the very end, but they must be preceded by a blank line.

Macros are usually stored in the Master Dictionary and can be created in one of two ways:

(1) Using any editing tool, the editor or Update Processor for example.

(2) Converting a TCL command into a macro.

A macro, like all system items in Advanced PICK, is identified by the contents of attribute 1. There are two possible options:

m when the macro is called, each command in the macro will be displayed on the screen, allowing it to be edited prior to being run

n when the macro is called, all commands will run without any user intervention being required

17.1.1 Create a macro with the Update Processor

The process is straightforward. Decide on the name of the macro and use the Update Processor to create it in the Master Dictionary of the account that is to use the macro. (See Chapter 10 for details on how to use the Update Processor.) Where parameters need to be fed to the TCL command, these are entered after the TCL command, but preceded by a value mark and Figure 17.1 gives some examples.

Example 1

```
:U MD MONTH.END
MD 'MONTH.END' NEW ITEM
01 N[CR]
02 SET-SCT[CR]
03 T-REW[CR]
04 ACCOUNT-SAVE SALES[CR]
05 RUN BP MONTH.END.SOP[CR]
06[CR]
07 Backup Sales account prior to running month end procedures[CR]
xf[CR]
MD 'MONTH.END' size = 51 filed
```

In this example a tape device is addressed, the physical tape rewound, an account-save of the account **SALES** is made before the month end program **MONTH.END.SOP** is executed

Example 2

```
:U MD COPY.SOP.ITEMS
MD 'COPY.SOP.ITEMS' NEW ITEM
01 N[CR]
02 COPY SOP.MASTER 1 2 3y[CR]
   4 5 6 [CR]
03 xf[CR]
MD 'COPY.SOP.ITEMS' size = 29 filed
```

In this example the items given by the item-id 1 2 and 3 are copied respectively to item-ids 4 5 and 6 in the file **SOP.MASTER**

Figure 17.1 Examples of macros created using the Update Processor.

17.1.2 Converting a TCL command to a Macro

There is a TCL command **CREATE-MACRO** which creates a macro from the last TCL statement. This is very useful if you have spent time creating a command to do exactly what you require and know that you will want to use it again at some point in the future, which is particularly the case with ACCESS statements. The format of the command is:

CREATE-MACRO *macro.name* {(*options*

where

macro.name is the name of the macro which will be stored in the Master Dictionary
options either **m** or **n** where

- **m** when the macro is called, each command in the macro will be displayed on the screen, allowing it to be edited prior to being run
- **n** when the macro is called, all commands will run without any user intervention being required

You need to remember that the **CREATE-MACRO** command only works on the last TCL command executed, therefore if you have forgotten to run the command after the TCL statement you wanted to 'capture' you will need to call it back from the TCL stack (see Chapter 21 Section 21.13). If you have had to use the TCL stack to recall your command you will first need to execute the command before you can use the **CREATE-MACRO** command. Figure 17.2 shows and example of its use.

:SORT CUSTOMER BY DEPT BY NAME BREAK-ON DEPT NAME TEL TOTAL SALARY
:CREATE-MACRO CUST.TEL
```
CUST.TEL created
```

A macro called **CUST.TEL** is created and stored in the Master Dictionary and contains the ACCESS statement previously typed at TCL. Since no option has been given the macro is created with **m** in attribute 1

Figure 17.2 Converting a TCL statement to a macro

17.2 Menus

In the early versions of PICK, PROCs were used extensively to build menu systems. In the past ten years or so application generators have come onto the scene and one of the tools in their kitbag has been a menu generator. Indeed even after the introduction of Advanced PICK which made the MENU processor available for the first time, companies have been promoting separate menu generator packages.

Since PROC is a complex function which uses buffers and tends not to be an end user tool, the MENU processor makes building menus a much more simple task, but as you will see it is far from being the ideal tool to build menus where consideration for appearance is important.

A menu is a displayed screen which provides the user with a selection of options to choose from. The user can therefore operate the application without having to have any knowledge of Advanced PICK or any of its command language.

Menu selections can execute any TCL command or macro or can call other menus which means a hierarchical tree structure of menus can be built. When considering building menus you should try to ensure that each menu contains no more options than can be displayed on a single screen. Whilst multi-page menus cannot always be avoided, they can sometimes fool users if they cannot immediately see the option they require when they call up a menu.

The name of the menu is stored in the Master Dictionary and is invoked by entering its name, just like the execution of any function stored in the Master Dictionary. The menu is then passed into the MENU processor which formats and displays the menu.

The first attribute of a menu item contains **ME** to tell AP that the item is a menu. The second attribute contains the menu description which is to be displayed above the menu options and describes the purpose of the menu. Each subsequent attribute is a separate menu option and is broken into three values, the description of the menu option, help text for the user on this option, and the function to be executed when menu option is chosen. The format of the menu item is as follows:

000	*Menu name*
001	**ME** *{comments*
002	*Menu Heading (to be displayed at the top of the screen)*
003	*menu option text (which user will see)*
	help message to be displayed (if requested)
	TCL statement (to be executed if user chooses this option)
004	*menu option text (which user will see)*
	help message to be displayed (if requested)
	TCL statement (to be executed if user chooses this option)

The help message is displayed if the user enters a question mark either directly prior to or directly following the menu option number chosen and then presses[CR].

The MENU processor gives no means of formatting the menu in any way. The MENU processor analyses the menu prior to its display and determines how it can divide the options into balanced columns of options. Hence if one menu description is particularly long, it means the options will be displayed in far fewer columns than if the descriptions are short.

The menu is displayed from the bottom of the screen upwards in teletype mode and is generally not the way users expect menus to be displayed. Equally, with Windows as a standard of operation, users will find the inability to use a mouse and to have to select menu options by number slightly antiquated!

Whilst the MENU processor is a significant step forward when comparing it to menus created using PROC, it is not the ideal way of displaying and building menus. Those concerned with creating menus with a modern look and feel will seriously consider the use of 4GL tools or even writing the menu structure in BASIC. Figure 17.3 gives an example of the creation of a menu using the Update Processor.

```
:U MD SLMENU
MD 'SLMENU' NEW ITEM
01 ME This is the main Sales Ledger menu[CR]
02 Sales Ledger Menu[CR]
03 Customer Enquiryv[CR]
   This option provides a Customer Detail enquiryv[CR]
   SLENQ[CR]
04 Transaction Menuv[CR]
   This option displays a list of the transactions that can be performed in the Sales
   Ledgerv[CR]
   STTRAN.MENU[CR]
05 xf[CR]
```

N.B. Notice that **v** *is used to insert a value mark and moves the cursor to the next line, but appends the contents of the next line to the current line preceded with a value mark.*

:SLMENU ◄———— **Invokes the menu**

```
                              Sales Ledger Menu

 1) Customer Enquiry             2) Transaction Menu


Enter number of choice, number? for Help, <RETURN> to exit menu, or verb:
```

Figure 17.3 The creation and presentation of a menu using the MENU processor.

18 The Procedure Language – PROC

TCL verbs and general commands covered in this chapter

LISTPROCS

18.1 An introduction to PROC

PROC the procedure language of the PICK R83 operating system, has in the main been superceded in Advanced PICK by the MACRO and MENU processors as described in the previous chapter. The PROC processor is included in this book for completeness. Many PICK systems still have extensive use of PROCs particularly for their menu systems and it is likely that you will encounter PROCS at some time in your use of PICK-based systems. If, however, you are not involved in taking over an existing system that uses PROCs, ignore this chapter altogether. PROCs, whilst quite powerful, involve learning both a new language and the concepts of using and manipulating data in a series of buffers. Whilst PROC has the ability to validate user input and branch accordingly, functions not available within MACROs and MENUs, this is not an appropriate reason to learn about PROCs – use MACROs and MENUs and handle data validation within a BASIC program.

The PROC language provides a powerful processor which provides a means of storing a number of commands together which can then be invoked from the terminal by a single command. Any sequence of commands that can be typed in at a terminal can be prestored using PROC. In addition, it is possible to take in input from the terminal and validate it, format screens (which makes it eminently suitable for building menu systems), run subroutines and set test conditions and branch in accordance with the results. In essence PROC is the equivalent of a powerful Job Control Language simplifying the day-to-day use of the system.

PROC is not a programming language and was never intended to be so, although it does offer some facilities, like conditional branching, found in programming languages. PROCs are held as items (records) in files and are interpreted at runtime. They are maintained via the system editor (**UP** or **ED**) and the single command name used to call the PROC must exist as an item in the master dictionary. To identify a PROC amongst the other items of the MD, attribute 1 of all PROCs must be PQ.

In order to determine all the PROCs in an account use the verb **LISTPROCS**. In PICK R83, this verb is itself a PROC. In Advanced PICK the PROC has been replaced by a program held in the file **dm,bp**. If the PROC is short, then its entire contents can be held in the master dictionary (MD). However, if the PROC is long and involved, the MD should just contain a pointer to the PROC and the PROC itself should be held in a separate file. The whole purpose of keeping large files outside the MD is to minimize the possibility of having the MD in overflow, the worst file of all to have in overflow.

Having the MD in overflow should be avoided at all costs because of the dramatic effect it has on response times. To store a pointer to a PROC in the MD uses just two lines, the first containing PQ and the second containing the name of the procedure file and the name of the procedure contained in parentheses (as shown in Figure 18.1).

PROC's power and flexibility is achieved by providing four buffers, each with a special purpose, in which data can be manipulated. These buffers are:

PRIMARY INPUT BUFFER	(**PIB**)
SECONDARY INPUT BUFFER	(**SIB**)
PRIMARY OUTPUT BUFFER	(**POB**)
SECONDARY OUTPUT BUFFER	(**SOB**)

As you can see there are two input buffers and two output buffers and all the processing handled by a PROC is handled within these buffers. However, only one input buffer and only one output buffer can be active and in use at any one time. There are commands in PROC to activate and deactivate each of these buffers and to pass information between them.

The primary input buffer is used to contain the exact and total contents of the command line that was typed at TCL to invoke the procedure and will automatically be selected as the current input buffer. If what was typed in at the TCL prompt was just the PROC name, such as **PROCl** then the primary input buffer would just contain the single word **PROCl**. If however the command was longer because it included parameters (extra data), required by the procedure then this would all be placed in the PIB. Hence invoking a procedure by typing in **PROCl A123 B456** would mean the PIB would contain **PROC1 A123 B456**. Each character string separated by a space is called a parameter and can be manipulated independently. Hence if the input buffer contains the string **PROCl A123 B456** it contains three parameters:

PR0C1
A123
B456

The secondary input buffer contains data subsequently input from the keyboard by the user in response to an **IS** command and is also used to hold data from several system processes, notably the spooler. The data is usually checked here before being moved to the secondary output buffer, referred to as ***the stack***. Subsequent data input to this buffer overwrites what was previously

:CT MD PROCl
```
PROC1
001 PQ
002 (PROCFILE PROC1)
```

Figure 18.1 The format of a PROC in the master dictionary.

held. As you may have now realized, the contents of this buffer are extremely volatile and should be viewed purely as a temporary storage area.

The primary output buffer is used to build up the command that will ultimately be executed at TCL. This is the only buffer that enables a new and future TCL command to be executed.

The secondary output buffer is referred to as ***the stack***. It has the ability to stack-up lines of data which can be passed to the procedure one at a time for processing. It is the only buffer whose data can be stacked up in this way.

Figure 18.2 shows how these buffers interrelate. Do remember that many PROC commands are designed to work on the currently active buffer, and only one input and one output buffer can be active at any one time. Thus, when

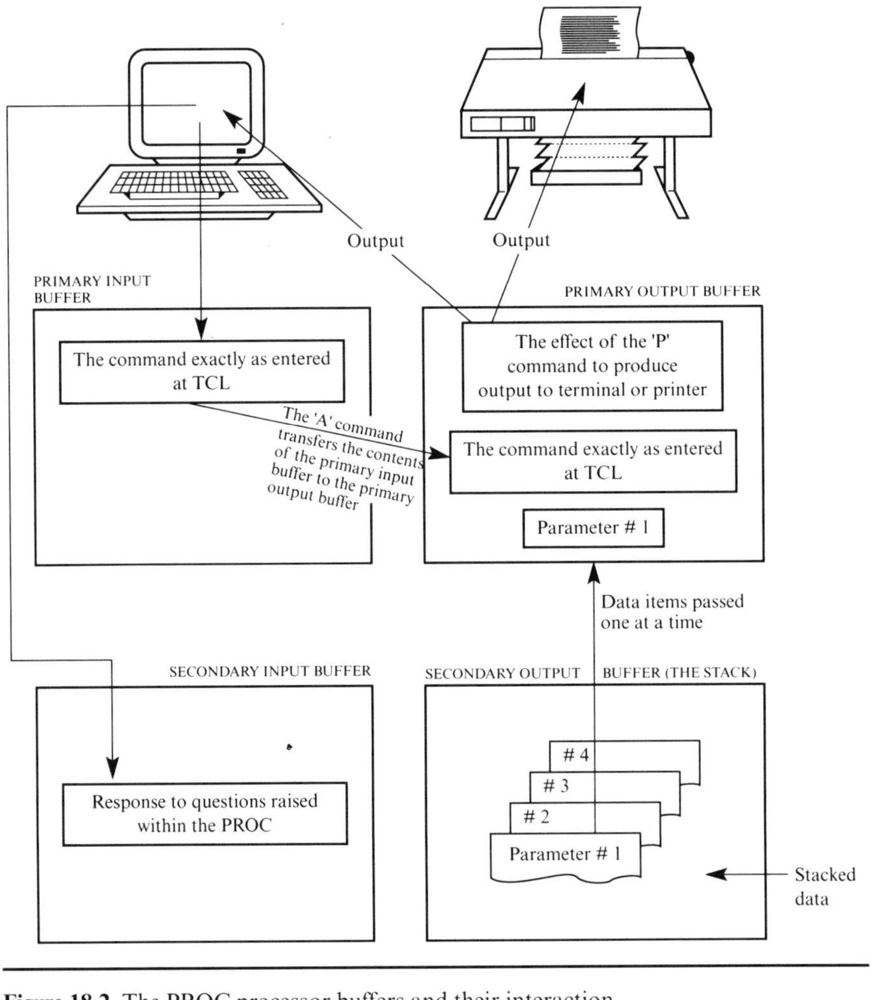

Figure 18.2 The PROC processor buffers and their interaction.

moving data between buffers, the source is the currently active input buffer and the destination is the currently active output buffer.

Another important aspect of the buffers worth noting is that they each have a pointer that points to the current position within the buffer. The purpose of these pointers is to point to a character position within the respective buffers enabling specific strings of characters to be moved to specific positions within the buffers, all of which will become apparent later on. A summary of PROC commands is shown in Figure 18.3.

Command	Description
A	Moves data from current input to current output buffer
B	Moves current input buffer pointer back one parameter
BO	Moves current output buffer pointer back one parameter
C	Comment
D	Display contents of current input buffer on terminal
F	Moves current input buffer pointer forward one parameter
G	Go to a specified statement label
GO	Go to a specified statement label
H	Moves text string to the current output buffer
IF	A test condition to execute specified commands
IH	Moves text string to the current input buffer
IP	Input from terminal into current input buffer
IS	Input from terminal to secondary buffer
IT	Input from tape label into current input buffer
O	Outputs text string on terminal
P	Execute command in primary output buffer
PH	As with P, but suppress the output produced by the command
PP	As with P, but also display contents of both output buffers
PW	As with PP, but wait for user response first
PX	As with P, but return to the TCL prompt not the PROC
RI	Clear (reset) both input buffers
RO	Clear (reset) both output buffer
S	Position the pointer in the current input buffer
SP	Select primary input buffer
SS	Select secondary input buffer
STOFF	Select primary output buffer (stack off)
STON	Select secondary output buffer (stack on)
T	Format output on the terminal
U	Exit to user-defined subroutine
X	Exit to TCL, or calling PROC
+n	Add a number to the parameter in the currently active input buffer
−n	Subtract a number from the parameter in the currently active input buffer
( )	Call another PROC
[ ]	Call subroutine, either local at a statement label or to an external PROC

Figure 18.3 The PROC processor commands.

18.2 A simple PROC using the C, H, P and STOFF commands

With so many commands in the PROC language, it is obviously not possible to cover them all here, although the most commonly used ones are explained. The easiest way to understand these is to see them in action; the others you will find detailed in EPICK (Encyclopedia **PICK** the book or online help facility of Advanced PICK) or if using R83 your PICK manual.

The **P** command will take the contents of the POB and pass it to TCL just as though it had been typed in at the terminal. After the command has been initiated, it will automatically clear both output buffers. A fairly obvious use of PROCs therefore is to hold frequently used and lengthy ACCESS commands. Not only does this speed up their execution, because you don't have to type in the commands each time, but it obviously removes the possibility of typing error! Figure 18.4 shows an example of a PROC containing an ACCESS statement. It also introduces the **C** command which is used to provide comments within the PROC.

Contents of a procedure called PROC1

PROC1

```
001 PQ  <----------------------------------  Defines this item as a PROC
002 C – ACCESS enquiry on STAFF <----------  Comment for clarity
003 HSORT STAFF BY NAME NAME AGE DEPT <----  ACCESS statement moved to POB
004 P <------------------------------------  Execute command in POB by passing
                                             it to TCL
```

The results of using PROC1

```
:PROC1 <-----------------------------------  Execute the PROC; results shown
                                             below

PAGE     1                                       11:42:44 24 OCT 1994

STAFF..  NAME           AGE       DEPT

002      Appleby, J     21        Accounts
011      Atkin, PL      24        Sales
171      Barnett, R     32        Accounts
 |
 v

35 ITEMS LISTED.
```

Figure 18.4 A simple PROC carrying out an ACCESS command.

Figure 18.4 shows how a simple ACCESS statement can be stored in a PROC. As we saw in Chapter 12 on ACCESS, it is important to realize that these statements can get very lengthy indeed. The **H** command for the POB places the buffer pointer at the very end of the string in the POB. This allows any subsequent **H** command to append data after it. The buffer pointer will then move to the end of the entire string. It is not until it encounters the **P** command that the POB contents will be sent to the TCL processor. Using this knowledge therefore we can build a PROC to handle lengthy ACCESS statements, an example of which is shown in Figure 18.5. Notice that the second and subsequent **H** statements are followed by a space. This is essential because each line is concatenated immediately onto the end of the previous one, and trailing spaces are ignored.

Contents of a procedure called PROC2

PROC2

```
001 PQ  <-------------------------------- Defines this item as a PROC
002 C - ACCESS enquiry on STAFF  <------- Comment for clarity
003 HSORT STAFF BY DEPT BY NAME  <------- ACCESS statement moved to POB
004 H BREAK-ON DEPT  <-------------+----- Continuation of the ACCESS
005 H NAME AGE DEPT                +----- statement (notice these start with a space)
006 P  <--------------------------------- Execute command in POB by passing it
                                          to TCL
```

The results of using PROC2

```
:PROC2  <-------------------------------- Execute the PROC; results shown
                                          below
```

```
PAGE    1                                     11:44:44 24 OCT 1994

STAFF..  NAME              AGE     DEPT

002      Appleby, J        21      Accounts
17       Barnett, R        32      Accounts
                                   ***

045      Johnson, JK       28      Administration
 |
 v

35 ITEMS LISTED.
```

Figure 18.5 A PROC to carry out a lengthy ACCESS statement.

18.3 The use of the stack

Within procedures there is often the need to pass parameters. Consider the TCL command COPY, which following its use, for example **COPY STAFF O2O**, will prompt with the question TO: and await input. We can handle this in a PROC by ensuring the necessary response is contained in the secondary output buffer, the place the procedure processor will first look for these answers. If it cannot find any data in ***the stack*** (the Secondary Output Buffer) then it will prompt for the data on the terminal. Figure 18.6 gives an example of the use of the stack. Notice that any input placed on the stack is followed by a < to simulate a carriage return. This is the normal keyboard symbol, for "less than" and does not use the control key.

PROC3	
001 PQ ←	Defines this item as a PROC
002 C - - TCL COPY command ←	Comment for clarity
003 HCOPY STAFF 010 ←	TCL COPY statement moved to SOB
004 STON ←	Turn stack on and make SOB active
005 H098< ←	Store data on stack – *notice* the <
006 STOFF ←	Turn stack off and make SOB active
007 P ←	Execute command in SOB by passing it to TCL
:PR0C3 ←	Execute the PROC; results shown below

```
1 010 to 098

1 ITEMS COPIED
```

Figure 18.6 A simple PROC using the stack.

PR0C4	
001 PQ	
002 C – - RUN PROGRAM PROGI ~-	
003 STON ←	Turn stack on and make SOB active
004 HA123< ←	Store data on stack – *notice* the <
005 HB456< ←	The second line on the stack
006 HC789< ←	The third line on the stack
007 HD012< ←	The fourth line on the stack
008 STOFF ←	Turn stack off and make POB active
006 HRUN BP PROGI ←	Write this statement into the POB
007 P ←	Execute command in POB by passing it to TCL

Figure 18.7 A PROC taking data from the stack.

Whilst Figure 18.6 just showed one line being added to the stack it is possible to add as many lines to the SOB as required. Assuming we were running a program that required four separate parameters, we could easily include these in a PROC and Figure 18.7 shows how this would be handled. Beware: when building your PROC to only build the stack relating to the next command to be executed using the **P** statement – the **P** command clears both output buffers.

18.4 Screen formatting and cursor control

Formatting a screen and controlling the cursor are handled by the **T** command. The command has the following format:

T {*function*}, {*function*}, ...

the **T** must be followed by one of the following options:

'*string*'	Displays the string of characters at the current cursor position
B	Sounds the terminal bell
C	Clear screen
Inn	Displays the integer character nn
Xnn	Displays the hex character nn
(*x*,*y*)	Positions the cursor at column *x*, row *y*
(-1)	Clears the screen
(-2)	Positions the cursor in the home position (0,0)
(-3)	Clears from cursor position to end of the screen
(-4)	Clears from cursor to the end of the line
(-5)	Starts blinking
(-6)	Stops blinking
(-7)	Starts protected field
(-8)	Ends protected field
(-9)	Backspace by one character
(-10)	Up one line

Figure 18.8 illustrates use of the **T** command. The result of Figure 18.8 is to produce a screen layout that offers text-processing options and which would be presented to the user as shown in Figure 18.9.

In Figure 18.8 we have been introduced to three commands which are relatively self-explanatory: **RI**, **RO** and **IP**. These stand for **R**eset (clear) **I**nput buffers, **R**eset **O**utput buffers and **I**n**P**ut to current input buffer, respectively. The **IP** command can optionally be followed by a character which represents the prompt character to be used. Hence **IP?** would cause a question mark to be displayed at the current cursor position and the cursor would await for data to be entered.

Data input by **IP** is placed in the PIB and replaces the parameter being pointed to, or if the pointer is at the end of the data, appends the inputted data to it.

```
TEXT-MENU
001 PQ
002 10C —- DISPLAY TEXT PROCESSING MAIN MENU
003 T (-1) ◄———————— Clear screen
004 T (25,0),"T e x t P r o c e s s i n g" ◄—— Display text for all lines beginning with T
005 T(0,3), "——————————————————————-"
006 T (0,5), "FILE MANAGEMENT"
007 T (20,5)" 1 : List Text Files"
008 T (20,6), " 2 : Create Text File"
009 T (20, 7), " 3 : Delete Text File"
010 T (0,9),'DOCUMENT MANAGEMENT"
011 T (20,9),"4 : List Documents"
012 T (20,10)," 5 : Word Process Document"
013 T (20,11), " 6 : Edit Document"
014 T (20,12)," 7: Copy Document"
015 T (20,13)," B : Delete Document"
016 T (20,14)," 9 : Print Document"
017 T (20,15),"10 : Merge & Print Document"
018 T (20,16),"11 : Runoff Document"
019 T (20,17),"12 : Merge & Runoff Document"
020 T (0, 19), "PRINTER CONTROL"
021 T (20, 19), "13 : List Printer Output"
022 T (20, 20), "14 : Kill Printer Output"
023 100 C —- INPUT OPTIONS
024 T (0,2), "SELECT MEMU OPTION                "(19,2)
025 RI ◄———————— Clear INPUT buffers
026 RO ◄———————— Clear OUTPUT buffers
027 IP ◄———————— Accept input from the terminal
```

Figure 18.8 Screen formatting within a PROC.

18.5 Moving parameters with the A command

The **A** command moves one parameter from the currently active input buffer to the currently active output buffer. The command has the following format:

A {*c*} {*p*} {,*n*}

where

c is the character that surrounds the parameter
p is the position of the parameter being moved
n is the number of characters to be moved

If the surround character is omitted, the parameter will be moved exactly as it is with surrounding blanks. If the surround character is a backslash (\), the

```
                    T e x t P r o c e s s i n g
                    ----------------------------

SELECT MENU OPTION __

     FILE MANAGEMENT                 1 : List Text Files
                                     2 : Create Text File
                                     3 : Delete Text File

     DOCUMENT MANAGEMENT             4 : List Documents
                                     5 : Word Process Document
                                     6 : Edit Document
                                     7 : Copy Document
                                     8 : Delete Document
                                     9 : Print Document
                                     10: Merge & Print Document
                                     11: Runoff Document
                                     12: Merge & Runoff Document

     PRINTER CONTROL                 13 : List Printer Output
                                     14 : Kill Printer Output
```

Figure 18.9 The screen presented to the user from the PROC listed in Figure 18.8.

surrounding blanks are omitted. If the position parameter is left out the parameter that will be moved is the one currently being pointed to. The surround character is extremely valuable in building an ACCESS statement where the input from the terminal has to be enclosed in double quotes.

After the execution of the **A** command the input buffer pointer points to the very next character after the string that was moved. Figure 18.10 shows an example of the **A** statement where input from the terminal is used to build an ACCESS statement.

18.6 Conditional operations with IF and GO

The IF statement allows you to test for a condition and take action dependent on the result. The format of the IF statement is:

IF [#]A–cmd PROC–cmd

where

equates to NOT
A–cmd is any valid form of the A command
PROC–cmd is any valid PROC command

The Go or G statement transfers control unconditionally to the PROC statement which starts with the label. The label must be a number and the statement containing the label must start with the label and can contrain any PROC command, but the command must follow on from the single space following the label number. If the label referenced does not exist, the PROC will continue to the next sequential statement following the branch command.

These two statements are used together and Figure 18.11 shows how they are used to check the validity of the department number input. This check is incorporated in the example of a PROC shown in Figure 18.10.

The IF statement can also be used to check for a specific pattern of characters in a string. The pattern specification is enclosed in parentheses and consists of any combination of the following:

- an integer number followed by the letter N which tests for that number of numeric characters;
- an integer number followed by the letter A which tests for that number of alphabetic characters;
- an integer number followed by the letter X which tests for that number of alphanumeric characters;

Hence IF # (2'–'3N) G 50 would go to the statement label 50 if the string was not in the format, two alpha characters followed by a hyphen followed by three numberic characters.

The **IF** statement allows you to test for a condition and take action dependent on the result. There are three possible formats of the **IF** statement as follows:

IF {#} **E** {*MESSAGE.NUMBER*} *PROC.COMMAND*
IF {#} **S** *PROC.COMMAND*
IF {#} **A**{*PARAM.NUMBER*}{,*n*} {*OPERATOR* {*MATCH.STRING*}}
PROC.COMMAND

In its first format, the **E** operand tests for a specified message number from the **dm,messages,** file (**ERRMSG** in PICK R83). If true, the specified PROC command given by *PROC.COMMAND* is executed. Hence you can check whether any system error has occurred without having to check for a specific error message number by using **IF E**. It is possible however to check for specific error message numbers by including the error message number in the statement. Thus **IF** *E* **1169 G 50** would go to statement label **50** if the error message 1169 (an illegal printer number) was encountered. This facility is often used to check the existence of a file (message number 201) or to check whether any items have been selected by ACCESS (message number 401) before a report is run. A complete list of error message numbers and their meanings can be found in Appendix A.

Another useful version of the **IF** command, is the second format with the **S** option. **IF S** is used to test for an active list and hence can be used after a **SELECT**, **SSELECT**, **QSELECT** or **GET-LIST** command and Figure 18.11 gives an example of its use.

The contents of a procedure called PROC5

```
PROC5
PQ                                      <---- Defines the item as a PROC
10 C------------DISPLAY MENU            <---- Comment for clarity
T (-1)                                  <---- Clear screen
C Display headings and display request' for dept
T (25,0),'E n q u i r y b y D e p t"
T (4,3),"------------------------------------------------------------"
T (10, 5), "Input Dept Number (001-012)"
STOFF                                   <---- Stack off, primary output buffer active
HSORT STAFF BY NAME WITH                <---- Start of ACCESS command
H DEPTNO =
C POB now contains 'SORT STAFF BY NAME WITH DEPTNO
T (38,5)                                <---- Position cursor ready for input of data
SP                                      <---- Select PIB as active
IP                                      <---- Data input moved into PIB
A"1                                     <---- Move 1st parameter of PIB to POB
                                              enclosed in double quotes
C POB = SORT STAFF BY NAME WITH DEPTNO = "nnn"
H NAME AGE DEPTNO                       <---- Remainder of ACCESS statement
P                                       <---- Execute command from POB
```

The results of using PROC5

```
:PROC5   <----   Execute the PROC; results shown below

                         E n q u i ry by D e p t
     ------------------------------------------------------------

                     Input Dept Number (001-012) 001

PAGE    1                                        11:42:44 24 OCT 1994

STAFF..  NAME            AGE       DEPT

002      Appleby, J      21        Accounts
171      Barnett, R      32        Accounts
  |
  v
12 ITEMS LISTED.
```

Figure 18.10 The use of the **A** command within PROC.

The last format of the **IF** statement tests the contents of the buffer location specified in the **A**{*PARAM.NUMBER*}{,*n*} expression with any logical or pattern matching operator, and performs the specified *PROC.COMMAND* command if successful. The optional **,n** argument allows only the specified number of characters to be compared.

The logical operators which are allowed in constructing PROC conditionals are as follows:

```
PQ
HGET-LIST  <------------------  Build up the TCL command
OENTER LIST NAME+  <----------  The + holds the cursor at the end of the word NAME
IP?  <------------------------  Input the list name
A
STON  <-----------------------  Turn Stack on and make SOB active
H
P  <--------------------------  Process the GET-LIST command
IF #S XNON EXISTENT LIST!  <--  If no list found eXit PROC with the message NON
                                EXISTENT LIST!
HSORT STAFF BY DEPT DEPT NAME TEL  <-  If an active list is found execute this
                                       ACCESS statement
P
```

Figure 18.11 Use of **IF** to check the existence of a list.

=	equal to
#	not equal to (the # character tests for the absence of the expression, when used on the left of the **A** command)
<	less than
>	greater than
[	less than or equal to
]	greater than or equal to

Whilst the pattern matching operators for composing 'match.strings' are as follows:

(*n***a**)	accepts *n* alphabetic characters only
(*n***n**)	accepts *n* numeric characters only
(*n***x**)	accepts *n* characters of any character
('*string*')	accepts the literal *string*

The *n* parameter in the pattern match string specifies the length of the match operator field. A length specification of zero (0) allows variable length input. The parentheses are required around the match.strings. Figure 18.12 gives some other examples of the **IF** conditional expression.

The **GO** or **G** statement transfers control unconditionally to the PROC statement which starts with the label. The label must be a number and the statement containing the label must start with the label and can contain any PROC command, but the command must follow on from the single space following the label number. If the label referenced does not exist, the PROC will continue to the next sequential statement following the branch command. The statement can also be used in conjunction with **A** statement to get the value from the input buffer. Hence **GO A1** means branch to the PROC statement with the number found as the first parameter in the input buffer.

IF E = 401 XNO ITEMS WERE SELECTED...
Checks for error message 401 and if found e**X**its the PROC with the message 'NO ITEMS WERE SELECTED'

IF A # (3N'-'2N'-'4N) OINVALID PART NUMBER
Checks for 3 numbers, a dash, 2 numbers, a dash, and 4 more numbers and if the input is not in this format Outputs the message 'INVALID PART NUMBER'

IF A = X XDONE.
Checks the currently active input buffer location for the presence of the letter X and if it is found e**X**its the PROC displaying the message 'DONE'

IF A = (0N) GO 10
Checks the currently active input buffer location for the presence of null or a number of any length and if a match is found, branches to the PROC statement given by the label **10**. Patten matches are the same as with the pattern match correlative

IF A1,1 = Q X
Checks the first character of the currently active input buffer location for the presence of the letter Q and if found e**X**its the PROC

IF # A1 GO 10
Checks for the absence of a value in the first location of the currently active input buffer and if nothing is there branches to the PROC statement given by the label **10**

Figure 18.12 Examples of the **IF** statement.

The two statements, **IF** and **GO**, are used together and Figure 18.13 shows how they are used to check the validity of the department number input.

18.7 Linking to other PROCs

18.7.1 Transferring control to another PROC

A command in one PROC can transfer control directly to another, which may be resident in any dictionary or data file. This is achieved by enclosing the location of the PROC in parentheses and has the general format:

({**DICT**} *filename* {*item-id*}) {*n*}

where

filename	is name of the file containing the PROC to which to transfer control
item-id	is the name of the PROC
n	is optional. If used, control is passed to the line whose label is n

Figure 18.14 shows an example of linking PROCs in this way. In this example, control is passed to the item in the file **MASTERPROCS** whose item-id matches the input from the **IS** command, providing it is in the range **001-080**.

```
        PROC5
PQ
10 C----------- DISPLAY MENU
RI
RO
T (-1)
T (25,0),'E n q u i r y b y D e p t"
T (4,3),"-------------------------------------
T (10, 5), "Input Dept Number (001-012)"
STOFF
HSORT STAFF BY NAME WITH
H DEPTNO =
T (38,5)
SP
IP
IF # A1 G 900 <----------  If parameter 1 is missing go to label 900
IF A1 < 001 G 900 <--------  Test value input for validity. Must be between 1 and 12
                             to be correct
IF A1 > 012 G 900
A"1
C POB NOW CONTAINS SORT STAFF BY NAME WITH DEPTNO = "nnn"
H NAME AGE DEPTNO
P        <-------------------Execute command from POB
G 999
900 T (38,10),"That number is out of range"
T (38,11),"Press RETURN to continue"
IP
G10
999 X
```

Figure 18.13 The use of conditional statements within a PROC.

```
PQ
10 T (-1)
T (0,2),"INPUT TASK TO BE RUN"
IS?
IF #A G 900
IF A < 001 G 900
IF A > 080 G 900
(MASTERPROCS#A)
900 XILLEGAL RESPONSE
G 10
```

Figure 18.14 Transferring control to another PROC.

18.7.2 Using another PROC as a subroutine

If instead of passing implicit control to another procedure, you require to use a PROC as a subroutine within another, the called PROC has to be enclosed in square brackets. Once the called PROC has completed, control is returned to the PROC that initiated the call. The general format of the command is:

[{**DICT**} *filename* {*item-id*}**]** {*n*}

where

filename	is name of the file containing the PROC to which to transfer control
item-id	is the name of the PROC
n	is optional. If used, control is passed to the line whose label is n

This principle is used extensively in menu systems where a main menu controls a series of submenus. When a program is run from a submenu and its operation is complete, the submenu is redisplayed. Pressing [CR] at the submenu recalls the main menu enabling an alternative submenu to be called. Figure 18.15 gives an example of this principle.

The PROC called **TEXT-MENU**

```
PQ
10 C     DISPLAY MENU
T (-1)                              Clear screen
T (25,0),"T e x t P r o c e s s i n g"
T (0,3),"------------------------------------------------------------
T (0,5),"PRINTER CONTROL"
T (20,6), "1 : List Printer Output"
T (20,7)," 2 : Kill Printer Output"
100 C----------INPUT OPTION
T (0,2),"SELECT MENU OPTION ",(19,2)
RI  <----------------------------------  Reset both input buffers
RO  <----------------------------------  Reset both output buffers
IP  <----------------------------------  Input response from terminal
IF #AI G 900  <------------------------  If null response, i.e. [CR] exit
IF AI = 1 G 500
IF AI = 2 G 500
G 100  <-------------------------------  If invalid response rerun PROC
500 C PROCESS OPTION
IF AI = 1 [PICK.UTILITY TEXT-OUTPUT]  <--  Call PROC TEXT-OUTPUT
IF AI = 2 [PICK. UTILITY TEXT-KILL]  <---  Call PROC TEXT-KILL
T (0,23),"Press Return To Continue "+  <--  Point at which called PROCs return
IP:
G 10  <--------------------------------  Rerun PROC
900 C  END TEXT PROCESSING
T (-1)  <------------------------------  Clear screen
OTEXT SYSTEM FINISHED  <---------------  Display message, return to TCL
```

Figure 18.15 The calling of PROCs as subroutines.

The PROC called **TEXT-OUTPUT**

```
PQ
HLISTPEQS
P
X ◄———————————————— Exit PROC, return to calling PROC
```

The PROC called **TEXT-KILL**

```
PQ
10 C--------DISPLAY SCREEN
T (-I)
T (13,0),"T e x t P r o c e s s i n g – Kill Printer Output"
T (0,3),"
100 C----------INPUT OPTIONS
T (20,5),"Printer Number 0"
T (35,5)
S1
IH0
IP
IF #AI G 900
500 C----------PROCESS
T (0,18)
RO
HSP-KILL
AI
P
X ◄———————————————— End of PROC return to calling PROC

900 C   EXIT
```

Figure 18.15 *Continued*

18.8 Printer control under PROC

Printers can be controlled within PROCs using information from the error message handler and the verb LISTPTR, both of which feed information into the secondary input buffer. Do remember that the information in the secondary input buffer is volatile. Hence, if the information needs to be held, it should first be saved.

Figure 18.16 shows the output from a typical **LISTPTR** verb and the data it passes to the secondary input buffer.

If you run into difficulties building procedures using these principles, the contents of the secondary input buffer can be displayed by including the statements **SS** and **D0** following the **P**. Hence the information shown in Figure 18.16 can be displayed using:

```
PQ
HLISTPTR
P
SS
D0
```

Normal output from LISTPTR

Type	Number	Output Queues	Page Skip	Dev or Line #	Status
SERIAL	0	0 2	0	0	INACTIVE
SERIAL	1	1	1	3	ACTIVE

Information passed to Secondary Input Buffer

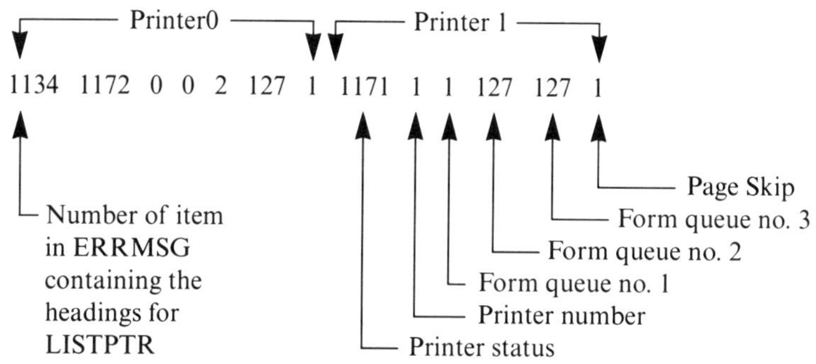

Note: a form queue number of 127 means that the form queue number has not been assigned

Figure 18.16 The data passed by **LISTPTR** to the SIB.

Checking the status of printers within PROCs can become necessary where a printer in general use has to be allocated to a specific task. Figure 18.17 explains the way in which this is handled.

PQ	
HSTOPPTR 0	Stop the printer
P	Execute the command
SS	Select secondary input buffer (SIB)
B	Move pointer for SIB back one parameter
10 IF #A G 30	If no more data go to label 30
IF A = 1171 G 100	If printer inactive go to label 100
IF A = 1174 G 100	If printer unallocated go to 100
IF A = 1172 G 20	If printer busy go to label 20
F	Get next parameter
G 10	Loop around the test
20 HSLEEP 5	Sleep for five seconds
30 HLISTPTR 3	List printer status
P	Execute LISTPTR command

Figure 18.17 The control of printers using PROC.

PROC statement	Explanation
SS	Select SIB
B	Move pointer for SIB back one parameter
40 IF A = 1134 G 10	Test for correct message number
IF # A G 999	Incorrect message number
F	Get next parameter
G 40	Loop around test
50 F	Get next parameter
IF # A G999	Nothing present
IF A = 1171 G 100	If printer inactive go to label 100
IF A = 1174 G 100	If printer unallocated go to 100
IF A = 1172 G 60	If printer busy go to label 60
XTHE BUFFER CONTAINS BAD DATA	An unknown printer status
60 OTHER PRINTER IS ACTIVE DO YOU WANT TO WAIT(Y/N)+	
SP	Set pointer to primary input buffer
IP?	Input response to question
IF A = Y G 20	Continue, pausing for 5 seconds
X	Exit PROC
100 HSTARTPTR 3,2,2,S2	Start printer as form queue 2
P	Execute the command
(remainder of PROC)	
999 OFINISHED	End of PROC

Figure 18.17 *Continued*

Whilst providing an extremely useful, flexible and powerful facility, the buffer principle of PROC is difficult to grasp and its language a little forbidding to the uninitiated! The MENU and MACRO processors of Advanced PICK coupled with the **EXECUTE** statement in BASIC obviates the need to learn PROC and for new incumbents to PICK this may be helpful. It should be borne in mind, however, that PROC is still a major element of the earlier PICK operating systems.

19 The OUTPUT PROCESSOR and RUNOFF

TCL verbs and general commands covered in this chapter are

OP	RUNOFF

19.1 An introduction to the OUTPUT PROCESSOR and RUNOFF

The OUTPUT PROCESSOR (OP) formats and prints text from commands embodied in the text of a document and is the successor to RUNOFF the R83 PICK utility that carried out a similar task. The OUTPUT PROCESSOR can be used to extract data directly from the PICK database, to format it and incorporate it within a document. It is the facility from within PICK that allows for the preparation of documents and manuals. It supports:

- automatic index and table of contents
- automatic numbering of chapters, sections, figures and tables
- boldfacing
- font control
- heading and footings
- proportional spacing (both horizontal and vertical)
- text formatting
- underlining.

The OUTPUT PROCESSOR has greatly enhanced the facilities which were available in RUNOFF. The control codes or commands mostly have both a long and abbreviated form and both are given in the command summary in Section 18.2. The OUTPUT PROCESSOR treats each attribute as a paragraph and control codes can be embedded anywhere in the text within that attribute. RUNOFF text was traditionally prepared using the Editor or a word processor such as JET but with the advent of Advanced PICK, text can also be input using the UPDATE PROCESSOR.

In the OUTPUT PROCESSOR the command is preceded with a space and a full stop and with RUNOFF they are preceded just by a full stop but the commands have to be on a line on their own. The commands within the text indicate such features as headings, footings, page numbering, bold text, underlined text and so on but in addition both the OUTPUT PROCESSOR and RUNOFF can compile a table of contents and an index, which makes them ideal for the preparation of manuals if you have no access to the standard DOS word processors. The use of both products is very straightforward. They require little discussion since from the summary of commands shown below their operation can be easily picked up with very little use. However, in addition to the summary of commands, this section does highlight some useful and not so obvious features. Since some of the RUNOFF commands are not the same as their replacements in the OUTPUT PROCESSOR the commands for each have been summarized separately.

19.2 OUTPUT PROCESSOR command summary

The format required to use the following command set is as follows:

<space> . <space> *command* {<space> or next *command*}

In other words the first OUTPUT PROCESSOR command must be preceded with a space, but can be immediately followed by other OUTPUT PROCESSOR commands which themselves may be preceded by a space, but this space character is optional.

*
The entire line following an asterisk is treated as a remark and ignored by the OUTPUT PROCESSOR.

.appendix *title*
.apx *title*
Alphabetically assigns letters to appendix titles and creates entries in the Table of Contents following those for chapters.

.begin page
.bp
Start at the top of the next page (begin a new page).

.block center
.bc
Centres all text following this command until an **.xblock center** or **.xbc** command is encountered

.boldface
.bf
Turns on the printer emboldening and all characters from this point will be emboldened until a **.xboldface** or **.xbf** command is encountered.

.box {*c1*,*c2*{,*c3*,*c4*}}
Draws a box starting a column position *c1* and ending in column position *c2*. The length of the box is determined by the text following the command, however any text in column *c1* and column *c2* will be overwritten by the box. If no parameters are specified the box is drawn on the left and right margins and the text margins are reduced to fit inside the box. If *c2* is not specified the right-hand side of the box is drawn on the right-hand margin.

A second box can be drawn alongside the first by specifying *c3* and *c4* in which *c3* must be greater than *c1* and *c4* greater than *c2*.

All text is enclosed in a box until a **.xbox** command is encountered. If two **.box** commands are encountered one after the other without an intervening **.xbox** then the second **.box** commands terminates that of the first and a new box with the parameters of the second **.box** command is started.

.break
.bk
Starts a new paragraph with the text immediately following the break command.

.cap sentences
.cs
Capitalizes the first letter of each sentence, leaving those already capitalised. The first letter of each attribute plus all those following a **.** (full stop) **?** (question mark) and **!** (exclamation mark) [only where each symbol is followed by a space] will be capitalized.

.center
.c
Centres the text on the line immediately following the command. Since this only works for text on the following line there is no command to turn off the centring. To centre more than one line use the **.block center** or **.bc** commands.

.chain {{**dict**} *file.name*} *item.id*
Start processing the text given by the file path in the **.chain** command. The OUTPUT PROCESSOR does not return from the 'chained' document, hence if you want to print multiple chapters a master item is set up with **.chain** commands for each chapter and the master item is processed in the TCL verb **OP** which invokes the OUTPUT PROCESSOR.

.chapter *title*
.ch *title*
Initiates the start of a new chapter which is started at the top of a new page. The chapter number is printed at the top of the new page after the word **Chapter** and the title printed two lines beneath that, both of which are centred

on the page. If you wish to use different layouts, the **.set chapter** command lets you determine these parameters. If chapter numbering is suppressed the chapter title is printed at the top of the page.

.char {*delimiter*} *characters* {*delimiter*}
This command is used to send a string of characters to the printer or terminal which is not interpreted as text to be printed. This is useful where you want to send printer set-up sequences to initiate special functions, such as different fonts, pitches or to turn the printer in landscape mode.

.col*n* *text*{**.col***n+1* *text*} {**.col***n+2* *text*} {..} {**.col***n+6* *text*}
Formats the *text* into columns whose width has already been set with a preceding **.columns set** or **.variable columns** command. A maximum of seven columns can be specified and each **.col** command must be followed by a number between **1** and **7** indicating the column in which the subsequent *text* is to be printed. Once a **.col** command is encountered where the column number specified is less than that of the previous **.col** command, the line of text is printed and a new one started.

.columns set *heading1,width1,space1*
{*;heading 2,width2,space2) (..)*
{*heading7,width7,space7*}
.columns *heading1,width1,space1*
{*;heading 2,width2,space2) (..)*
{*heading7,width7,space7*}
Specifies the column heading, column width and the spacing between the column and the next column. The *heading* text may itself contain OUTPUT PROCESSOR commands. The column heading is put at the top of each page after the header details and the output will continue in column mode until a **.xcolumns** command is encountered.

.crt
Directs all subsequent output to the terminal even if the OUTPUT PROCESSOR was invoked with the (**P** (printer) option. To redirect further text to the printer use **.line printer** and remember when mixing text between output devices that the OUTPUT PROCESSOR uses the TERM settings when working out its pagination.

.cursor {*column*}{*,row*}
Is used to place text at a specific column and row position. If either parameter is not specified in subsequent **.cursor** commands the values of the previous **.cursor** command is used. Since the OUTPUT PROCESSOR does not take these commands into account, pagination and line wrapping may be a problem.

.date
Outputs the current date in the format **month day, year** (i.e. May 8, 1995).

.default
.df
Sets the device to its default font setting. If the printer has no default font this command has no effect.

.em *n*
Is used for inserting spaces into text on laser printers to ensure the correct alignment. The command inserts one to the **em**th spaces into the text. Hence **.em 1** inserts a single space **.em 2** inserts $\frac{1}{2}$ a space, **.em 4** inserts $\frac{1}{4}$ of a space and so on.

.figure *text*
.fig *text*
This function sequentially numbers figures using the current chapter number followed by a dash and the next sequential number within that chapter. The *text* and sequential number are recorded in the table of contents under the heading **Figures**. If chapter numbers are suppressed, the figures are just given sequential numbers.

.font *n*
.f *n*
Selects the *n*th font defined for the device. This command has no effect on devices that do not support multiple fonts.

.font *orientation,symbolset,spacing,pointsize,pitch,style,strokeweight,typeface*
.f *orientation,symbolset,spacing,pointsize,pitch,style,strokeweight,typeface*
where the valid options are

orientation	**portrait** or **landscape**
symbolset	**ASCII** or **legal** or **roman8** or **linedraw**
spacing	**proportional** or **fixed**
pointsize	specify the point size required
pitch	specify the required pitch
style	**upright** or **italic** or **reverse**
strokeweight	**light** or **lightmedium** or **mediumlight** or **medium** or **mediumbold** or **boldmedium** or **bold**
typeface	any of the types defined in the devices file for the printer being used

.footing " {{*text* }{'*options*'}....}"
.ft " {{*text* }{'*options*'}....}"
Where *text* is the text to be printed at the foot of each page. If the line following the footing command is null the footing is suppressed. The valid options which are the same as those within ACCESS, BASIC and RUNOFF are as follows:

''	(Two single quotes). Outputs (one) single quote
'attr.name'	Inserts the value of 'attr.name'. Processes any conversion codes, but not correlatives in the attribute defining item.

b	Inserts the attribute name causing the break if the b option has been specified with 'roll-on' (in AP) or 'break-on' (R83 only).
c	Centres the output line.
d	Inserts the current date (format dd mmm yyyy).
f{*n*}	Inserts the file name; {in a field of 'n' blanks}.
j	Right-justifies the rest of the line. (AP only)
l	Issues a carriage return and line feed.
n	Prevents the pause at the end of each page (like NOPAGE modifier) (AP only).
p	Inserts the current page number, right-justified in a field of four blanks.
p*n*	Inserts the current page number, left justified. (R83 only)
p{*n*}	Inserts the page number, right-justified in a field of *n* blanks. (default *n*=4). (AP only)
r	Inserts the Roman numeral page number. (AP only)
s	Toggles on italics mode. (AP only)
t	Inserts the current time and date (format hh:mm:ss dd mmmyyyy).
u	Toggles on underline mode. (AP only)
v	Toggles on boldface mode. (AP only)
xc	Used with c to centre a segment. The xc delimits the end of the segment. (AP only)
xs	Toggles off italics mode. (AP only)
xu	Toggles off underline mode. (AP only)
xv	Toggles off boldface mode. (AP only)

.gohanging tab
.ght
Indents text to the position set by the previous **.hanging tab** command.

.hangingtab {*number*}
.ht {*number*}
Sets a tab at a specific column determined by *number*. To reset the margin place a **.ht** command at the appropriate column position.

.heading " {{*text* }{'*options*'}....}"
.hd " {{*text* }{'*options*'}....}"
Defines the heading to be printed at the top of each page. The list of valid *options* is shown in the **.footing** command.

.hilite *character*
.hi *character*
Prints the *character* in the right margin until a **.xhilite** or .**xhi** is encountered.

.indent {*n*}
.i {*n*}
Indents text *n* spaces from the left hand margin. If *n* is a negative number, the line begins *n* characters to the left of the previously set left-hand margin. If not specified *n* defaults to 1. If the command is in the middle of some text, the word following this command begins a new paragraph indented by *n* spaces.

.indent margin {*n*}
.im {*n*}
This has the same functionality as **.indent** except that the change to the left margin is permanent until the next **.indent margin** command is encountered.

.indent rmargin *n*
.irm *n*
The command is used to increase the right margin by *n* spaces. It will decrease the margin if *n* is a negative number. If the command is in the middle of some text, the word following this command begins a new paragraph with a right margin of *n* spaces. The command does not effect the left hand margin in any way.

.index{:} {'*main heading*'}'*phrase*' {'*phrase*'.....}
.ix{:} {'*main heading*'}'*phrase*' {'*phrase*'.....}
The **.INDEX** command is used to insert a phrase together with its page number into the index. If the colon (:) is not specified the phrase (which must be enclosed in quote marks) and its page number appear on the same line. To specify a subheading, where the main heading appears on the first line of the index entry and the subsequent text with its page number on the next line, insert a colon (:) immediately after the command name.

.index heading *heading text*
.ixh *heading text*
This will use the *heading text* (which should not be included in quote marks) as the header for the index pages.

.input
.in
This command accepts text input from the keyboard and inserts it into the main body of the text at the point of the command.

.italics
.it
Causes all text following this command to be italicized until a **.xitalics** or **.xit** command is encountered.

.justify
.j
All text following this command is right justified (by inserting extra spacing into the text line) until a **.xjustify** or **.xj** command is processed.

.left margin *n*
.lm *n*
Sets the left margin *n* spaces from the left margin and remains in effect until a **.indent margin** or **.im** or another **.left margin** or **.lm** or the command **.standard** or **.std** is processed.

.line length *n*
.ll *n*
Sets the line length to *n* characters from the left margin.

.line printer
.lp
Sends all subsequent output to the currently assigned line printer.

.lpi *n*
Sets the printer to *n* lines per inch.

.macro file *file.name*
.mf *file.name*
Specifies the name of the file containing items to be included in the document. The item-id of the macro must not contain any full stops, nor be any of the command names used in the OUTPUT PROCESSOR, since the item-id itself has to be preceded by a full stop (.) so that the OUTPUT PROCESSOR can differentiate it from normal text. Once the macro has been processed control returns to the original document item. Unless a *file.name* (which can be a file path, where the account containing the file is specified) is specified the macro must reside in the current file.

.over char *character*
.oc *character*
Whatever character is specified is used as an 'override' character to allow OUTPUT PROCESSOR commands to be treated as text. The default override character is the underscore (_).

.page length *n*
.pl *n*
Sets the page length to *n* lines.

.page number *n*
.pn *n*
Sets the current page number to *n* and numbers all subsequent pages from this number.

.paging
.pg
Forces a key to be pressed at the end of each page displayed on the terminal. This can be switched off by **.xpaging** or **.xp.**

.paragraph *n*
.p *n*
Specifies that each paragraph should have the first line indented *n* characters from the left margin, but will ONLY work where the first character of the paragraph is a space. If *n* is negative the first line is output *n* characters prior to the left margin setting.

.preface *text*
.pf *text*
This is the command to set automatic preface formatting where the *text* is centred at the top of the page and page numbering is reset to 1. Page numbers are set in the header or footer using the **r** option. In the table of contents preface numbering is shown in roman numerals.

.prefix page
.pp
The current chapter number is used as a prefix with the page number for each chapter starting at 1. Hence page numbers will be in the format *chapter number – page number*.

.print index
.pi
This command changes the tab settings and begins a new page. The index is sorted in alphabetical order and printed in two columns per page. The generated index will be lost unless a **.save index** or **.si** command is issued.

.print ptoc
.pptoc
This command prints a partial table of contents for all the **.appendix .chapter .figure .section** and **.table** commands used since the last **.print toc** or **.ptoc** command was issued.

.print toc
.ptoc
Prints a complete table of contents for all **.appendix .chapter .figure .prefix .section** and **.table** commands.

.prompt
.prm
Outputs the text shown on the line following this command, to the terminal. This is most commonly used with the **.input** or **.in** command to advise the user what input is expected of them.

.read {*(file.path.name*} *item.id*
.r {*(file.path.name*} *item.id*
Includes the contents of *item.id* as part of the current text. If the item is in a different file, a **(** must be included.

.readnext
.rn
Reads the next value from an active select list and places it in the current text. If there is no active list or when the list is empty the command is terminated and the OUTPUT PROCESSOR returns to the calling process.

.readnext null
Similar to the **.readnext** and **.rn** command but does not terminate if there is no active list or when the current list is exhausted.

.reset
.rst
Resets the printer to its initial state.

.right margin *n*
.rm *n*
Defines the right margin to be n spaces from the edge of the printable page and remains in effect until a **.indent rmargin** or **.irm** or another **.right margin** or **.rm** or a **.standard** or **.std** command is issued.

.save contents *item.id*
.sc *item.id*
Saves the table of contents into the item *item.id* in the current file.

.save index *item.id*
.si *item.id*
Saves the index into the item *item.id* in the current file. The index is saved in a single column form.

.section{*n*} *section.text*
.sec {*n*} *section.text*
Starts a new section with the section number *n* and displays the *section.text* alongside the section number. Both the section number and section text are included in the table of contents. If *n* is not specified the section is numbered as

section 1. Section numbers are incremented as each **.section** or **.sec** command is encountered.

.set chapter *options*
.sch *options*
This command sets the options for subsequent **.chapter** or **.ch** commands. The valid options which should be entered one after the other without intervening spaces or commas, are as follows:

b	boldface
i	italics
r	roman numerals for chapter numbers
s	suppress section numbers, which also suppresses the word **chapter** and its associated chapter number. The commands **.prefix page** or **.pp** are still valid
u	underline

.set section *options*
.ss *options*
This command sets the options for subsequent **.section** or **.sec** commands. The valid options which should be entered one after the other without intervening spaces or commas, are as follows:

b	boldface
i	italics
r	roman numerals for chapter numbers
s	suppress section numbers.
u	underline

.skip{*n*}
.sk {*n*}
Skips a certain number of lines dependent on the current line spacing, which can be altered using the **.spacing** or **.spg** command. If *n* is not specified then 1 line is skipped assuming single line spacing, 2 lines are skipped with double line spacing and so on.

.space *n*
.sp *n*
Skips a certain number of single lines, regardless of the line spacing that has been set.

.spacing {*n*}
.spg {*n*}
Sets the line spacing to *n* lines per line of text.

.standard
.std
Tells the OUTPUT PROCESSOR to use its default settings and can useful after various parameters have been modified. The standard settings being:

Block centre	Off
CRT output	Pause at end of page
Highlight character	Asterisk (*)
Hyphenation	On
Left margin	5
Line length	**TERM** setting less left and right margin
Override character	Underscore (_)
Paragraph mode	Off
Right margin	5
Text	Single spaced

.subscript
.sub
Moves text down one half line.

.superscript
.sup
Moves text up one half line.

.tab fill{"}*pattern*{"}
.tf {"}*pattern*{"}
Fills the space between the current position on the line to the next tab stop with the pattern specified. Quote marks are optional.

.tab left{"*phrase*"}
.tl {"*phrase*"}
Left justifies the last character of the *phrase* at the next tab position. Quote marks are only required where the phrase comprises more than one word.

.tab right{"*phrase*"}
.tr {"*phrase*"}
Right justifies the last character of the *phrase* at the next tab position. Quote marks are only required where the phrase comprises more than one word.

.tab rightm {"*phrase*"}
.trm {"*phrase*"}
Aligns the *phrase* with the right margin. Quote marks are only required where the phrase comprises more than one word.

.tab set *n,n,n...*
.ts *n,n,n...*

Sets a maximum of 20 tabs at the columns defined by *n,n,n...* Tab positions must be greater than zero and ever increasing. All tab settings are relative to the left margin and can be moved to by the **.tab left** or **.tl** and **.tab right** or **.tr** commands.

.table *text*
.tbl *text*
Numbers tables consecutively within a chapter by the numbering convention *chapter number – table number*. The text and table number are recorded in the table of contents.

.tc heading"{{*heading text*}{*'options'*}}"
.tch "{{*heading text*}{*'options'*}}"
Substitutes the *heading text* as the header for the table of contents. The *options* are the same as those give in the **.footing** command above.

.tcl *tcl.statement*
Executes the TCL verb *tcl.statement* putting the output from the statement into the current document at the current position.

.tcl box *tcl.statement*
.tclbox *tcl.statement*
Executes the TCL verb *tcl.statement* putting the output from the statement into the current document at the current position putting a box around the output. No box parameters can be specified, the width being determined by the left and right margin settings.

.test page{*n*}
.tp {*n*}
Tests to see if *n* lines are left on the page and if not throws to a new page before printing any further output. This prevents blocks of text which you want printed together from being broken up between different pages.

.underline
.ul
Underlines all text (including spaces) until a **.x .xul** or **.xuw** command is processed.

.underline words
.uw
Underlines all words (not the spaces between words) until a **.x .xul** or **.xuw** command is processed.

.variable columns *space,divisions,heading1,width1*
{*;heading2,width2* {*;...;heading7,width7*}}
.vcol *space,divisions,heading1,width1*
{*;heading2,width2* {*;...;heading7,width7*}}

This command is used to set the parameters for formatting text in multiple columns of variable widths, the parameters of which are used by subsequent **.column set** or **.columns** commands and should be used when the actual line length is unknown.

Space	specifies the number of spaces between each column
Divisions	specifies the number of sections into which to divide the current line and should be equal to or greater than the total of all the *width* parameters
Heading	the heading for the appropriate column
Width	the number of divisions to be included in the appropriate column

.x
Switches off boldface, underlining (including word underlining), and italics.

.xblock center
.xbc
Turns off block centre mode.

.xboldface
.xbf
Turns off boldface mode.

.xbox
Terminates a **.box** command and draws a bottom line.

.xcap sentences
.xcs
Terminates the capitalise sentence mode set by the **.cap sentences** or **.cs** command.

.xcolumns
.xcol
Turns off the column heading, width and spacing set by the **.columns set** or **.columns** command.

.xhilite
.xhi
Terminates the **.hilite** or **.hi** commands.

.xindex
.xix
Designates the end of an index entry initiated by a **.index** or **.ix** command.

.xitalics
.xit
Switches off italics mode.

.xjustify
.xj
Switches off the justification mode in current operation.

.xpaging
.xpg
Turns off the paging option so that output to the terminal no longer waits for a key to be pressed at the end of each page of screen output.

.xparagraph
.xp
Turns off paragraph mode.

.xpreface
.xpf
Turns off preface mode.

.xprefix page
.xpp
Turns off prefix page mode.

.xsubscript
.xsub
Turns off subscript mode.

.xsuperscript
.xsup
Turns off superscript mode.

.xuw
Terminates the mode of underlining of words.

.xul
Switches off the underline mode.

19.3 RUNOFF commands summary

RUNOFF commands are preceded with a full stop and like the OUTPUT PROCESSOR most have an abbreviated form. However, unlike the OUTPUT PROCESSOR the commands must be on a line on their own, and must start at the beginning of the line. It is possible to have a number of commands together on the same line, in which case no delimiter is required between them and one follows on immediately after the other. The summary of RUNOFF commands is as follows:

Command	Description
.*	Comment line – rest of text in the line is a comment only.
.BEGIN PAGE or **.BP**	Begin a new page.
.BOX *n,m*	Causes text following to be enclosed in a box starting at position *n*, ending at position *m*.
.BOX or .**BOX OFF**	Disables the BOX function and prints the bottom line of the box. Text to be put in a box is preceded with **.BOX** *n,m* and succeeded with **.BOX** or **.BOX OFF**.
.BREAK or **.B**	Causes any partially filled line to be output before processing next line.
.CAPITALISE SENTENCES	Automatically capitalizes the first letter after a full point, question mark or exclamation mark that is followed by a space. Also it follows these characters and the characters (:) and (;) by two spaces.
.CENTER or **.C**	Centres text found on the line following this command.
.CHAIN {*file*} *item*	Transfers control to a specified *item* name which may optionally reside in a different *file*.
.CHAPTER	Causes the subsequent text to be used as the chapter heading.
.CONTENTS	Outputs a table of contents based on previous **.CHAPTER** and **.SECTION** commands encountered.
.CRT	Directs output to the terminal.
.ENDCASE or **.EC**	Disables any previous **. LC** or **. UC** command.
.FILL or **.F**	Words are output one at a time until a line has been filled.
.FOOTING	Causes text found on line following this command to be printed at the foot of every page.
.HEADING	Causes text found on line following this command to be printed at the top of every page.
.HILITE*x*	Causes character *x* to be displayed at the extreme right-hand margin for every line until turned off.

.HIGHLITEOFF	Disables HIGHLITE.
.INDENT *n* or **.I** *n*	Indents following line by *n* spaces.
.INDENT MARGIN *n* or **.IM** *n*	Indents margin by *n* spaces. Causes break to occur.
.INDEX 'text'	Causes text, enclosed in single quotes, to be compiled into index together with current page number.
.INPUT	Prompts for text from the terminal which is then incorporated into the document.
.JUSTIFY or **.J**	Justifies to the right-hand margin.
.LEFT MARGIN *n*	Sets left margin to *n*.
.LINE LENGTH *n*	Specifies width of line, ignoring margin.
.LOWER CASE or **.LC**	Causes all subsequent text to be printed in lower case.
.LPTR	Directs output to the spooler.
.NOCAPITALISE SENTENCES or **.NCS**	Disables **.CAPITALISE SENTENCES**.
.NOFILL or **.NF**	Disables fill and justification and outputs tcxt cxactly as shown.
.NOJUSTIFY	Disables justification although line fill still or **.NJ** operates.
.NOPARAGRAPH	Disables PARAGRAPH function.
.PAGE NUMBER *n*	Sets page number to *n*, defaults to 1.
.PAPER LENGTH *n*	Sets page length to *n* lines. Unless specified, length used is as defined by the TCL TERM command.
.PARAGRAPH *n*. or .**P** *n*	Causes any blank line or line starting with a or space to be treated as the start of a new paragraph. A break occurs and text is indented *n* characters.
.PFILE *n*	Directs subsequent output to print file *n*.
.PRINT	Prints next line of text on users terminal.
.PRINT INDEX	Causes index to be printed in two-column output.

.READ {DICT} *{fname} {id}*	Causes RUNOFF to read the filename *fname* and the itemname *id*.
.READNEXT	Reads next item from a preselected list using **SELECT** or **SSELECT** ACCESS statements. Used for mailmerge techniques.
.SAVE INDEX *fname*	Causes index information to be saved in the filename *fname*. This filename must be different to the text filename containing the RUNOFF text.
.SECTION *n text*	Denotes next section at level *n*, which together with *text* is included in table of contents.
.SET TABS	Specifies tab settings.
.SKIP *{n}* or **.SK** *{n}*	Causes a BREAK after which *n* lines are skipped before printing continues.
.SPACE *n* or **.SP** *n*	Ignores SPACING after which *n* lines are skipped before printing continues.
.SPACING *n*	Sets standard line spacing. Hence double spacing means setting *n* to 2.
.STANDARD **.LINE**	Sets a series of default parameters: **.CS .F .J .UC .LEFT MARGIN 0 .CRT** **.HEADING .FOOTING .PARAGRAPH 5** **LENGTH 70.**
.TEST PAGE *n* or **.TP** *n*	Causes a BREAK and advances to a new page when there are less lines than *n* left on a page.
.UPPER CASE or **.UC**	Causes all subsequent text to be printed in upper case.

19.4 Special control characters in RUNOFF

RUNOFF handles underlining and bold print differently to the OUTPUT PROCESSOR. These special effects are handled by embedding special control characters into the body of the text. These characters are **&** for underlining and @ for bold. On their own they affect only the single character immediately following the control character. To underline or to embolden strings of characters these control codes should be placed at either end of the string, preceded by the up arrow (^) and followed by the backslash (\) as demonstrated in Figure 19.1.

Emboldened text which is also to be underlined has to use the combination of the two control codes, again encompassing a string of text with the up arrow and backslash characters. To be able to use the **@** and **&** as characters in their own right in the text, these special control characters have themselves to be preceded with a special control character, the underscore (_). The underscore denotes that the character following it is to be treated as text.

Two other useful control codes are the less than and greater than signs. Less than, <, denotes that the next word is to start at the next tab position whilst greater than, >, means that the word is to finish at the next tab position.

RUNOFF text	*Resulting output*
@A single bold character	**A** single bold character
@^A bold string@\	**A bold string**
&A single underlined character	A single underline character
&^An underlined string&\	An underlined string

Figure 19.1 RUNOFF control codes.

19.5 Using the OUTPUT PROCESSOR and RUNOFF

When using the OUTPUT PROCESSOR to produce manuals or lengthy documents it is usual to create a file to contain the documents and to create within it a separate item for each subject or chapter.

Make one of these items the master item containing a series of **.READ** commands, each relating to the separate items containing each subject or chapter in the OUTPUT PROCESSOR text. In the case of manuals, this master item would also contain the **.PRINT TOC** and **.PRINT INDEX** commands to generate the table of contents and the index. An example of this is shown in Figure 19.2 where the file WP contains four items, the first containing the master OUTPUT PROCESSOR control instructions and the other three, separate chapters of a book.

The entire manual would be output by the command **OP WP MASTER**, and would be suffixed with an **LPTR** or (**P** to produce the document on the printer rather than it being displayed on a terminal. The general format of the **OP** command is shown after Figure 19.2.

Contents of the file WP

Item-id *Contents*

MASTER
.READ CHAPTER1
.READ CHAPTER2
.READ CHAPTER3
.PRINT INDEX
.PRINT TOC

Contents of CHAPTER1, CHAPTER2 and CHAPTER3

CHAPTER1
.STANDARD
.HEADING
Introduction 'L'
.FOOTING
'L' The art of writing (c) R J Bourdon 'P'
.BOX 1,75.CENTER .BF I N T R O D U C T I O N . XBF .XBOX.J .CHAPTER .BF INTRODUCTION .XBF.SK2 .SECTION 1 An introduction to writing concepts SK2 This is the main body of the first chapter which will be right justified after the emboldened word **I N T R O D U C T I O N** which will be centred on the page in a box of 75 characters. A new chapter called 'Introduction' will be started on a new page and after a gap of two lines, the body text of this chapter will start as a new section at level 1 (i.e. if the chapter is numbered 1 then the section will be given as 1.1). The remaining text of the chapter continues from here

CHAPTER2

Contents of CHAPTER2 and CHAPTER 3 are similar to CHAPTER1 in that they contain text interspersed with OUTPUT PROCESSOR commands

CHAPTER3

Figure 19.2 typical OUTPUT PROCESSOR file.

OP *file.name* {*item.list*} {*(options)*}

where

file.name	is the name of the file containing the OUTPUT PROCESSOR documents
item.list	is the list of documents to be processed
options	are as follows
n{-*m*}	print the single page number *n* or the page range *n* to *m*
c	suppress the **.chain** and **.read** commands
d	double space document
f	suppress footings
h	suppress headings
j	suppress highlights
k	suppress legends
n	do not wait for key to be pressed at the end of each page output to the terminal
p	send document to currently assigned printer
s	suppress emboldening, underlining and fonts
t	triple space document
x	produce a word usage analysis for the documents in the file **WSYM**. Each word causes an individual entry in the file **WSYM** with the item-id *word:page.number:line number*. The analysis is produced as each word is output and there is no aggregate count, so if the same word appears multiple times it will have multiple entries in **WSYM**

The RUNOFF command format is very similar but it does not offer all the OUTPUT PROCESSOR options and has some others of its own. The general format of the command is shown below:

RUNOFF *file.name* {*item.list*} {*(options)*}

where

file.name	is the name of the file containing the OUTPUT PROCESSOR documents
item.list	is the list of documents to be processed
options	are as follows
C	suppress the **.chain** and **.read** commands
I	outputs the next item name. Useful for tracing when **.CHAIN** in use
J	suppress highlights
N	do not wait for key to be pressed at the end of each page output to the terminal
N*nn*	Indicates the number (*nn*) of times to overstrike on emboldening
P	send document to currently assigned printer
S	suppress emboldening, underlining and fonts
U	Forces all output into UPPER case

19.6 Some useful tips

19.6.1 The .box command

Text can be highlighted by enclosing it in a box. This is achieved by inserting a **.box** command before the text to be highlighted and a **.xbox** after it. The first **.box** command specifies the left and right margins for the box. The top and bottom lines of the box will be printed automatically on the line preceding and subsequent to the actual text being printer. If you require a blank line between the box lines and text you will have to force it using the **.SK** *n* command.

There is a difference in the ways in which RUNOFF and the OUTPUT PROCESSOR handle the **.box** command. If the box co-ordinates are too small to accommodate all the text, RUNOFF will truncate it, whilst the OUTPUT PROCESSOR will output the full text with the box superimposed over it. Neither takes note of the maximum number of print characters as defined by the TCL verb **TERM**, so it is up to you to ensure that your **.box** parameters are sensible. Figure 19.3 shows an example of its use.

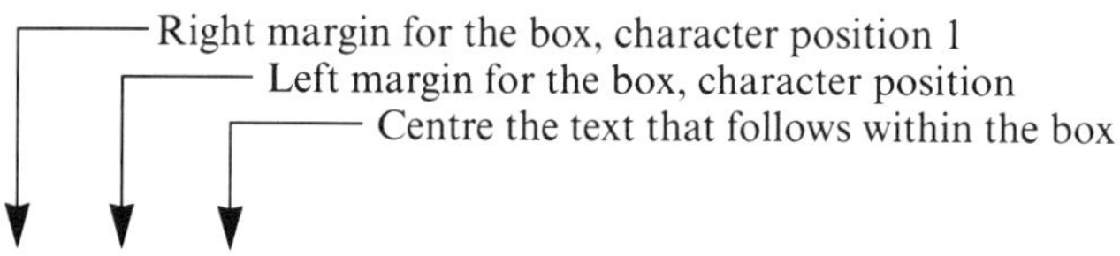

.BOX 1,50.CENTER
T H E T E X T P R O C E S S O R
.XBOX No resetting of justification required

The result:

```
T H E  T E X T  P R O C E S S O R
```

Figure 19.3 The use of the **.box** command.

19.6.2 Hanging tabs

If you need paragraphs of text to be numbered, where the numbers need to be 'hung' outside the text itself, use the **.ht** *n* command to set the start column for the text and then use the **.ght** command immediately prior to the text itself. Figure 19.4 shows this in operation.

The OUTPUT PROCESSOR text

.standard.ht 5
If problems occur try the following tests
1. .ght Make sure the printer is switched on and in a state ready to receive data
2. .ght Make sure you have defined the printer to the system using the .bf STARTPTR .xbf command and ensure you have defined its interface (serial or parallel) correctly
3. .ght Check the baud rate of the printer matches that of the speed for the line. Refer to your printer manual for the possible baud rate settings for your printer

The resulting output

```
If problems occur try the following tests
1. Make sure the printer is switched on and in a state ready to receive data
2. Make sure you have defined the printer to the system using the STARTPTR
   command and ensure you have defined its interface (serial or parallel)
   correctly
3. Check the baud rate of the printer matches that of the speed for the
   line. Refer to your printer manual for the possible baud rate settings
   for your printer
```

Figure 19.4 Hanging tabs with the OUTPUT PROCESSOR.

19.6.3 The .test page command

The **.test page** or **.tp** test page command enables a test to be carried out of the number of lines remaining on a page. If this is less than the number you specify, a page break will occur. This is invaluable where you wish to ensure that a specific part of a document be printed together and not split across two pages. It is frequently used where text is boxed, since the **.box** command will not recognize the bottom of a page and continues printing the sides of the box until a **.xbox** command is encountered. Figure 19.5 shows this in use.

19.6.4 The .fill, .nofill and .justify commands

The **.fill** command fills up the line with words from the text until there is no more room, without starting a new line. If the **.justify** command is also in effect, spaces are added at random between the words to create a straight right-hand margin. If justify is not in effect, the right-hand margin will be ragged.

The **.nofill** command not only cancels the effect of the **.fill** command but also the **.j** command. When **.nofill** is in effect, text is printed exactly as edited. In order to resume justification after this command, remember to issue a **.j** or **.justify** command.

```
.tp12                                              Test to ensure there are at least 13
                                                   lines left
.sk2                                          <--- Lines 1 & 2
.box 1,75                                     <--- Line 3
.nofill
.sk 1                                         <--- Line 4
INSERT(var,expl,exp2,exp3,new)                <--- Line 5
REPLACE(var,expl,exp2,exp3,new)               <--- Line 6
where- var is the name of the dynamic array   <--- Line 7
   - expl is the attribute position           <--- Line 8
   - exp2 is the multivalue Position          <--- Line 9
   - new is the new data to insert            <--- Line 10
.sk 1                                         <--- Line 11
.xbox                                         <--- Line 12
.fill.j
      This ensures all twelve lines are printed together
```

Figure 19.5 Use of the **.test page** command.

19.6.5 Working with columns

The OUTPUT PROCESSOR allows you to quickly and easily convert text into column form. The first stage is to set the columns together with their headings and then it is a simple job of placing **.col** commands in the text immediately prior to the text to be printed in one of the columns. Remember there is a maximum of seven columns and each **.col** command must reference an increasing column number until the start of a new line of data. Figure 19.6 shows how simple column output is with the OUTPUT PROCESSOR .

19.6.6 The .heading and .footing commands

The text output from the OUTPUT PROCESSOR can contain optional headings and footings text printed respectively at the top and bottom of each page output. This is achieved using the **.heading** and **.footing** commands. Following each of these commands can be one line containing a combination of text and special formatting characters. For a list of the formatting characters available please refer to the command summaries for both RUNOFF and the OUTPUT PROCESSOR at the start of this chapter. Remember to include some blank lines after your heading and prior to your footing to ensure they stand out from the main body of your document. Blank lines are output with the **L** option.

The OUTPUT PROCESSOR text

```
.standard
.heading "Staff list 'c'"
.sk 2
.columns set Name,20,2;Department,30,2;Telephone,15,2
.col1 Julie Riley .col2 Sales .col3 0121 355 6060
.col1 John Pike .col2 SW Support .col3 0121 359 6009
.col1 Ian Bright .col2 Administration .col3 01244 99933
.xcolumns.sk2
This is the remainder of the text of a document which starts with a
columnar list of staff
```

The results

```
                    Staff list

Name                Department              Telephone
Julie Riley         Sales                   0121 355 6060
John Pike           SW Support              0121 359 6009
Ian Bright          Administration          01244 99933


This is the remainder of the text of a document which starts with a
columnar list of staff
```

Figure 19.6 Column output with the OUTPUT PROCESSOR.

19.6.7 Producing an index

Any word or phrase can be stored in an index list by the command **.index**. The text to be indexed must be enclosed in single quotes. The word or phrase is put in a sorted index list which is printed out using the **.print index** command and which can be saved using the **.save index** command.

It is worth noting that each index column is just 25 characters wide, so the subject text for the index must be kept short, particularly where there are several page references to it!

The index can have subheadings, and these are denoted by multiple phrases in the **.index** command and by suffixing the **.index** command by a colon symbol. Figure 19.7 gives examples of the **.index** command.

19.6.8 Mailmerge techniques using .readnext and .chain

Whilst most people now use a DOS word processor for their day-to-day requirements, including its mailmerge facilities, for those without a DOS workstation it will be encouraging to know that mailmerging can be achieved by combining the facilities of the Update Processor or Editor, ACCESS and the OUTPUT PROCESSOR or RUNOFF.

The OUTPUT PROCESSOR text

.index 'Introduction'
.xindex

body text of the Introduction section

.index 'Advanced PICK – an overview'
.xindex
.print index

The results

```
Introduction .....................1
Advanced PICK - an overview ......7
```

The OUTPUT PROCESSOR text

.index: 'Introduction' 'Overview'
.xindex

body text of the overview
section of the introduction

.index 'How the system was developed'
.xindex

body text of the "how the system developed"
section of the introduction

.index 'Advanced PICK – an overview'
.xindex
.print index

The results

```
Introduction
Overview ... .....................1
How the system developed .........4
Advanced PICK - an overview ......7
```

Figure 19.7 Creating indexes with the OUTPUT PROCESSOR.

The technique requires the following steps:

(1) Create the letter, using the Update Processor or the Editor. The letter containing the merge commands can be placed in any file on your system. Place a **.readnext** command where text is to be merged into the letter. Remember to place two spaces immediately before and immediately after the **.readnext** command, otherwise the inserted text will not be delimited by a space character at all! At the bottom of the letter include a **.bp** to start the next letter on a new page and **.chain** *name*, where *name* is the name of the document being edited. This ensures that the OUTPUT PROCESSOR knows which document it should next print after throwing the page.

(2) Use ACCESS to select the relevant data from the file and save it in a list. This must be run immediately prior to executing the OUTPUT PROCESSOR. Alternatively the data from the ACCESS **select** statement should be saved in a list and the list retrieved immediately prior to running the OUTPUT PROCESSOR.

(3) Run the OUTPUT PROCESSOR for the letters using a special form of the command which specifies the dictionary and filename of the file on which the ACCESS was performed, this also being the dictionary which contains the master letter.

Figure 19.8 shows the preparation necessary before a mailmerge exercise can take place and uses the STAFF data files referred to in Section 12.3 on ACCESS. In order to display the salary details correctly, attribute 8 of the dictionary item SALARY is altered.

The preparation

1. The letter item-id **LETTER**

```
:U DOCUMENTS LETTER
DOCUMENTS 'LETTER' size = 336
01 .sk 8
02 Dear .readnext
03 Our records show that you are in the .readnext department which is being
transferred to our Bristol office next Spring. Your current salary of £ .readnext
will be incremented by £500 in consideration of any inconvenience this may cause.
04 .sk 2
05 Yours sincerely
06 .sk 4
07 M K L Chrochet
08 Personnel Officer
09 .bp
10 .chain letter
```

Figure 19.8 Mailmerge techniques for the OUTPUT PROCESSOR and RUNOFF.

2. Amend the dictionary definition of salary

(Adding the correlative in attribute 8 is necessary to force the decimal point to be printed within the OUTPUT PROCESSOR or RUNOFF)

```
:u dict staff salary
DICT staff 'salary' size = 54
01 A
02 6
03 Salary
04
05
06
07 mr2,
08 A;6(MR2,)
09 R
10 10
```

3. The ACCESS statement to select the required data

:sselect staff with dept = "02" fname dept salary

```
[404] 6 items selected out of 8 items
```

Only 2 items have been selected, but the list contains 3 attributes for each hence the count of 6.

4. The contents of the select list

```
GEORGE
ADMINISTRATION
12,500.00
IAN
ADMINISTRATION
12,400.00
```

Production of the letters

:op documents letter (p

```
Dear GEORGE
Our records show that you are in the ADMINISTRATION department which is
being transferred to our Bristol office next Spring. Your current salary of
£12,500.00 will be incremented by £500 in consideration of any inconvenience
this may cause.

Yours sincerely



M K L Chrochet
Personnel Officer
```

Figure 19.8 *Continued*

```
Dear IAN
Our records show that you are in the ADMINISTRATION department which is
being transferred to our Bristol office next Spring. Your current salary of
£12,400.00 will be incremented by £500 in consideration of any inconve-
nience this may cause.

Yours sincerely



M K L Chrochet
Personnel Officer
```

Figure 19.8 *Continued*

20 Security and Integrity

TCL verbs and general commands covered in this chapter

ACCOUNT-SAVE	ACCOUNT-RESTORE	ACCOUNT-MAINT	ADMIN.FILES
ADMIN.MAINT	ADMIN.TAPE	ADMIN.TAPE.SETUP	BREAK-KEY
BREAK-KEY-OFF	BREAK-KEY-ON	BRK-DEBUG	BRK-LEVEL
CHARGES	CHARGE-TO	CLEAR-FILE	DEBUG
FILE-SAVE	FLUSH	LIST-FILE-STATS	PASSWORD
SAVE	SEL-RESTORE	SET-HALF	SET-FLOPPY
SET-SCT	STARTLOG	STARTSCHED	STOPLOG
STOPSCHED	TANDEM	T-ATT	T-BCK
T-CHK	T-DET	T-EOD	T-EOF
T-FWD	TLOG-RESTORE	TXLOG	TXLOG-STATUS
T-RDLBL	T-READ	T-REW	

20.1 An introduction to security

On any multi-user system where a number of people can be accessing the system at any time, the subject of security becomes a major issue. It is important to ensure that those using the system are authorized users, and as such are only able to access the information they are entitled to. This becomes an even bigger problem where access to the system can be gained remotely over telephone lines. With the capabilities of todays's so-called 'hackers' it could be said that the only secure system is one that does not have electricity connected to it!

In managing the privacy and protection of your data, it is necessary to appoint a System Administrator to be responsible for setting up the necessary control procedures. Apart from the aspects of security of access, they should also ensure that regular backups are taken to ensure that the data of the system can be restored if necessary.

Whilst the security within Advanced PICK is not as far reaching as that offered by UNIX, the security is generally more than sufficient for most people. Indeed if UNIX level security is needed, Advanced PICK should be purchased for a UNIX implementation thereby giving the best of both worlds. PICK provides for security of access to the system in a number of ways:

- User identities with optional password and logon macro
- Optional account password
- File retrieval and update lock codes
- Privilege levels
- Port logon control
- Account logon macros

The various steps in implementing a secure system are firstly to put passwords on each user-id and each account. These passwords prevent unauthorized access to the system since if the password is typed in wrongly, the user is returned to the logon prompt. Once a user has access to an account, the files they can access can be restricted using retrieval lock codes, and the files they are permitted to update, by use of update lock codes. The user privileges assigned to a user when they log on, also restrict the facilities made available and a special logon process (a MACRO or PROC) can assist with the tailoring of a users environment. The final restrictions that can be applied are by removing specific TCL verbs from their account and preventing them access to TCL altogether which means they can only work within the confines of the application software. A further aid to the System Administrator is the provision of a comprehensive system history via a usage recording and reporting system and if you are worried about what a user is doing PICK provides a means of tapping into his line and getting an image of his screen on your own terminal regardless of where his terminal is located!

20.1.1 The users file

Advanced PICK separated the user from the account and has provided the option of putting passwords on each. The user logon record is held in the file **users** and creating the user record is the first important step in securing your system. Figure 20.1 provides the detailed layout of the user record.

ac..	**attribute-name**	**description**
0	item-id	User-id
1	name	User's name.
2	address	User's address.
3	zip	User's zip code.
4	phone	User's phone number.
6	keys	User's retrieval and update keys.
7	password	Optional logon password(s).
8	privilege	User privilege level.
9	options	User options:
	a (or u)	Updates accounting history file at logoff.
	d	Disables 'end' and 'off' commands from either debugger.
	r	Restarts logon procedure on any <break>+end.
	g	Stops at GFE's and offers the options to '(L)ogoff, (C)ontinue, or (Q)uit'.
	m	Invokes the automatic GFE handler at any GFE found.
12	macro	User logon macro. This is the same as a TCL macro without the macro type code, (in attribute 1) which is assumed to be 'n' (for 'non-stop'). Any number of TCL commands may be placed on attributes 12 and beyond. Each command will be executed before the user is logged on

Figure 20.1 The layout of the **users** file.

The attributes of the user record which are associated with security and the section of this chapter that covers them are as follows:

ac..	attribute-name	description	section
6	keys	User's retrieval and update keys	20.1.2
7	password	Optional logon password(s)	20.1.3
8	privilege	User privilege level	20.1.4
9	options	User options	20.1.5
12	macro	User logon macro	20.1.6

The user record is created using the Update Processor and a typical session is shown in Figure 20.2.

It is worth remembering that all Advanced PICK systems come with the user **dm** so the ***very*** first step in protecting your system is to ensure this record is password protected. This is done with the Update Processor by executing the command **u users dm** and pressing [CR] until you reach attribute 7 headed 'password'. At this point enter the password and press [CR] and you will see that the encrypted version immediately overwrites what you typed. This ensures that the password cannot be 'read' by anyone who happens to gain access to the user record. To change the password use the verb **password** as described in Section 20.1.3.

The Editor should not be used for changing user passwords as the encryption facility only works within the Update Processor. If you use the Editor the real, rather than encrypted, version of the password will be stored in the user record. Then when the user logs on the system will take the real version as the encrypted code and convert it to a 'real' password which it will then try to match to the password typed in by the user. The chances of the user getting it

```
:u users mike
users          'rjb' size = 158
name           Mike Brownxf
address
zip
phone
keys
password MJBUI <-------- after entering the password, the encrypted version
                         93B7E2E8 is displayed in its place
privilege      sys2
options
macro          term-type
10 sp-assign
11 brk-level
12 esc-data
13 set-sym gsym
14 speller-off
users          'rjb' size = 105 filed.
```

Figure 20.2 Creating a new user.

right are virtually nil and the result is that no-one will be able to use that user-id until the password has been changed properly using the Update Processor.

Please note that the password ***is*** case sensitive, even though the Advanced PICK environment is not. It is important to ensure that your users are aware of this.

Another point to note is that anyone with access to the Update Processor can change the password of any user record as the original password is not requested first. Hence you should consider putting retrieval and update lock codes on the **users** file definition record. The next section discusses the use of these codes.

20.1.2 Update and retrieval lock codes

These lock codes are provided to protect the most sensitive files of your system and provide for the most detailed level of security. The retrieval locks prevent a file being read, whilst the update locks prevent a file being updated. A retrieval access lock is therefore able to lock out any access to a file.

By using these codes, even an authorized user with sufficient technical knowledge to use file paths or create Q-pointers to other accounts, or even to the system dictionary (**mds**) itself, will be excluded from accessing confidential data.

These lock codes are placed in the definition items as follows:

definition item	**file secured**
mds	account
md	file dictionary
file dictionary	data file

The retrieval lock is placed in attribute 5 whilst the update lock is placed in attribute 6. These locks are compared with those of the user and provided they tally, the files can be read and/or updated. The user's codes are stored in attribute 6 of the users record in the file **users**. (In R83 the retrieval and update lock codes are held in attributes 5 and 6 respectively of the account entry in the system dictionary file SYSTEM.)

If you refer back to Section 6.2.1 about creating an account, you will notice that the retrieval and update lock codes were requested at the time the account was created. It is these codes that are compared to those assigned to the user to determine whether or not the user can access the account. In R83 in order to provide varying levels of access to the same account it is possible to create Q-pointer entries to an account which are held in the system dictionary and effectively creates user-ids (see Section 9.2).

The entire update or retrieval code given to a file, read left to right, must match completely all or part of the user's code. Hence if a file has a lock code of ABC anyone with that exact code will have access to the file as would anyone with a lock code which starts with ABC, i.e. ABC1, ABCD, etc.

However, anyone whose code is AB or BC or any other subset of the full code will not gain access.

To provide complete protection to the system dictionary these lock codes should be applied to both the **dm** and **sysprog** users in the **users** file and their respective records in the system dictionary (**mds**). You must take extreme care if you decide on this course of action, since to make a mistake could lock you out of the system dictionary and may require you to reload from a previous backup. As user logon is the first stage, effectively at the top of the Advanced PICK hierarchy, any security system must work down from there, moving through the file hierarchy starting with the system dictionary (**mds**).

Retrieval and Update lock codes can be multi-valued. If there is more than one, the first is known as the primary lock code and the second and subsequent codes are known as the secondary codes. The primary lock code prevents access to any file within an account which does not have the same lock code whilst the secondary lock codes allow the user to access any account or file that has one of these codes as its primary code.

Hence if account 1 has a primary lock code of ABC and no secondary lock codes and account 2 has a primary lock code of XYZ and a secondary lock code of ABC, a user with access to account 1 is locked out of the files within account 2 (because its lock code is not the same as the primary lock code of account 2), whilst users of account 2 can access files within account 1, because one of its codes (ABC) is the primary lock code of account 1.

A similar matching principle applies for the access to files by users whose lock codes are multi-valued. Creating multi-valued codes is achieved by entering ***v*** (control/v) between the codes when creating the user record with the Update Processor.

20.1.3 Password protection

The top level of security is that with users which can have their own passwords. These are input into attribute 7 of the user record in the **users** file using the Update Processor. As Figure 20.2 showed, when the actual password is input, the encrypted version immediately overwrites it.

Exactly the same happens when an account is created using the Update Processor (see section 6.2.1). If the Update Processor is not used, then a password can be added to either the user record or account with the TCL command **PASSWORD**.

This TCL command is normally restricted to the System Administrator and therefore generally only available from the **dm** account although if the verb is left in the NEWAC file (in which it resides by default) it will be available from all accounts. **PASSWORD** prompts for either the user-id or the account name and then asks for the password. An encrypted version of the password is then stored in attribute 7 of the defining item. This provides for a two level password capability, one at the user level and the other at the account level. Without giving the correct password to either the user password or account password the user is returned to the logon prompt.

Figure 20.3 shows how the **PASSWORD** verb works and how it affects the normal logon session.

As has been said earlier, it is obviously crucial to password-protect the standard user and account names such as **dm** and **SYSPROG**, otherwise anyone could freely gain access to all system utilities and password protection on any other account would be worthless! It is obviously equally sensible to change passwords from time to time and to avoid the use of obvious passwords such as user initials, Christian names or forenames, or two-character passwords, all of which can be readily broken. Any combination of characters is acceptable making password protection a realistic proposition. My recommendation would be a six character password which is a combination of both letters and numbers.

With the use of either the Update Processor or the editor and access to the system dictionary the encrypted password can be easily removed. It makes sense, therefore, to limit access to both of these facilities and if possible removing them totally from each user account. This is achieved by removing the verbs **ED**, **EDIT**, **U**, **UD**, **UP**, **UPDATE** and **PASSWORD** from their master dictionary and also from the file NEWAC if no new accounts are to contain these verbs. Doing so restricts access to the password utility to the **dm** account which itself should be restricted to the System Administrator by means of password protection.

```
:password
Change USER or ACCOUNT password (U,<A)>? u[CR]
Enter user name: rb[CR]

Enter new password (you will not see what you type):
Re-enter new password for verification (you will not see what you type):
:
:off

< Connect time= 0 Mins.; CPU= 31 Units; LPTR pages= 0 >
< logged off at 20:17:56 on 14 Oct 1994               >

20:17:56 14 Oct 1994
Advanced PICK O/S - Enter your PICK user id: rb
user password:
Term setting: 79,25,0,7,1,8,80,58,MM-MON

[1301] The Speller is off.
master dictionary:sb+
md password:
```

Figure 20.3 The implementation of passwords at the user and account level.

20.1.4 System privilege levels

A system privilege level is assigned to a user at the time their logon record is created and is stored in attribute 8 of the record. They can subsequently be amended by use of the Update Processor or the editor.

The privilege level limits of the user's access to the commands and facilities of the PICK environment. A privilege level is assigned to an account at the time it is created and that of the user prevails. Hence if an account has SYS2 privileges (the highest level) but the user has SYS0 privileges (the lowest level), when the user operates within the account their privilege level will be SYS0.

There are three privilege levels that can be used, the lowest level is SYS0, then follows SYS1 with SYS2 being at the top level. Obviously any System Administrator should be assigned SYS2 privileges as should that assigned to the account **dm**.

Those with SYS2 privileges have no restrictions. Those with SYS1 privileges cannot change or display anything from either the system or BASIC, can only use **CREATE-FILE DELETE-FILE CLEAR-FILE CREATE-INDEX DELETE-INDEX CLEAR-INDEX** file management verbs. All other file management verbs and many other verbs, such as, but not limited to **DUMP TANDEM** and **SP-KILL**, are also restricted from use. Those with SYS1 privileges can update file dictionaries and the MD, but cannot update the **mds** file (the system dictionary). They cannot start and stop printers, use the PICK assembler and nor use the FILE-SAVE and FILE-RESTORE processes although they can use peripheral storage devices such as floppy disks.

In addition to SYS1 restrictions, those with SYS0 privileges cannot create files, delete files or clear data from files and they are also not allowed to update the master dictionary.

20.1.5 Restricting TCL access and use of the user options flags

With anything other than the highest privilege level (SYS2), access to the system debugger and assembler is prevented. Further within an application program as we have seen, it is possible using the BREAK OFF statement in PICK BASIC to prohibit use of the BREAK key to get into the system debugger. Providing the application software is robust and proven and the system administrator is capable, there is no reason why a user should ever need to be given access to TCL.

If the user has SYS2 privileges, however, and the BREAK key is enabled, then by pressing the BREAK key or using CTRL/C the user gains access to the system debugger, denoted by an **!** or the BASIC debugger denoted by an *. By typing **END** to the debugger symbol the system will return to the TCL prompt : and thereafter the user can make use of whatever TCL facilities are available. It is possible, however, to stop people gaining access to TCL in this way, thereby confining them to the application software. This is achieved by using a security code (option code) which is placed in attribute 9 of the user record in the file **users**. The available user option codes are as follows:

a	Updates accounting history file at logoff.
d	Disables 'end' and 'off' commands from either debugger.
g	Stops at GFE's and offers the options to '(L)ogoff, (C)ontinue, or (Q)uit.'
m	Invokes the automatic GFE handler at any GFE found.
p	causes phantom processes initiated by this user to terminate and wrap up rather than simply going to sleep when a GFE is encountered. Needs AP version 6.1 and above.
r	Restarts logon PROC or MACRO on any <break>/end key combination.
u	Updates accounting history file at logoff.

The option attribute, attribute 9, can contain multiple option codes, which are placed side by side without a delimiter.

20.1.6 Logon PROC or MACRO

The logon PROC or MACRO is a series of commands which are executed by the PROC or MACRO. The PROC or MACRO resides in the MD and when a user logs to an account if either a PROC or MACRO exists with the same item-id as that of the user-id, it will be automatically executed. This can be very useful where different users need different menus or different environments to others using the exact same account. By setting attribute 9 in the users record to **r** this logon PROC or MACRO will be automatically invoked as soon as the user exits from the system or BASIC debug prompt with **END** or if the user tries to get to TCL by 'pushing' a level. The logon PROC or MACRO will generally set up the environment for the user, normally displaying a menu or security logon program. By re-executing the logon PROC or MACRO the user is kept from TCL thereby greatly enhancing system security.

20.1.7 The USER MACRO

The USER MACRO is the MACRO stored in the users logon record in the file **users**. The macro can be used to further customize the environment for the user. For example you could specify which printer the user is to default to, or specify special TERM characteristics. When a user is first set up the following macro lines, which are placed in attribute 12 onwards, are set up:

sp-assign	assign form queue 0 (zero)
brk-level	set break key to push a level instead of going to the debugger
esc-data	set the ESC key to send its value (char 27) rather than push a level
set-sym gsym	set access to the global synonym file
speller-off	switch off the spell checker

The MACRO is assumed to be type **n** which means no intervention is required during its execution (see Section 17.1 about MACRO types).

20.1.8 Control of the BREAK key

The BREAK key is the key that can stop execution of a process causing the system to display either the system debug symbol **!** (an exclamation mark) or the BASIC debug symbol * (an asterisk). The key is often labelled 'Break' but may not cause the break effect without being pressed in conjunction with the control key (Ctrl) or shift key. Sometimes the break sequence is the combination of the control key and the letter **C** depressed together. Whatever the sequence of keys, the break key provides access to the debugger and should be restricted from the hands of an inexperienced user.

There are specific commands which you can use to control use of the BREAK key and these can be added to the users logon macro (see Section 21.15). The TCL verbs available are:

Command	Description
BREAK-KEY {(*option*} where the possible options are **f** disables the break key **n** enables the break key **s** suppresses the status message	toggles the availability of the BREAK key
BREAK-KEY-OFF	disables the BREAK key on the current port`
BREAK-KEY-ON	enables the BREAK key on the current port
BRK-DEBUG	causes the BREAK key to invoke the debugger on subsequent use
BRK-LEVEL	causes the BREAK key to push a level on subsequent use

If when the **BRK-DEBUG** command is executed the current process is a PICK/BASIC program, the PICK/BASIC debugger is invoked and an asterisk displayed. In all other cases, the system (virtual) debugger is invoked and an exclamation mark is displayed

If the BREAK key is set to push a level, the debugger may be entered with the **debug** command. This then is another command to be aware of and to limit its availability, but do be aware that as a Systems Administrator you may need to access the debugger yourself.

On some systems, when the BREAK key is set to push a level, it is not possible to push a level while in the debugger in which case enter a colon (:) followed by either [CR] or <Enter>. You should also be aware that it is not possible to push a level whilst still at the TCL prompt : (colon) and at least one character has to have been entered at the TCL prompt before the BREAK key will push a level.

20.1.9 Restricting use of TCL verbs

If the user has access to TCL, it may be sensible to remove certain verbs from his account. The obvious verbs relate to the use of the Update Processor and the Editor, which, as was discussed fully in earlier chapters, allows the user access to any piece of data and the means to change it. Whilst the retrieval and update locks prevent access to confidential files, it is unlikely that all files in your system will use them. In that case any file without security lock codes is open to abuse. Be aware that neither the Update Processor nor the editor leaves an audit trail, so its use should be restricted to just those who need to use it.

Removing TCL verbs from an account is purely a matter of identifying those in question and deleting them using the **DELETE** verb (see Section 6.4.2).

20.1.10 The System Accounting History file ACCOUNTS

The System Accounting History file, called **accounts** (known as **ACC** in R83), records users' activities and is one of the mandatory files of the Advanced PICK system. It is activated by placing an **a** at the end of the options in the users' record in the **users** file. (In R83 place a U alongside the L or R in attribute 9 of the system dictionary entry for the account.) Once set, each time a user logs onto the system his connect time and CPU usage, together with the number of pages sent to the spooler, are recorded up to and including the time he logs off. This is an extremely useful mechanism for controlling security and the structure of the account is shown in Figure 20.4.

The information collected is contained in the display at the time a user logs off or logs to another account as shown below.

```
< Connect time= 0 Mins.; CPU= 102 Units; LPTR pages= 0    >
< logged off at 14:30:04  on 16 Oct 1994                  >
```

This charging information shown on the first line of the above display can be shown at any time by use of the command **CHARGES**. PICK maintains the

ac..	**attribute-name**	**description............................**
0	user	Item.id consists of 'users' id.
1	md	Name of md (item-id in mds file) for the accounting period.
2	l-date	Log date of the accounting data.
3	l-time	Log time of the accounting data.
4	acct-time	Accounting period to the second.
5	cpu	Central processing unit (cpu) execution time (in tenths of seconds) used by this process for the accounting period.
6	pages	Number of printer pages output for accounting period.

Figure 20.4 The structure of the ACCOUNTS file.

ACCOUNTS file and creates items within it which contain multi-values for each of its attributes built up as the user logs off or logs from account to account.

If a user wishes to charge his computer usage to another cost centre or project he can use the command **CHARGE-TO** followed by the cost centre or project name. PICK will create a new item on the **accounts** file which records activities from the time the **CHARGE-TO** command is entered to the time the user either logs off or enters a new **CHARGE-TO** command. The item-id of this new record is the concatenation of the user-id, an asterisk and the cost centre or project name. Producing reports from the **accounts** file is by use of the ACCESS processor which is described fully in Chapter 12. The **accounts**file dictionary names that can be used in the ACCESS statement, together with the attribute positions they define, are shown in Figure 20.4.

One great danger with the use of system accounting is to forget it is being used, since there is no automatic facility to clear it down. Provided the system accounting statistics are activated, entries will continue to be added to the **accounts** file until it uses all the spare disk space! Whilst the file has usually been sized to allow for a sensible number of entries, if it is overlooked it will link in additional frames to contain the history detail to an extent that will noticeably increase logon and logoff times and noticeably reduce the amount of free disk space.

The **accounts** file can be cleared down either completely or selectively. To clear it down completely use the **CLEAR-FILE DATA** verb which is described in Section 6.3.5. To clear it down selectively use the **DELETE** verb to delete the users details altogether. Figure 20.5 shows how these two options work.

Note however, that the deletion of records shown in Figure 20.5 removes the entire item containing ***all*** the information for a user. Since it is not possible to delete some of the multi-value accounting details within the user's record in the **accounts** file and that the only option is the removal of the entire item, in practice the accounting history file tends to be completely cleared out each time housekeeping takes place.

:CLEAR-FILE DATA ACCOUNTS	clears down the entire file
:DELETE ACCOUNTS RB	removes the user record RB

Figure 20.5 Removing items from the ACC file.

20.1.11 The TANDEM verb

Tandem is a means of finding out what is happening on another port by 'linking' into it. The process links your terminal to another such that what is typed on the other is displayed on yours – an effective way of spying without the other person being aware of it, providing you after you have made the link you do not use your keyboard, other than to exit the tandem process. The format of the command is given in Figure 20.6.

Since **TANDEM** links the current process to another process, i.e. it links your screen to that of another, any input or output to either screen affects both screens. The process initiating the tandem process is the 'master' with the process being attached to the 'slave' or 'target'.

If the slave process is a 'phantom' process, only output from the phantom is redirected to the master.

The target device must be available on the nominated port and may not be already attached to another process.

A 'hotkey' sequence disconnects the link which has a default of **<Esc>x**. However, if an **esc-data** command has not been issued previously, the process will issue it automatically, otherwise it would not be possible to cancel a tandem process. Figure 20.7 gives examples of the ways in which the **TANDEM** verb can be used.

:tandem *port.number* {(*options*}

where

port number is the port you wish to tandem to

options the selected options which can be as follows

d designates a sequence of (up to four) characters to terminate 'tandem' mode. Each character is provided in it's hexadecimal equivalent of it's ASCII value (see Appendix F for a list of valid ASCII and hexadecimal codes). Each character is separated by a comma. For example, 'd/41,42,43,44', indicates that an 'ABCD' will disconnect the link. The first two characters of the termination sequence must be different. For instance, it will NOT accept 'd/2b,2b,2b' (+++), but it will accept 'd/2a,2b,2b' (*++).

f turns off the ability to tandem on the current port. This keeps others from being able to tandem your terminal.

n turns on the ability to tandem on the current port. This gives others the ability to tandem your terminal. This option may NOT be used with the **u** option.

s suppresses the message when the process terminates. If this is used with the **d** option, the **s** option must precede the **d** option.

u unconditionally turns off tandem when used with the **f** option.

x terminates tandem mode on target device number.

Figure 20.6 The TANDEM verb.

:tandem 13	attaches the current process to port 13.
:tandem 33 (d/2a,2b,2b	attaches to port 3 and sets the hotkey sequence to *++.
:tandem (n	enables ability to be 'tandemed' on the current port.
:tandem 42 (uf	unconditionally disables 'tandem' capability on port 42.
:tandem 13 (x	terminates tandem on port 13.

Figure 20.7 Using the **TANDEM** verb.

There are some points to bear in mind. For example if the 'master' and 'slave' processes are different types of terminal using different TERM characteristics or terminal emulation the output to the 'master' screen may well turn out to be garbled.

If the 'master' and 'slave' processes are at different baud rates, the 'master' process may lock up, making normal termination impossible. Should this occur use the **LOGOFF** verb from another port to log off both the 'master' and 'slave' processes.

As mentioned earlier, it the current task has **esc-level** in effect, the tandem process automatically issues an **esc-data** command so that it can be terminated by **<Esc>x**. It does NOT, however, reset the **esc-level** upon termination, so this option must be manually re-executed in order to restore it to its previous state.

When a process pushes a shell to UNIX while being tandemed by another port, theoretically, the PICK process is suspended by UNIX and therefore the input from the master will not be processed by the PICK process until it is re-activated by UNIX.

20.2 An introduction to integrity

The integrity of the database is equally as important as its security if not more so. Integrity involves ensuring that what is contained within the database is a correct reflection of the masterfile data and its transactions. It means ensuring that adequate computer and manual systems exist to rebuild the database in the event of a system failure. It also means establishing, and where necessary carrying out, procedures at the time of a system failure to recover the database from previous backups and to bring the database up to date which in some cases may involve the re-input of transactions. In order for this to take place, manual procedures need to be developed that will enable the identification of those transactions which need re-processing.

To be able to recover from failure it is necessary to ensure that adequate backup copies of the database are taken. Whilst anyone would agree that the thought of losing their entire data is abhorrent, there are regretfully many companies who are either so convinced of the reliability of their hardware or generally relaxed and uncaring about their data or even too lazy to spend the time backing up, that a failure risks the loss of weeks of work. It is at times like these that the user realizes the value of support services and will place considerable and unnecessary pressure on the supplier to help them recover data! There can be no doubt that it is the responsibility of System Administrators to ensure that backups are carried out frequently enough to provide an adequate level of security for their company and each company's responsibility to recognize these responsibilities and to support the System Administrator when backup time conflicts with an 'urgent' task. No task can be more urgent than securing your data!

There are several ways in which the database can be secured:

(1) *System generation* – a complete save of all data including the operating system;
(2) *File save* – a complete save of all accounts;
(3) *Incremental save* – a save of changed items across individual or all accounts;
(4) *Account save* – a backup of specified accounts;
(5) *File backup* – a backup of specified files;
(6) *Save of item(s)* – a backup of one or a number of specified items;
(7) *Transaction logger* – the log of updates to another device.

The frequency and type of backup taken is very much a function of individual needs. Most people will take an account save once a day, with a complete file save being taken on a weekly and/or monthly basis. In each case several versions of the backup should exist, to protect against the unlikely but disastrous event that a backup tape is found to be corrupt.

The minimum backup should be carried out on what is known as a 'grandfather/father/son' basis where a cycle of three tapes is rotated. In this system, three tapes are used, labelled, for example, A, B and C. Today's backup is written to tape A, tomorrow to tape B and the day after to tape C. When all the tapes have been used once, the eldest (the grandfather), tape A, is reused, overwriting the oldest backup copy. In this way three independent backup copies are retained. This is not to say that three is all that is needed. For a nominal cost, particularly in relation to the value of the data, additional tapes can be added to the cycle, perhaps providing a complete set of backup tapes for each day of the working week, or even the working month with additional tapes being held for the weekly and/or monthly backups.

Whatever the number of tapes used, it will be essential to clearly identify and mark each tape and to keep a log of which tape was used, on which day and for which type of backup. In addition, all backup tapes and the log should be kept in a fireproof safe, with additional copies of the weekly, monthly or annual backups being kept off-site in a secure place, such as in a bank or with a security company. If all of this sounds dramatic, so is the loss of your data!

20.2.1 Working with backup devices

The original backup medium handling commands written for PICK were written for ½-inch magnetic tape and hence commence with the letter **T** (for Tape). As hardware evolved, other backup devices have been introduced, namely floppy disks, ¼-inch cartridge tape and dat tape. The original backup medium commands have not changed and are equally applicable to the other devices. In order to tell PICK which backup device you are addressing, these commands need to be preceded by a **SET** command, even when using $\frac{1}{2}$ inch tape. This **SET** command is followed by the device to be addressed. While these commands vary between implementations they are typically:

SET-FLOPPY	Floppy disk
SET-HALF	Magnetic tape (½-inch)
SET-SCT	Cartridge tape (¼-inch)
SET-8MM	8mm dat tape
SET-DAT	4mm dat tape

Once the backup device has been identified, any of the verbs shown in Figure 20.8 can be used. Whilst specifically referring to the tape unit, the commands will carry out the same function for all backup devices.

T-ATT {*blocksize*} {(*options*}

Attaches the tape or floppy device to the port number of the terminal carrying out the command. Only one port at a time can have access to the backup medium. If another port is using it, the message DEVICE ATTACHED TO LINE *n* will be displayed showing which terminal has control of the backup device. If they are no longer using it, either carry out a **T-DET** from the controlling terminal or a **T-DET (U** from your own terminal. The blocksize normally has a default when the device is attached. This can be overridden by specifying one here. Whilst the block size can be set at any number from 20 to 16384, the defaults are as follows:

floppy disk	500
half inch tape	8192
SCT (¼″ tape)	16384
8mm	16384

The options are as follows:

- **u** unconditionally attaches the tape and will 'steal' it from another port if necessary
- **z** unconditionally attaches the tape unless it is being used by the transaction logger

T-BCK {*nnn*} (not valid for cartridge tapes)

Move the tape back a specified number of blocks (nnn) or to the end of the previous file

Figure 20.8 Device-handling commands.

T-BSF {*nnn*} (not valid for cartridge tapes)
Backspaces a given number of files, but if no number is given the command behaves like **T-BCK**

T-BSR {*nnn*} (not valid for cartridge tapes)
Backspaces a given number of records, but if no number is given the command behaves like **T-BCK**

T-CHK {(*options*}
Check current tape file for parity errors. When the **A** option is omitted the current file is checked. The possible options are

- **a** check to the end of the tape
- **l** displays label data if one is found after an end-of-file mark
- **p** directs output to the printer

T-DET {(*options*}
Detaches the device from the current process making it available to others. The options are:

- **u** detaches the tape unit from any port except the Spooler, which detaches automatically at the end of each job. This option requires **SYS2** privileges
- **z** Unconditionally detaches the tape, except if the tape is attached to the transaction logger

T-EOD
Moves the tape forward to the end of the data on the tape. The last file on the tape is marked with two EOF marks and is considered the end of the data

T-ERASE
The **T-ERASE** command performs two functions. It re-tensions the tape and in the process erases all data on it

T-FSF{*nnn*}
Spaces forward a given number of files. If a number omitted the command acts as a **T-FWD**

T-FSR{*nnn*}
Spaces forward a given number of records. If a number is omitted the command acts as a **T-FWD**

T-FWD {*nnn*}
Moves the tape forward to the next file or a specified number is of blocks. If no number is specified, one is assumed

T-RDLBL {(*options*)}
Reads a tape label from the attached magnetic media and initialises the internal label storage area. The options are

- *nnn* reel number
- **a** allows for beginning at 'any' reel number rather than processing sequentially

Figure 20.8 *Continued*

T-READ {(*options*)}
Reads a records from the attached magnetic media device and displays its contents. The available options are:

nnn{-*nnn*} reads a specific block or range of block numbers counting from the current tape position

a	displays EBCDIC data in ASCII format
n	suppresses pause at end of each page on the terminal
p	sends display to the printer
x	outputs the display in hexadecimal

T-RET
Invokes the **T-RETEN** verb to re-tension the tape

T-RETEN
Re-tensions the tape by forwarding to the end of tape and then rewinding. It is a recommended procedure which is incorporated into the **FILE-SAVE** and **ACCOUNT-SAVE** procedure and does not affect the data on the tape in any way

T-REW
Rewinds the attached media to the start or 'load point' and should always be used before data is saved or retrieved from magnetic devices

T-SELECT
The **T-SELECT** verb attaches a 'tape' device to the current process. These devices include floppy diskettes, streaming cartridge tape (sct), half-inch and 'pseudo-floppies' such as communication ports and inter-virtual-machine files. This verb is the root command from which **SET-FLOPPY**, **SET-SCT** and **SET-HALF** operate. If no options or parameters are specified, **T-SELECT** displays all devices defined for the system and prompts for a selection. The general format of the command is as follows:

:**t-select**
:**t-select** {*device*} {(*options*)}
:**t-select** {*keyword*} {(*options*)}

where

device	is a device number from 0 to 15 corresponding to a pre-defined tape device
keyword	may be any combination of characters (except numeric integers between 0 and 15) appearing in the TYPE, DENSITY or DEVICE NAME columns of the **T-STAT** verb. These keywords are used to try to pinpoint the desired device from a captured list. On some systems there may be more than one of a particular device (two $5\frac{1}{4}''$ floppies, for example). If there is not sufficient uniqueness in the parameters, the process will always find the first floppy On UNIX implementations, if there is more than one floppy drive, and one of them is a $5\frac{1}{4}''$ floppy, the $5\frac{1}{4}''$ is always designated as drive A. If no other parameters but FLOPPY are given, the verb will assume drive A, $5\frac{1}{4}''$ high density floppy

Figure 20.8 *Continued*

options	is one of the following
3	$3\frac{1}{2}''$ floppy
5	$5\frac{1}{4}''$ floppy
9	9-track, $\frac{1}{2}''$ tape
a	$5\frac{1}{4}''$ floppy
b	$3\frac{1}{2}''$ floppy
c	Changes the 8mm tape block size. The current tape block size is displayed and the operator is prompted for the new block size (0 or 512). On AP/Unix Systems, the default block size is set to 0 (zero) at install time. Zero means variable-length
e	Selects 2.88mb floppy. (AP 5.2.5 and higher only)
f	Floppy ($3\frac{1}{2}''$ or $5\frac{1}{4}''$ as default)
h	High density (1.44M for $3\frac{1}{2}''$ floppy, 1.2M for $5\frac{1}{4}''$ floppy, 6250 bpi for 9-track tapes, 150M for Quarter Inch tapes)
i	Suppresses display of devices after the command is complete and useful for MACROs
k	Hard disk 'pseudo' tapes. These devices are removable or fixed hard disks or regular Unix files. Their size is fixed and determined by the device or by the maximum file size for a user. The main usage for these devices is for small, fast t-dumps/saves, transaction logging or incremental saves
l	Low density (720K for $3\frac{1}{2}''$ floppy, 1600 bpi for 9-track tapes)
m	Medium density (720K for $5\frac{1}{4}''$ floppy, 3600 bpi for 9-track tapes)
n	Network 'pseudo' tape. This device has an 'infinite' size. It is assumed another system is reading the data at the 'other end' of the network
q	Quarter Inch tape
r	Prevents an automatic rewind on the device. This option must be used to set the device to a floppy with an unformatted floppy disk in the drive
s	Standard density (360 for $5\frac{1}{2}''$ floppy, 60M or 120M for quarter- inch (SCT) tapes

T-SPACE {*nnn*}
Moves the attached media forward a specified number of files, displaying each tape label as it is encountered

T-STATUS
This command displays the current settings of the peripheral storage device characteristics consisting of its type, density and drive number of the most recently used T-ATT device. The media does not have to be attached to the current process in order to use this command

T-UNLOAD
Rewinds, unloads and detaches the attached tape

Figure 20.8 *Continued*

T-WEOF
Writes and 'end-of-file' (EOF) marker at the current tape position on the currently attached device after a flush of the last buffer written. Writing two EOF markers creates and 'end-of-data' (EOD) mark

T-WTLBL
Writes a PICK format 80 character tape label at the current position on the currently attached device

Figure 20.8 *Continued*

Advanced PICK introduced the command **SET-DEVICE** a more generalized version of the **SET-*xxxx*** where the device can be expressed as a number, relating to the number assigned to a given backup device. If a system has two identical devices, two 3½″ floppy drives , for example, the other **SET-*xxxx*** options will select only the first. The format of the **SET-DEVICE** verb is given in Figure 20.9.

:**set-device** {*nnn*} {(*options*}
:**set-device** {*device*} {(*options*}
:**set-device** {*keyword*} {(*options*}

where

nnn	is the device number numbered from 0 to 9 as they appear in the configuration file.
device	is a device number from 0 to 15 (displayed if the command **SET-DEVICE** is executed without any further arguments).
keyword	is one of the following. **720K** **1.2M** **1.44M** **3½** **5¼** **FLOPPY** **8MM** **HALF INCH**
options	is one of the following.

3	3½″ floppy.
5	5¼″ floppy.
9	9-track, ½″ tape.
a	5¼″ floppy.
b	3½″ floppy.
c	Changes the 8mm tape block size. The current tape block size is displayed and the operator is prompted for the new block size (0 or 512). On AP/Unix Systems, the default block size is set to 0 (zero) at install time. Zero means variable-length.
e	Selects 2.88mb floppy. (AP 5.2.5 and higher only).
f	Floppy (3½″ or 5¼″ as default).
h	High density (1.44M for 3½″ floppy, 1.2M for 5½″ floppy, 6250 bpi for 9-track tapes, 150M for Quarter Inch tapes).

Figure 20.9 The format of **SET-DEVICE**.

i	Suppresses display of devices after the command is complete (useful for MACROs).
k	Hard disk 'pseudo' tapes. These devices are removable or fixed hard disks or regular Unix files. Their size is fixed and determined by the device or by the maximum file size for a user. The main usage for these devices is for small, fast t-dumps/saves, transaction logging or incremental saves.
l	Low density (720K for 3½″ floppy, 1600 bpi for 9-track tapes).
m	Medium density (720K for 5¼″ floppy, 3600 bpi for 9-track tapes).
n	Network 'pseudo' tape. This device has an 'infinite' size. It is assumed another system is reading the data at the 'other end' of the network.
q	Quarter Inch tape.
r	Prevents an automatic rewind on the device. This option must be used to set the device to a floppy with an unformatted floppy disk in the drive.
s	Standard density (360 for 5½″ floppy, 60M or 120M for quarter-inch (SCT) tapes.

Figure 20.9 Continued

With floppy disks, there is one additional command to be aware of, and it is the one to format the physical diskette. Nowadays it is possible to purchase ready formatted diskettes and for the little extra it costs, it is well worth considering. No floppy disk can be used until it has been formatted so if you do not purchase your diskettes ready formatted you will have to format the diskette immediately before it is used for the very first time. Again the verb to perform this function can vary dependent on the PICK implementation but under Advanced PICK it is **FORMAT** but other licencee implementations allow:

FORMAT-FLOPPY
FORMAT-DISKETTE
FFORMAT

20.2.2 System generation backup and restore processes

A system generation tape is a copy of the entire data on your disk including the PICK operating system. This facility is generally only available from licensees and not with versions of R83 and Advanced PICK supplied direct from PICK Systems. If such a facility exists, it is obviously advisable to take such a backup upon receiving your system and at regular intervals thereafter. Since this is not a generally available facility you will have to follow the instructions in your operations manual to perform this process. If you are unable to create a system generation backup then you will only have ***one*** copy of PICK, which should naturally be treated with every precaution. If this copy gets lost or damaged and you need to recover, the only way would be by a replacement set, which could involve costly delays.

The method of restoring the system from a system generation tape is to reboot the system with the system generation tape/diskette loaded in the system. Once the operating system has been loaded from the backup, you will be prompted whether or not you wish to restore from the backup or just execute the PICK environment. If the file system is satisfactory take the execute option, otherwise restore the entire file system too.

20.2.3 The FILE-SAVE backup and restore processes

Saving the file system

The FILE-SAVE procedure will place on a backup medium a copy of all data, with the exception of the PICK database/operating system. This process is normally handled by a program in the **dm** account which ultimately executes the **SAVE** verb. The **SAVE** verb is common to the file-save process as well as that for backing up an individual account and handling an incremental file save. See Figure 20.10 for full details on the **SAVE** verb and its options.

SAVE {(*options*}

where

- **b** Saves the b-tree indexes; prevents having to regenerate them after a file-restore.
- **c** Creates R83-compatible file-save tapes, generating a file-save media that will restore on R83 machines. AP files have dictionary codes that are not recognized by R83 and vice versa. Accounts should be 'updated' when restored. This option does not work with incremental saves, only file and account saves. **dl**, **dp**, and **ds** pointers are saved as normal D-pointers. **dc** and **dy** pointers are saved as they are. Binary items are properly dumped as R83 **CC** pointer items. Items larger than 32K and not in **dc** files are skipped, with a message displayed. Binary code items not in **dc** files are also skipped.
- **f** Displays the file names as they are saved. If omitted, only the **mds** file and individual Master Dictionary names are listed.
- **g** Displays GFEs (group format errors) when found, but skips the group and continues the save. Errors are logged in the file **errors** in the **dm** account attributes 14, 15, and 16 of the error item. Attribute 14 is the save date, 15 is the primary group fid (from gfe.sr), and 16 is the 'account > dict > data' display information. At the end of the save, a message displays indicating the total number of gfe's encountered, if at least one was found.

Figure 20.10 The **SAVE** verb.

i Individual master dictionary save. The system prompts for the account name, if it is not specified at TCL. Using the **i** option with an active list generates multiple account-saves. If a list is active and the **i** option is specified, the system generates a tape that may be restored with the **restore-accounts** command.

k Reorganizes all 'file-of-files' numbers sequentially on the tape. This is also useful when frame one is corrupted or some file numbers are negative. The incremental restore will abort with negative file numbers. (AP 6.0 and higher only.)

l Each file may have a list of specific item-ids within the file to save. This option saves only the list of item-ids provided in the associated item for the given file, located in the FILE-OF-FILES, beginning at attribute 25. Any number of item-ids may follow in attributes 26 and beyond. An '*' (asterisk) in attribute 25 saves all items in the file. If there is no list, only the file defining item is saved, as if the file had a **dy** d/code. In addition, the **l** option does not 'unmark' (clear 'dirty' bits) items that have changed. These items will be saved on subsequent incremental file-saves or account-saves. This is similar to the **v** option for the full file-save.

m This is the same as the **l** option, but it additionally 'unmarks', or 'clears' the 'dirty' bits.

p Directs console listing to the printer, via the Spooler.

q Changes the terminal display from hierarchical format to indented format. This is the 'old' (R83) save display format.

r This is the same as the **l** and **m** options, except the list is also saved with the file as a separate item in the FILE-OF-FILES.

s This option generates additional statistics available with the verb **list-file-stats**.

t Outputs to the 'tape' (magnetic media) which has been previously attached to the process. If the **t** option is not specified, **save** does all the processing, but nothing is written to the media. The system prompts for the file-save tape label which is written on the tape as part of the tape label. Omitting the **t** option is useful for re- generating system statistics and/or for finding gfe's, and is the basis of 'dummy' saves.

u Performs an 'incremental' file-save or account-save. This saves all file items and data items that have changed since the last full file-save or account-save.

v Performs a 'full' file-save, but does not 'unmark' the items that have been changed. These items will continue to be saved on subsequent incremental file-saves. Unless the **i** or **u** options are specified, the system does a 'full' file-save.

w Unmarks, or clears, 'dirty' bits 'on-the-fly'. Normally, this occurs at the end of the save. This additionally causes update locks to be placed on the groups as they are saved and updated, in addition to the 'read' locks which are normally set during a save.

x Saves files with a 'd-pointer' type of 'dx'.

y Saves files with a 'd-pointer' type of 'dy'.

Figure 20.10 *Continued*

R83 'save' options:

The following options were available on all R83-compatible, pre-AP releases. Some of the option characters are used in AP, but their functionality has changed.

d	Saves data files.
f	Outputs filenames. When omitted, only system-level names are displayed.
g	Handles gfe's encountered during save. Rather than stopping and waiting for a response, it skips the rest of the current group and proceeds to the next group. Logs entries in the STAT-FILE when used with the 's' option.
n	No overflow space is required.
p	Directs the report output (not the saved data) to the printer, via the Spooler. If 'p' is not specified, output is displayed to the terminal.
s	Creates file statistics in STAT-FILE.
t	Outputs to the 'tape' (magnetic media) which has been previously attached to the process. If the **t** option is not specified, **save** does all the processing, but nothing is written to the media. The system prompts for the file-save tape label which is written on the tape as part of the tape label. Omitting the **t** option is useful for re-generating system statistics and/or for finding gfe's, and is the basis of 'dummy' saves.

Figure 20.10 *Continued*

The file-save program will handle all aspects of the backup process through a question and answer session after which a security copy of your data will be created. During the procedure, file statistics are recorded in a file called FILE-OF-FILES. Whilst one of the file-save options allows for the statistics to be printed as part of the file-save process, they can be reproduced thereafter by the command **LIST-FILE-STATS** or by use of a simple ACCESS enquiry. In order to establish the dictionary items available for use in your ACCESS enquiries, carry out the command **SORT ONLY DICT FILE-OF-FILES** which will list them for you.

The FILE-OF-FILES provides useful information about file sizes which enables the System Administrator to keep a watchful eye on files which may need resizing. Additionally, of course, it will show up files that are bigger than they should be, typically word-processing files because they contain unwanted items have not been removed.

Figure 20.11 shows typical output from the **LIST-FILE-STATS** command. Some of the information from the file statistics report is an invaluable aid in determining incorrectly sized files. The specific column headings are as follows:

r#	the reel or volume number that the file resides on
seq#	the file sequence number within the file-save
file#	the file sequence number in the MD
fname	the file name

mod	file modulo
bytes	the number of bytes in the file i.e. the file size
items	the number of items in the file
ovfitems	the number of items residing in overflow frames
frames	the total number of frames used by this file
ptr-fms	the number of pointer frames used by this file

PAGE 5 ** FILE STATISTICS REPORT ** 22 Oct 1994
Account: dm

r#	seq#.	file#	fname.......	mod.....	bytes.....	items..	ovfitms	frames..	ptrfms
0	7	43	newac newac	23	45610	808	201	56	
0	8	44	newac rs6000	3	668	10	3		
0	9	45	newac system	7	2590	18	7		
0	66	98	pibs	3	3957	25	6	6	21
0	67	99	pibs pibs	37	288	6	37		
0	71	103	users users	23	711	6	29	6	
0	52	84	words	1	597	1	2	1	
0	53	85	words words	1	1	1			
	*** dm				4565612	12100	4966	5813	3108
					4566805	12108	4966	5819	3110

[405] 73 items listed out of 2184 items.

Figure 20.11 Output from the **LIST-FILE-STATS** command.

Since a file save operation can be a highly time-consuming exercise, there may be certain accounts or certain files you may not wish to back up each time. These accounts can be marked with a DX in attribute 1 of the system dictionary item, whilst the files not to be backed up need to have a DX in attribute 1 of the master dictionary item. Whilst this is an extremely useful facility to reduce backup times, it can be dangerous in that should the system need to be recovered from the file save tape, the contents of the file save tape are used to *completely* overwrite the file system. Hence any files or accounts not included on the file save tape will not be restored and will, therefore, no longer exist. In certain situations unless other copies of the Dxed files have been kept it could mean that valuable data is lost forever!

There are valid reasons for DXing accounts, for example where the account rarely changes and adequate backups already exist, typically application program accounts or accounts containing static data, such as a postcode database. It is also possible to use DY in place of DX in file definition items which means that the files will be restored empty of data following a file restore process. This process has its uses for certain types of transaction file. File definition item types are discussed further in Section 7.1.3.

The order of saved data on the tape

During the file-save process, PICK displays a list of the data saved and an example of a typical display is shown below:

```
1      35 > dm
1      36 > dm > newac
1      37 > dm > newac > newac
```

Although the display shown above suggests that the **dm** file (a level 1 file , or MD) is saved before the **dm** > **newac** file (a level 2, or dictionary file) which itself is saved before the **dm** > **newac** > **newac** file (a level 3, or data file) this is not what actually happens. In fact, the D-pointers to the **dm** account and **dm** >**newac** are saved, but not the data within them. The data file is saved ***first*** followed by its dictionary and the data from the MD is saved ***last***. This enables PICK to rebuild the account properly with new file sizing when the file system or an account is restored.

Restoring the file system

To reload the file system from backup, reboot the system with the PICK System diskette or tape loaded. This initiates a cold-start process which will prompt

```
Options: K)ill F)ile only, A)BS only, X) eXecute
```

When this message is displayed, place the latest file save backup in the machine (this could have been a system generation backup tape from which the system was booted), and take the F option. The entire file system will be re-built and if any files have had their re-sizing parameters set, the files will be restored with their new modulos.

20.2.4 Verifying the data secured

Once the data has been backed up it should be checked to see that the copy contains readable data. Under R83 this was achieved by using the **SEL-RESTORE** command, but in Advanced PICK a new command **t-verify** was introduced and is an option provided during the **file-save** process. If it is selected, errors are logged to the **tv.log** file which will be created when it is required. The **t-verify** command is far more thorough than **SEL-RESTORE** in its checking process because it compares the contents of the backup with the actual contents of the hard disk. It does mean, of course that changes cannot be made to the database until the backup and verify processes are complete, but in honesty this is only sensible anyway. Whilst the verification effectively doubles the backup time, it can save a lot of heartache and wasted time when things go wrong and the backup tape has to be relied on to recover data. Since most backups are performed unattended overnight, this is rarely an issue. Figure 20.12 gives details of the **t-verify** command and its options.

---

t-verify {(*options*}

where the possible options are

- *nnn* a number indicating the 'choke' count. This specifies the maximum number of errors allowed before the procedure is aborted. If this occurs the tape is left at the abort point.
- **?** displays brief on-line help.
- **a** validates an account-save and verifies all accounts until the 'end of save' mark is encountered. This option is useful for file-save reels other than reel 1 (one).
- **d** suppresses display of duplicate item-ids in a group. (R83 only).
- **e** displays errors only.
- **f** displays all file names found on the tape in hierarchical format. If used with the **I** option, item-ids are also displayed.
- **g** suppresses group 'hashing'. Skips hashing test on all items. No errors will be found if items are in the wrong group. This item is especially useful when going from AP to R83 (using the **c** option with the **save** command), where case sensitivity could generate error messages for all lower-case items. The most likely use for this option is on R83 systems only.
- **i** displays all items found on the tape in file hierarchy format. The display is 'in place' for each file (i.e. all items for that file display on the same line). If used with the **f** option, items are displayed in the 'form-feed' format, showing each item on a new line.
- **l** logs errors to a log file. Attribute 1 of the log file is the error message from the **messages** file in the **dm** account. Attribute 2 is the element that caused the error, in hierarchical form. The **l** option prompts the operator for the log file name.
- **n** activates 'nopage' function on output to terminal.
- **p** directs output to printer, via the Spooler.
- **q** queries operator on each error found. The operator gets a choice to either continue, quit or skip file system comparisons for the current file.
- **t** verifies contents of tape only.
- **x** displays index b-trees found on tape. This is useful for determining if the indices were saved with the file system. See the b option in the save command for saving indices (refer to Figure 20.10)

Figure 20.12 The **T-VERIFY** command and its options.

20.2.5 Incremental saves

An incremental save is one of the new features of Advanced PICK and is a save of the changes made to all the file definition and data items that have changed since the last full file-save. An incremental save can be processed for an individual account or for the entire file system, i.e. at the file-save level.

PICK knows whether or not an item has changed since the last full file-save because it sets a flag when it has. Each item has an 8 byte header, one of which, byte 6 contains item flags which tells the system its state and what kind of record it is. One of the bits of the item byte indicates whether the item has been updated since the last file save and another indicates whether the item has been deleted. These status bits are known as the 'dirty bits'.

Incremental file saves, by virtue of only saving changes, do not take a great deal of time, so you can schedule these at much shorter and more regular intervals. Do be aware that an incremental save contains the changes since the last full file-save, not since the last incremental save, so on a very active transactional system, incremental saves will take longer and longer each time they are run until the next file-save is complete. To restore using the incremental system, means first restoring from the latest file or account save and then applying the last incremental save.

The commands to perform incremental saves are as follows:

SAVE (UT)	an incremental file save
SAVE (IT)	an incremental account save

At the end of the **SAVE** process (unless the **V** option is taken) these 'dirty bits' are reset and the system displays the message 'clearing dirty bits' followed by the frame numbers being examined and updated. This process can take a while on a system with a large disk, so please be aware it will happen and be patient!

You should be aware that if a file has a **dx** or **dy** code and an item in it is updated, that item will not be marked as changed when it is filed. Therefore, even if the 'x' or 'y' is removed before the save process, that item will not be saved by an incremental file-save.

The save process locks groups as it saves them. While the group is locked, no process may access any item in that group. Locking groups prevents spurious Group Format Error messages that would occur if another process changed an item while it was being saved.

Up to four groups may be locked at one time these being:

- the mds dictionary pointer
- the md pointer
- the file dictionary pointer
- the group for the data currently being saved.

An update lock is attempted before a group is cleared of 'deleted' items. As locked groups are not permitted to shift, any deleted items cannot be removed immediately. They are 'marked' as 'updated-and-deleted', and will be removed later by other processes.

Any changes made to the file system during the save (either a change or a deletion) are ***not*** written to the save. This is yet another reason why the save process should be carried out without anyone using the system.

20.2.6 The ACCOUNT-SAVE backup processes

The **ACCOUNT-SAVE** verb is controlled by a PICK BASIC program which issues a **SAVE** command in order to save all the data of an individual account to tape or diskette. The program has no tape-handling commands included in it, so you should attach and rewind the backup device prior to carrying out an account save.

The format of the **ACCOUNT-SAVE** verb is shown in Figure 20.13 and a sample account save dialogue is given in Figure 20.14. In order for the incremental account save to work, the system marks any item that is changed. This mark is normally cleared by a complete file-save; however, when using the **ACCOUNT-SAVE**, the marks indicating changed items are not cleared.

ACCOUNT-SAVE {*account.name*} {*account.name...*} {(*options*)}
file-save tape label = {*tape.label*}
account name = *account.name.reply*

where

account.name	is the name of the account to save. If more than one account is specified, each must be separated by a space. If the account name is not specified, the system prompts for the account name.
options	any of the options applicable to the **SAVE** verb can be applied (see Figure 20.10 for a list of these). The account-save process saves the entire account unless the **u** option (incremental save option) is specified.
tape.label	is an optional 48-character character string which is written into the tape label area at the beginning of each reel or volume of the save and is only requested if an account name has not been specified on the command line.
account.name.reply	is the name of the account to be saved and will only be prompted where the account name has not previously been specified.

Figure 20.13 The **ACCOUNT-SAVE** verb.

```
:set-floppy (ah   <-  indicates the backup device and its density
Block size: 500
[1088] Tape device is assigned to 3½" high density (1.44M) floppy using drive 'A '.
:t-rew   <-  rewinding the device before its use
Block size: 500
[96] bot
:account-save sb+
Block size: 500
1  123  > SB+
1  124  > SB+ > DMDIARY
1  125  > SB+ > DMDIARY > DMDIARY
1  126  > SB+ > DMDIARY.ARCHIVE
1  127  > SB+ > DMDIARY.ARCHIVE > DMDIARY.ARCHIVE

1  136  > SB+ > DMDIARY.FINAL
1  137  > SB+ > DMDIARY.FINAL > DMDIARY.FINAL
:t-rew
:t-verify (elnp
```

Figure 20.14 The **ACCOUNT-SAVE** dialogue.

20.2.7 Restoring an individual account

The **ACCOUNT-RESTORE** command reverses the save processes of **FILE-SAVE** and **ACCOUNT-SAVE** and will restore an account from a security backup. The account must not already exist on disk otherwise the message **EXISTS ON FILE** will be displayed. This is a protection mechanism to prevent you from overwriting a working account. If the account you are restoring is still resident on your hard disk, you will first need to remove it using the **DELETE-ACCOUNT** verb discussed in Section 6.2.2. You can also use the account restore process to restore the account under a different name, which can be useful where you want to create a copy of the account for training or testing purposes. Remember too that if you are restoring an account that has been saved on a system with a different frame size to the one used by your system, you will need to state the frame size of the source computer as one of the options at the command line. This is so PICK can create a file of the correct modulo, otherwise too little space or too much space will be allocated because PICK will use exactly the same modulos when restoring an account of those of the file at the save time, unless told otherwise.

The general format of the command is given in Figure 20.15, whilst a typical dialogue is shown in Figure 20.16. In this figure the account **RBACCOUNT** is restored from a backup stored on floppy disk under the name **RB.BACKUP**.

:account-restore *account.name* {(*options*)}
`account name on tape :` *acount.name.reply*[CR]

where

account.name	is the name to be given to the account being restored	
account.namereply	is the name of the saved account being restored	
options	are as follows	
	nnn	is the frame.size, as an integer number, of the source system which created the backup and is only required where the frame size of the source and target systems differs. This option automatically affects modulos, which are either divided or multiplied by the given number, according to the data frame size on the target machine (the **what** command shows the frame size under the heading **dfsize**). This file resizing operation occurs after the reallocation parameter has been checked, unless file resizing has been disabled during the initial boot process.
	a	indicates that the tape is already positioned at the data section of the correct account. This means that it is positioned past the label, right at the beginning of the data. For example, if a **t-fwd** command was executed to position the media to the right spot on the tape, a **t-rdlbl** command would have to be executed to be positioned at the beginning of the data. (R83 only)
	a	account-save tape verification. This verifies all accounts until an 'end of save' mark is found on tape. It first forwards to the beginning of an account and verifies its contents which is useful for verification reels other than reel one. (AP only)
	c	stands for compatible tape and is used on tapes produced on 'licensee' systems such as Ultimate, McDonnell Douglas, ADDS, General Automation, etc.) The restore process runs noticeably slower. (AP only)
	d	data-sensitive files. All files except the md will be restored as ds-type files (case sensitive). (AP only)
	n	disables file reallocation process.
	s	ignores tape label information. (R83 only)
	s	suppresses messages on txlog tapes. (AP only)
	z	bypasses prompts for restore from incremental or transaction logs. (AP only)

Figure 20.15 The format of the **ACCOUNT-RESTORE** command.

Additional changes saved on a transaction log and/or incremental save tape may also be applied, once the account/master dictionary has been restored and these two options are requested by default.

```
:set-floppy (ah ◄──── indicates the backup device and its density
Block size: 500
[1088] Tape device is assigned to 3 1/2' high density (1.44M) floppy using
drive 'A '.
:t-rew ◄──── rewinding the device before its use
Block size: 500
[96] bot
:account-restore rbaccount
account name on tape: rb.backup
rb.backup
1  > rbaccount 77177,37  ◄──── creating the account's MD
1  > rbaccount > SAHELP 77215,23  ◄──── a file with a dictionary level only
1  > rbaccount > SAPROCESS 60076,1
1  > rbaccount > SAPROCESS > SAPROCESS 77239,23
1  > rbaccount > SA.PRODUCT 60087,3  ◄──── the dictionary of the file SA.PRODUCT
1  > rbaccount > SA.PRODUCT > SA.PRODUCT 77263,3 ◄── the data of the file SA.PRODUCT
1  > rbaccount > SADEFN 77267,23
1  > rbaccount > SA.PROVINCE 77291,7
1  > rbaccount > SA.PROVINCE > SA.PROVINCE 60097,1
1  > rbaccount > SA.PCODE.INDEX 60104,1
1  > rbaccount > SA.PCODE.INDEX > SA.PCODE.INDEX 77299,53
│
▼
1  > rbaccount > SA.SOURCE > SA.SOURCE 77648,1
1  > rbaccount > SA.COUNTY 77650,11
1  > rbaccount > SA.COUNTY > SA.COUNTY 77662,3
1  > rbaccount > SAWORK 77669,1
1  > rbaccount > SAWORK > SAWORK 77671,37
  Restore from incremental save tape (y/n)? n
  Restore from transaction log tape (y/n)? n
restore completed
:
```

Figure 20.16 The **ACCOUNT-RESTORE** dialogue.

Do be aware that the **account-restore** process may be started from any tape of a multi-tape **file-save** which could save considerable time in a multi-reel situation. You can determine which reel contains the account by examining your file statistics report, providing the **file-save** has been performed with the **s** option. Similar to the file restore process, PICK will recreate the index files once the restore is complete.

20.2.8 Restoring multiple accounts

Whilst it is possible to restore several accounts from a single backup tape by performing multiple **ACCOUNT-RESTORE** commands, it means that you will need to sit through the restore process to execute the **ACCOUNT-RESTORE** command after each account has been loaded. Equally you will have to know which order the accounts were stored on the tape and that's not always the case.

The simple solution is to use the **RESTORE-ACCOUNTS** verb which restores all accounts from the backup medium which do not already exist on the system. This can be done from either a full file-save tape or a tape containing multiple account saves. This command is most frequently used after upgrading the operating system, when only the initial PICK file system has been loaded and all user data accounts need to be restored.

There are two options to be aware of and both would follow the verb preceded with a left parenthesis

c used with tapes created on Ultimate systems
u indicates the tape label is in Ultimate format

20.2.9 Backing up individual files

An individual file may be backed up by means of the **T-DUMP** command, which was briefly discussed in Section 12.6.3 on ACCESS. This command is also used to selectively back up records from a data or dictionary file since the command can optionally include selection criteria. Without any qualification (selection criteria), the entire file will be backed up. It is important to remember that the data and dictionary portions of a file are separate files. Hence, to back up an entire file, the dictionary file must be dumped in the same way, and as well as its data portion, and similarly it must be restored separately. Figure 20.17

```
:set-floppy (ah
Block size: 500
[1088] Tape device is assigned to 3 1/2' high density (1.44M) floppy using
drive 'A '.
:t-rew
Block size: 500
[96] bot
:t-dump dict stratum,slmaster,
     1 NAME
     2 TEL
     3 REGION.CODE
     |
     |
    23 FAX
    24 ADDRESS
    25 CURRENT.BALANCE
[802] 25 items dumped.
:t-dump stratum,slmaster,
     1 2298
     2 1663
     3 2934
     |
     |
   373 1279
   374 2550
   375 2297
[802] 375 items dumped.
:
```

Figure 20.17 Using **T-DUMP** to backup a file.

illustrates a typical T-DUMP process where the file SLMASTER in the account STRATUM, is backed up to floppy disk.

20.2.10 The file restore process using T-LOAD

The T-LOAD process is the reverse of T-DUMP and can only be used from a T-DUMP backup. In exactly the same way as with T-DUMP, the **T-LOAD** statement can contain selection criteria to qualify the records of a file that is restored.

Without this qualification, all records are restored. The file must already exist in the account you are working in otherwise the error message [10] The file name missing will be displayed. If the item being restored already exists on the file, a message will be displayed to that effect; the original item will not be overwritten.

If the file being restored does not exist it will have to be created using the **CREATE-FILE** command, which is described in Section 6.3.1. These **T-DUMP** and **T-LOAD** commands can be used to create test data in test accounts, which contain a subset of the live data. Figure 20.18 shows a typical dialogue from the use of the **T-LOAD** command.

```
:set-floppy
Block size: 500
[1088] Tape device is assigned to 3 1/2' high density (1.44M) floppy using
drive 'A '.
:t-rew
Block size: 500
[96] bot
:t-load dict slmaster
BLOCK SIZE 1000
1 ADDRESS
2 NAME
3 CRLIMIT
...
...
10 item(s) loaded.
:t-load slmaster
BLOCK SIZE 1000
1 A0007
2 C0018
3 A0003
4 D0003
5 D0004
  |
  v
53 item(s) loaded.
```

Figure 20.18 Using the **T-LOAD** command.

20.2.11 Selective restores

Selective accounts can be restored from a file save tape using the standard **ACCOUNT-RESTORE** command. In the case of an extreme emergency you might like to know that it is possible to restore an account from a system generation tape, again using the **ACCOUNT-RESTORE** verb, but after having **T-FWD**ed past the ABS frames at the beginning of the tape. PICK will look consecutively through the tape from start to finish, so in order to save wasted time rewinding and researching through the tape, accounts selected for restore should be selected in the order in which they were originally saved and the file statistics report will give you this information. Remember too, that accounts can be restored from a full file-save tape.

Individual files and items may be selectively restored from a file-save, account-save, incremental-save or transaction-log tape. The means of doing this is with the **SEL-RESTORE** command. The selective restore can be initiated from any tape of a multi-tape backup, which saves wasting time searching from the start of the first tape produced. Again the statistics file report will enable you to determine which volume the data is held on. However at any point, the media may be **T-BCK** (*n* or **T-FWD** (*n* to reposition it (assuming the media device supports these commands).

Finally, selected records may be restored to a file based on the selection criteria of the ACCESS command **T-LOAD**. Hence all records whose name starts with the letter **R** could be restored from a **T-DUMP** backup, using the command **T-LOAD SLMASTER WITH NAME = "R]"**.

As with any of the file or item restore processes, do remember that the file you are accessing must already exist in the account in which you are working. The format of the **SEL-RESTORE** command is shown in Figure 20.19.

20.2.12 Controlled shutdown

The way in which the system is shut down is extremely important. The PICK system is a virtual memory system and frequently frames of data are held in memory for long periods before they are written away to disk. This means that simply powering off the system could mean a substantial loss of data.

Until release 6.1 of Advanced PICK, which introduced the feature called 'halt tolerance', PICK users risked severe problems by just turning off their systems without following the controlled shutdown procedure. Whilst PICK would carry out automatic and routine flushes of 'write required' frames to disk, if the system was unplugged prior to this happening, at best the system would suffer from GFEs and at worst would power up with the message 'referencing illegal frame abort' and also need the ABS area rebuilt.

If you are working on Advanced PICK 6.1 and above, then you can just power off your system, but even so it is advisable and recommended to follow the controlled shutdown procedure. The normal command for this is **SHUTDOWN** but licencee versions can vary, so do make sure you know the command to use. Once executed, the procedure will ask you to confirm whether or not you wish to continue with the message

```
Do you wish to continue (Y/N/0)?
```

:SEL-RESTORE *file* {*item.list*} {(*options*)}
`Account name on tape:?` *account.name*
`File Name:?` *tape.file*

where

file	indicates the file to restore into.
item.list	designates which items to restore from tape. A null list (i.e. ignore this option) restores all items.
account.name	indicates the name of the account on the media used for the restore process.
tape.file	indicates the name of the file on the media used for the restore process. If a null is entered, the account's master dictionary is restored.

N.B. The specified *account.name* and *tape.file* must match exactly with the appropriate names on tape.

options

a	Indicates that the media is already positioned at the correct account. The **a** option is used to avoid rewinding and searching. If the order of the files on the tape is known (from the file-stats report normally generated following the save) then multiple files may be restored without rewinding the media. After the first file is restored on the account, the next **sel-restore** is done using the **a** option. The **sel-restore** process prompts directly for the file. The system next prompts for full, incremental, or transaction restore. As the tape is searched, the file names on it are printed, along with the file numbers. Names are indented one space for account names, two spaces for dictionaries, and three for data file names. At the completion of the restore, the system again prompts for incremental and transaction restore.
c	Causes every item before the next end of file to be a candidate for restore. This ensures that data can be restored even if a D-pointer is damaged on the tape. This option is used with the **n** option.
f	Displays all file references for all accounts and is not compatible with the **n** option.
i	Item-ids of the restored items are not to be printed.
n	Restores a file by its number. The process prompts for the number of the file to restore. This option is particularly useful for restoring from a multi-reel backup media, so that the restore can begin from the reel where the file resides (or begins). The file number can be found on the file statistics report.
o	Overwrites, if a duplicate item-id is found on disk. D-pointers are protected from being overwritten.
s	Suppresses the *'item-id'* exists on file message.

Figure 20.19 The **SEL-RESTORE** command.

where 0 (zero) means only shutdown the system if the process is executed from line zero. Versions of AP before 5.2.5 lacked the '0' option. On UNIX platforms of AP version 5.1.0 onwards, this same functionality could be handled with the **EXIT** command on line 0.

In the rare instances that the manufacturer has no recommended procedure to follow, ensure that all other users are logged off the system and if your implementation has the **FLUSH** verb use this to flush the 'write required' frames to disk. If this verb does not exist then allow five minutes to pass before powering off. Following these procedures you will be able to shutdown your system in the secure knowledge that the integrity of the database has been protected.

21 Managing your System

TCL verbs and general commands covered in this chapter

ACCOUNT-MAINT	ACCOUNT-SAVE	ADMIN	ADMIN.CONTROL
ADMIN.FILES	ADMIN.MAINT	ADMIN.STATUS	ADMIN.TAPE
ADMIN.TAPE.SETUP	BREAK-DEBUG	BREAK-KEY	BREAK-LEVEL
CONFIG.MENU	COMPARE	DATE	DEBUG
DEFINE-TERMINAL	DUMP	ECHO	ECHO-ON
ECHO-OFF	END	ESC-DATA	ESC-LEVEL
ESC-TOGGLE	FLUSH	FREE	GROUP
HASH-TEST	HELP	ISTAT	ITEM
LERRS	LISTABS	LIST-JOBS	LIST-LINES
LIST-PIBS	LOGON	LOGOFF	LU
MAXUSERS	MESSAGE	MOVE-FILE	MSG
OVF	POVF	PRIME	REBOOT
RECOVER-FD	RECOVER-ITEM	RESET-PORT	SAVE
SEARCH-FILE	SEARCH-SYSTEM	SEL-RESTORE	SEND-MESSAGE
SET-BAUD	SET-DATE	SET-DATE-EUR	SET-DATE-STD
SET-KBRD	SET-OVF	SET-OVF-RESERVE	SET-SYM
SET-TERM	SET-TIME	SHUTDOWN	SM
SP-ASSIGN	SP-KILL	SP-STATUS	STAT
STARTPTR	STEAL-FILE	TANDEM	TCL
TERM	TERM-TYPE	TIME	VERIFY-SYSTEM
WHAT	WHERE	WHICH	WHO
XCS-ON			

21.1 The role of the System Administrator

This section summarizes the role of the System Administrator in managing a PICK-based system. Whether PICK is the database or primary operating system, there are tasks that must be undertaken to ensure the integrity of the system and to sort out the day-to-day problems that may arise with its use. In earlier chapters we have reviewed the structure of the PICK database and covered, in detail, the functional workings of its various facets. Undoubtedly you will have realized that this is a substantial product whose strengths can best be realized by a detailed understanding of its operation. In this respect, as with all other computer systems, at least one person, whom I have called the System Administrator, needs to gain at intimate understanding of PICK to be the person others can turn to in time of difficulty.

This chapter summarizes the role of the System Administrator. It encompasses several functions not discussed earlier and also those referenced in earlier chapters. It is intended that the System Administrator should be able to use this chapter to answer problems, either directly or by reference to other chapters.

21.2 System start up and close down

The first aspect of managing your system is being able to start up and close down your system in a controlled manner. These functions are mostly implementation-dependent and you should refer to your manual for those specific to your system. Few problems should be experienced in this area if you follow the instructions properly. For information on typical procedures refer to Section 4.1.

Do remember that the start-up and close-down messages are displayed on the terminal plugged into port 0 and that unless you have a special close-down procedure provided by your supplier, you must wait a few minutes after all others have logged off or, if available on your implementation, carry out a **FLUSH** command, to flush the memory to disk, before powering off (see Section 19.2.12). The cold-boot mechanism provides the means to restore the complete file system. This is touched on in Section 4.1.1 and discussed more fully in Section 19.2.3.

21.3 Logging on and logging off

Logging on and off the system is a simple process provided the necessary users have been set up and all required accounts exist and any passwords to them are correctly entered. The setting up of users is discussed in Section 6.1 whilst Section 4.2 discusses the procedure of logging on and logging off.

The other aspect of logging on is that of security and the use of passwords which is discussed in detail in Section 20.1.3. There are three levels of general access known as the System Privilege level, a topic covered in Section 20.1.4, and Section 20.1.5 continues the theme looking at security codes that can be set in the users record in the file **users**. Section 20.1.6 discusses the use of the logon PROC or MACRO and how that can be used to limit the users access within an account. Section 20.1.7 talks about the function of the users macro in the **users** file and Section 20.1.8 the means of restricting use of the break key, which unless switched off gives a user access to the system debugger.

21.4 Setting the date and time

Since many applications make use of the systems internal clock, before using the system, it may be necessary to set the date and time. On most systems these days a battery-backed clock is provided, and this process will generally be unnecessary on a day-to-day basis. Even so, at some stage you will need to make changes, even if it is just to cater for British Summer Time! The command **TIME** displays the current date and time whilst **SET-DATE** and **SET-TIME** change the date and time, respectively, as Figure 21.1 illustrates. In R83 only there is an option (**U** for updating the real-time clock when setting

```
:time
09:35:15 28 May 1995 Sunday
:set-time 10:32:00
:set-date 29MAY1995
:time
10:32:17 29 May 1995 Monday
```

Figure 21.1 Changing the date and time.

either the date or time. This is handled automatically in Advanced PICK and hence this option no longer exists.

If you find the format of date incorrect, in that it presents the day and month in the wrong order then there are two commands you should be aware of:

set-date-eur	which sets the date to the form dd/mm/yy
set-date-std	which sets the date to the form mm/dd/yy

Whilst neither of these commands will affect the way in which the time and date are displayed from the **time** command, it does affect the way in which dates are displayed from application programs.

There is one useful option available with the **date** command within Advanced PICK (not R83), the *c* option for outputting a calendar as shown below:

```
:date (c
May 29, 1995; Monday internal: 10011 julian: 149

 +----------------------------------------+
 |    M a y                 1 9 9 5       | 10:35:12
 | SUN | MON | TUE | WED | THU | FRI | SAT |
 |     |   1 |   2 |   3 |   4 |   5 |   6 |
 |   7 |   8 |   9 |  10 |  11 |  12 |  13 |
 |  14 |  15 |  16 |  17 |  18 |  19 |  20 |
 |  21 |  22 |  23 |  24 |  25 |  26 |  27 |
 |  28 |  29 |  30 |  31 |     |     |     |
 |     |     |     |     |     |     |     |
 +----------------------------------------+

 (D=Prev Month, F=Next Month, X=Exit)
 (Y=Prev Year, U=Next Year )
```

21.5 Control of terminals

Provided terminals are plugged in, switched on and operating with the correct terminal type, at the correct baud rate, they will rarely give any problems unless they develop a hardware fault. However, when you decide to purchase additional terminals you need to know how to link them to the system.

There are six tasks involved in the configuration of terminals:

(1) Setting up the terminal characteristics within the terminal itself (adjusting the contents of its PROM).
(2) Assigning the correct PICK terminal driver (or writing a fresh one).
(3) Connecting the terminal to the system with a properly configured cable.
(4) Setting the baud rate within PICK to match that set within the terminal PROM (as in step 1).
(5) Amending the PIBS file (the ACC file in R83) to reflect the characteristics of the total system configuration.
(6) Amending the coldstart MACRO (a PROC in R83) to reflect the characteristics of the total system configuration.

21.5.1 Terminal setup

Most terminals in common use today can emulate the operations of a wide variety of different terminals. In other words inside the Programmable ROM within the terminal is a series of programs capable of handling the cursor addressing functions identical to those of the original manufacturers of terminals such as the Wyse 60, Wyse 50, Televideo 925 and DEC VT100.

PICK supports a number standard terminals, each of which is assigned a terminal driver/definition. These definitions are held in a file called DEVICES in the DM account (a file called CURSOR in the SYSPROG account under R83). A terminal driver is software within PICK that enables data to be displayed 'properly' on a VDU, by virtue of the specification of a series of parameters to control the terminal's cursor addressing and characteristics such as emboldened text, reverse video and blinking. PICK supplies terminal definitions for many terminals. The following terminal definitions are supplied by Advanced PICK and will cover the majority of terminals in use today. Although there is a facility to generate a new terminal driver, you are highly unlikely to have to create one. If the terminal you wish to purchase cannot emulate one of the terminals listed below, you are probably best to purchase an alternative!

A ADDS580	G GTC	M MIME	*W wy-50-link
A ADM-11	*G IBM3161	*N WY-100	*W wy-50132
A ADM3A	G IBM3164	P PERTEC	W WY-60
A CIE-ANT	G mn3161	Q QVT102	W wy50-132
B AMPEX210	G mn3161-132	R R25	W WY60
B BEEHIVE	H HONEYWELL	S ansi.c	W wy60.1
B IBM3151	I AT.MON	S SOROC	X DATAGRAPHIX
B ibm3151-132	I IBM	T TEC	x xterm
B mark	I IBM3010	T TV920	x xterm-dim
B mn3151	I MM-MON	T TV950	Z ANSI

C DTC	I port-mon	V VP	Z att605
C VT-52	J VT100	V VP-60	Z att705
D DATAMEDIA	J vt100-dim	V VP-A2	Z HFT
D dg	J vt320	W link	Z rt.console
E EMULOG200	K prism	W link125	Z RT.MON
E EX-34	L LSI	W w	Z Z
F TV910	M AMPEX-D80	W WY-50	
G g	M AMPEX.D80	W wy-50-132	

The first letter denotes the device driver used by the particular terminal, whilst the description next to it is the item-id of the record to be found in the DEVICES file. If you examine attribute one of the DEVICES record for your terminal you will see the driver letter shown as one of its values.

One of the setup parameters of your terminal will be terminal emulation. You will need to refer to your terminal manual to determine how to get into the terminal setup display. Most terminals have a special key marked 'setup' that needs to be pressed. In some cases this may be all that needs to be pressed, in other cases you may find you also need to hold down the control key, shift key or both the control and shift key.

Terminal emulation is not the only characteristic that is important within the setup routine which will also allow you to specify the speed of the line, number of data bits, number of stop bits, the parity, handshaking and so on. If these terms are unfamiliar to you they are described in the Glossary of Terms at the end of this book.

One of the most important parameters is that of baud rate, the speed at which data is transferred to and from the terminal. This only applies to the serial ports and not PCs connected as workstations over a network and NOT the PC monitor if PICK is running on a PC. By default the baud rate is set to 9600. Dependent on the quality of the serial card it is possible to operate at speeds of 19,200 baud or even 38,400. Whilst processing of data will not be quicker, screen refresh most certainly will be and because the screen displays fill up much more quickly the user feels the system is working faster!

21.5.2 Assigning the correct PICK terminal driver

A terminal driver needs to be assigned to each port when the system is powered up. Details of the driver, denoted by an alphabetic device name, together with other characteristics such as the page width and depth is held in the PIBS file (the DICT portion of the ACC file in R83). The contents of the PIBS file is discussed further in Section 21.5.5, but if you look at attribute 2 of any PIBS record (or ACC record in R83) you will see the string of parameters displayed by the **TERM** command.

If you find the terminal display completely mixed up, the chances are the terminal driver is incorrect. You can check the setting of the terminal without examining the PIBS record by executing the TCL command **TERM**, which gives a display similar to the following:

```
terminal name: mm-mon
product name: IBM VIDEO
terminal        width: 80        printer width: 80
                depth: 25                depth: 64
lineskip:          0
lf delay:          7
ff delay:          1
back space:        8
```

If you are not sure of the device driver (denoted by a single alphabetic character), you can find this from attribute 1 of the record in the DEVICES. In R83 the **TERM** command displayed the terminal driver under the heading TERM TYPE.

If for whatever reason the terminal driver is incorrect it can be reset using the **TERM** command. The general format of the command is as follows:

:TERM *sw,sd,ls,lf,ff,bs,pw,pd,tt*
where

sw	is the terminal screen width in columns; defaults to 79
sd	is the terminal screen depth in lines; defaults to 24
ls	is the terminal line skip in lines, defaults to 0. The sum of sd and ls must equal the number of lines of the VDU
lf	is the number of delay characters output after a linefeed. This is for terminals that require a pause after such an operation because they cannot cope with the speed the processor sends data
ff	is the number of delay characters output after a top-of-page is encountered. This affects both terminals and printers
bs	is the backspace character
pw	is the page width of the printer in columns; defaults to 132
pd	is the page depth of the printer in lines; defaults to 64
tt	is the terminal type or driver which defines the way in which the cursor addressing is to handled. If this is incorrect, the information will be displayed in a jumbled form on the screen. Whilst these vary from implementation to implementation they are defined by a single letter and listed in Section 21.5.1

It is possible to change only some of these characteristics by typing in the relevant number of commas. Hence

:term ,,,,,,,66

will change the number of lines per page for printed output to 66 and

:term wy-50

will change the terminal driver to the Wyse 50 driver. PICK is able to distinguish alphabetic characters and in recognizing a terminal driver does not need the preceding commas defined.

The **set-term** command updates the default characteristics for each port until the system is powered off, when these settings are lost and the system reverts to those set by the coldstart procedure.

The TCL command to reset the ports' characteristics back to those contained in the PIBS (or ACC) file is **TERM-TYPE**. Sometimes you may find that the correct terminal type is not set properly during the logon process and executing a **TERM-TYPE** command is a useful way to correct this. A useful tip is to include this command in user's logon MACRO/PROC.

There is a utility for defining a new terminal driver invoked with the **DEFINE-TERMINAL** command. When run, it prompts you to specify the parameters of the terminal. It asks questions relating to the size of the screen (width in characters, depth in lines) and cursor addressing. It requires an intimate understanding of your terminal, so if you are uncertain about your terminals characteristics and if your terminal can emulate one of the standard defaults, you may find it easier to set its emulation to one of those.

If you do need to define your own terminal driver, cursor code strings are specified as expressions which produce the control and escape sequences used by the terminal being defined. The terminal definition is effectively 'compiled' once all the 40 parameters are complete, and any errors displayed during this process.

Cursor code strings may consist of any of the following, separated by blanks or colons:

- Defined control character (e.g. ESC, BS, DEL etc.)
- String literal in quotes (e.g. "A", '[O' etc.)
- Character function (e.g. CHAR(21) etc.)
- Hexadecimal string (e.g. HEX(1B41) etc.)
- String function (e.g. STR(NUL,5), STR(CHAR(12),X00))
- Cursor address variable (e.g. X,Y or Z)

The cursor address variables cause the specified address to be inserted into the control string at the specified position.

X	represents the COLUMN position
Y	represents the ROW position
Z	represents the ROW PREVIOUSLY referenced

It is highly unlikely that you will need to produce a new driver, but if you do the PICK manual provides adequate instruction. Indeed, before embarking on such a task you should examine some of those already defined by looking at existing definitions.

21.5.3 Connecting the VDU using an RS232 cable

Having set the correct parameters within the terminal setup process and having assigned the correct terminal driver, the next stage is attaching the terminal to the computer using an RS232 cable.

The cable is made up of several separate individually coloured wires, covered in a protective sheath, and has a connector at each end. The connector will either be a male or female connector with either 9 or 25 pins. A male connector is one where the pins are prominent, a female connector is one with holes for the male connector plug to fit into.

The connectors, known as 'D' connectors because of their shape are likely to have 9 pins for the serial ports on the motherboard on a PC or for the serial port on a serial/parallel card, but are more likely to have 25 pins on the expansion cards.

Regardless of whether the connectors are male or female, the connections are the same. Each of the 9 or 25 pins are numbered, although often very difficult to read, and the multi-wired cable is connected to some of the numbered pins at either end. There are a number of different wiring options and the PICK installation guide will advise on these, but the most common configurations are:

25 Pin to 25 Pin Connector	Pin 2	to	Pin 2
	Pin 3	to	Pin 3
	Pin 7	to	Pin 7
9 Pin to 25 Pin	Pin 2	to	Pin 2
	Pin 3	to	Pin 3
	Pin 5	to	Pin 7

In some cases it may be necessary to cross over pins 2 and three by connecting pin 2 to pin 3 and pin 3 to pin 2 and to 'jumper' pins 4,5 and 6 at the computer end. This means linking pins 4, 5 and 6 together with solder.

21.5.4 Setting the baud rate within PICK

As has been mentioned earlier, it is possible to operate serial ports at speeds above the 9600 baud default, the speed each port is set to when PICK is first loaded.

Changing the baud rate of the terminal within the terminal setup is only part of the story. The terminal will not operate, if its baud rate is different to that set within PICK, so obviously the method of changing the baud rate is to change the baud rate within PICK *before* changing the baud rate within the terminal setup.

Changing the baud rate within PICK is achieved by the **SET-BAUD** command, operated at TCL. The format of the command is:

SET-BAUD	*line number, {baud rate}*
:SET-BAUD 1,19200	which sets the baud rate of line 1 to 19,200

In Advanced PICK (not R83) the **SET-BAUD** command can also change the parity, stop bits and word length by adding these parameters to the end of the above command. Hence

:set-baud 1,19200,n,1,8	additionally sets **no parity, 1** stop bit and **8** data bits

Since the command specifies the line (or port) whose speed is to be changed, it is possible to run this command from any terminal. Whilst you can set the baud rate permanently in the terminal, you need to modify the procedure which initiates the line at the correct speed when the system is powered up. This is a MACRO or PROC called **USER-COLDSTART**.

21.5.5 Amending the PIBS file

The PIBS file contains a record for each port of the system and attribute 2 contains the parameters given by the TCL command **TERM.** In R83 PICK this information is held in the Dictionary portion of the ACC file. If we review the **TERM** command we will see it reflects the size and shape of the VDU and printer configured for the port as well as specifying its' terminal driver.

```
terminal name: mm-mon
product name: IBM VIDEO
terminal        width: 80        printer width: 80
                depth: 25                depth: 64
lineskip:          0
lf delay:          7
ff delay:          1
back space:        8
```

If we look at the corresponding PIBS entry for port 0 we would see the following:

```
001
002 79,25,0,7,1,8,80,58,MM-MON
```

The configuration of the DICT of ACC under R83 is slightly different in that it specifies the device driver letter and not the device name (such as MM-MON) since the file DEVICES is one of the new files to be found with Advanced PICK.

```
001 Memory Mapped Monitor
002 79,24,0,2,2,8,80,64,I
```

In the DICT of ACC each port is specified by a two digit number, thus to edit the characteristics of port zero you would need to type in the TCL statement

>ED DICT ACC 00

In both Advanced PICK and R83 attribute 1 contains a description of the port, which you could change to denote the name of the user or user department. Attribute 2 contains the important **TERM** characteristics which you should ensure you change correctly. It is unlikely you will have to change the entry for port 0, the memory mapped monitor, unless you are using JET version 2.0 and above, which requires the number of lines for the monitor to be 25 and not 24. The monitor will operate other software properly when set to 25 lines, so you may decide to make this a change one of your operational standards.

On the other asynchronous ports you will need to set up the appropriate definitions ensuring the correct driver is assigned. Equally, the number of columns and rows on your printer may well need to be set to something other than 80 and 64. If your printer is generally used as a 132 column printer, you should change the 80 to read 132.

When these entries have been set, they will only become effective when the system is powered up, or when the command **TERM-TYPE** is executed, so don't expect them to become operational the moment you make the changes.

21.5.6 Changing the power-up MACRO or PROC

When the system is first powered up Advanced PICK runs a MACRO called **system-coldstart** which carries out the initialisation procedures. The macro is to be found in the **dm** account and is as follows:

```
n
run dm,bp, setpib0
term-type (s
run dm,bp, start.rtc
run dm,bp, start.ss
initovf
coldstart.log
run dm,bp, cleanpibs
:reset-async
set-abs dm,abs, (s
maxusers (mql
rem verify.system
run dm,bp, start.dos.printer.p0
run dm,bp, clear.unix.printers
coldstart   <----------
off
```

this executes the program **user.coldstart** which calls the MACRO or PROC **USER-COLDSTART**

In R83 the PROC in the SYSPROG account is called **COLDSTART** in the file SYSPROG-PL and is as follows:

```
001 PQ
002 C Executed by BOOT process
003 C
004 C *** (C) Copyright 1986 Pick Systems ***
005 C
006 HINIT-CURSOR CURSOR *
007 P
008 HTERM-TYPE
009 P
010 HSET-SYM PSYM
011 P
012 HSELECT ACC WITH NAME
013 STON
014 HB/ADD DICT PROCLIB :DEL<
015 H'ACC' *<
016 PH
017 C Setting the system TIME & DATE from the Real Time Clock
018 HSTART.RTC
019 PH
020 20 C
021 HSTARTPTR 0,0,0,P0
022 PH
023 O
024 (SYSPROG-PL USER-COLDSTART)
```

In both cases the final task is that of running a PROC called **USER-COLD-START**, which is a PROC set aside for user-specific parameters and options. You should not change any of the system coldstart MACROs or PROCs. Any changes you make to specify requirements to suit your system configuration should be made within **USER-COLDSTART**. It is in this PROC that you can set the baud rate for specific terminals.

The coldstart PROC in PICK R83 leaves the internal clock in USA format so if you are in a European country you will need to add the command **SET-DATE-EUR** to your **USER-COLDSTART** PROC. If when running R83 in European date format, you occasionally find a corruption of the system date (i.e. finding it reset it to day 0 the 31st DEC 67) then change the **COLDSTART** PROC shown above to add the following two lines prior to line 18/19 (i.e. prior to the START.RTC command and the two lines after as follows).

```
HSET-DATE-STD
P
START, RTC
P
HSET-DATE-EUR
P
```

The standard **USER-COLDSTART** contains nothing other than a couple of comment lines telling you where to put your commands, and a log off command (**OFF**) to ensure that all users have to go through a log on procedure.

The **USER-COLDSTART** PROC is used to specify changes specific to your configuration, such as changes to baud rates, the specification of printers other than parallel printer 0 (which is handled in automatically in the PICK coldstart procedures) and any other pertinent parameters which may need setting.

21.5.7 Terminal echo

There is one other problem that may arise and this will undoubtedly confuse you the first time it happens. A user may tell you that although he is typing his commands into the terminal, the cursor is not moving and no characters are appearing on the screen! Whilst this can be a hardware failure, it is more likely to occur because the terminal echo, which echoes (redisplays) the characters typed in onto the screen, has been turned off. Although the echo is turned off the system will react to the instructions in exactly the same way, the only difference being that you cannot see what you've typed in! The echo can be toggled on and off with the commands **ECHO ON** and **ECHO OFF** and in Advanced PICK you can also use the **echo** command which toggles echo alternatively off and on.

21.6 Configuring printers

In a similar way to the setting up of terminals, difficulties will generally only arise when adding new printers or moving printers around on the system. There are seven aspects in the configuring of printers:

(1) Setting up the printer characteristics within the printer itself.
(2) Assigning the printer to the system.
(3) Assigning the appropriate printer to each user.
(4) Connecting the printer to the system with a cable configured properly.
(5) Setting the baud rate within PICK to match that set within the printer (as in step 1).
(6) Amending the ACC file to reflect the characteristics of the total system configuration.
(7) Amending the power-up PROC to reflect the characteristics of the total system configuration.

21.6.1 Setting the printer characteristics

Most printers available today can link to your computer in one of two ways, either as a serial printer connected to a serial line or as a parallel printer connected to a parallel port. Providing your printer has both interfaces built into it, you can decide which to use. In R83, each serial device was considered a user, so connecting printers to parallel ports was an attractive proposition. Under Advanced PICK only serial terminals are considered users and you can add as many serial printers as you wish without affecting your PICK licence.

Whilst serial ports can be used to support either terminals or printers, the same is not true of the parallel port which can ONLY be used to support parallel devices (normally printers) and most definitely NOT VDUs.

The maximum number of printers supported is 20 under R83 and 50 under Advanced PICK. In both cases the maximum number of parallel printers is four.

The capabilities of printers vary enormously. Some only work as parallel printers and others need a serial option before they can work on serial ports. Most of the faster and higher quality printers have both a serial and parallel port. Those that do have both options can normally be connected to either the serial or parallel port without any configuring. However you should read the manual carefully to check that there are no dip switches that need to be set first.

You may also find that there are dip switches to be set in order to change the baud rate. Most printers these days operate as a default at 9600 baud, but again you may find this not to be true of your particular printer. If you have a use some older printers, you may find their maximum speed to be 2400 or 4800 baud.

One other area of printers to mention is the ability to work with a variety of fonts, pitch settings (cpi) and maybe even spacing (lpi). These will again be mentioned in the printer manual and may also require the setting of dip switches.

Most laser printers provide a series of emulation's, similar to the principles of terminal emulation's. The most common of these being the HP Laserjet, so if your laser can work in this emulation, it would be best to set it to do so. With laser printers, all settings are handled through software, so you need to attach and configure the printer within PICK first, before worrying about its emulation.

21.6.2 Assigning the printer to the system

If the printer is other than the first parallel printer, which is configured for you automatically, you will need to tell PICK about the printer. In order to do so, you will need to understand a little about the PICK spooler which is described in detail in Chapter 22.

Each printer used is assigned a number, with printer number 0 (zero) normally being used as the default or system printer and initially configured as a parallel printer. Each printer must have a form queue number assigned to it, which represents a specific printer with specific stationery. Where a system has a number of the same printers each using the same stationery then all printers can be given the same form queue number.

Mostly you will need to assign different form queues to each printer, for example form queue 0 for the matrix printer (the system printer and nominated as printer 0) and form queue 1 for the letter quality printer (printer 1). Where possible assign each printer the same form queue number as given to the printer itself since many of the spooler commands refer to the form number rather than printer number and it is far easier to know what response to give if you know they are both the same!

To assign a printer use the command **STARTPTR** (described in Section 22.2.1) and to remove a printer use **SP-KILL D*n*** (Section 22.2.3).

21.6.3 Assigning the appropriate printer to each user

If there is only one printer on your system, the selection of printer for each user is not an issue. Each time you log to any account the system automatically assigns printer 0 (i.e. the system printer).

To assign different printers to different users is a question of either providing a printer selection menu which carries out the appropriate **SP-ASSIGN** command, to amend the users logon MACRO/PROC or to add the **SP-ASSIGN** command to the users record in the USERS file.

LISTABS is a very useful command when things start to go wrong. If reports are being printed on the wrong printer, or do not start printing at all, this command helps you to find out why since it shows the print queues assigned to each port. Using this information with that of **SP-STATUS,** the printers associated with each user can readily be established. A complete description of all these SPOOLER commands can be found in Chapter 22.

21.6.4 Cabling the printer to the system

When using a parallel printer you will need to purchase a parallel printer cable which will connect to the 25 pin connector on the PC and the standard parallel connector on the printer. You will find that there is generally a limit of around 6–7 metres for the length of a parallel cable unless you buy line boosters, which is one reason why some people run printers on the serial ports. There is debate of the maximum length of cable for a serial printer. Generally this can be in the order of 100 feet, but boosters can be purchased to extend the distance further.

Connections for serial cables are as described in Section 21.5.3 on cabling for terminals.

21.6.5 Setting the baud rate within PICK

Setting the baud rate for a printer port is no different to setting the baud rate for a terminal. Refer to Section 21.5.4 for a detailed explanation of this task.

21.6.6 Amending the PIBS file

The PIBS file (DICT of ACC in R83) specifies the size and shape of the printed page. As a default the printer width is set to 80 columns and the number of lines on the page to 64. To enable the output to be printed up to 132 columns wide, it is necessary to change these parameters. This can be handled for the current logon session with the **SET-TERM** command or it can be changed permanently by changing the PIBS (or DICT ACC) entry from 80 to 132. See Section 21.5.5.

21.6.7 Changing the power-up MACRO or PROC

The final stage of configuring the printers on the system, is to amend the power-up MAVRO or PROC and Section 21.5.6 describes this in detail. Having changed this, do remember to take a copy for safe keeping, so that if necessary it can be re-instated with ease.

21.7 Configuring keyboards

The PC version of PICK provides a keyboard definition function for the PC monitor. This enables the support of a wide variety of different keyboard layouts in many foreign languages. Two standard UK formats are already defined, these being for 84, and 101 key keyboards. By default, the keyboard is assumed to be a 101 key USA keyboard, so for those in Europe a new layout definition has to be invoked. For those of you in the UK two definitions are provided **BRITISH-84** and **BRITISH-101**. which can be found in the KEYBOARDS file. The command to invoke a new keyboard definition is **SET-KBRD** and this command is followed by the file name and item in that file that contains the keyboard definition. Typically the command would bc:

:SET-KBRD KEYBOARDS *name*

> where *name* is the item name in the KEYBOARDS file which defines the required keyboard layout (such as BRITISH-84 for an 84 key keyboard, BRITISH-101 for a 101 key keyboard)

21.7.1 Changing the coldstart PROC

The USA-101 keyboard is the default layout which is activated each time the system is booted. To change this to an alternative, you need to modify the **USER-COLDSTART** PROC (see Section 21.5.6) by adding the lines:

S2
IHKEYBOARDS *name* ◄———— where *name* is the keyboard name
HRUN SYSPROG-BP SET-KBRD
P

21.7.2 Modifying a keyboard definition item

If you find that none of the keyboard definitions match exactly to your requirements then you can set up your own. For example in the BRITISH-*nn* keyboard definitions the " and @ symbols are the wrong way round and the **£** symbol above the **3** key prints as a hash sign.

To produce your own keyboard definition, first find a keyboard layout nearest to the one you want. own. For safety's sake, and so that you can retain the original to refer to, it is best to copy one of the British definitions (BRITISH-84 or BRITISH-101) in the KEYBOARDS file to a new item and modify the new item. For example:

:COPY KEYBOARDS BRITISH-101
TO: **BRITISH-102**

The keyboard definition item contains details of the values to be transmitted when each key is pressed. The values are stored in hex (refer to Appendix G for the ASCII and hex table), and each key is represented by two hex characters.

If you look at a keyboard definition item, for example BRITISH-101, it is obvious it defines far more keys than that of any normal monitor keyboard. The reason for this is that it holds a definition for each of four possible key combinations:

- On its own (i.e. lower case)
- SHIFT/Key (i.e. upper case)
- CTRL/Key (i.e. concurrently with the CTRL key)
- ALT/Key (i.e. concurrently with the ALT key)

Effectively, therefore the keyboard is defined four times over. If we look at the BRITISH-101 item, we can see how this works – notice also, it is the upper case definitions which are represented first.

```
BRITISH-101
*  Define BRITISH 101-key keyboard
*
*  Note: X'FF' means ignore this keystroke
*
*
*  Upper case definitions
*
FF1B21402324255E262A28295F2B08FF  <—— Hex 40 is the @ symbol while
                                       hex 23 produces a # symbol
51574552545955494F507B7D0DFF4153
444647484A4B4C3A227EFF7C5A584356  <—— Hex 22 produces a " symbol
424E4D3C3E3FFF2AFF20FF5051525354
5556575859FFFF3738392D3435362B31
3233302EFFFFFF5A5BFFFFFFFFFFFFFF
FFFFFFFFFFFFFFFFFFFFFFFFFFFFFFFF
FFFFFFFFFFFFFFFFFFFFFFFFFFFFFFFF
*
```

```
* Lower case definitions
*
FF1B313233343536373839302D3D0809
71776572747975696F705B5D0DFF6173
646667686A6B6C3B2760FF5C7A786376
626E6D2C2E2FFF2AFF20FF4041424344
4546474849FFFFFF1AFF2D15FF062BFF
0AFFFFFFFFFFFF4A4BFFFFFFFFFFFFFF
FFFFFFFFFFFFFFFFFFFFFFFFFFFFFFFF
FFFFFFFFFFFFFFFFFFFFFFFFFFFFFFFF
*
* Control key definitions
*
FF1BFF00FFFFFF1EFFFFFFFF1FFF7FFF
11170512141915090F101B1D0AFF0113
040607080A0B0CFFFFFFFF1C1A180316
020E0DFFFFFFFFFFFF20FF2021222324
2526272829FFFFFFFFFFFFFFFFFFFFFF
FFFFFFFFFFFFFF2A2BFFFFFFFFFFFFFF
FFFFFFFFFFFFFFFFFFFFFFFFFFFFFFFF
FFFFFFFFFFFFFFFFFFFFFFFFFFFFFFFF
*
* Alternate key definitions
*
FFFFFFFFFFFFFFFFFFFFFFFFFFFFFFFF
FFFFFFFFFFFFFFFFFFFFFFFFFFFFFFFF
FFFFFFFFFFFFFFFFFFFFFFFFFFFFFFFF
FFFFFFFFFFFFFFFFFF20FF3031323334
3536373839FFFFFFFFFFFFFFFFFFFFFF
FFFFFFFFFFFFFF3A3BFFFFFFFFFFFFFF
FFFFFFFFFFFFFFFFFFFFFFFFFFFFFFFF
FFFFFFFFFFFFFFFFFFFFFFFFFFFFFFFF
*
```

Changing the keyboard layout specification is therefore just a matter of determining the whereabouts of the current code is held in the keyboard definition item and changing it with the Update Processor or Editor.

Whilst swapping the hex 40 and hex 22 codes around is relatively straightforward, the hex code 23 needs to be changed to 9C (the hex code produced by holding down the Alt key whilst typing in 156).

Although this will change the keyboard definition you need to run the command **XCS-ON** to tell PICK to enable the extended character set, which means that the high order bit of the character is not stripped out and means that any character in the range 128 through to 255 can be used. Once you have established this is needed you should add the command to you coldstart PROC. Remember that **XCS-ON** has to be set for *each* port requiring the extended character set so add the command **XCS-ON** *n* (where *n* is the port number) for each port using the extended character set.

21.8 Monitoring and controlling disk usage

Perhaps one of the main tasks of the System Administrator is the control of the files within the database. The control and monitoring of disk usage can be a severe management task in a volatile system with limited disk space. Fortunately, disk capacity these days is extremely cheap, and should not be a problem. The first step, of course, is to keep a regular eye on the amount of free disk space and how it is organized.

One of the new commands with Advanced PICK is **free**, a command which gives a pictorial representation of disk usage and monitors the available space. An example of the output from this command, together with that from the **WHAT** command is given in Figure 21.2.

The command **WHAT** performs an analysis across the entire system giving information about lock tables, printer status and the execution status of tasks in process. To limit the output from this command use the options **lsw**, which focuses on the disk and memory statistics as shown below:

:what (lsw

```
16:58:04 11 Jun 1995
memory   pibs    pcb0    sysbase/mod    maxfid    available    dfsize
  1040k     6    2048      2078    7    102400        13794      1000
```

In addition to giving information about the spare disk space, Figure 21.2 shows how other system status information is displayed. For example it also shows the amount of memory on the system (1040K) and the number of pibs (6). In R83, the word pibs is replaced with the word lines, but do remember in each case this will not be the number of physical ports because phantom processes and the Spooler are included in these numbers. The display also shows the frame number which is the location of the start of the system files (SYSBASE) and it also displays MAXFID, the maximum number of frames on the disk. In Advanced PICK since each frame is 1K bytes it is a simple job to determine the disk size from the command **what**. Indeed it is even easier using the command **free**. In R83 you can determine the disk size by multiplying the number of ABS frames by 2048 bytes and adding the remainder of frames multiplied by 512 bytes. Given the display in Figure 21.2 under R83 the disk capacity would work out at ((1023x2048)+((102400-1023) x 512)) = 54,000, 128 bytes or approximately 53 Mbytes.

A disk should not operate at more than 80% of its capacity as PICK needs space for sorting, file resizing, the spooler and other temporary files. If you find your system working regularly above this figure you should seriously consider a disk upgrade.

Having established the amount of spare space available, it is important to find out how it is distributed on the disk. Spare frames scattered all over the disk

```
:free
Disk Available

0....1....2....3....4....5....6....7....8....9....100%
*******

                                        MB         Bytes      Frames
Maximum disk space        100%     102   102,400,000     102,400
System usage                2%       2     2,078,000       2,078
Data usage                 85%      86    86,546,000      86,546
Available disk space       13%      14    13,776,000      13,776

:what                                                   Available disk frames
16:58:15 11 Jun 1995
  memory    pibs   pcb0       sysbase/mod      maxfid   available    dfsize
 1040k        6    2048         2078    7      102400       13776      1000

System Locks
   0   1   2   3   4   5   6   7   8   9   A   B   C   D   E   F
0 ### ### ### ### ### ### ### ### ### ### ### ### ### ### ### ###
1 ### ### ### ### ### ### ### ###

Basic Locks
   0   1   2   3   4   5   6   7   8   9   A   B   C   D   E   F
0 ### ### ### ### ### ### ### ### ### ### ### ### ### ### ### ###
1 ### ### ### ### ### ### ### ### ### ### ### ### ### ### ### ###
2 ### ### ### ### ### ### ### ### ### ### ### ### ### ### ### ###
3 ### ### ### ### ### ### ### ### ### ### ### ### ### ### ### ###

Spooler Locks
  mq  iq  fq  peq
0 ### ### ### ###

Group Locks       PIB#   Lvl     Type     Filename

Item Locks        PIB#   Lvl     Hash     Item-id            Filename

*000 000800   FF10 000018   ws.where1:000   ws.whatwhere:236 ws.whatrtn:037

 003 000803   BF10 000018   P sp.sleep:027   sp.spoolout:07A
 005 004734   BF10 000018   P pp.sched:02A

The spooler is inactive.

Printer # 0 is parallel, inactive, and on line.
The printer is defined as parallel printer # 0.
Assigned output queues: 0 .
The number of inter-job pages to eject is 0.
```

Figure 21.2 Reviewing available disk space.

in small groups cause the condition known as fragmentation. Fragmentation will lead to long response times and may restrict the use of the system, particularly where new files are concerned, since new files have to have the required initial allocation of frames provided as a contiguous block.

In R83 the only command available was **POVF** and an example of its output is given in Figure 21.3. In Advanced PICK **POVF** gives a summary display, whilst **ovf (a** equates to the R83 **POVF** command.

From Advanced PICK

:povf

```
overflow: 26512 reserve: 1024 blocks: 81 b-tree levels: 1 leaves: 1
```

:ovf (a

```
3957- 4163 :       207    9829- 10215 :      387
13262- 13268 :       7    13276- 13276 :     381
13303- 39212 :   25910

overflow: 25488 reserve: 1024 blocks: 81 b-tree levels: 1 leaves: 1
```

From R83 PICK

>POVF

From FID location
To FID location
Spare frames

```
3957- 4163 :       207    9829- 10215 :      387
13262- 13268 :       7    13276- 13276 :     381
13303- 39212 :   25910

Total number of contiguous frames: 26512
```

← Total number of spare frames

Figure 21.3 Free frame analysis from Advanced PICK and R83.

In R83 PICK the overflow table can normally only hold 32 entries. When the table is full, the last entry is used to chain together references to all other spare frames and the system is then said to have 'linked overflow'. This demonstrates a severely fragmented system which should be immediately reorganized by performing a FILE-SAVE and restore. You should also be aware that GFEs are far more likely to occur when the system has linked overflow. Linked overflow is signified from the POVF command by virtue of the first entry showing a number in parentheses, that number being the number of linked frames. Figure 21.4 gives an example of this.

In Advanced PICK the entries in the overflow table are unlimited, so although a linked overflow situation cannot develop, it does not stop the system becoming heavily fragmented and the number of entries displayed by **ovf (a** gives a good indication. One other notable change with Advanced PICK is the ability to set a reserve of frames to ensure the disk never gets completely full. This stops a situation occurring where you cannot even list files or accounts because the disk is full and there is no work space to hold these display files. The reserve is set with the command **set-ovf-reserve**.

```
34179 (     17)
14936- 14967 :    2  14983- 14984 :      2
15003- 15004 :    2  15040- 15044 :      5
15057- 15057 :    1  15059- 15059 :      1
15061- 15061 :    1  15068- 15068 :      1
15073- 15073 :    1  15084- 15084 :      1
15098- 15200 :  200  15902- 15902 :      1
16298- 24021 : 7724  24157- 24157 :      1
35899- 35899 :    1  36328- 36328 :      1
36852- 36852 :    1  37888- 37889 :      2
37892- 37892 :    1  38177- 38177 :      1
38346- 38346 :    1  38529- 38529 :      1
38785- 38787 :    3  40000- 40000 :      1
40004- 40005 :    2  40328- 40340 :     13
40351- 40479 :  129  52444- 52444 :      1
52447- 52447 :    1  52884- 52884 :      1
53165- 80109 :26945
Total number of contiguous frames: 34981
```

Figure 21.4 An example of linked overflow under R83.

21.8.1 Files to monitor

There are a number of files on your system which the System Administrator should monitor regularly. These files, some of which do not exist in R83, will continue to grow unless concerted action is taken to clear them out or archive the records they contain.

One such file is the system accounting history file **accounts** (called **ACC** in R83), which can optionally record system logon sessions. The recording mechanism is switched on by adding the letter **a** to attribute 9 of the **users** file (in R83 add the letter **U** to the item in the SYSTEM file). If switched on, this file will just grow and grow and once you have the information you require the file should be cleared out.

Another file which will just grow and grow is the file containing the TCL stack for each user. This file (**tcl-stack**) is a new file and first introduced with the launch of Advanced PICK. It contains a record for each user-id which is built attribute by attribute to contain details of each command used. Whilst this is obviously useful for a user who can cruise backwards and forwards through the TCL commands executed, if ignored the item can grow very substantial in size.

The **POINTER-FILE** is a file found in both Advanced PICK and PICK R83 and is used to store lists which are items containing the item-ids satisfying selection statements. This is an area often forgotten, but lists can in themselves be quite large.

The file **clashes** is an Advanced PICK file which holds details of the items removed from the **md** of an account that is upgraded to Advanced PICK from a different PICK flavour (such as PICK R83, or a licencee version such as that from Adds Mentor or General Automation). It will hold these definitions indefinitely so again they need to be cleared out. Be aware that **clashes** holds multiple data level files, one for each account that is updated, so to remove the details for a specific account run the command **:delete-file clashes**,*acct.name* where *acct.name* is the name of the account that was updated.

The **jobs** file, another non R83 file, holds details of all background processes that have been executed. Since the **verify.system** process which checks the validity of the ABS area, is a background process executed each time you boot the system, you will soon find this file growing bigger than you want. The file is valuable in telling you the status of a background job whilst it is executing, but of little value thereafter, so you may want to consider clearing out the file on a regular basis.

The **errors** file (**SYSTEM-ERRORS** in R83) contains a variety of messages from the PICK system manager for detected hardware faults and log messages. There is no automatic cleardown process for this file, so make sure you examine it and remove unwanted messages on a regular basis.

Also keep a watchful eye on word-processing files, which users rarely tidy up behind them. All these could be using considerable disk space completely unbeknown to you. The **STAT** verb (see Section 12.6.3) will tell you the size of a specific file, whilst the file statistics produced from a file save operation will give you a complete analysis of your files (see Section 20.2.3).

21.8.2 File sizing and resizing

If a file grows considerably it will link on additional frames as required, gradually causing a degradation in response each time the file is accessed. In these circumstances it is essential to resize the file and organize the data in a larger file.

The file statistics report is an invaluable guide to the files which are both too small and too large. Where you decide a file needs resizing, the existing distribution of data can be checked using **ISTAT** (Section 7.3) and new file sizes tested, before they are created using **HASH-TEST** (Section 7.3). This testing of alternatives enables file sizes to be optimized, from which the physical reorganizing, described in Section 7.4, can be carried out.

A new facility was introduced for Advanced PICK which enables file resizing to be done on-line. The **resize** verb, unlike any previous resizing utilities allows the size of the file to be altered even while the file is in use. It does not require a completely new block of overflow with a size equal to the new file modulo. Instead it allocates a new file 'segment' which is the difference in size between the new and old modulos and 'maps' this segment onto the existing file. Do be aware that you cannot use the **resize** verb to shrink a file in size.

The other important aspects of disk usage management are the control of accounts, their creation and deletion (covered in Sections 6.2.1 and 6.2.2) and the management of data files (explained in Section 6.3).

21.9 Optimizing response time

Response times are affected by either hardware or software. On the hardware side, apart from hardware failures such as hard disk errors causing the system to force the Winchester disk controller to continually retry to read the data until it is read successfully, the two main factors affecting response are the available RAM and the hard disk speed.

Since PICK is a virtual memory system, it will use the spare space on the hard disk as an extension of its real memory and it will 'page' information out of real memory when it needs the space to work on something else. Hence, the more memory it has available, the more information it can retain before 'paging' data to disk and working from real memory is a great deal faster than having to access data from disk – from RAM access is virtually instant!

Paging information to and from disk is a fundamental function of PICK. Apart from this, PICK itself and all of the data it works on is stored on disk. It is fairly obvious, therefore, that the speed at which the disk works is an important factor in system performance.

Whilst the hardware elements are important, invariably poor response is caused by software. This can be a function of the application software in handling excessively large items or making more disk accesses than are necessary, but more often than not is caused by poorly sized files or a fragmented disk. The previous section has dealt with how to recognise and correct disk fragmentation.

Poorly sized files can have a dramatic effect on response. If response times seem to be slowing down you should look very carefully at all the files on the system, *including* the master dictionary. Since the master dictionary is the central reference point for all activities within an account, the file that will have the greatest impact on response time, if wrongly sized, is the master dictionary. File sizing and optimizing is covered in Sections 7.3 and 7.4.

21.10 Dealing with system hangs and locked terminals

This section covers what to do in the event of terminal and system hangs, system crashes and disk crashes. A 'hung' terminal is one which appears not to be responding to key depressions whilst others on the system do. A system hang is one whereby no terminal on the system seems to respond to key depressions, whilst a system crash is one whereby an error message indicating a system failure is displayed on a terminal or system console (the system may or may not have hung in the process). A disk crash is where the symbol '&' appears on the screen or where disk errors are displayed.

21.10.1 Terminal hangs

A terminal will hang for a variety of reasons. The most common of which is a conflict in the data flowing between the terminal and the computer. There are two data flow protocols known as 'data terminal ready' and 'xon/xoff'. Whichever method is used, the purpose is to ensure that data is not sent by or received by a VDU until the device at the other end has had time to process it.

A 'stop sending me data' signal can be simulated by pressing s (ctrl/s). The effect of this can be seen by issuing the command:

:LIST MD (N

and pressing s (ctrl/s) during the display. The terminal then appears to have hung but can be freed by issuing a **q** (ctrl/q). Thus issuing the control sequence **q** (ctrl/q) is the first thing to be tried if a terminal appears to have hung.

The next step is to use the command reset-port n where n is the number of the port to which the hung terminal is attached. Unfortunately this command is not available in R83. This will cure 99% of all terminal hangs, but there will be some instances where the line is so severely road blocked that even more drastic action is required.

In both the above cases no characteristic of the terminal is changed and neither will it affect the information being processed on the terminal. If the terminal fires back into life, it will continue at exactly the point at which it stopped.

If the data being processed is critical and you want to save the work being processed there is one further option open to you before taking the more drastic action of trying to log off the terminal and clear the line, and that is to 'break' the process on the line and restart it. This can be done by using the 'break' key. The break key varies terminal by terminal but is either a key marked break, or invoked using that key in conjunction with the shift, alt or control key. Sometimes c (ctrl/c) will also achieve a break. When you break successfully you will see a debug symbol (the * or !). If you get either of these then enter a **G** (the GO option).

If the terminal still does not respond try turning the power on and off (be careful if the terminal is a PC in terminal emulation mode as you may lose other data, like word processing documents). If the terminal is still locked then pull out the RS232 connector from the back of the terminal for a moment. After you have plugged it back in, press the RETURN key several times, try to 'break' once more and see whether you can get a debug symbol. If you get either of these then try the **G** option. If the terminal locks up again, get back to debug and log the terminal off, with the **OFF** command at the debug prompt.

If none of these have been successful, the next step is to try the command **LOGOFF** (see Section 4.2.2) from another terminal. This command may not be in the account you are working in, but is definitely a verb of the **dm** (SYSPROG in R83) account.

If the terminal is still stuck it will only be released when the system is coldstarted. You should first get all other users to save their work and logoff before either powering down the system (see Section 4.1.2) and restarting it (Section 4.1.1) or use the **reboot** command which will execute a controlled shutdown and power-up in one step.

21.10.2 System hangs

A system hang is potentially extremely serious and is a situation which can cause GFEs to occur although with release 6.1 of Advanced PICK onwards, GFEs are a thing of the past, but more of that later. A system will generally hang because of a hardware failure, although a serious breakdown in the system's operating system can equally be to blame.

If the system really has hung there is only one option, that of rebooting the system. Unless the reboot is done in a controlled way (using the **REBOOT**, **POWER-OFF** or **shutdown** verbs), there will be a strong possibility of GFEs. For this reason all attempts should be made to prevent an uncontrolled reboot or system reset.

The first step is to try and find a terminal that is operational, or to get one to respond by undertaking the steps discussed above. If you can get into the system then the first step is to flush the system's memory with the **FLUSH** verb. Not all systems support this command and those that do often only have the command in the **dm** (**SYSPROG** in R83) account, so log to that account and try the command to see if it exists. If your system does support this verb, it might be worth adding it to all your existing accounts and adding it to NEWAC so that it gets added to all new accounts that get created in the future. This means that you can execute the command from any account and don't run the risk of the system hanging during the process of logging from the user account to **dm** (or SYSPROG).

The next step is to kill any print jobs using the **SP-KILL** verb (see Section 22.2.3) and using the same command delete any printers from the system.

Then try logging off as many active terminals as possible with the **LOGOFF** command (Section 4.2.2) On some systems the system or monitor port (port 0) is the only one that can reboot the system and that is the case, try logging this on from the active terminal by use of the **LOGON** command. In PICK R83 the command just requires to know the port to logon and the account to which it should be logged. In Advanced PICK it also needs to know the user-id and any relevant passwords. The general format of the command is as follows:

:logon *port,user-id,user password,account name,account password*

If all else fails, **WAIT A COUPLE OF MINUTES** to allow all activity on the system to cease then reboot/reset the system using the **ctrl/alt/del** keys on your PC or the reset key on any other system. This should awaken the PICK flush process which will flush any write required frames to disk before the system is re-booted.

21.10.3 System crashes

A system crash is where an abnormal error message such as 'memory parity error' suddenly appears and is most likely to be associated with a problem with your hardware. The first task is to diligently record the message shown, together with the date and time the problem occurred. Also record the processes that were being performed at the time. This log may well help your hardware engineer but in any case you may find it useful to track down what is causing the problem if it is of an intermittent nature.

By examining the **errors** file (**SYSTEM-ERRORS** in R83) you may well find messages relating to the system failure experienced. After you have recorded all the details, treat the situation as a system hang and try to reboot the system as the error may be transitory and resetting the system may cause it to go away.

If the problem continues your only software alternative is reloading the operating system. If the problem still persists you will need to call a hardware engineer.

21.10.4 Disk crashes

A disk crash is of two types, a soft crash and a hard crash. A 'soft' crash is indicated by ampersands (**&**) appearing across the screen (although this may also occur with a hard crash) and a 'hard' crash when the disk will not spin up (which could be the power supply or hard disk controller) or when the heads physically touch the surface of the disk and eradicate the information contained on it.

When ampersands occur immediate action is needed. Log everyone off the system as quickly as possible and reload the ABS part of the operating system. If this has not solved the problem reload the entire operating system using the **K**(ill) option which will cause the PICK partition to be reformatted, but first remember to deactivate any software with 'lives' – such as Compusheet+.

If you are running PC PICK you could try reformatting the entire disk with a low level formatter and then rebuild the entire disk. If this fails then the hard disk is faulty and as with a hard disk crash, will mean getting the disk replaced.

21.11 Group format errors

21.11.1 What is a GFE and why does it occur?

Group format errors (GFEs) occur when PICK detects a fault in the structure of a group within a file. (see Sections 7.2.4 and 7.2.5 for a detailed explanation of frame/group formats). GFEs are a rare occurrence and normally associated with a hardware failure. Even so they come without any warning, are often difficult to resolve with restoring from backups and more importantly are very time consuming to eliminate.

In order to rid PICK of these problems a new storage method was introduced with Advanced PICK version 6.1 and from this version onwards, GFEs are a thing of the past. The new storage method means taking an image of a group and updating this copy with new and amended items. Only when this has been done successfully does PICK link in this group to the file in place of the old one. It means that even if power is switched off to the system and the contents of RAM lost, system data integrity will be maintained. As a side issue, the copying process does have implications on response times where groups are large in size.

If you do experience a GFE it will come without any prior warning and will happen when one of the following conditions occurs:

(1) The actual size of an item in a group differs from that recorded by the item header which precedes the item data.
(2) A terminator is of the wrong type or is missing.
(3) Backward frame linkages are incorrect.
(4) Forward frame linkages are incorrect.
(5) The item body is corrupt.
(6) The item is hashed to the wrong group.

21.12 What to do when a GFE is encountered

The ***very very*** first step when a GFE is encountered is to stop ***everyone*** on the system from doing anything else. That means stopping input at whatever point users are at. ***Do not*** under any circumstances let people save their data, nor log off. This could only exacerbate the situation, particular where file linkage errors have been detected. Just get everyone to down tools and take a break whilst you sort out what to do.

When a GFE occurs there are several courses of action open to you.

(1) Restore the corrupt file from a backup.
(2) Save as much of the current system as possible and rebuild your system from the save tape and backup tape(s).
(3) Restore your entire system from a backup.
(4) Truncate the GFE and lose data.
(5) Fix the GFE using the System Debugger.

When a GFE occurs the following message is displayed

****gfe encountered @** *.nnnnn.nnnn text*
F=fix item/T=truncate group & quit/Q=just quit/<cr>=go to debugger?

where *nnnnn.nn* is the frame location and offset
text is a text message giving details of the type of GFE

Sometimes the GFE message does not give you a frame location, just stating something like **gfe encountered @ gfe.scr bad count field**. A frame location will at least gives you a starting point, but whether or not you have a frame location specified in the GFE message, you need to know the file(s) in which the GFE(s) reside. Quite frequently the reported GFE is not the only one, particularly where the forward and backward links are corrupt, it just happens to be the first one encountered.

At the terminal with the GFE message, press [CR] which will display the **!** exclamation mark, the symbol of the System Debugger and then type END to get to the TCL prompt. The next step therefore is to assess the damage, so you need to carry out a dummy save across your entire system and see just how many there are and determine the files in which they are located. A dummy save is performed with

save (fsg (in PICK R83 **SAVE (FDSG**).

The save would skip through the GFEs although they would be reported on the screen or printer and recorded in the **errors** (**STAT-FILE** in R83). Figure 21.5 gives an example of the file save listing.

Once recorded in the **errors** file (the **STAT-FILE** in R83) they can be listed out to determine their file path. The standard **list errors** does not show the file path of the files with the GFE so you need to list the comments field as shown in Figure 21.6. In R83 the command **LIST-FILE-STATS** has a separate column against each file showing the number of GFEs in each file.

```
0 3230 > admin > AD.CMP
0 3231 > admin > AD.CMP > AD.CMP
0 4184 > admin > DEPT
0 4185 > admin > DEPT > DEPT
0 3232 > admin > AD.LAB
0 3233 > admin > AD.LAB > AD.LAB
0 5255 > admin > PC.CL.DATA.INDEX
0 5256 > admin > PC.CL.DATA.INDEX > PC.CL.DATA.INDEX
0 4182 > admin > STAFF
0 4183 > admin > STAFF > STAFF
*** GFE Encountered @gfe.sr - Bad count field

0 3234 > admin > AD.LABELS
0 3235 > admin > AD.LABELS > AD.LABELS
0 3236 > admin > AD.NOTES
0 3237 > admin > AD.NOTES > AD.NOTES
0 3238 > admin > TR.BP
0 3239 > admin > TR.BP > TR.BP
0 3240 > admin > AD.PRODUCT.INDEX
0 3241 > admin > AD.PRODUCT.INDEX > AD.PRODUCT.INDEX
0 3242 > admin > TR.DIARY.XRF
0 3243 > admin > TR.DIARY.XRF > TR.DIARY.XRF

1 gfe(s) encountered.
:
```

Figure 21.5 An example of a GFE being located during a file-save.

:list errors

```
Page 1       errors                              22:01:32 11 Jun 1995

date. time. r mode-addr........... pib/user md........... error.........

28/09 13:17   sv.srch.grp:2E8        0 dm dm                 gfe count
28/09 13:17   gnseqids:16D           0 dm admin              gfe count

[405] 2 items listed out of 2 items.
```

:list errors comment

```
Page 1       errors                                   22:01:18 11 Jun 1995

errors.... comment..................................

1002478779 admin,STAFF,STAFF
1002478634 admin,STAFF,STAFF

[405] 2 items listed out of 2 items.
```

Figure 21.6 The location of files containing GFEs.

Once you know the files containing the GFEs you can decide the course of action to take. If they are in static files, such as files containing look-up tables, then delete the file and restore it from a backup tape using the **SEL-RESTORE** command (see Section 20.2.11). If the file(s) relate to a certain portion of the application which contains transaction data, then you should save the current state of the account to tape using the **ACCOUNT-SAVE** command with the **G** option. Please note you cannot save a GFE to tape, so that file can safely be restored without the worry of recreating the GFE. In fact when it is restored the file containing the GFE will contain all records up to the point that the GFE was encountered and all records from that point on will be lost. The reason for saving and restoring the account is to ensure it is completely free of GFEs. You can then delete the file(s) that contained the GFE and all those that are affected by the transactions that need to be re-input. Once deleted they can all be restored from your backup using **SEL-RESTORE** and the appropriate transactions re-input.

The one certain way to ensure you have rid yourself of all GFEs is to restore the entire file system from a previous file-save tape. This means you will need to re-input all the data and transactions input since that save was taken and whilst this may seem a dreadful loss, in many cases it is the quickest means of recovery. Without doubt it is the safest.

When the GFE message is displayed the two options **F** for fix or **T** for truncate will repair the group, by truncating it at the point the GFE is found or by trying to patch up the group, fixing the GFE. In either case data will be lost and the state of the file unknown. For those reasons neither of these options are sensible unless you are working in a test or development account and do not care what state the files are in.

21.12.1 Forward and backward link errors

GFEs can also occur because of corruption in the forward and/or backward links which are stored in the first 12 bytes of each frame (see Section 7.2.4). These occur for similar reasons to the other types of GFE and make themselves known by a message similar to

forward link zero;reg 9
abort @
!

leaving the system in the debugger. This occurs because PICK is trying to read a number of bytes greater than that left in the current frame and when it goes to get the next frame in the chain it finds the frame number is zero. A similar situation happens when it reads back through the chain and hence causes a backward link error. When this happens the chances are your system has really got itself into a mess and the only way out is a complete system reload from the backup tape.

To check the forward and backward links use the **DUMP** command with the **L** option as shown in Figure 21.7. This show you the forward and backward linkages of a group whose first frame is specified as part of the command.

Another message that may be encountered, again requiring technical help, is **Referencing illegal frame**. This message occurs when a frame links to one which is below 0 or above MAXFID, i.e. a frame that does not exist on the system. This generally needs a reload of the ABS area and file system and if the problem persists you need to call in your hardware engineers.

:DUMP 10318 L

Backward link FID
Forward link FID
FID

← The same table in hexadecimal format →

```
+ fid:  10318 :  0 10340  0         0  (  284E :  0 2864  0     0  )
+ fid:  10340 :  0 10341  10318     0  (  2864 :  0 2865  284E  0  )
+ fid:  10341 :  0 10342  10340     0  (  2865 :  0 2866  2864  0  )
+ fid:  10342 :  0 10343  10341     0  (  2866 :  0 2867  2865  0  )
+ fid:  10343 :  0 10344  10342     0  (  2867 :  0 2868  2866  0  )
+ fid:  10344 :  0 10345  10343     0  (  2868 :  0 2869  2867  0  )
+ fid:  10345 :  0 0      10344     0  (  2869 :       0  2868  0  )
```

Figure 21.7 Checking the linkages of a group.

21.12.2 Useful commands in locating GFEs

There are two useful commands that will help in the location and correction of GFEs, particularly if you want to dump the contents of a frame. When you know the GFE is in a particular file, but are not sure of the frame number in which the item(s) resides use **GROUP** to display the base FID of each group of the specified file and **ITEM** to provide information about the frame number and offset at which the items reside within the frame. These commands are illustrated in Figure 21.8.

:GROUP STAFF

Frame & its offset
Item length
Item-id

```
 65778.0000      009C  2395
 65778.009C      0090  4018
 65778.012C      0078  1313
 65778.01A4      00B0  2936
 65778.0254      008E  13
 65778.02E2      00DA  1854
 65778.03BC      00AE  3477
7 items 1130 bytes 1/130 frames in group 65778

 65779.0000      00A2  14
 65779.00A2      00AE  1314
 65779.0150      00A0  1855
 65779.01F0      0090  2396
 65779.0280      008A  2937
 65779.030A      00A0  3478
 65779.03AA      0046  4019
7 items 1008 bytes 1/8 frames in group 65779
```

The number of bytes in the last frame of the group
The number of full frames in the group
The size of the group in bytes
The number of items in the group

The **ITEM** command provides exactly the same information as the group command, but only for the group in which the specified item is located.

: ITEM STAFF 2936

```
 65778.0000      009C  2395
 65778.009C      0090  4018
 65778.012C      0078  1313
 65778.01A4      00B0  2936
 65778.0254      008E  13
 65778.02E2      00DA  1854
 65778.03BC      00AE  3477
7 items 1130 bytes 1/130 frames in group 65778
```

Figure 21.8 The **GROUP** and **ITEM** commands.

The final stage is to repair the GFE, an option which is only open to experienced and highly skilled PICK technicians who know PICK intimately and are competent in the use of the System Debugger. If you are unsure of what you are doing, do not under any circumstances try to fix a GFE as you can bring down the entire system and even corrupt PICK. If you have fixed GFEs under R83 the following section explains how to do so under Advanced PICK.

```
:set-sym psym

:list staff
*** GFE Encountered @gfe.sr - Bad count field
F=fix item/T=truncate group & quit/Q=just quit/<CR>=go to debugger ?[CR]

!/GFE.SR .000000004CF6=
!*GFE.SR;6 .000000007300=
!END
```

By dumping the frame containing the GFE we can see the item count in question hex 73 (representing an item of 115 bytes), should actually be 71 as the item in question (the first in this group) is actually only 113 characters long.

```
:DUMP 19702 X
fid: 19702 :   0        0        0 0 ( 4CF6 :  0 0 0
0000 00000000 73001001 303034FE 4841524C 000 :....s...004^HARL:
0010 4F572C4D 49434841 454CFE35 3820464F 016 :OW,MICHAEL^58 FO:
0020 554E5441 494E204C 414E45FD 42494C4C 032 :UNTAIN LANE]BILL:
0030 45524943 4159FD45 53534558 20434D31 048 :ERICAY]ESSEX CM1:
0040 32203348 46FE3031 34373420 33343432 064 :2 3HF^01474 3442:
0050 3535FE31 31FE5351 55415348 FD4D5553 080 :55^11^SQUASH]MUS:
0060 4943FE31 32393030 3030FE39 383938FE 096 :IC^1290000^9898^:
0070 FFFF0000 00007100 10013030 35FE4D4F 112 :__....q...005^MO:
0080 52524953 2C4A494D FE333320 4D494C4C 128 :RRIS,JIM^33 MILL:
0090 204C414E 45FD4C4F 4E444F4E 20FD5355 144 : LANE]LONDON ]SU:
00A0 52524559 20524833 20385658 FE303138 160 :RREY RH3 8VX^018:
00B0 31203334 35203534 3534FE31 33FE5351 176 :1 345 5454^13^SQ:
00C0 55415348 FD425249 444745FD 52414C4C 192 :UASH]BRIDGE]RALL:
00D0 59494E47 FE313535 30303030 FE393930 208 :YING^1550000^990:
00E0 32FEFFFF 00000000 6D001001 303036FE 224 :2^__....m...006^:
00F0 42524947 48542C49 414EFE31 3231204A 240 :BRIGHT,IAN^121 J:
0100 4F494E45 5253204C 414E45FD 57454C57 256 :OINERS LANE]WELW:
0110 594EFD48 45525453 20534731 20314444 272 :YN]HERTS SG1 1DD:
0120 FE303132 34342039 39393333 FE3032FE 288 :^01244 99933^02^:
0130 4B415241 5445FD4D 41525449 414C2041 304 :KARATE]MARTIAL A:
0140 525453FE 31353430 303030FE 39393333 320 :RTS^1540000^9933:
0150 FEFF0000 00002900 10013030 37FEFEFE 336 :^_....)...007^^^:
```

The end of the item at byte 113

```
:debug

I ut.go.debug:07E
!x19702.0004;1 .73=71
!end
:
```

Figure 21.9 Repairing a GFE.

21.12.3 Repairing a GFE

The first step is set up the symbol table to be used by the debugger. At the TCL prompt type **set-sym psym**. Then locate the GFE by listing or counting the contents of the file. Once found the command **/GFE.SR** (which must be entered in upper case) will display the frame and offset of the GFE and ***GFE.SR;6** will display the pointer to the GFE. Figure 21.9 shows this in operation.

21.12.4 GFEs and system security

Fortunately all these errors are rare and not impossible to resolve. If they do occur it is generally because of a hardware fault, so if they start to occur regularly you should call in a hardware engineer.

It is this type of problem, which comes without giving any sort of warning, which emphasizes the importance of adequate backup procedures. It is worth repeating, without wishing to sound over dramatic, that only you can determine the frequency and type of backups that should be taken to secure your own system. It's at times like this that you realize just how important regular backups, whether full file saves, account saves or incremental saves, really are.

21.13 The TCL stack

The TCL stack is another of the new features introduced with Advanced PICK and provides the means of browsing through a list of previously executed TCL commands and re-executing them or modifying them prior to execution.

This time saving feature uses the Update Processor to enter and modify the current TCL line and has a series of its own commands to move through and retrieve commands from the stack.

21.13.1 Modifying a TCL command

When the command is first entered at the TCL prompt the TCL editor is in overtype mode, hence changing a typing mistake is simply a question of moving to the incorrect text and typing over it. If you need to insert some text type r̲ (ctrl/r) which in exactly the same way as the Update Processor moves the text from the cursor to the end of the line onto the next line, leaving you in insert mode. When all the text has been inserted, type another **r̲**.

21.13.2 Processing through the TCL stack

The TCL stack is stored in the file **tcl-stack** in the **dm** account with the commands executed stored as attributes in an item with the item-id being that of the logged on user as given in the **users** file. Hence the TCL stack in Advanced PICK is user and not port related.

Edit commands for the TCL stack

b	Up one line
e	Delete to end of line
g	Move to end of line
h	Backspace, replacing character with a space
i	Tab forward
j	Cursor left
k	Cursor right
l	Delete character
m	Insert mode at end of line and inserts <cr>/lf when within the line
n	Down a line
o	Delete to end of word
r	Toggle insert mode
t	Move to start of line
u	Move to next word
w	Insert a single space
x	Return to the TCL prompt
y	Move back one word
zz	Undo last delete

Changing any part of the TCL command displayed will cause the amended command to be moved to the top of the stack, which means the most recently executed commands stay at the top. However, as was stated earlier, there is no limit to the size of the items within the stack file and it should be reviewed and cut down in size at regular intervals. One way to shrink it is to clear out the file completely. Whilst this has the desired effect, it may not make you too popular with your users, who may have some large ACCESS statements floating around. The alternative is to go into each item and delete all but the first *n* attributes of each item. Most users would accept that having access to the last 100 TCL commands for example is entirely reasonable.

The three most valuable commands are **d** to retrieve the previously entered command or to work backwards through the stack, **f** to work forward through the stack and **a** which if entered immediately after a string of characters will search for that string of characters anywhere in the stack. It will retrieve the first command it finds that contains the string *somewhere* in the command; the command does not have to commence with the string, it just has to contain the string. The **a** command works forwards through the stack, but to work backwards use **za** (ctrl/z a). Overleaf is a summary of the commands that can be used to help you retrieve and execute commands in your stack.

From Advanced PICK version 6.2 the TCL stack can also be accessed using the 'dot stacker'. This means that commands from the stack can be retrieved and edited using commands that begin with a dot or full stop. This type of TCL stack processor was implemented on a number of licencee implementations and was included in Advanced PICK by PICK Systems to provide compatibility to licencee versions. For those of you not familiar with the dot processor, the following summarizes the available commands:

Retrieving and executing commands in the TCL stack

a	Searches forwards in the stack looking for a given string of characters
cp	(cut and pop). Put current TCL line at the top of the stack
d	Move back a line through the stack
e	Deletes to the end of the command. If the line is left blank the command is deleted from the stack
f	Move forward a line through the stack
p	Make a copy of the TCL command and put it on the top of the stack
x	Clear the command line and put the pointer back to the top of the stack
z	Goes to the command at the top of the stack
za	Searches backwards in the stack looking for a given string of characters

The dot stacker commands

.?	Displays a list of available commands
!*string*	Searches forwards in the stack looking for a given *string* of characters
.C{O} *n*{,*m*}	Create a macro from line(s) *n* {to *m*} {overwriting if **O** option used}
.DE {*n*}	Delete the top entry on the stack. If *n* is entered the top *n* commands are removed from the stack
.DE *n*/*string1*	Delete the top *n* commands from the stack which contain the string *string1*
.L	Lists the commands in the stack
.L*n*{-*m*}	Lists the first *n* {through *m*}commands in the stack
.R	Display the top entry in the stack
.R *n*	Displays the *n*th entry in the stack
.R{*U*} *n*/*string1*/*string2*	Replaces the first occurrence of *string1* with *string2* in the *n*th command in the stack. If the **U** is included it replaces all occurrences of *string1* with *string2*
.X	Execute the command on the top of the stack
.X {file} name	Execute the macro called *name* {in the file *file*} created by a **.C** command

21.14 The background processor

The background processor is one of the features introduced with Advanced PICK. It enables tasks to be set in motion which will operate without tying up a terminal and the user who spawns the task then carries on with other processing while the background process continues. One background or phantom process is allowed for each eight-user Advanced PICK licence purchased, but this does not limit the number of background tasks being initiated. If insufficient phantom ports are available for the number of background tasks that have been initiated the background tasks will be queued until a phantom port becomes available.

When a phantom process is initiated an item is written to the **jobs** file and to the queue of jobs for the job scheduler. When the scheduler is ready to process the task, it changes the status of the job in the **jobs** file to 'running' which is changed to 'done' was the job is complete.

The job scheduler is a process which has to be initiated if background processing is required. This is part of the normal coldstart procedure, but can be initiated separately with the **startsched** command. The scheduler normally runs on the very last phantom port of the system.

21.14.1 Initiating a background or phantom process

Setting a task to run in background is very straightforward, just precede the command with a **z**. Adding the letter **h** will hold all terminal output to a hold file, whilst adding an **s** will suppress error messages, which otherwise would be displayed on the terminal. The **z** verb can have any combination of the options **h** or **s** added to it. Hence **z**, **zh**, **zs** and **zhs** are all valid options. Figure 21.10 shows a typical background process being initiated, together with the contents of the **jobs** file.

```
:z count md
[438] Job #1003616694 submitted.
:
04:38:14 23 Jun 1995 from user Roger line 4
[407] 977 items counted out of 977 items.

:list jobs
Page 1       jobs                                      04:38:24 23 Jun 1995

user-md...... ln. pib status...... start-dt... stop-dt... tcl-command.....

Roger DM       0   4 done(4)       23/06 04:38 23/06 04:38 count md
Roger DM  1003616694 sched id(10)  23/06 04:38

[405] 4 items listed out of 4 items.
```

Figure 21.10 The background processor.

21.14.2 Killing a background process

A background process is killed using the **end** command. The purpose of this command is to terminate a process on another port and is not available under R83. The process to be terminated by the **end** command can either be a background process, a process active on another port or a task pushed to another level (level pushing is covered in the next section). The general format of the command is

end {*port.number user.name*}

21.15 Level pushing

It is possible to work on more than one task at a time, by suspending the current command or program and pushing a level. When this is done, the number of colons (the TCL prompt symbol) will increase by one indicating the level at which you are working. In all you can push up to 16 levels, although you are unlikely to require more than a couple. If, for example, you are in the process of restoring a large account and you run out of disk space, you might want to see if there is an account or some files you can delete to allow the restore to complete. In such a situation by pushing a level you suspend the restore and are given full and normal access to the system as you would if at the TCL prompt at the normal level. You can then explore the system, delete the required files and/or accounts, return to level one and tell the system to continue.

There are two keys you can use to act as the level pushing key, the break key or the escape key. In both cases they can be set to act in their normal capacity or to act as the level pushing key.

If you wish to use the break key as the level pusher, ensure that it is first enabled by pressing it to see what happens. Whilst an active break key is usual, the command **break-key-off** will disable it for the current port and **break-key-on** will enable it again. However, there is a system wide command to disable the break key, which is as follows:

break-key {(*option*}
where valid *option* is

f	disables break key
n	enables break key
s	suppress display of status message

The commands available for setting the functions of the escape and break keys are as follows:

brk-level	causes break key to push a level
brk-debug	causes break key to invoke the debugger
esc-data	causes escape key to send its ASCII code as data
esc-level	causes escape key to push a level
esc-toggle	causes escape key to toggle its function between **esc-data** and **esc-level**

When working at a lower level there are two ways in which you can return to the previous level, by pressing [CR] the carriage return key or by entering **end**. Beware however, that entering **end** will cause any active list at the previous level to be lost.

21.16 Sending messages

It is possible to send messages to other users on the system. Under R83 the only command available was **MSG** but in Advanced PICK you can also use

message, **send-message** or **sm**. These commands enable messages to be sent to all users, users on a specific port or users operating with a specific user-id (in a R83 this would send messages to a specific account). Whilst this has its uses, it immediately interrupts the user with the message, rings the VDU bell and in the process disturbs the position of the cursor which is moved to the end of the displayed message. Since this disturbs the data on the user's screen, they are often thrown by it, not being sure whether the message will be considered as part of the data being input, which of course, it is not.

To send a message to all users, known as an all-ports broadcast, use the verb followed by an asterisk followed by the text of the message.

```
send message * The system will be unavailable between 1pm and
2pm today
```

If the asterisk is replaced by an exclamation mark, the message will also be sent to all serial printers too. For messages to a specific port the asterisk is replaced with an exclamation mark, followed by the port number, such as

```
send message !2 Please would you log off
```

For messages to a nominated user (a user logged on to a specific account under R83) the asterisk is replaced by the user-id (the account name in R83)

```
send message dm Can you help sort out my printer problem?
```

21.17 The EPICK account

The EPICK (Encyclopedia PICK) account is an account which contains an electronic cross-referenced copy of the Advanced PICK Reference Manual. Whilst it is retained centrally, EPICK contains an installation option to enable access from any account on your system. The installation in an account takes very little space, so it is worth installing it in the prime accounts on your system.

The EPICK system enables you to quickly locate a topic and to display on-line help on the subject. The display is an exact replica of the page from the Advanced PICK Reference Manual but with the advantage that you can immediately access related topics or search on specific words or phrases.

Each topic is broken into a number of areas:

token	the subject matter or topic
category	the part of PICK the topic relates to, such as ACCESS, BASIC, TCL, etc.
type	the topic type, such as verb, modifier, user exit, relational operator, etc.
description	text describing the topic in detail

syntax	the full syntax of the topic (where appropriate)
options	the available options (where applicable)
compatibility	the 'flavours' of PICK to which the topic is applicable, such as R83, AP, APDOS, etc.
see also	related topics which may prove helpful in understanding the topic in question
examples	examples of the use of the topic in question
warnings	areas to take care about

If EPICK is initiated in your account you can go directly to a topic by typing **help** followed by the topic, such as **help delete**. This will bring up the first topic which starts with the word delete. If this is not the correct one, press **f** (ctrl/f) to move forwards and **d** (ctrl/d) to move backwards alphabetically through the topics.

If you wish to choose a different topic overwrite the topic displayed with the new topic, press **e** (if applicable) to clear the remaining text on the line and then press **f** to move to the first reference with that new topic name.

You can also 'zoom' to related subjects when the cursor is in the **category**, **type** or **see also** attributes by pressing **gg** (two consecutive ctrl/g). When you have finished in this related topic you can return to the original one with **xe** and a further **xe** will exit the help facility altogether.

If you hadn't already realized, EPICK uses Update Processor commands to get around and those applicable are as follows:

EPICK command summary

a	Search for phrase or repeat last search.
b	Move cursor up one line.
d	Cruise backward on indexed attribute or move to previous sentence in a text attribute.
e	Erase to end of line.
f	Cruise forward on indexed attribute or move to next sentence in a text attribute.
g	Move to end of attribute (paragraph).
gg	Zoom to related subject.
n	Move cursor down one line.
m	Move to next paragraph.
p	Move to next page. (the page up key also works on the PC monitor)
t	Move to top of item.
xe	Exit item.
ze	Move to end of document.
zy	Move to previous page.

21.18 Some useful commands

There are a few commands that as the System Administrator you might find useful. Firstly there are a number of commands which invoke a menu to handle specific tasks and saves having to know the TCL command and syntax to perform that task.

account-maint	to create, modify, rename or delete user accounts	
admin	a system admin menu, which calls other menus, which can be called separately in their own right. These menus are:	
	admin.files	a menu to handle backups and restores
	admin.status	a menu for information about the status of the system including user status and system locks
	admin.control	a menu to set the system date and time, to send messages and to log off processes
	admin.maint	a menu for creating and maintaining users and accounts
admin.tape	a menu for listing and attaching devices	
admin.tape.setup	a menu to assign various devices for use	
config.menu	a menu to configure UNIX/AP systems	

Other commands you might find useful are as follows:

compare	compares the contents of two items in either the same or different file(s)
lerrs	a MACRO which produces a detailed report on system errors
list-jobs	a list of all items in the **jobs** file, which are tasks executed by the phantom processor
list-lines	list the status of all attached ports (serial or networked)
list-pibs	a list of all active ports
lu	a list of logged on users
maxusers	displays the number of licenced PICK users
move-file	moves a file from one MD to another
prime	calculates prime numbers
recover-fd	recovers the last item deleted within the EDITOR
recover-item	recovers the last item deleted within the UPDATE PROCESSOR
reset-port	resets a 'hung' port
search-file	searches a file for specified string(s)
search-system	searches every file on the system for specified string(s)
steal-file	steals a file from another account and puts it in the currently logged on account
tandem	links current port to another so that any input or output on either screen is reflected on the other
tcl	suspends operation of current task and pushes a level executing the task given after the **tcl** verb
where	displays the status of all processes
which	displays details of the version and release of PICK in use
who	displays details of the port executing the command

21.19 Security, integrity and backup procedures

This chapter concludes with the most important task of the System Administrator, that of the security and integrity of the system. Once the security systems have been established they rarely need changing, other than for the regular change of passwords and the removal of user-ids after staff leave the company. For full details on the security facilities available in Advanced PICK, refer to Chapter 20.

The System Administrator should ensure that regular backups are taken to secure the company's database. These procedures should ensure that several copies of the backup are rotated. This is to protect against the extremely unlikely circumstances of needing to recover from the backup tape and finding the tape unreadable. In addition, at regular, perhaps monthly, intervals, a copy of the database should be placed outside the company, perhaps in a bank or at another branch, to protect against fire damaging the computer and all its backup copies.

22 The Control of Printers using the Spooler

TCL verbs and general commands covered in this chapter

ASSIGNFQ	LISTABS	LISTPEQS	LISTPTR	SETUP-PRINTER
SP-ASSIGN	SP-CLOSE	SP-EDIT	SP-KILL	SP-OPEN
SP-STATUS	SP-TAPEOUT	STARTPTR	STARTSHP	STARTSPOOLER
STOPPTR				

22.1 An introduction to the Spooler

The Spooler deals with the need for users in a multi-user environment to produce printed documents and to use any of the printers attached to their system. PICK has always recognized the need to support multiple printers (on the PC implementation it supports up to 50 serial and 4 parallel printers) allowing concurrent printing of documents (the Spooler controls up to 600 printed documents at any one time) and controlling functions such as multiple copies, paper alignment, re-directed output and producing output on magnetic media.

The Spooler (Simultaneous Peripheral Output and On-line Error Recovery) is an output management system and deals with two classes of peripheral device:

(1) a save device, such as the floppy disk or tape unit;

(2) one or more printers.

The Spooler, therefore, controls backup procedures (as described in Chapter 20), as well as the control of printers (to which this chapter is devoted). One of the important considerations of any multi-user system is the control of printing, where one or more printers is to be shared amongst a number of users. No user wishes to be constrained by what is being currently printed. When a user is ready to produce a report that is the time they wish to send the report for printing and once this has been done they do not want to wait until their report has finished printing before being able to use their terminal again.

The PICK Spooler provides a powerful and extensive facility for controlling all printed reports. Once a report has been generated, from whatever process, it is stored on disk and PICK creates a control record which refers to it. The Spooler then takes over and fully controls the printing process. By producing reports in this way the user is held up for only the time required to prepare a copy of the report on disk and is able to produce reports freely regardless of whether or not a printer is available for immediate use. Thereafter, whilst the report is printing or awaiting its turn in the queue, the user's terminal is free to carry out any other task.

The Spooler runs as a separate process in the system although it is called a 'phantom' process since it is treated as the last and non-physical port on the system. In addition to actual ports, a system may have a number of 'background' or 'phantom' processes as well as the Spooler. Hence in a three-user system there maybe the monitor, two serial ports, two background or phantom processes and the Spooler. This would mean a total of six PIBs (Process Identification Blocks), one for each process on the system.

The Spooler is started automatically by an option in the system coldstart procedure, a program called **start.ss**, which starts the Spooler and phantom processor. To initiate the Spooler the program invokes the TCL command **STARTSPOOLER**. A file restore process will also automatically initiate the Spooler and phantom scheduler.

There is no command to stop the Spooler and indeed there is no real need to do so. It sits in the background and awaits jobs to process. Individual printers can be stopped and re-started, but the only command available to you which affects the total Spooler functionality is **STARTSPOOLER** a command to re-start the Spooler and a command of last resort, since it causes all spooled reports to be lost.

The Spooler can control up to 50 serial and four parallel printers at any one time, maintaining up to 600 reports scattered amongst them. The key features of the Spooler are shown in Figure 22.1.

- Up to 600 print files may be retained and controlled.
- Up to 60 print files may be produced simultaneously.
- Up to 125 output queues may be defined. (An output queue identifies a specific printer loaded with a particular type of stationery.)
- Up to 125 copies of a report can be requested at a time.
- Up to 50 serial printers can be defined.
- Up to 4 parallel printers can be defined.
- Print files can be transferred to and from storage media such as tape, floppy or hard disk.

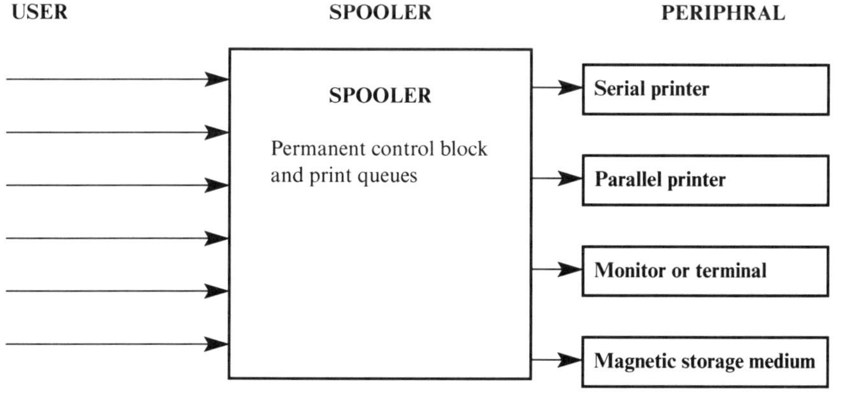

Figure 22.1 Features of the Spooler.

Each printer on the system is assigned a number, with printer number 0 (zero) normally being used as the default or system printer. Unless specified to the contrary, each users output will automatically be sent to printer 0. To make use of a printer other than printer 0, the user will have to specifically assign that printer for their use. This assignment performed with the TCL verb **SP-ASSIGN** has to be carried out from the line that requires the assignment as remote line assignments are not possible. In general therefore, printer assignments are carried out in logon macros or logon procs. What is not generally made clear, however, is that a specific printer assignment is lost as soon as the user logs to another account and, unless a further printer assignment is made, all subsequent reports will then, by default, be produced on the system printer!

Each printer must have a form queue number assigned to it, which represents a specific printer with specific stationery. Where a system has a number of the same printers each using the same stationery then all printers can be given the same form queue number, e.g. zero. All reports have to be directed to a form queue and it is the job of the Spooler to match a spooled report to the right form queue. Where there are several printers with the same form queue the Spooler will take each report in the spool queue and direct it to the first available printer. It is rarely that simple, however, since most companies have a mixture of printers, some laser, some matrix, and will also have a number of different types of stationery to print on.

If some printers are letter-quality printers and others are fast dot-matrix printers, then you would want to ensure that outside correspondence was produced on the letter-quality printer and lengthy draft reports on the matrix printer. In this situation you need assign different form queues to each printer, for example form queue 0 for the matrix printer (the system printer and nominated as printer 0) and form queue 1 for the letter-quality printer (printer 1). In this example each printer on the system is given the same number as its form queue number, form queue 0 to printer 0, form queue 1 to printer 1 and so on. This situation is preferable since many of the Spooler commands refer to the form number rather than printer number and it is far easier to know what response to give if you know they are both the same!

To enable the use of special stationery, however, each printer can be allocated up to three different queue numbers. This means that for any single printer you can send reports which can be segregated into three separate queues. For instance one queue might handle normal reports using plain stationery, the second, invoices on pre-printed invoice stationery, whilst the third may require that reports be printed on four-part plain stationery. Unless you have a dedicated printer for each of these different requirements, an existing printer will have to be used and by separating the reports into identifiable queues is the way in which PICK helps you deal with these sorts of requirement.

To handle a situation that requires the use of special stationery (for special read different) for a printer that is being used for other work you will need to undertake the following steps:

(1) Assign a unique form queue number in the range 0–125 for the special stationery. Use the command **STARTPTR** described in Section 22.2.1. If you are using preprinted stationery ensure you set the **A** (alignment) option with the **STARTPTR** command.

(2) Before running the program that uses special stationery, assign the form queue number using the hold options **HS**. This is achieved with the **SP-ASSIGN** command described in Section 22.6.

(3) When the program has finished its output will be held on the spool queue under a spool queue number. Once the printer has been loaded with the special stationery, release the output from the spool queue by use of the **SP-EDIT** command described in Section 22.3.

22.1.1 Spooler options

Many of the verbs used to control the Spooler share a common options handler and are therefore treated in the same manner. The verbs affected are:

ASSIGNFQ	SETUP-PRINTER		STARTSHP
STARTSPOOLER	SP-EDIT	T-ATT	T-RDLBL
DUMP	SP-KILL	T-BCK	WHAT
LISTABS	SP-STATUS	T-DET	WHERE
LISTPEQS	SP-TAPEOUT	T-FWD	WHO
LISTPTR	STOPPTR	T-READ	

22.1.2 The LISTPTR, LISTPEQS, SP-STATUS and LISTABS commands

The first step in taking control is to find out what printers are known by the system and what state they are in. There are a number of useful commands that explain which printers are already configured and available to the system and give information about the state of the Spooler. Firstly **LISTPTR** lists the printers available, their type and the line to which they are attached. The **LISTPEQS** command produces a list of all the entries on the Spooler and gives information on each, whilst the **SP-STATUS** command provides useful status information on all Spooler controlled devices. Another helpful command is **LISTABS**, which provides a list of the form queues associated with each physical line on the computer.

Figure 22.2 shows a typical display from the **LISTPTR** command. It shows there are two printers attached to the system, one a parallel printer the other attached serially. Only one, printer number 1 on line 1, is currently in use. The **LISTPTR** verb, like most Spooler commands, has a number of options which follow the verb (Table 22.1).

:LISTPTR

```
Page Dev or
Type Number Output Queues  Skip Line  #     Status
parallel      0  0                          0           0      inactive
serial        1  1                          1           1      active
```

Figure 22.2 Output from **LISTPTR.**

Table 22.1 The **LISTPTR** options.

n(-rn)	A range of printers from number n to rn
B	Reports on all possible printers regardless of whether they are in use or not. This may list some as 'unallocated', a situation which can occur if the printer has never been started, if it has been deleted using the **SP-KILL (D** command or has been lost because of a system error.
N	The NOPAGE option, displaying in continuous mode on the terminal
P	Produces the output on the printer rather than the terminal

Hence, the command **LISTPTR 1** would produce a report of printer status and queue allocation information for printer number 1 only, whilst **LISTPTR 1P** would send the same report to the printer. Notice that no (is required for the options, although they will work equally as well with the (present. The **LIST-PEQS** command illustrated in Figure 22.3, has even more options (Table 22.2):

Table 22.2 The **LISTPEQS** options.

n(-m)	A range of print file numbers from number n to m
A	Outputs the status of all reports generated on the account to which you are logged
C	Outputs a count of the number of spooled reports and the amount of storage space they are using
E	Displays the frame location of the spooled entries
F	Displays the entries on the Spooler in form queue order (~125)
H	Displays 'hold' files only
L	Displays reports that have been deleted, in addition to the current ones
P	Causes the output from the command to be sent to the printer rather than terminal
'account'	Displays the status of all reports produced from the account called *account*
'user-id'	Displays the status of all reports produced by the user with the id *user-id*

:listpeqs

```
Spooler Queue Elements.                               22 Apr 1995 14:53:26
Job Stat Lnk Line Status     Copies Form Frames     Date     Time     User

 1 A285       0  o p c so l      1   0       2  22/04/95  14:52:23  dm
 2 8088       0  p l             1   0       2  22/04/95  14:58:28  dm

 2 Queue Elements.                           4 Frames in use.
```

:listpeqs l

```
Spooler Queue Elements.                               22 Apr 1995 14:53:26
Job Stat Lnk Line Status     Copies Form Frames     Date     Time     User

 1 A285       0  h c             1   0       2  22/04/95  14:52:23  dm
 2 8088       0  a (h c l)       1   0       2  22/04/95  14:58:28  dm
 3 8088       0  c h             1   0       1  22/04/95  14:52:39  dm
 4 A548       0  c  l op s       1   0       1  22/04/95  14:53:18  dm

 4 Queue Elements.                           6 Frames in use.
```

:listpeqs (e

```
Spooler Queue Elements.                               22 Apr 1995 14:53:26
Job Stat Lnk Frms Cdsp      BegFID   Form  Frames     Date     Time     User

 1 8088        0001 00004835 00004835 0      2  22/04/95  14:52:23  dm
 2 8088        0001 00004836 00004836 0      2  22/04/95  14:52:28  dm
 3 8088        0001 000068E6 000068E6 0      1  22/04/95  14:52:39  dm
 4 A548 6   1- 0001 0000483A 0000483A 0      1  22/04/95  14:53:18  dm
 5 A548     2- 0001 000068BA 000068BA 1      2  22/04/95  14:54:10  dm
 6 8548        0001 000068D7 000068D7 0      2  22/04/95  14:54:19  dm

 6 Queue Elements.                          10 Frames in use.
```

Figure 22.3 Output from the **LISTPEQS** command.

The first example of Figure 22.3 shows that two reports have been spooled from the **DM** account which have been given the Spooler references (entry numbers) 1 and 2. These numbers can be used within the command **SP-EDIT** which is a versatile command enabling you to manage reports in the spool queue. The status codes show that the first entry on the Spooler is being printed on form queue 0, and in each case just one copy of the report has been requested. The status codes that may be encountered are shown in Table 22.3.

Figure 22.4 shows the output from the **SP-STATUS** command which gives a self-explanatory status report of the up-to-date position on each printer. This general overview first indicates whether or not the Spooler is active. It then shows the number of frames taken up by any spooled report, the form queues assigned to each printer and the physical line to which each printer is attached.

Table 22.3 The **LISTPEQS** status codes and their meanings.

A	Indicates that the control block is available for use. These are shown when the **L** option is used. This will occur when several reports have been spooled and an earlier one printed. The earlier control blocks will be reused before additional ones are allocated
C	Indicates the print file is closed. If this code is not shown it means that the report is being generated or that an **SP-OPEN** condition exists
G	Indicates the control record references a phantom print file being the alignment segment of another print file which was aligned
H	Specifies the entry to be a hold file by virtue of the **SP-ASSIGN**ment under which it was created or because it was dequeued by **SP-KILL F***n* (where *n* is the entry number) or due to the occurrence of a cold start
I	Specifies that immediate printing of the report was requested by virtue of the **SP-ASSIGN I** option being taken
L	Indicates the record is locked and cannot be **SP-EDIT**ed. It is locked when it is available, open, spooled, being output or while it is being **SP-EDIT**ed
N	Indicates that the print file was generated under an **SP-OPEN** condition
O	The report is being output
P	Indicates the output is to go to the printer
R	Indicates the entry has been **SP-EDIT**ed and sent to the printer
S	Indicates the report has been spooled using **SP-EDIT**
T	Indicates that the report has been sent to the storage medium (tape, floppy, etc.)
X	Indicates the report was aborted using **SP-KILL**

:sp-status

```
The spooler is active.

Printer # 0 is parallel, active, and on line.
[1219]** The printer cable is off! **
The printer is defined as parallel printer # 0.
Print file being output is element 4, a closed file for line # 0
Generated on account dm , which is 1 frames long.
Assigned output queues: 0 .
The number of inter-job pages to eject is 0.


Printer # 1 is serial, active, and on line.
The printer is running on line 1.
Print file being output is element 5, a closed file for line # 0
Generated on account dm , which is 2 frames long.
Assigned output queues: 1 .
The number of inter-job pages to eject is 1.
```

Figure 22.4 Output from **SP-STATUS.**

Figure 22.5 shows the typical output from the **LISTABS** command, a very useful command when things start to go wrong. If reports are being printed on the wrong printer, or do not start printing at all, this command helps you to find out why since it shows the print queues assigned to each port. Using this information with that of **SP-STATUS** the printers associated with each user can readily be established.

Figure 22.5 shows that lines 0, 1 and 5 are using form queue 0, whilst lines 4, 6 and 7 are using queue number 1. Lines 2 and 3 are the printers themselves.

LISTABS status codes (Table 22.4) are based on options taken when the printer is assigned using the **SP-ASSIGN** command and are explained in full in Section 22.2.6.

:listabs

```
Line#     Status   Copies    Form#   Device
    0       P          1        0
    1       H          1        0
    2                  0        0
    3                  0        0
    4       P          1        1
    5       P          1        0
    6       P          1        1
    7       P          1        1
```

Figure 22.5 Output from **LISTABS.**

Table 22.4 The **LISTABS** status codes.

C	Choke the creating process to printer speed
H	Create and keep a copy on hold
I	Immediate output
0	Keep the print file open at completion
P	Output to the printer
T	Output to the tape

22.2 Adding and removing printers

22.2.1 The STARTPTR command

The PICK system allows printers to be added and removed from a system configuration with very little effort. The command **STARTPTR** is used to add a printer to the system. The same command is used to assign a further form queue to an existing printer or restart an existing printer that has been stopped with the **STOPPTR** command. The general format of the command is shown in Figure 22.6.

Figure 22.7 gives some examples of its use, the first of which shows the addition of a new printer to the system. The serial printer, number 1 attached to line 4, is given the form queue number 3 with two pages being specified to be thrown between each report printed.

:STARTPTR *n{,formq,eject,typeN,{A} {(options}}*

where

n	is the actual printer number (0 is system printer); this can be a number between 0 and 49
formq	the form queue number in the range 0 to 125. It is possible to assign up to three form queues per printer. If more than one is assigned, these are separated by commas and enclosed in parentheses, i.e. (0,2,3) assigns form queues 0, 2 and 3
eject	the number of blank pages to eject automatically between reports
type	the printer type, where **S** = serial and **P** = parallel
N	the line number to which the printer is attached if a serial printer, or the device number for a parallel printer
A	the alignment option for preprinted stationery. Causes the prompt **LINES?** asking for the number of lines for each alignment test. After each trial the prompt **AGAIN(Y/T/N)** will be displayed. In response **Y** continues the alignment trials, **T** stops them and **N** allows a different number of lines to be input. During the alignment process the printer is not considered attached to the Spooler, so cannot receive print jobs
options	Other options such as

B	for serial printers where the line feed and form feed delays are assigned as those of the initiator
S	to suppress first form feed on serial printers
X	followed by a number to specify the lines per page for serial printers. If the number of lines is not specified, 66 is assumed

---

Figure 22.6 The general format of **STARTPTR**.

Allocate printer 1
Assign form queue 3 to the printer
Eject 2 blank pages between each report
Printer is serial and attached to line 4
Set the alignment option

:startptr 1,3,2,s4,a

Set two form queues for printer 1

:startptr 1,(2,3),2,s4

A simple 'restart' of printer 1 after use of **STOPPTR**

:startptr 1

Figure 22.7 Use of the **STARTPTR** command.

The second example in Figure 22.7 shows the same printer being added to the system, but this time the form queue numbers 2 and 3 are assigned to it.

On the final example in Figure 22.7 the same printer is restarted after it had previously been stopped by the **STOPPTR** command. Since the printer has only been stopped from printing and its other details (such as line number and form queue numbers) are unchanged, it only requires a simple re-start instruction. The **STOPPTR** command is explained next.

22.2.2 The STOPPTR command

The **STOPPTR** command does not remove a printer from the system configuration nor does it stop the Spooler. Its effect is to stop the printer after it has finished the report it is currently printing. **STOPPTR** therefore only stops a particular printer, and only when the report in progress on that printer has been completed. As with most PICK commands there are a number of options that can be used and these are explained in Figure 22.8. However, the user of this command must have **SYS2** privileges, the highest system privileges. For further information on privilege levels see Section 20.1.4.

Examples of the use of the **STOPPTR** command are shown in Figure 22.9. Having used the **W** option, all subsequently produced reports will hold on the spool queue until released by a **STARTPTR** command (see Figure 22.8). The **W** option is of particular importance when handling the Spooler within a PROC or Macro. The **STARTPTR** command will not work if the printer is still active, hence within a PROC or Macro the **STOPPTR** command should always contain the **W** option.

:STOPPTR {*options*}

where valid *options* are

n{-*m*}	where *n* and *m* are valid printer numbers in the range 0 and the maximum printer number, normally 54. Where a number is not specified, PICK stops printer zero
B	will stop all printers
D	deletes specified printer(s) or all printers if used with the **B** option
S	suppresses display of error messages
W	will cause the Spooler to finish printing the reports in the spool queue and stops the printer immediately they are complete. The terminal that carries out this command is returned to TCL after printing is complete

Figure 22.8 General format of **STOPPTR**.

:STOPPTR 1	Stops printer number 1
:STOPPTR 1-3	Stops printers in the range 1 to 3
:STOPPTR B	Stops all printers
:STOPPTR 1W	Stops printer 1 and waits until printer 1 is inactive before returning terminal to TCL

Figure 22.9 Examples of **STOPPTR.**

22.2.3 The SP-KILL command

The command **SP-KILL** can be used to perform one of three separate functions. These are to:

(1) Immediately terminate a report that is being printed.

(2) Remove a printer from the Spooler system.

(3) Remove entries from the Spooler queue.

If no options are specified this command aborts the current print job on printer zero. Unless the user has **SYS2** privileges only print files generated by the current user-id (or within the current account if using R83) can be aborted. The general format of the command is shown in Figure 22.10.

Terminating reports

The **SP-KILL** verb will stop a report from printing ‘immediately’. The word immediately is enclosed in quotes because the Spooler stops sending data to the

SP-KILL {*options*}

where the valid *options* are

n{-m}	where *n* are valid printer numbers in the range 0–50. This kills the spool queue entry for the report being produced on logical printer number *n*, and optionally through to printer number *m*
A	kills reports produced by the current user-id (or current account in R83)
B	kills all possible Spooler entries. If you have **SYS2** privileges this kills everything; if not it kills all reports on all printers created on the account to which you are logged When used with the **D** option this kills all printers. When used with the **F** option it kills all open jobs
C	kills all copies of the spooler entry or entries rather than just the current copy (available from version 6.1.0 onwards)
D*n*{-*m*}	deletes printer(s) *n* to *m* from the system and treats their line(s) as a logon port, if the printer is a serial printer
F*x*{-*y*}	changes status of any spool queue entry in the range 0 to 600, not currently being printed, to a hold file
N	suppresses the **ABORT!** message
O	removes from Spooler queue the report currently being printed and converts it to a hold file
S	Suppresses the system message (see **N** option)
U	Used with the **D** option, this deletes printer zero only
W	waits until all processes have finished. Using this option is identical to **STOPPTR D***n* returning terminal to TCL

Figure 22.10 The general format of **SP-KILL**.

printer immediately, but the printer memory buffers have to empty first before the printer itself will stop printing and in most cases this will take a while. Usually you can only kill the jobs generated on the account you are working within if you use SP-KILL for the purpose. Again only the highest privilege level (**SYS2**) allows printing to be stopped on any printer (even if the job being output belongs to another account).

The verb requires that the logical printer number printing the report be quoted and will cause **ABORT** to be printed one line after the point where the text of the report was terminated. This indicates that the report was abandoned part way through. The abort message can be suppressed if the **N** option is used.

The report will be released from the Spooler unless action is taken to convert it to a hold file (see the next section). The printer will start printing the next report from its assigned queues unless a **STOPPTR** has been executed.

22.2.4 Removing a printer from the Spooler system

The **SP-KILL** with the **D** option and followed by the printer number is used to delete a printer from the Spooler system. Carrying out the command whilst the printer is still working can cause all sorts of problems, so it is wise to ensure that the printer is stopped in a controlled manner (use **STOPPTR** followed by **SP-KILL** *n* [*n* being the printer number] where the report is a lengthy one). Only then is it safe to remove the printer from the system configuration.

If the printer is a parallel printer it will just become inactive. If, however, the printer is a serial printer the port the printer is attached to is sent the logon banner and can then have a terminal connected to it if required.

22.2.5 Removing entries from the Spooler queue

Printed reports which are to be removed from the Spooler queue are accessed by their entry number, the number displayed on the screen at the time the report was produced. If these have been forgotten, a full list of Spooler entries can be gained using the command **LISTPEQS** (Section 22.1.2).

Only those with the highest privilege level (**SYS2**) are permitted to dequeue any report whilst others can only remove the reports they generated under their user-id or from the account onto which they are logged.

Either way, reports are removed from the spool queue by using the **SP-KILL** with the **F** option followed by the entry number. When used successfully, this will convert the report to a 'hold' file which is then available to be **SP-EDIT**ed. One of the options of **SP-EDIT** (see Section 22.3) is to delete the report entirely.

If the report is currently being output and you require to keep the report, then neither **SP-KILL** *n* where *n* is the printer number which will lose the report nor **SP-KILL F***n* where *n* is the entry number will work. If the report is already being printed you need to combine the **O** option with the **F** option. Hence the command becomes **SP-KILL FO***n* where *n* is the entry number in which case the report is converted to a hold file which can then be manipulated with the command **SP-EDIT** (see Section 22.3).

SP-KILL – *its format and examples of its use*

Whilst Figure 22.10 shows the general format of the **SP-KILL** command, Figure 22.11 gives examples of its use. The **SP-KILL** command is used in many situations but naturally, as its name suggests, it needs to be used wisely and carefully. If a report has taken considerable time to send to the Spooler, you won't want take the wrong option and end up respooling it.

If after having spooled a report to a printer, you realize it was sent to the wrong printer or wrong form queue, you can use the **SP-KILL** command to take one of two courses of corrective action. If the report is being printed you can kill the printer, thereby removing all reference to it on the Spooler. This will require the report to be respooled. Otherwise if the report is lengthy an alternative to deleting it from the spool queue and respooling it for output to a different printer, is to use the **F** option to convert it to a hold file. Once in this state it can be manipulated by the command **SP-EDIT** (covered in Section 22.3).

:SP-KILL 1	immediately stops the report being printed on printer number 1
:SP-KILL 1-3	immediately stops the reports being printed on printers number 1, 2 and 3
:SP-KILL B	stops printing immediately on all printers on the system
:SP-KILL 1N	immediately stops the report being printed on printer number 1 and suppresses the abort message
:SP-KILL D1	will remove printer 1 from the system configuration, and will treat the line as a logon port, i.e. for use by a terminal, providing printer is a serial printer
:SP-KILL BD	removes all printers from the system configuration, and leaves their serial lines ready for use by terminals
:SP-KILL F4	changes Spooler queue entry number 4, not currently being output, into a hold file
:SP-KILL FO4	changes Spooler queue entry number 4, currently being output, into a hold file

Figure 22.11 Examples of **SP-KILL.**

SP-EDIT enables you to direct 'held' reports to other printers, take extra copies of reports and even convert them back into a data file on disk. Another use of the **F** option in **SP-KILL** is to take entries in the spool queue which are queued to a busy printer and reassign them to one that's free, which evens out the printing load and cuts down waiting time. The way to do this is covered in Section 22.3.4.

22.2.6 Directing printer output with SP-ASSIGN

Reports are produced on the printer by taking the appropriate menu option within an application package or by adding **LPTR** or **(P** to the end of an ACCESS command or **(P** to the end of any other TCL command. Unless some previous action has been taken, reports, by default, will be produced on the printer controlling form queue 0 and hence referred to as the 'system' printer.

Each user can modify his device assignment by use of the **SP-ASSIGN** verb. On its own, without any options, it will assign the system printer (printer zero), but reports can be sent to any printer on the system and may also be spooled to magnetic tape or diskette. The **SP-ASSIGN**ment is made to a specific form queue, which is again why form queue numbers tend to be the same as the printer numbers. The general format of the command is given in Figure 22.12.

SP-ASSIGN {*options*}

where valid *options* are:

n	where *n* is the number of copies of the report to print (must be between 1 and 125)
?	outputs the current assignments for the port executing the command
A	output is passed to the alternate port of the VDU. Useful where the terminal has an auxiliary port, but requires that the auxiliary on and auxiliary off commands are contained in the **devices** file
C	choke the printer process to printer speed. This *must* be used with the **I** option and *cannot* be used with the **H** option. The **C** option ensures that the minimum of disk space is taken up when producing the report and is useful for the production of large reports where little spare disk space remains. The maximum number of frames used at any one time is 20. However only one copy of a report can be printed at a time
D	delays sending the report to the spool queue until the file is closed. This option may not be used with the **I** option
F*n*	directs all future output to the form queue *n*. The default is zero and the maximum number is 125. The form queue number immediately follows the **F** without a space
H	causes the output to be retained as a hold file
I	outputs the report immediately without waiting for the report to be spooled first. This option must be used with the **C** option
M	causes the suppression of message 1151, "Entry # *n*"
O	keeps the print file open upon completion of the current report. This is useful where a number of reports need to be kept together and this option prevents anyone else spooling a report on the printer until an **SP-CLOSE** for the current port is encountered
R*n*	used in conjunction with PICK BASIC where a program opens more than one printer. This option opens a print file with the specifications given by the other options. The number *n* is the number used in the BASIC statement **PRINT ON *n***
S	suppresses output to the printer
T	assigns output to the currently attached media

Figure 22.12 The format of the **SP-ASSIGN** function.

Before looking to take any re-assignment action we need to know whether the printer currently allocated to us is the one we want to use and whether the correct number of copies will be produced. As we saw, **LISTABS** gave the form queue assignments for all users and provided you know which port you are using (the command **WHO** will give you this if you are unsure), then you can establish which form queue your report will go to. Another way to find out details of your printer assignment is to use **SP-ASSIGN ?** which gives this information for the terminal (or line number) which executed the command.

As with so many PICK commands, there are numerous options which can be applied to **SP-ASSIGN** and these are shown in Figure 22.12. Examples of the various ways in which the **SP-ASSIGN** command can be used are given in Figure 22.13. It is important to become familiar with the use of the **SP-ASSIGN** command, particularly when your system has more than one printer.

:SP-ASSIGN ? ← What are the current Spooler assignments?

```
Line#     Status   Copies   Form#    Device
0           p           1       0
```

The user is on line 0, with output going to the printer. One copy of each report will be produced on form queue 0

:SP-ASSIGN H ← Print the report, but also produce a hold file on disk containing this report

:SP-ASSIGN HS ← Produce the hold file, but do not print the report

:SP-ASSIGN F1 ← Print all future reports on form queue 1

:SP-ASSIGN 3 F1 ← Print 3 copies of all future reports on form queue 1

:SP-ASSIGN CIF1 2 ← Print 2 copies of all future reports on printer 1, start printing immediately, but constrain the Spooler to printing at the speed of the printer using no more than 20 frames on disk

:SP-ASSIGN HSR1 ← Causes the print file generated by a **PRINT ON 1** statement in a succeeding BASIC program to be made into a hold file, with out any output being produced

---

Figure 22.13 Examples of the use of **SP-ASSIGN.**

22.3 Manipulating the Spooler with SP-EDIT

Any item on the spool queue with a hold status can be accessed by a very useful command **SP-EDIT**, enabling the manipulation of these reports on the Spooler. The **SP-EDIT** verb provides all the facilities needed for the System Manager to take complete control of spooled reports. Once entered on the spool queue as a 'held' report, the print file can:

- be produced on another printer;
- have as many further copies produced as are required;
- be reprinted from any point;
- be removed from the spool queue altogether;
- be spooled to tape or diskette;
- be converted into a data file.

It is important to realize that only reports produced as 'held' reports can be manipulated in this way. It is the **SP-ASSIGN** command which not only assigns a particular printer to a user but also determines whether or not the reports are to be given 'hold' status. Any report on the spool queue can be converted to a hold file using **SP-KILL** (see Section 22.2.3).

The **SP-EDIT** command is very powerful and has options too numerous to discuss in great detail. All of these will be found in your manual, and provided you understand the principles of the **SP-EDIT** command these options will present you with no difficulty. The most common uses of this command are to remove reports from the print queue, to redirect the report to a different printer and to restart the report at a specific point.

There are two parts to **SP-EDIT**; firstly, the selection and manipulation options which form part of the command line and, secondly, an interactive session to determine the action to be taken on the reports selected.

22.3.1 SP-EDIT options

Using the command on its own without any options, will allow the manipulation of all the hold files which have been produced by the user (based on their PICK user-id) or if used in R83 PICK those produced on the account to which the user is currently logged. In both cases it deals with the reports which are not being output. Anyone with **SYS2** privileges can use the **U** (Universal) option to access all hold files or can follow the command by a user-id or account name, enclosed in single quotes, which will allow access to all print jobs produced by that user or account. The full list of **SP-EDIT** options is shown in Table 22.5.

Figure 22.14 give examples of the more common and useful combinations of options with the **SP-EDIT** verb.

22.3.2 The interactive session of SP-EDIT

The initial **SP-EDIT** verb executed states which reports you which to process. For each of these **SP-EDIT** will ask a series of questions. This interactive session enables you a number of options for the processing of each individual report. The interactive dialogue is shown in Figure 22.15 together with the meaning of each question and the relevant responses.

Table 22.5 SP-EDIT options.

Option	*Meaning*
Account Name	Selects reports generated from the specified account. **SYS2** privileges are required in order to use this option
User-id	Selects reports generated by the specified user
n or *n-m*	Selects report number *n* or reports *n* to *m* on the spool queue (the numbers must be in the range 1–600)
B	Suppresses the '.bp' and '.nf' commands which are included in the report when it is spooled to a file (using the **F** option). Not available in R83
C	Places the entire report in a single item when spooled to a file (using the **F** option). If this option is not used the report is broken into multiple items each 'chained' together
D	Deletes each report selected
F*n* or **F***n-m*	Selects reports on specified form queue or range of form queues (must be in the range 1–125)
H	Suppresses the label when the report is output to diskette or tape. This requires the **T** option on **SP-EDIT** or **SP-ASSIGN** to be effective
L	Looks at the contents of the reports on the Spooler. The first 500 characters are displayed. If you require to look at more use the T option
MD	Allows multiple reports to be deleted without the 'confirm' message being displayed. Without such opportunity for intervention this option is obviously dangerous in inexperienced hands since it will delete all held reports in the specified range without displaying an options at which to change your mind. The **D** option on its own does ask for confirmation that the report should be deleted
MS	Allows multiple reports to be spooled without intervention at each prompt. All held reports will be printed
N	The 'no pause' option and thus only effective with output to terminals. This causes the display to run continuously, ignoring page breaks
O	Used in conjunction with the **L** option to look at reports being printed
P	Directs the report to the currently assigned printer and overrides the **SP-ASSIGN** parameters
R	Changes the original output parameters (form queue and number of copies) to those of the current **SP-ASSIGN**. The form queue number and number of copies are changed permanently
T{W}	Directs the output to diskette or tape and waits for the device to be ready, if it is not already. Whilst the **W** (wait) here is strictly optional, it makes great sense to use the two together
U	Accesses all reports on the Spooler. **SYS2** privileges required
V	Converts the held report to a data file without removing trailing blanks or blank lines

:sp-edit	Retrieves all hold reports generated by the current user-id (from the current account if you have PICK R83)
:sp-edit u	Retrieve and edit all hold reports, regardless of the user-id (account in R83) that produced them. The person executing the command must have **SYS2** privileges
:sp-edit 10-20	Obtains any hold files with entry numbers in the range 10 to 20 produced by the same user as that executing the command
:sp-edit f2md	Deletes all the reports in form queue 2 produced by the same user as that executing the command
:sp-edit 'rb' msp1-10	Prints any hold file entries in the range 1 to 10 created by the user 'rb'. This requires the person executing the command to have **SYS2** privileges.
:sp-edit mud	Unconditionally deletes all hold reports

Figure 22.14 Examples of the **SP-EDIT** command.

22.3.3 Removing reports using SP-EDIT

Provided the report is already on the spool queue as a hold file, removing it is a simple job. Figure 22.16 shows how to remove print file number 4 from the spool queue which has been created by the same user-id (contained in the file **USERS**) as the user executing the command. (In R83 the person executing the command must be in the same account as the account in which the report was generated.)

A slightly more complicated series of commands is required if the report to be removed is on the spool queue but not as a hold file. Figure 22.17 shows how the report is first converted to hold status, using the **SP-KILL** verb and then removed using **SP-EDIT**. Remember if the report is currently being output you would need to add the **O** option to the **SP-KILL** command. Hence in the example in Figure 22.17, the command would be **SP-KILL F4O**.

22.3.4 Redirecting reports with SP-EDIT

Sending reports to a different printer than the one to which it was originally assigned is a two-stage process. The first step is to assign to yourself the printer on which the report is to be printed. This is achieved with the **SP-ASSIGN**. The second stage is to use **SP-EDIT** to carry out the spool to printer function. Figure 22.18 shows this in operation where report number 4, originally spooled to form queue 0, is redirected to form queue 1 and assumes the report is not currently being output. If it is being output use the **SP-KILL F*n*O** command first.

Meaning of options

```
ENTRY # nnn
DISPLAY (Y/N/S/D/X/(CR))?-
```

Y	Display the first 500 bytes of the record
N	Skip to **STRING** question
S	Skip to **SPOOL** question
D	Skip to **DELETE** question
X	Terminate **SP-EDIT** and return to the TCL prompt
[CR]	Skip to next print file

Any other response will skip to the **STRING** question

```
STRING:-
```

text	Scan report for first occurrence of *text*
[CR]	Skip to **SPOOL** question

```
SPOOL (Y/N=CR/T/TN/F)?-
```

Y	Spool the report
N	Skip to **DELETE** question
[CR]	Skip to **DELETE** question
T	Output the report on the terminal a page at a time
TN	Output the report on the terminal without stopping at the end of each page
F	Convert the report into a data file. This will then prompt for the file name and initial item name. If the **C** option is not taken, the report will be broken into multiple items each around 2K. The first item will have the name input by the user, the others will have a 4 digit sequential number appended to them and each will chain to the other with a '**.chain**' command being added as its last line.

```
DELETE (Y/N=CR)?-
```

Y	Remove the report from the Spool queue
N	Do not delete the report and move onto the next selected report and restart this dialogue

Figure 22.15 The interactive session of **SP-EDIT**.

:SP-EDIT 4

```
ENTRY # 4
DISPLAY (Y/N/S/D/X/(CR))?-D
DELETE (Y/N=CR)?-Y
END OF REQUESTED PRINT FILES.
```

Figure 22.16 Removing a spooled 'hold' report.

```
:SP-KILL F4
PRINT FILE #4 WAS UNLINKED AND IS AVAILABLE AS A HOLD FILE

:SP-EDIT 4
ENTRY # 4
DISPLAY (Y/N/S/D/X/(CR))?-D
DELETE (Y/N=CR)?-Y
END OF REQUESTED PRINT FILES.
```

Figure 22.17 Removing a 'non-hold' file from the Spooler.

```
:SP-ASSIGN F1
:SP-EDIT R4
ENTRY # 4
DISPLAY (Y/N/S/D/X/(CR))?-S
SPOOL (Y/N=CR/T/TN/F)?-Y
END OF REQUESTED PRINT FILES
```

Figure 22.18 Spooling a report to a different printer.

22.3.5 Restarting reports with SP-EDIT

Within the interactive session of **SP-EDIT** it is possible to restart a held report at any point by locating a specific string of characters. The report can be spooled to the printer from the point at which the string of characters is located.

Before restarting the report make sure that your printer assignment (**SP-ASSIGN**) has no hold status otherwise the following error message will be displayed and the report will not be spooled:

> [1160] Your output specification is 'no output'.
> Reassign your line if you wish to output a holdfile.

Figure 22.19 shows the procedure for restarting a report and what to do when the printer you want to use has the hold option set. Such an error is corrected by an **SP-ASSIGN** command, after which the report can be spooled correctly.

Do note from Figure 22.19 that the exact string of characters entered (case sensitive) must exist in the spooled report before you can progress further. You should also be aware that **SP-EDIT** locates the first occurrence of the specified string within the report. It is therefore important that the string of characters entered be long enough to uniquely identify the point at which the report is to be restarted. Since the report has 'hold' status, once the reprinting is finished, the report will remain on the spool queue.

:SP-EDIT 4
```
ENTRY # 4
DISPLAY (Y/N/S/D/X/(CR))?-N
STRING:-IF this fails to work
STRING NOT FOUND  <------ Note the string is not found because IF was typed
                          instead of If
STRING:- If this fails to work
SPOOL (Y/N=CR/T/TN/F)?-Y
 [1160] Your output specification is 'no output'.
 Reassign your line if you wish to output a holdfile.
```

:SP-ASSIGN F1

:SP-EDIT 4
```
ENTRY # 4
DISPLAY (Y/N/S/D/X/(CR))?-N
STRING:-If this fails to work
SPOOL (Y/N=CR/T/TN/F)?-Y
END OF REQUESTED PRINT FILES
```

Figure 22.19 Restarting printing from a specific point.

22.4 How to handle Spooler and printer problems

If problems appear to occur within the Spooler there are a number of checks that should first be made before taking the option of last resort that of re-initializing the Spooler.

- Make sure the printer is switched on in a 'ready' state.
- Make sure the printer is not out of stationery or in the case of laser printers, not out of toner or needs the drum changed.
- Make sure the printer cable is properly attached.
- Make sure you have defined the correct printer type, i.e. serial or parallel.
- Check that the baud rate of the printer matches that of the speed of the line. Refer to your printer manual for the baud rate for the printer. Unless the **SET-BAUD** command has been used to change the line speed (see Section 21.5.4), the speed of the line should be 9600 baud. You can check the state of the line with the command **LIST-LINES** (or **LIST-PORTS** if you have an R83 system).
- Make sure the printer is known to the system by using the **LISTPTR** command. If not, use the **STARTPTR** verb.
- Make sure the printer is connected to the port as stated in the **SP-STATUS** command. If not, either connect the printer to the correct

physical port or change the system configuration with the commands **SP-KILL** and **STARTPTR**.

- Make sure the report has been sent to the spool queue by using the **LISTPEQS** command.
- Create a 'hold' report and try manipulating it with **SP-EDIT.** If problems still occur re-initialize the Spooler.

The **STARTSPOOLER** command will re-initialize the Spooler at the TCL prompt without going through the normal coldstart procedures. The general format of the command is:

STARTSPOOLER *{port}* *{options}*

where

port	the port number to initialize	
options	the valid options which are as follows	
	c	clears all form queue assignments, kills the printer, clears input and output queues and converts any existing print files to hold files. Use as the penultimate option
	d	used in conjunction with the port number to enable the debugger on the port
	i	starts and initializes the Spooler from scratch. All disk space previously used by the Spooler is lost until the next file restore and all spooled reports will be lost. This is the option of last resort

Using the command without any options will re-initialize certain Spooler controls, leaving it for use in the normal way. If this fails to work, the next option is to use the **C** option to clear all control blocks with the exception of the permanent master control record. Finally, if all else fails, the **I** option should be used:

:STARTSPOOLER
:STARTSPOOLER C
:STARTSPOOLER I

In each case the message SPOOLER STARTED will be displayed. Using the command with either the **C** or **I** option will lose the printer assignments for all terminals and will remove all printers from the system configuration. Using the I option will also clear out all reports from the Spooler.

22.5 Control of the printer via PROC

Chapter 18 is devoted to PROC, a procedure language which allows the user to prestore a complex series of operations that can be invoked by a single command. It also explains how the Spooler can be manipulated within a PROC.

23 PICK and Application Generators

23.1 An introduction to application generators

Historically PICK's superb and efficient, variable length database integrated within the operating system encouraged the development of application generators more than any other operating system. However even working with PICK as a database, software companies are still producing development toolsets many of which are marketed and sold independently. All application generators, often referred to as fourth-generation application generators, fourth-generation languages or 4GL products, require a powerful database or ISAM (Indexed Sequential Access Method) file system to be able to operate.

A fourth-generation language is merely a development aid, but a development aid that permits people, often without data processing experience, to develop computer applications. Dependent on the features of individual 4GL products, these could develop merely skeletal systems requiring considerable work to complete or entire systems without the need for any further development or programming.

The computing industry has come a long way since the early 1950s when highly skilled specialists programmed huge electronic-valve-based computers in machine code, a language of noughts and ones. In the late 1950s electronic valves were replaced by transistors and then in the late 1960s by micro-miniaturized circuits which today have been replaced with VSLI (Very Large Scale Integration), often containing tens of thousands of circuits on an individual chip with enormous computing power way and above that of the mainframes of a decade earlier.

Developments in software have been just as impressive as those in hardware. Machine code languages were replaced with second-generation assembler languages, to be followed by the third generation of high-level languages like Pascal, COBOL and FORTRAN, many of which are still widely used today. In the early 1980s, 4GL products grew in number, acceptance and use.

Historically, computer users have suffered from being at the mercy of data processing specialists; data processing specialists who spoke a technical language of their own, who were unable to understand a problem sufficiently to develop a system exactly as the user required, whose developments were rigid and always behind schedule and who were either not keen or unable to change an existing development without the user incurring significant delay and/or significant cost.

It is hardly surprising, therefore, that users have pressed for development aids. These originally came in the form of report generators and developed in sophistication to include simple data entry facilities. At the same time programmer aids were also being developed in order to speed up the production of working lines of program code. Finally, with the introduction of database technology fourth-generation application generators came of age.

Whilst 4GL products enable non-experienced users to develop application software, invariably there will be a need to resort to a small amount of 'programming' particularly within sophisticated, multi-file, transaction processing systems. Whilst these tools have gone a long way to placing the power of the computer in the hands of the user, there remains a misconception that they can produce miracles. Regardless of how clever the application generator, users still have to understand their applications sufficiently to define them in terms of 'files' and 'data relationships'. In other words, these 4GL products are no different from the earliest software development languages in that they still require systems to be 'designed' – something of which not everyone is capable. If you know what you want from a system, these tools enable you do develop it, simply, easily and in a fraction of the time taken using conventional third-generation programming languages. If you don't know what you want or you have not analysed the problem properly, then your application will still be a failure, but by using a 4GL product you will know about it sooner!

23.2 How the PICK 4GL products work

Whilst each generator has its own idiosyncrasies, all start off by providing a simple means of creating files and building dictionaries. These facilities, as with its others, are generally hidden behind a series of menus and question and answer proformas which ultimately produce a working application. The additional facilities these products offer include producing data entry screens, creating reports, building menus, defining multi-file updating procedures, and producing system documentation and operating manuals.

There are primarily, two types of generator: those that generate parameters from the user's responses and those that generate program code.

Those that generate parameters enable systems to be developed extremely quickly, since the users' responses are converted into a series of parameters which are interpreted immediately at runtime. The advantage of this type of generator is the speed at which systems can be developed and subsequently modified, enabling and encouraging the prototyping of systems. Once a change has been made to the parameters, the change can be tested immediately, without the need to generate and compile source code. The main disadvantage of this method is that the developed application is generally slower in operation than a compiled program, a degradation in response which is noticeable most when in use by a large number of users.

In contrast, a system that generates source code will be faster in operation but, since source code must be generated and compiled for *every* change, however minor, development is much longer. In addition this type of approach tends to discourage prototyping and specifically discourages minor modifications. Further to cope with the enormous variety of possible application requirements, source code generators tend to produce voluminous code, making them less efficient and requiring more disk storage than specifically written programs.

There are many products which have arisen since the early eighties, the prime ones being: *ALL*, *APPGEN*, *CREATOR*, *CUEBIC*, *EZ PROCESSOR*,

FORGE, GHOSTWRITER, G/CODE, LIBRA, NEXTGEN, OHM TOOLS, SB+, SYSTEM BUILDER, SYSTEM PAINTER, TPS, UPDATE, WIZARD, and X-Y-Z (3D).

Only a handful have survived commercially and these have been those capable of meeting the increasing demands for more sophisticated facilities such as pull down menus, pop up windows, active function keys and most importantly the ability to provide true GUI (Graphical User Interface) capability.

SB+, the product with which the author is most familiar has not only survived but is seen as a market leader. It is also one of the few to offer both interpretative and compiled methods of operation. *SB+* is the successor to the highly successful *System Builder* + package originally the product of the *SB+* Corporation but now part of the UniData organization since their takeover of the *SB+* Corporation in October 1995. Whilst I am not trying to promote *SB+* above other 4GL products, it is an outstanding product, I am familiar with it, and for that reason I am using it here in order to demonstrate the typical facilities offered by this type of product.

SB+ is far more than an application generator. It has in-built user security encompassing logon passwords, application system access and TCL command restriction. It has a full system administration module enabling the System Administrator or any other user to perform their regular tasks using menu driven question and answer sessions rather than the native database commands. This administration system encompasses activities such as print management (the Spooler), file management (including file resizing), media management and general system functions which would otherwise have to be operated using TCL commands. It also includes a full office automation suite including diaries, messaging, activities, to-do lists and a calculator. Another important part of *SB+* is a pseudo-TCL environment limiting user access to specified TCL commands. The 'Logto' option of *SB+* enables you to log between accounts. However the remainder of this section will focus on the application development tools.

When you purchase *SB+* and load it onto your system you will be presented with a starting (logon) menu as shown in Figure 23.1. This is the default menu system, but everything in *SB+* including this menu is 'soft' and hence configurable by the developer. As you develop applications from the 'tools' menu the finished software is attached to a menu system behind the 'runtime' option. This entire menu system can then be re-organized to provide a menu system compatible with the style with which users are currently familiar or would wish to see.

Each of the tools provides the developer with the means to build a facet or a 'building brick' of an entire application. Each of these 'building bricks' is called a 'process' within *SB+* and these processes can be utilized as frequently as required during the use of the application. For example a data input screen is a process, an enquiry screen is a process, a report is a process and so on. Each process is given a unique name so that it can be referred to whenever required. Hence a report can be attached to a function key on a data entry

A/W
Screen
dump

Figure 23.1 The tools menus of SB+.

screen and called during the middle of data entry by the user. Further the report could be displayed within a window on the screen if required and whilst within the report the user could 'jump' to another process, let's say an enquiry screen and then return back via whence they came to the original data entry screen. These processes are core to *SB+* and are what make it such a powerful development environment.

Each of the individual menu options of the *SB+* tools lead to a proforma screen, sometimes via other menu options or alternatively subsequent to prompting the developer for the name of the database on which they wish to operate.

Figure 23.2 examines the first menu option in more detail, showing the results of creating a file. As may be apparent, *SB+* calculates the modulo size of both the dictionary and data portions of the file from the answers given by the developer, which it then passes to the **create-file** command. This results in the file being created and the standard PICK message being displayed, after which control is returned to *SB+* and the application developer.

If we consider the way in which fields (attributes) are defined, using *SB+*, again it will be apparent that it is a user front end to building dictionaries, which otherwise would have to be created using the Update Processor or the Editor. *SB+* creates two dictionary items, the normal dictionary item and one of the same name preceded with a full stop, which contains various parameters needed by *SB+* to perform such tasks as default and validation functions. Whilst in general use each dictionary item generally contains ten attributes, the *SB+* dictionary item uses up to 19 attributes, but since the standard PICK dictionary is created, the use of *SB+* does not affect the normal use of the file for any of the standard PICK functions such as ACCESS, the Update Processor or Editor.

A/W
Screen
dump

Figure 23.2 Creating a file using the *SB*+ 4GL

Figure 23.3 examines the final proforma screen for creating a data field, resulting in the production of PICK dictionary items.

A/W
Screen
dump

Figure 23.3 Building a dictionary with the *SB*+ 4GL.

In the simple example in Figure 23.3 we saw how *SB+* is able to accept PICK correlative codes and it can equally accept PICK conversion codes. *SB+* does not expect the developer to know these codes providing context sensitive 'intuitive' help to derive the codes required. Equally you will notice a **M**: in the validation code, which makes the field mandatory. This is just one of numerous complex validations which *SB+* can handle and these too are built using the *SB+* intuitive help feature invoked by pressing the F3 function key.

Intuitive help is a major feature of *SB+* and is available throughout. Being context sensitive means that the help it provides relates to the current question being asked. Hence on the field validation the F3 would display the following options:

A/W
Screen
dump

If you selected the 'Key on Another File' option *SB+* would display a further proforma for completion as follows:

A/W
Screen
dump

and it would provide further intuitive help for the 'File Name' with a list of available files to choose from and on 'Fld Name to Display' with a list of valid fields from the chosen file.

All of these additional features in defining a field and in particular the system-wide intuitive help feature are aimed at enabling a person who knows what he wants from a computer system to be able to develop it without having to resort to programming.

In a similar way to creating files and building dictionaries, *SB+* allows data capture and enquiry screens to be produced. *SB+* produces a proforma screen, in this case a blank screen, onto which the defined fields and any headings and text are 'painted'. This simple process enables the screen to be used for the full file maintenance functionality of creating, amending and deleting of records, records a development, which takes a matter of a few minutes in SB+, is an exercise that could readily take upwards of half a day using conventional methods!

Each screen comprises two parts, the parameters associated with the running of the screen and the layout of the screen itself. The parameters define such elements as the screen co-ordinates, screen colours and what processes are to be run at various stages of the execution of the screen, such as before the screen is displayed, after data has been entered, after the relevant files have been updated and if the user escapes from the screen before filing the data record.

The screen painter enables the developer to paint text, graphics and fields on the screen (whether or not the fields have already defined). Behind each field is a set of field parameters defining its use in that particular screen, which may be different to that of its standard definition defined within the field definition tool. Apart from defining its physical screen position, these parameters determine amongst others, whether or not the field is mandatory, whether data can be entered into the field or whether it is for display purposes only and importantly the processes to be called before and after data has been entered into the field. Figure 23.4 shows an example of the development of a screen used for capturing car details and shows the field parameters screen for the registration number.

Apart from the obvious productivity benefits of using 4GLs for this sort of exercise, it is far easier to work with a screen image than it is in PICK BASIC code where just to display the fields would comprise of a series of **print @** statements using mnemonic variable names and a differing format codes. A properly structured program for such a screen could readily comprise in excess of 500 lines of code and have little chance of compiling and working first time. But that is just the first step. If the program then needs to be modified and has

A/W
Screen
dump

Figure 23.4 Building a screen using the *SB*+ 4GL

to be modified by someone other than the originator, many hours can be spent just understanding the logic constructed into the program by the original developer and all for what might be just a simple change.

SB+ provides a consistent standard for development, working with visible 'objects' that once developed work first time. They can be changed with the minimum of fuss, the minimum of time and hence with the minimum of cost.

The production of complex reports under *SB+* is almost identical to that of screens in that there are two parts to report development, the report parameters and the report itself. Again the report is developed by 'painting' the fields on the report where they are required and each field has its separate field definitions to determine its requirements for that specific report, such as its length and format and whether or not it contains data to be totalled (such as in the case of monetary amounts). The report writer enables a report to be defined into sections so that processing for headings, the main body of the report, sub-totals and grand totals can be defined independently.

For simple ACCESS style reports *SB+* has second report writer tool which is a simple proforma screen which by virtue of the intuitive help facility, can be taught to end users in no more than a couple of hours and Figure 23.5 gives and example of such a screen. Once developed the report can be run as a one-off report or the parameters saved to the menu system so the report can be run at any time in the future without the need to redefine its parameters.

Once familiarity has been gained with these 'foundation' tools, which enable simple systems to be built to handle file maintenance, enquiry and reports, *SB+* enables the developer to advance into sophisticated multi-file transactional processing systems, all built in the same proforma or question and answer fashion. Transactional systems are those which take in one set of data and use it to update several files. For example, the information on an invoice would typically be used to maintain information on the customer file, the salesman file (for commission calculations), the sales analysis file and so on.

A/W
Screen
dump

Figure 23.5 The creation of an ACCESS report using the *SB+* 4GL.

As you can see, therefore, 4GL products are extremely valuable development aids, which when used in conjunction with the PICK database generate flexible documented systems, capable of being developed and modified even when 'live' with the minimum of fuss and effort. In addition they give a useful introduction to the concepts of the PICK database for those who move on to use it, since many of its features have been 'incorporated' in a user-oriented shell.

23.3 GUI presentation of 4GL software

With the Windows standard being adopted by most organizations, the production of character-based software is less acceptable to users regardless of its quality and functionality. End-users have come to expect a familiar, graphical desktop environment. The day-to-day products they use, such as word processors and spreadsheets, have set a standard for ease-of-use, aesthetic appeal and functionality.

Software companies worldwide are now facing up to the reality that a prerequisite for long-term survival in their competitive marketplace lies in embracing (or at least accommodating) this new standard.

There are a number of intelligent terminal emulators which effectively 'spraypaint' a GUI veneer onto the application. So, while they have the advantages of supporting legacy code, allowing some piecemeal conversion and providing an entry-level GUI front end, they fall far short of a true Windows look and feel, both in terms of aesthetic appeal and functionality. Many of these 'easy' GUI options currently available fall into this 'spraypainting' category. Indeed PICK Systems themselves started to develop such a product which they called GraPICK and some early copies came to market. However, realizing they were only reproducing what other companies had already developed and indeed were behind in their development schedule, set the product aside in favour of a joint marketing arrangement with UniData and its **wIntegrate** product.

The route taken by UniData for its *SB+* product is very different. Using special software at the client end (originally called Termulator but now referred to as SB/Client) sequences sent from the host computer are translated into graphical elements on the PC. Converting an application to run in this way is an automated process and importantly this environment supports both PCs and dumb terminals; the same application can run ***simultaneously*** in GUI mode on the PC and in character mode on the dumb terminal.

The SB/Client software is a Microsoft validated product generating an application presentation as good as any running in the Windows environment. It preserves the developer's investment in legacy code, retaining all the functionality and sophistication of the host-based application and, because the conversion to GUIs is automated, there is minimal need for re-coding or re-engineering.

Further, part of the *SB+* toolset is a GUI screen painter (Figure 23.6), operating in a similar fashion to the screen development tool described above. For programmers familiar with *SB+* there is no need to learn a new language; they can continue to develop in an environment that is familiar and comfortable without the need for retraining and without having to sacrifice experience

A/W
Screen
dump

Figure 23.6 The *SB+* forms painter (shown here in black and white).

gained over the years. Furthermore, they now have the option of developing in *either* character mode or GUI mode.

Automated conversion and built-in graphical tools provide the quickest route to full GUItization for character-based *SB+* applications. As can be seen from Figures 23.7–23.9, an elcgant Windows look and feel can be created and this can be achieved in as little as a few seconds, while added functionality and fully customized graphical elements can be added within a matter of minutes.

A/W
Screen
dump

Figure 23.7

A/W
Screen
dump

Figure 23.8

A/W
Screen
dump

Figure 23.9

Figure 23.7 shows a typical character-based application (in this example for a car rental company) developed using the UniData 4GL, *SB*+. Figure 23.8 shows the same application after automatic conversion to a graphical interface. In this example, converting the process from character to GUI took less than

10 seconds. Figure 23.9 shows the same screen after about 10 minutes of enhancement; adding bitmaps to buttons, background colours, patterns and multimedia capability.

23.4 The case for fourth generation languages

23.4.1 Advantages of fourth generation languages

- Applications can be developed very quickly, in fractions of the time taken with traditional programming methods. Using an application generator, typically what takes 1–2 days to develop using conventional programming, will take less than an hour.
- The application will conform to standards imposed by the 4GL making subsequent modification simple for anyone with knowledge of the 4GL, whereas a program is highly individual making subsequent amendment very difficult other than by the originator (and in some cases even the originator has problems!). This does not mean that you do not need to develop in house standards, but they are less voluminous, being limited to such things as file and field naming conventions, the colour scheme, window sizing and positioning and so on.
- Customizing or changing the application is very easy. This is for two reasons. Firstly, the PICK database system, being dictionary-driven, enables systems to be modified even when 'live'. This is because a simple change to the dictionary definition item, even to the key of the file, is instantly reflected throughout the system. Secondly, because 4GL products themselves have been designed to handle such changes, they can be made speedily and easily. These facilities, coupled with the speed of initial development, encourage prototyping. This gives greater credibility to the application, enables early discussion on user requirements and shows up problems and potential problems far quicker.
- Maintenance of the application is substantially easier. This is because either the source code generated is written to a common format, or there is no source code to maintain at all!
- The completed application works reliably, immediately it has been developed. There is no time wasted in 'debugging' programs.
- Applications can be developed by inexperienced non-data processing professionals, with a minimum of programming effort.
- Application generators are easy to learn and easy to use which means that development staff need less training and are more productive than those using conventional programming languages.
- Application generators provide a useful introduction to the facilities within PICK, by incorporating many of its features in a user-oriented shell.

23.4.2 Disadvantages of fourth generation languages

- Application generators are rarely able to develop an entire application, leaving a small, and often minute, part of the system to be programmed in PICK BASIC.
- Application generators will not improve the design and workings of an application. A poorly designed system will remain a poor system in operation.
- The completed application may run less efficiently and/or utilize greater disk space than customized BASIC programs.
- Some application generators are not portable between hardware suppliers.
- Multi-user use of the software may degrade response.
- There is a learning curve required with any 4GL product, regardless of how easy it is supposed to be.

23.5 Summary

None of the above drawbacks outweigh the advantages of using 4GL products. Conventional programming methods are now seen to be outdated, and users are pressing for 4GL tools, to develop their own applications and reduce their reliance on data processing professionals.

Whilst application generators do not solve every problem, they are well suited to most commercial applications. In addition they provide users with a simple and easy method of developing speedily and with the minimum of programming by non-DP specialists.

24 PICK on the IBM PC and Compatibles

TCL verbs and general commands covered in this chapter

COLOR	COPYDOS	COPYPICK	EXPORT
FDISK	FORMAT	FFORMAT	IMPORT
MONO	PRINT@	POWER-OFF	REBOOT
SET-BAUD	SET-FLOPPY	SET-DEVICE	SET-FUNC
SET-KBRD	SET-SCT	SHUTDOWN	T-STATUS
XCS-ON			

24.1 An introduction to PC PICK

The implementation of PICK for the IBM PC in the early 1980s was significant for a number of reasons:

(1) It was the first implementation to be sold directly by PICK Systems.
(2) It enabled the product to be made more widely available and hence increased market awareness.
(3) It was only operating system at that time that made the PC multi-user.

IBM first launched the IBM PC in 1981 which they thought would primarily be used as workstations for their mainframe systems. The very first systems came with 128KB up to 640KB RAM with one or two 360KB floppy disks, 4.77 MHz processor and a monochrome or colour monitor. It was nearly two years later before the system began shipping with a hard disk, and even then it was only of 10MB capacity with a very slow 70 ms access speed. I am sure many of you will remember the PC-XT, I certainly do. It was noisy and slow, but heralded a significant breakthrough in personal computing. It was not until the availability of the hard disk version of the PC-XT that PICK were able to implement their system for the PC. In those early days the implementation was a full version of the PICK R83 operating system exactly the same as those available on minicomputers from the licencees. This brought the power of PICK to those previously unable to afford it. On the original IBM PC-XT a total of three users were supported, albeit very slowly.

At that time the PICK R83 operating system co-resided on the fixed disk with up to three other operating systems. The disk was partitioned into sections with each operating system resident in its own section on the disk, each with is own area of contiguous disk space. The operating system to be used was marked 'active' by the **FDISK** command within the respective operating system and then the 'active' operating system invoked by rebooting the machine.

Whilst this was not a problem for the larger user sites that would dedicate a PC for the running of PICK, for the smaller number of users, notably the single user systems, switching between PICK and DOS was a sheer nuisance.

During 1985 PICK Systems modified their product to support some of the IBM clones and the 8086 processor (the chip at the heart of the PC-AT) and by the mid 1980s the PICK PC could support over 100MB of disk which could use then tape as its backup medium. There were three versions of PICK, for one to three users, one to six users and for one to ten users, with prices for the entire operating system starting at around £495, little more than the price of any other single-user database manager! By this time, therefore, the PICK system was a practical option for the small business and at a very affordable price. Needless to say, the system was sold in significant volumes.

As the power of the PC grew, so did the number of users that PICK supported. It went up initially to 17 users, but in 1989 version 3 of PC-PICK was released and this was the first version to use the extended memory on the PC (the memory above the base 640KB) as a memory cache. Now the supported users grew to a staggering 33 users on a single 386 processor and sales of PC PICK systems continued to soar starting to eat into the low end minicomputer sales of the PICK licencees.

At the beginning of 1990, as PICK Systems began to reposition their product as a database rather than operating system, they announced the first implementation of Advanced PICK for the PC which used SCO UNIX as the base operating system. This brought a new release of power to the PC because SCO UNIX had the ability to address all available memory directly and suddenly thc number of supported Advanced PICK users shot up to 129.

It was about this time that even more dramatic progress was being made with hardware. PCs could be purchased with multiple processor cards, disk capacities grew to two gigabytes and memory capacities of 32MB and 64MB were readily available. What was even more significant was that prices for PC hardware started to fall.

In 1991 PICK Systems released the first version of AP/DOS, a full version of Advanced PICK which could be run from within DOS. No longer did the hard disk need partitioning and no longer was it necessary to alternate between partitions to run PICK and DOS. Even better, PICK could be run from within Windows enabling all the standard Windows facilities including the ability to cut and paste PICK data into Windows products using the Windows clipboard. The only limitation with this version is that it is limited to three users, the main monitor and two other users connected to the PCs standard serial ports.

As acceptance of Advanced PICK grew, PICK Systems announced they would cease developing PICK R83 and since Advanced PICK is totally R83 compatible and a far superior product this was an understandable move. It is worth noting that should you still be using R83 and decide to use it on a Pentium or subsequent generation of processor you will need a special version, since the standard versions only support 286, 386 or 486 processors.

Both Advanced PICK products for the PC (AP/Native and AP/DOS) are restricted to using the standard 640Kb memory of a PC as real memory, using extended memory as a disk cache. In early 1995, PICK Systems released a product called AP/PRO (Advanced PICK protected mode) a means of offering substantial performance benefits. In protected mode operation, each job has its own piece of RAM which is 'protected' and is not used by any other job running at the same time. In addition protected mode operation makes use of the full RAM in the machine rather than being limited to just 640Kb. This means that jobs are not continually swapped in and out of RAM as they get processed and it enables the support of up to 257 users on a single PC!

Whilst the pure power of PICK was amazing, connection to the central database was still through serial ports, limited to a speed of 9600 or 19,200 baud. During the 1990s networks were becoming more and more established as the office standard and Windows the most widely used PC environment. PCs were linked together on a peer-to-peer basis using products like Windows for Workgroups or as a LAN (local area network) using products like Novell Netware, IBM Token Ring and Banyan Vines. Whilst many established computer multi-user systems still operated on serial cables with 'dumb' VDUs most new PCs came with Windows and because the price of PCs fell so dramatically, to not much more than the price of a VDU, many companies went through a program of replacing their VDUs with PCs running a terminal emulator (a piece of software that enable the PC to act as a VDU).

PICK Systems recognised they needed to address the network arena and reached an agreement with Modular Software Corporation which enabled PICK to include a copy of PicLan with each copy of AP/PRO. PicLan is a software product originally developed by Modular Software Corporation in the late 1980s which enables a PC running PICK R83 or Advanced PICK to be connected to a network. The PicLan software provided the same capability for the Sanyo/Icon UpBoard and systems from General Automation and Alpha Microsystems

Once AP/PRO with PicLan was released PICK Systems announced the cessation of development of AP Native, with AP/PRO taking over as their flagship product for the PC.

24.2 Selecting and maintaining your PC hardware

One of the most important aspects of administering a PC-based PICK system is an understanding of the hardware itself. Most people working with equipment from a PICK Licencee such as Adds Mentor, General Automation, C-Itoh, etc., are protected and in fact precluded from getting involved with their hardware by virtue of the support service offered by their supplier. With PC PICK, particularly as a dealer, it is often necessary to configure the hardware, make changes to dip switch settings, and to add/swap boards within the machine. Whilst you would be strongly recommended to purchase your PC from a recognized PC PICK supplier who understands what's possible and what's not possible, with a limited amount of knowledge those who wish to can take care of most of their hardware requirements.

As soon as the IBM PC product was released in 1984, PICK Systems was faced with the difficult problem of support for PC compatibles and quite rightly explained that their product was developed for, and hence supported on, the IBM PC. For that reason and in view of the myriad of compatibles, so-called compatibles and add-on cards and disks, PICK Systems gave the warning *caveat emptor* – let the buyer beware! It adopted the view, and quite rightly so, that provided a 'compatible' system was truly IBM compatible, it *should* work with PC PICK. They did, however, test their product on a number of alternative systems and have from time to time published details of their findings. This is a never-ending task, but as more and more hardware standards develop, so hardware becomes less of an issue.

The BIOS, tape drives and hard disk technology were the areas that caused the greatest problems in the early days and even now, SCSI disks are only supported under Advanced PICK (Native or AP/PRO). Do remember that AP/PRO requires a minimum of 20MB and since PICK will grab the remaining free space on your disk which is not part of another operating system partition, you may need to check the available space on your system using **FDISK** under DOS first.

24.2.1 The external features of your PC

(1) **Power switch**

Turns the computer on and off. Before turning on the system, turn on power to the peripherals first. DO NOT turn the computer off until you have flushed the memory, a process handled automatically by the 'power-off' or 'shutdown' command.

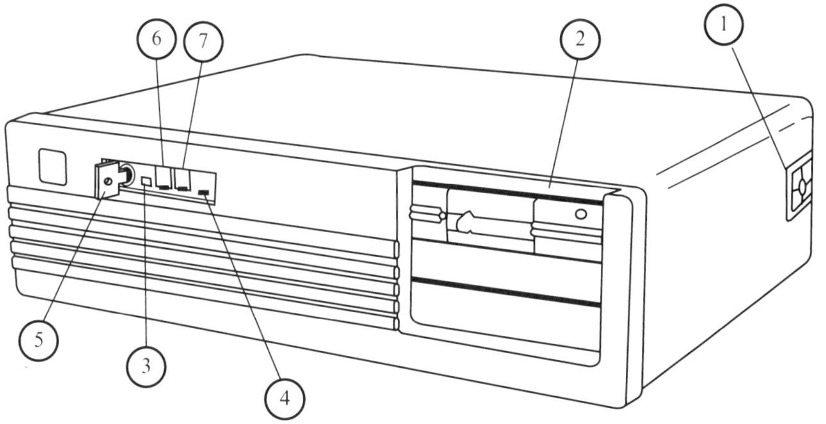

Figure 24.1 (a) PC external features (front); (b) PC external features (rear); (c) serial/parallel adaptor; (d) keyboard connector jack; (e) monitor and connector.

(2) **Floppy disk drive**
PICK supports both 3.5" and 5.25" drives, either of which can be the primary drive. PICK now make a surcharge for supplying their product on 5.25" diskettes so it is best to make the 3.5" drive the primary drive. PICK will support a mixture of drive sizes and recognises drives 'a', 'b' and 'c".

(3) **Hard disk drive status indicator**
When PICK reads from or writes to the hard disk this indicator lights up. Should the hard disk fail, this light will fail with a pattern of long and short pulses giving a meaningful code to your hardware maintenance company.

(4) **Power status indicator**
Lights when the computer is turned on.

(5) **Key Lock**
When this key is turned to LOCK position the monitor keyboard cannot be used. The lock has no effect on other terminal keyboards attached to the system. It just prevents unauthorized access to the system unit.

(6) **Reset button**
Resets the computer when it 'hangs' or needs to be re-booted and is not found on all PCs. Whenever this button is pressed the computer will begin to execute the self-diagnostic tests and then will 'boot up' into the 'active' partition. If working within PICK when users are active pressing this button will cause data to be lost and with certain implementations of PICK Group Format Errors are likely to occur.

(7) **Turbo switch**
Some PC compatibles have this switch to enable the processor to run at a higher speed than the standard IBM PC. Some DOS programs do not operate correctly at high speed hence the reason for the switch. PICK, however will run perfectly well at these higher speeds so this switch if available, should always be depressed.

Sometimes you will find a jumper setting on the motherboard which will fix the processor to operate continually at the higher speed. Unless you are using your PC to run applications that you know will not run at these speeds, it is perfectly safe to set the jumper for a PICK-based system.

(8) **Cooling fan**
Protects the computer against overheating. Do not block this ventilation opening by positioning the computer too close to a wall or some other object which might block the intake of air to the computer.

(9) **AC power inlet**
This is generally a three pin 'kettle' socket into which an AC power lead from the mains is inserted.

(10) **AC power outlet**
A power lead to a peripheral unit may be plugged into this outlet. The power to this outlet is controlled by the power switch and is turned on and off automatically when the computer is switched on or off. It is normally used for connection to the monitor screen and should never be used for anything needing high levels of power or you will overload the power supply of your PC.

(11) **Parallel printer port**
A Parallel (centronics) cable may be connected from this socket to a parallel printer. Normally PCs are supplied with one 25-pin female parallel printer port but more may be added. PC PICK supports a maximum of four parallel ports.

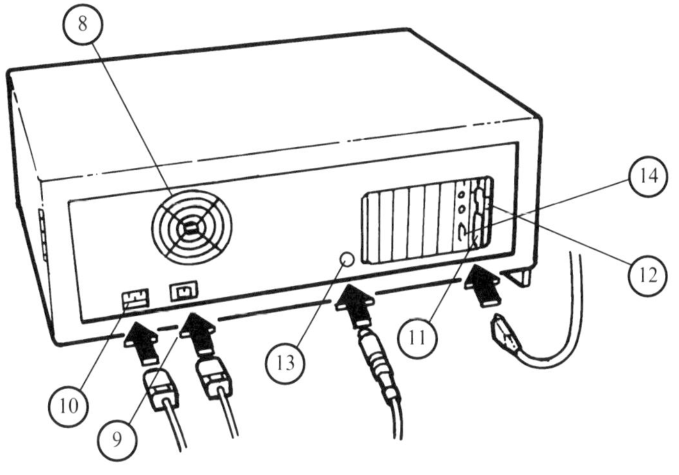

Figure 24.1(b)

(12) **RS232C serial ports**
There may be one or more of these ports and which may have 9-pin or 25-pin connectors. Normally a PC will contain one of each type of connector and possibly in addition, a games port. Cables may be attached from these connectors to a variety of input/output devices. The games port cannot be used under PICK and 'dumb' terminals are most frequently connected to the serial ports, although serial ports can also support serial printers, bar-code readers, other PCs, etc.

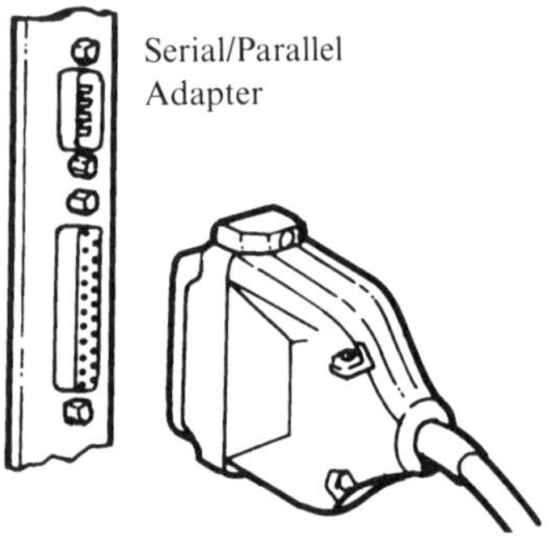

Figure 24.1(c)

(13) **Keyboard connector jack**

A Cable is connected from this socket to the keyboard for the monitor – PICK recognizes this keyboard and the monitor as user number 0 (zero).

Figure 24.1(d)

(14) **Monitor connector**

This is a 9-pin socket into which the monitor screen cable is connected. The connector illustrated is for a colour monitor and all PCs these days come with a colour monitor. If you have a monochrome monitor you may find its connector sited just above the parallel printer port.

Figure 24.1(e)

24.2.2 The internal features of your PC

If you open the case of a PC you will see the following components.

The motherboard or system board

This is the circuit board that lies in the bottom of your PC (Figure 24.2). On this board are mounted the main processor (Intel 286,386, 486, Pentium etc.), keyboard connector, the main system RAM (memory) the battery (to support the real-time clock), various jumpers and the expansion slots.

Expansion slots

These vary from system to system dependent on the size of the case. A slimline case may only contain a couple of expansion slots, whilst on the large systems, tower or mini-tower units you may find as many as eight or twelve expansion slots. These slots are used to support a number of different cards to provide a number of hardware options. These slots are numbered consecutively from left to right with the highest numbered slot normally containing the disk drive controller board. The remainder can be used as required, although if you examine them you will notice that some are longer than the others. The longer ones are called 'full slots' whist the shorter ones are known as 'half slots". Some cards require a full slot, so it is best to use half slots where possible to save having to re-organise your cards at a later date.

The BIOS

The BIOS of a computer is the heart of the system. BIOS stands for Basic Input Output System, in other words it is the primary mechanism by which the

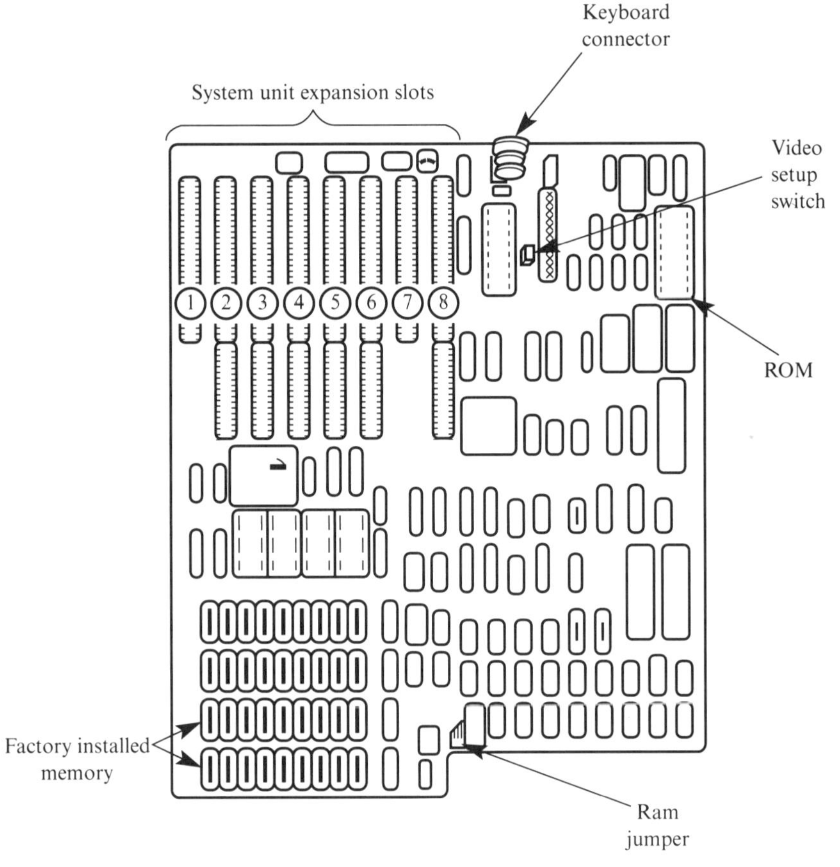

Figure 24.2 Motherboard or system board.

data in the computer is processed and it is one of the most important considerations when buying a PC to run PICK. You should ensure your system has one of the following three BIOSs:

- Phoenix Computer Products
- AMI (American Megatrends Inc.)
- Award Software Inc.

The BIOS name will appear on the top line of the monitor screen when the system is booted (whether in DOS or any other operating system). PICK uses the BIOS extensively for controlling the various peripherals – the diskette, the tape drive, the parallel printer ports and the serial ports. If the BIOS is incompatible with PICK then serious problems arise most likely during the loading process when the message 'Protection violation' will be displayed. Other typical BIOS problems are that you will continue to experience problems using backup devices or that some of the devices are omitted from the configuration information which is automatically displayed when PICK is initiated

The bus

This is the channel joining together the individual components of your system and along which data is transmitted. There are a number of these you may encounter, VESA, EISA, ISA, MCA or PCI. You should avoid MCA for a PICK-based system and PCI if you are using PICK R83.

RAM (Random Access Memory)

Even though the early PC-XT processors could support 1MB RAM, the majority of PCs were supplied with just 640KB. Under DOS, only 640KB was intended to be used as system memory, any extra being allocated to the screen, expansion ROMs and the system BIOS. Nowadays the minimum RAM supplied is 4MB and systems increasing require 8MB or even 16MB to process applications at a reasonable speed.

PICK works significantly faster with extra RAM and with the advent of AP/PRO support was made available for up to 4GB using memory in 'protected' mode. In protected mode operation, each task executed by PICK has its own piece of RAM which is 'protected' and is not used by any other job running at the same time. In addition protected mode operation makes use of the full RAM in the machine rather than being limited to just 640KB which means that jobs are not continually swapped in and out of RAM as they get processed.

There are a number of references to different categories of RAM you may come across:

- Shadow RAM
  The memory that lives between 640KB and 1MB
- Extended RAM
  This is IBM's term for memory above 1MB
- Expanded RAM
  Another term for extended memory, originally devised by Lotus, Intel and Microsoft and often called the LIM standard, where additional memory is allocated in 'pages'.

Floppy disk drives

PICK supports a mixture of both 3.5″ and 5.25″ drives operating in both standard and high density mode and any manufacturers drives will work satisfactorily. The 3.5″ drive is the obvious standard and these are not only more reliable, but hold more data than their larger and outdated 5.25″ counterparts. The normal capacity of these drives being:

3.5"	Standard density 720KB High density 1.44MB
5.25"	Standard density 360KB High density 1.2MB

The normal flat cable connecting the floppy disk drive and the controller has a second connector attached to it, making the addition of a second floppy disk drive relatively straightforward. If your system only has one connector on the cable you will need replace it with one that has the second connector 'daisy-chained' onto it.

The first connector in the 'chain' will determine which is the primary floppy drive and where possible you should ensure that the 3.5″ drive is the primary one. If at any time you need to make the second drive the primary one, it is simply a job of swapping over the connectors.

As an alternative to adding the floppy drive internally, an external floppy disk drive can be purchased that runs from a separate controller card. Operationally the drives will work the same as if it is connected internally, however it will cost you more (you have to buy a controller card as well as the drive) and it takes up what can sometimes be a valuable expansion slot.

Hard disks

The range of hard disks supported is extensive although only a maximum of two hard disks is permitted. Using AP/PRO you can support most MFM, RLL, ESDI, IDE or SCSI drives. A hard disk comprises of cylinders, sectors and heads and the maximum for each of these is as follows:

Cylinders	1024
Sectors	64
Heads	256

This means the maximum disk capacity of a single disk is 8GB hence the maximum disk capacity under AP is 16GB. If your disk driver exceeds the above parameters, typically it will be because your hard disk has more than 1024 cylinders it may be possible to 're-map' the disk, by telling the controller it has 1023 cylinders or less but that the number of heads or the number of sectors per track is greater than it actually is. Most disk controllers these days have this 'translation' capability but if you need to purchase one, then look to DPT, Tekram, UltraStor or Alpha Research.

The recommended controllers for AP support are:

Adaptec AHA-1542C SCSI (ISA)
BusLogic BT542B SCSI (ISA)
DPT PM2021 (with or without cache) SCSI (ISA)

For IDE drives larger than 540MB use Alpha Research or Tekram DC-600C/CF IDE caching controller which handles re-mapping to less than 1024 cylinders.

Providing you are using version PICK R83 2.2 and above then any MFM, RLL or ESDI drive is supported. For all other releases (XT/AT) then any MFM disk with 17 sectors per track is also supported. Please note that PICK R83 does not support SCSI drives.

Serial port cards

Whilst PICK R83 supports specific user configurations (1,2,3,6,10,17,25,33 users) up to a maximum of 33 users, Advanced PICK (Native and AP/PRO) support significantly more. On a standard PC the memory mapped monitor is always port 0, whilst the two serial ports can be used for terminals, printers and modems.

These two serial ports use two standard interrupts known as IRQ3 and IRQ4 and if you are going to add serial expansion cards then disable one (or both) of these interrupts and add the serial card(s) set to the disabled interrupt(s). With the release of version 3.0 R83 PICK in 1989 which expanded the maximum number of users from 17 to 33, two further interrupts were made available, namely IRQ2 and IRQ7 although these two interrupts are not supported on the IBM PS/2.

Initially serial cards supported either 4 or 8 ports and with only two interrupts available the maximum number of users was limited to 17 (2 x 8 ports plus the monitor). With the additional interrupts and the availability of 16 port cards and those that could be 'piggy-backed' together in clusters containing up to 128 serial ports all taking the same interrupt, the number of supported users under Advanced PICK expanded significantly.

Under Advanced PICK port numbers are assigned to interrupt channels allocated to serial I/O devices in the following order:

IRQ2 IRQ3 IRQ4 IRQ7 IRQ10

with IRQ10 generally being used for the PicLan Ethernet card.

The standard serial cards mentioned above operate by interrupting the CPU each time a character is entered on a keyboard. This character is 'confirmed' by the CPU and the character sent back down the line and displayed on the screen. You can imagine the level of interrupts generated on a busy multiuser system!

The load on the CPU can be greatly reduced by use of 'intelligent' I/O. This means that all terminal I/O is handled by a serial port board with its own processor and local RAM. The purpose of the processor is to buffer the character interrupts and only interrupt the central processor when a terminal 'message' is complete, i.e. at the time the user presses the [CR] key.

In most cases these 'intelligent' expansion cards are not necessary, particularly if your system has fewer than 25 users. Since these frequently need special device driver software to be loaded independently of PICK itself you run the risk of the cards not being supported with the release of new versions of PICK where the serial card supplier has not updated their driver software.

Intelligent cards are recommended for AP/Citrix and AP/SCO where most SCO supported cards will work perfectly well with PICK.

The Installation Guide, supplied with each copy of PC-PICK, gives a detailed explanation of the dip switch settings for a wide variety of serial I/O cards. Equally you should find the manuals supplied with these serial devices give clear details of how to set the appropriate interrupts, so installation is not so daunting as it may at first appear.

Parallel ports

A parallel port is used to support printers and has the advantage that it is not considered one of the 'users' of an R83 licence and does not take up a serial port. Whilst most printers have both serial and parallel interfaces, quite often the serial version is more expensive. If you have a printer with both interfaces you may find there are dip switches or jumpers to be set, so check the manual carefully before connecting it.

Although parallel printers do not take up one of your valuable serial ports, they have the disadvantage that they cannot be placed more than 30 or so feet from the PC without line boosters apart from which the cable is much thicker and more expensive.

PICK supports up to three parallel printers but with the IRQs disabled. For this reason a parallel printer IRQ located on a:

- Monitor card
- Parallel card
- Serial/Parallel card
- Motherboard

must have its IRQ disabled. Failure to disable IRQs may well lead to conflict with other devices, particularly the tape drive which uses IRQ5 (the IRQ most commonly assigned to parallel cards) which needless to say will lead to unpredictable results. You may find the tape drive hanging, generating parity errors or you may find the printer prints garbage.

Tape drives

Tape options for PICK R83 and AP/Native used the QIC02 interface a standard that ceased to be available in 1995. These drives could copy up to 250MB on a single tape which in its day seemed more than adequate. These days disk sizes of 500+MB are commonplace and not only is this tape capacity insufficient, but PICK has to support the SCSI (Small Computer Systems Interface) hardware standard which it does in AP/PRO and AP/SCO. For those people still using R83 and AP/Native support is available for QIC36 and QIC02 tape controllers. You will need third party software for support of SCSI tape drives, including higher capacity $\frac{1}{4}''$ tape units and DAT devices which can back up many gigabytes of disk on a single tape.

The installation of the tape drive is relatively straightforward providing the drive is given the interrupt IRQ 5. Any difficulties experienced tend to relate to the issue of compatibility.

It is worth noting that the tape format changed from PICK R83 version 2.2 onwards, so if you are using data from one of these old releases you will need to use the **R** option in the **SET-SCT** command. Whilst the new versions of PICK can read the old format, they *cannot* write tapes in the old format.

On the subject of the physical media you should buy the best quality available and replace them on a regular basis (at least once a year) since tapes will stretch in continual use and may then give parity errors when used for data recovery. These tapes are your insurance in the event of a major computer failure. They contain the total data on which your company's operation are entirely dependent and are all you will have to rely on in the event of a major disaster. If you need to make savings this is not the area to find it. The importance of regular backups cannot be stressed too highly but all this effort is wasted if the media is worn out and you are unable to recover your data.

Uninterruptible power supply (UPS)

A UPS ensures power to your system in the event of a power failure. The length of time these units can supply power during a power failure is dependent on the quality of the unit itself, although it is rarely less than about 10 minutes, sufficient to power down the system in an orderly manner. Whilst use of a UPS is less important with the later versions of PICK (AP/PRO onwards) which have fault tolerance, it is imperative to use one with all other versions. This is because of PICK's virtual memory management the contents of which will be 'lost' in a power failure and will undoubtedly result in GFEs.

On any computer system you should consider use of a power conditioner, which will protect it from power 'spikes' and other fluctuations, particularly if you know you are in an industrial area affected by these electrical variances. They can also be found where the system shares the same circuit as heavy machinery or other office equipment such as photocopiers. Where possible your system should be on a dedicated power line installed by a qualified electrician.

Installing boards in your PC

There are 10 golden rules to ensure the successful changing or addition of boards in your PC.

(1) ALWAYS power-down the operating system in a controlled manner, turn off the power and disconnect the power lead from the PC before opening the cover.

(2) NEVER attempt to modify the power supply or cables connected to it.

(3) ALWAYS leave the monitor adaptor board in the first slot.

(4) Other boards can be put in any of the remaining spare slots, although some boards will need to use the longer expansion slots.

(5) NEVER touch the components of the boards directly.

(6) NEVER touch the gold connector strip directly.

(7) ALWAYS hold the board at the edges and ensure the board is aligned properly before pushing it firmly into its expansion slot.

(8) ALWAYS ensure the board is pushed fully into the expansion slot. This may well mean exerting even pressure at both ends of the board before it will fit into place.

(9) When removing a board try to lift it from the slot by exerting pressure at both ends of the board.

(10) When storing boards, ALWAYS leave them in anti-static bags, NEVER place boards on top of each other and NEVER place other items on top of them.

24.3 PC-specific software features

24.3.1 Memory mapped monitor

There are a number of new software options developed for the PC. Firstly, since the standard IBM monitor differs from standard asynchronous terminals attached to RS232 ports, in that it is a memory-mapped monitor, a special terminal device driver has been written and added to the list of term types. The term type for the memory mapped monitors is **I** and uses the Advanced PICK device driver **MM-MON** from the file **devices**.

24.3.2 COLOR and MONO verbs

Two new verbs, **COLOR** (spelt the American way) and **MONO** were supplied with the R83 version of PICK to support the two types of IBM monitor (colour and monochrome). Neither of these verbs work under Advanced PICK, so to maintain compatibility ensure colours and terminal attributes are set using the '**PRINT @**' functions described in the next section. If you wish to use these commands their general format is shown in Figure 24.3.

24.3.3 The PRINT @ functions

New functions have been added to the **PRINT @** statement in BASIC and the **T** command in PROC to support memory-mapped monitors. These statements can set foreground and background colours in the same way as defined by a **COLOR** statement using the negative integer concept. A full list is given in the Figure 15.13 in the chapter on BASIC. The **PRINT @** functions specifically for the memory mapped monitor are shown in Figure 24.4.

COLOR *{foreground colour,background colour}* *{switches}*

where supported colours are:

BLACK	RED
BLUE	MAGENTA
GREEN	BROWN
CYAN	WHITE

and supported switches are:

/B	or	/BLINK	Set character blinking
/NB	or	/NOBLINK	Cancel character blinking
/F	or	/FULL	Set foreground in full intensity
/H	or	/HALF	Set foreground in half intensity
/R	or	/REVERSE	Set reverse video
/NR	or	/NOREVERSE	Cancel reverse video

MONO *{switches}*

where supported switches are as above with the following additions:

/U	or	/UNDERLINE	Set underlining
/NU	or	/NOUNDERLINE	Cancel underlining

Examples of their use

COLOR RED	Set foreground colour to red
COLOR,GREEN	Set background colour to green
COLOR BLUE,WHITE	Set foreground colour to blue, and the background white
COLOR BLUE,WHITE /R /H	Set foreground colour to blue, the background colour to white, activate reverse video and set the foreground colour in half intensity
MONO /U /B	Set screen to monochrome, and activate underlining and blinking

Figure 24.3 The **COLOR** and **MONO** verbs.

If you wish to use these functions within a PROC use the **T** function and drop the @ symbol. Hence to activate the colour/graphics mode and set the foreground in blue and the background in white use the following:

PQ
T(-93),(-47),(-33)

Functions @(-33) through @(-40) set colour terminals background colours.

@(-33) Set Background Colour = WHITE
@(-34) Set Background Colour = BROWN
@(-35) Set Background Colour = MAGENTA
@(-36) Set Background Colour = RED
@(-37) Set Background Colour = CYAN
@(-38) Set Background Colour = GREEN
@(-39) Set Background Colour = BLUE
@(-40) Set Background Colour = BLACK

Functions @(-41) through @(-48) set colour terminals foreground colours to a full-intensity colour.

@(-41) Set Foreground Colour = WHITE
@(-42) Set Foreground Colour = BROWN
@(-43) Set Foreground Colour = MAGENTA
@(-44) Set Foreground Colour = RED
@(-45) Set Foreground Colour = CYAN
@(-46) Set Foreground Colour = GREEN
@(-47) Set Foreground Colour = BLUE
@(-48) Set Foreground Colour = BLACK
@(-49) through @(-56) (Reserved)

Functions @(-57) through @(-64) set colour terminals foreground colours to a low-intensity colour.

@(-57) Set Foreground Colour = WHITE
@(-58) Set Foreground Colour = BROWN
@(-59) Set Foreground Colour = MAGENTA
@(-60) Set Foreground Colour = RED
@(-61) Set Foreground Colour = CYAN
@(-62) Set Foreground Colour = GREEN
@(-63) Set Foreground Colour = BLUE
@(-64) Set Foreground Colour = BLACK
@(-65) through @(-88) (Reserved)
@(-89) Activate monochrome monitor to 80x25 mode.
@(-90) through @(-92) (Reserved)
@(-93) Activate colour monitor to 80x25 mode.
@(-94) Activate colour monitor to 80x25 B&W mode.
@(-95) through @(-99) (Reserved)
@(-99) Embedded Visual Attributes.
'0' = Visual Attributes are 'hidden'.
'1' = Visual Attributes are 'embedded'.
@(-100) Sets the foreground brightness to half-intensity.
@(-101) Sets the foreground brightness to full-intensity.

Figure 24.4 The **PRINT @** functions for the memory mapped monitor.

In BASIC the statement would be:

PRINT @(-93):@(-47):@(-33)

In PICK R83 there is a program in the SYSPROG-PL file within the SYSPROG account called DEMO which demonstrates the extended support provided for the memory-mapped monitors. It is worth bearing in mind that these functions only work for the memory-mapped monitor and will not function on standard asynchronous terminals linked to the PC in multi-user mode.

24.3.4 Redefining the keyboard layout

The PC version of PICK provides a keyboard definition function for the PC monitor. This enables the support of a wide variety of different keyboard layouts in many foreign languages. Two standard UK formats are already defined, these being for 84, and 101 key keyboards. By default, the keyboard is assumed to be a 101 key USA keyboard, so for those in Europe a new layout definition has to be invoked. For those of you in the UK two definitions are provided **BRITISH-84** and **BRITISH-101**. which can be found in the KEYBOARDS file. The command to invoke a new keyboard definition is **SET-KBRD** and this command is followed by the file name and item in that file that contains the keyboard definition. Typically the command would be:

:SET-KBRD KEYBOARDS *name*

where *name* is the item name in the KEYBOARDS file which defines the required keyboard layout (such as BRITISH-84 for an 84 key keyboard, BRITISH-101 for a 101 key keyboard)

The USA-101 keyboard is the default layout which is activated each time the system is booted. To change this to an alternative, you need to modify the **USER-COLDSTART** macro with the command:

set-kbrd keyboards *name* where *name* is the keyboard name

If you are using PICK R83 you can add the following lines to your PROC:

S2
IHKEYBOARDS *name* ◄——— where *name* is the keyboard name
HRUN SYSPROG-BP SET-KBRD
P

Modifying a keyboard definition item

If you find that none of the keyboard definitions match exactly to your requirements then you can set up your own. For example in the BRITISH-*nn* keyboard definitions the " and @ symbols are the wrong way round and the **£** symbol above the **3** key prints as a hash sign.

To produce your own keyboard definition, first find a keyboard layout nearest to the one you want. own. For safety's sake, and so that you can retain the original to refer to, it is best to copy one of the British definitions (BRITISH-84 or BRITISH-101) in the KEYBOARDS file to a new item and modify the new item. For example:

```
:COPY KEYBOARDS BRITISH-101
TO: BRITISH-102
```

The keyboard definition item contains details of the values to be transmitted when each key is pressed. The values are stored in hex (refer to Appendix G for the ASCII and hex table), and each key is represented by two hex characters.

If you look at a keyboard definition item, for example BRITISH-101, it is obvious it defines far more keys than that of any normal monitor keyboard. The reason for this is that it holds a definition for each of four possible key combinations:

- On its own (i.e. lower case)
- SHIFT/Key (i.e. upper case)
- CTRL/Key (i.e. concurrently with the CTRL key)
- ALT/Key (i.e. concurrently with the ALT key)

Effectively, therefore the keyboard is defined four times over. If we look at the BRITISH-101 item, we can see how this works – notice also, it is the upper case definitions which are represented first.

```
    BRITISH-101
001 * Define BRITISH 101-key keyboard
002 *
003 * Note: X'FF' means ignore this keystroke
004 *
005 *
006 * Upper case definitions
007 *
008 FF1B21402324255E262A28295F2B08FF  <—— Hex 40 is the @ symbol while
009 51574552545955494F507B7D0DFF4153       hex 23 produces a # symbol
010 444647484A4B4C3A227EFF7C5A584356  <—— Hex 22 produces a " symbol
011 424E4D3C3E3FFF2AFF20FF5051525354
012 5556575859FFFF3738392D3435362B31
013 3233302EFFFFFF5A5BFFFFFFFFFFFFFF
014 FFFFFFFFFFFFFFFFFFFFFFFFFFFFFFFF
015 FFFFFFFFFFFFFFFFFFFFFFFFFFFFFFFF
016 *
017 * Lower case definitions
018 *
019 FF1B31323334353637383930 2D3D0809
020 71776572747975696F705B5D0DFF6173
021 646667686A6B6C3B2760FF5C7A786376
022 626E6D2C2E2FFF2AFF20FF4041424344
023 4546474849FFFFFF1AFF2D15FF062BFF
024 0AFFFFFFFFFFFF4A4BFFFFFFFFFFFFFF
025 FFFFFFFFFFFFFFFFFFFFFFFFFFFFFFFF
026 FFFFFFFFFFFFFFFFFFFFFFFFFFFFFFFF
```

```
*
* Control key definitions
*
FF1BFF00FFFFFF1EFFFFFFFF1FFF7FFF
1117051214191509 0F101B1D0AFF0113
040607080A0B0CFFFFFFFF1C1A180316
020E0DFFFFFFFFFFFF20FF2021222324
2526272829FFFFFFFFFFFFFFFFFFFFFF
FFFFFFFFFFFF2A2BFFFFFFFFFFFFFFFF
FFFFFFFFFFFFFFFFFFFFFFFFFFFFFFFF
FFFFFFFFFFFFFFFFFFFFFFFFFFFFFFFF
*
* Alternate key definitions
*
FFFFFFFFFFFFFFFFFFFFFFFFFFFFFFFF
FFFFFFFFFFFFFFFFFFFFFFFFFFFFFFFF
FFFFFFFFFFFFFFFFFFFFFFFFFFFFFFFF
FFFFFFFFFFFFFFFF20FF303132333334
3536373839FFFFFFFFFFFFFFFFFFFFFF
FFFFFFFFFFFF3A3BFFFFFFFFFFFFFFFF
FFFFFFFFFFFFFFFFFFFFFFFFFFFFFFFF
FFFFFFFFFFFFFFFFFFFFFFFFFFFFFFFF
*
```

Whilst this series of tables may look a little daunting it is not difficult to understand.

(1) Any line (attribute) starting with * is a comment line.

(2) Any line not starting with an * is a data line and all data up to the first space encountered will be used. The rest of the line is ignored and therefore can be used to contain comments.

(3) The data must consist of *exactly* 174 key definitions grouped into three groups of 58 characters each.

(4) Each group is divided into four lines and represents a keyboard row.

(5) Each character definition is composed of two ASCII hexadecimal characters (see Appendix G).

(6) A definition of **FF** or **00** means that nothing is displayed when the key is pressed.

(7) Key definitions **01** to **1F** will display unusual looking characters, such as happy faces, hearts and diamonds.

Changing the keyboard layout specification is therefore just a matter of determining the whereabouts of the current code is held in the keyboard definition item and changing it with the Update Processor or Editor.

When setting up your own keyboard definition item remember the following:

(1) Definitions are in hexadecimal not decimal. Appendix G contains a full list of hex characters.

(2) Set them up carefully and ensure there are exactly 174 character definitions.

(3) It is probably easiest to copy an existing definition and modify it, rather than start from scratch.

(4) Use comments freely – they may be very useful later on!

Whilst swapping the hex 40 and hex 22 codes around is relatively straightforward, the hex code 23 needs to be changed to 9C (the hex code produced by holding down the Alt key whilst typing in 156).

Although this will change the keyboard definition you need to run the command **XCS-ON** to tell PICK to enable the extended character set, which means that the high order bit of the character is not stripped out and means that any character in the range 128 through to 255 can be used. Once you have established this is needed you should add the command to your coldstart PROC. Remember that **XCS-ON** has to be set for *each* port requiring the extended character set so add the command **XCS-ON** *n* (where *n* is the port number) for each port using the extended character set.

Modifying the function keys

This is a function purely for the memory mapped monitor and will not work for any other keyboard that may be attached to a dumb terminal. To modify the function key values for a dumb terminal (VDU) refer to the terminal manual.

The function keys are set by use of the command **SET-FUNC** referring to an item in the file **FUNCKEYS**. The means of using and modifying function keys is similar in principle to that for the keyboard. In the file **FUNCKEYS** are a number of items defining the function key values. The default item is as follows:

DEFAULT

```
*
* Define default function keys
*
505152535455565758595A5B  function key + shift
404142434445464748494A4B  function key only
202122232425262728292A2B  function key + ctrl
303132333435363738393A3B  function key + alt
*
* Define function key lead in character
*
02                        lead in character = STX
*
```

Typically the command would be

:SET-FUNC FUNCKEYS *name*

where *name* is the item name in the **FUNCKEYS** file which defines the required values to apply to the function keys

The rules for defining a function key's item are very similar to those in setting up a keyboard definition:

(1) Any line (attribute) starting with '*' is a comment line.

(2) Any line not starting with an '*' is a data line and all data up to the first space encountered will be used. The rest of the line is ignored and therefore can be used to contain comments.

(3) The data must consist of exactly 40 key definitions grouped into four lines of 10 characters each.

(4) Each character definition is composed of two ASCII hexadecimal characters (see Appendix G).

(5) A definition of **FF** or **00** means that nothing is displayed when the key is pressed.

(6) Key definitions **01** to **1F** will display unusual looking characters, such as happy faces, hearts and diamonds.

24.3.5 Setting baud rates

Baud rates cannot be changed for the memory mapped monitor which always operates at 9600 baud. Section 21.5.4 explains how the baud rate can be altered for any of the serial ports.

24.3.6 Using tapes and floppy disks

Newly purchased floppy disks must be formatted before they can be used on the PC. Once they have been formatted under PICK they can be reused time and time again without reformatting. Ready formatted diskettes can be purchased from many diskette suppliers and although these are advertised as DOS formatted they will work on PC-PICK. Once used for PICK they cannot then be used for DOS without first being formatted under DOS, but the reverse is does not apply. Any DOS formatted disk, whether blank or containing data can be used to record PICK data.

If you do not have formatted diskettes then you will need to perform a formatting operation. For anyone still using a PC-XT with the XT version of PC-PICK you have to use the **FFORMAT** verb, all other PC-PICK implementations (R83 on the 286 processor and above, AP/Native, AP/DOS and AP/PRO) use the **FORMAT** verb.

Before using the floppy drive for any task first attach it to your port with the **SET-FLOPPY** command specifying the drive letter and drive density.

A – drive A
B – drive B
H – high density (1.2MB for 5.25″ and 1.44MB for 3.5″)
S – standard density (360K for 5.25″ and 720K for 3.5″)

Hence **SET-FLOPPY** (AH will format a diskette in drive A to high density format. The default setting is drive A in high density. If you have not used the

SET-FLOPPY command for standard density floppies the diskette may appear to work initially and but will then given parity errors. If you are getting parity errors whilst using floppy disks then check the current settings for the drive are correct. To check the current settings use the command **T-STATUS**. The commands to switch between using floppy disk and $\frac{1}{4}''$ tape are:

SET-SCT
SET-FLOPPY

Advanced PICK introduced the command **SET-DEVICE** a more generalized version of the **SET-*xxxx*** where the device can be expressed as a number, relating to the number assigned to a given backup device. If a system has two identical devices, two 3.5″ floppy drives , for example, the options will select only the first. The format of the **SET-DEVICE** verb is given in Figure 24.5.

24.3.7 Moving data between PICK and DOS

There are sets of verbs for transferring data between the two operating environments, PICK and DOS:

IMPORT	imports a DOS file into a PICK item
EXPORT	exports a PICK item to a DOS diskette
COPYPICK	transfers data from the PICK partition to the DOS partition
COPYDOS	imports a DOS file into a PICK item

There is a slight difference between the operation of these two sets of commands. Firstly **IMPORT** and **EXPORT** were only introduced with Advanced PICK, so R83 users have to use the **COPYPICK** and **COPYDOS** commands. Secondly **COPYPICK** being a DOS program has to be separately purchased from your PICK supplier and is not part of the standard PICK system.

Transferring data from PICK to DOS using export

The **export** utility transfers data from the PICK database to a DOS diskette; it is not possible to export PICK data directly to the hard disk as you can with **COPYPICK**. The general format of the command is as follows:

export *file.name* [*item.id* | *] {*options*}
to: {*DOS.path.name*}

where

file.name	is the name of the file containing the data to be transferred	
item.id | *	is the item-id of the item to export (* means all items)	
options	the transfer options, which can be any of the following	
	A	appends a segment mark at the end of each item
	C	concatenates the items into one DOS file
	D	displays diagnostic information during the transfer process

:set-device {*nnn*} {(*options*}
:set-device {*device*} {(*options*}
:set-device {*keyword*} {(*options*}

where:

nnn is the device number numbered from 0 to 9 as they appear in the configuration file

device is a device number from 0 to 15 (displayed if the command **SET-DEVICE** is executed without any further arguments)

keyword is one of the following

720K **1.2M** **1.44M** **3 1/2** **5 1/4** **FLOPPY**
8MM **HALF INCH**

options is one of the following

3	$3\frac{1}{2}''$ floppy.
5	$5\frac{1}{4}''$ floppy.
9	9-track, $\frac{1}{2}''$ tape.
a	$5\frac{1}{4}''$ floppy.
b	$3\frac{1}{2}''$ floppy.
c	Changes the 8mm tape block size. The current tape block size is displayed and the operator is prompted for the new block size (0 or 512). On AP/Unix Systems, the default block size is set to 0 (zero) at install time. Zero means variable-length.
e	Selects 2.88mb floppy. (AP 5.2.5 and higher only).
f	Floppy ($3\frac{1}{2}''$ or $5\frac{1}{4}''$ as default).
h	High density (1.44M for $3\frac{1}{2}''$ floppy, 1.2M for $5\frac{1}{2}''$ floppy, 6250 bpi for 9-track tapes, 150M for Quarter Inch tapes).
i	Suppresses display of devices after the command is complete and useful for MACROs.
k	Hard disk 'pseudo' tapes. These devices are removable or fixed hard disks or regular Unix files. Their size is fixed and determined by the device or by the maximum file size for a user. The main usage for these devices is for small, fast t-dumps/saves, transaction logging or incremental saves.
l	Low density (720K for $3\frac{1}{2}$' floppy, 1600 bpi for 9-track tapes).
m	Medium density (720K for $5\frac{1}{4}$' floppy, 3600 bpi for 9-track tapes).
n	Network 'pseudo' tape. This device has an 'infinite' size. It is assumed another system is reading the data at the 'other end' of the network.
q	Quarter-inch tape.
r	Prevents an automatic rewind on the device. This option must be used to set the device to a floppy with an unformatted floppy disk in the drive.
s	Standard density (360 for $5\frac{1}{2}$' floppy, 60M or 120M for quarter-inch (SCT) tapes.

Figure 24.5 The format of **SET-DEVICE.**

E	appends a specified terminator at the end of each item
I	includes the item-id as the first field in the DOS files
N	sorts the item-ids numerically before the export process
O	overwrites the DOS file if it already exists
P	directs output to the printer
S	creates a DOS file with same name as the PICK item-id
T	translates specified characters to another specified character

DOS.path.name the name of the DOS path and file name

Transferring data from PICK to DOS using COPYPICK

The **COPYPICK** utility allows data in the PICK database to be transferred directly into the DOS partition. Since the transfer is performed from the DOS partition, a separate DOS diskette is required (available from your PICK distributor). It comprises two utilities, BRIDGE.EXE and BASRUN.EXE, which are copied to the hard disk with the command **COPY A:*.* C:** and then executed with the command **COPYPICK**. The command brings up a menu for transferring both R83 and Advanced PICK data. Since each of PICK's attribute marks (hexadecimal FE) are replaced with line feeds (hexadecimal 0A), it effectively means that each PICK attribute becomes a DOS record.

The options available with this utility are as follows:

D	displays diagnostics during the transfer process
I	includes the item-id as the first field in the DOS files
N	transfers all items within a given range of item-ids

Transferring data from DOS to PICK using IMPORT

The **import** utility transfers data a DOS file into a PICK item. If no item name is given the DOS file name is used. The general format of the command is as follows:

import *DOS.path.name* {*options*}
`to:` (*file.name* {*item-id*}

where

DOS.path.name is the name of the DOS path and file name
options the transfer options, which can be any of the following

C	no conversion of cr/lf to an attribute mark
M	creates multiple PICK items
O	overwrites the PICK item if it already exists
T	translates specified characters to another specified character

file.name	is the name of the PICK file to contain the data being transferred
item.id	is the item-id of the item to be created from the imported data

Transferring data from DOS to PICK using COPYDOS

The **COPYDOS** utility is the reverse of **COPYPICK** in that it allows data from the DOS partition to be transferred to an item in the PICK database. The general format of the command is as follows:

COPYDOS *DOS.path.name* {*options*}
`to`: (*file.name* {*item-id*}

where

DOS.path.name	is the path and name of the file containing the data to be transferred
options	the transfer options, which can be any of the following

D	displays diagnostic information during the transfer process
F	flags specified characters with hex '00'
L	creates a list item (R83 version 2.2)
M	creates multiple PICK items
O	overwrites the PICK item if it already exists
P	directs output to the printer
R	indicates the DOS file is in random order
S	indicates the DOS file is in sequential order
T	translates specified characters to another specified character
X	creates a hexadecimal image of the DOS file

file.name	is the name of the PICK file to contain the data being transferred
item.id	is the item-id of the item to be created from the imported data

The general rules applied are as follows:

(1) If neither **S** nor **R** is specified, then **S** (sequential) is assumed.

(2) If neither the **F** nor **T** option is specified, the DOS hex string 0A (line feed) is converted to hex FE (attribute mark), meaning that each DOS line becomes a PICK attribute.

(3) If the DOS file is too large to fit into a PICK item and the **M** option has not been specified, the data will be split across several items each numbered sequentially: **itemname1**, **itemname2**, **itemname3** and so on.

(4) No item is created with the name given in the command line. A number is always appended to the item name.

The **M** option enables the item size to be regulated. If the option is specified a secondary prompt will be given:

ENTER LENGTH OF RECORD (OR Dn):

The response can either be a number, to indicate the number of bytes in length to make each PICK item, or a **D** followed by a number, indicating the number of PICK attributes there should be in each PICK item. Using the ***Dn*** option will cause PICK to translate linefeeds as attribute marks.

All items created are given an item-id, equal to the item name given in response to the `TO:(`prompt, concatenated with the next in the sequence of numbers starting at 0, i.e. *itemname0, itemname1, itemname2* and so on. No item is created using just the item name alone.

If the **T** option is chosen up to 16 different hex bytes can be translated. The system will respond alternately with `REPLACE:` and `WITH:` until a carriage return is given to a `REPLACE:` prompt after which an `OKAY(Y/N):` is offered so that the translate specifications can be re-entered if an error has been made.

The **F** option enables up to 16 different hex bytes to be flagged by placing the hex string '00' in front of them. If the **F** option is taken, following the response to the TO:(prompt, the system will display `REPLACE:` and await a response. After entering the hex character to translate or pass, the system displays `WITH FLAGGED:`. Upon entry of the same character or a replacing one, the system will prompt for a replacing flag up to a further 15 times.

24.3.8 Powering off and rebooting

The PC implementation has a special verb, **shutdown** which should be used before the system is closed down. This disables all users, causes the memory buffers to be flushed to disk and halts the system. Under R83 and AP/Native the command **POWER-OFF** should be used. Once shutdown the system can be switched off or rebooted using the **CTRL/ALT/DEL** keys (all three keys being depressed at the same time).

If you need to reboot the system when it is still active use the command **reboot**. This is a useful facility after the active partition has been altered using **FDISK** and you now wish to return to a non-PICK operating system or where a port is roadblocked and the only way of releasing it is a complete system re-initialization.

24.4 Installing and making PICK work on a PC

Advanced PICK is supplied on a number of diskettes, and should be used in the following order:

	System 1	Contains the PICK monitor (the interface with the hardware and the operating system)
	System 2	Contains many of the device drivers
	ABS 1 and ABS 2	Contains the PICK virtual or the operating system/database manager
	Data 1 to Data 5	Contains all the primary files and the initial accounts, such as **dm**, **pa** and **qa**.
	EPICK1 and EPICK2	Contains the online PICK encyclopedia
*	PicLan host	Contains the PicLan software that resides on the PICK host
*	PicLan workstation	Contains the PicLan software that resides on the DOS workstations

* *these diskettes are only supplied with AP/PRO systems*

Whilst you can install AP/DOS from either drive A or drive B, it is important to be aware that you can only install AP/Native and AP/PRO from drive A, so ensure your diskettes are of the correct size. Whilst all new systems now use 3.5″ floppy disks, there are still many systems around that have 5.25″ floppy drives and your PICK licence will be supplied on 3.5″ floppies unless you state otherwise.

The installation guides provide most of the information you require to successfully install PICK on your PC, so the following sections are dedicated at highlighting the more important points and the less obvious installation issues.

24.4.1 Installing AP/DOS

AP/DOS sits on your hard disk in the same way as any other DOS application and hence you do not need to partition your disk further. You should use MS-DOS version 3.3 and above, although version 5 and above is strongly recommended. You should have at least 10MB available in one of your logical drives and be running on a 286 processor and above. Before use you should ensure you have the following parameters set in your **config.sys** file and if you have to change **config.sys** to accommodate these, then reboot your system.

```
files=20
buffers=20
stacks=0,0
device=c:\dos\himem.sys
DOS=HIGH
```

Whilst AP/DOS use a file system of just over 2MB, the minimum disk size you can allocate is 10MB. In reality this is likely to be substantially more and whilst the installation procedure gives you standard allocations for AP/DOS up to 105MB, you can select a customised installation option which will allow you to allocate as much disk space as you need.

The limitations of AP/DOS are that it supports a maximum of three users (the monitor and two serial ports), extended memory requires MS-DOS 5 or above and when extended memory is available the maximum supported is 4MB. It should also be noted that AP/DOS does not use the usual DOS tape backup devices and is restricted to a number of ¼" devices.

One important point to note with AP/DOS is to do with the keyboard. If you find your keyboard is not responding in AP/DOS as you would expect, exit AP/DOS and return to the DOS prompt. From within the AP/DOS directory on your hard disk, execute the command **picknat** and take the AP/Native and R83 keyset. You will only have to do this once during the lifetime of your use of AP/DOS but if you ever need to reload from scratch you will have to re-run the command.

24.4.2 Installing AP/Native

AP/Native has to reside in its own partition on your hard disk. It can either take up the entire disk or co-reside with other operating systems. When installing AP/Native on the PC it becomes an operating system rather than a database. If SCO is the native operating system and you wish to run AP as the database you will need a copy of AP/SCO. AP/Native and AP/SCO can reside on the same hard drive *only* if AP/SCO is installed *within* SCO UNIX. If you attempt to load AP/Native on a drive in which AP/SCO is installed as a separate partition, AP/Native will erase the AP/SCO data.

AP/Native, PICK R83, DOS and UNIX can all co-reside on your hard disk but they need to occupy their own dedicated partitions. AP/Native can co-reside with a maximum of three other partitions. Since AP takes up the remaining unallocated spare space on your disk, ensure all other operating systems are loaded or at least ensure the partitions have been allocated **prior** to loading AP. It requires as a minimum a 286 PC, 512KB RAM and 20MB of hard disk. These days such a low specification of PC is impossible to purchase, but the information is given here for completeness or for those wishing to try PICK out on one of their older and maybe no longer used PCs.

The installation of AP/Native and AP/PRO is much longer than that of AP/DOS because it has to format the disk prior to installation and during this process it looks for disk defects flagging and removing bad tracks from its use.

To carry out the installation procedure, insert the PICK System #1 diskette into the floppy drive A and boot the machine. After a few seconds the system will display the following options:

```
PICK's AP/AT-Native 5.2.#.M#     DD MMM YY

Monitor options

E  -  Extended Memory ......................... enabled
F  -  Forced SCT recognition .................. disabled
M  -  Multi-sector hard disk operations ........ enabled
P  -  PICK disk driver (vs Bios) .............. disabled
R  -  Reset hard disk after disk error ......... enabled
S  -  Short disk format ....................... disabled

Press letter of option to toggle :

Press <enter> to continue ...
```

Providing you are using the default SCT address, which is probable, then you should toggle the **F** option and you should only switch off use of extended memory if you don't want to use it (highly unlikely) or if you know you have a memory fault in your computer. Whilst using the short disk format will halve the formatting time, since this is done only once, it is worth leaving this option disabled. In essence you are unlikely to need to change these standard settings. From this point on you will be prompted for other installation information, including your name and that of your company. This security information is written onto System diskette #1 to preclude them being copied and used on another system. Each time you boot your system these details will be displayed and once you have told PICK you have typed them in correctly you will not be able to change them, so take extra time to make sure you have the details accurately recorded.

Once the system diskettes have been loaded, you will be asked to configure any serial ports, whether these be the standard ones that come with each PC or whether they be expansion cards (intelligent or non-intelligent). This procedure is straightforward and invariably PICK will have correctly detected the boards in your system, so it is just a case of confirming them to be correct.

Once this has been done you will be prompted to load the two ABS diskettes (using the **A** {ABS} option) and then the four Data diskettes (using the **F** {File} option). If this is a virgin install make sure you reply **n** to the questions 'Restore from incremental tape (y/n)' and 'Restore from transaction log (y/n)' otherwise you are likely to corrupt the system and have to start again.

Please note too that on some earlier implementations of AP the **:files** verb was not available and the only way to perform a file restore was to reboot AP from the System #1 diskette and reply **F** when prompted with the message:

```
OPTIONS: K)ill, F)ile, A)BS only, X)eXecute =
```

You need to reboot from the PICK disks if you add or change the serial expansion cards on your machine as this is the only way to invoke the Serial Driver Installation program and sometimes you also need to reboot from the PICK disks when upgrading to a new release as you may find you it is not possible to perform the upgrade without performing a file-save and file-restore. Regardless of whether or not this applies in your case, you should always ensure you have a valid file-save before making any changes to the operating system and for safety's sake it is well worth taking two verified file-saves just in case you have a problem with one of them.

Do make sure that your monitor, abs and data files are of the same revision. Do not upgrade the system by reloading the monitor and abs and then restoring the file system from your file-save tape. First load the monitor, abs and file system from the new diskettes and then perform a **restore-accounts** from your file-save ensuring that all your application accounts are restored. You will then have to modify any configuration parameters in the user coldstart proc (**md user-coldstart**) and restore/re-create all your user records from the **users** file.

For this reason it is worth spending a few moments prior to launching into a system upgrade to determine the whereabouts of customized items in the **dm** account and then to back up these files/items separately, which saves you significant time over the alternative, that of performing **sel-restore**'s from your file-save. The primary files to review for changes are **bp devices pibs** and **tcl-stack**.

AP/Native comes already configured to support 65 users but that does not mean you can automatically connect 65 active users without purchasing the appropriate licences. To increase users in earlier releases of PICK, namely PICK R83, it was necessary to exchange your PICK disks for new ones and to perform a complete system reload. Now it is possible to increase the number of users by using your original diskettes and getting a new authorization code over the telephone.

Another change that came with AP/Native was the way in which the maximum number of users could connect to the system. In PICK R83 if you had a 10 user licence the first 10 ports on your system were active and hence PICK could only be made available to nominated individuals. In Advanced PICK it is possible to connect as many users as you require (up to a maximum of 65) with the first *n* users that log on (where *n* is the number of users of the licence you have purchased) gaining access to the system. Hence on a 10 user licence you could connect up to 65 people to the system with the first 10 that logon getting into the system. To determine the maximum number of users of your system use the TCL verb **maxusers**.

Whilst the loading and configuration process is straightforward and PICK Systems provide a detailed installation guide you may find that you encounter installation problems. Whilst there is a section in the installation guide on the possible error messages and their meaning it is not always clear as to what the problem might be and how to get around it. Invariably the problem will be to do with your hardware and the BIOS is the most important consideration. When purchasing your PC ignore those from companies that have their own BIOS. Try stripping down the machine to its minimum configuration, removing all unnecessary PCBs, tape drives, etc. Once you have got PICK loaded then start adding the card(s)/tape drive(s) one by one to determine what is giving you the problem and also check that you have loaded the correct serial drivers.

24.4.3 Installing AP/Pro

Installing AP/Pro is very similar to that of AP/Native so it is worth reading through the previous section first if you are about to install AP/Pro. AP/Pro requires at minimum a 386 PC with 4MB RAM and a 20MB hard disk, again a specification far below any new computer you are likely to purchase.

AP/Pro has to reside in its own partition on your hard disk. It can either take up the entire disk or co-reside with other operating systems. When installing AP/Pro on the PC just as with AP/Native, it becomes an operating system rather than a database. Hence planning the layout of your disk is identical to that of AP/Native in that multiple operating systems can reside on the same hard disk at the same time, but remember AP/Pro can only boot from the first hard disk if you have more than one in your computer.

The maximum number of users concept is the same as AP/Native in that you can have many more people connected to the computer with only the licenced number getting **concurrent** access to PICK itself. Whereas 65 users could be connected under AP/Native, AP/Pro is delivered with 257 PIBS set up, allowing for up to 257 connections to your system.

The installation step is to insert the PICK System #1 diskette in your A drive and boot the machine. The following installation screen will then be displayed.

```
PICK's AP/AT-Prot 6.1.#.M#      DD MMM YY

Monitor options

Q  -  Quick install
C  -  Configuration of serial drivers .......... disabled

D  -  Protected Mode disk I/O .................. disabled
F  -  Forced SCT recognition ................... disabled
R  -  Reset hard disk after disk error ......... enabled
S  -  Short disk format ........................ disabled
V  -  Protected Mode Bios Video ................ disabled
W  -  Hard disk Wait and Post .................. disabled
T  -  Third party SCSI devices ................. disabled

Press letter of option to toggle :

Press <enter> to continue ...
```

The Quick option bypasses the screen which prompts for information on serial cards and leaves PICK to determine these for itself. If for whatever reason you need to configure these yourself then enable the **C** option.

Once the Monitor has been loaded, follow the prompts to load the ABS and file system and ensure on the initial installation you answer **N**(o) to the prompts **Restore from incremental tape (y/n)** and **Restore from transaction log (y/n)** otherwise you will be prompted to load further media and even breaking out of the system at this point will cause system corruption and you will need to re-do the installation.

Once AP/Pro is loaded you are in a position to load PicLan from the diskettes supplied, but if you only intend to use serial connections and have no network in place then this is completely unnecessary.

If you are upgrading from a previous release you will need to ensure you have first saved, and after the upgrade restore, items in the following files which you may have added or customized in the **dm** account.

```
bp
devices
pibs
tcl-stack
users
```

One other point of which to be aware is that of third party SCSI drivers. Although SCSI drivers were supposed to be available for AP/Pro it took nearly a year from its release before these drivers became available and in the interim third party SCSI drivers were introduced. These software drivers enabled the use of SCSI tape devices which otherwise could not be used, devices such 4 mm DAT and 8 mm Exabyte drives which back up several gigabytes of data on one tape. If you are using third party drivers, such as those from The Computer Clinic, ensure the **T** option is set after booting from the PICK System #1 diskette.

25 Networking and Communications

25.1 Introduction

Until the introduction of Advanced PICK the greatest perceived weakness of a PICK system was its communication capability. In the early days even the porting of software from one PICK computer to another could present serious difficulty as there were no TCL verbs or BASIC commands to communicate with serial ports. In some cases software was moved from one machine to another by 'printing' from one computer and 'capturing' this output in another by fooling the second computer that it was 'talking' to a dumb terminal.

A number of PICK licencees developed their own software to address these problems notably Adds Mentor General Automation, Prime and Ultimate. Whilst these suppliers offered completely viable solutions, they were unique to that vendor. Hence buying from anyone of these locked you into their hardware and their PICK implementation and still meant you couldn't network systems from other PICK suppliers.

A number of companies provide 'black box' solutions with appropriate software to enable PICK systems to communicate. These are mostly needed for minicomputers and mainframes which communicate by sending blocks of data. PICK systems serial communications involve the transmission of individual characters of data, so these intelligent black boxes which plug into the PICK system's serial port are essential to work with block mode protocols such as 3270, 2780/3780, X25 or SNA

During the period up to the release of Advanced PICK software companies developed independent software packages for PICK-to-PICK and PICK-to-DOS communications. The release in the early 1980s of the **COPYPICK** and **COPYDOS** utilities within PICK for the PC enabled data to be transferred as ASCII text between the PICK and DOS partitions on a PC, but if you were not working with a PC and using one of the more commonplace minicomputers these utilities were of no use. The only way to move data into DOS was to use a terminal emulation package with PICK-to-DOS and DOS-to-PICK routines. Indeed, even today, these products still form one of the main methods of moving data between these two environments. For PICK-to-PICK communications one of the most commonly used products is **Infolinke** from Sables Associates in Phoenix Arizona. This product enables items, files or entire accounts to be transferred between computers using a serial cable. As far as emulators are concerned there are a wide number that also offer data transfer facilities. The leading products (in alphabetical order) being:

Product	*Supplier*
MacToPic	Carnation Software
PFX	Landa Systems Software
PL-TERM (part of PicLan)	Modular Software Corporation
PK Harmony	Synex Systems Corporation
SB/Client	System Builder Technologies now part of Unidata
TERMiTE	Pixel Innovations
Via Express	Via Systems
vxConnect for Windows	Cambridge Computer Corporation
W/Integrate	Unidata

Advanced PICK completely opens up the communications arena. It provides the TCL verb **converse** to communicate with a serial port and the incorporates the BASIC commands **get** and **send** to retrieve and send characters on a nominated port.

Another important aspect of Advanced PICK is that it can work as a database under other native operating systems, in particular UNIX, which support network protocols and machine to machine communications. The Protected mode version of Advanced PICK for the PC, incorporates PicLan, a software system originally developed by the Modular Software Corporation, which enables a PICK-based computer to be directly connected to a network. PicLan had been available prior to the 'bundling' agreement with Pick Systems and is still available as a separate product from Modular Software Corporation for the following PICK implementations:

- PICK R83
- Advanced PICK native
- Seattle Lab UPBOARD
- Alpha Microsystems Pick/64
- General Automation R91
- ADDS PC/OS

Since PicLan is such an important and strategic product to Advanced PICK, the remainder of this chapter is dedicated to its installation and use.

25.2 PicLan

25.2.1 Introduction

PicLan is a software package that enables a PICK-based computer to be directly connected to a network and as such is treated as any other server linked to that network. DOS workstations can access the PICK server and any VDU directly connected to one PICK server can also link to any other PICK server on the same or bridged network. Figure 25.1 gives an example of the network possibilities with PicLan.

The PicLan software comes in two parts, the software which resides on the server and the software for each DOS workstation. PicLan uses the IPX (Internetwork Packet eXchange) network protocol, the protocol most commonly used by Novell NetWare networks, but it also supports a wide number of other networks. The most commonly supported networks being:

- Novell NetWare
- NetWare Lite
- Personal NetWare
- Artisoft Lantastic
- Microsoft Lan Manager

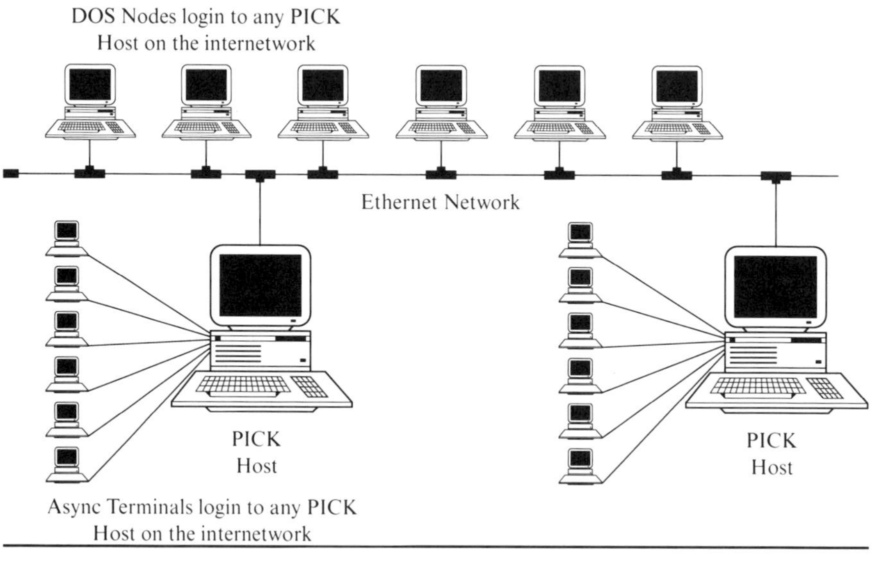

Figure 25.1 PicLan network schematic.

- Microsoft NT
- Microsoft NT Advanced Server
- Microsoft Windows for Workgroups
- IBM Lan Server
- IBM Token-Ring
- Banyan Vines

However, PicLan can operate a PICK environment as a stand-alone network, without having it connected into one of the above mentioned networks. In this way links can be made to the PICK server(s) either serially or over Ethernet. The biggest problem in operating this way is in the initial set-up. If after loading the PicLan software you cannot make connection to the PICK host you have no network debugging tools to help you. Connecting to an existing network means that you at least have a working configuration and can monitor the packets travelling round the network.

On a stand-alone PicLan network once the software is loaded the network should spring into life and if it doesn't you need to explore both ends of the network to determine the problem. If this happens first look for hardware conflicts by removing all unnecessary PCB cards from either end and then add them back gradually until you locate the card that is giving you the greatest difficulty and go forward from there.

Under PicLan DOS workstations connected to the network can operate up to eight simultaneous sessions and can access any server (PICK or otherwise), and any VDU connected to one PICK system can logon to any other PICK system connected to the network. It is possible to initiate PICK-to-DOS and PICK-to-PICK transfers although the PICK-to-PICK transfers are at the file or item and not the account level.

With PicLan any printer on the network, whether connected directly to a DOS PC, connected to the PICK server or directly connected to the network can be used by any user on the network regardless of whether the user is a DOS workstation or VDU. This is handled by a PicLan function known as the DOS Services Gateway.

In essence, PicLan provides a powerful networking and communications environment enabling data transfer rates at over 20 times that possible using serial lines even when the speed of the serial line is operating at 19,200 baud.

25.2.2 Installing PicLan

PicLan is supplied with a detailed installation guide, but there are a number of points to be borne in mind the first of which is to ensure you have Advanced PICK installed and working on your PC before embarking on the installation of PicLan. The next step is to install the network card. PicLan works with two different styles of Ethernet adaptor for which many clones are available. The two original adaptors are:

- Western Digital WD8013
- Novell/Eagle NE2000

However, although the WD style adaptor is preferred because it is more efficient, results in lower system overhead and is considered better tested, the original model WD8013 is no longer available. There are however a number of others which you can use, these being:

Compex ENET-M
Compex ENET-U
Compex ENET16-U
Compex ENET16-P
Compex ENET16-V
SMC Elite/16
SMC Elite/A (a microchannel adaptor)

Whilst cards which support the NDIS2 standard are fine for the PICK host you may well find that the DOS workstations which support certain networking protocols, Windows for Workgroups being one of them, require a network card to the NDIS3 standard.

The next concern is to avoid any clashes with I/O addresses and IRQs used by other devices on the PICK host. The PicLan documentation strongly recommends I/0 Address 380 and Interrupt 10 although you will come across several machines where IRQ 10 is reserved and does generate a conflict. Further, some modern Ethernet cards do not offer I/O address 380 as an option.

It is up to you to determine the IRQ and I/O address which does not conflict with other adaptors in your system. It really does not matter which ones you use providing the combination of IRQ and I/O address are unique and do not conflict with those used elsewhere. If, after setting a unique IRQ and I/O address you still find you are not getting a response from the system, try moving the Ethernet card to a different slot. It really should not make a difference which slot the card is seated in, but I have known instances where it does.

It is also worth noting that although the PicLan documentation says that if you boot the PICK system under DOS and are able to access a Netware file server then the configuration is set properly to operate under Pick, this is not always the case. It is mostly true but it is not always true. The most important aspect to focus on is that of the interrupts and I/O addresses.

25.2.3 Configuring the network card

The stages involved are as follows.

- Begin by shutting down Pick and turning off the power to the computer, removing the power cable.

- Then install the Ethernet card in the Pick host. Follow any installation guide supplied with the card, although Ethernet cards generally are self-setting and do not require any jumpers to be altered or any dip switches to be set.
- Connect the Ethernet card to the ethernet network using an appropriate cable.
- Boot the Pick host into DOS using a DOS bootable floppy diskette.
- Exchange the DOS boot diskette for the Ethernet set-up diskette. (A useful tip for the technical amongst you, is to create a bootable network set-up diskette, which saves having to find a DOS boot diskette when you need to reconfigure the card!)
- Run the appropriate set-up routines as given in the installation instructions.
- Change the IRQ and I/O address.
- Set the transceiver type which is normally BNC, but choose TP if using twisted pair cabling.
- The Boot ROM base address and Turbo mode should be disabled.
- Save the configuration and back at the main menu choose the option to test the adaptor. Only if everything passes can you continue. At this point the most likely failure will be the Interrupt Test which tests both I/O address and IRQ so you may need to change one or both of these until the all the tests work successfully.

25.2.4 Configuring PicLan

Having set up the network card the next step is to see if PicLan can access it, which can be determined by performing the following:

- Boot up the Pick system and if it is configured to start up PicLan automatically interrupt the auto load process.
- Log to the PicLan account and from the menu displayed, choose the configure PicLan software option

```
PicLan v 1.1.0.29    Account maintenance menu    11 RB PIC-LAN

      1. Display/Print Installation Notes
      2. Re-execute initial install.
      3. Configure PicLan software
      4. Setup another account with PicLan verbs
      5. PicLan status display

      TCL - Access TCL
      OFF - Logoff

 Enter selection ===>
```

followed by that to configure PicLan hardware

```
PicLan Pick Host Configuration Utility

      1 - Configure PicLan License
      2 - Configure PicLan Hardware
      3 - Configure PicLan Software

      S - Save current configuration and exit
      X - Exit without saving

Enter Selection :
```

and change the I/O Address and the IRQ to match those of the configured card.

```
PicLan Pick Host Configuration

      PicLan Hardware Configuration

 System uses NE2000 adapter.
      Base I/O Address      = 300
      IRQ                   = 3

      Network Number (hex)  = A0A0A0A0
      Ethernet format       = 802.3

      Retry time            = 500 ms
      Auto XOFF time        = 0 sec
      Watchdog time         = 5 sec

        Is data ok (Y/N/X) :
```

In the above example, the A0A0A0A0 is a Novell network number. If Novell is not in use this number relates to the PICK host number and is normally set to one.

- The Ethernet format will normally be 802.3 for Novell and Ethernet-II for Windows for Workgroups.
- Save your changes and shutdown Pick and reboot.
- As PicLan auto loads it will show various parameters on the screen and the one to watch for is the node address. This is a unique address hard-coded into the Ethernet card. If this shows the correct address followed by 'Done' then you may continue. If this shows an incorrect address, for example FFFFFFFF or the machine hangs then there is a conflict and you need to go back a step and re-configure the card using a different I/O address and/or IRQ.

Assuming everything has worked so far the final step is to configure the software on the DOS workstation.

25.2.5 Configuring a DOS workstation

Configuring the DOS workstation is relatively straightforward and described quite clearly in the PicLan installation guide. The process varies depending on the type of network and type of drivers in use. In essence the steps to undertake are as follows:

- Insert the Ethernet card and connect the workstation to the network.
- Configure the I/O address and IRQ of the Ethernet card.
- Install and configure networking client software (if applicable).
- Install PicLan client software.

Once this is complete you should be able to make connection to the PICK host and log on from the DOS client workstations.

Additional configuration information

For those not familiar with networks there are some other steps to be undertaken from those published in the PicLan manual if you are using Novell or Windows for Workgroups version 3.11. The changes to the documented procedures are underlined and those only relating to Novell are also italicized.

- <u>Install, configure and test the Ethernet card in the workstation</u>
- Install Windows For Workgroups 3.11(WFW) onto your DOS system
- After WFW is installed go to 'Windows Setup' and select the 'Change Network Settings' option
- Highlight the LAN adaptor driver that you are using and select Drivers
- Select 'Setup' to change the driver options
- Select 'Real Mode' driver
- Save your changes
- Reboot the system
- <u>Install the PicLan client software by inserting the PicLan/DOS disk, exit windows, and at the DOS prompt enter A:\INSTALL.EXE</u>
- Edit your SYSTEM.INI file in your windows directory and look for the [network drivers] section.
- This section should look something like:

```
[network drivers]
devdir=c:\windows
loadRMDrivers=Yes
netcard=smcac.dos        (note this filename – the name of the
                          netcard driver)
transport=*netbeui,ndishlp.sys
```

- Copy the DIS_PKT.DOS file from \PICLAN\NDIS to your C:\WINDOWS directory
- Insert the following command into your CONFIG.SYS file after the ---.DOS LAN driver is loaded:

  DEVICE=\WINDOWS\DIS_PKT.DOS (or alternative path)
- add the [PKTDRV] section to your PROTOCOL.INI file:

```
[MS$3C509]                    (or similar)
...
[PKTDRV]
drivername=PKTDRV
bindings=MS$3C509
intvec=0x61
```

- The 'binding' field should point to the NDIS driver that you are actually using
- Change the 'netcard' line in the [network drivers] section of the SYSTEM.INI file to read

  netcard=smcmac.dos,dis_pkt.dos
- Edit the PL-CFG.INI file and make the following amendments:

```
[general]
user=xxxxxx          (where xxxxxx is a unique name for each
                     client)
DefHost=APPRO        (or whatever name is given to Pick Host)
....
[System]
...
EnetIrq=0xnn         (where nn is the IRQ of the Ethernet card)
EnetIO=0xnnn         (where nnn is the I/O address of the Ethernet
card)
Enet RAM=0xnnn       (some, but not all, cards need memory
                     addressing set)
Enetnet=0xnnn        (where nnn is the Novel network number)
...
EnetFrame=Ethernet-II
...
Fastini=No           (*** see notes below on Fastini)
[Function Keys]
DefPc_Consolekeys=SB+
```

- Make a Windows group for Piclan and an item which uses the appropriate emulator.
- Change the path in the [general] section of \PICLAN\PICLAN.INI to PICLAN
- Copy \PICLAN\PICLAN.INI to \WINDOWS

- Amend AUTOEXEC.BAT to execute pl-dev e.g. C:\PICLAN\PL-DEV.EXE (*this is only required if you are not using PL-TERM*)
- Add PICLAN to the path in AUTOEXEC.BAT e.g. SET PATH = %PATH;C:\PICLAN
- Reboot the system and verify that your network is still functional

The Fastini configuration option

The **pl-cfg.ini** file comes with **Fastini** set to **yes**. This means that the first time you use PicLan and it reads the **pl-cfg.ini** file it compiles the file to a file called **pl-cfg.$$$** which speeds up the loading of the configuration options. Whilst this may seem like a good idea, it means that every time you make a change to the **pl-cfg.ini** file you need to remember to delete the **pl-cfg.$$$** file otherwise you will still be loading the old configuration. Since there is no noticeable difference in loading the configuration interpretatively rather then compiled (certainly not on the new 486 and Pentium chips) you may decide to change the fastini option to **no**. However, for those of you with inquisitive users, if you do use Fastini set to **yes** it means that you can delete the **pl-cfg.ini** file and know that no-one can tamper with your configuration settings.

25.2.6 Installing PicLan with Windows 95

- Install PicLan on the PICK host
- Install Windows 95 on the client workstation
- Change the Windows 95 network driver in the control panel/network option from the 32 bit NDIS driver to the 16 bit NDIS driver
- Restart Windows 95 on the workstation
- Install PicLan on the workstation and ensure you have installed the NDIS packet drivers.
- Assuming PicLan is installed in the **c:\piclan** directory and Windows 95 is installed in the **c:\windows** directory, copy the **DIS_PKT.DOS** file from **c:\piclan\ndis** directory to the **c:windows** directory
- Amend the **protocol.ini** file by adding the following section

```
[PKTDRV]
drivername=PKTDRV
bindings=MS$NE2CLONE
intvec=0x61
```

- Add the following lines to the **autoexec.bat** file

```
set pl-cfg.ini=c:\piclan\pl-cfg.ini
c:\piclan\pl-dev
pause
```

- Amend the **pl-cfg.ini** file to ensure the **EnetIrq**, **EnetIO** and **EnetRAM** settings match your network card and that the **EnetNet** and **EnetFrame** parameters are set for NDIS
- Attach the packet driver to Windows 95 by clicking on Start/run and enter REGEDIT. Locate **NETCARD** then add **,DIS_PKT.DOS** to the end of the line.
- Shutdown and restart Windows 95. You should see the following messages
  Reading configuration.........
  DRV_EPKT has been loaded and bound to MAC/DIS converter
  DRV_MAIN,nnnn bytes, DOS memory segment 0xNNNN
  DRV_EPKT, nnnn bytes, DOS memory, segment 0xNNNN

  If you don't see these, in particular the first message where DRV_EPKT is *bound* to MAC/DIS review the above procedures for correct operation.

25.2.7 The DOS Services Gateway

The DOS Services Gateway provides additional file transfer and printer sharing capability between the PICK and DOS environments. Whilst it is an integral part of the PicLan software bundled with AP/Pro, it is an optional extra for all other platforms (PICK R83, AP/Native, UPBOARD, Alpha Microsystems PICK/64 and General Automation R91). The gateway is a PC which can either be a dedicated system or an existing user's PC with the gateway option switched on, which executes the following tasks:

- Import and export of DOS files

  PICK applications can import and export DOS files that are accessible to the DOS Services Gateway computer. These can be files on the local hard disk of the DOS Services Gateway computer or those stored on a network file server.

  Any PICK process (connected either asynchronously or over the network) can perform these data transfers utilizing the PicLan DOS Services Gateway. File transfers take place at network speeds allowing for large amounts of data to be efficiently moved between the two environments. PICK to DOS file transfer services include several industry-standard format conversion functions for rapid conversion of PICK-formatted data into DOS data structures, and vice versa.

  DOS users can perform file transfers to and from PICK file systems allowing DOS applications to import and export PICK data and utilize the same file transfer formatting functions available to PICK users who initiate data transfers. The PicLan DOS Services Gateway is not required when initiating transfers from within DOS.

- Printing
  The PicLan DOS Services Gateway enables PICK printing to occur on either DOS-connected printers (COM1 through to COM4 or LPT1 through to LPT3) or through NetWare print queues.

25.2.8 PicLan printing options without the DOS Services Gateway

With PicLan, users may share printers among multiple PICK host systems enabling PICK applications to spool a print job to be printed on a printer connected to a different PICK system. PicLan provides for setting destination form queues, copy counts, and hold files. The manipulation of printers is fully compatible with standard PICK applications.

PicLan's printer support extends to allow DOS workstations to utilize the PICK spooler to print DOSgenerated jobs. DOS users (particularly those without NetWare access) can utilize shared PICK printers without special printer-sharing hardware.

25.2.9 Using the DOS workstation under PicLan

The PicLan emulator is invoked on the DOS workstation using the command **PL-TERM** from within the PicLan directory. This will invoke a screen image with three options, **Session Transfer** and **Window** from which the **Session** option should be taken. The Session menu is used to open and close sessions on the network, for which up to eight at any one time can be open.

```
Session          Transfer          Window

Open
Connect
Close            Ctrl+F4

Execute DOS

Exit             Alt+F4

About
```

From this menu select the Open option which invokes a terminal emulation session and enables you to set the parameters for the session, such as the virtual screen size, emulation mode and keyboard set-up. In the main these will not need to be changed.

```
                    Open Session
  Cols                  Emulation
  [80          ]        ( ) VT-100
                        ( ) Regent
  Rows                  (X) PC Console
  [24          ]        Keys
     (X) Zoom           PC Console
                         REGENT
                         SB+
                         VT-100
  <OK>                  <CANCEL>
```

Having selected the emulation characteristics the next step is to select the server to connect to which can be handled either asynchronously (via RS232) or using PicLan (over the network).

```
                              Connect Session
                                  Server
                              AP/PRO
                              GA/R91                      Port No.
  Medium
  (X) Pic-LAN
  ( ) Async.        Device     Parity                     Flow Control
                               ( ) None                   ( ) None
                               ( ) Even                   ( ) XON/XOFF
                               ( ) Odd                    ( ) RTS/CTS
                               ( ) Mark                   ( ) DTR/DSR
  <OK>              Baud       ( ) Space

                               Data        Stop           [ ] Outbound
  <CANCEL>                     ( ) 7       ( ) 1
                               ( ) 8       ( ) 2          [ ] Pacing
```

From this point you should be connected to the server and be able to operate as a normal user.

25.2.10 Remote printing from PicLan

All PicLan remote printing functions are implemented within the PicLan SERVER-PROCESS which runs as a background task and every 30 seconds looks to see whether or not there is a print job in the PICK spooler. If so it determines on which printer it is to be printed, transfers the printing to that printer and deletes the job from the PICK spooler.

If you require the job to be printed immediately run the command **pl-kick-server** which forces the SERVER-PROCESS to examine the spooler immediately and deal with any print jobs it finds. Thereafter it resumes its 30 second review cycle.

The SERVER-PROCESS is automatically started during the coldstart procedure and stopped during the shutdown process. However, should you need to carry out these tasks manually use the commands:

pl-start-server
pl-stop-server

The command **pl-stop-server** should always be used where you are unable to carry out the standard PICK shutdown procedure and you are trying to shut the system down in an orderly fashion before carrying out a system reset or reboot.

To see how the SERVER-PROCESS works, its operation can be monitored with **monitor-server** command as shown in Figure 25.2.

If you are going to use the PicLan remote printing options you must ***not*** have PICK servicing the print queues and hence you should ***not*** use the **startptr** command. If you want to set up PicLan to control a PICK printer use the **pl-assign** command, which is effectively a replacement for the PICK **startptr** command. The general format of the **pl-assign** command together with examples is given in Figure 25.3.

```
PicLan SERVER-PROCESS Monitor

Press X to eXit
      L to toggle Log flag (currently OFF)
      V to toggle Verbose flag (currently ON)


13:46:01 EVENT: 602,,CHECK SPOOLER,.
13:46:02 EVENT: 597,38,OUTBOUND PRINT JOB,1.90421.BAC.APT_LON/PLAIN:0.1..32.
         CL..
13:46:02 EVENT: 597,38,OUTBOUND PRINT JOB,1.90421.BAC.APT_LON/PLAIN:0.1..32.
         CL..
13:46:02 EVENT: 597,38,OUTBOUND PRINT JOB,1.90421.BAC.APT_LON/PLAIN:0.1..32.
         CL..
13:46:02 EVENT: 597,38,OUTBOUND PRINT JOB,1.90421.BAC.APT_LON/PLAIN:0.1..32.
         CL..
13:46:02 EVENT: 597,38,OUTBOUND PRINT JOB,1.90421.BAC.APT_LON/PLAIN:0.1..32.
         CL..
13:46:02 EVENT: 597,38,OUTBOUND PRINT JOB,1.90421.BAC.APT_LON/PLAIN:0.1..32.
         CL..
13:46:02 EVENT: 597,38,OUTBOUND PRINT JOB,1.90421.BAC.APT_LON/PLAIN:0.1..32.
         CL..
13:46:02 EVENT: 597,38,OUTBOUND PRINT JOB,1.90421.BAC.APT_LON/PLAIN:0.1..32.
         CL..
13:46:02 EVENT: 598,,DELETE TEMP PRINT FILE,O*24.
13:46:02 EVENT: 599,38,ACTIVITY,.
13:46:02 EVENT: 598,,DELETE TEMP PRINT FILE,O*24.
13:46:31 EVENT: 600,,CHECK SPOOLER,.
13:47:01 EVENT: 601,,CHECK SPOOLER,.
```

Figure 25.2 The **monitor-server** command.

pl-assign *queue=dsg.ref!printer.ref* (*options*

where

queue	is the PICK form queue number
dsg.ref	is the DOS Services Gateway name
printer.ref	is the destination printer identifier
options	**p** for print **s** to suppress the display of assignments

pl-assign 3=DB!LPT1: Assign PICK form queue 3 to the printer known as **LPT1** on the DOS Services Gateway known as **DB**

pl-assign 2=RB!APT_LON/JET:0 Assign form queue 2 to the printer which is served via the DOS services gateway known as **RB** and is on the Novell server and known by the identity **APT_LON/JET:0** where APT_LON is the Novell system reference, JET is the printer reference and 0 is the form queue number

Figure 25.3 The general format and use of **pl-assign.**

25.2.11 Using and administering PicLan from the PICK server

The primary PicLan account is called **pic-lan** and the software can be administered direct from this account. If you wish to use the PicLan commands from another account, take the 'Setup another account with the PicLan verbs' option on the main menu of the **pic-lan** account. Once the host is set up there is nothing to do unless something goes wrong. Then the first step is ensure the SERVER-PROCESS is running and to establish the current PicLan status via the **pl-stat** command. This displays the status of the network and an example of the output is given in Figure 25.4.

The first part of the display in Figure 25.4 identifies the servers which are accessible on the network, whilst the lower part of the display shows the PICK port number (Pib#) of the users connected to the network together and whether or not their network node is acting as a DOS Services Gateway. This report can be very useful in isolating network cabling and workstation problems and can also be of assistance during installation.

If you use **pl-stat** with the **r** option, i.e. **pl-stat (r** you will be presented with any driver error statistics that exist. If you see a count in the **transmit timeouts** field, this is an indication of a conflict of IRQs. Alternatively if there is a number in the **discarded packets** field and nothing in the **broadcasts received**

```
PicLan Network Servers                                    13:30:25 16 Nov 1995

 Name     TP    Version     PicLan SN    Net #         Node #         Imm. Node #

*APPRO    07    1.1.0.29    11000233     [A0A0A0A0]    [ E8CB4701]
 BAC      34    1.1.0.29                 [A0A0A0A0]    [ 20AF0FB65C]

PicLan Connection Status Display     SERVER = APPRO       13:30:25 16 Nov 1995

                           |------ connected to ------|------- activity -----
Ch# Pib# type         st er | type          name     p#  |  inbound      outbound
                           |                             |
 2    9   Term Host 01 00 | DOS Term      RB        0 |       72          7481
25   32   Term Host 01 00 | DOS Term      DW        0 |     2499        815553
45   39   XFR Node  01 00 | DOS Gateway DB            |        0             0
```

Figure 25.4 The **pl-stat** command.

field you might find that the PICK host is configured with an incorrect Ethernet frame type.

Next perform a **list-jobs** to see if the SERVER-PROCESS is active and you should see this as the tcl-command **run pl-bp server-process (e**. You can ensure this is active by checking the output from the **where** command. If all this looks alright, then the PICK host is working properly and you need to ensure the DOS client workstations and DOS Services Gateways are properly setup and defined. To do this you need to check the PL-CFG.INI files on the respective PCs and remember if a PC is acting as a DOS Services Gateway, it has to be switched on and running the PicLan software even if the person who normally uses it is absent. Do also remember the issue of the Fastini parameter as described in Section 25.2.5.

Next review the current print queues currently defined using the command

pl-assign

If it looks as though there is a problem with an existing print queue, it can be deleted with the command

pl-assign *n*=[CR]   (where *n* is the print queue number)

and then re-assigned using **pl-assign**. If things still do not seem to be operating properly, try stopping and starting the server using **pl-stop-server** and **pl-start-server** and if for whatever reason this has not resolved the problem it is time to reboot the machine.

If the PicLan connection becomes completely 'hung' use the command **pl-kill** which will prompt for the connection to be 'killed'. If the connection is a terminal session the session is disconnected but the port is not logged off giving the user an opportunity to reconnect to the PICK Host and continue processing from where they left off at the time of the hang. If a data transfer was in progress, the connection is closed.

Two other useful commands are **pl-logoff** and **pl-logon**. The **pl-logoff** verb is used to ensure that a specified port is logged off if the connection is broken between the user's workstation and the PICK host. The verb has several formats based on whether or not you wish this feature to apply to all ports, nominated ports or all ports with nominated exceptions. Examples of the verb, which can either be run at TCL or included in the coldstart macro, are as follows:

pl-logoff all
pl-logoff none
pl-logoff include 2,3,6,7
pl-logoff exclude 3,4,5

The **pl-logon** verb is used to automatically log on specific users to specific accounts. The format of the command is as follows:

pl-logon user=*user.name,user.password,md,md.password*
where

user.name	is the user-id as held in the **users** file
user.password	is the user password (if applicable)
md	the name of the account to log to
md.password	the name of the account password (if applicable)

Both the **pl-logon** and **pl-logoff** verbs require the SERVER PROCESS to be running.

25.2.12 Data transfers using PicLan

There are a number of ways of transferring information with PicLan. The first and perhaps simplest way involves using the **Transfer** option on the main screen presented when **PL-TERM** is initiated:

```
Session          Transfer          Window
                 Receive File
                 Transmit file
```

The transfer option enables data to be transferred between PICK and DOS provided the PICK systems are running PicLan. The options are:

PICK to DOS	–	Receive file option
DOS to PICK	–	Transmit file option.

Each of these options present a dialogue screen requesting details of the location of the source data and the location to which the data is to be transferred. The download process which uses the SERVER-PROCESS occurs independently of any open session and does not require the initiator to be logged on to the PICK host or use a PICK port.

An alternative method is use the DOS based command **pl-copy.exe**. This command can be invoked completely independently of PL-TERM and has the advantage over other terminal emulators that data is transferred over the network at network speeds as opposed to transferring data over serial cables, which is considerably slower.

On the PICK Host system you can import data from DOS or export data to DOS with the commands:

pldos-import
pldos-export

where data is moved between PICK items and DOS files. If you want to move data between two PICK systems, use the **pl-copy** command, but do be aware it does not work for BASIC object code or other list items. The use of these commands is well documented in the PicLan manual.

The final means of data transfer is to write BASIC programs. In line with other terminal emulators, PicLan provides the developer with a number of BASIC subroutines which can be called in order to access network functions and handle data transfers.

26 PICK in the Commercial World

26.1 The problems besetting the businessman

Historically the data processing (DP) function has been a centralized operation with DP specialists charged with the corporate responsibility of developing and installing management information and control systems. As well as this, DP departments have been responsible for the operation of the computer, including all aspects of its security and integrity.

Once in place, these systems have tended to need additional work, either by changing its functionality to cater for misunderstandings in design, or to incorporate additional facilities or to satisfy the need for *ad hoc* management information. In this respect it is not uncommon for centralized DP departments to be months, if not years, behind in fulfilling user requirements.

The advent of a vast range of low-cost powerful multi-user computers is bringing computing to the fingertips of the mass market and distributing computing power throughout companies. Whilst these systems are also purchased by central DP departments, they are mainly finding their way onto the desks of the users. Users are now much more 'computer-literate' than ever before and are able to build their own financial models and use enquiry languages to produce their own *ad hoc* reports. They buy computers for the very reasons they were bought in the past :

- better control of their business
- simplified administration
- elimination of errors
- reduction in paperwork
- receipt of better and more timely information
- better decision making resulting from all the above

Experience in practice demonstrates reasonable levels of attainment in all these areas, so you could be forgiven in thinking that these installations have been a success. However in a large number of cases this success is coupled with a feeling of being let down and by frustration with the limitations and restrictions that have been found. Contrary to general belief this is not primarily associated with the quality of the application software, but in much more common-sense areas frequently overlooked.

The businessman expects that it should be easy to put information into his system. He expects the system to recognize and cope with his information that varies in size, in shape and in form. He becomes a little unhappy when he realizes that to make real progress with his system he has to understand new terms such as files, fields, records and so on.

The user expects that the system will take care of everything within itself and he expects to be able to develop his system at his own pace. He still views it as the cure to all his problems – a miraculous tool. He becomes disappointed when he realizes he must understand the aspects and importance of file structure, file maintenance and file security. He gets very upset when he discovers that he should have got everything worked out at the beginning and not as he goes along, which is the way he expected to implement his systems. In some cases he may find it bordering the impossible to develop his system the way he wanted because of something not considered at the beginning.

He also finds it strange that the computer that he purchased as his business system doesn't understand the peculiarities of his business, a business that has its own terminology, its own peculiarities and its own idiosyncrasies. The computer requires that his business conforms to its design and to its need to call each piece of information by just one name.

He further believes that if he has put the information in once, then it really should be there for all other purposes. In many systems, however, he soon discovers that he is putting in the same information more than once. It gradually begins to dawn on him that files have a discreet nature; that the operating system is not the same, and has nothing to do with, a database management system, and that neither of these have anything to do with report generation.

It's with output when for him everything starts to go wrong. The whole essence of the computer system was to get vital control information from which he was hopefully going to run his business more efficiently. Having made extreme efforts to get his information in, he now realizes that if he didn't define a report in the first place, which he's suddenly realized he should already have thought of, he may be involved in new programs, additional cost and undoubtedly delay. Further if the information he requires is contained in two separate files, the costs and delays he incurs could escalate dramatically.

All this indicates is that the businessman requires and should be given control of the computer systems necessary to manage his business, for them to be implemented at his pace and in his way.

26.2 The problems besetting the computing industry

The computing industry has seen tremendous change over the last thirty years such that today's pocket calculator is more powerful than the world's largest computer of 1954. With the development of hardware, which has become smaller, more powerful and cheaper, has culminated changes in software, from machine-specific operating systems and machine-specific programming languages to standards being established for both. The industry has seen a move from specialized, tailored software towards packages, database management systems and program and application generators. The intention being that software and its development should be brought to those people who use it and who know what they want. For those reasons software development tools have to be more powerful and easy to use.

It is hardly surprising to find that four major problems have beset the computing industry and are still there today:

- meeting project deadlines
- recruiting
- predicting future technology
- maintaining existing programs

The computing industry has to cater for the needs of the businessman. As we have discussed, the businessman is becoming far more 'computer aware' and as such expects far more from his system. The software, if developed centrally, has to be developed or tailored to suit his needs, modified simply and quickly to meet the changing needs of his business and be sufficiently flexible to grow as his business grows. It also needs to be able to work in a way that requires the minimum of development effort, support and maintenance resources.

All this indicates the wider use and acceptance of software development tools, the so-called application generators, 4th generation languages (4GL products), generally associated with powerful database management systems.

26.3 What PICK and 4GL products provide

It is apparent that the PICK open database and operating system complied with fourth generation application generators like SB+ satisfy the needs of both the businessman and the computing industry. PICK uniquely puts control in the hands of the businessman. It eliminates all the limitations, all the restrictions, all the difficulties mentioned earlier. It makes it easy for the businessman to relate to it, because it relates to his business. It takes account of the peculiarities of his business and he can progress on a step-by-step basis.

It accepts and stores information in its natural form. It understands the end of one thing and the beginning of the next, by something similar to punctuation marks, and we are all accustomed to those. There is no inherent restriction on the size, shape or form of information; it is always there in its natural, readable form. There is no conversion to, or from, a whole series of terminology like binary, binary coded decimal, hexadecimal, packed decimal and so on. The individual pieces of information are referred to by names, within the computer itself, that have actually been defined by him and the people who work for and around him. The sales department can refer to 'models' whilst the production department can refer to 'products' and the service department can refer to 'parts'. In each case the element of information is stored once and referred to by each of these names.

In its natural form data varies in length. Addresses, for example, can be long or short, each line of which is normally a different length. The PICK system readily copes with these, and allows them to be added, deleted or changed at will. PICK allows data to expand and contract in line with business demands.

The PICK system breaks away from convention in a way which is important to both the businessman and the computing industry. The businessman is not only interested in standard software systems – the accounting, stock, order processing systems. He frequently only needs to control information which has to be kept up-to-date and from which management information can be retrieved and reported. This needs to be done, simply and easily. The new generation of software products, fourth generation application generators like SB+, enable the businessman, without previous DP experience to create and maintain these files and to produce the required reports, simply and easily and without the need for costly experienced DP resources.

26.4 PICK the right approach?

Hopefully by now, you too will be convinced that PICK is the right approach for the commercial world, whether it be for the Data Processing department or the businessman himself. Its friendly, flexible approach makes it a winner to all who come in contact with it. To summarize its benefits, therefore, I would say that PICK:

- OFFERS HARDWARE INDEPENDENCE
  There are now over 20 manufacturers offering PICK on their systems, from the single terminal PC, to several thousand terminals linked to mainframes. This provides the user security and protects his software and technical investment in the event he decides to change his hardware.
- OFFERS EFFICIENT SYSTEM USAGE
  The PICK system has generally been optimized to the hardware on which it runs. In addition it offers virtual memory management and stores data in variable length, using a powerful database manager. This efficient use of variable length data alone offers savings in the size of disk that may be required. The overall environment is one that enables bigger applications with many more terminals to be run on smaller, less powerful and hence less expensive equipment.
- OFFERS UPWARD COMPATIBILITY
  PICK applications are portable to the extent that should you need to upgrade your system, or even have to buy a system from a different supplier, you will always be able to find a system to run your software without having a major conversion exercise to undertake.
- USES THE TERMS OF THE BUSINESS
  PICK's powerful dictionary driven system enables the terms of the business to be adopted. New terminology can be added at will. No longer need the businessman conform to the terms of the system. It can talk to him in terms he understands.

- ACCOMMODATES VARIATION IN DATA
  PICK not only facilitates data entry, by taking in and storing data in its raw form, but it is designed to accommodate variations in form, shape and length of information. It recognizes that some addresses have more lines than others and that some of these lines are longer than others. It does not force information to be entered in a fixed space, with the inherent wasted space and inefficient data handling that fixed length data handling implies.

- ENABLES SPEEDIER DEVELOPMENT AND EASIER MAINTENANCE
  PICK provides a complete environment to allow systems to be developed and maintained, simply and easily. The increased use of 4GL tools encourage this environment even further. This helps remove the substantial maintenance headaches that have beleaguered the computing industry.

- ENABLES SYSTEMS TO BE DEVELOPED AT THE BUSINESSMAN'S PACE
  Since all data is held in a common format, integration of applications is far simpler. Additionally the data dictionary concept enables new data elements to be readily defined and existing ones amended. All of this, coupled with an easy-to-use enquiry language for regular or *ad hoc* reports, provides an environment in which the businessman can build his systems in way he wants and at the pace he is able to cope with.

- PROVIDES A COMPREHENSIVE REPORTING SYSTEM
  The most important part of any system is its output. Having put the information in, it is essential to get management information out. PICK's ACCESS report utility is one of its' most powerful and beneficial features. It provides an easy-to-use enquiry system allowing regular and ad hoc reports to be produced using an English-like enquiry language. By use of such vocabulary, users with little training can soon produce their own enquiries and reports.

IN SHORT, PICK PRODUCES CONTROL BY PROVIDING CONTROL.

All these issues prove adequately and without doubt, the value and significance of the PICK system to the businessman, the computing industry and the commercial world. There is no doubt in my mind that PICK is the right approach.

26.5 The future of PICK

Pick Systems have been highly successful in the positioning of Advanced PICK as a leading database. For many it continues to serve as a comprehensive, yet easy to use operating system, but its future surely lies as a powerful database management system capable of residing on all the leading operating systems and hardware platforms.

As you would expect, Pick Systems is continuing to improve its product. They have addressed issues such as SQL, ODBC and GUIs (graphical user interfaces) and are looking to broaden the open systems nature of the product by being able to work alongside other mainstream databases.

The launch of Advanced PICK was a major step forward which incorporated new communication facilities, the integration with network protocols. By virtue of its integration with both DOS and UNIX, a vast range of industry standard applications, such as word processors and spreadsheets, can now be used with PICK.

The future of PICK is in my view assured. It will continue to grow from strength to strength gaining wider acceptance and use as it becomes available on a wider range of computers. It has set a standard which others can only hope to follow. At long last we have a system that recognizes what the data processing industry is all about, that of processing data and processing it in a way that we, mere mortals, can readily understand and control.

Appendix A – The Messages File

This appendix lists the error messages from the file **messages** (**ERRMSG** in PICK R83). It is helpful to see the sort of problems and status messages reported by PICK. Since these can vary implementation by implementation, you can view the ones on your system with the command:

ct messages *nnnn* (where *nnnn* is the message number)

System messages

0	atp error *
2	Uneven number of delimiters (‘ “ \)
3	The verb’
4	Syntax error
5	The word *xxxx* is illegal
6	Six**
7	A value must follow the heading, footing, tag or grand-total connective
8	A window specification string must follow the ‘window’ connective
9	System dl/id missing
10	The file name is missing
11	The frame is locked at location x’
12	Input conversion ‘N’ must be replaced by ‘V0’, and ‘SV’ replaced by ‘V1’
13	The data level descriptor (file-name in dictionary) is missing
14	Unable to open a bridge file
15	The file-name is preceded by an illegal connective
17	‘WITHIN’ is valid only in count/list/sum or stat statements
18	The last word may not be a connective
19	A value without an attribute name is illegal
20	Error in the ‘using’ syntax
21	The item-id is meaningless in the statement
22	A ‘to’ before an item-id is valid only in a change statement
23	The word *xxxx* cannot be found in the attribute list
24	The word *xxxx* cannot be identified
25	The connective ‘with’ may not immediately precede a value
26	Attribute values may not both precede and follow an attribute name
27	‘Sampling’ must be followed by a positive number
28	Tape attached to line *n*
29	At least one item-id must be specified for a ‘within’- type statement
30	The verb definition is bad
31	Transaction logger must be stopped
32	Tape attached block size:*nnnn*
33	Exceeded the maximum number of 32767 file opens
34	Corrupted file# in file control block, need to do full save
35	Option conflict in ‘save’ with regards to clearing dirty bits
36	File Q-pointer must point to another file or file Q-pointer

37 File definition item'
38 *xxxx* must be a Q-pointer item to an account
39 Used Q-pointer to access system dictionary is illegal
40 *xxxx* is an illegal Q-pointer type within the dict of a file
41 File definition item *xxxx* cannot be used for get-list or qselect
42 File definition item *xxxx* cannot be deleted
48 Data area not on file
50 Columns attribute must follow the 'ss' connective
51 Two comparable values must follow the 'ss' connective
52 Attribute for selected total must follow the 'ss' connective
53 Item list required for 'WITHIN' connective
54 Incorrect item specification
55 This is an invalid use of the ss connective
56 No logical connectives allowed with 'ss' connective
57 Invalid comparable values with 'ss' connective
58 The maximum number of 'ss' clauses is 8
59 Block size:*nnnn*
60 DX or DY files cannot be transaction logged
62 Source and destination files must be at same file leve l
67 System error detected while processing item
68 Dependent attribute has more values than its controlling attribute
69 Bad group
70 Too many values in dependent attribute
71 An illegal connective modifies the word *xxxx*
72 The value *xxxx* is meaningless
73 Invalid 'id' conversion specified, use the default date and sequence id's instead
74 Cross-reference pointers are still present, unable to delete item
75 No duplicate found for cross-reference items, unable to delete item
76 Illegal format in bridge correlative
77 Columnar fields exceed terminal width
78 An i-input conversion has failed compilation
79 The number of separate 'AND' clause sets cannot exceed 9
80 A system error has occurred in mode:5
81 Syntax: {MDS,}account-name or {SYSTEM,}account-name expected
82 Your system privilege level is not sufficient for this statement
83 All defined attributes are 'display-only'; unable to edit item
85 File *xxxx* does not exist
91 End tape check – files(s)
92 End of recorded data – file(s)
93 Attach the tape unit!
94 End of file
95 Tape attached to line *nn*
96 Bot
97 End of tape

98 Parity error
99 Block transfer has not completed
101 Duplicate definitions for attribute:
102 Controlling attribute must be defined before its dependent attributes
103 Error in controlling-dependent specification
104 Illegal specification of attribute 0 used without i-option
105 Invalid attribute name *xxx* used in heading option
106 Attribute name *xxxx* is not a valid attribute definition item
107 File *xxxx* is update protected
108 Data file is update protected, dictionary not deleted
109 Bad PCB fid detected for port
110 Overflow runaway limit set to *nnnn* frames
111 Item *xxxx* is not on file
112 User exit *xxxx* is not valid
113 The item *xxxx* is not in the file-of-files
114 Overflow runaway limit cannot be negative
115 Overflow runaway limit set too low
120 Negative balance is not permitted
130 Line *n* has en illegal EQUATE statement
158 An illegal connective of the form *xxxx* modifies *yyyy*
160 File *xxxx* in the process of being deleted
161 An a-correlative must be specified after file-name
162 Error in icode conversion: *xxxx* index not found
163 An a-, f-, or t-correlative has failed compilation
164 A-code operand *xxxx* cannot be used to define index
165 Illegal bridge-correlative: *xxxx*
166 The a-correlative attribute name *xxxx* is illegal
167 Missing terminal quote ("/") in a-correlative: *xxxx*
168 Illegal A-correlative.: *xxxx*
169 Missing left parethensis in A-correlative: *xxxx*
170 Missing right parenthesis in A-correlative: *xxxx*
171 Index already exists
172 Index not found
173 Missing semi-colon in A-correlative
174 Index deleted
175 Index corrupted; must regenerate it
176 Index verifies
177 Total of *nnnn* frames counted
178 No index defined in file defining item
179 Index *xxx* in file *xxxx* has invalid version
180 Error in sub-index code: *xxxx*
181 Exceeded the maximum 7 levels of the N conversion
182 An attribute specification must follow the 'total' connective
183 Illegal o-correlative: *xxxx*
190 *xxxx* is a function not accessible from TCL

191 *xxxx* object revision is incompatible with system revision – please recompile
192 *xxxx* is a subroutine, not accessible from TCL
193 *xxxx* is a BASIC object pointer and cannot be copied
194 Cannot copy to the same item in the same file
195 *xxxx* is not a list
196 *xxxx* is too large to be an item
197 There is a problem with the statement: *xxxx*
198 The list pointed to by pointer item *xxxx* is defective
199 Insufficient work space for item *xxxx*
200 File name?
201 *xxxx* is not a file name
202 *xxxx* not on file
203 Item name?
204 File definition *xxxx* is missing
205 There are no statements to be assembled
206 *xxxx* assembled
207 Undefined symbols
208 Error in item-id list
209 Columns must be in the range 1–80
210 File *xxxx* is access protected
211 Mode *xxxx* no assembled code can be found
212 Mode *xxxx* has no frame statement
213 Mode *xxxx* location counter error at line no *nnn*
214 Mode *xxxx* overflows frame at line *nnnn*
215 Mode *xxxx* hex error at line no *nnnn*
216 Mode *xxxx* loaded; frame = *nnnn* size = *nnnn* cksum = *nnnn*
217 Mode *xxxx* verified; frame = *nnnn* size = *nnnn* cksum = *nnnn*
218 Mode *xxxx* frame = *nnnn* has *nn* mismatches
219 Illegal command:
220 *xxxx* exited
221 *xxxx* filed
222 *xxxx* deleted
223 *xxxx* exists on file
224 Checksum mismatch; absload aborted
225 *xxxx* exited
226 Tape format error
227 Frame #*nnn* – verified
228 Frame #*nnn* – *nnn* mismatches
229 *xxxx* is not a valid md name
230 *xxxx* references Q-pointers which reference each other
231 Endless loop encountered updating ACCESS(3)
232 Card reader ebcdic error
233 Card reader hopper empty
235 Attempt to write into update protected file

238 No selection criteria allowed with ‘nselect’ with an active list
239 List *xxxx* in file *xxxx* saved
240 A ‘select’ or ‘sselect’ must be used preceding a ‘save-list’ statement
241 Successful compile
242 *xxxx* decatalogued
243 List saved – *nnnn* frames used
244 *xxxx* catalogued
245 *xxxx* deleted
246 List *xxxx* decatalogued
247 *xxxx* is a basic object pointer and cannot be edited
248 Flash cannot be run with the (i option
250 *xxxx* failed
251 Done
253 *xxxx* recovered
254 No item to be recovered
260 Invalid batch lock command
265 Proc stack overflow
267 Proc transfer to *xxxx* cannot be completed
268 The destination of the proc ‘go’ statement
269 Input buffer overflow!
270 Format error in the proc statement
271 Item is not a PROC
272 A value exists for the attribute referenced by the element
273 Error in column-number/field-width or format specification at
281 d1 must have y11 storage correlative ... error at : *nnnn*
282 Invalid parameter for select list
289 *(the errmsg item that displays the output to the TCL verb TERM)*r
290 The range of the parameter *xxxx* is not acceptable
291 *xxxx* file-definition is missing
293 *(the errmsg item that displays the output to the TCL verb OVF)*
298 Format error in specifications
299 Invalidly specified structure code
300 *xxxx* verifies
301 *xxxx* has *nnnn* mismatches
302 *xxxx* linked
303 *xxxx* loaded
304 *xxxx* linked & verifies
305 *xxxx* linked & has *nnnn* mismatches
306 *xxxx* linked & loaded
307 Missing or invalid abs item ‘%abs%’
308 Monitor link format error
309 Cannot execute an ABS of different implementation type
310 ABS does not verify *nnnn* frame(s) corrupted: Reload of ABS strongly recommended
311 ABS frame record(s) missing; loading not recommended

312 Verifying ABS from file *xxxx*
313 No ABS area exists for ABS file *xxxx*
314 *xxxx* corrupted; Expected *xxxx* actual *xxxx*
315 Frame record *nnnn* missing
316 Numeric parameter is missing
317 *nnnn* frame(s) corrupted
318 ABS file *xxxx* verifies
319 Destination ABS are incompatible with current ABS – EXEC aborted!
331 The account file is missing
332 The file-of-files is missing
333 The file of files cannot be cleared or deleted
335 *(the PICK logon banner)*
336 < logged off at
337 User is not logged on
338 Account file statistics were not updated due to either
1. insufficient work-space to contain the account file item, or
2. system dictionary changed while you were logged on
340 *(system accounting statistics message when logging off an account)*
341 System verifies
342 *** System does not verify! ***
367 Illegal if-correlative.: *xxxx*
390 *xxxx* loaded
391 *xxxx* verified
398 The file or dl/id requires a v(ertical) correlative for this statement
399 The maximum of 20 levels for a 'within'-type statement has been exceeded
401 No items present
402 'dict' cannot be specified in this statement
403 End of list
404 *nnnn* items selected out of *nnnn* items
405 *nnnn* items listed out of *nnnn* items
406 (*ISTAT statistics message*)
407 *nnnn* items counted out of *nnnn* items
408 One item counted
409 *xxxx* is not on file
410 A synonym (q-type) file cannot be specified in this statement
411 'dict' or 'data' must be specified in a clear-file statement
412 Insufficient contiguous disk space available for the file
413 The file name already exists in the master dictionary
414 Illegal or missing modifier used in defining the file area(s)
415 *xxxx* exists on file
416 Range error in modulo parameter
417 File *xxxx* created; base = *nnnn* modulo = *nnnn*
418 File definition item *xxxx* cannot be copied or overlayed
419 The specified file cannot be renamed, cleared or deleted!

420 Dictionary file deletion cannot be done without deletion of data-section(s) first
421 Statistics of *xxxx* total = *nnnn* average = *nnnn* count = *nnnn*
422 Byte statistics for :*xxxx* total/average/maximum/minimum
423 Total of *xxxx* = *nnnn*
424 Frame id: *nnnn* device address *nnnn* unit number..*nnnn* cylinder...*nnnn* head..*nnnn* sector...*nnnn*
425 Invalid frame-id request
426 Data file already exists!
427 There is no data section for this file
428 *xxxx* object pointer not found
429 *xxxx* program object verifies
430 *xxxx* program object does not verify
431 Unable to copy out of a pointer file!
432 *xxxx* item-name used in program-file dictionary, compile aborted
433 *xxxx* is a file definition item and should not be edited
434 *xxxx* is a file pointer and cannot be edited
435 Item *xxxx* deleted
436 *xxxx* command not allowed at current level
437 *xxxx* – a file pointer cannot be T-DUMPed or overlaid by T-LOAD
438 Job #*nnnn* submitted
439 Must specify line number as part of option parameters!
440 Error! Attempting to monitor initiating process
441 The line to be monitored is uninitialized
442 Last TCL stack entry is not available for macro
443 You must give a non-null name for your macro
444 *xxxx* is a binary item and should not be edited
445 Unable to load ABS to BOOT-ABS; BOOT-ABS base is invalid or ABS overflows BOOT-ABS area
446 BOOT-ABS area overlays PCB0
447 Boot-ABS base: *nnnn* Size: *nnnn* Frames added: *nnnn*
448 The object size of program *xxxx* exceeds the maximum 64K. Compile aborted
449 Binary object code cannot be displayed
450 Frame locked at: *nnnn* (hex)
451 *nnnn* is an invalid frame
452 Verb options are incompatible
453 Macro lookup has encountered recursive loop condition. Macro aborted!
454 Item *xxxx* unlocked
455 Group *xxxx* released
456 Cannot convert non-hex data
457 Division by zero illegal
458 Need fid number with Z-option
459 Illegal hotkey conversion in TCL-STACK d-pointer

460 Illegal or missing account name
461 Master dictionary files cannot be specified in this statement
462 Tape type is set to Cipher with slow T-FWD capability
463 Tape type is set to Kennedy with fast T-FWD capability
464 Tape format is set to Microdata with 50-byte label size
465 Tape format is set to standard Pick with 80-byte label size
466 One of the following options must be used:

- (M) for Microdata format: label size = 50 bytes
- (P) for standard PICK format: label size = 80 bytes
- (C) for Cipher-type T-FWD. This is slow but will not have problems when T- FWDing across reels
- (K) for Kennedy-type T-FWD. This is used if you have a Cipher tape drive and want to simulate the Kennedy fast forward

467 Group *xxxx* is not locked
497 Illegal use of 'WITHIN' clause
498 Destination ABS size specified is too small
499 Source file is not a valid ABS file
500 System configuration indicates invalid number of PIBS
501 The 'jobs' file for phantom processing is missing
502 Need to start transaction logger
503 Unable to deal with the binary item *xxxx*
505 Insufficient input data to continue process
507 Scheduler started
508 Unable to start scheduler
509 The scheduler needs to be started
510 Scheduler disabled
520 BLOCK-PRINT needs an argument
521 There are too many characters in word to block
522 BLOCK-CONVERT file is missing or improperly defined
523 Block output exceeds page width
524 The letter *x* is missing from the BLOCK-CONVERT file
525 Input character *x* is improperly formatted in BLOCK-CONVERT file
529 Already logged off, but process did not respond
530 The line is already logged on
531 Logoff successful, but process did not respond
532 Unsuccessful logon
533 LOGON successful
534 logoff successful
535 Line specified is unavailable – try another
536 Already logged off
537 Process disabled
538 The first parameter must be numeric, specifying a valid line number
539 Invalid line number
540 The user specified does not match the user of the target line
541 The target line failed to respond appropriately

542 Invalid input parameter list
543 Sorry. You can't logoff/logon your own line
544 The target line is roadblocked
545 The number separators are setup
546 Process in the debugger
547 Cannot TCL to your own line
548 Line *n* is a memory mapped device and process information is unavailable
549 Process has corrupted workspace
550 A required numeric parameter is missing or invalid
551 Specify number of lines to skip
552 Item *xxxx* has invalid format
560 No available print queue elements
598 Footer/Legend/Header too big for page size-Abort
599 OP font queue overflow abort!
600 OP item stack overflow abort!
601 Unable to detach transaction logger from tape
602 The transaction logger is disabled
603 Unable to disable transaction logger
604 Transaction logger already disabled
605 The transaction logger is active
606 Backup media needs to be specified for transaction logger
607 Transaction logger started
608 Unable to start transaction logger
609 Transaction logger not started
610 The transaction logger is inactive
611 Unable to disable transaction logger
612 Transaction logger not attached to tape
613 Transaction log error: unsuccessful device assignment
614 Transaction Logger Queue released to overflow
615 Transaction logger waiting for next reel
616 Transaction log tape not ready
617 Transaction log error: tape unit not ready
618 Transaction log error: unrecoverable parity error
619 Transaction log error: block transfer error
620 Transaction logger has been killed
630 stop' in effect. Use 'resume'
631 Spooler is waiting for printer cable to be attached
632 Spooler is waiting because the printer is off-line
633 Spooler is waiting for the tape to be detached
634 Spooler is waiting for the printer to be detached
635 Spooler is waiting because the the tape is off-line
636 There was a parity error on writing a spooled file
637 The spooler needs the next reel of tape to continue
638 The spooler is writing a file on tape
640 The spooler is printing a file on the printer

641 Hold file £*nn* added
644 An open file for line #*n* is being processed
645 A closed file for line #*n* is being processed
646 The current job has been aborted
651 Spooler is not active
652 Too many pages
653 No file is being output, or file originated
654 Illegal output string length!
655 Not attached
656 End of spool queue
657 Not a hold file
658 Illegal number! Use sp-status
659 Line printer ready
660 Insufficient privileges; or device is attached to a spooler
700 Run-time f-correlative abort
701 Invalid F-correlative definition
702 No index generated for attribute *xxxx*
703 Invalid C-conversion/correlative definition
704 E Function correlative stack error: *xxxx*
705 Illegal conversion code : *xxxx*
706 The translate subcode *xxxx* is illegal
708 *xxxx* cannot be converted
720 Too many items with same key, must rebuild index with a different key
779 Item *xxxx* was not locked
780 Item *xxxx* not on file
781 *xxxx* added
782 *xxxx* updated
783 *xxxx* deleted
784 File *xxxx* deleted
790 Number of licensed users
791 Already in single user mode
792 Already in multi-user mode
802 *nnnn* items dumped
803 *nnnn* item(s) loaded
804 *nnnn* item(s) read
805 *nnnn* item(s) copied
806 *nnnn* item(s) updated
808 System Priorities *nn* Interactive priority *nn* Batch priority *nn* Super-hi process *xxx* Timeslice MS, *nnn*
809 *nnnn* item(s) deleted
820 Creating Flash BASIC Object (Level *nn*) ...
821 Flash BASIC compilation Error; Phase nn, Code xx
822 Retrying Flash BASIC compilation at Level *nnnn*
823 Failed to create Flash device *xxxx*
824 Waiting for availability of Flash BASIC compiler

861 *** end of instruction diagnostic *** no errors detected ***
862 *** end of instruction diagnostic *** instruction errors have been detected ***
863 *xxxx* required for error logging is missing
876 Flash object of program *xxxx* was created on a different machine – please recompile
877 Flash object revision of program *xxxx* is incompatible with system revision – please recompile
878 Insufficient space to load Flash version of *xxxx*. Please run without optimization
879 Insufficient space to run Flash version of *xxxx*. Please run without Flash
880 Missing TOC for program *xxxx* – please recompile
881 Undefined external in program *xxxx*. Please recompile
950 Linkfield error – group at *nnnn* – frame *nnnn* links *xxxx*
951 Illegal forward link. Group at *nnnn* frame *nnnn* links *xxxx*
952 Illegal backward link. Group at *nnnn* frame *nnnn* links xxxx
953 Should link back to: group at *nnnn* frame *nnnn* links xxxx
954 New error items created in DICT TSYM
990 Error in abs-dump frame limits specifications
991 *xxxx* exists on file
992 *xxxx* items have been restored
993 Account name must be specified
994 Account not found
995 N option must be used to specify file number
996 *(abs analysis)*
997 Waiting owner fcb group
998 Ln PCB PIB ABS Stat R1 & Return stack contents
999 Memory pibs pcb0
1000 Abs file must have dict and data level. Cannot be dict level only
1001 Abs size specification required. Format: CREATE-ABS filename (size)
1002 Item %ABS% is not on file in source abs file
1003 Destination %ABS% item points to boot-abs
1004 *xxxx* is not on file
1005 Abs file creation successfully completed
1006 Destination file abs-size is too small. It must be at least the size of the source file abs-size
1007 Data terminal ready is high
1008 Data terminal ready is low
1009 Unable to set DTR signal
1011 Error in the selection processor. Try to generate a reproducible case. Call your software support group
1020 Line number : *nnn* Baud rate: *nnnn* Parity:*nnn* Stop bits *nn* Word length: *nnnn*
1021 Unsuccessful; Error code=*xxxx*
1022 Illegal specification *xxxx*

1025 Printer *nn* Delay = *nnn* Burst = *nnn* Slice = *nnnn*
1026 Printer *nn* is busy
1027 Printer *nn* is in an error mode
1028 *nnnn* characters poked
1029 Missing 'text' from the command line
1050 This is an obsolete BASIC verb (RUN or CATALOG). Please obtain the current verb
1051 This is a program catalogued under pre-R80 protocols. Please recatalogue the program
1070 A DMA channel number is required for this verb
1071 Legal DMA channel numbers are 1,2,3,5,6 and 7
1072 Settings: DMA channel *nn* port address *nnnn*
1073 The port address has been reassigned
1074 Illegal port address
1075 Failed to change settings
1076 Settings: Timeout *nnnn* seconds
1078 All write-required buffers have been flushed to disk
1079 Illegal tape command for current tape type
1080 Tape device code is illegal
1081 Tape device is assigned to half inch tape
1082 Tape device is assigned to quarter inch Streaming Cartridge Tape (SCT)
1083 Tape device is assigned to low density (320K) floppy
1084 Tape device is assigned to std. density (360K) floppy
1085 Tape device is assigned to high density (1.2M) floppy
1087 Tape device is assigned to 3 1/2" std. density (720K) floppy
1088 Tape device is assigned to 3 1/2" high density (1.44MB) floppy using drive *nn*
1089 Tape device is assigned to 3 1/2" extra density (2.88MB) floppy using drive *nn*
1090 Assignment successful
1091 Invalid floppy driver parameter
1092 Invalid floppy media type parameter
1093 Requested floppy drive is not installed
1094 Requested floppy drive not supported by PICK
1095 Cannot set high density media in standard density drive
1096 Streaming Cartridge controller is not installed
1097 Cypher Tape controller is not installed
1098 Streaming Cartridge tape is being used by host operating system. Delete device in host operating system
1099 Hold entry #*nnnn*
1100 Start code locked
1101 Null printer number
1102 Printer number too big
1103 Illegal print files
1104 Illegal character

1105 Printer must be stopped
1106 Form number too big – exceeds 125
1107 Too many pages in the page skip – exceeds 9
1108 Negative number
1109 No form number
1110 Illegal printer type – not P or S
1111 Illegal line number or parallel printer number
1112 Illegal parallel printer number
1113 Illegal serial printer number
1114 The device or line which you specified is being used as another printer on the system
1115 Allocation attempted on uninitialized printer
1116 There is no job enqueued for output on the forms you specified. Therefore alignment is impossible
1117 Your align was just aborted by someone. You must start the align process over
1118 Printer *nn* control block initialized
1119 You are attempting to start printer *nn* on line *nn* which is not stopped
1120 Printer £*nn* is started
1121 You are improperly logged on
1122 Your output specification is 'no output'. Reassign your line if you wish to output a holdfile
1123 Line #*nn* is already logged on
1124 Unable to start printer *nnn*
1126 Printer #*nnn* control block damaged. It has been cleared to null.
1127 Illegal printer number, must be 0–n
1129 *nnn* form q elements unlinked
1130 Job Stat Lnk Line Status Copies Form Frames Date Time User
1131 Job Stat Lnk Frms Cdsp CurFID BegFID Form Frames Date Time User
1132 *nnnn* Queue elements
1133 *nnnn* frames in use
1134 Type number output Queues Page Skip Dev or Line £ Status
1135 Spooler queue elements
1136 Spooler Form Queue £*nnn*
1137 The spooler is initialized
1138 The spooler jobs are cleared
1139 The spooler is started
1140 Your open files were closed
1141 Line£ Status Copies Form£ Device
1142 Printer *nnn* has been deleted, but it's process is already logged off
1143 Align terminated; printer stopped
1144 Tape unit did not respond
1145 Illegal specification number: *nnnn*
1146 No physical line/Not attached/Not initialized

1147 Not attached
1148 Tapeout terminated because of assign T or null assignment
1149 Fatal Spooler abort!
1150 There is something wrong with the syntax of your verb's options
1151 Entry # *nnnn*
1152 Verb issued on your own process/device is not allowed
1153 Process is not in Tandem/Converse/Mirror mode
1154 Process is already in Tandem mode
1155 Process is already in Converse mode
1156 Process is already in Mirror mode
1157 Process is currently busy or road-blocked
1158 The file dm,cap-file, is missing
1159 Process not currently linked to a device
1160 Your output specification is no output. Reassign your line if you wish to output a hold file
1161 End of requested print files
1162 End of print file control block
1166 Your choke limit is currently set to *nnnn* frames
1167 Parameter error. Must be numeric, range: 2–1000
1169 Illegal printer number. Must be between 0 and 7 inclusive
1170 Printer #*nnn* set to stop
1171 Printer £*nnnn* is stopped already
1172 Printer £*nnnn* is set to stop, but is active
1173 Printer £*nnnn* is set to stop already, but is active
1174 Is unallocated
1175 Parallel printer £*nnn* has been deleted
1176 Serial printer #*nnnn* has been deleted, and its process sent to logon
1177 Printer #*nnnn* is idle
1178 The job being output on printer #*nnnn* is not your print file
1179 Job aborted on printer #*nnnn*
1180 Print file #*nnnn* was not unlinked because it is being output
1181 Print file #*nnnn* was not unlinked because it is unused
1182 Print file #*nnnn* was not unlinked because it is not spooled
1183 Print file #*nnnn* was not created on the account onto which you are now logged
1184 Print file #*nnnn* was unlinked and is available as a hold file
1185 Printer £*nnnn* does not exist
1186 All print files reported
1187 Printer £*nnnn* control block damaged. It has been cleared to null
1188 Print file £*nnnn* was aborted and is available as a hold file
1189 Print file £*nnnn* was not unlinked because it is open
1191 The specified printer already exists on another line or port
1192 Cannot find file dm,pibs
1193 Process item not found in the dm,pibs file
1194 Cannot find file dm.devs

1195 Device item not found in the dm,devs, file
1196 Target device is not available
1197 Frame size out of range
1198 Target device is not previously attached
1199 Unable to close linked tty
1200 The spooler is inactive
1201 The spooler is active
1202 Needs to start printers
1203 Needs to log disk errors
1205 The spooler needs to be started
1206 Printer *nnnn* has not been started
1208 Neither a global nor a local PCTL spooler control file can be found. Check with your System Administrator
1209 The control block for printer #*nnnn* is in an ambiguous state. Delete the printer from the spooler system
1210 Printer #*nnnn* is *nnnn*
1211 Unallocated
1212 Serial
1213 Parallel
1214 , inactive+
1215 , active+
1216 , stopped+
1217 , and on line
1218 , and off line
1219 ** The printer cable is off **
1220 Printer *nnnn* – no controller is installed
1221 The printer is defined as parallel printer £*nnnn*
1222 The printer is running on line *nnnn*
1229 Print file being output is element *nnnn*
1230 Open file for line #*nnnn*
1231 Closed file for line #*nnnn*
1232 Generated on account *xxxx*
1233 , which is *nnnn* frames long
1234 And the output is choked
1235 .
1239 Erroneously, the printer has no output queues assigned to it
1240 Assigned output queues: *nnnn*
1241 , *nnnn*
1242 , *nnnn*
1243 The number of inter-job pages to eject is *nnnn*
1300 The speller is on
1301 The speller is off
1302 Legend output is active
1303 Legend output is supressed
1304 TCL header output is active

1305 TCL header output is supressed
1306 The time-date display is on
1307 The time-date display is off
1308 The tcl-stack is on
1309 The tcl-stack is off
1310 Data carrier detect is on
1311 Data carrier detect is off
1312 Type-ahead is on
1313 Type-ahead is off
1314 xon/xoff is enabled
1315 xon/xoff is disenabled
1316 The break-key will level push
1317 The break-key will go onto debug
1318 Case sensitive
1319 Case insensitive
1320 R83 output for WHO display specified
1321 PICK output for WHO display specified
1322 Break key enabled
1323 Break key disabled
1324 Update-logging is on
1325 Update-logging is off
1326 The overflow protection scheme is enabled and active
1327 The overflow protection scheme is disabled and inactive
1328 Data terminal ready is on
1329 Data terminal ready is off
1330 Cannot rebuild overflow because scrubber never completed
1331 BASIC compilation protection is on
1332 BASIC compilation protection is off
1333 Global update protection is on
1334 Global update protection is off
1350 Group locks PIB£ Lvl Type Filename
1351 Item locks PIB£ Lvl Hash Item-id Filename
1352 Group locks Owner Pib£ Lock Level Lock Type
1501 'D' type item expected
1502 Illegal file level for 'D' pointer
1503 Illegal file ID for 'D' pointer
1504 Illegal character count for 'D' pointer
1505 Character count too small for 'D' pointer
1506 Item ID too large for count field in 'D' pointer
1507 Item ID too small for count field in 'D' pointer
1510 'D' pointer missing 'D' in attribute one
1511 Non decimal base for 'D' pointer
1512 Non decimal modulo for 'D' pointer
1513 MDS 'D' pointer expected
1514 Bad MDS 'D' type item

1515 Illegal file level for MDS 'D' pointer
1516 Mismatching MDS 'D' pointer
1520 Non hexadecimal file ID
1521 Bad group found
1522 Item with bad count field found
1523 Count field too small for item
1524 Item ID too large for count field
1525 Non hexadeciaml binary code block count
1526 Attribute mark missing after item ID
1527 Count field missing
1530 Character count too large for item
1531 Premature end of file
1532 Tape label missing
1534 Tape verifies
1536 Tape does not verify, *nnnn* errors found
1537 Node(s) missing in index
1538 File Mark missing at end of save data
1539 Bad descriptor type found
1540 Too many Nodes in B-tree on tape
1541 Bad data in root node on tape
1542 Specific node missing from tape
1543 'D' pointers mismatch
1544 Incomplete node found on tape
1545 Bad data in node on tape
1546 Account not on disk
1547 DICT level not on disk
1548 Data level not on disk
1549 File on tape not on disk
1550 File on tape is an item in a file
1551 Code missing on tape
1552 Binary code missing inter-block delimiter
1553 Binary code missing final segment mark
1556 Items mismatch
1557 Item not on file
1558 Binary pointers mismatch
1559 Object code items mismatch
1560 *nnnn* index corruption(s) encountered
1561 Item in MDS file not on tape
1562 DICT file not on tape
1563 Data level not on tape
1564 Item not on tape
1565 Data level file is in the process of being deleted
1566 Dictionary is in the process of being deleted
1567 Account is in the process of being deleted
1581 D pointer cannot be overlayed by sel-restore

1588 Label missing
1590 Unknown file id found
1591 Illegal file ID of zero
1592 Stopped at MDS file
1593 Illegal file number for B-tree
1594 Index will not restore, different frame size
1595 Data corruption in index
1596 Index b-trees mismatch
1597 T-VERIFY OPTIONS......A=... E=.... etc
1598 *nnnn* gfe(s) encountered
1599 Warning! *xxxx* greater than 32k
1602 Tape device is assigned to 8 mm Data Cartridge Tape
1606 Error in file open table
1607 Transaction log error in attempt to close file
1610 Quit tape operation
1613 Could not T-FWD to end of file
1650 Illegal Copies parameter
1651 Error! Choke option implies one copy
1652 Error! Invalid form queue name. Must be 50 characters or less, no embedded spaces or hyphens
1660 Tape error
1661 Tape not attached
1662 Null variable
1663 Attempt to write null string
1664 Tape error
1665 End of tape encountered
1666 Tape write protected
1667 Tape unit not ready
1668 Unrecoverable parity error
1669 Block transfer error
1670 Binary item read
1671 Tape record truncated
1672 Unrecoverable write error. Please enter 'nat-help' for more info
1673 Unrecoverable read error. Please enter 'nat-help' for more info
1674 No tape media inserted
1675 Tape subsystem not ready. Please try a 'set-ect'
1676 Tape error
1677 Tape error
1678 Tape error
1679 Tape error
1680 Tape error
1681 Tape error
1700 You are not currently attached to any tape device
1701 Tape device is assigned to 3 1/2" high density (1.44M) floppy using drive 'B'
1702 Tape device is assigned to high density (1.2M) floppy using drive 'A'

1703 Tape device is assigned to 3 1/2" std density (720K) floppy using drive 'B'
1704 Tape device is assigned to std density (360K) floppy using drive 'A'
1705 Tape device is assigned to a hard disk file (pseudo floppy)
1706 Tape device is assigned to system network (pseudo floppy)
1707 Tape is assigned to low density quarter inch tape (SCT)
1708 Tape device is assigned to standard quarter inch tape (SCT)
1709 Tape deviced is assigned to medium density quarter inch tape (SCT)
1710 Tape deviced is assigned to standard density quarter inch tape (SCT)
1711 Tape deviced is assigned to half inch tape 1600 BPI
1712 Tape deviced is assigned to half inch tape 3200 BPI
1713 Tape deviced is assigned to half inch tape 6250 BPI
1714 Tape deviced is assigned to 8 mm tape
1715 End of tape copy. Input blocks: *nnnn* Byte count *nnnn* Output blocks *nnnn*
1716 Tape device is assigned to 4 mm DAT
1720 That index does not exist
2000 *nnnn* out of *nnnn* item(s) found
2001 No search strings entered
2002 No items selected
2003 *** search verb help menu ***
2004 Null item-id is illegal for list name
2005 Help is not available
2006 Duplication of 1st disconnect character is not allowed
2210 *xxxx* filed; size = *nnnn*
2211 Filed
2221 Deleted
2389 Remote phrase definition item *xxxx* is illegal
2390 Remote phrase*xxxx* missing
2391 Assumed *xxxx* is an item-id, or modifies the item-id
2392 Assumed *xxxx* is a print-limiter which modifies *xxxx*
2393 Assumed *xxxx* is a value used as a selection criteria on attribute *nnnn*
2394 Assumed *xxxx* is a value used as selection criteria on attribute *nnnn*
2395 Assumed *xxxx* is a value used to modify the sort clause on attribute *nnnn*
2396 Assumed *xxxx* is a value used as selection criteria on attribute *nnnn*
2398 Circular phrase definition encountered in phrase *xxxx*
2399 Uneven number of delimiter ("') in phrase *xxxx*
3126 No ABS area exists for ABS file *xxxx*
3136 Type SET-FLUSH with no parameters for help. Parameters must be numeric. Some examples SET-FLUSH 6,32 flush every minute in 64K chunks SET-FLUSH 30,512 flush every 5 minutes in 1Meg chunks
3137 Invalid parameter 1. SET-FLUSH with no parameters for help
3138 Invalid parameter 2. SET-FLUSH with no parameters for help
3139 *(the SET-FLUSH help message)*
4000 Units conversion set

4001 Dozens conversion set
4002 Decimals conversion set
4003 Thousands conversion set
4041 *nnnn* items selected
4042 *nnnn* items selected out of *nnnn* sampling items
4051 *nnnn* items selected
4052 *nnnn* items selected out of *nnnn* sampling items
4060 *(Hash-test statistics)*
4071 *nnnn* items counted
4072 *nnnn* items counted out of *nnnn* sampling items
4322 Incremental save is not currently implemented
4323 Line is roadblocked
4324 Line status: DTR: *xxxx* RTS *xxxx*
4325 Line is busy. Retry later
4326 Not supported on this implementation
4327 Device is in a busy state
4328 Invalid baud-rate
4329 Not supported on this implementation
4334 Tandem terminated
4335 Converse terminated
4336 Tandem on pib *n* is on
4337 Tandem on pib *n* is off
7021 No *xxxx* index generated
9999 *(Monitor activity statistics)*

PICK BASIC error messages

B0 Catalogued
B1 Line *nnnn* : Run-time abort
B10 Line *nnnn* : Variable has not been assigned a value; zero used
B11 Line *nnnn* : Tape/diskette record truncated to tape block size
B12 Line *nnnn* : File has not been opened
B13 Line *nnnn* : Null conversion code is illegal; no conversion done
B14 Line *nnnn* : Bad stack descriptor
B15 Line *nnnn* : Illegal opcode: *xxxx*
B16 Line *nnnn* : Non-numeric data when numeric required; zero used
B17 Line *nnnn* : Array subscript out-of-range
B18 Line *nnnn* : Attribute number less than 1 is illegal
B19 Line *nnnn* : Illegal pattern
B20 Line *nnnn* : col1 or col2 used prior to executing a field statement; zero used
B21 Line *nnnn* : MATREAD: number of attributes exceeds vector size
B22 Line *nnnn* : Number of parameters passed to subprogram *xxxx* does not match
B23 Line *nnnn* : Common area in subprogram *xxxx* mismatches with main program

B24 Line *nnnn* : Divide by zero illegal; zero used
B25 Program *xxxx* has not been catalogued
B26 Line *nnnn* : UNLOCK *xxxx* attempted before LOCK
B27 Line *nnnn* : RETURN executed with no GOSUB
B28 Line *nnnn* : Not enough work space
B29 Calling program must be CATALOGed
B30 Line *nnnn* : Array size mismatch
B31 Line *nnnn* : Stack overflow
B32 Line *nnnn* : Page heading exceeds maximum of 1400 characters
B33 Line *nnnn* : Precision declared in subprogram *xxxx* is different from that declared in the mainline program
B34 Line *nnnn* : File variable used where string expression expected.
B35 Line *nnnn* : Subroutine *xxxx* object revision isincompatible with system revision – please recompile
B36 Line *nnnn* : Second parameter of KEY function must be of root-type
B37 Line *nnnn* : Program *xxxx* is not a subroutine, not accessible from CALL
B38 Line *nnnn* : A symbol table in object code is required to clear variables
B39 Line *nnnn* : Dynamic array is not dimensioned
B40 Line *nnnn* : Mismatch in passing parameter type
B41 Line *nnnn* : Mismatch named common size
B42 Line *nnnn* : Zero or negative dimension of array is illegal
B43 Line *nnnn* : Named common is not declared
B44 Line *nnnn* : Invalid CALL arguments abort – a variable was specified more than once and/or a COMMON variable was specified, ie. CALL(X,X,...)
B45 Line *nnnn* : Subroutine *xxxx* causes descriptor table overflow
B46 Line *nnnn* : Calling argument parameters *xxxx* and *yyyy* are duplicated data pointers and cannot be passed to the subroutine
B47 Line *nnnn* : Subroutine argument parameter *xxxx* is defined as common data in both the subroutine program and the calling program
B50 Line *nnnn* : Illegal descriptor in an array element passing to C function
B54 Line *nnnn* : Unknown built-in C function call
B56 Line *nnnn* : Not enough contiguous space to hold parameters for C function
B57 Line *nnnn* : Frame fault occurs during parameter passing to C function
B58 Line *nnnn* : Fails to pass a parameter to C function because of zero core link
B59 Line *nnnn* : Variable is not a valid C pointer to a string descriptor
B60 Line *nnnn* : String descriptor has a null length
B65 Line *nnnn* : Illegal values for PWR function; zero returned
B66 Line *nnnn* : Illegal value for SQRT function; zero returned
B67 Line *nnnn* : Illegal value for LN function; zero returned
B100 Line *nnnn* : Compilation aborted; no object code produced
B101 Line *nnnn* : Missing 'END', 'NEXT', 'WHILE', 'UNTIL' 'REPEAT' or 'ELSE'; compilation aborted, no object code produced
B102 Line *nnnn* : Bad statement
B103 Line *nnnn* : Label *nnnn* is missing

B104 Line *nnnn* : Label *nnnn* is defined more than once
B105 Line *nnnn* : *xxxx* has not been dimensioned
B106 Line *nnnn* : *xxxx* has been dimensioned and used without subscripts
B107 Line *nnnn* : THEN/ELSE clause missing.
B108 Line *nnnn* : Variable *xxxx* is defined as a subroutine parameter more than once
B109 Line *nnnn* : Variable missing in NEXT statement
B110 Line *nnnn* : END statement missing
B111 Line *nnnn* : 'UNTIL' or 'WHILE' missing in 'LOOP' statement
B112 Line *nnnn* : REPEAT missing in LOOP statement
B113 Line *nnnn* : Unrecognized code at end of statement
B114 Line *nnnn* : Maximum number of variables exceeded
B115 Line *nnnn* : Variable *xxxx* is used before the EQUATE statement
B116 Line *nnnn* : Variable *xxxx* is used before the COMMON statement
B117 Line *nnnn* : Variable is missing a subscript list
B118 Line *nnnn* : Variable *xxxx* is the object of an EQUATE statement and is missing
B119 Line *nnnn* : Precision out of range
B120 Line *nnnn* : Multiple precision statements
B121 Line *nnnn* : *xxxx* is a constant and cannot be written into
B122 Line *nnnn* : Label *xxxx* is improper type
B123 Line *nnnn* : DIM variable *xxxx* has a zero subscript
B124 Line *nnnn* : Variable has literal subscripts out of range
B125 Line *nnnn* : Label *xxxx* has a jump which exceeds 32k byte limit
B126 Line *nnnn* : Attribute name does not exist in dictionary or numeric value required
B127 Line *nnnn* : Multiple '*' cannot be used
B128 Line *nnnn* : Internal function variable is multi-defined
B129 Line *nnnn* : Label *xxxx* goes to an infinite loop
B130 Line *nnnn* : Function *xxxx* has not been defined
B131 Line *nnnn* : REPEAT or NEXT is missing with EXIT statement
B132 Multiple '*' cannot be used
B133 Line *nnnn* Invalid INCLUDE statement
B134 Line *nnnn* : Variable *xxxx* is the named common variable and cannot be used as an equated variable
B135 Line *nnnn* : Variable *xxxx* is used before the named common
B136 Line *nnnn* : Label *xxxx* is not allowed to resize in passed dynamic array
B137 Line *nnnn* : Variable *xxxx* is the named common variable and cannot be passed as a parameter
B138 Line *nnnn* : C function is not defined
B139 Line *nnnn* : Commons must beallocated before simple variables
B154 Line *nnnn* : NEXT statement is missing
B155 Line *nnnn* : Invalid file name used with FILE statement
B156 Line *nnnn* : illegal to ENTER a subroutine
B198 The compiler BNF is incompatible with the system revision, please update BNF

B199 Format error in source file definition
B200 Line *nnnn* : Illegal use of ACCESS function
B201 Line *nnnn* : File name in INCLUDE does not exist
B202 Line *nnnn* : Item name in INCLUDE does not exist
B203 Line *nnnn* : INCLUDE is more than five levels deep
B204 Line *nnnn* : File name is invalid
B205 Line *nnnn* : Dictionary of item id does not exist
B206 Line *nnnn* : Protected attribute definition type in DICT file
B207 Line *nnnn* : Invalid attribute definition type in DICT file
B208 Line *nnnn* : Invalid attribute mark count in DICT file
B209 Line *nnnn* : File is update protected
B210 Line *nnnn* : File is access protected
B211 Line *nnnn* : TCL level-push limit exceeded
B212 An a- or f- correlative of an item failed compilation
B213 Line *nnnn* : File variable is doubly defined in external function
B214 Line *nnnn* : DIM variable is defined more than once in external function
B215 Line *nnnn* : External function variable is multi-defined
B216 Line *nnnn* : Illegal assignment to access(3) called from file defining item
B217 Line *nnnn* : Illegal to ENTER a program from a subroutine
B218 Line *nnnn* : Illegal to ENTER a subroutine
B220 Line *nnnn* : CSYM is not a file name or needs a data level
B221 Line *nnnn* : Maximum number of item locks exceeded
B222 Line *nnnn* : This ACCESS() function must be used with the Update Processor only
B230 Line *nnnn* : Invalid port specified or port not attached
B300 Line *nnnn* : Illegal code for KEY function
B400 Line *nnnn* : Common area in subprogram *xxxx* mismatches with main program
B875 Line *nnnn* : Subroutine *xxxx* must be compiled with Flash
B876 Line *nnnn* : Flash object of subroutine *xxxx* was created on a different machine – please recompile
B877 Line *nnnn* : Flash object revision of subroutine *xxxx* is incompatible with system revision – please recompile
B878 Line *nnnn* : Insufficient space to load subroutine *xxxx*. Please run without Flash
B879 Line *nnnn* : Insufficient space to run subroutine *xxxx*. Please run without Flash
B880 Line *nnnn* : Missing TOC fro subroutine *xxxx* – please recompile
B881 Line *nnnn* : Undefined external in subroutine *xxxx* – please recompile
B882 Line *nnnn* : Common area in subprogram mismatches with main program
B883 Line *nnnn* : Cannot continue after abort in Flash BASIC
B884 Line *nnnn* : Gosub stack overflow
B885 Line *nnnn* : Variable is defined as a recursive equate

Appendix B – Table of Prime Numbers

This table comprises the prime numbers between 1 and 32K (32,768) and should be used for the modulos when creating and resizing files. Advanced PICK contains the TCL verb PRIME which will create the nearest prime numbers to a number that is input and a copy of the program is included at the end of this appendix.

1	2	3	5	7	11	13	17	19	23	29
31	37	41	43	47	53	59	61	67	71	73
79	83	89	97	101	103	107	109	113	127	131
137	139	149	151	157	163	167	173	179	181	191
193	197	199	211	223	227	229	233	239	241	251
257	263	269	271	277	281	283	293	307	311	313
317	331	337	347	349	353	359	367	373	379	383
389	397	401	409	419	421	431	433	439	439	443
449	457	461	463	467	479	487	491	499	503	509
521	523	541	547	557	563	569	571	577	587	593
599	601	607	613	617	619	631	641	643	647	653
659	661	673	677	683	691	701	709	719	727	733
739	743	751	757	761	769	773	787	797	809	811
821	823	827	829	839	853	857	859	863	877	881
883	887	907	911	919	929	937	941	947	953	967
971	977	983	991	997	1009	1013	1019	1021	1031	1033
1039	1049	1051	1061	1063	1069	1087	1091	1093	1097	1103
1109	1117	1123	1129	1151	1153	1163	1171	1181	1187	1193
1201	1213	1217	1223	1229	1231	1237	1249	1259	1277	1279
1283	1289	1291	1297	1301	1303	1307	1319	1321	1327	1361
1367	1373	1381	1399	1409	1423	1427	1429	1433	1439	1447
1451	1453	1459	1471	1481	1483	1487	1489	1493	1499	1511
1523	1531	1543	1549	1553	1559	1567	1571	1579	1583	1597
1601	1607	1609	1613	1619	1621	1627	1637	1657	1663	1667
1669	1693	1697	1699	1709	1721	1723	1733	1741	1747	1753
1759	1777	1783	1787	1789	1801	1811	1823	1831	1847	1861
1867	1871	1873	1877	1879	1889	1901	1907	1913	1931	1933
1949	1951	1973	1979	1987	1993	1997	1999	2003	2011	2017
2027	2029	2039	2053	2063	2069	2081	2083	2087	2089	2099
2111	2113	2129	2131	2137	2141	2143	2153	2161	2179	2203
2207	2213	2221	2237	2239	2243	2251	2267	2269	2273	2281
2287	2293	2297	2309	2311	2333	2339	2341	2347	2351	2399
2411	2417	2423	2437	2441	2447	2459	2467	2473	2477	2503
2521	2531	2539	2543	2549	2551	2557	2579	2591	2593	2609
2617	2621	2633	2647	2657	2659	2663	2671	2677	2683	2687
2689	2693	2699	2707	2711	2713	2719	2729	2731	2741	2749
2753	2767	2777	2789	2791	2797	2801	2803	2819	2833	2837
2843	2851	2857	2861	2879	2887	2897	2903	2909	2917	2927
2939	2953	2957	2963	2969	2971	2999	3001	3011	3019	3023

3037	3041	3049	3061	3067	3079	3083	3089	3109	3119	3121
3137	3163	3167	3169	3181	3187	3191	3203	3209	3217	3221
3229	3251	3253	3257	3259	3271	3299	3301	3307	3313	3319
3323	3329	3331	3343	3347	3359	3361	3371	3373	3389	3391
3407	3413	3433	3449	3457	3461	3463	3467	3469	3491	3499
3511	3517	3527	3529	3533	3539	3541	3547	3557	3559	3571
3581	3583	3593	3607	3613	3617	3623	3631	3637	3643	3659
3671	3673	3677	3691	3697	3701	3709	3719	3727	3733	3739
3761	3767	3769	3779	3793	3797	3803	3821	3823	3833	3847
3851	3853	3863	3877	3881	3889	3907	3911	3917	3919	3923
3929	3931	3943	3947	3967	3989	4001	4003	4007	4013	4019
4021	4027	4049	4051	4057	4073	4079	4091	4093	4099	4111
4127	4129	4133	4139	4153	4157	4159	4177	4201	4211	4217
4219	4229	4231	4241	4243	4253	4259	4261	4271	4273	4283
4289	4297	4327	4337	4339	4349	4357	4363	4373	4391	4397
4409	4421	4423	4441	4447	4451	4457	4463	4481	4483	4493
4507	4513	4517	4519	4523	4547	4549	4561	4567	4583	4591
4597	4603	4621	4637	4639	4643	4649	4651	4657	4663	4673
4679	4691	4703	4721	4723	4729	4733	4751	4759	4783	4787
4789	4793	4799	4801	4813	4817	4831	4861	4871	4877	4889
4903	4909	4919	4931	4993	4937	4943	4951	4957	4967	4969
4973	4987	4993	4999	5003	5009	5011	5021	5023	5039	5051
5059	5077	5081	5087	5099	5101	5107	5113	5119	5147	5153
5167	5171	5179	5189	5197	5209	5227	5231	5233	5237	5261
5273	5279	5281	5297	5303	5309	5323	5333	5347	5351	5381
5387	5393	5399	5407	5413	5417	5419	5431	5437	5441	5443
5449	5471	5477	5479	5483	5501	5503	5507	5519	5521	5527
5531	5557	5563	5569	5573	5581	5591	5623	5639	5641	5647
5651	5653	5657	5659	5669	5683	5689	5693	5701	5711	5717
5737	5741	5743	5749	5779	5783	5791	5801	5807	5813	5821
5827	5839	5843	5849	5851	5857	5861	5867	5869	5879	5881
5897	5903	5923	5927	5939	5953	5981	5987	6007	6011	6029
6037	6043	6047	6053	6067	6073	6079	6089	6091	6101	6113
6121	6131	6133	6143	6151	6163	6173	6197	6199	6203	6211
6217	6221	6229	6247	6257	6263	6269	6271	6277	6287	6299
6301	6311	6317	6323	6329	6337	6343	6353	6359	6361	6367
6373	6379	6389	6397	6421	6427	6449	6451	6469	6473	6481
6491	6521	6529	6547	6551	6553	6563	6569	6571	6577	6581
6599	6607	6619	6637	6653	6659	6661	6673	6679	6689	6691
6701	6703	6709	6719	6733	6737	6761	6763	6779	6781	6791
6793	6803	6823	6827	6829	6833	6841	6857	6863	6869	6871
6883	6889	6907	6911	6917	6947	6949	6959	6961	6967	6971
6977	6983	6991	6997	7001	7013	7019	7027	7039	7043	7057
7069	7103	7109	7121	7127	7129	7151	7159	7177	7187	7193
7207	7211	7213	7219	7229	7237	7243	7247	7253	7283	7297

7307	7309	7321	7331	7333	7349	7351	7369	7393	7411	7417
7433	7451	7457	7459	7477	7481	7487	7489	7499	7507	7517
7523	7529	7537	7541	7547	7549	7559	7561	7573	7577	7583
7589	7591	7603	7607	7621	7639	7643	7649	7669	7673	7681
7687	7691	7699	7703	7717	7723	7727	7741	7753	7757	7759
7789	7793	7817	7823	7829	7841	7853	7867	7873	7877	7879
7883	7901	7907	7919	7927	7933	7937	7949	7951	7963	7993
8009	8011	8017	8039	8053	8059	8069	8081	8087	8089	8093
8101	8111	8117	8123	8147	8161	8167	8171	8179	8191	8209
8219	8221	8231	8233	8237	8243	8263	8269	8273	8287	8291
8293	8297	8311	8317	8329	8353	8363	8369	8377	8387	8389
8419	8423	8429	8431	8443	8447	8461	8467	8501	8513	8521
8527	8537	8539	8543	8563	8573	8581	8597	8599	8609	8623
8627	8629	8641	8647	8663	8669	8677	8681	8689	8693	8699
8707	8713	8719	8731	8737	8741	8747	8753	8761	8779	8783
8803	8807	8819	8821	8831	8837	8839	8849	8861	8863	8867
8887	8893	8923	8929	8933	8941	8951	8963	8969	8971	8999
9001	9007	9011	9013	9029	9041	9043	9049	9059	9061	9091
9103	9109	9127	9133	9137	9151	9157	9161	9173	9181	9187
9199	9203	9209	9221	9227	9239	9241	9257	9277	9281	9283
9293	9311	9319	9323	9337	9341	9343	9349	9371	9377	9391
9397	9403	9413	9419	9421	9431	9433	9437	9439	9461	9463
9467	9473	9479	9491	9497	9511	9521	9533	9539	9547	9551
9587	9601	9613	9619	9623	9629	9631	9643	9649	9661	9677
9679	9689	9697	9719	9721	9733	9739	9743	9749	9767	9769
9781	9787	9791	9803	9811	9817	9829	9833	9839	9851	9857
9859	9871	9829	9833	9839	9851	9857	9859	9871	9883	9887
9901	9907	9923	9929	9931	9941	9949	9967	9973	10007	10009
10037	10039	10061	10067	10069	10079	10091	10093	10099	10103	10111
10133	10139	10141	10151	10159	10163	10169	10177	10181	10193	10211
10223	10243	10247	10253	10259	10267	10271	10273	10289	10301	10303
10313	10321	10331	10333	10337	10343	10357	10369	10391	10399	10427
10429	10433	10453	10457	10459	10463	10477	10487	10499	10501	10513
10529	10531	10559	10567	10589	10597	10601	10607	10613	10627	10631
10639	10651	10657	10663	10667	10687	10691	10709	10711	10723	10729
10733	10739	10753	10771	10781	10789	10799	10831	10837	10847	10853
10859	10861	10867	10883	10889	10891	10903	10909	10937	10939	10949
10957	10973	10979	10987	10993	11003	11027	11047	11057	11059	11069
11071	11083	11087	11093	11113	11117	11119	11131	11149	11159	11161
11171	11173	11177	11197	11213	11239	11243	11251	11257	11261	11273
11279	11287	11299	11311	11317	11321	11329	11351	11353	11369	11383
11393	11399	11411	11423	11437	11443	11447	11467	11471	11483	11489
11491	11497	11503	11519	11527	11549	11551	11579	11587	11593	11597
11617	11621	11633	11657	11677	11681	11689	11699	11701	11717	11719
11731	11743	11777	11779	11783	11789	11801	11807	11813	11821	11827

11831	11833	11839	11863	11867	11887	11897	11903	11909	11923	11927
11933	11939	11941	11953	11959	11969	11971	11981	11987	12007	12011
12037	12041	12043	12049	12071	12073	12097	12101	12107	12109	12113
12119	12143	12149	12157	12161	12163	12197	12203	12211	12227	12239
12241	12251	12253	12263	12269	12277	12281	12289	12301	12323	12329
12343	12347	12373	12377	12379	12391	12401	12409	12413	12421	12433
12437	12451	12457	12473	12479	12487	12491	12497	12503	12511	12517
12527	12539	12541	12547	12553	12569	12577	12583	12589	12601	12611
12613	12619	12637	12641	12647	12653	12659	12671	12689	12697	12703
12713	12721	12739	12743	12757	12763	12781	12791	12799	12809	12821
12823	12829	12841	12853	12889	12893	12899	12907	12911	12917	12919
12923	12941	12953	12959	12967	12973	12979	12983	13001	13003	13007
13009	13033	13037	13043	13049	13063	13093	13099	13103	13109	13121
13127	13147	13151	13159	13163	13171	13177	13183	13187	13217	13219
13229	13241	13249	13259	13267	13291	13297	13309	13313	13327	13331
13337	13339	13367	13381	13397	13399	13411	13417	13421	13441	13451
13457	13463	13469	13477	13487	13499	13513	13523	13537	13553	13567
13577	13591	13597	13613	13619	13627	13633	13649	13669	13679	13681
13687	13691	13693	13697	13709	13711	13721	13723	13729	13751	13757
13759	13763	13781	13789	13799	13807	13829	13831	13841	13859	13873
13877	13879	13883	13901	13903	13907	13913	13921	13931	13933	13963
13967	13997	13999	14009	14011	14029	14033	14051	14057	14071	14081
14083	14087	14107	14143	14149	14153	14159	14173	14177	14197	14207
14221	14243	14249	14251	14281	14293	14303	14321	14323	14327	14341
14347	14369	14387	14389	14401	14407	14411	14419	14423	14431	14437
14447	14449	14461	14479	14489	14503	14537	14543	14549	14551	14557
14561	14563	14591	14593	14621	14627	14629	14633	14639	14653	14657
14669	14683	14699	14713	14717	14723	14731	14737	14741	14747	14753
14759	14767	14771	14779	14783	14797	14813	14821	14827	14831	14843
14851	14867	14869	14879	14887	14891	14897	14923	14929	14939	14947
14951	14957	14969	14983	15013	15017	15031	15053	15061	15073	15077
15083	15091	15101	15107	15121	15131	15137	15139	15149	15161	15173
15187	15193	15199	15217	15227	15233	15241	15259	15263	15269	15271
15277	15287	15289	15299	15307	15313	15319	15329	15331	15349	15359
15361	15373	15377	15383	15391	15401	15413	15427	15439	15443	15451
15461	15467	15473	15493	15497	15511	15527	15541	15551	15559	15569
15581	15583	15601	15607	15619	15629	15641	15643	15647	15649	15661
15667	15671	15679	15683	15727	15731	15733	15737	15739	15749	15761
15767	15773	15787	15791	15797	15803	15809	15817	15823	15859	15877
15881	15887	15889	15901	15907	15913	15919	15923	15937	15959	15971
15973	15991	16001	16007	16033	16057	16061	16063	16067	16069	16073
16087	16091	16097	16103	16111	16127	16139	16141	16183	16187	16189
16193	16217	16223	16229	16231	16249	16253	16267	16273	16301	16319
16333	16339	16349	16361	16363	16369	16381	16411	16417	16421	16427
16433	16447	16451	16453	16477	16481	16487	16493	16519	16529	16547

16553	16561	16567	16573	16603	16607	16619	16631	16633	16649	16651
16657	16661	16673	16691	16693	16699	16703	16729	16741	16747	16759
16763	16787	16811	16823	16829	16831	16843	16871	16879	16889	16901
16903	16921	16927	16931	16937	16943	16963	16979	16981	16987	16993
17011	17021	17027	17029	17033	17041	17047	17053	17077	17093	17099
17107	17117	17123	17137	17159	17167	17183	17189	17191	17203	17207
17209	17231	17239	17257	17291	17293	17299	17317	17721	17327	17333
17341	17351	17359	17377	17383	17387	17389	17393	17401	17417	17419
17431	17443	17449	17467	17471	17477	17483	17489	17491	17497	17509
17519	17539	17551	17569	17573	17579	17581	17597	17599	17609	17623
17627	17657	17659	17669	17681	17683	17707	17713	17729	17737	17747
17749	17761	17783	17789	17791	17807	17827	17837	17839	17851	17863
17881	17891	17903	17909	17911	17921	17923	17929	17939	17957	17959
17971	17977	17981	17987	17989	18013	18041	18043	18047	18049	18059
18061	18077	18089	18097	18119	18121	18127	18131	18133	18143	18149
18169	18181	18191	18199	18211	18217	18223	18229	18233	18251	18253
18257	18269	18287	18289	18301	18307	18311	18313	18329	18341	18353
18367	18371	18379	18397	18401	18413	18427	18433	18439	18443	18451
18457	18461	18481	18493	18503	18517	18521	18523	18539	18541	18553
18583	18587	18593	18617	18637	18661	18671	18679	18691	18701	18713
18719	18731	18743	18749	18757	18773	18787	18793	18797	18803	18839
18859	18869	18899	18911	18913	18917	18919	18947	18959	18973	18979
19001	19009	19013	19031	19037	19051	19069	19073	19079	19081	19087
19121	19139	19141	19157	19163	19181	19183	19207	19211	19213	19219
19231	19237	19249	19259	19267	19273	19289	19301	19309	19319	19333
19373	19379	19381	19387	19391	19403	19417	19421	19423	19427	19429
19433	19441	19447	19457	19463	19469	19471	19477	19483	19489	19501
19507	19531	19541	19543	19553	19559	19571	19577	19583	19597	19603
19609	19661	19681	19687	19697	19699	19709	19717	19727	19739	19751
19753	19759	19763	19777	19793	19801	19813	19819	19841	19843	19853
19861	19867	19889	19891	19913	19919	19927	19937	19949	19961	19963
19973	19979	19991	19993	19997	20011	20021	20023	20029	20047	20051
20063	20071	20089	20101	20107	20113	20117	20123	20129	20143	20147
20149	20161	20173	20177	20183	20201	20219	20231	20233	20249	20261
20269	20287	20297	20323	20327	20333	20341	20347	20353	20357	20359
20369	20389	20393	20399	20407	20411	20431	20441	20443	20477	20479
20483	20507	20509	20521	20533	20543	20549	20551	20563	20593	20599
20611	20627	20639	20641	20663	20681	20693	20707	20717	20719	20731
20743	20747	20749	20753	20759	20771	20773	20789	20807	20809	20849
20857	20873	20879	20887	20897	20899	20903	20921	20929	20939	20947
20959	20963	20981	20983	21001	21011	21013	21017	21019	21023	21031
21059	21061	21067	21089	21101	21107	21121	21139	21143	21149	21157
21163	21169	21179	21187	21191	21193	21211	21221	21227	21247	21269
21277	21283	21313	21317	21319	21323	21341	21347	21377	21379	21383
21391	21397	21401	21407	21419	21433	21467	21481	21487	21491	21493

21499 21503 21517 21521 21523 21529 21557 21559 21563 21569 21577
21587 21589 21599 21601 21611 21613 21617 21647 21649 21661 21673
21683 21701 21713 21727 21737 21739 21751 21757 21767 21773 21787
21799 21803 21817 21821 21839 21841 21851 21859 21863 21871 21881
21893 21911 21929 21937 21943 21961 21977 21991 21997 22003 22013
22027 22031 22037 22063 22067 22073 22079 22091 22093 22109 22111
22123 22129 22133 22147 22153 22157 22159 22171 22189 22193 22229
22247 22259 22271 22273 22279 22283 22291 22303 22307 22343 22349
22367 22369 22381 22391 22397 22409 22433 22441 22447 22453 22469
22481 22483 22501 22511 22531 22541 22543 22549 22567 22571 22573
22613 22619 22621 22637 22639 22643 22651 22669 22679 22691 22697
22699 22709 22717 22721 22727 22739 22741 22751 22769 22777 22783
22787 22807 22811 22817 22853 22859 22861 22871 22877 22901 22907
22921 22937 22943 22961 22963 22973 22993 23003 23011 23017 23021
23027 23029 23039 23053 23057 23059 23063 23071 23081 23087 23099
23117 23131 23143 23159 23167 23173 23189 23197 23201 23203 23209
23227 23251 23269 23279 23291 23293 23297 23311 23321 23327 23333
23339 23357 23369 23371 23399 23417 23431 23447 23459 23473 23497
23509 23531 23537 23539 23549 23557 23561 23563 23567 23581 23593
23599 23603 23609 23623 23627 23629 23633 23663 23669 23671 23677
23687 23689 23719 20741 23743 23747 23753 23761 23767 23773 23789
23801 23813 23819 23827 23831 23833 23857 23869 32873 23879 23887
23893 23899 23909 23911 23917 23929 23957 23971 23977 23981 23993
23993 23981 23993 24001 24007 24019 24029 24043 24049 24061 24071
24077 24083 24091 24097 24103 24107 24109 24113 24121 24133 24137
24151 24169 24179 24181 24197 24203 24223 24229 24239 24247 24251
24281 24317 24329 24337 24359 24371 24373 24379 24391 24407 24413
24419 24421 24439 24443 24469 24473 24481 24499 24509 24517 24527
24533 24547 24551 24571 24593 24611 24623 24631 24659 24671 24677
24683 24691 24697 24709 24733 24749 24763 24767 24781 24793 24799
24809 24821 24841 24847 24851 24859 24877 24889 24907 24917 24919
24923 24943 24953 24967 24971 24977 24979 24989 25013 25031 25033
25037 25057 25073 25087 25097 25111 25117 25121 25127 25147 25153
25163 25169 25171 25183 25189 25219 25229 25237 25243 25247 25253
25261 25301 25303 25307 25309 25321 25339 25343 25349 23557 25367
25373 25391 25409 25411 25423 25439 25447 25453 25457 25463 25469
25471 25523 25537 25541 25561 25577 25579 25583 25589 25601 25603
25609 25621 25633 25639 25643 25657 25667 25673 25679 25693 25703
25717 25733 25741 25747 25759 25763 25771 25793 25799 25801 25819
25841 25847 25849 25867 25873 25889 25903 25913 25919 25931 25933
25939 25943 25951 25969 25981 25997 25999 26003 26017 26021 26029
26041 26053 26083 26099 26107 26111 26113 26119 26141 26153 26161
26171 26177 26183 26189 26203 26209 26227 26237 26249 26251 26261
26263 26267 26293 26297 26309 26317 26321 26339 26347 26357 26371
26387 26393 26399 26407 26417 26423 26431 26437 26449 26459 26479

26489 26497 26501 26513 26539 26557 26561 26573 26591 26597 26627
26633 26641 26647 26669 26681 26683 26687 26693 26699 26701 26711
26713 26717 26723 26729 26731 26737 26759 26777 26783 26801 26813
26821 26833 26839 26849 26861 26863 26879 26881 26891 26893 26903
26921 26927 26947 26951 26953 26959 26981 26987 26993 27011 27017
27031 27043 27059 27061 27067 27073 27077 27091 27103 27107 27109
27127 27143 27179 27191 27197 27211 27239 27241 27253 27259 27271
27Z77 27281 27283 27299 27329 29337 27361 27367 27397 27407 27409
27427 27431 27437 27449 27457 27479 27481 27487 27509 27527 27529
27539 27541 27551 27581 27583 27611 27617 27631 27647 27653 27673
27689 27691 27697 27701 27733 27737 27739 27743 27749 27751 27763
27767 27773 27779 27791 27793 27799 27803 27809 27817 27823 27827
27847 27851 27883 27893 27901 27917 27919 27941 27943 27947 27953
27961 27967 27983 27997 28001 28019 28027 28031 28051 28057 28069
28081 28087 28097 28099 28109 28111 28123 28151 28163 28181 28183
28201 28211 28219 28229 28277 28279 28283 28289 28297 28307 28309
28319 28349 29351 28387 28393 28403 28409 28411 28429 28433 28439
28447 28463 28477 28493 28499 28513 28517 28537 28541 28547 28549
28559 28571 28573 28579 28591 28597 28603 28607 28619 28621 28627
28631 28643 28649 28657 28661 28663 28669 28687 28697 28703 28711
28723 28729 28751 28753 28759 28771 28789 28793 28807 28813 28817
28837 28843 28859 28867 28871 28879 28901 28909 28921 28927 28933
28949 28961 28979 29009 29017 29021 29023 29027 29033 29059 29063
29077 29101 29123 29129 29131 29137 29147 29153 29167 29173 29179
29191 29201 29207 29209 29221 29231 29243 29251 29269 29287 29297
29303 29311 29327 29333 29339 29347 29363 29383 29387 29389 29399
29401 29411 29423 29429 29437 29443 29453 29473 29483 29501 29527
29531 29537 29567 29569 29573 29581 29587 29599 29611 29629 29633
29641 29663 29669 29671 29683 29717 29723 29741 29753 29759 29761
29789 29803 29819 29833 29837 29851 29863 29867 29873 29879 29881
29917 29921 29927 29947 29959 29983 29989 30011 30013 30029 30047
30059 30071 30089 30091 30097 30103 30109 30113 30119 30133 30137
30139 30161 30169 30181 30187 30197 30203 30211 30223 30241 30253
30259 30269 30271 30293 30307 30313 30319 30323 30341 30347 30367
30389 30391 30403 30427 30431 30449 30467 30469 30491 30493 30497
30509 30517 30529 30539 30553 30557 30559 30577 30593 30631 30637
30643 30649 30661 30671 30677 30689 30697 30703 30707 30713 30727
30757 30763 30773 30781 30803 30809 30817 30829 30839 30841 30851
30853 30859 30869 30871 30881 30893 30911 30931 30937 30941 30949
30971 30977 30983 31013 31019 31033 31039 31051 31063 31069 31079
31081 31091 31121 31123 31139 31147 31151 31153 31159 31177 31181
31183 31189 31193 31219 31223 31231 31237 31247 31249 31253 31259
31267 31271 31277 31307 31319 31321 31327 31333 31337 31357 31379
31387 31391 31393 31397 31469 31477 31481 31489 31511 31513 31517
31531 31541 31543 31547 31567 31573 31583 31601 31607 31627 31643

31649	31657	31663	31667	31687	31699	31721	31723	31727	31729	31741
31751	31769	31771	31793	31799	31817	31847	31849	31859	31873	31883
31891	31907	31957	31963	31973	31981	31991	32003	32009	32027	32029
32051	32057	32059	32063	32069	32077	32083	32089	32099	32117	32119
32141	32143	32159	32173	32183	32189	32191	32203	32213	32233	32237
32251	32257	32261	32297	32299	32303	32309	32321	32323	32327	32341
32353	32359	32363	32369	32371	32377	32381	32401	32411	32413	32423
32429	32441	32443	32467	32479	32491	32497	32503	32507	32531	32533
32537	32561	32563	32569	32573	32579	32587	32603	32603	32611	32621
32647	32653	32687	32693	32707	32713	32717	32719			

Program to provide prime numbers

Supplied courtesy of PICK Systems

```
program prime
* find the next prime number from a given point
*
casing off
equate true to 1, false to 0
*
prompt ""
tclread cmnd.tail
base = field(cmnd.tail, ' ', 2) ;*pull from tail
input.required=(base='')
*
if input.required then
  print ;print "PRIME - computes the next greater prime number "
  print ;print "Enter a positive integer = ":
  input base
end
print
if not(num(base)) then stop 550
origbase = base
*
gosub primehigh
if origbase = 2 then base = 2;n=4
*
if origbase = n-2 then
print base:" is a prime number"
   base = base + 1
   gosub primehigh
   print "The next highest prime number is = ":n-2
 end else print "The next highest prime number is = ":n-2
 gosub primelow
 if origbase = 3 then n = 0
 print "The next lowest prime number is = ":n+2
 stop
 *
 primehigh: *
 base=base + not(rem(base,2))
```

```
 prime=false
 for n=base to n+2 step 2 until prime
  denom=3
  max.div=int(sqrt(n))+1
  loop
   prime=(denom >= max.div)
   norml=not(rem(n,denom))
  until prime or norml do
   denom=denom+2
  repeat
 next n
 return
loop
   prime=(denom >= max.div)
   norml=not(rem(n,denom))
  until prime or norml do
   denom=denom+2
  repeat
 next n
 return
 *
 primelow: *
 base=origbase + not(rem(origbase,2))-2
 prime=false
 for n=base to n-2 step -2 until prime
  denom=3
  if n le 0 then n = 1
  max.div=int(sqrt(n))+1
  loop
   prime=(denom >= max.div)
   norml=not(rem(n,denom))
  until prime or norml do
   denom=denom+2
  repeat
 next n
 return
```

Appendix C – Alphabetical List of TCL Verbs

!	Creates UNIX shell and issues command
.	Invokes DOS shell
:absload	Reload abs section from file-save media
:bootstrap	Verb called from 'bootstrap'
:files	Restores entire file system from 'file-save' media
:reset-async	Resets current or all ports
:shutdown	Activates system shutdown sequence
:startspooler	Total spooler initialization; only use in an emergency
:swd	Switches 'e' pointer(s) to 'd' pointer(s)
:swe	Switches 'e' pointer(s) to 'd'-pointer(s)
:swx	Switches 'd-pointer' to 'dx-pointer'
:swz	Switches 'd-pointer' to 'dz-pointer'
:taskinit	Allocates workspace for execute
abs-dump	Dumps the abs file to tape
abs.fid	Displays current abs information
absdump	Dump the abs file to tape
account-maint	Invokes account maintenance menu
account-restore	Restores one account
account-save	Saves one account to magnetic media
add	Adds integer numbers
add-font	Adds printer font
addx	Adds hexadecimal numbers
admin	Invokes system administrator menu
admin.control	Invokes system administrator menu
admin.files	Menu for saves and restores
admin.maint	Menu for maintaining accounts
admin.status	Menu for various system reports
admin.tape	This menu on the dm account is used for tape control
admin.tape.setup	This menu on the dm account allows assigning the various types of tape devices
assignfq	Assigns a printer device driver to a spooler form queue
b/list	Formats and displays PICK/BASIC source listings
basic	Invokes 'compile' with upper / lower case insensitivity
basic-prot	Displays status of or toggles PICK/BASIC object protection
basic-prot-off	Turns off PICK/BASIC object protection scheme
basic-prot-on	Invokes PICK/BASIC object protection scheme
beep	Beeps until any key is pressed
bformat	Reformats a PICK/BASIC source item
blist	Formats and displays PICK/BASIC source listings
block-print	Produces banner on CRT or printer
bootstrap	Reloads O/S from an operational system
break-key	Enables or disables break key
break-key-off	Invokes 'break-key' with 'f' option
break-key-on	Invokes 'break-key' with 'n' option
brk-debug	Causes the break key to enter the system or PICK/BASIC debugger

brk-level	Causes the break key to push a level
buf-map	Displays a map of the buffers
buffers	Displays virtual memory buffer status
buffers.g	Produces histogram of system performance
bulletin.board	Displays 'bulletins' during logon sequence
capt	Enables or disables TCL command capturing
capture-off	Disables TCL command capturing
capture-on	Enables TCL command capturing
case	Toggles effect of upper/lower case sensitivity
case-file	Converts case of item-ids in file
case-off	Invokes 'case' command with 'f' option
case-on	Invokes 'case' command with 'n' option
cat	Displays size and fid of object pointers
catalog	Creates 'verb' item for a PICK/BASIC program
cf	Invokes 'create-file' command
charge-to	Terminates charges accumulation on current process
charges	Displays total time logged on and CPU activity statistics
check-account	Performs dummy save
check-dx	Checks entire file system for 'dx', 'dy' or 'dl' files
check-files	Performs 'dummy' account-save
check-ws	Checks workspace for specified port
chg-device	Changes a device
chksum	Creates check-sums for all or selected items in a file
choose.term	Selects terminal type
cl	Invokes 'copy-list' command
cleanpibs	Clears tandem connects for all ports
clear-basic-locks	Invokes command: 'clear-locks (b'
clear-file	Clears dict or data section of specified file
clear-index	Clears all but null root of specified b-tree index
clear-locks	Clears locks
clock	Displays and updates the hardware and software clocks
cls	Clears screen
cmdu	Shows last command for each user
coldstart	System coldstart procedure
coldstart.log	Logs coldstart status
compare	Compares items
compare-list	Compares two lists for intersections
compile	Compiles with upper/lower case insensitivity
compile-catalog	Compiles and catalogues PICK/BASIC program
compile-run	Compiles and runs a PICK/BASIC program
compile.catalog	Compiles and catalogues PICK/BASIC program
config	Invokes configuration menu
conv-case	Converts item-ids to upper/lower case
converse	Connects current process to given process
copy	Copies items to output devices or between files

copy-list	Copies previously saved lists
copydos	Invokes program 'import.pick' and copies and converts DOS data to PICK files
count	Displays a count of number of records that meet a specified criteria
cp	Copies items to printer
create-account	Creates a new account
create-bfile	Creates 'dc'-type file pointer for PICK/BASIC source and object code
create-file	Creates a new file
create-index	Creates new b-tree index
create-macro	Creates macro from 'top' (last) command on TCL stack
cross-index	Generates assembler cross-reference index
cs	Clears display screen
ct	Copies items to terminal
date	Converts dates to various formats
db	Invokes 'debug' command
dcd	Toggles dcd
dcd-off	Invokes 'dcd' command with 'f' option
dcd-on	Invokes 'dcd' command with 'n' option
debug	Enters virtual or PICK/BASIC debugger
decatalog	Decatalogues PICK/BASIC program(s)
define-terminal	Adds or modifies terminal types and drivers
define-up	Front-end for defining your keyboard for the update processor
delete	Deletes item(s) from file
delete-account	Procedure to remove account
delete-file	Deletes file from account
delete-index	Deletes b-tree index
delete-list	Deletes previously saved lists
detach-floppy	Detach the floppy diskette
detach-sct	Detaches the SCT
dev-att	Attaches a port to the current port
dev-det	Detaches a device from the current port
df	Invokes 'delete-file' command
dir	Executes a 'dir' command on a DOS diskette
div	Divides integer numbers
divx	Divides hexadecimal numbers
dl	Invokes 'delete-list' command
dos	Invokes DOS shell
download	Downloads fonts to a laser printer
dtr	Converts a value to a specified radix
dtr-off	Drops dtr
dtr-on	Brings up dtr
dtx	Converts decimal number to hexadecimal

dump	Dumps frame(s) to screen or printer
echo	Toggles terminal echo
ed	Invokes line editor
edit	Invokes line editor
edit-list	Edits saved list using line editor
el	Edits saved list using Update Processor
end	Ends process
epson	Sets up Epson printer characteristics
esc-data	Makes escape key behave normal
esc-level	Makes escape key push a level
esc-toggle	Toggles between esc-level and esc-data
exchange	Swaps item-ids
exec	Changes to specified abs area
exit	Logs off process and disconnects
export	Exports PICK item(s) to UNIX or DOS file(s)
f-resize	Resizes files
fc	Displays status of flow control
fc-off	Disables flow control
fc-on	Enables flow control
fdisk	Activates partition manager menu
fid	Display frame information
file-save	System backup process
filecomp	Compares two files
find	Searches and selects items containing specific strings
fl	Forms single list from two lists
flush	Flushes write-required frames to disk
font-parms	Utility to transform font parameters
format	Formats floppy diskette
frame-fault	Tests write frame faults
free	Displays available disk space for PICK and UNIX
fuser	Display ownership information on a device
get-list	Retrieves previously saved list
get.pick	Gets name of program currently executing
gl	Invokes 'get-list' command
group	Displays group statistics
halt-system	Immediately shuts down system
hash-test	Performs distribution analysis on file with test modulo
help	Description of 'help' system
hush	Toggles terminal echo
import	Imports UNIX or DOS file(s) to PICK item(s)
indexer	Creates b-tree indices for account
init-abs	Initializes abs area
init-ovf	Writes PICK signature on every available frame
inter	Displays or changes interactive timeslice setting
iselect	Selects items from group using 'item' verb

isselect	Selects and sorts items from group using item verb
istat	Performs distribution analysis on existing file modulo
item	Displays group to which item hashes
kill	Front end to UNIX 'kill' command
l	Synonym for 'list'
ld	Displays sorted file dictionary
ldf	Displays attribute summary descriptions
legend	Toggles status of 'legend' output
legend-off	Invokes 'legend' command with 'f' option
legend-on	Invokes 'legend' command with 'n' option
lerrs	Produces reports from the 'errors' file
lf	Invokes 'list-files' command
lfd	Lists file descriptions from specified file
lfs	Produces file statistics report
li	Invokes 'list-item' command
link-pibdev	Links the port to the device#
link-ws	Relinks process workspace(s)
list	Outputs a list of the contents of items in a file in the order in which they are stored
list-abs	Produces report from 'abs' file
list-acc	Invokes 'listacc' command
list-commands	Sorts and displays verbs from specified md (account name)
list-device	Lists UNIX devices used as 'tapes'
list-errors	Sorts contents of the 'errors' file
list-file-stats	Generates file statistics report
list-files	Lists files in specified account
list-item	Displays the contents of selected items in order in which they are stored in the file
list-jobs	Displays information about phantom processes
list-label	Outputs the specified contents of selected items in label format
list-lines	Lists all port baud rates, parity, bits setup
list-lists	Sorts saved-lists in 'pointer-file'
list-lockq	Display processes waiting to lock a frame
list-locks	Displays status of all locks
list-logoffs	Lists history of logoff commands
list-macros	Displays macros from specified (md) filename
list-menu	Displays PICK 'menu' items
list-menus	Lists menus from specified filename
list-obj	Output descriptive internal information about compiled Flash BASIC or PICK/BASIC programs
list-pibs	Sorts and displays information from pibs file
list-ports	Displays port communication parameters
list-procs	Invokes 'listprocs' command
list-system-errors	Produces report from the 'errors' file

list-users	Displays currently active users
list-verbs	Invokes 'listverbs' command
listabs	Lists current spooler assignments for each port
listacc	Displays system usage report
listbi	List built-in C functions
listc	Lists item-ids in four-column format
listconn	Displays connectives in account
listdict	Displays sorted file dictionary
listf	Invokes 'list-files' command
listfiles	Lists file pointers from specified file/account
listpeqs	Lists all entries in the spooler queue
listprocs	Displays procs in specified file
listptr	Lists printer status for all printers
listverbs	Invokes 'listverbs' command
lm	Invokes 'list-menu' command
lock-frame	Core locks specified fid
log-msg	Logs message(s) to errors file
log-status	Displays status of transaction logger
logoff	Terminates session on specified port
logon	Initiates process on specified port
logto	Logs to another account
loop	Loops continuously on any TCL command
loop-on	Invokes 'loop' command
lp	Invokes 'list-pibs' command
lq	Invokes 'listpeqs'
lu	Invokes 'list-users' command
maxusers	Displays/sets maximum number of PICK users
mirror	Directs output from 'master' to one or more 'slave' terminal
mlist	Formatted assembler listing utility
mload	Loads assembled object code
mmvideo	Utility to test memory mapped monitor
modem-off	Invokes 'xonoff' command with 'f' option
modem-on	Invokes 'xonoff' command with 'n' option
monitor-status	Gets monitor statistics and buffer table information
move-file	Moves file from one account to another
mul	Multiplies integer numbers
muld	Multiplies two integer numbers
mulx	Multiplies hexadecimal numbers
mverify	Validates assembler code integrity
nframe-index	Displays total number of frames used by index or indices
node	Identifies network node
off	Terminates session
okidata	Okidata printer setup menu
op	Invokes OP on specified item(s)
overflow	Displays the total number of available frames

p	Toggles terminal output
password	Modifies user/account password(s)
pc	Invokes DOS or UNIX shell
phantom-status	Displays all phantom lines
pibstat	Returns settings of PIB Status bits
pick	Front end to (UNIX) 'ap' command
pick-setup	Sets administrative aspects of system
pid	Displays selected pid
pitch-compile	Compiles font pitch table
pitch-table	Builds pitch table
poke	Sends input to another port
power-off	Performs orderly system shutdown sequence
ppcp	Copies item(s) between PICK Virtual Machines
prime	Displays prime number
print-err	Displays effect of error message
print-error	Prints error message from stacked data statements
printronix	Sets vertical form length on Printronix printers
prio	Displays activation parameters
psh	Execute a UNIX command and capture the results
psr	Gets process status
pverify	Verifies PICK/BASIC object code
qselect	Creates active list from item(s)
r83.setup	Sets user options to r83 defaults
reboot	Forces system restart
rebuild-ovf	Rebuilds overflow table
recover-fd	Recovers deleted item
recover-item	Recovers last item delete by update processor
reformat	Enables selected items to be output in a different item structure
rename-file	Changes filename and updates pointers
renumber	Renumbers a source program
reset-port	Initializes specified port
reset-user	Reinitializes a process
restore-accounts	Restores accounts which don't already exist
ri	Invokes 'recover-item' command
rnf	Invokes 'rename-file' command
rtd	Converts radix to decimal
run	Activates compiled PICK/BASIC program
run-list	Runs series of programs
runoff	Invokes Runoff processor for output
save	Invokes backup process
save-list	Saves active list
search	Searches file for items containing specific string(s)
search-file	Searches file for up to 15 different strings
search-system	Searches entire file system or files in a given account items containing specific string(s)

sel-restore	Restores item(s) from save media
select	Creates a list of item-ids of selected items
send-message	Sends messages to other users
set-8mm	Selects/attaches 8 mm cartridge
set-abs	Link the ABS file to the boot ABS area
set-baud	Adjusts baud rate for specific port
set-break	Sets the value of break character for the current process
set-cmem	Sets the memory size used for basic/c
set-date	Changes system date
set-date-eur	Toggles date display to dd/mm/yy format
set-date-format	Changes date display/input format
set-date-std	Toggles date display to mm/dd/yy format
set-device	Attaches device (sct/floppy/half) on AIX
set-dptr	Set D pointer attributes
set-esc	Sets the value of escape character for the current process
set-file	Creates temporary 'q-pointer' called 'qfile'
set-floppy	Attaches floppy diskette drive to current process
set-flush	Sets the flush period
set-func	Assigns function keys on port 0
set-func.sco	Sets PC keyboard for SCO/ATT/UNIX
set-half	Attaches half-inch tape drive to current process
set-imap	Sets an input/output translation table
set-kbrd	Defines keyboard type for port 0
set-kbrd.sco	Sets PC keyboard for SCO/Unix
set-keys	Sets keyboard keys on port 0
set-lptr	Adjusts communication parameters for parallel printers
set-num-format	Designates currency sign locally or globally
set-ovf-local	Manipulates the local overflow cache
set-ovf-reserve	Reserves extra overflow space
set-port	Adjusts baud rate and communication parameters for a specific port
set-runaway-limit	Sets/displays runaway overflow limit
set-sct	Attaches streaming cartridge tape to current process
set-sct-dma	Sets dma channel for sct
set-shutdown-delay	Sets system shutdown delay
set-sound	Sets console sound level
set-sym	Designates symbol table to use with virtual debugger
set-tape-type	Indicates type of half-inch tape drive
set-term	Sets default system terminal and printer characteristics
set-time	Sets system clock
setpib0	Resets port 0 terminal type
setport	Sets all ports except 0 to 9600 baud, no parity, 1 stop, 8 bits
setup-printer	Downloads the fonts for a form-queue and/or printer
sh	Invokes DOS or UNIX shell
shell	Invokes DOS shell

shl	Invokes DOS shell
shp-kill	Kill a shared printer
shp-status	Display shared printer status
shpstat	Manipulates shared program status
shutdown	Invokes orderly system shutdown procedure
sl	Invokes 'save-list' command
sleep	Suspends processing for a specific amount of time
slice	Sets timeslice
sort	Outputs the specified contents of a file in a sorted order
sort-item	Displays the contents of selected items in a sorted order
sort-list	Retrieves, sorts and rewrites previously saved list
sortc	Sorts item-ids in four-column format. Invokes program 'listc'
sp-assign	Sets spooler output assignment
sp-close	Closes a print file left open by a 'sp-open' command
sp-edit	Enables access to entries in the spooler queue to facilitate changes to their status
sp-kill	Aborts spooled process or removes printer device from the Spooler
sp-open	Keeps access to the spool queue open to ensure print reports are kept together
sp-status	Displays status of all spooler controlled devices
sp-tapeout	Retrieves reports spooled to tape for output to the printer
speller	Toggles spelling checker on or off
speller-off	Invokes 'speller' command with an 'f' option
speller-on	Invokes 'speller' command with an 'n' option
sreformat	Enables selected items to be sorted and output in a different item structure
sselect	Creates a sorted list of item-id's of selected items
stack	Toggles TCL command stack on or off
stack-off	Invokes 'stack' command with an 'f' option
stack-on	Invokes 'stack' command with an 'n' option
startlog	Invokes the transaction logger utility
startptr	Initializes use of a printer
startsched	Starts the phantom scheduler
startshp	Starts shared printer under UNIX
steal-file	Moves file from another account to current account
stoplog	Stops transaction logger
stopptr	Stops the output to a printer after current report has been printed
stopsched	Deactivates the phantom scheduler
strip-source	Removes assembler source from object
sub	Subtracts integer numbers
subd	Subtracts two integer numbers
subx	Subtracts hexadecimal numbers
system-coldstart	Performs startup commands after booting PICK

t-att	Attaches magnetic media unit to current process
t-bck	Moves magnetic media back one or more records
t-bsf	Backspace file(s)
t-bsr	Backspace record(s)
t-chk	Checks tape for parity errors
t-det	Detaches tape or diskette drive
t-eod	Moves magnetic media to end of data
t-erase	Erases all data on a tape
t-fsf	Forward space file(s)
t-fsr	Forward space record(s)
t-fwd	Moves forward to next end of file mark
t-link	Cascades one tape device to another
t-rdlbl	Reads label from magnetic media
t-read	Reads and displays contents of magnetic media
t-ret	Invokes 't-reten' command
t-reten	Retensions sct
t-rew	Rewinds magnetic media
t-select	Attaches a 'tape' device
t-space	Moves media forward 'n' files
t-stat	Reports the current attachment status of all tape devices
t-status	Displays magnetic media attachment status
t-unld	Detaches half-inch tape from take-up spool
t-unload	Detaches half-inch tape from take-up spool
t-verify	Validates contents of save tape
t-weof	Writes eof on magnetic media
t-wtlbl	Writes label on magnetic media
ta	Displays status of type-ahead buffer
ta-off	Invokes 'type-ahead' command with an 'f' option
ta-on	Invokes 'type-ahead' command with an 'n' option
tabs	Defines tabstops for use with line editor and the Update Processor
tandem	Logically link two devices to the same process
tcl	Executes a TCL command on another port
tcl-hdr	Toggles or displays status of default TCL header on Spooler output
tcl-hdr-off	Invokes 'tcl-hdr' command with an 'f' option
tcl-hdr-on	Invokes 'tcl-hdr' command with an 'n' option
term	Displays or changes current terminal or printer characteristics
term-type	Sets terminal and printer characteristics automatically
test-cursor	CRT visual effects demo
time	Displays time and date
time-date	Toggles display of time and date at TCL
time-date-off	Disables time and date display at TCL
time-date-on	Invokes 'time-date' command with an 'n' option
timedate	Toggles display of time and date at TCL

timedate-off	Invokes 'time-date' command with an 'f' option
timedate-on	Invokes 'time-date' command with an 'n' option
tlog-restore	Restores the transaction log records
to	Logs to another account
touch	Touch all items in a file or in all files in accounts
txlog	Invokes transaction logger menu
txlog-off	Turns off transaction log enqueuing for the current process
txlog-on	Turns on transaction log enqueuing for the current process
txlog-status	Displays status of transaction logger
type-ahead	Toggles type-ahead on or off
type-ahead-off	Invokes 'type-ahead' command with an 'f' option
type-ahead-on	Invokes 'type-ahead' command with an 'n' option
u	Invokes the 'update' verb
ud	Updates dictionary of given file
unix	Invokes UNIX 'sh' command
unlock-frame	Unlocks core locked buffer
unlock-group	Clears group locks
unlock-item	Clears item locks in specified file
up	Invokes the 'update' command
update	Invokes Update Processor
update-account	Invokes 'update-md'
update-accounts	Updates mds after system upgrade
update-logging	Toggles transaction log or displays status
update-md	Updates an account to AP
update-prot	Displays status of or toggles update protection
update-prot-off	Disables the global file update protection scheme
update-prot-on	Invokes global file update protection scheme
user-coldstart	Invokes user-defined coldstart sequence
verify-abs	Invokes 'verify-system'
verify-index	Verifies b-tree indices
verify-system	Verifies PICK system software
what	Combines output of 'what', 'where', 'list-locks' and 'sp-status' commands
where	Displays system execution information
wheres	Displays execution status and last command for each process
which	Displays system/release information
which-line	Returns current port number in PROC PIB
who	TCL command which shows the port number, the user id and the account name
wlist	Same as 'list', but uses indices if present
wselect	Same as 'select', but uses indices if present
wsort	Same as 'sort', but uses indices if present
wsselect	Same as 'sselect', but uses indices if present
x-ref	Assembler cross-reference utility
xcs	Toggles status of extended character set

xcs-off	Disables extended character set
xcs-on	Enables extended character set
xonoff	Toggles xon/xoff or data set ready
xref	Proc to drive assembler cross-reference utility
z	Invokes phantom process

Appendix D – List of TCL Verbs by Function

ACCESS

cl	Invokes 'copy-list' command
copy-list	Copies previously saved lists
count	Displays a count of number of records that meet a specified criteria
delete-list	Deletes previously saved lists
dl	Invokes 'delete-list' command
edit-list	Edits saved list using line editor
el	Edits saved list using Update Processor
fl	Forms single list from two lists
get-list	Retrieves previously saved list
gl	Invokes 'get-list' command
isselect	Selects and sorts items from group using item verb
l	Synonym for 'list'
ld	Displays sorted file dictionary
legend	Toggles status of 'legend' output
legend-off	Invokes 'legend' command with 'f' option
legend-on	Invokes 'legend' command with 'n' option
li	Invokes 'list-item' command
list	Outputs a list of the contents of items in a file in the order they are stored
list-item	Displays the contents of selected items in order in which they are stored in the file
list-label	Outputs the specified contents of selected items in label format
listc	Lists item-ids in four-column format
qselect	Creates active list from item(s)
reformat	Enables selected items to be output in a different item structure
save-list	Saves active list
select	Creates a list of item-ids of selected items
sl	Invokes 'save-list' command
sort	Outputs the specified contents of a file in a sorted order
sort-item	Displays the contents of selected items in a sorted order
sort-list	Retrieves, sorts and rewrites previously saved list
sreformat	Enables selected items to be sorted and output in a different item structure
sselect	Creates a sorted list of item-ids of selected items
wselect	Same as 'select', but uses indices if present
wsort	Same as 'sort', but uses indices if present
wsselect	Same as 'sselect', but uses indices if present

Accounts

admin.maint	Menu for maintaining accounts
check-account	Performs dummy save
create-account	Creates a new account
delete-account	Procedure to remove account
restore-accounts	Restores accounts which don't already exist

Assembler

cross-index	Generates assembler cross-reference index
mlist	Formatted assembler listing utility
mload	Loads assembled object code
mverify	Validates assembler code integrity
strip-source	Removes assembler source from object
x-ref	Assembler cross-reference utility
xref	Proc to drive assembler cross-reference utility

BASIC

b/list	Formats and displays PICK/BASIC source listings
basic	Invokes 'compile' with upper / lower case insensitivity
basic-prot	Displays status of or toggles PICK/BASIC object protection
basic-prot-off	Turns off PICK/BASIC object protection scheme
basic-prot-on	Invokes PICK/BASIC object protection scheme
bformat	Reformats a PICK/BASIC source item
blist	Formats and displays PICK/BASIC source listings
cat	Displays size and fid of object pointers
catalog	Creates 'verb' item for a PICK/BASIC program
compile	Compiles with upper/lower case insensitivity
compile-catalog	Compiles and catalogues PICK/BASIC program
compile-run	Compiles and runs a PICK/BASIC program
compile.catalog	Compiles and catalogues PICK/BASIC program
create-bfile	Creates 'dc'-type file pointer for PICK/BASIC source and object code
decatalog	Decatalogues PICK/BASIC program(s)
list-obj	Output descriptive internal information about compiled Flash BASIC or PICK/BASIC programs
pverify	Verifies PICK/BASIC object code
renumber	Renumbers a source program
run	Activates compiled PICK/BASIC program
run-list	Runs series of programs

Files and items

case-file	Converts case of item-ids in file
cf	Invokes 'create-file' command
clear-file	Clears dict or data section of specified file
clear-index	Clears all but null root of specified b-tree index
compare	Compares items
compare-list	Compares two lists for intersections
conv-case	Converts item-ids to upper/lower case
copy	Copies items to output devices or between files
create-file	Creates a new file
create-index	Creates new b-tree index
delete	Deletes item(s) from file
delete-file	Deletes file from account
delete-index	Deletes b-tree index
df	Invokes 'delete-file' command
exchange	Swaps item-ids
f-resize	Resizes files
filecomp	Compares two files
hash-test	Performs distribution analysis on file with test modulo
indexer	Creates b-tree indices for account
istat	Performs distribution analysis on existing file modulo
ldf	Displays attribute summary descriptions
lf	Invokes 'list-files' command
lfd	Lists file descriptions from specified file
lfs	Produces file statistics report
list-files	Lists files in specified account
listdict	Displays sorted file dictionary
listf	Invokes 'list-files' command
listfiles	Lists file pointers from specified file/account
move-file	Moves file from one account to another
rename-file	Changes filename and updates pointers
rnf	Invokes 'rename-file' command
set-dptr	Set D pointer attributes
set-file	Creates temporary 'q-pointer' called 'qfile'
sortc	Sorts item-ids in four-column format Invokes program 'listc'
steal-file	Moves file from another account to current account
ud	Updates dictionary of given file

General-purpose utilities

block-print	Produces banner on crt or printer
capt	Enables or disables TCL command capturing
capture-off	Disables TCL command capturing

capture-on	Enables TCL command capturing
case-off	Invokes 'case' command with 'f' option
case-on	Invokes 'case' command with 'n' option
check-ws	Checks workspace for specified port
cls	Clears screen
cs	Clears display screen
ct	Copies items to terminal
date	Converts dates to various formats
dir	Executes a 'dir' command on a DOS diskette
echo	Toggles terminal echo
find	Searches and selects items containing specific strings
frame-fault	Tests write frame faults
free	Displays available disk space for PICK and UNIX
fuser	Display ownership info on a device
get.pick	Gets name of program currently executing
group	Displays group statistics
help	Description of 'help' system
hush	Toggles terminal echo
init-abs	Initializes abs area
init-ovf	Writes PICK signature on every available frame
lerrs	Produces reports from the 'errors' file
link-ws	Relinks process workspace(s)
list-abs	Produces report from 'abs' file
list-acc	Invokes 'listacc' command
list-commands	Sorts and displays verbs from specified md (account name)
list-device	Lists UNIX devices used as 'tapes'
list-errors	Sorts contents of the 'errors' file
list-file-stats	Generates file statistics report
list-jobs	Displays information about phantom processes
list-lists	Sorts saved-lists in 'pointer-file'
list-logoffs	Lists history of logoff commands
list-macros	Displays macros from specified (md) filename
list-menu	Displays PICK 'menu' items
list-menus	Lists menus from specified filename
list-pibs	Sorts and displays information from pibs file
list-procs	Invokes 'listprocs' command
list-system-errors	Produces report from the 'errors' file
list-verbs	Invokes 'listverbs' command
listbi	List built-in C functions
listconn	Displays connectives in account
listprocs	Displays proc's in specified file
listverbs	Invokes 'listverbs' command
lm	Invokes 'list-menu' command
log-msg	Logs message(s) to errors file
log-status	Displays status of transaction logger

loop	Loops continuously on any TCL command
loop-on	Invokes ‘loop’ command
lp	Invokes ‘list-pibs’ command
maxusers	Displays/sets maximum number of PICK users
mmvideo	Utility to test memory mapped monitor
monitor-status	Gets monitor statistics and buffer table information
nframe-index	Displays total number of frames used by index or indices
overflow	Displays the total number of available frames
p	Toggles terminal output
pc	Invokes DOS or UNIX shell
pibstat	Returns settings of PIB Status bits
pid	Displays selected pid
poke	Sends input to another port
ppcp	Copies item(s) between PICK Virtual Machines
prime	Displays prime number
print-err	Displays effect of error message
print-error	Prints error message from stacked data statements
prio	Displays activation parameters
psh	Execute a UNIX command and capture the results
psr	Gets process status
r83.setup	Sets user options to r83 defaults
rebuild-ovf	Rebuilds overflow table
send-message	Sends messages to other users
shl	Invokes DOS shell
shpstat	Manipulates shared program status
sleep	Suspends processing for a specific amount of time
slice	Sets timeslice
speller	Toggles spelling checker on or off
speller-off	Invokes ‘speller’ command with an ‘f’ option
speller-on	Invokes ‘speller’ command with an ‘n’ option
ta	Displays status of type-ahead buffer
ta-off	Invokes ‘type-ahead’ command with an ‘f’ option
ta-on	Invokes ‘type-ahead’ command with an ‘n’ option
tabs	Defines tabstops for use with line editor and the Update Processor
tcl	Executes a TCL command on another port
term	Displays or changes current terminal or printer characteristics
test-cursor	CRT visual effects demo
time	Displays time and date
time-date	Toggles display of time and date at TCL
time-date-off	Disables time and date display at TCL
time-date-on	Invokes ‘time-date’ command with an ‘n’ option
timedate	Toggles display of time and date at TCL
timedate-off	Invokes ‘time-date’ command with an ‘f’ option

timedate-on	Invokes 'time-date' command with an 'n' option
type-ahead	Toggles type-ahead on or off
type-ahead-off	Invokes 'type-ahead' command with an 'f' option
type-ahead-on	Invokes 'type-ahead' command with an 'n' option
unix	Invokes UNIX 'sh' command
update-prot	Displays status of or toggles update protection
update-prot-off	Disables the global file update protection scheme
update-prot-on	Invokes global file update protection scheme
what	Combines output of 'what', 'where', 'list-locks' and 'sp-status' commands
where	Displays system execution information
wheres	Displays execution status and last command for each process
which	Displays system/release information
which-line	Returns current port number in PROC PIB
who	TCL command which shows the port number, the user id and the account name
wlist	Same as 'list', but uses indices if present

Logging on, off and logging to

!	Creates UNIX shell and issues command
.	Invokes DOS shell
dos	Invokes DOS shell
exit	Logs off process and disconnects
logoff	Terminates session on specified port
logon	Initiates process on specified port
logto	Logs to another account
off	Terminates session
pick	Front end to (UNIX) 'ap' command
power-off	Performs orderly system shutdown sequence
reboot	Forces system restart
set-shutdown-delay	Sets system shutdown delay
sh	Invokes DOS or UNIX shell
shell	Invokes DOS shell
shutdown	Invokes orderly system shutdown procedure
to	Logs to another account

Mathematical functions

add	Adds integer numbers
addx	Adds hexadecimal numbers
div	Divides integer numbers

divx	Divides hexadecimal numbers
dtr	Converts a value to a specified radix
dtx	Converts decimal number to hexadecimal
mul	Multiplies integer numbers
muld	Multiplies two integer numbers
mulx	Multiplies hexadecimal numbers
rtd	Converts radix to decimal
sub	Subtracts integer numbers
subd	Subtracts two integer numbers
subx	Subtracts hexadecimal numbers

Saves, restores and device control

:absload	Reload abs section from file-save media
:bootstrap	Verb called from 'bootstrap'
:files	Restores entire file system from 'file-save' media
abs-dump	Dumps the abs file to tape
absdump	Dump the abs file to tape
account-restore	Restores one account
account-save	Saves one account to magnetic media
admin.files	Menu for saves and restores
admin.tape	This menu on the dm account is used for tape control
admin.tape.setup	This menu on the dm account allows assigning the various types of tape devices
bootstrap	Reloads O/S from an operational system
check-files	Performs 'dummy' account-save
chg-device	Changes a device
detach-floppy	Detach the floppy diskette
detach-sct	Detaches the SCT
dev-att	Attaches a port to the current port
dev-det	Detaches a device from the current port
file-save	System backup process
format	Formats floppy diskette
save	Invokes backup process
sel-restore	Restores item(s) from save media
set-8mm	Selects/attaches 8 mm cartridge
set-device	Attaches device (sct/floppy/half) on AIX
set-floppy	Attaches floppy diskette drive to current process
set-half	Attaches half-inch tape drive to current process
set-sct	Attaches streaming cartridge tape to current process
set-tape-type	Indicates type of half-inch tape drive
t-att	Attaches magnetic media unit to current process
t-bck	Moves magnetic media back one or more records
t-bsf	Backspace file(s)

t-bsr	Backspace record(s)
t-chk	Checks tape for parity errors
t-det	Detaches tape or diskette drive
t-eod	Moves magnetic media to end of data
t-erase	Erases all data on a tape
t-fsf	Forward space file(s)
t-fsr	Forward space record(s)
t-fwd	Moves forward to next end of file mark
t-link	Cascades one tape device to another
t-rdlbl	Reads label from magnetic media
t-read	Reads and displays contents of magnetic media
t-ret	Invokes 't-reten' command
t-reten	Retensions sct
t-rew	Rewinds magnetic media
t-select	Attaches a 'tape' device
t-space	Moves media forward 'n' files
t-stat	Reports the current attachment status of all tape devices
t-status	Displays magnetic media attachment status
t-unld	Detaches half-inch tape from take-up spool
t-unload	Detaches half-inch tape from take-up spool
t-verify	Validates contents of save tape
t-weof	Writes eof on magnetic media
t-wtlbl	Writes label on magnetic media
touch	ouch all items in a file or all files in accounts

Spooler and printer functions

:startspooler	Total spooler initialization; only use in an emergency
add-font	Adds printer font
assignfq	Assigns a printer device driver to a spooler form queue
download	Downloads fonts to a laser printer
epson	Sets up Epson printer characteristics
font-parms	Utility to transform font parameters
listabs	Lists current spooler assignments for each port
listpeqs	Lists all entries in the spooler queue
listptr	Lists printer status for all printers
lq	Invokes 'listpeqs'
okidata	Okidata printer setup menu
pitch-compile	Compiles font pitch table
pitch-table	Builds pitch table
printronix	Sets vertical form length on Printronix printers
set-lptr	Adjusts communication parameters for parallel printers
setup-printer	Downloads the fonts for a form-queue and/or printer
shp-kill	Kill a shared printer

shp-status	Display shared printer status
sp-assign	Sets spooler output assignment
sp-close	Closes a print file left open by a 'sp-open' command
sp-edit	Enables access to entries in the spooler queue to facilitate changes to their status
sp-kill	Aborts spooled process or removes printer device from the Spooler
sp-open	Keeps access to the spool queue open to ensure print reports are kept together
sp-status	Displays status of all spooler controlled devices
sp-tapeout	Rtrieves reports spooled to tape for output to the printer
startptr	Initializes use of a printer
startsched	Starts the phantom scheduler
stopptr	Stops the output to a printer after current report has been printed
tcl-hdr	Toggles or displays status of default TCL header on Spooler output
tcl-hdr-off	Invokes 'tcl-hdr' command with an 'f' option
tcl-hdr-on	Invokes 'tcl-hdr' command with an 'n' option

System accounting

charge-to	Terminates charges accumulation on current process
charges	Displays total time logged on and cpu activity statistics
listacc	Displays system usage report

System management functions

:reset-async	Resets current or all ports
:shutdown	Activates system shutdown sequence
:swd	Switches 'e' pointer(s) to 'd' pointer(s)
:swe	Switches 'e' pointer(s) to 'd'-pointer(s)
:swx	Switches 'd-pointer' to 'dx-pointer'
:swz	Switches 'd-pointer' to 'dz-pointer'
:taskinit	Allocates workspace for execute
abs.fid	Displays current abs information
account-maint	Invokes account maintenance menu
admin	Invokes system administrator menu
admin.control	Invokes system administrator menu
admin.status	Menu for various system reports
beep	Beeps until any key is pressed
break-key	Enables or disables break key
break-key-off	Invokes 'break-key' with 'f' option

break-key-on	Invokes 'break-key' with 'n' option
brk-debug	Causes the break key to enter the system or PICK/BASIC debugger
brk-level	Causes the break key to push a level
buf-map	Displays a map of the buffers
buffers	Displays virtual memory buffer status
buffers.g	Produces histogram of system performance
bulletin.board	Displays 'bulletins' during logon sequence
case	Toggles effect of upper/lower case sensitivity
check-dx	Checks entire file system for 'dx', 'dy' or 'dl' files
chksum	Creates check-sums for all or selected items in a file
choose.term	Selects terminal type
cleanpibs	Clears tandem connects for all ports
clear-basic-locks	Invokes command: 'clear-locks (b'
clear-locks	Clears locks
clock	Displays and updates the hardware and software clocks
cmdu	Shows last command for each user
coldstart	System coldstart procedure
coldstart.log	Logs coldstart status
config	Invokes configuration menu
converse	Connects current process to given process
copydos	Invokes program 'importpick' and copies and converts DOS data to PICK files
cp	Copies items to printer
create-macro	Creates macro from 'top' (last) command on TCL stack
db	Invokes 'debug' command
dcd	Toggles dcd
dcd-off	Invokes 'dcd' command with 'f' option
dcd-on	Invokes 'dcd' command with 'n' option
debug	Enters virtual or PICK/BASIC debugger
define-terminal	Adds or modifies terminal types and drivers
define-up	Front-end for defining your keyboard for the update processor
dtr-off	Drops dtr
dtr-on	Brings up dtr
dump	Dumps frame(s) to screen or printer
ed	Invokes line editor
edit	Invokes line editor
end	Ends process
esc-data	Makes escape key behave normal
esc-level	Makes escape key push a level
esc-toggle	Toggles between esc-level and esc-data
exec	Changes to specified abs area
export	Exports PICK item(s) to UNIX or DOS file(s)
fc	Displays status of flow control

fc-off	Disables flow control
fc-on	Enables flow control
fdisk	Activates partition manager menu
fid	Display frame information
flush	Flushes write-required frames to disk
halt-system	Immediately shuts down system
import	Imports UNIX or DOS file(s) to PICK item(s)
inter	Displays or changes interactive timeslice setting
iselect	Selects items from group using 'item' verb
item	Displays group to which item hashes
kill	Front end to UNIX 'kill' command
link-pibdev	Links the port to the device#
list-lines	Lists all port baud rates, parity, bits setup
list-lockq	Display processes waiting to lock a frame
list-locks	Displays status of all locks
list-ports	Displays port communication parameters
list-users	Displays currently active users
lock-frame	Core locks specified fid
lu	Invokes 'list-users' command
mirror	Directs output from 'master' to one or more 'slave' terminals
modem-off	Invokes 'xonoff' command with 'f' option
modem-on	Invokes 'xonoff' command with 'n' option
node	Identifies network node
op	Invokes OP on specified item(s)
password	Modifies user/account password(s)
phantom-status	Displays all phantom lines
pick-setup	Sets administrative aspects of system
recover-fd	Recovers deleted item
recover-item	Recovers last item delete by update processor
reset-port	Initializes specified port
reset-user	Reinitializes a process
ri	Invokes 'recover-item' command
runoff	Invokes Runoff processor for output
search	Searches file for items containing specific string(s)
search-file	Searches file for up to 15 different strings
search-system	Searches entire file system or files in a given account for items containing specific string(s)
set-abs	Link the ABS file to the boot ABS area
set-baud	Adjusts baud rate for specific port
set-break	Sets the value of break character for the current process
set-cmem	Sets the memory size used for basic/c
set-date	Changes system date
set-date-eur	Toggles date display to dd/mm/yy format
set-date-format	Changes date display/input format
set-date-std	Toggles date display to mm/dd/yy format

set-esc	Sets the value of escape character for the current process
set-flush	Sets the flush period
set-func	Assigns function keys on port 0
set-func.sco	Sets PC keyboard for SCO/ATT/UNIX
set-imap	Sets a input/output translation table
set-kbrd	Defines keyboard type for port 0
set-kbrd.sco	Sets PC keyboard for SCO/UNIX
set-keys	Sets keyboard keys on port 0
set-num-format	Designates currency sign locally or globally
set-ovf-local	Manipulates the local overflow cache
set-ovf-reserve	Reserves extra overflow space
set-port	Adjusts baud rate and communication parameters for specific port
set-runaway-limit	Sets/displays runaway overflow limit
set-sct-dma	Sets dma channel for sct
set-sound	Sets console sound level
set-sym	Designates symbol table to use with virtual debugger
set-term	Sets default system terminal and printer characteristics
set-time	Sets system clock
setpib0	Resets port 0 terminal type
setport	Sets all ports except 0 to 9600 baud, no parity, 1 stop, 8 bits
stack	Toggles TCL command stack on or off
stack-off	Invokes 'stack' command with an 'f' option
stack-on	Invokes 'stack' command with an 'n' option
startlog	Invokes the transaction logger utility
startshp	Starts shared printer under UNIX
stoplog	Stops transaction logger
stopsched	Deactivates the phantom scheduler
system-coldstart	Performs startup commands after booting PICK
tandem	Logically link two devices to the same process
term-type	Sets terminal and printer characteristics automatically
tlog-restore	Restores the transaction log records
txlog	Invokes transaction logger menu
txlog-off	Turns off transaction log enqueuing for the current process
txlog-on	Turns on transaction log enqueuing for the current process
txlog-status	Displays status of transaction logger
u	Invokes the 'update' verb
unlock-frame	Unlocks core locked buffer
unlock-group	Clears group locks
unlock-item	Clears item locks in specified file
up	Invokes the 'update' command
update	Invokes Update Processor
update-account	Invokes 'update-md'
update-accounts	Updates mds after system upgrade
update-logging	Toggles transaction log or displays status

update-md	Updates an account to AP
user-coldstart	Invokes user-defined coldstart sequence
verify-abs	Invokes 'verify-system'
verify-index	Verifies b-tree indices
verify-system	Verifies PICK system software
xcs	Toggles status of extended character set
xcs-off	Disables extended character set
xcs-on	Enables extended character set
xonoff	Toggles xon/xoff or data set ready
z	Invokes phantom process

Appendix E – BASIC Functions and Operators

$include	Alternate method of 'include'
$insert	Inserts object module within object module
$insert$	Alternate method of 'insert' (or 'include')
%	Defines built-in C function
% accept	Accept a connection on a socket
% alarm	Sends SIGALRM to calling process after given delay
%bind	Binds a name to a socket
%chdir	Changes the current directory
%chmod	Changes mode of given file
%chown	Changes owner and group ID
%close	Closes a Unix file
%close.apdos	Closes an MS-DOS file
%connect	Establishes a connection with a host through sockets
%creat	Creates new Unix file, or rewrites to existing file
%dup	Returns new file descriptor
%fclose	Closes stream
%fdopen	Associates stream with a file descriptor
%fgetc	Gets a character from a stream
%fgets	Reads a C string from a stream
%fopen	Opens a stream
%fprintf	Writes formatted string on a stream
%fputc	Puts a character on a stream
%fputs	Writes a string on a stream
%free	Frees memory
%freopen	Reopens a stream
%fsize	Gets the size of a file
%getenv	Gets Unix environment variable
%gethostid	Gets the unique identifier of the current host
%getpgrp	Gets group id
%getpid	Gets Unix Process id
%getppid	Gets parent PID
%ioctl	Special IO control
%kill	Sends signal to process ID
%listen	Listens for incoming connections and limits the backlog of incoming connections
%lseek	Sets Unix file pointer
%lseek.apdos	Sets MS-DOS file pointer
%malloc	Allocates memory
%memccpy	Copies memory up to a delimiter
%memcpy	Copies memory
%memxcpy	Copies memory and converts to hexadecimal
%open	Opens a Unix file for reading or writing
%open.apdos	Opens an MS-DOS file for reading or writing
%pause	Suspends calling process until signal received
%pclose	Closes a stream

%pgetpid	Gets a PICK process PID
%popen	Creates pipe between calling process and command
%putenv	Assigns value to environment variable
%rdhex	Reads a Unix file and translates to hexadecimal
%read	Reads from a Unix file
%read.apdos	Reads from an MS-DOS file
%semctl	Performs semaphore control operations
%semget	Creates a semaphore set
%setflush	Sets flush period
%shmat	Attaches to a shared memory segment
%shmdt	Detaches from a shared memory segment
%shmget	Creates shared memory segment and returns identifier
%socket	Creates a socket
%ttyname	Returns a pointer to a terminal name
%unlink	Removes a directory entry
%wait	Waits for termination of child process
%whex	Writes to a Unix file, converting into binary
%write	Writes to a Unix file
%write.apdos	Writes to a DOS file
!	Logical ‘or’ operator and remark line indicator
’	String delimiter
#	‘not equal to’
&	Logical ‘and’ statement
’	String delimiter
(	Open parentheses
)	Close parentheses
*****	Arithmetic operator (multiply) and remark line indicator
+	Arithmetic operator (add). Also unary plus
–	Mathematical operator (subtract). Also unary minus variable
/	Mathematical operator (divide)
:	Concatenation operator
;	Program source line delimiter
<	‘Less than’ operator and symbol denoting the start of a dynamic array
<=	‘Less than or equal to’ operator
<>	not equal to
=	Logical ‘equal’ operator or variable assignment
>	‘Greater than’ operator and symbol denoting the
><	Logical ‘not equal’ operator
>=	‘Greater than or equal to’ operator
@	Special cursor addressing functions
[	Substring extraction, assignment, or field store
****	String delimiter or arithmetic operator
]	Substring, or text string extraction
^	Mathematical operator (exponent)

abort	Terminates program and PROC{s}
abs	Returns absolute value
access	Interface between access and PICK/BASIC
alpha	Determines if string is alphabetic
and	Boolean operator
ascii	Converts ebcdic to ascii
assigned	Determines if variable has been assigned a value
assignment	Assigns value to variable
begin case	Start of a case function
break	Enables or disables the break key
break off	Disables break key
break on	Enables break key
call	Calls external PICK/BASIC subroutine
capturing	Toggles output capturing
capturing off	Disables output capturing
capturing on	Enables output capturing
case	Initiates the case statement
casing	Enables or disables case sensitivity
casing off	Disables case sensitivity
casing on	Enables case sensitivity
cat	Concatenates string expressions
cfunction	Declare a list of C functions
chain	Transfers control to executable TCL expression
char	Returns ascii character of numeric expression
clear	Initializes all variables
clearfile	Clears specified file variable
close	Closes file
col1	Returns beginning position derived from last 'field' function
col2	Returns ending position derived from last 'field' function
com	Alternative to 'common'
common	Declares common variables
convert	Converts characters
cos	Returns cosine of numeric expression
count	Counts number of occurences of string with string
crt	Outputs expression to crt
data	Stacks strings for subsequent input(s)
date	Returns system date in internal format
dcount	Returns count of strings delimited by a given delimiter
debug	Invokes PICK/BASIC debugger
del	Alternate method of 'delete'
delete	Deletes element from an array or an item from a file
dim	Declares a dimensioned array
dimension	Alternative to 'dim'
do	Part of 'loop' construct
dtx	Converts decimal to hexadecimal

ebcdic	Converts ascii to ebcdic
echo	Toggles terminal echo
echo off	Turns off terminal character echo
echo on	Turns on terminal character echo
else	Part of an IF statement
end	The end of a program or a the end of a series of program statements
end case	Terminates case construct
enter	Transfers control to catalogued program
eq	Equal
equ	Alternative to 'Equate'
equate	Declares constants at compile time
error	Displays error message
error()	Returns TCL command line used to activate the program
execute	Performs TCL command expression
execute.apdos	Executes DOS command from PICK/BASIC
execute.unix	Executes Unix command from PICK/BASIC
exit	Forces early exit from 'loop' or 'for ... next' construct
exp	Returns exponent from numeric expression
extract	Extracts element from array
field	Returns substring from string expression
file	Opens file and dimensions array
fold	Folds string
footing	Defines report footing
for..next	Incremental loop function
for..next..until	Incremental loop function
for..next..while	Incremental loop function
ge	'Greater than or equal to' operator
get	Gets raw characters from another port
go to	Transfers execution to statement label
gosub	Transfers control to local subroutine
gt	'Greater than' operator
heading	Defines report heading
iconv	Input conversion function
if	Initiates logical expression
in	Inputs single character
include	Includes object module within object module
index	Returns numeric starting position of string within string
input@	Stops program to accept input
inputerr	Used with 'input' to display error message on status line
inputnull	Defines null input character for input @
inputtrap..gosub	Sets trap for input@ statement subroutine branches
inputtrap..goto	Sets trap for input@ statement subroutine branches
ins	Alternative method of 'insert'
insert	Inserts element into array

int	Returns integer portion of numeric expression
key	Locates item-id in a b-tree index
le	'Less than or equal to' operator
len	Returns number of characters in a string expression
let	Optional assignment indicator
ln	Returns natural log of numeric expression
locate	Locates element in string expression
lock	Sets execution lock
locked	Takes 'locked' path when group/item lock encountered
loop	Conditional loop function
loop..until	Loops 'until' condition is met
lt	'less than' operator
mat	Assigns data to a dimensioned array
matbuild	Converts dimensioned array to dynamic array
match	Pattern matching function
matches	Alternative to 'match'
matparse	Converts dynamic array to dimensioned array
matread	Reads item into dimensioned array
matreadu	Reads item into dimensioned array and locks item
matwrite	Writes dimensioned array to file
matwriteu	Writes dimensioned array to file, releasing lock
mod	Returns remainder from dividing two numbers
ne	'not equal to'
next	Terminates for..next loop
not	Negates a logical expression
null	No operation
num	Determines if string is numeric
occurs	Locates strings which occur certain number of times
oconv	Output conversion function
on..gosub	Calculated gosub
on..goto	Calculated goto
onerr	Takes 'error' path when media error encountered
open	Opens file for input and output
or	See !
out	Outputs single character
page	Forces page eject
precision	Defines precision for calculations
print	Outputs expression to printer or crt
print on	Directs output to specific report
printer	Toggles CRT/Spooler output or closes entry
printer close	Closes print file
printer off	Directs 'print' statement output to crt
printer on	Directs 'print' statement output to Spooler
procread	Reads primary input buffer
procwrite	Writes primary input buffer

program	First line in a PICK/BASIC program
prompt	Defines input prompt character
pwr	Exponentiates numeric expression
read	Reads item into dimensioned or dynamic array
readnext	Retrieves the next item-id from an active list
readt	Reads one tape record
readtl	Reads label from magnetic media
readtx	Reads one tape record and displays in hexadecimal
readu	A version of 'read' which locks the record
readv	Reads one attribute and assigns to value
readvu	A version of 'readv' that locks the record
release	Releases group/item lock(s)
rem	Calculates remainder of two numeric expressions or defines a user-specified remark
repeat	part of a 'loop' function
replace	Replaces element in string expression or maintains integrity of item bridges
return	Returns control from a local or external subroutine
rewind	Rewinds magnetic media
rnd	Generates random number
root	Loads the root variable with the root FID of the specified index; effectively an 'open' on an index file
rqm	Suspends processing for a specific amount of time
select	Creates internal active list
send	Sends output to a specific port
seq	Converts ascii expression to numeric equivalent
sin	Calculates sine of angle
sleep	Suspends processing for a specific amount of time
sort	Sorts a string of attributes or values
soundex	Returns soundex value for specified string
space	Generates string of spaces
sqrt	Calculates square root
stop	Terminates program
str	Generates string of characters
subroutine	Defines program as external subroutine
sum	Returns the sum of a list of numbers
system	Displays status of system-controlled variables
tan	Calculates tangent of angle
tcl	Performs TCL command expression
tclread	Reads TCL command string into variable
time()	Returns current time in internal format
timedate	Returns time and date
trim	Trims leading and trailing spaces from string
unlock	Resets execution lock
until	Part of 'loop' and 'for ... next' constructs

weof	Writes an end-of-file mark to tape
while	Part of 'loop' and 'for ... next'
write	Writes dynamic array to file
writet	Writes a string to magnetic media
writeu	See 'write' or 'matwrite'
writev	Writes one attribute
writevu	Writes one attribute, without unlocking
xtd	Converts hexadecimal number to decimal

Appendix F – Formatting Program for PICK BASIC

PROGRAM FORMAT

```
***********************************************************
* THIS PROGRAM FORMATS A DATA/BASIC PROGRAM TO *
* DISPLAY BLOCK STRUCTURING BY INDENTING LINES   *
***********************************************************
*——— DEFINITIONS
10      SP = 6    ;* LEFT MARGIN COLUMN NUMBER
        ID = 3    ;* NUMBER OF SPACES TO INDENT
*——— INITIALIZATION
        SPX = SP
        LINE.NO = 0
*——— INPUT FILE NAME AND PROGRAM NAME
        PRINT; PRINT
        PRINT "BASIC FILE NAME— "::INPUT FILE
        IF FILE = "" THEN STOP
        OPEN "",FILE ELSE
        PRINT "CANNOT OPEN FILE — ":FILE
        GOTO 10
        END
        PRINT "BASIC PROGRAM NAME — "::INPUT NAME
        IF NAME = "" THEN GOTO 10
        NEWITEM = ""
        READ ITEM FROM NAME ELSE
        PRINT "CANNOT FIND THAT PROGRAM"
        GOTO 10
        END
*——— GET NEW LINE, IF NONE THEN DONE
100     LINE.NO = LINE.NO + 1
        LINE = EXTRACT(ITEM,LINE.NO,0,0)
        IF LINE = "" THEN
        WRITE NEWITEM ON NAME
        PRINT; PRINT; PRINT "——DONE—— "; GOTO 10
        END
        LABEL = ""
*——— STRIP OFF LEADING/TRAILING SPACES
200     IF LINE[1,1] = " " THEN LINE = LINE[2,32767]; GOTO 200
210     IF LINE[LEN(LINE),1] = " " THEN LINE = LINE[1,LEN(LINE)-
        1];GOTO 210
*——— LOOK FOR A COMMENT ( '*' , '!' , OR 'REM' )
        IF LINE[1,1] = "*" THEN GOTO 1500
        IF LINE[1,1] = "!" THEN GOTO 1500
        IF LINE[1,3) = "REM" THEN GOTO 1500
*——— LOOK FOR 'FOR'
        IF LINE[1,4]= "FOR " AND INDEX(LINE,"NEXT ",1) > 0 THEN
        GOTO 2000
```

```
      IF LINE[1,4]= "FOR " AND INDEX(LINE,"NEXT ",1) = 0 THEN
      GOTO 1000
*——— LOOK FOR 'END'
      IF LINE = "END" THEN GOTO 1100
      IF LINE[1,4] = "END " THEN
      IF LINE[LEN(LINE)-4,5] = "ELSE" THEN GOTO 1200
      END
*——— LOOK FOR 'NEXT'
      IF LINE[1,5] = "NEXT" THEN GOTO 1100
*——— EXTRACT LEADING NUMERIC LABEL
      IF LINE[1,1] MATCHES 1N THEN
      L = 2
300   IF LINE[L,1] MATCHES 1N THEN L=L+1; GOTO 300
      LABEL = LINE[1,L-1]
      LINE = LINE[L,32767]
      GOTO 200
      END
*——— LOOK FOR LINE ENDING IN ELSE OR THEN ( IF OR READ )
      X = LINE[LEN(LINE)-4,5]
      IF X =" THEN" THEN GOTO 1000
      IF X =" ELSE" THEN GOTO 1000
*——— THIS IS JUST ANOTHER LINE, THEREFORE NO CHANGE
      GO 2000
*——— INDENT ON SUBSEQUENT LINES
1000  SP = SP + ID
      GOTO 2000
*——— OUTDENT ON THIS AND SUBSEQUENT LINES
1100  SP = SP – ID
*——— OUTDENT THIS LINE ONLY
1200  SPX = SPX – ID
      GOTO 2000
*——— PRINT WITH NO INDENTATION
1500  SPX = 0
*——— WRITE NEW LINE
2000  NEW.LINE = LABEL : STR(" ",SPX-LEN(LABEL)) : LINE
      PRINT NEW.LINE
      NEWITEM = REPLACE(NEWITEM,LINE.NO,0,0,NEW.LINE)
      SPX = SP
      GOTO 100
END
```

Published courtesy of Pick Systems

Appendix G – Table of ASCII Codes

ASCII	*Decimal*	*Hexadecimal*	*EBCDIC*
NUL	0	00	00
SOH	1	01	01
STX	2	02	02
ETX	3	03	03
EOT	4	04	37
ENQ	5	05	2D
ACK	6	06	2E
BEL	7	07	2F
BS	8	08	16
HT	9	09	05
LF	10	0A	25
VT	11	0B	0B
FF	12	0C	0C
CR	13	0D	0D
SO	14	0E	0E
SI	15	0F	0F
DLE	16	10	10
DC1	17	11	11
DC2	18	12	12
DC3	19	13	3A
DC4	20	14	3C
NAK	21	15	3D
SYN	22	16	32
ETB	23	17	26
CAN	24	18	18
EM	25	19	19
SUB	26	1A	3F
ESC	27	1B	27
FS	28	1C	1C
GS	29	1D	1D
RS	30	1E	1E
US	31	1F	1F
	32	20	40
!	33	21	5A
“	34	22	7F
#	35	23	7B
$	36	24	5B
%	37	25	6C
&	38	26	50
‘	39	27	7D
(	40	28	4D
)	41	29	5D

ASCII	*Decimal*	*Hexadecimal*	*EBCDIC*
*	42	2A	5C
+	43	2B	4E
,	44	2C	6B
–	45	2D	60
.	46	2E	4B
/	47	2F	61
0	48	30	F0
1	49	31	F1
2	50	32	F2
3	51	33	F3
4	52	34	F4
5	53	35	F5
6	54	36	F6
7	55	37	F7
8	56	38	F8
9	57	39	F9
:	58	3A	7A
;	59	3B	5E
<	60	3C	4C
=	61	3D	7E
>	62	3E	6E
?	63	3F	6F
@	64	40	7C
A	65	41	C1
B	66	42	C2
C	67	43	C3
D	68	44	C4
E	69	45	C5
F	70	46	C6
G	71	47	C7
H	72	48	C8
I	73	49	C9
J	74	4A	D1
K	75	4B	D2
L	76	4C	D3
M	77	4D	D4
N	78	4E	D5
O	79	4F	D6
P	80	50	D7
Q	81	51	D8
R	82	52	D9
S	83	53	E2

ASCII	*Decimal*	*Hexadecimal*	*EBCDIC*
T	84	54	E3
U	85	55	E4
V	86	56	E5
W	87	57	E6
X	88	58	E7
Y	89	59	E8
Z	90	5A	E9
[	91	5B	80
/	92	5C	E0
]	93	5D	90
^	94	5E	5F
_	95	5F	6D
‘	96	60	79
a	97	61	81
b	98	62	82
c	99	63	83
d	100	64	84
e	101	65	85
f	102	66	86
g	103	67	87
h	104	68	88
i	105	69	89
j	106	6A	91
k	107	6B	92
l	108	6C	93
m	109	6D	94
n	110	6E	95
o	111	6F	96
p	112	70	97
q	113	71	98
r	114	72	99
s	115	73	A2
t	116	74	A3
u	117	75	A4
v	118	76	A5
w	119	77	A6
x	120	78	A7
y	121	79	A8
z	122	7A	A9
{	123	7B	C0
|	124	7C	6A
}	125	7D	D0

ASCII	*Decimal*	*Hexadecimal*	*EBCDIC*
~	126	7E	A1
DEL	127	7F	07
	128	80	04
	129	81	06
	130	82	08
	131	83	09
	132	84	0A
	133	85	13
	134	86	14
	135	87	15
	136	88	17
	137	89	1A
	138	8A	1B
	139	8B	20
	140	8C	21
	141	8D	22
	142	8E	23
	143	8F	24
	144	90	28
	145	91	29
	146	92	2A
	147	93	2B
	148	94	2C
	149	95	30
	150	96	31
	151	97	33
	152	98	34
	153	99	35
	154	9A	36
	155	9B	38
	156	9C	39
	157	9D	3B
	158	9E	3E
	159	9F	41
	160	A0	42
	161	A1	43
	162	A2	44
	163	A3	45
	164	A4	46
	165	A5	47
	166	A6	48
	167	A7	49

ASCII	Decimal	Hexadecimal	EBCDIC
	168	A8	4A
	169	A9	4F
	170	AA	51
	171	AB	52
	172	AC	53
	173	AD	54
	174	AE	55
	175	AF	56
	176	B0	57
	177	B1	58
	178	B2	59
	179	B3	62
	180	B4	63
	181	B5	64
	182	B6	65
	183	B7	66
	184	B8	67
	185	B9	68
	186	BA	69
	187	BB	70
	188	BC	71
	189	BD	72
	190	BE	73
	191	BF	74
@	192	C0	75
A	193	C1	76
B	194	C2	77
C	195	C3	78
D	196	C4	8A
E	197	C5	8B
F	198	C6	8C
G	199	C7	8D
H	200	C8	8E
I	201	C9	8F
J	202	CA	9A
K	203	CB	9B
L	204	CC	9C
M	205	CD	9D
N	206	CE	9E
O	207	CF	9F
P	208	D0	A0
Q	209	D1	AA

ASCII	*Decimal*	*Hexadecimal*	*EBCDIC*
R	210	D2	AB
S	211	D3	AC
T	212	D4	AD
U	213	D5	AE
V	214	D6	AF
W	215	D7	B0
X	216	D8	B1
Y	217	D9	B2
Z	218	DA	B3
]	219	DB	B4
\	220	DC	B5
]	221	DD	B6
^	222	DE	B7
_	223	DF	B8
‘	224	E0	B9
a	225	E1	BA
b	226	E2	BB
c	227	E3	BC
d	228	E4	BD
e	229	E5	BE
f	230	E6	BF
g	231	E7	CA
h	232	E8	CB
i	233	E9	CC
j	234	EA	CD
k	235	EB	CE
l	236	EC	CF
m	237	ED	DA
n	238	EE	DB
o	239	EF	DC
p	240	F0	DD
q	241	F1	DE
r	242	F2	DF
s	243	F3	E1
t	244	F4	EA
u	245	F5	EB
v	246	F6	EC
w	247	F7	ED
x	248	F8	EE
y	249	F9	EF
z	250	FA	FA
[	251	FB	FB

ASCII	*Decimal*	*Hexadecimal*	*EBCDIC*	
/	252	FC	FC	SUBVALUE mark
]	253	FD	FD	VALUE mark
^	254	FE	FE	ATTRIBUTE mark
_	255	FF	FF	SEGMENT mark

Appendix H – List of Frames for R83 PICK

Reproduced by courtesy of Pick Systems

When an error occurs, it is very useful to know what PICK function is in progress. The output from WHAT, which lists the user activities, which whilst referred to by function name in Advanced PICK is referred to by frame number in PICK R83. For those using PICK R83 this list will direct you to the likely function in operation. You should be aware that this list will not hold true for all implementations.

Frame name	*Number*	*Function*
DB01	001	DEBUG TRAPS
TCL2	002	TCL
DISK2	003	FILE MANAGEMENT
TCL.INIT	004	TCL
TCL1	005	TCL
TERMIO	006	TERMIO
DISK1	007	FILE MANAGEMENT
SS1	008	NUMERIC
SS2	009	TERMIO
WRAPUP1	010	TCL
WRAPUP2	011	FILE MANAGEMENT
WRAPUP3	012	TCL
EDIT1	013	EDITOR
EDIT2	014	EDITOR
EDIT3	015	EDITOR
EDIT4	016	EDITOR
EDIT5	017	EDITOR
EDIT6	018	EDITOR
EDIT7	019	LIST-MANAGEMENT EDITOR
EDIT8	020	EDITOR
SYSTBL3	021	TABLES:DISK ERROR
GAF	022	ASSEMBLER
PASS1	023	ASSEMBLER
ASTAT	024	ASSEMBLER
MACRO	025	ASSEMBLER
ALIGN	027	ASSEMBLER
PASS2	028	ASSEMBLER
GETOP	029	ASSEMBLER
ADDLAB	030	ASSEMBLER
LOADER	031	ASSEMBLER
MLIST	032	ASSEMBLER
OF2	033	OVERFLOW MANAGEMENT
OF1	034	OVERFLOW MANAGEMENT

Frame name	*Number*	*Function*
TAPE1	035	TAPE
TAPE2	036	TAPE
TDUMP	037	SYSTEM UTILITY
EBCDIC	038	UTILITY
SORT	039	UTILITY
LOGON	040	TCL: ACCOUNTING
PROC1	041	PROC
PROC2	042	PROC
PROC3	043	PROC
PROC4	044	PROC
PROC5	045	PROC
PROC6	046	PROC
ABSL1	047	RESTORE
GLOCK	048	FILE MANAGEMENT
LOGOFF	050	TCL: ACCOUNTING
SS3	051	TERMIO
MSG	052	UTILITY
MD3	053	ACCESS
SETHDR	054	ACCESS
MD4/5	055	ACCESS
MD6	056	ACCESS
MD7/8/18	057	ACCESS
ECHECKSUBS	058	ACCESS
MD9/10	060	ACCESS
MD12	062	ACCESS
A.CORR	063	ACCESS
A.CORR1	064	ACCESS
BLOCK.LETTERS	065	UTILITY
DUMP1	066	UTILITY
DUMP2	067	UTILITY
MD20X	068	ACCESS
MD19	069	ACCESS
MD20	070	ACCESS
MD300	071	ACCESS: LIST
MD310	072	ACCESS: LIST
MD125	073	ACCESS: LIST
MD128	074	ACCESS: LIST
MD126	075	ACCESS: LIST
MVVL	076	ACCESS: LIST
MD145	077	ACCESS: LIST
GOSORT	078	ACCESS: SELECTION
SUM/STAT	079	ACCESS: UTILITY

Frame name	*Number*	*Function*
BATCH1	080	BATCH
BATCH2	081	BATCH
BATCH3	082	BATCH
BATCH4	083	BATCH
BATCH5	084	BATCH
BATCH6	085	BATCH
BATCH7	086	BATCH
BATCH8	087	BATCH
BATCH9	088	BATCH
DBY	089	DEBUG: SET Y: ARITHMETIC
CONV	090	ACCESS: CONVERSION
IDATE	091	ACCESS: CONVERSION
IDATEX	092	ACCESS: CONVERSION
ODATE	093	ACCESS: CONVERSION
MASKC1	095	ACCESS: CONVERSION
CHARGES	096	TCL: ACCOUNTING
CB2	097	ACCESS: LIST
CB1	098	ACCESS: LIST
FUNC2	099	ACCESS: CONVERSION
SAVE.LIST	100	LIST MANAGEMENT
FUNC1	101	ACCESS: CONVERSION
MD1011	103	ACCESS: SELECTION
MD1012	104	ACCESS: SELECTION
MD30	105	ACCESS: SELECTION
ISTAT	106	ACCESS: UTILITY
COPY.LIST	107	EDITOR: LIST MANAGEMENT
DELETE.LIST	109	LIST MANAGEMENT
MD147	111	ACCESS: LIST
UEX1	112	ACCESS: CONVERSION
FUNC3	113	ACCESS: CONVERSION
UEX2	114	ACCESS: CONVERSION
TLOAD	115	TAPE LOAD
TAPEITEM	116	ACCESS
GOSELECT	118	ACCESS: SELECTION
MASKC2	120	ACCESS: CONVERSION
WHERESUBS	121	UTILITY
SLEEPERS	122	UTILITY
VARIOUS	123	ACCESS: CONVERSION
ISOS	124	ACCESS: UTILITY
MAIL.LABEL	125	ACCESS: LIST
SYSTBL2	126	FILE MANAGEMENT
STSTBL1	127	OVERFLOW TABLES

Frame name	*Number*	*Function*
TABSUBS	128	TERMIO
CONV2	129	ACCESS: CONVERSION
DBBRK	131	DEBUG: SET BREAKS
DBPARSE	132	DEBUG: COMMAND PARSE
DBSYM	133	DEBUG: SYMBOL CHECK
DBDISP	134	DEBUG: DISPLAY
DBOUT	135	DEBUG: OUTPUT
DB06	136	DEBUG: RUNNING
DBA	137	DEBUG: UTILITY
DBADDR	138	DEBUG: ADDR GEN
DBDOY	139	DEBUG: RUNNING TRACE
COPY1	140	FILE MANAGEMENT
FILEUT1	141	FILE MANAGEMENT
COPY2	142	FILE MANAGEMENT
FILEUT2	143	FILE MANAGEMENT
WSPACES2	144	UTILITY
XREF	145	ASSEMBLER
CROSS	146	ASSEMBLER
ASEXT2	147	ASSEMBLER
OPEN	148	FILE MANAGEMENT
ASEXT3	149	ASSEMBLER
ASEXT	152	ASSEMBLER
TAPE3	153	TAPE
TAPE4	154	TAPE
PT2.PT	156	TAPE
DBOTH	157	DEBUG: UTILITY
SS5	158	UTILITY
SS4	159	UTILITY
ARITH	160	UTILITY
NEW.EDIT2	161	SPOOLER: EDIT
TAPEHDLR2	162	SPOOLER: TAPE
EOJ.GNJ	163	SPOOLER: PRINTER
NEW.CLS	164	SPOOLER: TERMIO
WORKING.SET	165	SPOOLER: PRINTER
MSGS	166	SPOOLER
ASSIGN	167	SPOOLER
TAPEHDLR	168	TAPE
NEW.EDIT	169	SPOOLER: EDIT
LOCKS	170	SPOOLER: PRINTER
GENLPEQ	171	SPOOLER
WSPACES	172	UTILITY
GOSTOP	173	SPOOLER

Frame name	*Number*	*Function*
PTRABS	174	SPOOLER
INIT	175	SPOOLER: INIT
INIT2	176	SPOOLER: INIT
INIT3	177	SPOOLER: INIT
START2	178	SPOOLER
START3	179	SPOOLER
TAPEHDLR3	180	SPOOLER: TAPE
LPEQS	181	SPOOLER
GETLIMS	182	SPOOLER
MSG2	183	SPOOLER
SERIALPTR	184	SPOOLER
SCHEDULE	186	SPOOLER
CONFIG	187	UTILITY
COM9	188	BASIC COMPILER
COMC	189	BASIC COMPILER
COM0	190	BASIC COMPILER
COM1	191	BASIC COMPILER
COM2	192	BASIC COMPILER
COM3	193	BASIC COMPILER
COM4	194	BASIC COMPILER
COM5	195	BASIC COMPILER
COM6	196	BASIC COMPILER
COM7	197	BASIC COMPILER
COM8	198	BASIC COMPILER
COMU	199	BASIC COMPILER
SAVE.GZ.1	200	SAVE
DDUMP1	201	SAVE
DDUMP2	202	SAVE
DDUMP3	203	SAVE
DDUMP4	204	SAVE
DDUMP5	205	SAVE
DDUMP6	206	SAVE
ABSDBIN	207	SAVE: BINARY
ABSLBIN	209	RESTORE: BINARY
ABSL2	210	RESTORE
ABSL3	211	RESTORE
DLOAD1	212	RESTORE
DLOAD2	213	RESTORE
DLOAD3	214	RESTORE
DLOAD4	215	RESTORE
SEL.RESTORE	216	RESTORE
OLOAD1	217	RESTORE

Frame name	*Number*	*Function*
GFE	218	FILE MANAGEMENT: GFEs
RECOVER	219	RESTORE
ACTIVATE	220	RESTORE
CAT.PVER	224	BASIC: UTILITY
BCALL	225	BASIC: RUN TIME
ERRMSG	226	BASIC: RUN TIME
DYNAMIC	228	BASIC: RUN TIME
BSTORAGE	229	BASIC: RUN TIME
BRP00	230	BASIC: RUN TIME
BRP01	231	BASIC: RUN TIME
BRP02	232	BASIC: RUN TIME
BRP03	233	BASIC: RUN TIME
BRP04	234	BASIC: RUN TIME
BRP05	235	BASIC: RUN TIME
BRP06	236	BASIC: RUN TIME
BRP07	237	BASIC: RUN TIME
BRP08	238	BASIC: RUN TIME
BRP09	239	BASIC: RUN TIME
BRP10	240	BASIC: RUN TIME
BRP11	241	BASIC: RUN TIME
BRP12	242	BASIC: RUN TIME
BRP13	243	BASIC: RUN TIME
BRP14	244	BASIC: RUN TIME
BRP15	245	BASIC: RUN TIME
BRP16	246	BASIC: RUN TIME
BRP17	247	BASIC: RUN TIME
BRP18	248	BASIC: RUN TIME
BNF0	250	BASIC: BNF
BNF1	251	BASIC: BNF
BNF2	252	BASIC: BNF
BNF3	253	BASIC: BNF
BNF4	254	BASIC: BNF
BNF5	255	BASIC: BNF
BNF6	256	BASIC: BNF
BNF7	257	BASIC: BNF
BNF8	258	BASIC: BNF
BNF9	259	BASIC: BNF
BNF10	260	BASIC: BNF
BNF11	261	BASIC: BNF
BNF12	262	BASIC: BNF
BNF13	263	BASIC: BNF
BD:00	264	BASIC: DEBUGGER

Frame name	*Number*	*Function*
BD:01	265	BASIC: DEBUGGER
BD:02	266	BASIC: DEBUGGER
BD:03	267	BASIC: DEBUGGER
BD:04	268	BASIC: DEBUGGER
BD:05	269	BASIC: DEBUGGER
BAUD	270	UTILITY
NEW.VERB	271	UTILITY
BD:06	273	BASIC: DEBUGGER
BD:07	274	BASIC: DEBUGGER
OPCODES	275	BASIC: RUN TIME
FILEUT3	277	FILE MANAGEMENT
DIAG3	282	ATP
POINTER.DMP/LD	288	UTILITY: DUMP/LOAD
CHECK.SUM	289	UTILITY
WP1	291	WORD PROCESSING
WP2	292	WORD PROCESSING
WP3	293	WORD PROCESSING
WP4	294	WORD PROCESSING
WP5	295	WORD PROCESSING
WP6	296	WORD PROCESSING
WP7	297	WORD PROCESSING
WP8	298	WORD PROCESSING
WP9	299	WORD PROCESSING
REFORMAT	300	ACCESS: UPDATE
MSG1	301	UTLITY: DB-MSG
MSG2	302	UTILITY: LOAD-MSG
MSG3	303	UTILITY: EDIT-MSG
MSG4	304	UTILITY: SPOOL-MSG
MSG5	305	UTILITY
MSG6	306	UTILITY: TAPE-MSG
MSG7	307	UTILITY: MISC-MSG
MSG8	308	UTILITY: RESPONSE
MSG9	309	UTILITY: BDB-MSG
MSG11	311	UTILITY: ENG-MSG
02.EXIT	314	UTILITY
ID.TAPE.PT	315	TAPE OVERFLOW
HT.TAPE.PT	316	TAPE
ID.TAPE2.PT	317	TAPE: FORMAT-FLOPPY
XP.EXITS2	335	S/1
XP.EXITS1	337	S/1
MLIST2	338	ASSEMBLER
	340—372	(USED BY JET IF SUPPORTED)

Frame name	*Number*	*Function*
COMPARE1	381	UTILITY
COMPARE2	382	UTILITY
MON.LOAD	394	
TST.LOADER	395	ASSEMBLER
ASM.UEX	396	ASSEMBLER USER EXITS
COLDDUMP	398	SAVE
SYSTEM.CURSOR	399	TERMIO

Appendix I – PICK Licensees

Direct PICK licensees

Fujitsu Espana SA

General Automation

NCE Computer Group (Sanyo/Icon implementation)
Sequoia Systems Inc

Siemens Nixdorf

Stratus Computer Inc

SunRiver Corporation (ADDS)

Tau Engineering

PICK-related licensees

Cosmos Inc.	Revelation (an emulation of PICK under DOS, also available as a networked version)
Unidata Corporation	Unidata (a UNIX database capable of supporting the PICK database structure)
V-Mark Corp.	Uni-Verse (an emulation of PICK under UNIX)

Other PICK suppliers

McDonnell Douglas Information Systems	Reality Sequoia

This version of PICK was originally written by Dick Pick and later became the property of Microdata, now known as McDonnell Douglas Information Systems. It has been considerably enhanced and contains differences to those versions supplied by the direct licensees.

Appendix J – Glossary of Terms

ABS frame	One of the frames within the first group of frames of the system known as the ABS section. These frames contain the object code of the PICK operating system.
ACCESS	The information retrieval language of the PICK system.
AMC	Abbreviation for Attribute Mark Count, the second attribute of the dictionary definition item, defining the attribute position.
ANSI	An acronym for 'American National Standards Institute'.
ASCII	An acronym for 'American Standard Code for Information Interchange'. Established by ANSI in 1963, it is one of the standards used to represent alphanumeric characters.
Abort	The termination of a computer function in the event of a hardware or software malfunction.
Access time	The time taken to reference a piece of information.
Accoun	A group of logically related files defined by a single master dictionary. Can also define a user logon name.
Address	A way of referencing a memory location or a part of a disk.
Algorithm	A set of rules for solving a task.
Alphanumeric	A string of characters which can contain any combination of letters, numbers and symbols.
Applications	Software programs that perform specific tasks such as accounting, stock control, etc.
Array or **matrix**	A whole set of variables identified by a single name.
Asynchronous	A means of communication between terminals and the computer, sometimes referred to as 'async'.
Attribute	A specific element of data, often referred to as a 'field' in other systems. This data element can be subdivided into values and subvalues.
Attribute Mark	A reserved character used to separate attributes in an item and has the ASCII value 254 (hexadecimal FE).
BASIC	An abbreviation of 'Beginners All-Purpose Symbolic Instruction Code', a popular and easy-to-learn programming language.
Background	*See* Foreground.
Backup	The means of copying the database to be able to recover its contents in the event of a hardware or software malfunction.
Base FID	The first of a block of frames making up a file.
Batch	A method of processing data in which work is grouped together in batches for processing, rather than each item being worked on individually in an interactive way.
Baud	The capacity of a communications line, often synonymous with bits per second. Terminals and printers typically operate at a speed of 9600 baud.
Binary	A method of representing numbers to the base of two using the numbers '0' and '1'.

Bit Contraction of the words 'binary digit'. This is the lowest level of data storage in the computer, each bit being represented as either a '0' or a '1'.

Bootstrap The process of starting a computer from powerup.

Buffer A place where information can be stored temporarily.

Bug An error of programming logic.

Byte A character of data made up of eight bits.

CPS An abbreviation of 'characters per second'.

CPU An abbreviation of 'central processing unit', the heart of the computer system, where processing is carried out.

CRT An abbreviation for cathode ray tube and used to refer to terminals, the means of communicating with the computer.

Channel Another name for 'port', the connection on the computer that links to peripheral devices.

Checksum A clever means of verifying data by carrying out a calculation of its content and comparing the result to that expected, the expected value normally being held elsewhere on the disk.

Coldstart The procedures undertaken once the initial program load has taken place.

Command An instruction given to the computer to carry out a task.

Compiler A means of translating a source program into object form, the form which enables it to be used.

Concatenate Join together side by side without an intervening space.

Connect tim The length of time that a user is connected to the system.

Conversion The processing of data in ACCESS and BASIC to convert data held in internal format to that known as external format or vice versa.

Correlative A processing function enabling values to be computed at runtime rather than being held as a data element on the database. A derived value.

Cursor The means of indicating the position on a terminal at which the next input/output is expected.

D-pointer A dictionary record that defines a file.

Data Information or the information stored in a computer.

Data dictionary A necessary requirement of any database system, which enables the structure and form of the database to be defined.

Data processing The input, output and processing of information.

Database A collection of data in an organized form, enabling ready storage and updating of information shared centrally.

Deadly embrace A situation where two or more processes control information needed by the other in such a way that no process can proceed.

Debug The process of removing errors of logic from a program.

Debugger A software tool to enable the corrections to program logic to be made. It allows programs to be executed step by step

	and information, such as the contents of variables, to be displayed.
Default	An action or value presented automatically unless other instructions are explicitly given.
Degradation	A slowing down in the response from a computer as it is given more work to perform.
Delimiter	A character used to separate data elements. Some special characters, known as 'system delimiters' are used by PICK. These are attribute marks, value marks, subvalue marks and segment marks.
Diagnostics	A series of routines designed to locate hardware or software errors.
Dictionary	A file that holds records defining the structure of the next level file in the PICK hierarchy.
Disks	Magnetic media shaped like circular discs which are used for storing information.
DM	The prime data manager account in Advanced PICK which contains special facilities for managing the computer system and corresponds to **SYSPROG** in PICK R83.
EBCDIC	An acronym for 'Extended Binary Coded Decimal Interchange Code', a standard for representing alphanumeric characters.
Editor	A program for editing data.
End user	The person who ends up using the computer.
FID	A contraction of the words 'frame id' denoting the logical address of the frame on the disk.
Field	A single element of data, referred to in PICK as an 'attribute'.
File	A collection of logically related items of data.
Firmware	A series of operating instructions (software) fixed in ROM (Read Only Memory). ROM is a hardware 'chip' on a PCB (printed circuit board).
Floppy disk	A flexible single disk used for storing information.
Foreground	Foreground is the task that has the highest priority in a situation where several tasks are run concurrently at a terminal. The other tasks are known as background tasks.
Frame	The smallest element of data storage on a PICK disk – 512 bytes.
Function key	A key that performs a special function.
GFE	An abbreviation of 'Group Format Error', an error condition within a group of data frames.
Global variable	A variable that is available to all users of a program.
Group	The name given to a frame or series of linked frames in a file.
Handshaking	A term which indicates that two processes involved in some kind of communication have a means of controlling and confirming the receipt of data sent by each other.

Hard copy Printed output from a computer.

Hardware The physical computer equipment.

Hashing The processing of an item-id by an algorithm to locate the position of data in a file.

Hexadecimal A method of representing numbers to the base of 16. Sometimes abbreviated to hex.

Holdfile A temporary file used to store a print file.

I/O An abbreviation of the term 'input/output', which relates to the way in which data can be input to or output from the computer.

Initialize To reset the system or a process to its starting point.

Interface A link between systems or processes. Can be either software or hardware.

Interpreter A software program that translates a program (in source or part compiled form) into machine code instructions which are then executed.

Interrupt A temporary suspension of computer activities caused for a variety of reasons.

Item A collection of logically related attributes; often referred to as a record on other systems.

Item-id A contraction of 'item identifier', the key of a file item. This record key is always stored in attribute 0.

Job A specific function made up of one or more programs run one after each other.

Justification The method of aligning data either to the right, the left or central on a page.

K Symbol for 'kilo' – a thousand. Using binary notation this works out to 1024.

Kbyte or **KB** Kilobyte – 1024 bytes.

Key The code by which a record can be identified and which makes it unique from other records in its file.

Key in To use the keyboard to enter data into the computer.

Label An identifier made up of alphanumeric characters.

Language A programming code of a particular type, such as COBOL, BASIC, FORTRAN or Pascal.

Licensee A hardware manufacturer who has purchased and maintains the source code to PICK which is implemented on their systems for resale.

Line The connection between the computer and its peripheral devices, such as VDUs or printers.

Linkage The first 12 bytes of a frame used to define forward and backward links to other frames.

Local variable A variable that is only available to the specific user running the program.

Logoff The process of ending a working session on the computer.

Logon	The process of gaining access to the computer.
Loop	A series of program instructions which may be executed more than once before the program continues.
MD	An abbreviation of 'Master Dictionary', the primary file for each account which defines all files, procs, verbs and pointers.
Machine code	A programming language using 0s and 1s only and, hence, the lowest level programming language available.
Main memory	*See* Memory.
Master Dictionary	The primary file for each account which defines all files, procs, verbs and pointers.
Matrix	*See* Array.
Mega	A term meaning 'million'.
Mbyte or MB	One million bytes. Typically used to define the size of disk storage.
MDS	The primary file of Advanced PICK which is at the top of the file hierarchy and contains records to all accounts on the system and is equivalent to **SYSTEM** under PICK R83.
Memory (RAM)	RAM (Random Access Memory) is the physical hardware capable of storing information.
Microcomputer	A small computer, capable of handling more than one user.
Millisecond	A thousandth of a second.
Minicomputer	The next stage up from microcomputers, both in size and the number of users it can handle – often up to 12 or maybe 64 terminals.
Modulo	The number of groups in a file.
Monitor	The special software written for each implementation to control the input and output devices.
Numeric	Comprising numbers only.
OEM	An abbreviation for 'Original Equipment Manufacturer' and relates to someone who incorporates componenets or subsystems from other manufacturers into their own systems.
Online	The position of being connected to a computer system.
Option	Characters enclosed in brackets to denote the provision of additional functionality.
Overflow	The amount of available (unused) frames on the disk.
PC	An abbreviation for 'Personal Computer', a system that is for use by one person at a time.
PCB	An abbreviation for 'Primary Control Block', the working storage area allocated to each port.
POB	Abbreviation for 'Primary Output Buffer', used in PROCs.
PROC	A means of storing a series of commands which can be initiated by a single command name.
PROM	Abbreviation of 'Programmable Read-only Memory', typically used to store program instructions on an integrated circuit board.

Package	A piece of software written to handle a specific task and made generally available with the purpose of many people being able to use the software with little or no modification.
Paging	The process of transferring blocks ('pages') of information to and fro from disk.
Parameter	A piece of information which can be given a specific value to suit the task in hand.
Pascal	A popular programming language.
Password	A series of characters which need to be input correctly before access to the system is provided.
Peripheral	A device connected to the computer system. This could relate to VDUs, printers, magnetic tape units and so on.
Pointer	An element of data that contains the address where other data resides.
Port	The connection on the computer to which the terminals, printers and other peripheral devices are attached.
Privilege level	A security code given to each user which can be used to limit access to certain facilities.
Processor	*See* CPU.
Program	A sequence of instructions, written in the programming language, to perform a given task.
Protocol	A series of rules for defining the exchange of data.
Q-pointer	A type of file pointer enabling alternative access to a file; often referred to as a synonym.
RAM	Abbreviation of 'Random Access Memory', the physical memory of the computer system.
Record	A collection of related information and known as an 'item' in PICK terminology.
Reset	The same process as initialization.
Routine	A small number of program instructions.
RUNOFF	A text formatting utility within PICK
SIB	An abbreviation for 'Secondary Input Buffer', used in PROCs.
SOB	An abbreviation for 'Secondary Output Buffer', used in PROCs.
SYSPROG	The system programmers account in PICK R83 which contains special facilities for managing the computer system.
SYSTEM	The primary file of the PICK R83 system which is at the top of the file hierarchy and contains records to all accounts on the system.
Scroll	The process of displaying the next or previous screen of information.
Segment mark	The special character used to separate items held on disk and whose value is ASCII 255, or FF in hexadecimal.

Select list	A list of items that have been selected from ACCESS using the commands SELECT or SSELECT.
Separation	The number of frames in a group in a file.
Software	Computer programs.
Sort	The means of placing information in a specified sequence according to the contents of particular parts of a record.
Spooling	A technique for temporarily storing output on disk.
Stack	A small area of memory allocated for holding data where information added to the stack pushes down the information already held.
Subroutine	A series of instructions performed frequently that can be executed anywhere within a main program and, once performed, enable the main program to continue from the instruction immediately following the branch instruction.
Subvalue	The subdivision of a value.
Subvalue mark	The special character delimiting subvalues and whose value is 252 in ASCII or FC in hexadecimal.
Syntax	The rules for the formulation of program and ACCESS statements.
System	A term often used as synonymous with the computer, or the computer and its peripherals.
TCL	Abbreviation of 'Terminal Control Language', the command language of PICK.
TTY	Abbreviation for teletype.
Terminal	*See* VDU.
Timeslice	The number of milliseconds of processing given to each task during its processing cycle.
Transfer rate	The rate at which information is transferred between peripheral devices, including disks and tapes, and main memory.
User-id	A unique name given to a user to enable him to access the computer system.
VDU	An abbreviation of 'Visual Display Unit', the terminal used to commun-icate with the system.
Validation	The process of checking data to ensure its accuracy.
Value	The first subdivisions of an attribute.
Value mark	The character used to delimit values and whose ASCII value is 253 (FD hexadecimal).
Variable	A data element that can be assigned a number of values.
Virtual memory	A means of making available more memory for processing than the physical RAM available. It is achieved by using the spare space on disk and treating it as an extension of RAM.
WPM	'Words per minute'.

Winchester disk A form of disk technology, where the disk is contained in a sealed and non-removable unit.

Word processing The processing of text by use of an editor and a process to format and print the edited text.

Workspace An area of disk of memory set aside for work associated with a specific task or user.

Index

In general, Advanced PICK is case insensitive, which means that commands can be executed in upper case, lower case or mixed case without affecting the functionality of the process being executed. This contrasts with the earlier version of PICK, known as R83, where all commands had to be entered in upper case. This index contains entries in both upper and lower case.